Diabetes Ignored: Krystin's Life

Krystin Engstrand

Assembled by and with commentary from
Gary Engstrand

Copyright © 2019 by Gary Engstrand

All rights reserved. No part of this book may be reproduced or used in any manner without written permission of the copyright owner except for the use of quotations in a book review.

For more information, address: garyengstrand@gmail.com

FIRST EDITION

This book is dedicated to Krystin, to all children who are diagnosed with Type 1 diabetes, and to the medical staff of the University of Minnesota Hospitals and Clinics, whose extraordinary care and attention gave us Krystin for an additional five years.

Contents

Prologue	i
People	v
Introduction	vii
Krystin Life Events	xiii

Part I:

Living Life and Ignoring Diabetes: Life at Home and Abroad

1 Young Years: Through Middle School	1
2 High School Years	27
3 The College Years: University of Minnesota Morris	65
4 The College Years: Scotland and Treatment	135
5 The College Years: University of Minnesota Twin Cities	179
6 An Interim Year After College	189
7 Teaching and Traveling in South Korea	199
8 An Interim Year Between Korea and Transplant	239

Part II:

Paying the Consequences: The Downhill Slide	263
Prologue to Part II	265
9 Journey to Transplant	269
10 Kidney Transplant	365

11 Kitties and Hospital Visits 393

12 Hospital Visits and Another Transplant 447

13 No Diabetes, Losing the Cats, and Opioid Addiction 485

14 Miscellaneous Months of Medicine and More 557

15 Pancreas Rejection 615

16 Three Months in the Hospital 673

17 Life at Logan House 715

Tod und Erinnerung: Death and Remembrance 801

Prologue

Dear young, naive Krystin of the past,[*]

There's a series of movies called Final Destination, in which someone will have a premonition of a horrible, bloody accident that is about to happen, in which many people die. That person will then do something to keep themselves and a number of other people out of the accident. By cheating death, throughout the rest of the movie they all die anyway, because Death comes after them to claim them, as he should've done in the original accident. The lesson of the story, essentially, is that there is no cheating death.

This will be similar to your life. You will keep cheating death, over and over. And you never learn your lesson after each escape. You continue to take your life for granted. Most people lock their door from the grim reaper with bolts and chains and deadlocks. But you leave yours wide open, every day, finally closing it when the grim reaper has already stepped one foot inside. Well, each time he comes around, he's able to creep in a little more. By 2016, he will have had his hands around your wrists, leading you out the door, at least 4 times. And those are only the times you know about. The only reason you'll be able to escape his grip is because someone was there to save you, to pull you back in, to bring you to the hospital.

Let me tell you, in the best order I can, what you will endure if you don't get your ignorant head out of the clouds and start managing your diabetes like you need to.

-- Painful neuropathy in your feet that will feel like you're stepping on sharp, scalding needles; especially when you lie down. You will even stupidly get a foot tattoo, that will get infected and end up looking like shit.
-- Lethargy, causing you to not excel in school as well as you could, and skipping out on many activities with friends because you're too tired.

---

[*] I discovered this "letter to herself" on her laptop after her death, written sometime during 2016, apparently.

- Visit #1 from the Grim Reaper your sophomore year of college when you end up in the CCU with DKA.
- Visit #2 from the Grim Reaper your junior year of college when you end up in the hospital in Paris, again with DKA. You will just have spent 26 hours on a bus ride from Warsaw, puking your guts out the entire ride. Mom will be so mad, she won't even want to come see you. She'll want to finish out the trip to Paris and return to our short-term home in Edinburgh with dad and Elliott, and let you figure out your own way back once you're released. It E@ [probably "will"] be dad who convinces her to come.
- Summer of 2006 you will spend in and out of an eating disorder program, because your endo thinks you are restricting your insulin to control your weight. Nov. 2006 – March 2007 you will be at a residential ED [eating disorder] place in Arizona, where you will be when your mom tells you she's leaving your dad.
- March 2007 your parents will divorce. We will forever be convinced that we had a part in it.
- 2012 you will find out that your kidneys are failing and you will need a kidney transplant.
- Between the beginning of 2013 – spring 2016, you will go through the following:
- Cataract surgery in both eyes.
- Gallbladder removal.
- Gastric stimulator placed in stomach due to very poor stomach motility.
- Fistula placed in left arm in case dialysis is needed.
- Severe diabetic gastroparesis.
- Kidney transplant.
- Tube placed in your stomach so you can do tube feedings because you can't stay properly nourished on your own.
- Visit #3 from the Grim Reaper during a 2 week hospital stay because you contracted both EBV and CMV viruses, an infection, and mild pneumonia, all at once.
- Pancreas transplant.
- Addiction to and abuse of narcotics, resulting in you not ever being allowed narcotics again, even when in the hospital, no matter how much pain you're in.

- Pancreatitis and pancreas rejection.
- Approximately 25 esophageal procedures, meaning stents and dilations, because your esophagus is damaged by all the acid your stomach is producing in an attempt to break down and push through food. Your esophagus will develop strictures and you will forever have issues swallowing without a stent being in there.
- Numerous hospital stays for numerous reasons.
- Put on a permanent soft mechanical diet, so you don't further damage your esophagus.
- Visit #4 from the Grim Reaper when you end up in the hospital for what ends up being 3 months. That time, no one will expect you to survive. On your medical chart the docs will enter "failure to thrive", which is a nice way of saying they've done all they can do and are waiting for you to die. But somehow, despite all odds, you pull through.
- Daily, chronic pain that you'll have to deal with because you don't get anything for it due to your history.
- Moving into a group home and losing all sense of independence, but finally getting the help you need to deal with all your medical issues.

You may take some of this to heart, but it won't change anything you do. I know this because I AM you. We're stubborn, and think that nothing bad will happen to us. But it will. Continue on the path you're on and you're headed for a whole lot of bad. Not just in the distant future, but soon. You'll notice the downward spiral start in college. You'll be tired all the time. You'll skip classes. You'll spend less time on homework and studying. You'll even get an F on what should've been an easy paper for you, due to plagiarism. All so that you can sleep.

So keep telling yourself you'll be alright, and that you have time to turn things around. Time will catch up with you quicker than you think. Modern medicine is wonderful, and as of 2016 has kept you alive, but not without consequences. Not without a lot of pain and suffering. And not just for you. You feel the pain and suffering physically, every day beginning after your first transplant, but your family and friends feel it every day in their hearts already, because they can already see what's happening to you at such a young age.

They see the effects the diabetes non-compliance is starting to have. Effects you choose to ignore because you don't care. You don't care what happens to you, because you don't care about yourself. I see that now, in hindsight, and it breaks my heart that no one helps you find your self love, your self respect, your sense of pride in who you are and accepting the unfortunate hand of cards you've been dealt.

Even into our 30s, we will still have a fear of losing one of our parents. We still don't know how to exist in a world that they aren't in. Luckily, knock on wood, we still have many years with both of them. But what about from their end? Do you think they're ready to lose their only daughter? They've been fearing for our life since freshman year of high school, when your endocrinologist at the time told them they needed to let me take the reins on my diabetes. They were scared as hell. And you will continue, for the next 17 years, to keep that fear in their hearts until you finally, at age 31, accept the help that you have needed for so long. You finally let them breathe. But you don't realize, until my time, how much permanent emotional damage you've done to them. For someone who cares so much about making them proud, you fail to do the one thing that will make them the most proud, and that is take care of yourself.

People

Krystin (Stephens Hermanson) Engstrand
10/30/1984 – 10/17/2017

Gary Engstrand, Dad
1951-

Pat (Stephens) Engstrand, Mom
1957-

Kathy Jensen, Stepmom (informally, not legally)
1956-

Elliott (Stephens Miller) Engstrand, Brother
1990-

Christine Hinz Lenzen, a best friend
1984-

Peggy Hinz, Christine's mom and a best friend

———

Many other friends as well as many medical staff at the University of Minnesota

Introduction

This is Krystin's story. It is the story of a life that ended too soon, of a life of someone diagnosed with diabetes at age 4, of a life illuminating what happens when diabetes is ignored. But it is also the story of a life that was filled with fun and travel and friends in between the pain and fatigue of the disease. Krystin managed to get through college, teach abroad, and find a job at her alma mater, the University of Minnesota, all the while contending with the complications of diabetes ignored *and* her inability to assume responsibility for the management of the disease. (As the timeline of her life reveals, after she returned from teaching in South Korea in the summer of 2011, she was treated at the University of Minnesota hospital 66 times before she died—and an additional five times at other clinics for eye treatments and surgery.) The disease finally killed her, but not before she lived about as full a life as a 32-year-old middle-class American kid could.

People do not live their lives in chapters but often, long after the fact, we recognize that there were periods or segments of our lives marked by changes at the beginning and the end of each. In Krystin's case, many of the chapters, the segments, correspond to her location: growing up at home, high school, at college, in Scotland, at home and in college again, in South Korea, at home, in her apartment, in the hospital and then Logan House. Those are fairly neat breaks in Krystin's life, so that's how the chapters are organized.

This book has several goals. As she got older, Krystin wanted others to know of the consequences of ignoring diabetes. She had a short piece published and she repeatedly sought ways to inform people. Her objective is the primary focus of this volume. There are other foci, however, that I include in order to capture Krystin's life: the point of view of parents of a recalcitrant child with diabetes, her quirky sense of humor (often in the face of daunting and painful medical conditions), her travels, and other aspects of her life that round out her personality. It is worth noting the difference between the often cheery Facebook posts and the sometimes depressing entries in her blog about her journey as a transplant patient.

There are aspects of Krystin's life which will not show up here, primarily in the interest of brevity. She had a terrible time handling money (she spent it faster than she had income to spend, and eventually declared bankruptcy) and it was a thorn in her side until the last year and a half of her life. She was a liberal Democrat and not bashful about saying so (e.g., on Facebook). She enjoyed music and had a wide range of artists to whom she listened, including going to their concerts (e.g., Lady Gaga). She read a lot and was fond of the Harry Potter novels, Lord of the Rings, and British and Scandinavian detective novels—in addition to British history. She also loved competing in ice hockey and soccer when she was a youngster—and played on one of the teams the first year the Minneapolis Park and Recreation Board offered girls ice hockey.

The first chapter will contain more of my voice, her father's, because obviously a young child does not write. Krystin's mother, Pat, declined to participate in the preparation of this book because recalling the events of Krystin's life was too painful for her, a decision I respected. On occasion, however, Pat's voice will appear in the form of email messages or other notes. Krystin's voice comes through clearly as well. As with all of the text, the chapter will draw almost exclusively on contemporary letters, messages, and other documents. I am at heart an archivist, so I kept many of the communications that went back and forth and other items that instinct told me to retain. It is true that history must be written from the records available, and what I have in my files is not the entirety of what Krystin, I, and others wrote during her early life. Nonetheless, what survives provides a full picture.

The last chapter records Krystin's prescience and her death, and the reactions to it by her many friends. Even after a discount for social niceties, their statements reflect the deep attachment they had to her.

Everything in between the first and last chapter is largely Krystin's voice.

Krystin loved to write. Her ambition in life was to be a writer, and she wanted to start with the *New Yorker*. Even though she was never published, except on one website devoted to diabetes, she nonetheless wrote extensively on her blogs, on Facebook, in her diaries, and in her emails to me. It is her writing, lightly edited, that comprises the majority of the narrative.

I want to extend my deep thanks to my editor, Leah Reinert, who carefully went through all 1700+ pages of Krystin's writing and who was instrumental in reducing the scope as well as shaping the narrative. This volume would not have been possible without her help.

A few notes are in order.

When drawing on Krystin's writing, I have corrected typos. Krystin often wrote extemporaneously (e.g., on Facebook, in emails), and (like most of us) did not try to ensure those postings and messages met a standard worthy of publishing. She was ferocious about good writing, however, so would be dismayed were I to leave typos and other minor errors in the text, errors that she certainly would have corrected if she knew the writing were going to be published.

Bracketed comments appear throughout the text. Those are explanatory narratives from me.

Some of the photographs are not high quality, but they're as good as the original (mostly cell phone) photos that I had to work with.

Krystin's Facebook posts frequently elicited comments from friends and family, sometimes many, many comments, expressions of sympathy, or good wishes. Except in a few cases, those comments have been omitted; I left them in when friends' comments elicited further responses from Krystin. Anyone curious enough to want to see them all may do so by going to her Facebook page, which is memorialized, at https://www.facebook.com/krystin.engstrand/about. Except in a couple of cases in the aid of clarity, I made no changes to the spelling or punctuation in Facebook posts from Krystin's friends.

One dilemma I faced shortly after Krystin's death was whether or not I should read her diaries. There are websites with discussions about reading the diaries of deceased family members, but none that I could find that addressed the specific question of reading the diaries of one's deceased adult child. I wrote to a number of friends who are intelligent, thoughtful, and ethical people to ask their opinion. As I expected, the replies were indeed thoughtful. Only one person advised against reading them; the others thought I should, but raised questions and caveats. Was it too soon after her death? What would Krystin want? What if I read something that altered my opinion of her? Should someone else read them first? As my son and her brother Elliott wrote to me, "I doubt there's anything in there that would be really terrible for anyone to read."

After further reflection, I concluded that I would read them. The most compelling reason was that I was certain that Krystin would have wanted most of the content included in any collection of her writing. I posed a question to a friend who knew Krystin: "Would she want me to destroy them unread and unused?" The friend's response: "Oh, no!"

I thought my friend was right. Given how much she loved to write, it would be a travesty to simply toss out all the work, thought, and heart she presumably put into the diaries. So I think she'd probably want something done with them, if possible--which, of course, meant reading them.

The other persuasive argument (for me) came from another friend: "By default, you may be her literary executor, so to speak." I agreed, but also accepted the suggestion that it would be best to have someone else read them before me, to ensure that there was nothing that would hurt me or that Krystin obviously would not have wanted me to see. Kathy took on the task, and after reading them told me that Elliott was correct. So about six months after her death, I read and transcribed the diaries.

Some of the diary entries have been omitted. Not everything one writes in a diary are germane to the story of one's life. I have also deleted those (very few) entries that could cause embarrassment to people as well as entries that Krystin herself clearly would not have wanted made public. Those deletions, however, constitute only a small fraction of the total; Krystin's thoughts and feelings are not compromised.

In the case of a few diary entries, I realized after a sentence or two that Krystin had written explicitly and graphically about her sexual activities. I closed the journal and did not continue reading those entries, but with a smile. Smile, first, because I was amused that Krystin wrote about *everything* in her life, and second, because I was glad that she had been able to experience intimacy.

During one of the sessions with one of the several therapists that Krystin saw, sometimes with us present, the therapist told us that "you'll have her until she's 30." What the therapist meant was that Krystin would not be mature enough to be completely out from parental responsibility until age 30. Retrospectively, it became a chilling forecast of her lifespan.

What saddens me as much as anything was how much I came learn about my daughter only after her death, as I edited all her writing. I didn't see her sense of humor as much as I should have, I didn't realize the depth of her friendships with many people and the extent to which they admired her, and I didn't fully understand how reflective she was. With her family, of course, her medical conditions were (far too) often the focus of our interactions; we didn't see the "whole Krystin" as much as we should have. That is my great regret. There was nothing left unsaid between us—we both affirmed that many times to one another, and on that score I have no regrets—but at the same time there wasn't enough said (on topics other than medicine).

In the end, I can be glad about how Krystin viewed our relationship. Here's a message she sent to me at some point during 2017 (it wasn't dated):

Dad,

I'm writing to say thank you. Not just for being my dad. Thank you for being my advocate, my support beam, my sound board. Over the last number of months, feeling like no one was on my side, you've been there for me. Even if our opinions on some things differed, you still understood and respected my point of view. All your support, and all the times you visited, meant (and still means) so much to me; more than I will ever be able to express. I know parents can feel helpless sometimes, when there's nothing they can do to help their child's situation, but believe me when I say that even if it feels like you haven't done much, that you actually have, through your actions and words. You have been so helpful, and I appreciate more than words could express. Love you so much, always & forever. [3 hearts] KE

What parent would not be thrilled to receive such a message?

-- Gary Engstrand

Krystin's Life

Travel, Medical, and Other Significant Events

1984	Oct 30	born at Fairview Hospital (Riverside Avenue, Minneapolis)
1986	summer	Pat's family gathering, Virginia Beach, VA
1987	summer	Pat's family gathering, Ogdensburg, NY
1988	summer	Pat's family gathering, Chautauqua Lake, NY
1988	Dec 22	diagnosed with Type 1 diabetes
1989	summer	Pat's family gathering, Virginia Beach, VA
1990	summer	Pat's family gathering, Green Lake, MN
1990	Sept	started at Michael Dowling elementary school, Minneapolis
1991	summer	Pat's family gathering, Virginia Beach, VA
1992	summer	Pat's family gathering, Smith Mtn Lake, VA
1993	summer	Pat's family gathering, Green Lake, MN
1994	summer	Pat's family gathering, Virginia Beach, VA
1995	summer	Pat's family gathering, Green Lake, MN
1996	summer	Pat's family gathering, Kill Devil Hills, NC
1997	summer	Pat's family gathering, Green Lake, MN
1997	Sept	started at Anwatin Middle School, Minneapolis
1998	summer	Pat's family gathering, Lake Patoka, IN

1999	July	Martha's Vineyard, Philadelphia, Washington D.C., and N. Myrtle Beach (with dad and Christine Lenzen, ending at Pat's family gathering)
1999	Sept	started at South High School, Minneapolis
2000	July	Maine, Prince Edward Island (week with family)
2001	Apr 6-14	London (with mom, dad, Christine Lenzen)
2001	June 29-July 7	Vancouver/Vancouver Island (week with family)
2003	Mar 13	admitted to the University of Minnesota, Morris
2003	June	graduated from South High School
2003	summer	Pat's family gathering, North Myrtle Beach, SC
2003	Sept	started at Morris
2003	Dec 20-27	Cancun (week with family)
2004	June 11-15	New York City (with family)
2004	Nov	to ICU, released Thanksgiving
2005	Oct 14-22	Florence & Rome (with mom & dad)
2006	Jan-May	Scotland/Europe (with family)
2006	April	Hopital Tenon (DKA after bus ride from Warsaw, in hospital a week)

2006	May-summer	program at Methodist Hospital & Anna Westin House
2006-07 Nov 30-Apr 1		Remuda Ranch, Wickenburg, AZ
2007	May	Job in Research Animal Resources, U of M (through August)
2007-10		Worked at University of Minnesota bookstore, Coffman Union (student job, ended 1/30/10)
2008	summer	Pat's family gathering, Glenwood, MN (grandmother's funeral en route)
2009	June	graduated from the University of Minnesota, Twin Cities (B.A., History)
2009	summer	Pat's family gathering, Glenwood, MN
2009	summer	San Francisco (with Elliott to celebrate graduations)
2010	Feb	Arizona (week with friend Rachel)
2010	summer	Pat's family gathering, Glenwood, MN (grandfather's funeral en route; the last time she attended the family gathering)
2010-11		teaching in Cheonan, South Korea (July 2010 – August 2011)
2012	Jan	cataract surgery
2012	Apr	started work at Sponsored Projects Administration office (SPA), University of Minnesota, Minneapolis
2012	Oct 7-9	U Hospital (dehydration)

2012	Nov 27	U Hospital (beginning of eye shots)
2012	Dec 4	U Hospital (fistula surgery)
2012	Dec 6	U Hospital (ER, incision swelling)
2012	Dec 19	Eye clinic (first of 6 laser eye treatments)
2013	Jan 22	Fairview Southdale Hospital (cataract surgery)
2013	Jan 29	Fairview Southdale Hospital (cataract surgery)
2013	Jan 30	U Hospital (fistula surgery)
2013	Feb 4	U Hospital (fistulagram)
2013	Feb 22	U Hospital (ER, seizures/blacking out)
2013	June 1-8	U Hospital (kidney transplant)
2013	June 17-20	U Hospital (dehydration)
2013	June 27	U Hospital (ER, med problem)
2013	July 4	U Hospital (low blood pressure)
2013	Aug 2-3	U Hospital (pancreas transplant, but donor pancreas damaged)
2013	Sept 1	moved into apartment
2013	Sept 12, 18	got Gabi and Molly the cats
2013	Oct 7-8	U Hospital (viral pharyngitis)
2013	Oct 11-15	U Hospital (infection, abscess)
2013	Nov 1-5	U Hospital (gastric pacer surgery)

2013	Nov 11-19	U Hospital (mono, cytomegalovirus, esophagitis, slight pneumonia)
2013	Dec 28-29	U Hospital (GI virus)
2014	Feb 14-15	U Hospital (gall bladder removal)
2014	May 5-8	U Hospital (insulin drip)
2014	July 1-2	U Hospital (DKA)
2014	July 28	U Hospital (Rituxan, anaphylactic shock)
2014	Aug 1-3	U Hospital (endoscopy)
2014	Aug 5	U Hospital (endoscopy, second try)
2014	Aug 21	U Hospital (stent)
2014	Aug 24	U Hospital (mild DKA)
2014	Sept 5	U Hospital (ER, abdominal pain)
2014	Sept 14-25	U Hospital (pancreas transplant)
2014	Sept 26-Oct 1	U Hospital (feeding tube, dehydration)
2014	Oct 2	U Hospital (stent)
2014	Oct 8-15	U Hospital (GJ feeding tube)
2014	Nov 14	U Hospital (ER, vomiting)
2014	Nov 17-20	U Hospital (vomiting, depression)
2014	Nov 27-Dec 2	U Hospital (diarrhea, dehydration)
2014	Dec 4	Her cats move to Peggy to foster

2015	Jan 12	U Hospital (dilation, stent)
2015	Mar 18-19	U Hospital (stent removal)
2015	April 2	U hospital (dilation)
2015	April 9-10	U Hospital (sleep study)
2015	April 21-22	U Hospital (stent)
2015	April 23-24	U Hospital (vomiting, nausea)
2015	May 26-29	U Hospital (tube placement)
2015	June 11-18	U Hospital (stomach issues)
2015	July 17	U Hospital (ER, nausea, enema)
2015	Aug 7-12	U Hospital (liver biopsy, pain)
2015	Aug 16-17	U Hospital (ER, diarrhea and dehydration)
2015	Sept 28-Oct 7	U Hospital (GJ tube, stomach)
2015	Oct 23	U Hospital (ER, pain med)
2015	Oct 27-Nov 4	U hospital (colon, intestine issues)
2015	Nov 12-17	U Hospital (colon issues)
2015	Nov 24	U Hospital (ER, pain, in and out)
2015	Nov 25	U Hospital (pancreas biopsy, in and out)
2015	Dec x-4	U Hospital (stent)
2016	Jan	leave of absence from SPA
2016	Jan 4-13	U Hospital (stent removal, pancreas rejection)

2016	Jan 13	Moved back to dad & Kathy's house
2016	Jan 24-26	U Hospital (high BG, pancreas rejection)
2016	Feb 16-May 19	U Hospital ("failure to thrive")
2016	Feb 18	"Acknowledgement of notice to vacate" apartment
2016	May 16	Bankruptcy hearing (in hospital, later approved)
2016	May 19	to Logan House (group home in Brooklyn Center, Minneapolis suburb)
2016	May 27-June 7	U Hospital (stent problems)
2016	June 10-13	U Hospital (dehydration, bowel obstruction, tachycardia)
2016	June 17	U Hospital (ER, blood pressure)
2016	July 19-29	U Hospital (thin blood, stent)
2016	Nov 2-14	U Hospital (psychiatric ward)
2016	Dec 14-16	U Hospital (fever, vomiting, creatinine level)
2017	Jan 1-Feb 23	U Hospital (intestinal surgery) then Texas Terrace (transitional care facility)
2017	Mar 20	Returned to job at U (SPA) part time
2017	June 12-	U Hospital (stent repositioning)
2017	June 30-July 3	U Hospital (CT scan, nothing wrong)
2017	Aug 2	U Hospital (stent migration)

2017   Oct 5   U Hospital

2017   Oct 16-17   U Hospital (died during surgery)

Part I

Living Life and Ignoring Diabetes: Life at Home and Abroad

Chapter 1

Young Years: Through Middle School

Dad's initial narrative:

As with anyone, Krystin's story begins at birth. Before getting to the story, you should understand that some of the reports and exchanges in the story seem grim, and they were at the time. But Krystin matured and many of the issues identified in the psychologists' evaluations, for example, were addressed or faded as time passed. I am comfortable including even the unpleasant elements of Krystin's life for three reasons. One, if she were writing this as autobiography, she would include them. She was forthright about almost everything in her life. Two, her life turned in positive directions with respect to just about everything related to her personality and behavior, so the negatives you read about here demonstrate just how much she changed as she became an adult. Three, both the good and bad illustrate what a challenge it was to be her parents.

Reviewing all the material I had available, and recalling many of the events, I am even more proud of Krystin than I was before, because she transformed herself between her middle school years and adulthood into a person who many admired and loved.

Parent and Other Writings

Krystin was contrarian from the very beginning: she wouldn't be born. Pat was overdue. It was clear that Krystin was full term, but she declined to come out. I received a call in my office from Pat, perhaps Thursday or Friday October 25 or 26, 1984; she told me that the physicians had determined that they should do a C-section if Krystin wasn't born soon, and they would schedule it for the following Wednesday. To her astonishment, I said, in vigorous terms, "absolutely not!" Pat was taken aback. "Did you look at the calendar," I asked? "If the date is going to be a matter of choice, I do *not* want to her birthday to be Halloween!" Pat hadn't realized that. As it turned out, Krystin finally decided to be born on October 30.

Recollections prepared in 1999 for Krystin's therapists.

1. Pat:

When Krystin was born after a very fast labor and delivery, her 2-minute APGAR was 2 and she was immediately surrounded by a team of medical staff. Her 5-minute APGAR was 8. She improved in those first 10 minutes, but not enough for me to hold her in my arms. They whisked her away to the Preemie Nursery. It was 3 hours after birth before I saw her.

At 4lbs 12oz, she was unable to hold her body temperature to an acceptable level, so she was placed in an incubator. The first time I saw her, she was full of tubes. She remained that way for 7 days.

When I went to the nursery, I was not able to hold her. She needed to stay in her "warming bed." If I looked at her through the glass, I wept, so I stayed away because it was too hard to watch her. She was tube-fed her first 3 days. In the meantime, I expressed milk in the solitude of a separate room. She was getting breast milk, but not directly from me. On her fourth day, she was able to drink from a bottle with a large hole in the nipple. Only then was I able to hold her in my arms and give her my milk via an artificial source. It worked, but this was not what I imagined motherhood to be.

After eight days she was allowed to go home. I took her home, with instructions to keep her little hat on her head and make sure her nursery room was no less than 80 degrees.

Once we were home, I tried to nurse her, but she would only nibble at my nipple and cry because nothing came out. I tried forever to make this work. In frustration, I called the pediatrician and explained the difficulties we were experiencing. He told me at once that I could not let her cry that hard at feeding time. She needed to get calories IN, not burn them off. So I had to quit trying to nurse. Expressing was not pleasurable for me (in fact, it was downright painful), so I decided if I could not nurse her directly and if she was destined to a bottle, she'd have to get by on formula. So that was how we started.

Her first three months were difficult. She went from being an underweight infant to an overweight baby. Suddenly the same pediatrician who once told me to feed her on demand to get her weight up was now telling me she was too fat and needed to be restricted on her formula intake. I was confused and scared.

From birth on, Krystin preferred to be left alone to calm herself. Close contact from us seemed to over-stimulate her and put her into an emotional crisis. At bedtime, we would just lay her down and let her cry for a little bit before she fell asleep. If we held her or walked with her, the crying would continue as long as we held her. But if we put her in her crib, the crying always stopped within a couple minutes. So that's what we did.

We had a lot of problems with Krystin during [her first two years]. She would wake every morning crying. She was always crying. I couldn't deal with the crying. I remember talking to the pediatricians about the constant crying, but don't remember getting any good advice on how to make it stop. The more she cried, the more frustrated and angry I became. The more frustrated and angry I became, the more she cried.

When Krystin was 3, I remember talking to Don (our counselor at the time). I told him that when I'd put Krystin in a time out, she'd leave the spot. He instructed me to put her back there and restart the time. I did, and she'd leave again. A two-minute time out could drag on for 45 minutes. Soon I was sitting on her to make her stay put for her time out. She screamed the whole time.

I remember sending her to her room and she'd come back out. Back to her room and out she'd come. She'd come back to my heels and kick and scream. I didn't know how to deal with that. Don told me that if Krystin wouldn't honor the time out from me, I was to time myself out from Krystin. He told me to put MYSELF in the bathroom and close the door so she couldn't get to me. I remember sitting on the bathroom floor with my head in my hands, sobbing, while she stood outside the bathroom door and kicked and screamed. I really don't remember now what the purpose of all that was. I only remember it didn't seem to be working.

I also remember her crying so much and misbehaving so much that I'd grab her by the arm and drag her down the stairs to the lower level study. I simply needed her to be a distance away from me while she was constantly crying. I'd tell her she could come up when she was done crying. I'd go back upstairs to the kitchen and hear her coming after me crying. I was sure that being consistent in my discipline was critical, so I'd meet her half way and return her to the room where I'd placed her initially. This would go on for an hour or more. I was sure that if I gave in she'd become a spoiled, undisciplined child.

Removing her from me was not always my initial reaction. I'd try to sit with her and calm her, but the more I held her and talked to her, the more hysterical she'd become. I simply did not know what I was supposed to do.

This type of interaction continued for most of her toddler-hood. [In the] fall of 1988 . . . Krystin had just turned 4. Two months later, she was diagnosed with diabetes, on December 22, 1988.

[At this same time] we needed to move and we were preparing a "garbage house" for sale [the home of my great-aunt Inez; more on this in a few pages]. We decided to buy it from the estate, and moved in in February, 1989. The house, however, needed more work than we imagined. Our first four months there were constant cleaning and minor remodeling projects. Krystin, just diagnosed with a chronic illness, was tossed between diabetes education/training and house cleaning. She came to hate the house, at the time, and not want to go there, because she knew we would do nothing but work (although she likes it perfectly well now and has for many years).

In the summer of 1989, Gary's mother was diagnosed with cancer--two months after his great-aunt had died in May. His mother died three months later. As we noted in our 1989 Christmas letter, this was the year from hell for us (December 1988 – September 1989).

We were just getting our lives pulled back together in 1990 (we were finally settled in our own house again, the trauma of family deaths was receding) when I found out I was pregnant again. This was wonderful, because I knew I always wanted Krystin to have a sibling. Unfortunately, I was put on total bed rest at 28 weeks, just one week after Krystin started kindergarten.

It was a two hard months for all of us, but I think more for Krystin, because I was not able to do anything for her. She was not interested in laying on the couch with me. She wanted to be on the go all the time. I, however, was not able to follow her. So she left me behind.

Then came the big blow for her: the birth of Elliott. Right from the start she resented him and was not shy about telling us it was time we took him back.

2. Gary:

From the start, we have to acknowledge that we were never particularly enthusiastic about spending time doing kid activities with the kids when at home, during the normal week. We still aren't. In

Krystin's case, this may have "hurt" her. In Elliott's, it seems not to matter; he amuses himself endlessly. (I have asked him many times what's wrong with his life and what he'd like changed; he always says it's great and he likes things just the way they are. He told me last week that second grade seemed like it was only two or three weeks; it went by really fast because he had a great time.) Krystin was never able to amuse herself. One thing we did was rent A LOT of movies for her when she was young.

I think Krystin's first few years were not particularly happy for her, although the natural process of memory, making gentle that which was not and blurring or blotting out the unpleasant, might not lead her to that same conclusion. Unfortunately, we probably treated her more as a burden than as the gift of a bright and lively little girl, and she may well have sensed that, however inchoately.

There has been, all these years, the interaction of "inattentive parents" and a prickly personality. Even though we have made sporadic attempts to be closer to Krystin, or to "do things" with her, they were not particularly successful. The behavior or interaction pattern that evolved between Krystin and us was one of distance and continued guerilla combat, interrupted by occasional periods of calm and closeness. It may be that her behavior problems stem, at least in part, from this situation at home.

* * *

An aside on Krystin's circumstances immediately after birth. One of her friends, who read an earlier draft of this chapter, commented as follows:

You said Krystin cried constantly from birth to early toddler years, and that human touch would not soothe her. After reading about her entry into the world and how she was not able to be lovingly caressed but immediately whisked away by people who were not her family to be poked and prodded and stuck with needles and tubes, I can imagine that had to have left some type of traumatic imprint on her.

As a teacher, I have seen students who behave a certain way in class, and I can usually tell if they were born early or if they were born with the cord around their neck. I have never read any studies, but it amazes me from what I have seen in my own experience as a teacher how some kids still have lasting behavior that seems to be left over from a reaction to a traumatic birth.

I am completely shocked that Krystin's teachers didn't seem to notice her talent, and it makes me so sad that she wasn't in some kind of Gifted and Talented Program. When kids are GT and they are not put in with kids that are like them, they will usually have failing grades or be so bored with the material that they will fail. She doesn't mention any teacher as having given her support, or any teacher that she had a deep conversation with about her future. Maybe she did and it just wasn't in there, but as an educator it infuriates me that a teacher didn't single her out to try to mentor her.

These comments prompted me to forward them to a friend on the faculty, one of the University's distinguished faculty in child development, to ask about the birth events. She wrote back to me:

Here is what we know. Premature babies often have a narrow range of acceptable stimulation. Too little, they don't arouse, too much, they are overstimulated. For stable babies (who do not have their blood pressure plunge when touched), neonatal massage has proven helpful in stimulating weight gain.

The weight gain issue is a major one that docs are concerned about now. It is pretty common to go from needing to get weight up to overweight.

The pain issue is a real one, and may contribute to the sensitivity to touch. When your daughter was born, the issue of neonatal pain was just beginning to be addressed. Now there is tremendous concern about reducing pain for premies undergoing medical procedures. There is also a much greater sensitivity to getting parents involved in the premie's care and with touch as an important thing for premies.

So, your daughter's need to self-sooth and reduce stimulation makes sense to me.

Even though Krystin was not a premie, she had to be treated like one because of her low birthweight. We can never know the nature or extent of the effect of her having been in an incubator for the first week, but it cannot have been positive.

* * *

January 10, 1989 Letter
[The first few paragraphs of the letter relate that on December 22, 1988, I had spent the entire day having my great-aunt Inez (to whom I had been close all my life) involuntarily admitted to the psychiatric ward of the University of Minnesota hospital, a long, trying day but a story not germane to Krystin's—except that Pat and I ended up buying and moving into the house we moved Inez out of, and it was the house that Krystin grew up in from age four and a half. Pat had taken Krystin to the doctor that same day. The following paragraphs are excerpts from the letter.]

Gary to friends:
That night [December 22]—I was out playing bridge—I called Pat to find out how a doctor's appointment for Krystin had gone and to tell her about Inez. Pat told me that the doctor had made a preliminary diagnosis of diabetes—which just made my day. We had set up an appointment for Krystin because we were bothered by her toilet training problem—she is forever still wetting her pants, at age 4—and wanted to find out if there was some infection or neurological problem.

The urine test showed very high levels of blood sugar. At some point in the next day or so we had Krystin back to the doctor for additional testing. We went up to (my brother) Tracy and Joan's in Wisconsin for Xmas Eve; Joan, who is a Med Tech, did a blood sugar test and the results were not particularly high (just at the top of the normal range). Then on the next Tuesday we took her in because over Christmas Day (Sunday) and Monday she was getting lethargic and mildly feverish (she didn't want to eat and said she'd rather take a nap than go sledding—both of which are drastic behavior changes for her).

After the visit to the doctor Tuesday night, we went to a specialist (in pediatric endocrinology) Wednesday night. During the day on Wednesday I had talked to a faculty friend who is an MD and whose research specialty is diabetes; in a roundabout fashion, one of his colleagues found out about Krystin and called me to ask if we would be willing to have her participate in a study of children who had just been diagnosed as diabetic. I said we'd talk about it and get back to him; then, talking to the pediatric endocrinologist (Dr. [physician]), she said that the research project required a blood sample and if we came immediately out to the clinic that afternoon she would have it drawn; it would also give her the chance to meet Krystin and us. So Wednesday afternoon we went trooping out to the clinic.

While at the clinic, [physician] lent us this little electronic/computerized gadget that is used to check blood sugar levels. We checked Krystin's blood sugar levels that Wednesday night and then again Thursday morning. The blood sugar—glucose, actually—levels for a normal individual range from 60 to 100. Krystin's Wednesday night was 262; Thursday morning it was 257. [I'd write this a little differently today: "levels for a person who does not have diabetes. . . ." "In the U.S., blood sugar is normally measured in milligrams of glucose per deciliter of blood (mg/dl). A milligram is very little, about 0.00018 of a teaspoon. A deciliter is about 3 1/3 ounces." https://www.diabetesselfmanagement.com/ A high number indicates glucose levels that are doing damage to tiny blood vessels in the eyes, organs, and extremities. The normal range for someone without diabetes is 60-140, with the high number expected after a meal. For people with diabetes, the desirable range is 80-180, which must be achieved with the injection of insulin in some fashion.] I phoned those numbers in to [physician]'s nurse; within 30 seconds of hanging up the phone [physician] called back and said she wanted Krystin in her office within an hour because the kid would go into shock if she didn't get insulin. So in we went Thursday morning, gave her insulin, and then spent the next five hours there meeting with the doctor and other staff members to learn about diabetes.

Krystin appears to be very sensitive to insulin; her blood sugar levels dropped dramatically (from 257 to about 130) after a dose that was $1/8^{th}$ to $1/10^{th}$ as much as would be administered to someone her weight who is a diagnosed diabetic. Since all seemed to be developing as a case of the disease, however, we bought syringes, insulin, a little spring-loaded doohickey that pricks your finger to draw blood, the chemical strips, and our own blood-testing device. We were told that henceforth, for at least the foreseeable future, we have to test Krystin's blood four times a day.

Back to the doctor on Friday morning of that week—now we're up to December 30—(supposedly a holiday for us) to meet again with the doctor, more evaluation, and more learning. By Friday night her glucose level had climbed to 303; we talked to the doctor, who told us to administer a small dose of insulin. We did, and the blood sugar level dropped back down again.

Through the next Wednesday we did not have to administer insulin again. A couple of times her glucose levels went over 200—but never near 300 again—but most of the time ranged from 75 to 175. Those were all acceptable numbers, as far as the doctor is concerned; there was nothing threatening about them.

By the end of New Year's weekend—and long before that—Pat and I were psychologically and emotionally weary to the point of exhaustion. [During this same time we had been cleaning out Inez's house and threw out about 20 lawn bags of garbage.] It didn't help to have the doctor tell us, the Friday before New Year's, that most parents who are told their child has diabetes go through a mourning or grieving process—they have lost a child. She said that the carefree and unrestrained little girl we had before was gone forever; for the rest of her life she must exercise very careful control over her diet and exercise and must daily test her blood levels to be sure she is OK. Both Pat and I have, over the past couple of weeks, been in tears on a couple of occasions. I almost burst into tears at our friends Joe and Genie Dixon's annual New Year's Eve dinner when I was telling those present about all this. (Fortunately, I didn't.) [I thought at the time, and have thought ever since, that that was a dreadful thing for a physician to say to parents about a child diagnosed with diabetes. The important contents of the message could have been conveyed in a far more graceful and considerate fashion.]

For the last week or so Krystin's blood sugar levels have been all over the place. Yesterday was the worst yet—by late afternoon she was up to 398, or between 6 and 7 times as high as normal. We have been giving her insulin now, off and on, although part of the time it seems as though the insulin causes her glucose levels to go up rather than down. Tomorrow we start a new regimen, which combines short-term impact insulin (2-3 hours) with a long-term impact insulin (8-10 hours) to try to control these wildly gyrating numbers. For the most part it isn't yet troublesome—at least to [physician]—because the damage from diabetes is over the long haul. (High levels of blood sugar eventually wear down and wear out the blood vessels in the eyes and the kidneys and the extremities, but this doesn't happen over the course of a week or two.)

We've no idea how this developed. [Physician] said it is probably about 2 parts genetic predisposition and 3 parts environmental insult—the weakness was there, and then an otherwise innocuous virus attacked the pancreas, apparently inexorably wiping out Krystin's ability to produce insulin. (And without insulin, we have learned, your body cells are unable to absorb the sugar—food they need—in your blood, which is why it spills out into the urine and remains in the bloodstream.) There is no history of diabetes in either Pat's or my family back for at least four generations that we know of, so where the genetic weakness arose is a complete mystery.

The one person who has actually made this more bearable than might otherwise be the case is Krystin herself—she has reacted like a little trooper. Although at first she cried a lot and resisted every time we had to prick her finger to draw blood to test the glucose levels, in the past couple of weeks she has gotten into the pattern of getting out the glucometer, setting up the stuff we need, and choosing which finger she wants to use. At the last minute she sometimes still pulls back from the thing, but she pretty much does it without fuss now—then afterwards she gets to hold the cotton ball and put on a bandaid (which she usually pulls off within an hour or so). Despite the fact that we have been forced to basically make her life miserable, compared to three weeks ago, she's handling it very well. She also tells the teachers at her daycare center that she can't things with sugar in them, and goes off quite proudly to the office to have the director do her blood test before lunch (she has to be tested before every meal and just before bedtime).

Unfortunately, Pat and I have to deal with the long-term consequences. As my M.D. friend said, one can be guardedly optimistic about the possibilities in the future, but it is nonetheless a nasty, nasty disease that one cannot be positive about. As I said, eventually diabetes can attack the eyes and the kidneys. The eyes, he told me, can be fixed—if she has a good ophthalmological exam every year, they can immediately arrest any eye deterioration at the point it is detected. The kidneys, however, are a different problem; about 20-25% of diabetics have kidney failure, and at the present state of knowledge they have no idea why those who have it do—there is nothing to predict kidney failure. Kidney transplants, he said, are a much more benign operation than they were 20 years ago—but they still require lifetime reliance on an immunosuppressant (so the body won't reject the transplanted kidney)—and those immunosuppressants, such as prednisone and cyclosporine, are steroids and they have terrible side effects. [Physician] also told us we could consider alternate day administration of prednisone now, because it has been shown to have a repressive effect on the evolution of diabetes in children and with substantially reduced side effects, but we're going to wait on that because the drug is otherwise so toxic.

Pat commented to me last Friday that she was having problems at work if she was confronted with any intellectual challenge greater than tying her shoes—I know exactly how she feels because I feel the same way.

July 8, 1992 Letter
Dad to Krystin [Written before I went in for spinal column surgery, just in case anything happened. I am not certain that Krystin ever saw this letter; it was intended to be one that I added to over the years—but I only added two more segments in September, 1992—and that I then would give to her when she was old enough to appreciate it. It wasn't written at a level that a 7-year-old would understand.]

I have great hopes for you as you get older. Even though you are now sometimes difficult to deal with--because you are so accursedly independent-minded--I nonetheless love you very, very much and believe that you are an extremely bright girl who has the potential to go far.

My one regret about you and your mother and me is that we never spent enough time with you when you were very small. This is one of those chicken-and-egg questions (which came first?), though, for which I have no answer. You were a tough baby to love--you didn't like to be held and resisted warm, fuzzy attention--but we also tended to ignore you too much in favor of our own activities.

I have been hoping all along that we could, as you get older, dissolve some of the distance that has grown up between you and your mother and me. Thus far I haven't seen that happen much, but you're also too young to understand the issues, at least on an intellectual level. I do think, however, that as we have done things together recently, it's been a little easier to have fun with you--and for you to have fun. At least I hope so, and I try for that.

One of the problems your mother and I have had all along is that we are not REALLY all that fond of babies and kids. In some ways your mother is more tolerant (she's better able to play games and color with you than I) and in some ways I'm more tolerant (I demand less of you, and let you get away with more). I now realize that my folks were the same way (I don't know about [your mother's parents]. Actually, I've gotten more attached to you kids as I've gotten older--but I've also come to like you more as you've gotten older, just because you're now more of a little human being who can reason and understand things.

September 2, 1992
    Your mother and I talked recently about your grandparents and how little they are affectionate or involved with their grandchildren--they are not at all like the ideal image of grandma and grandpa.
    One of your most striking characteristics--and this has been true for a couple of years--is your utter inability to amuse yourself and your constant need to have someone to play with. You are constantly calling up friends or going outside to find somebody. I can't tell if that's because your mother and I tend not to do a lot of stuff with you or if it's because you just want something to do every waking moment.
    Sometimes I think your mom and I spend too much time on house cleaning and house maintenance tasks (painting, lawn-mowing, etc.) and not enough time with you and Elliott. Other times, though, I think we could not possibly spend enough time with you--no matter how much, as soon as we weren't, you'd be looking for someone to play with. Most of the time, when you ask if you can call someone, we just say "I don't care." (I have come to think we say "I don't care" to far too much of what you ask of us--we probably seem to be telling you we aren't interested in what you do. It isn't true, but we tend to spend time on our activities, rather than yours, and we are sometimes frustrated by your constant need for activities. On the other hand, you do sometimes go upstairs and watch movies.)

September 29, 1992
    Seems like in the last few weeks you have not cared for my company; I'm not sure why, and you aren't saying anything. Perhaps I imagine things. But I do feel that I haven't done much with you lately, so I told your mother that you and I are going out to do something tonight.
    You had Kristen Kramer up to the lake with you last weekend, when Ann and Denise also came up, and we closed it up. Your mother and I have very much enjoyed going up there, but you have not--because often you are bored. Elliott, of course, doesn't care, because he doesn't care where he is any of the time. At least not yet. I told you last night that next year you could have friends up more often.
    I often think that you might come to hate your little brother, because it seems like a lot of the time we yell at you for making him

upset or making him start crying--sometimes even when it isn't your fault. But you don't seem to be holding it against him, and you really do try to treat him as nicely as you can. Sometimes you just don't know how to play with him, however--that may be a skill that comes, if ever, only when one is older.

July 1994 Psychologist's report
[Krystin was 9 years, 9 months old and had completed 3rd grade. We brought her in for psychological testing because of "ongoing behavior management concerns. A more comprehensive evaluation was undertaken at this time because of recent escalation in both the frequency and seriousness of behavior concerns." The psychologist had Krystin complete a number of tests, as did Pat and I. Excerpts from the report follow.]

I had Krystin complete the Child Depression Inventory. Her score on this inventory was 7, which is well within the normal range.

Krystin endorsed very few items (3) on the Child Depression Inventory, and her scores were well below the clinical average . . . Krystin reported moderate to high self-concept in all areas.

Krystin scored at or above grade level in all academic areas . . . except the humanities area, where she scored approximately one grade below grade level. Despite her slow reading, her basic reading skills . . . were excellent, and two or more years above grade level on average.

Krystin's responses on the Roberts Apperception Test (where the task is to make up a dramatic story about a series of pictures) reflected strong skills in identification of problem situations, but with relatively weak ability to solve problem situations. The primary affect portrayed by the characters in the stories was anxiety (fear, self doubt, and guilt), and to a lesser extent, but still clinically significant, anger and depression. Story themes included concerns about parental divorce, the importance of peer relationships, the mother figure's offering and the child's ability to receive warmth and support, and a father figure that is more imposing and emotionally distant.

While Krystin came willingly to testing, and fulfilled all requests, she was defensive, emotionally distant, and it was more difficult to establish a personal connection with her than is typical of most children her age. This is consistent with the parents' description of Krystin and indicates that helping parents to develop ways to have positive interactions with Krystin even though she is not a demonstrative child, will be an important therapeutic issue.

Krystin is a bright girl with academic achievement at or above her current grade level. There is no reason to suspect that learning disabilities are a contributing factor to her current behavior problems.

Krystin has a strong need to appear good. This is evidenced by her high self ratings on the Self Perception Profile. . . . In contrast, feelings Krystin expressed . . . include a predominant emotion of anxiety, and to a lesser extent, anger and depression. This would indicate that Krystin feels self-doubt, guilt, and shame over misdeeds, but professes that she is blameless or doesn't care as a defense.

Finally, Krystin's anti-social acts . . . are not fully explained by the assessment data . . . It is possible that Krystin generally exerts a great deal of effort to control her behavior, but that this control is punctuated by episodes of significant lack of control.

Summer 1995 Camp counselor report, summer YMCA camp

Krystin was always willing to share herself and her ideas with the group. It was a great help on the first day when she was eager to share her stories. Krystin was great, and it was fun to see her work well with the other girls in the cabin and at camp. Krystin was a joy to have in the cabin and we were very impressed at how well she handled her health and were very proud and excited to have her in our cabin.

Krystin's Writings

Late 2006
[Krystin labeled this as a draft of her life story; this is the first part of her narrative.]

October 30, 1984. I was born in Minneapolis, MN at 7:21 a.m. Although I was not premature, I was considered a premie because I was so small. I think I had a pretty normal childhood. We moved 2 times, the last time to my current home in south Minneapolis in the perfect neighborhood.

In 1988, right after my 4th birthday, I was diagnosed with diabetes. I don't remember the early years of my diabetes, but I know that from early on I insisted on doing my own shots. My parents would draw up the insulin, but I wouldn't let anyone else poke me with a needle. If it hurt, I'd be less likely to kick myself in the face than if my parents had done it and I got to kick them—I'm sure they appreciated it as well.

On November 3, 1990, when I was 6, my brother Elliott was born. I was not happy about this. I had been an only child thus far in my life, and who was he to change that? So he and I got off to a bad start. When I was 8 years old, I started both ice hockey and gymnastics. After not very long, I dropped gymnastics and focused on hockey. Too much leotard and not enough aggression for me. I played for the Minneapolis Park and Recreation board, and we played against other park teams in the city. I also started playing soccer not long after, with the same girls that I played hockey with in the winter, including my best friend Christine [Lenzen]. Whom I actually met at daycare back when we were 2.

The 2 of us were troublemakers. We always had to be separated at naptime at daycare because we couldn't keep quiet, we ran through houses naked covered in dirt, and ran around poking holes in waterbeds with tacks. We were 2 of a kind.

We stopped playing hockey and soccer for park board around age 12, but I continued playing soccer into high school.

At a young age I developed a bad habit: stealing. Whether it was money or things, it didn't matter. I don't know why I did it. It's not like I needed the money, and it's not like I needed the object, it was more [that] I wanted it. I stole from my parents. From other family. From friends, and from friend's [sic] parents. Even from people at school. And it is this that changed my life. It was in 6th grade, which then was still elementary school. Prior to this time, I was a very different person. I was the kind of person I wish that I could be again. I was extraverted, energetic, a social butterfly, a rebel, a wild child. I was fun, and I had a lot of friends. But I was different. I was also "nerdy." I had the big glasses, the "unstylish" baggy clothes, the not-yet-developing-physically appearance. And when I got caught in 6th grade with a stolen item from a classmate, my other classmates took the opportunity and ran with it. I was teased, made fun of, called names, and all-around emotionally stomped on. I was beginning to believe that I had no worth, that I was a waste of space on this earth. I hated myself, and I thought everyone hated me. I became reserved, withdrawn, quiet, and shy. Why would anyone wanna socialize with and be friends with me? This only continued into 7th and 8th grade, because many of the kids in my class in 6th grade went to the same middle school, and they were more than willing to share with everyone else all the gossip on me. Now I began getting crap from new kids as well. I made a couple friends though, a couple of whom I am still friends with today. Friends who like me for me and didn't let the teasing influence their opinion of me.

I hated middle school. They were the worst 2 years of my life. I never told my parents or anyone about all this until later, after I was in high school. I was so glad when middle school was over and I entered high school. I loved high school. Everyone seemed to have matured, it was way less clique-y, and best of all, a majority of my classmates from middle school went to a different high school. I continued playing soccer for my school freshman and sophomore year, but stopped after that. I knew I loved to play but wasn't the most exceptional player, and hated to practice, so I ended my soccer career. I tried out for a city hockey team my freshman year, but was the worst one at the tryouts because I hadn't played in a couple years. So on the first day of tryouts, which also happened to be my birthday, at break time I faked a migraine and called my parents and told them I was ready to go. So we went out to dinner.

During the first couple years of high school I made many new friends, and I think my self confidence and self esteem even went up a little, since I no longer had to put up with verbal abuse on a daily basis. But although I wasn't getting it [the abuse] at all any more, it still stuck with me in my mind, and still does to this day. I will never be able to go back to being the kind of person I was before because I was just emotionally damaged too much.

My junior year I decided to try the insulin pump, a small device a little bigger than a pager that had a tube coming out of it, going into me somewhere on my body (which I would change every few days) and administered insulin slowly 24 hours a day. It was much easier and more efficient than doing shots, but I hated it. It would beep in the middle of class, due to being low on insulin or a kink in the tubing, and I hated having something connected to me and in me 24/7. It was basically like a permanent IV. Ick. So I stopped wearing it, sometimes for days at a time. At school it would sit in my locker. This is how my eating disorder started. Over a period of months of not getting a sufficient amount of insulin, I noticed that I was still eating whatever I wanted and in whatever quantity, but my weight wasn't going up. Actually, it was doing down. Not having insulin in my body meant nothing to break down the sugars in food and get rid of the bad stuff and keep the good nutrients. So although I was eating (and quite a lot actually), I was starving my body because it would all go in and right through and out. I started dropping pounds quickly. And I liked the way I looked, because all the other girls in my class (it seemed) were thin with flat stomachs and lean legs, and with the right clothes I could pretend that underneath them I could look like that too. I would look like the kind of girl that wouldn't have been teased and made fun of in middle school. Now if only I could go back to all those jerks and say "ha ha, look at me now." But even though I couldn't, I felt better about myself. I continued this pattern through high school.

January 2014 The Rope
[Krystin wrote a long summary of her life. The following 12 paragraphs are an excerpt from "The Rope," that narrative. The title is taken from a short story she wrote for an 11th grade creative writing class.]

I had always been a bed/clothes wetter as a child. While in preschool, my mom would come home with two or three bundles of wet shorts/underwear almost every day. When I was four, my mom was reading a book to me on our living room couch, and when I got up at the end of the story, the couch was soaked. She was both sad and a little angry. The bathroom was right there, 20 feet away. Why hadn't I gotten up and gone? My parents had been seeing a therapist, and during one visit my mom brought up my bed/clothes wetting issue, and inquired if this was another power struggle of mine. The therapist said that it was something we'd work on, but in the meantime, it would perhaps be a good idea to take me in to be checked out to make sure there wasn't something medically wrong, like a defective bladder or something. When she took me in, my urine showed high levels of sugar.

In December of 1988, at the age of four, I was diagnosed with type 1 diabetes. December 21, to be exact. Aside from the bed/clothes wetting, I hadn't shown any signs or symptoms of diabetes. It was because of the therapist's recommendation to take me in that my diabetes was discovered. Most kids get sicker and sicker and sicker and end up going to the hospital, but my parents learned of it long before it got to that point. Call it dumb luck, if you will, that it was discovered before I started showing any severe symptoms. It turns out that many kids were diagnosed with diabetes towards the end of 1988. My endocrinologist at the time said she's had more kids diagnosed with diabetes at the end of that year than she had ever seen in her whole career. A particular flu strain that was going around that year looked very similar to the pancreatic cells. When my white blood cell armies went in to kill off the flu bug, they couldn't tell the flu cells from my pancreatic cells, and ended up killing both. Either many kids, including myself, had very confused white blood cells, or it was a very clever flu strain.

We had plans to go to my aunt and uncle's house in Wisconsin for Christmas. My doctors at the time said absolutely not, but my aunt convinced them that I would be taken to the Rice Lake Clinic (where my aunt worked) if I showed any signs of distress. The docs agreed, and so we went. My aunt had to hide all the Christmas candy and cookies out on the porch so that I wouldn't be tempted to eat them.

All of the responsibility of caring for me and my diabetes was on my parents, so for many years it was never an inconvenience for me. When I was first diagnosed, my parents had to go to educational classes for three hours, three days a week. My mom had just started a new job that September, and three months later was already having to ask for time off to take the diabetes education classes. Luckily her boss told her not to worry about it; they would figure out vacation/sick time later. My parents had to learn how to be my nurse, my nutritionist, my therapist, my guardian angel, and my travel advisor. During the lessons on how to inject insulin, my mom would inject saline injections into an orange, and then into her leg. My dad was too scared to do it on himself. It was a lot for them to absorb, but it had to be done.

Even if my parents were doing all the work, it was still more of a struggle for me than it was for them, because they had to say "no" so much. In 1988, insulins were not as flexible as they are in recent years. I would receive a dose of long-acting insulin in the morning, and it would do its own thing on its own timeline, sometimes 7-10 hours later. It was hard to know, at 8am, what would be happening at 4pm.

In elementary school, at the beginning of each school year the school nurse, my mom, and I would give a small presentation to my class about diabetes. They got to see me do a blood test, draw up my insulin into a syringe, and show them how I would give myself a shot. Everyone thought it was so cool, and there were arguments over who got to go to the nurse's office with me before lunch. It wasn't every day that a classmate got to accompany me to the nurse, so when a day came that the teacher would allow it, everyone wanted to go and watch me poke my finger. To a 3rd grader, it was pretty fascinating.

Up through middle school, my parents did most of the work for me at home. When it was time to do a blood stick or take an insulin injection, they got my monitor and syringe ready and all I had to do was be there to do it. Same with at school: I went to the nurse every day before lunch to do a blood test and take insulin. Both at home and at school, therefore, I had someone holding me accountable and monitoring all my blood tests and my injections. Middle school is where everything changed.

Sixth grade (which, at that time, was the last year of elementary school) was a really bad year for me. Kindergarten - 5th grade were great, as far as I can remember. I had lots of friends, I was an extrovert, a social butterfly, unlimited self-esteem and total confidence in myself and everything I did. Then in 6th grade everything changed. I became your classic example of a victim of bullying. Not physically, but mentally. Emotionally. It's hard to imagine that in 6th grade there would be such a thing as the cool and popular kids, but there were. They teased me, made fun of me, made jokes at my expense. I was a very late bloomer in life, so even in 6th grade I still didn't brush my hair, I had dorky glasses, I wore the same clothes for probably 3 or so days in a row. It was really easy to target in on me as the one to bully.

During that year, the person I was disappeared, and I became more of an introvert, withdrawn, self-conscious, and had no self-esteem or confidence at all. I was afraid that anything I said or did I would be judged for or made fun of for. Since a handful of my 6th grade classmates ended up going to the same middle school, that teasing and bullying followed me. I wasn't made fun of for my diabetes, but my diabetes was no longer cool. In fact, I think most of my classmates, aside from those whom I was friends with, didn't even know I was diabetic. I didn't flaunt it like I used to, and the fact that it no longer brought me positive attention made me start to resent it.

7th and 8th grade were the worst years of my life. Suddenly new classmates who hadn't even gone to elementary school with me were teasing me. I did anything and everything to avoid attention being drawn to me. I still went to the nurse every day before lunch, but classmates were no longer allowed to join me. I was friends with a lot of the popular kids, but I wasn't popular. I would sit with them at lunch, but didn't participate much in conversation. I knew they were talking about me and teasing me behind my back; it was only a brave few who actually teased me to my face.

Beginning with my teen years, I was not very good at taking care of myself. The defiance I showed as a kid began to transfer over into my diabetes care. If there were a Diabetics Anonymous group for people with diabetes who fail to make peace with and acknowledge their illness, I would be the head honcho; a fact that I am not proud of.

1999 sometime during the school year
[These notes were written by Krystin.]

WHY SCHOOL SUCKS
-- I'm not popular
-- I'm diabetic
-- I have glasses
-- Whatever clothes are in style I don't have
-- I'm not a big extravert at school so I don't talk out much
-- I sit by myself at lunch
-- I'm not invited to any parties
-- I have no friends at school
-- Someone has spread rumors about me so no one wants to hang out with me

Transition into High School

January 20, 1999 Email
Dad to Krystin:
Dear Krystin,
There is a hard lesson for you in what I need to tell you. I hope you will learn it, but I am afraid you may choose not to. You do need to pay attention, however.

I spoke with Mr. Gahm at Anwatin today. He looked at your grades for this year and last year and said there was no possibility you would be admitted to the liberal arts program at South. He is sending me a copy of your grades.

I think you have no alternative, now, to the comprehensive program at Roosevelt. You remember the woman at South said that education gives people more choices. The reverse is also true: a lack of education (or a lack of performance in education) will take away choices. This is what has happened now. You have lost a choice, and must accept Roosevelt.

I worry that you think only about the immediate present, and almost never about your future. You spend much time on your TV shows, on chat lines, on your clothes and hair, talking with friends, watching movies--all things that are of <u>very little importance</u> in the long run of your life.

The <u>most important</u> thing to the future of your life, your education, you choose to pay very little attention to, and you choose to do as little as you can get away with. You talk about going to an Ivy League college, or a selective private college in Minnesota, but you are not putting in the effort that will get you into a third-rate community college. You would not be admitted to the University of Minnesota with your grades.

<u>You have done nothing so far that will affect your college plans.</u> Colleges do not look at grades before high school. Going to Roosevelt and doing well will get you into any college you want to go to. But if you continue to pay so little attention to your studies, then you will have far fewer choices in college than you will if you do well.

I should point out one other thing. You have also talked about marrying someone who is going to do well. You probably will not meet that person until you are in college. (Or at least I hope you don't.) Guess where the best and the brightest boys go to college. It's the University and the private colleges and such places. If you want to meet someone who is going to be successful, you have to be able to put yourself in a place to meet them. Going to a mediocre community or other kind of college will not do that.

I'm sorry that you will be in this position, and I am sorry I have to tell you this. But maybe, for the next 4 years, you can get yourself on track and get things really going well. This will take an effort on your part, and a clear decision (by you) that this is what you are going to do. If you don't want to do that, it is up to you.

Love you.

February 15, 1999 Email [a series of exchanges]
Krystin to dad:
Hey Dad-

How is work going? I am VERY bored today, since I have no money and I can't drive. I wanted to come to work with you today. You could've just put Elliott at a friend's house or something. It is so boring here. . . . Are we doing anything tonight? We should after a long boring day stuck here in the house with nothing to do. We should go to the mall or something. Like to Camp Snoopy or something. It can be a Valentine's gift to Elliott and me. What time are you going to be home?

Love, Krystin
Dad to Krystin:
Krystin:

About tonight, I think you better focus on your homework.

I have been thinking a lot about the letter I prepared to send to South. I do not believe I can send it. The grades you received the 2nd quarter basically wiped out the argument I was making in the letter. I said that you didn't do well last spring because you had high blood sugars. Dr. [physician] agreed, and she also wrote a letter for you. I will not send a letter making an argument that I do not believe and that is not supported by the fact. I think that if you had had good grades the 2nd period—as good as you did last fall—then I probably could have made a strong argument to get you into the liberal arts program. That is no longer possible.

In your most recent grades, in a couple of classes it says you have "missing assignments." There is simply no excuse for that. I can't say that that is caused by diabetes. And you said you didn't know what grades you were getting in your course. If getting into South was all that important to you, and I were you, I would have been making VERY SURE all along this year that I was getting good grades. Since you didn't seem to care enough to monitor your own performance, I can only assume that you really don't care that much about getting into South.

You remember how the woman who runs the liberal arts program at South said that education gives you more choices? The opposite is also true: NOT getting an education (which is what low grades are) means you have FEWER choices. In this case, I am very sorry that you have eliminated choices you might have had. . . . [several more paragraphs]

Krystin to dad:
   Thanks a lot for ruining my day. How do you know I'm not trying my hardest in school? I have been trying my hardest, and maybe I'm not as smart as you think I am, and maybe I can't do as well as you THINK I can. I am trying as hard as I can in school. All you really care about is my school work and how well I'm going to do in life, and what college and high school I'm going to. That's all you're concerned about! You've never asked me if I'm trying my hardest, and I don't think you understand that I am! I mean, maybe I wasn't meant to be in IB. And like I told mommy, I have been doing homework for like 2 hours already today, and I will prove it to you when you come home today. I'll see you tonight.

Dad to Krystin:
   Thanks a lot for ruining my day. How do you know I'm not trying my hardest in school? Missing assignments is not trying your hardest.
   I have been trying my hardest, and maybe I'm not as smart as you think I am, and maybe I can't do as well as you THINK I can. Krystin, you have already DEMONSTRATED that you can do very well. All I have to do is look at your fall grades for the past two years!
   I am trying as hard as I can in school. All you really care about is my school work and how well I'm going to do in life That last part is absolutely true—that is what ALL parents who love their children mostly care about.
   and what college and high school I'm going to. I only care about this because I know how well you want to do in life, and how well I want you to do in life, and if you muck things up too much in high school, then things will be a lot harder for you. I'd rather not see that happen.
   and like I told mommy, I have been doing homework for like 2 hours already today, and I will prove it to you when you come home today. That's VERY, VERY good, Krystin, and I'm proud of you.
   Love you, Dad

Dad to Krystin
[responding to a missing response to the preceding email]:
   And maybe you should be caring about more than just my grades. Maybe you should also care about me, I do. One way I do is by caring about how you do in school.
   everyone's grades are dropping, except those that don't have a life and spend 5 hours a night studying! . . . I can't handle that! I am willing to work on homework for 1-2 hours a night, If you did that, and extra when you have projects due, then you should be able to do fine. (And by the way, I know perfectly well that you're SMART enough to do well—remember me? I know you pretty well. I don't believe you have received any homework that you could not handle, with a little concentrated attention. Your school does not give out work that's too hard for you to do. You can make that argument, but I'm going to flatly disagree.)
   but I also have an outside life, and I don't want to spend the rest of my schooling life studying 24 hours a day! Krystin, I don't disagree. What I was telling you is that your "outside life" has been getting more attention than your academic life. Or so it appears.
   At least not until college, or next year. No. These habits are not suddenly changed on a whim. You need to be starting them now—and working to where you need to be for high school.
   have been trying as hard as I can, and I want you to understand that! I wish I could believe that.
   And the only reason I may have missing assignments is because either the teacher loses them, which does happen, [or] I forget to put my name on it and it's in the no-name pile, These problems you should be able to fix, quickly.
   or the work was too hard for me and it was too hard to do! I know you're going to say I should've come to you, and I don't know why I didn't, but those are the only reasons! Because it's too hard. Like I said, I just don't believe this. If you were a low IQ kid, who was having a hard time reading and writing, I'd be understanding. But you're not. Anybody who can send me the kinds of emails you've just been sending me today CERTAINLY has the ability to handle 8th grade in Mpls Public Schools and do very well at it. . . .

Dad to Krystin:
   May I show copies of all these emails between you and me to Nicole? She might be able to help you think about this stuff, too, and she's seen you work on homework.
Krystin to dad:
   Yes, you have my permission to show them to Nicole. We've been e-mailing back and forth today I've told her most of this, but there's probably stuff in the emails she doesn't know about, so yes you can show them to her. It will probably be good for her to see them anyway. She would be a good counselor. Tell her she's ½ the reason I'm feeling better, and if you want, you can tell her she should know what the other reason is, if she read my most recent email. Are you coming home before you go play bridge? I was just wondering, sometimes you do and sometimes you don't. Well either way, I'll see you tonight-
Krystin

p.s. After 3 hours, I am done with my homework. happy?

Dad to Krystin:
   She has them. . . .
   p.s. After three hours, I am done with my homework. happy?
If it's done, and done WELL, then yes, I'm happy. Congratulations. I'll give you your money for watching Elliott when I get home. Love you.

Krystin to dad:
. . .
p.s. Of course I did my homework well! See what I mean? I did my best, and that should be good enough.

February 23, 1999 Letter
[asking that Krystin be admitted to the Open program despite erratic academic performance in middle school; the letter noted the nexus between blood glucose levels and academic performance, and the fact that glucose levels fluctuate widely during the onset of puberty. Her grades were very good in fall of 1997 and again fall of 1998 but then dropped significantly.]

Gary to counselor at South High School [excerpt]:
   There is a significant psycho-social element to our request. Krystin very much enjoyed school in grades K-6; she made friends

with whom she remains in contact, and she did well academically. She also made friends playing ice hockey (which she wants to continue to play). We picked Anwatin Middle School for Krystin (with her consent) because we believed it had the best curriculum. . . . The experience has not been wholly positive, although through no fault of the Anwatin staff. Krystin is far from all her friends, and has not had an easy time making new friends at Anwatin. In combination with the fact that she is "different" because of her diabetes (and "different," as I am sure you know, in teenage girls is akin to death), her self-confidence and self-image have declined. She is desperate to once again be in a school setting with the friends she has known, friends who do not think anything about her diabetes. Those friends are all selecting South—and have the grades to be admitted. In my judgment, Krystin needs to be where she not only has friends who treat her as such without regard to her condition, but also where she has friends with whom she can study and work on projects and collaborate in academic pursuits.

A final note on this chapter. Even though it presents a gloomy and depressing picture, there were also many, many good times with Krystin when she was growing up (as the photographs in the last chapter illustrate). We cheered her and her teams in hockey and soccer (and brought her to countless practices), we had birthday and other parties, we read books together, we took her to playgrounds, we traveled with her, and we spent many hours in activities together. It was sometimes a troubled childhood—but it also had weeks and days and hours of joy and fun.

South High School admitted Krystin to the Open program.

Chapter 2

High School Years

[The first entry in this chapter predates Krystin's graduation from high school. It records the trouble we were having with stealing and other behavioral issues as she finished middle school.]

March 8, 1999 Fax to therapists from Gary and Pat

Approx Age	Activity
Birth-5	Woke every morning crying. Would never stay in crib/bed and do "self" play.
3-4	Stole small items from daycare
5	Stole item from store; we made her return it, pay for it, and apologize
6-7	Would steal items from around our home and lie about it. Always had unfamiliar items in her room; declared that her friends "gave them" to her.
7-8	We started getting calls from other parents and relatives that "things/$" were missing from their homes after Krystin had been there.
8	Stole $100 bill from a friend's dad. Made her return it and apologize.
9	Stole engagement ring from friend's mom. Made her return it and apologize.
10	Stole money from 3 male cousins at week long family reunion with Pat's family. They all confronted her and she returned the money. By end of week, she stole from them again. Krystin saw Pat totally traumatized. She never said a thing.
11	Made a very lengthy obscene phone call to friend's mother. Very sexual in nature. Continues to steal $ from brother and parents.
11-12	Stole a total of about 30 Beanie Babies from friend and

	4 stores at the Mall of America. Returned the 13 or so to the friend, and the dad (a lawyer) took her aside and explained the wrongs of stealing. Returned the rest to the 4 stores at the MOA. Made her return them, pay for them, and apologize. She promised never to do that again.
12 items	Continues to steal $ from parents and brother. Has in her room that she cannot show receipts for; swears she "bought" the stuff. We cannot allow her to babysit outside our home because we know she'll steal from them as well. When asked by mothers why she doesn't babysit, she blames it on Pat, stating that "my mother won't let me."
13	Got a call from [ ] that items were missing from their home after we visited. We found them in her room. Confronted her to no avail.
14 announces	Steals $ and mother's gold necklace and then she "got it from a boyfriend." Hundreds of $s in charges turn up on the VISA and Pat's TCF Bank Card from Internet usage (for web site access and the such). Pat's wallet has not been stolen and neither Pat nor Gary have ever put credit card/bank card numbers out on the Internet, so it seems odd that someone (other than someone within the home) could have access to both account numbers simultaneously. Krystin denies all charges, despite the fact that she is warned that the VISA people are on the phone and will begin investigations at our signal. We give the approval for investigation. No findings to date.

General Observations
(These observations include things we've heard from counselors over the years.)

Krystin:
-- shows no remorse
-- is much more "impulsive" than the norm, and much less "reflective" than the norm.

-- has a hard time making friends/nurturing friendships. [As her later life demonstrated, the lack of ability to make friends and nurture friendships at age 14 was replaced by an outgoing, gregarious woman who had a wide and also deep circle of friends.] For example, she currently has 2 friends: Christine, whom she has known since age 2 at daycare, and Erin, whom she met in 3rd grade. On her 14th birthday, she invited 7 girls to her party. No one came except Christine. . . .
-- can't nurture relationships.
-- thinks others are "mean" to her.
-- is extremely sensitive to animals that are suffering. [This sensitivity to/affection for animals showed up dozens of times in her Facebook posts about animals (not all of which are included in this volume) and in her time volunteered for the Animal Humane Society.]
-- does not make the connection between negative response from peers and her negative treatment towards them.
-- believes that everything is always someone else's fault.
-- has very low self esteem; has become shy and withdrawn, has no confidence, while in the past she was quite confident and the life of the party.
-- wants to be the best (at sports and in school) but resists practice/study.
-- lies to our face (and gets angry over the fact that we don't believe her) on issues even when she's caught red-handed.
-- as an infant always "pushed away" from human contact. This was noted by her maternal grandmother and maternal aunt within her first month of life.
-- displays the behavior of a sociopath.
-- simply cannot control her negative behavior.
-- has a family history of depression.

What We Need
[help, fast; testing; put her on an antidepressant for a trial period; therapy frequently]

Where We Are
    After 14 years and continued bouts of counseling to address the same issues, we have determined that Krystin: [is a thief, liar, can't handle relationships, etc.]

We have to help Krystin. We think [the physicians and counselors] should be able to read her medical/behavioral history for the past 14 years in the medical charts, consider our observations and comments, and agree that this child needs prompt and vigorous professional psychological intervention.

We, as parents, are having a hard time dealing with Krystin, in her current state, in our home without more aggressive treatment. We do not want to live in a household where we have to lock up our wallets and jewelry, the food, and anything of value. We are wary about leaving Krystin home as babysitter to Elliott, because we cannot be sure she will treat him well. We are tired of having the only unpleasant or ugly part of Elliott's life be his interactions with his sister (we know there are usual sibling differences and arguments, but we think the pattern here is beyond the norm). We know we cannot trust her to make the right decision or choice, if left alone at home; she'll invariably do SOMETHING stupid, dangerous, or malicious. Despite REPEATED (25 or 50 times) admonitions not to do something (e.g., eat or drink in front of the computer, pick her clothes up from the bathroom), she continues to do exactly the same thing—we can't tell if it's simply to irritate us or because she doesn't remember or because she just doesn't care. We have often reflected that the household would be a much more pleasant place were Krystin not in it. We do not want her gone, but she's pushing the limits on our tolerance. We very much want Krystin's life turned around, because she's our daughter and because right now she's on a path where she won't have to worry about college—she'll be in jail before she ever gets there. The word that comes to mind when contemplating her character and behavior is sociopath.

At the same time, Krystin's a bright kid, she can be very charming (we are told that she is when at other people's homes), and if she were heading in the right directions in life, would have a lot going for her. We cannot figure out how effectively to steer her in those directions—either we do not know how or she is determined to resist us.

Since about age 8 or 9, Krystin started focusing on the negatives in life, rather than the positives.

As quickly as possible, we want consideration given to drug therapy for depression (e.g., Prozac), combined with intensive psychotherapy for this child.

We might add that we would find it troubling to be told that we have driven Krystin to this behavior. Her younger brother, who has a more keenly-developed sense of responsibility at 8 than Krystin does at 14, is (for an 8-year-old) well-behaved, considerate, helpful, and a pretty sensitive little guy. He's nearly the opposite of Krystin in every major character and personality respect. It is not evident to us that we have raised the two any differently—but we would be the first to acknowledge that any parent, any human, will respond positively and warmly to positive and warm behavior. Krystin, unfortunately, only rarely demonstrates such behavior, despite attempts on our part to encourage it and give it.

It may be that Gary has sometimes been too hard on her, in the sense of setting expectations that were too high (e.g., in school).

May 23, 1999 Gary message to therapist
[excerpts; sent in advance of a meeting with the therapist]:

There is something wrong in this family for Krystin. I do not place blame. But the combination of her genetics, our parenting, her and our temperaments, the presence of a nearly-angelic younger brother (at least by comparison), are all conspiring, in some way, to make life for Krystin not what it should be. I am convinced that if the path Krystin is on continues, she will be pregnant and/or on drugs and/or in a juvenile detention center by the time she's 16. As you can guess, that saddens me a great deal, but the dynamics of this family seem to be leading her in that direction.

I do not claim we are great parents. We are OK parents, but we do (like both of our own sets of parents) have a rather hands-off approach to parenting. For Elliott, this seems to be ideal; he entertains himself, enjoys himself, likes his life. For Krystin, it has not worked.

[Several paragraphs outlining why it might be a good idea for Krystin to stay with another family for a year, with friends who lived in Texas at the time and who we believed to be superb parents. Krystin went to visit the family in June for two weeks.]

As for Elliott, I think he'd be better off with Krystin out of his life for awhile. The only source of irritation in his life is his sister, and he complains about her to me a fair amount.

In my judgment, not only might this divert Krystin to a better direction in life, I think it might also fend off what might ultimately develop into permanent alienation between us and Krystin. I think her feelings toward us vary between love and dislike and sometimes hate—with the latter two coming to predominate. If she can get some perspective on us and herself, the future relationship would be much better.

June 3, 1999 Email from Nicole to Gary
[Nicole's email transmitted a message she had received from Krystin, who had read my May 23 message to the therapist.]

Krystin to Nicole [excerpts]:
    Did I tell you I was going to Texas for 2 weeks?!? Or did my dad? Well, if no one has, I am. . . . The reason I'm going to Texas is because my mom and dad agreed I need to get out of the house for a while away from the family (mostly Elliott). Both of them have discussed that there is something wrong in this family for me, and I guess I do kinda agree. I mean, I love my family and all, it's just something isn't right I guess. They said that if this 2 week trip to Texas works out and I have a good time, the people who I'm staying with are going to ask me to stay there for a year, through 9th grade! I know this because I printed a letter off the computer that my dad typed to a psychologist about me. My dad doesn't know I have it, and I'm not sure if I want to tell him or not that I do.

Gary to therapists [on receiving the message from Nicole]:
    What Krystin read, clearly, is what I faxed to you about the possibility of her going to Texas. I am not certain what to do. For the time being, I do not intend to let Krystin know that I know she knows. ("Oh, what a tangled web we weave When first we practise to deceive!") I did, however, forward Nicole's email to [my friend in Texas] so she is aware. (Nicole, incidentally, read the fax the same day I sent it to you, because I wanted her to be aware of what was going on. Nicole has tried, in a small way, to be a good role model for Krystin, and I've been grateful to her for that.)

June 14, 1999 Email
Krystin, in Texas, to mom [excerpts]:
Mom—
    Hi! I miss you already too. I wish you were here! But it's also fun already and great weather!
    I will have a good dinner tonight, you too! I will also say hi to everyone for you. I'm sleeping in [ ]'s room, she has a cool room!
    Yes, they have lots of bikes! [ ] mentioned it to me on the way home from the airport, and she said if I was interested in biking with them, I could. Yippee!

Well, I have to go. . . . and I still have to email daddy to let him know I'm here.
I LOVE YOU LOTS AND I MISS YOU!!

June 14, 1999 Email
Krystin, in Texas, to dad [excerpts]:
Yes, I made it! I'm sorry I didn't e-mail you. The reason I e-mailed her first is because when I got here I went into my e-mail account and was going to write to you because you asked me to write to you when I got here right? So anyway I had an e-mail from mommy so I replied to her and that was longer than I thought. [Related doings, such as going to stables, swimming, eating out with the family.]
So I'll be going now. Off to do something! I'm going to send an e-mail that's for Elliott k? Print it out and give it to him, and let him read it. You might have to help him though if he asks for help. I love you and I miss you!

June 14, 1999 Email
Gary to faculty colleague/friend in Virginia:
Pat was initially dead-set against the whole idea, and said she would certainly not send Krystin to Texas kicking and screaming (neither would I); the more she's thought about it, talked with friends, and talked with the therapists, she's now concluded that if Krystin does NOT go, SHE (Pat) will be kicking and screaming—and SHE (Pat) may go to Texas for the year. Krystin is now in Texas, flew down this morning for 2 weeks, and emailed Pat that she's already having a great time. (K comes back for 36 hours, and then goes off to two weeks of Spanish camp. She's then home one week, after which she and I and a friend [Christine Lenzen] leave on our driving trip for two weeks, ending up in Myrtle Beach for another week. With diabetes camp thrown in the end of August, Krystin will be home about 3 and ½ weeks this summer. She loves it. So does Elliott.)

June 15, 1999 Email
Krystin to Elliott:
Hi, Elliott!
How have you been doing? I am doing pretty good. Texas is fun. Guess what! David has Super Smash Bros, and he has all 4 of the hidden people you can get! . . . He also has Banjo-Kazooie and has beaten the witch! . . .

I miss you, too, but I am having fun. I go swimming almost every day. It is very hot here. . . .

Well, I have to go now. Give Millie and Cody and Vickie [the two dogs and the cat, respectively] a big hug for me ok? But since Vickie isn't very big, you might not want to hug her too hard, or you may squeeze her insides out. Don't kill my kitty kitty! Ok so I love you and I miss you a lot! Talk to you later.

Elliott to Krystin [his formatting; Elliott was 8½ years old]:
Dear Krystin,

    I liked your E-mail message but you made a few mistakes.
It's Ness, not Nell. And you said Captain Falco.
And you said Squiggly Puff, it's Jiggly Puff. I just
wanted to let you know about that. I got Captain Falcon back too.
And don't worry I won't "KILL" Vickie. Then again, I MISS YOU! !
!!!

Love, Elliott

June 15, 1999 Email
Krystin to mom:

Hi, mom! I don't really have much to tell you because nothing has really happened. . . . I just really wanted to write you and let you know I miss you so much and I love you so much! I love you I love you I love you I love you I love you I love you I love you I love you I love you I love you I love you I love you I love you [four lines worth] I love you soooooooo much ! ! ! ! ! ! And I think about you a lot too. I am having a lot of fun, but I still wish you were here! I want to cry. I love you I love you I really miss you a lot, even though it's only been 2 days. I guess just knowing I'm going to be away 2 weeks makes me miss you more and more. I love you so much mom, and when I get off the plane next Saturday either if you're there or not, I'm going to give you a great big hug! . . . [There were almost daily emails back and forth between Krystin and her mom and me while Krystin was in Texas, mostly relating events taking place in each other's lives. Eating, shopping, walking the dogs, weather, etc.]

June 18, 1999 Email
Gary to faculty colleague/friend in Virginia:
[my colleague asked: "How does Elliott handle all this? Sounds like he can use some undivided attention."]

    He gets quite a bit of it. He's of mixed mind about his sister's absence. I asked him last night if he liked it better with her gone or better with her home; he said he couldn't answer, because it was some of both.

June 18, 1999 Email
Gary to mom/friend in Texas:
[citing email from Krystin to Pat earlier in the week]

    Krystin continued: "Especially if y'all are expecting me to come back here for 9th grade. Which by the way I found a down side to that. Here, 1-6 graders are in elementary, then 7-9 is middle school, and 10-12 is high school, so I'd still be in middle school! I think I'm ready for high school, and ready for South."

    Well—I can hardly imagine any point upon which Pat and I would disagree more with Krystin than this. Apart from what we see as your enormous virtues as a surrogate mom, the most compelling reason for K to stay with you for a year is so that she is NOT in 9th grade in a senior high, but rather in a middle school with younger kids. The opportunities for her to go astray are MUCH more limited in a junior/middle school that in a senior high—we know perfectly well that there are a lot of fast-talking 16-17-year-old (males), and since Krystin really has no moral compass of her own, she could go down the wrong garden path immediately.

    What we find odd about this entry from K is that we specifically TALKED with her about 9th grade being in middle school in Texas, and how we worried about her going into a senior high and the problems that could come up. This conversation must have gone on for 15-20 minutes—but she apparently heard none of it!

June 29, 1999 Message
Gary to therapists:
[excerpts, summarizing a conversation I had had with one of them]

    (We agreed to continue with two therapists at least until after Krystin's summer travels are done and the recommended psychological testing had been done.) The goal is to have Krystin on a positive trajectory, but it will not be a straight line—there will be downturns. We cannot let those downturns blow us out of the water. The hope is that the downturns will be less frequent and intense, and that we will be able to get through them more quickly.

(Texas was out as an option for the following year; the mom suspects that she has either fibromyalgia or MS, so could not take on Krystin.) [The therapist] and I had reached the same conclusion: that Krystin could start at South, but that if we discovered trouble, she would be removed. [The therapist] agreed that that is probably the best approach, at this point, and to talk with Krystin about this. [Discussion of different school options if not South, including both Lutheran and Catholic high schools.]

Per [our mom friend in Texas], Krystin has to make decisions over and over and over. Her example was the grocery store: Krystin would go with [the friend] down the aisles, and would point to things and say "I want that but I can't have it" over and over. Krystin needs to make that decision EACH TIME, rather than do what most of us do, which is make the decision once. [Our friend] said she'd be exhausted from going to the store if she had to approach things the way Krystin does. Krystin needs help in figuring out how to make these decisions.

July 1999 Emails interlude
[during a two-week trip that I took with Krystin and Christine Lenzen to Martha's Vineyard, Philadelphia, Washington D.C., and then to join Pat's annual family gathering at Myrtle Beach, SC for a third week]

July 21 Krystin to mom
[There was evidently a message or messages preceding this one. Millie was one of our dogs; she "leaked" all over the house, so Pat decided she had to get rid of her. Krystin was so distraught—prior to her first email reprinted here—that she slept with in my bed with me while we were visiting our friends Burt & Eileen Shapiro at their house on Martha's Vineyard. Needless to say, she hadn't slept with me or her mother since she was a tiny tot. Unfortunately I don't have emails from the visit to Martha's Vineyard, where the two girls had a wonderful time, including going on a trip to get fresh lobster and seeing all the pastel houses of Oak Bluff. We were there when John F. Kennedy, Jr.'s plane crashed in the water near Martha's Vineyard, July 16, 1999, so part of the island was

closed to us. I also don't have emails from the day I took them to New York City on the train from Philadelphia.]

Mom-

I love you too, very much. Why Millie? How is she? Did you get to see her again before you left the vet? Are they going to tell you if they find a home for her? I never even said good-bye! I wasn't worried because I could just say bye and hello when we got home, but now I never get to see her again, and I never even said goodbye. I miss her so much already. Why her?! I'm going to miss her so much. She was the best. We will never find another dog like her. Plus, she doesn't get to go to the DP [dog park, an area by the Mississippi River set aside for dog owners to let them romp] anymore? Poor Millie. I think her life is going to be terrible in another home, but we won't think about that k? Daddy told me the Monday after we get back we're going out to look for another dog. Are we going to the Humane Society? Do you have any kinds or types of dogs in mind? I think we'll have to do what we did before, just go and look.

July 26 Mom to Krystin:

Krystin, the hobby farm lady couldn't take Millie. I'm sad about that.

I told the vet last week that our decision was if the hobby farm lady couldn't take her, that we wanted to put her down.

The vet begged me today to give her another chance to find Millie a home. Millie is such a good dog, and she's sure that there are people out who would love to have her and be willing/able to put the money into her medical needs. . . .

I could make this decision on my own, and then just tell you the hobby farm lady took her, but I value your opinion and respect your decision. I think that you should have a vote on what happens to her. She was your doggie too.

So, should I tell the vet to still put her down, or should we trust her to find her a good home. . . . She wants so much to have another chance. She's just sure she can do it. . . .

What do you think? I trust this vet, and think it's worth a try to find her a good home. But if you feel strongly the other way, I'll honor your decision.

July 26 Krystin to mom:
Mom, we just talked on the phone, so you know what my opinion is, and I think we should trust the [vet's] nurse. [Krystin was concerned that "bad people" would get Millie and mistreat her; Pat had assured her that bad people weren't going to take a dog that had medical problems.] But the vet won't let that happen. She'll get a good history and story from the family. I trust her, and hope that either way, Millie is happy. . . .

August 10, 1999 "Personality evaluation," psychologist
[excerpts; testing done over three days in early July; the psychologist came recommended from faculty colleagues as the best in the metro area.]

Referral Question: Krystin was referred for personality testing by her parents and their therapist. She has been exhibiting troublesome behavior at home, including lying and stealing. A personality evaluation was sought as a means to better understand the nature and extent of any underlying difficulties she may be struggling with. [The therapist reviewed Krystin's birth issues, family tensions, diagnosis of diabetes, history of stealing.]

Test Behavior: Krystin is an attractive 14 year old girl who appeared for testing dressed in age-appropriate summer make-up and clothing. Her demeanor was casual and friendly, apparently unconcerned about the reason for her visit. She was cooperative with all testing demands and produced an adequate amount of data.

Evaluation Results: Results of this evaluation point to a complex array of strengths and weaknesses in Krystin's character. In her favor, she is a bright, usually responsive and socially motivated child who has developed a strong empathy for vulnerable creatures, shown in her interest in and love of animals. This appreciation of vulnerability in other creatures reflects a positive aspect of her own self esteem.

However, there are also significant problem areas in Krystin's development. While she is a bright child, her thinking is notably immature and marked by a simplistic understanding of causation, a wish for easy or magical answers, and avoidance of complex or threatening material. Early on, perhaps in response to some of the challenges in her young life, she developed a coping style of denial and avoidance. As she became older, she was unable to let go of these immature ways of coping and failed to practice more adult ways of responding. As a result, she is quite inflexible and immature in her ability to manage challenging situations. Her judgment is poor and she has great difficulty considering her own negative behavior and taking responsibility for it. Beneath a superficial unconcerned attitude, she harbors a deep longing for care and closeness but lacks an understanding of her true needs and how she might go about obtaining the care she so desires. Instead, what she wishes for are magical or fantasy solutions which require little action on her part. When Krystin feels especially needy or vulnerable, she is more likely to avoid her true painful feelings, and behavior in socially inappropriate ways, such as stealing or lying. Because this is a habit she has practiced for some time now, she faces greater difficulty in changing it.

Diagnosis: Krystin's situation is unique and at her age she is quite vulnerable to further acting out. For purposes of clarification, I discuss each possible diagnosis separately.

Depression: None of the testing material suggests that Krystin is currently depressed. However, she has limited internal resources to cope with complex troublesome situations and is vulnerable to feelings of inadequacy and helplessness.

Generalized Anxiety Disorder: Again, as with depression, there are few overt signs of pervasive anxiety in Krystin's profile. Still, at times in the testing situation, when confronted with ambiguous or threatening material, Krystin's responses were characteristic of someone avoiding overwhelming worries. . . .

Conduct Disorder: The fairly extensive history of stealing and lying does point to a diagnosis of Conduct Disorder. However, Krystin's behavior is not characterized by other relevant features of that diagnosis, namely, a more aggressive and antisocial personality type. Apart from stealing, her behavior has been with the normal range of social conformity.

Kleptomania: With one important exception, this diagnosis of kleptomania most closely describes Krystin's behavior. It is her primary symptom; she is not particularly planful nor successful in her attempts at theft; and it appears that she often commits these thefts when she is tense. For behavior to be fully consistent with this diagnosis, however, the items taken usually are of little monetary value. Krystin often takes items that have substantial monetary value. It may also be noted that there is a quality of compulsivity or lack of logical planfulness in the stealing that Krystin does. She steals from friends and family, is often caught and is subjected to angry criticism from those whose opinions she values.

[Treatment recommendations were included in the report, including intensive psychotherapy to address the behavior problems. "In addition, it is recommended that her family be engaged in regular family therapy for two purposes. The first purpose is to assist the family in creating a more harmonious relationship with Krystin, a goal that she strongly wishes for. The second purpose of family therapy is to support the family as they go through this next challenging period in their lives."]

January 2014 The Rope
[as noted earlier, Krystin's story of her life; this is the high school portion.]

When I started high school, my parents were told by my doctors that it was time they let go of the leash and let me do it; "it" being managing my diabetes on my own, since they would not be able to take care of me forever. I suddenly had this newfound freedom and control over my diabetes. No one to prep everything for me, no one to confirm that I had actually done my blood test and injection, no one to hold me accountable anymore. This does not mean that my parents didn't check in frequently to ask how my blood sugars were. It means that I began lying about it, and somehow I didn't even feel guilty about lying.

I never did quite grasp the whole concept of taking responsibility for myself. Instead, I began to neglect the illness, treating it as if it weren't there. Diabetes was an inconvenience, a hassle, a burden; it was a "problem" with me that I came to loathe. Like addicts have a problem with alcohol, and shopaholics have a problem with shopping, I had a problem with diabetes, and like other holics, should've sought help. However, that would've meant acknowledging that I actually had a problem. That's the first step though, isn't it?

In high school, a time when judgment from peers is cruel, and self-critique is even crueler, all I wanted was to fit in. I pretended that I was "normal," that there was nothing different about me. Although the bullying and teasing had stopped, the past had already done its permanent damage on me. I didn't want to leave class ten minutes early anymore to go to the nurse's office. I didn't want to do anything that I thought would draw negative attention to me, and that's just how I saw it: Diabetes would make me an outcast, and at a time in life when fitting in was all that mattered, I would do anything to make sure that happened, even if it meant putting my health on the line. I stopped going to the nurse before lunch, and like everyone else, ate whatever I wanted from the lunch line, but without covering it with an insulin injection. I lived by the theory that I was still young, it would be years before any complications started, or if anything else went seriously wrong, the medics would be able to save me. I had time. Not the best motto to live by, but in my rebellious teenage years, I used it to get by.

I tried using an insulin pump while in high school, but that didn't work out too well. In fact, that's what brought that negative attention in classes that I was trying so hard to avoid. There were no silent settings on the pump, so any time is had a warning to give me, it warned the whole classroom. Low battery? BEEP BEEP. Low insulin levels remaining? BEEP BEEP. Something blocking the tubing? BEEP BEEP. I want to make Krystin feel awkward when weird beeping noises start coming from mysterious areas around her? BEEP BO BEEP DA DA DA BEEP BEEP. I swear the thing had it out to get me from the very beginning. Solution? Take it off and stash it in my locker when I got to school and put it back on when I got home. That is, if I remembered to grab it out of my locker at the end of the day. I hated my pump and the stinging it caused when it delivered insulin into my stomach. I resented it, and through transference, more and more I continued to resent my diabetes as well.

Eventually this self-talk became not just an idea in my head, but a lifestyle. Everyone around me saw my health declining. I saw it and felt it, too, but I continued to ignore it, telling myself that if I didn't acknowledge my failing health, it might not be true. Nobody ever told me to my face how unhealthy I looked. I would find out later from my mom that a cousin or an aunt would inquire if I had been sick lately. They could see it in my face, in my eyes that no longer shined, in the bubbliness that no longer existed in my personality. I let the illness begin to define me: I was no longer Krystin, but Krystin the Bad Diabetic. Even if no one said it out loud, I assumed they were all thinking it.

Four years of high school. Four years is a long time; plenty long enough for a habit to develop that became impossible to break. Over the years, after high school and into college, even with all the emotional pain it caused my family and friends to watch me struggle to be healthy, I let diabetes win. I no longer cared about the illness, or myself. I had somehow convinced myself that it wasn't worth taking care of; that I wasn't worth taking care of. Younger, defiant Krystin had her hold, and wasn't going to let adult, more responsible Krystin take responsibility.

Perhaps I had been on my parents' leash for too long, been under the care of them and my doctors for too long, and I had become too comfortable being taken care of. Even though I was enjoying the freedom of no longer being on my parents' ball and chain, if you will, I had no idea the damage I was doing to my body by not taking my insulin, and how within a couple years, the consequences would confront me in a way that could not be ignored.

December 3, 1999 Email
Mom to Krystin [excerpts]:

Krystin, I just wanted to say how proud I am of you for doing so well at your school work. You were right when you said you didn't need us to "check you in and check you out" and I should have trusted you. I'm glad we asked [one of the therapists] to let us try without it and I'm glad you proved me wrong. You've done a terrific job and I like that we don't have that stress in our lives with me have to be on your case all the time.

I feel like things have been going smoother for us lately. Do you feel the same way? I know we will always have our "moments" where we don't agree with the other one, but that's normal. . . . Your school work has improved, your [blood glucose] numbers are getting better, Elliott has stopped sniffling [a habit of his that drove Krystin to distraction], our dog is beautiful, you are beautiful. Is this great, or what?

Krystin to mom:

Elliott is still sniffling, and I wish I could prove to MYSELF that I'm beautiful. You just have to say that cause you're my mother! You and daddy keep saying that in a few years I will be a beautiful young woman . . . how do you figure? [Krystin was correct: we did say that. And we were right.] I haven't really matured yet, and I don't see many people at school that haven't either. I feel like a baby still there! Like nothing has happened to me yet, and I feel like no boys would like me either. I even feel weird walking with Chris! I feel like her little tag-a-long kinda person, you know?

[Krystin reported her grade expectations, with two C's and the rest B's or higher.] That's going to affect my options for college isn't it? Starting high school was a big change for me, but do you think that now I'm used to it and kinda settled in, if I do better next trimester and the rest of high school (let's just say) do you think that'll still be ok? I know A's and B's are good, but having two C's, what'll that do? Because I don't wanna ruin my chances for anything.

Mom to Krystin:

Two C's in 9th grade are NOT going to keep you from most colleges. It's true, the higher the overall GPA (grade point average), the more CHOICES for college you'll have, but decent grades will still hold many doors open for you. The most important thing, Krystin, is that you do your BEST work and try hard at it. That's your biggest (and only, really) job right now. It will be your ticket to freedom when you become an independent adult. . . .

And why do you say you aren't beautiful? Of course you are! I think you are far prettier than just about ANY of your friends. . . . As far as being physically developed, sure you're on the slower end of the scale, but so what? You can't change it, so fussing over it doesn't pay. Just be confined in who you are now and trust me that WILL develop in time. Have you ever seen an adult who looks 12? . . .

So boys aren't interested in you now. That's an ADVANTAGE!! If you start dating now, you'll be bored with "just walking and holding hands" before too many years go by, and then what happens? Just like [ ]. She had boyfriends since 7th grade. She has never felt that she was anybody without being attached to someone else. That's so sad. Take advantage of this time to develop your inner mental values and worry about boys later.

March 20, 2000 Email
Krystin to dad:

Of course this means I'm not playing softball. I was CUT. And you know what? [ ] made it. She hurt herself Tuesday, the second day, she sat watching every other day. How are they going to put her on a team? . . . And then [ ] was rubbing it in all day, you and mommy both know I have a soft heart and I cry easily, and I was trying not to all afternoon, but it wasn't working, and I feel really mad and sad, more sad. I looked dumb as heck crying in front of everyone. Not really crying like bawling my eyes out, but you know, tears coming down. I tried my hardest and I don't know how they cut people. Even [ ] was a lot better than me, and she's been playing for like 7 years, and she got cut, too. EVERYONE of my friends who tried out got on. [List of 11 girls.] And I feel dumb and rejected. I hate this!

September 25, 2000 Email
Krystin to mom:

well I don't really have much to say. Obviously all I do is little to what you tell me to do, and push a little button and my life is perfect. [That is what she wrote. I can't make it understandable.] Well, it's not. People have no idea how hard it is to be a teenager with diabetes. I don't have a normal life, and I can't remember ever having a normal life. I never will have a normal life. It's so hard walking through school with kids asking you what's that bulky thing on you? what's diabetes? Ewww it's in your butt? People shiver and squiggle when I tell them I have a tube in me 24/7. Now I'm sure to that you'd say it's more like 20/6 or something. . . . I am trying to maintain my blood sugar average. But, I can't have it on during gym (5th hour) and I can't wear it during soccer, so the reason my blood sugars at dinner are up, is because I've practically had my pump off most of the afternoon. Gym is an hour, and soccer is 2 hours. That's 3 hours w/o my pump, with one hour in between. And yes, I do bolus during that hour, but one hour with the pump can't make up for 3 without. And if I do extra units in that hour, it will just go low, and that would not be good during a soccer game or practice, especially since we haven't gotten any food in my bag yet. I know my pump is being left out. There is nothing I can say about that. I can say oh I'll do better or oh I won't leave it out any more, but obviously I can't make those kind of promise because you always point out that I'll just break it.

November 20, 2000 Email
Mom to Krystin:
Krystin,

We need to sit down, the three of us, and discuss some concerns. I'm sending you an email first because I want you to print it would and spend some time thinking about it before we talk. Something is going on, and I don't know what it is.

1. You sent me a lovely message last week stating that you were really going to try to do better with your diabetes. You thought that once you got the longer sets, things would be much better. I got you the longer sets and new batteries for your remote [for her insulin pump] and things have gotten worse. You average only 2 tests a day instead of 4, and the numbers you do are very high. What's up?

2. Your number last night at 8:30pm was 500+. [Recall that the desirable range for people with diabetes is 80-180. 500 was an extremely high number.] I was concerned that maybe your pump line was kinked. I asked you to bolus and then do another test before you ate anything/went to bed. You then came upstairs with a box of Cheez-its and some raspberry water. I asked you if you had your test bag upstairs. You got irritated with me, like you were saying, "I can do this, mom. You can stop bugging me." I see this morning you didn't do a test at all. Krystin, what's going on?

3. You check the phone messages, but then don't tell us that they are there. Krystin, either write them down or save them as new. It's not acceptable that two weeks go by with a saved message from the doctor's office and I don't even know it's there. . . .

4. I understand that you were supposed to turn in a bunch of forms for Costa Rica last Friday. So what's up with that? What forms? Are you going on this trip?

5. I made arrangements to take Tuesday morning off of work so we could get your passport. Now I hear that you have arrangements Tuesday to drop off some project for school that you didn't turn in on time? And when is it you were going to complete this project? You work Monday night and will be with me Tuesday morning. Yet it was OK to play all weekend and not say anything about this project that was overdue?

Krystin, you can't continually drop the ball on everything you do and then expect that we're going to pick up all the pieces for you. What's the scoop? Do you think it's OK that mom and dad constantly invest money in things for you and then you just let them fall? I find that very disrespectful, and very disturbing.

Pat to Gary:
[The email to Krystin is a good agenda for a meeting with the therapist.]

    Krystin seems to have the same attitude in every aspect of her life. We're supposed to do everything and she's not supposed to be responsible for anything. I know that's probably a normal default for kids, but I need to know how much we need push and how much we need wait for her to "catch up." Everyone tells us she's developmentally slow, and we can't expect the same from her as other kids her age because she's "just not there yet." But how much CAN and SHOULD we expect from her? . . .

    I'm really angry at her that she continues to treat her diabetes like a joke and am about to halt ALL outside activities in her life until she realizes the importance of this. That's one thing I need to talk to [the therapist] about. Where is the line between what she should be doing and what she is emotionally capable of doing?

December 11, 2000 Email [an illustrative interlude]
Krystin to dad:
Dad-

    I'm in 2nd hour right now and all we're doing is finishing and turning in some journals which I finished on Friday, so I'm all done and have nothing to do, so I came down to the computer lab to write you an e-mail, because I guess I have an issue to talk to you about. On Saturday, you know I had $15 in my wallet, right? Well, I wanted to borrow $5 because there was something I knew I wanted that cost $20. Then later you gave me $15 more. When I got to Chris's house, I looked and saw that I accidentally took your $50 bill. I didn't spend it downtown because I knew I was going to give it back to you, I just didn't know how, without you thinking I took it, which I didn't. And when you came into the study and said you were missing $50, I didn't know what to say or how to react because I didn't believe I had borrowed $50. I know that you pretty much think I stole the $5, but I didn't, I only borrowed and WAS going to tell you, I really was going to say I borrowed $50, but when you said you were missing $50, I didn't know what to say, so I didn't say anything then because I'm sure you'd be mad, and I'm sure you are anyway. But anyways, this morning I looked in my wallet because I was going to put it on the table with a note for you, because it's easier for me to say things in a note than in person, and it was gone. I don't know if Zack [a friend of Elliott's who visited the house often. Zack would never have taken any money] took it, or if you or mom did, but if either of you did, then that makes me mad of course because it's invading my privacy. I had to return the money on my own, instead of you finding it or Zack taking it, that's not how I wanted it to be because that would just make it look worse. I was going to tell you, I was just hoping it wouldn't have to be this way. Of course I'm sorry it happened, and of course I know you're mad, but I am too. I'm also sure you don't believe me huh? Well, it's true. And I guess I don't know what else to tell you, so I'll have to leave it at that.

Dad to Krystin:

We did look in your wallet, since you left it lying around. We also looked in Elliott's pants pockets.

I am glad you wrote to me about this. I will accept your explanation of what happened. [But I did not really believe her.] But I do want to INSIST on something: if you want to borrow a few bucks from me from time to time, I'll usually be glad to help you out. But DON'T take money out of my wallet unless I say it's OK!!!!

And by the way, you should understand that while kids are generally entitled to privacy (or at least good parents give good kids privacy most of the time), they do not always get it. For example, if a parent thinks one of their kids is using drugs, they may very well search a room or read emails. If they think the kid is having a problem or doing something wrong (or, more important, something that will harm themselves), most parents I know will intervene. Since we have had problems in the past, we have to find out what is going on to be sure that we can deal with anything that continues. But I'll assume from your message to me that we don't really have a problem any more that that this was just a big mistake. I do want to emphasize, however, that you should NOT take money from me or your mother without first asking if you can have it.

Thank you for being honest about this. I appreciate it.

Krystin to dad:
Hi dad-

I didn't get to talk to you after work because I ran late, and it's not morning yet (even though it will be when you get this) but I don't really talk to you in the morning since we have different schedules, but I wanted to say thank you for understanding about the money. I don't know why I ever take things. I just don't understand. I mean, I have a job now, and I always had money (at least an allowance) so I had it, so I don't understand why I had to TAKE it. [The two therapists] and everyone said it could have been to get attention, but that's not true, I don't need any, or I have as much as I need. And that kind of attention I don't think is the kind of attention one wants, ya know? Maybe we should talk to [one of the therapists] about that. I have no problems about now that I want to discuss, I mean about the past, why I would do it.

September 10, 2001 Email
[I wrote to a friend who'd inquired about how Krystin was doing. This message from me probably represents a good summary of how things stood with Krystin at that point.]

Terrible. She got so mad at us yesterday that she slept overnight at a friend's house. But, since she needed to change her schedule (because she was not put in an English class of any kind), I picked her up this morning and got her to school early so she could be first in line to get a
change. . . .

And mid-morning she called me, civil and friendly, and asked if I could come to the school to sign a form allowing her to be a teacher's aid (for credit!) instead of taking English, and that she would have 2 English courses next semester. So I did. Maybe she'll even come back home tonight.

Last night came on the heels on Friday of my finally seeing her transcript. She had an A, 3 C's, a D, and an F last semester. In the fall she had an A, 2 B's, a C, and a D. (In contrast, fall of her sophomore year [fall 2000] she had 4 A's, a B, and a C—so I know perfectly well, as I have all along, that she's capable of doing the work. Easily.) But now she's at risk, and with another earlier F, she's behind in credits.

She's not playing soccer. The coach won't (probably can't) let her. It's a big disappointment both for her and for us.

She lives in a fantasy land. She talks about going to medical school; she's going to be lucky to graduate from high school at the rate she's going. She prefers to believe she does not have diabetes—so she doesn't have it (and her blood sugar numbers were astronomical, until, the Friday before Labor Day weekend, I unilaterally declared the "experiment" by the medical team, to let Krystin control her own diabetes, a failure; since then we have been in her face (as politely as we are able) about doing tests and taking insulin—and her numbers have come back down to normal.)

But I also wrote her a little note about grades (we have learned that Krystin absorbs things much better if they are written down, either in an email or in a note—oddly, [our Texas mom/friend] noticed the same thing when Krystin visited them last summer). In it I pointed out that competition to get into medical school was extremely intense, that she was not on track to be able to get into a good college or university, much less medical school, and that her current trajectory was to graduate from high school (maybe) and end up with a job at Walmart, maybe get married and have a family (very high risk with uncontrolled diabetes) and live with a very modest income that she would not like. I told her I'd do anything to help her—but I can't learn for her.

Well—that note, plus the fact that we would not let her go to Target last night at 7:30, after she had been gone most of the day Sunday and most of the day Saturday, with friends, sent her into a surly mood that ended in the house only when she left to stay overnight at her friend's.

This morning I called Holly [my sister] and asked her to talk with her husband about whether they'd like to take on a boarder (and Krystin go to Oakdale HS). For some strange reason, Krystin has always liked Holly and John [Holly's husband] (even though she has not seen them much in recent years, until they moved back to the Twin Cities from Texas last year). She has spent a couple of overnights there in the last few months and always has a good time. . . .

Holly of course was startled (we had never mentioned this possibility to them when we were talking to [our friends in Texas]). But she said she'd talk to John and also talk to the school about how Krystin would get in. So we'll see. We see Krystin's therapist on Thursday afternoon; we'll bring this up with her, too. Since Krystin learned (I think by going into my email files and reading my messages) about the possibility of staying with [our Texas friends] when she wasn't supposed to know, but was sort of keen on the idea, she may think it's an attractive idea to stay with Holly and John.

There's something toxic in the family dynamics in our house for Krystin (has been for years) and we just can't seem to deal with it. I told Holly that Krystin (at least to start) would probably do voluntarily and cheerfully for them (with both diabetes and school) what she spends every ounce of her energy resisting in us.

Holly asked me if we had a "Plan B": I said we did not—but that's our problem, not hers. I don't know what Plan B would be; we can't really afford a boarding school, at 25K per year or more. But she's making all of our lives miserable. Elliott loves her dearly (or so he shows signs of doing some of the time, on the rare occasion when she's in a good mood) but he can hardly wait until she's gone to college and she won't be there to abuse him in daily life.

Mid-year 2001 Notes on Krystin living elsewhere
[As noted in my message to my friend, in September 2001 we had lengthy discussions with my sister and brother-in-law about Krystin moving in with them. They lived in Oakdale, a suburb of St. Paul. In the course of thinking about her living elsewhere, we put together a table. My files have 13 pages of email messages back and forth between Pat and me and Holly and John. We discussed everything from driving to computer use to studying to visiting friends to health insurance.]

Living Somewhere Else

Krystin:

Pros:
new school
new friends; wouldn't know about past, start clean
new room?
no more annoying brother
new job
still get to go on vacation with family and do stuff
get into different activities at school; new sport teams
might get better grades
different boys to scope out (all at South are dumb)

Cons:
miss friends/parents/pets
harder to get to doctor appointments
home wouldn't be "home" anymore
would eventually miss brother
new job
wouldn't see parents and friends as often

Pat:

Pros:
no arguments with Elliott
Krystin says she'd be happier
boarding school might better prepare for college
one less person for bathroom time

Cons:
I'd miss you; I'm not ready for you to leave
very expensive
I'd miss your soccer games
who'd take you to doctor and Ellie?
you'd have to change schools
who'd teach you to drive?
could you have a part-time job?
would have to be a boarding school; we can't ask family unless we're dead and leave an estate to cover costs

Gary:

Pros:
away from Elliott fights/sniffling (pro for Krystin)
Krystin must always be at her social best
no fights for Elliott (pro for Elliott)
Gary/Pat not argue with Krystin
Gary/Pat not have Krystin laundry or bed linens to do

Cons:
cost – big bucks
Krystin must always be at her social best
Gary/Pat not take to doctor, etc.

Gary/Pat not involved in Krystin's school
Gary/Pat not see Krystin much
Krystin not see South friends
not have love/care of real parents

[After several discussions, including with Krystin, we decided not to pursue the option of her living with my sister and brother-in-law. Years later, Pat recalled that "we pulled the plug on her living with H/J because they demanded we give up all control and decision making. They would be her parents and would expect from her same as they expected from their own. That shocked us (don't think we were expecting that, not from them or anyone else). We weren't prepared to give up that much, especially the part about them raising her as their own." That coincides with my memory. We were not prepared to give up our daughter to that extent.]

After October 30, 2002 Psychologist's report
[We brought Krystin to a psychiatrist in the summer of 2002 because we were concerned about her thinking, behavior, and diabetes; the psychiatrist referred Krystin to a psychologist who administered a battery of eight tests. The psychologist's report refers to Krystin as "an 18-year-old high school senior at South High School in Minneapolis, Minnesota. She lives at home with her parents, Gary and Pat Engstrand, and her younger brother, Elliott (age 11), in Minneapolis." The report from the psychologist contained several lists of test scores. Excerpts from his report follow.]

Krystin was referred for psychological testing . . . for depressive symptomatology. She was diagnosed with Dysthymic Disorder. [From the Mayo Clinic website: "Persistent depressive disorder, also called dysthymia (dis-THIE-me-uh), is a continuous long-term (chronic) form of depression. You may lose interest in normal daily activities, feel hopeless, lack productivity, and have low self-esteem and an overall feeling of inadequacy. These feelings last for years and may significantly interfere with your relationships, school, work and daily activities."] In addition, her parents expressed concerns regarding her memory and ability to follow through with expectations. She has also had compliance problems managing her diabetes.

Krystin responded to these self-report measures as an adolescent endorsing no clinically significant syndromes, but low self-esteem, feelings of inadequacy, and problems interacting with her parents.

The Millon Adolescent Clinical Inventory is a norm-referenced personality and clinical assessment well standardized for use with adolescents.... On the Millon, Krystin responded in a manner typical of an adolescent who is significantly depressed with anxious and insecure feelings. She tends to be dependent and submissive in family and peer relationships, putting her at risk for negative peer influences. She may feel lonely and isolated, fueled by insecurity and fear of abandonment. By submerging her individuality, subordinating her personal desires, and submitting at times to potential abuse and intimidation, she hopes to avoid total abandonment. Krystin's fatigability and depression create an ever-present feeling of weariness and apathy, often feeling like daily tasks take more energy than she has available. In addition, Krystin sees her home life as significantly discordant. Many of these issues culminate in Krystin feeling unattractive, self-demeaning, and hypersensitive to her own shortcomings. She yearns for acceptance if not affection, from others, although her hope appears to be waning. [To jump ahead in the narrative: The description of Krystin in this worrisome summary may have been accurate at the time, but was not as she grew older and matured.]

December 8, 2002 Diary
[The first diary entry that we have. They will continue through the remainder of the narrative.]
Today I went shopping at the MOA [the Mall of America, in Bloomington, MN] with my aunt and uncle (Marcie and Jeff). I got a lot of my Christmas shopping done. First we saw 'Harry Potter and the Chamber of Secrets.' I already saw it before but I love it enough it's still as good the second time around. I decided to get this journal at Barnes and Noble. Apparently journals are good for the soul. So, here I am. Anyway, we bought things for people from the Macy's Giving Tree, which always feel good (to give) and know I'm making someone's Christmas brighter.... Then we ate dinner at Tony Roma's then I came home! So all in all it was a good day. Nothing too big or bad happened, but that will change. Good night!

December 9, 2002 Diary
    Today was just another ordinary day. Nothing too exciting at school. I went to Sylvan for my ACT class and found out I got a 21 on my practice test. I got 23 last time, so hopefully I can get a 23 or higher on the real thing when I take it on Sunday.

December 12, 2002 Diary
    After school I took the bus to Highland and got job applications from Bruegger's and Barnes and Noble. . . . Then later tonight I got all my college applications ready to mail and got the checks all made out. All I need is the transcript, but I don't really trust Dan to send it all in. . . . So tomorrow I'm making an appointment to talk to Dan about it all. Wish me luck.
    I'm done with ACT class now, so hopefully I'll do good on the real thing! Nicole told me she got a 23 and still got into UMD.

December 15, 2002 Diary
    Today I took my ACT test at Eddy Hall at the U of M. 8 IN THE MORNING! Honestly, I don't think I did very well, and it's too late to take again. But maybe I did OK. I just don't know. I got done about a quarter to 12 (11:45) and my mom picked me up. We went to Mervyn's and mom got butter spreaders for dad for Christmas, then over to Highland and I turned in my application at Bruegger's. I don't think they're hiring even though the guy thought they were, so I'll call on Wednesday and tell them I'm interested if and when they're hiring. . . . Anyway, after I got home I worked on homework. I got done almost all my homework this weekend! Go me.
    Tomorrow I'm going to Dan and giving him my college apps and he'll fill in the transcript part and then send them in for me. I'm crossing my fingers so hard for UMD. He's not very trustworthy though so hopefully he won't forget to do it.

December 16, 2002 Diary
    Sometimes I really can't stand my mom. Every time I bring up something about what Elliott's doing that I don't like, she brings up some shit about how I did something similar when I was younger, and it pisses me off. It's not about me, it's about Elliott in the present and now. I already hate Elliott, and I've always had problems with my mom. And in situations like this my dad just sits there like he's deaf and like nothing's happening. My whole family sucks.

I really, really need a job. I hate not having money! I'm working on Bruegger's and if that doesn't work out I'll find someplace else.

December 17, 2002 Diary

Today I went and saw Dan at 11 a.m. to give him my college apps. I told him about Sylvan and he looked at my transcript and said I was doing pretty good, so I really think he'll put in a good word for me. Now all I have to do is wait. This is the hardest part. I know I probably won't hear anything for more than a month, but I won't be able to help checking the mail every day! I know for sure I can get into [U of Wisconsin] River Falls, but I really, really want to get into UMD.

I really want to fake sick tomorrow, but I think my mom is catching on. Hmm. . . . I'll let ya know what happens. That's it for now. Goodnight.

December 18, 2002 Diary

Vickie peed in the living room again. My dad said he thinks it's time to put her down. I'm really sad. I love my kitty and will really miss her. The only good news is that we'd get two new kittens. I dunno how I feel. I really don't want Vickie to go. ☹

December 19, 2002 Diary

Tomorrow is the last day of school before a two week break! And I'm not even going to be there the first two hours. We (my dad and I) are taking Vickie to the vet ☹ She's getting tested for diabetes and kidney failure. To do that they need a urine sample, so they have to squeeze her to make her pee! Poor kitty. If it's only an infection, my parents will buy antibiotics, but if it's serious, we have to put her down. I think I mentioned this last night. And I thought we'd get kittens soon, but my parents said not for awhile, so I'm really sad about that.

So today I had an appointment with Ellie [therapist, the one who once told us that "you'll have her until she's 30"] and my mom dropped a big bomb on me. Starting middle of February, my parents aren't going to drive me ANYWHERE any more. Not Sylvan, not doctor, anywhere. So I have until then to get my license back. Wish me luck.

Tomorrow I'm bringing all my presents for people to school! I'm excited to give people their gifts. I probably won't get many in return, but whatever, at least I'm ready for it. Time to go to bed now. Goodnight.

December 20, 2002 Diary

So much to say about today. This morning my dad and I took Vickie to the vet in St. Louis Park. My parents let me miss the beginning of school to go in case anything happens. Vickie had to ride in the kitty carrier on my lap, and she barfed all over in it. She was good at the vet, but they couldn't get any pee out of her so they had to keep her. They still couldn't by the afternoon so they have to keep her overnight. My poor kitty.

I guess that's it for now. Tomorrow we go to Owatonna for Christmas with my mom's side, and I have to go to Sylvan while someone goes to pick up Vickie. I want my kitty! But, the sooner I go to bed, the sooner it will be tomorrow and the sooner Vickie will be home. Goodnight.

December 21, 2002 Diary

-No Sylvan for 2 weeks! 😊

We got Vickie this morning around noon, and I guess not a whole lot is wrong with her but she did get a pill she has to take once a day, but shoving it down her throat. [?] Then we went to Owatonna for Xmas with my mom's side, and guess who was there—aunt Joey! Jeff had bought her a ticket to fly here, and no one knew about it except Marcie and Jeff. So that was a nice surprise.

December 24, 2002 Diary

Today we went and saw the Lord of the Rings movie—it was SO good! Better than the first one. Then when we got home we had spaghetti for dinner then opened presents! It was kinda a dud for me. My dad did the shopping for me this year instead of my mom. I got a necklace from The Museum Company—pearls. I dunno if I like it or not. I'm not really a pearl person. Then from Eddie Bauer I got a blue shirt and a jean pull-over vest. I'm returning both. And lastly I got a black hat and some really cute, warm mittens that I will be keeping! My mom said next year she'll be doing my shopping. I feel bad for my dad, but I love him for trying. I did see some of his receipts though, and he got a $20 AE gift card and the GAP striped scarf! Those are from grandpa and I'll be getting them tomorrow. So then at 11:30 Elliott and I snuck down to see what was in our stockings—all school stuff! Tape, scissors, whiteout, mechanical pencil, etc. Elliott got address labels! Oh well. Now it's time to go to bed. Merry Christmas Eve!

January 1, 2003 Diary
HAPPY NEW YEAR 2003
SIX MONTHS TILL GRADUATION!

My New Years Resolutions:
- Be nice to my brother
- Eat healthy and get in shape
- Do all tests and insulin to get my license back
- Get a job

January 2, 2003 Diary
   Right before I ate dinner I saw a letter from St. Cloud State on the table. We didn't think it could be an acceptance letter yet, but it was. I didn't get in. I tried not to let it show that I was upset, because I was. I didn't really wanna go there anyway, but St. Cloud isn't as good a school as UMD. So if I couldn't get into St. Cloud, I probably can't get into UMD. This is very depressing for me. I didn't get in because I'm not in the top 50% of my class and I didn't have an ACT score of 25 or higher. I don't even know what my ACT score is! I'd like to know my score before I get college letters. DAMN!

January 5, 2003 Diary
   I GOT A 23 ON MY ACT!! I was so happy. I got a 25 on English and Reading, a 20 on science reasoning and 21 on Math. So that averages 23. Go me!

January 8, 2003 Diary
COUNTDOWN TO GRADUATION: 106 DAYS!
   Today in Economics we did our presentation on Dream Cones. We did pretty good: 98%! We got 118/120. Go us! The rest of the day was pretty usual and boring.

P.S. Yesterday I turned in my app. to Barnes and Noble!

January 17, 2003 Diary
COUNTDOWN TO GRADUATION: 97 DAYS!
Tuesday starts the new semester, here are my classes, in order:

1. Adv. Biology   4. Myths & Legends/short stories
2. Ceramics   5. Alg 2/Trig

3. Psych./Soc   6. Yearbook

I like the schedule, so it should be a fun and easy end to the school year! I have Sylvan tomorrow then I'm hoping my mom will take me to Galyans to get a new school bag. Now I must go to bed. Goodnight.

January 18, 2003 Diary
COUNTDOWN TO GRADUATION: 96 DAYS!
   Today after Sylvan I went to the dog park with my mom. It was fucking cold as hell. When we got home, I had a letter for me from UW-River Falls. It didn't come with a folder or anything so I was nervous. I was right too. I didn't get in. I don't really know why though, I was sure I could get in there. So I spent like an hour in my room crying. My dad came up and said he could help me, if I got him my grades on Tuesday, he would write to the admissions people. So now I only have UMD left, and I'm thinking if I didn't get into River Falls, I probably won't get into UMD. I think the AmeriCorps are looking better and better.

January 19, 2003 Diary
COUNTDOWN TO GRADUATION: 95 DAYS!
   Today I actually slept most of the day. I don't know why I was so tired. My blood sugar isn't high or anything. Hmmm. Oh well. So because of that I didn't do anything. Tomorrow I have a meeting with the dentist about getting my wisdom teeth pulled. Then at 5 (before Sylvan) we have a meeting AT Sylvan with Jill. I have a feeling it'll be all good things to say! I'm excited that Tuesday is the beginning of a new semester at school.

January 22, 2003 Diary
COUNTDOWN TO GRADUATION: 92 DAYS
   On Monday I went to the dentist and got a filling! I thought it was the consultation for getting my wisdom teeth removed, but I guess that's not until Feb 23. So they gave me a shot in my gums and the whole left side of my face was numb for hours! It sucked. Then yesterday at school I started a new semester!
   Yesterday I got a letter from UMD. They haven't rejected me yet—my application is going to be individually reviewed by an admissions committee. So at least I know they're taking time to decide if they want to take a chance on me! I'm also sending UWRF this

quarters grades. So I guess I do still have a chance. Time for bed now. Goodnight.

January 24, 2004 Diary
COUNTDOWN TO GRADUATION: 90 DAYS!
   Yesterday, I wrote a letter to the UMD Director of Admissions telling her I'd rather be admitted to the Liberal Arts college instead of the College of Science and Engineering, which is where I'd go for pre-med. So maybe I'll have more luck now. So now it's even more waiting . . . oh boy. I'm tired as hell now, so I have to go to bed cause I have Sylvan tomorrow morning! Goodnight.

January 27, 2003 Diary
COUNTDOWN TO GRADUATION: 87 DAYS!
   I decided I really, REALLY need to go on a diet. I look and feel awful in like all my clothes. I'm not gonna starve myself, but I'm going to eat a lot less.

January 31, 2003 Diary
COUNTDOWN TO GRADUATION: 83 DAYS!
   I decided I'm going on a very strict diet. I weigh like 142 pounds, and I want to weigh 130. I also want a flatter stomach. I see all these girls with flat stomachs, and I'm jealous because I have to suck it in and I still have a stomach sticking out. I feel gross in all my shirts. All I want to wear is sweatshirts. So I'm going to eat less, eat smarter, and exercise. It's been hard to discipline myself, but I definitely am now. I want to feel comfortable with myself. I need to look good come prom, graduation, and summer! I also need to get a job, then I'm going to go tanning too. Yeah. So that's my plan.
   Nothing really happened at school today, it was just a normal Friday. On Monday I have a doctor appointment with [nurse dietitian] and Dr. [ ]. I don't think my A1C will be down to 10 but I'm sure it will be down some! My license will come soon enough. I just hate the wait! [The A1C measures blood glucose levels for the preceding three months or so; a high blood glucose number means that there are too many blood sugar molecules in the blood stream. Those large sugar molecules do damage to tiny blood vessels in the eyes, digits, organs, etc. Non-diabetics run about 6.5. At one time Krystin was 13, an astronomically high number. Even 10 is dangerously high for someone with diabetes—or anyone else.]

February 1, 2003 Diary
COUNTDOWN TO GRADUATION: 82 DAYS!
Here's what I ate today:
- toast w/peanut butter & banana
- cream of mushroom soup
- yogurt
- bread crumb chicken & an orange
- peach
- toast w/peanut butter & banana <u>again</u>
- yogurt <u>again</u>

I guess that's pretty good! Of course I'm still hungry but I'm not going to eat. I still need to do crunches too.

I also picked up an application to Tobac and News that I'll turn in tomorrow. Hopefully I've finally have a job! Now I'm tired so I'm going to bed. Goodnight

February 4, 2003 Diary
COUNTDOWN TO GRADUATION: 79 DAYS!

Today I stayed home from school because I was sick. I felt horrible, I slept all day. My mom even came and got me early from Sylvan yesterday. On the up side though, I had a doctor appointment yesterday and Dr. [ ] said she'd sign my driver license form! YAY! My mom got the form from the DMV today, brought it home over lunch for me to sign, and faxed it to [physician] to fill out and send to the DMV, so I should be driving again by this weekend! I'm so excited! It'll be like getting my license for the first time. It'll be great because I know my friends are getting tired of driving me around everywhere.

I know this is short but I absolutely have to go to bed so I can get over this cold. I'm tired anyway. To bed now. Goodnight.

February 5, 2003 Diary
COUNTDOWN TO GRADUATION: 78 DAYS!

Tonight my dad and I went over to Highland. I turned in my application to Tobac & News. I think I have a good chance of getting a job there. I'll call in a few days if I haven't heard anything.

Then at about 8:45 a lady from UMD called and wanted to make sure I'm sending in my mid-year report. Then when they get it they'll make a decision and notify me right away. I'm so nervous!

Now I have to go to bed so I can finally get over this damn cold! Goodnight

February 8, 2003 Diary
COUNTDOWN TO GRADUATION: 75 DAYS!

Today was a pretty exciting day. At Sylvan, I switched the days I go from Mondays to Tuesdays, so I can be with Amy again! I get to drive there now, that's why I did it. Then Maria and I decided to go shopping. We got so much shit! We went to Southdale, and from American Eagle I got a pair of pants, underwear, two shirts and a cool belt. For Maria I got two belts and a hat. Then from JCPenney I got a pair of pants. Then we went to Lunds. Then we went over to Snyders and got a box of Crest white strips, two boxes of metabo-loss, Sharpie markers, hair clips, and hair bindies. Overall it was a very good and successful trip! Then Maria came over and we ate food and made Valentine's cards!

I have so much homework though I don't know when I'm going to do it. I don't want to let school stress me out, but I have a feeling it will.

My dad is really bugging me to apply to Morris. He's convinced he can get me with a snap of his fingers. Whatever. I don't really want to go there though. I don't think I can handle the hard work. Even if I got into both UMD and Morris, I'll still go to UMD, even if it disappoints my dad. It's my choice anyway, not his. [The University of Minnesota at Morris is a small (~1900 students) and somewhat selective liberal arts campus in western Minnesota. Krystin's grades in high school were such that she would only be able to get into a community college. I could not snap my fingers (or do anything else) and get her admitted, but fortunately for Krystin Morris happened to have an enrollment slump at that time so they were looking for students. They admitted Krystin, but under ordinary circumstances they might not have done so.]

February 15, 2003 Diary

Yesterday was Valentine's Day, and nothing too exciting happened at school. I gave out my cards and got only one sucker from Kelsey and Allison, and that was it. Sad huh? I went on the wheel in ceramics for the first time though! Mr. Sponsler helped me and practically did the whole thing for me. He ended up smashing it in the end though. Oh well, I'll try again on Tuesday.

Today after Sylvan my parents went to Southdale, so Elliott and I went to Cub and got groceries. Only $177 worth! Not too bad. I love grocery shopping with blank checks. I can basically get whatever I want.

February 17, 2003 Diary
COUNTDOWN TO GRADUATION: 66 DAYS!

Today we had school off, so my dad and I drove 3 hours up north to the U of M-Morris campus. We left about 7 am and got to the campus around 10:15 because we had to get breakfast. First we got a tour of the campus from Ann. The campus is pretty cool. Very small! I really liked the dorm rooms though. Then I met with one of the professors, Paula something. We just talked about what there is to do around the campus. Throughout the rest of the day I met with 4 other faculty members, ate lunch in the café, and sat in on a psychology class. Plus I got a sweatshirt from the bookstore! So it was a pretty good visit.

March 1, 2003 Diary
COUNTDOWN TO GRADUATION: 59 DAYS!

Today Joel and I went out! I thought it would never happen, but it finally did. We met at the Oakdale theater by Holly and John's, and saw 'Old School.' It was pretty funny, it was Joel's 2nd time seeing it. I put my hand down on the seat by my leg hoping we would hold hands, but unfortunately it never happened! Joel did buy my movie ticket though. Aww. . . ☺ I had a good time. I was so nervous the whole time. His hair is so long! It's longer than mine. Oh well, he's still cute. I wish something more would've happened, but of course I was too chicken to make a move. Maybe next time. I e-mailed him and said we should do something again soon. So we'll see!

March 6, 2003 Diary
COUNTDOWN TO GRADUATION: 57 DAYS!

Again, sorry I haven't written [in] so long! Not much has happened. I found out I didn't get into UMD though ☹ I still have Morris to hear from though. Everyone's crossing their fingers or toes for me, including me! Supposedly I'm supposed to find out this week, but it's already Thursday and I haven't anything yet so. . . . I guess we'll see tomorrow! If I don't get in Morris my dad said he'll start pulling some strings for me. [An idle promise, I confess now. I don't know what I would have done.] Cool.

March 13, 2003 Diary
COUNTDOWN TO GRADUATION: 53 DAYS!

Today I faked sick. I worked on biology, because I had Chrystalynne's notebook, and some math. Also, biggest news of the day: I GOT INTO MORRIS!! How exciting! My dad quickly checked the mail when he came to get me for Ellie, and there was a big envelope! YAY! I had to go to Sylvan afterwards, and my mom called and had one of the workers come give me a hug! How silly. So, yeah, I'm pretty excited about that.

March 20, 2003 Diary
COUNTDOWN TO GRADUATION: 48 DAYS!

Tomorrow my mom and dad and I are going to Morris for a new-student day and so my mom can have a tour of the campus.

[Krystin graduated from South High School in June 2003.]

Chapter 3

The College Years: University of Minnesota Morris

Late 2006 <u>DRAFT</u> <u>Life Story</u>
[Krystin's label; this is the second and final part of her narrative]

I graduated and started my freshman year of college in Fall 2003 at the University of Minnesota-Morris. I loved college even more than high school, even though I wanted to go home every weekend. I loved independence but missed home and my parents. My diabetes management got worse in college. I was no longer under the supervision of my parents or doctors, so I didn't feel as guilty about not doing my insulin.

In November 2004 it all caught up with me. It was the weekend before Thanksgiving and I was at home. I was feeling sick all weekend and by Sunday I was too sick to drive back to school. I stayed overnight with the intention of going back Monday morning in time for classes (school was ~3 hours from home). At 2 a.m. Monday morning, I was throwing up constantly, and was having breathing troubles, so I decided to go wake up my mom to bring me to the hospital. She thought I just didn't want to go back to school, but she called urgent care, and when she told the nurse my symptoms, the nurse told her to get me to the ER right away. The whole drive there I was getting worse. We walked into the ER, I plopped down into a wheelchair, and my mom went to check me in. The next thing I knew I was being whisked back and was stripped of my clothes and put into a hospital gown. They started up 2 different IVs, one insulin drip and one fluid drip. I don't remember anything of this, and I don't remember anything until about Tuesday, because I was in a mild coma-like state. Turns out I went into diabetic ketoacidosis, where ketones have built up in the blood and have started spilling out into my system, poisoning my body and shutting it down. The doctor said I was very lucky, because if I hadn't come in when I did, I would've died within an hour probably. I was in the hospital for 5 days and released on Thanksgiving day. [See below, "DKA, Round One," for more details of this episode.]

I did well with my management for awhile, but slowly started to decline again. I made it through 2 more years of school, just getting by with grades, considering I was sleeping more than anything. I still loved college and all the people I lived in the dorm with. In spring of 2006, my dad got a 4½ month leave to study at the University of Edinburgh in Edinburgh, Scotland. So my parents and brother and I packed up and moved over there. I even got to invite a school friend, so my friend Mike came along too. He and I did a lot of traveling around Europe on our own. We hit about 11 countries all together. And for 4½ months I didn't do my insulin. Maybe a few shots a week. On one of my last trips, Mike and I were in Warsaw, Poland, and I was leaving to go to Paris to meet my parents, who were already there, and Mike was going to continue traveling on his own to more of Eastern Europe. I left Warsaw on a Monday morning, and that whole weekend I had been feeling sick. It was starting again. I could tell as I got on the bus for the 25 hour ride to Paris. The whole ride I was shutting down. I was back and forth to the bus bathroom every hour, throwing up. I was supposed to meet my parents at the Louvre at 1 pm Tuesday afternoon when I arrived, but I never made it. When I got to the Paris bus station, I was so exhausted and dying that I just laid down on a bench, convinced it was going to be my final resting place. Luckily, a guy sensed something was wrong, because he came up and asked me, in English, if I needed a doctor. I nodded yes, and away he went. Within 10 minutes, the paramedics were there lifting me off the bench and bringing me to the ambulance. I don't remember the ride, the sirens, the IVs going in. Not at all. Again I was in the critical care unit, within less than an hour this time of losing my life, and my parents and brother were sitting at the Louvre wondering where I was. [We weren't; we just figured the bus was probably late so we went to do a little more touring in Paris that afternoon.] The hospital was able to get a message to the apartment that my family was in, and they did come to see me that night. [We took a long and expensive cab ride to the hospital during the Paris rush hour. Her much more detailed story about the bus ride and hospital stay in Paris comes later.]

I was in the hospital until that next Monday. We came home in mid-May, and that's when I found that what I was doing (or not doing) with my insulin was considered an eating disorder. This is also when I began the long journey of treatment, with 5 trips to an inpatient E.D. program at a hospital in the Twin Cities, and a 1-month period at a residential program, which didn't really work out for my situation. My parents and I decided that I wasn't going to return to school in the fall, and that I would look into other residential programs. We only started looking at Remuda in November, and the process to get me there was very quick. 2 days after my phone assessment, I was on the plane to Wickenburg, AZ.

And here I am today, very committed and very motivated for treatment and recovery, and looking forward to a life of freedom and health.

The Rope
[again, Krystin's narrative of her life]

Even when I went off to college, the habit continued. [She is referring to the preceding paragraphs in her narrative about the habit of ignoring her diabetes.] No blood tests, no insulin shots. All my friends knew I had diabetes, and they didn't like me any less. I didn't get teased for it, they didn't look at me like I had some contagious, deadly virus. Unlike in middle school and even a lot of people in high school, by college age, most people know what diabetes is and understand the basics of it. Nobody cared that I had diabetes, but after four years of ignoring it and living like I didn't have the illness, it had become a lifestyle. One that I didn't even try to break, because it wasn't even at the front of my mind as something that I *needed* to break.

DKA, Round One
[This is the more extended story about her DKA around Thanksgiving 2004]

Diabetic Ketoacidosis, also known as DKA, is a medical emergency which results in the body not having a sufficient amount of insulin, causing the body to start burning fat and muscle. This produces ketones (acid) that enter the bloodstream and essentially poisons the body. Think industrial-strength glue; you know, the kind that melts plastic. Symptoms of DKA include vomiting, dehydration, deep gasping breathing, confusion and disorientation, fatigue, and decreased consciousness. If not treated quickly, DKA progressively worsens until the body starts shutting down and every function ceases, resulting in death. For some people with diabetes, DKA can occur after a short period of time of mismanagement, around a week or two; for others, a month or more. It occurs quicker for diabetics who have had much better, tighter control over their diabetes, so as soon as their blood sugars start to get out of control, their body reacts quickly. Although I had avoided DKA up until this point, I had not been taking care of my diabetes for years, which means my body had become accustomed to always having high blood sugars, and it was going to take a lot to finally sound the alarm.

It all started my sophomore year of college, when I woke up feeling crummy Saturday morning the 20th of November, 2004. My first mistake was not taking my once-a-day insulin dose that slowly releases itself into my system throughout the day. I felt crummy all day Saturday and all day Sunday, although I still went out and about. I didn't take any insulin either of those days, because I hadn't eaten anything. I had a bowl of cereal Saturday morning, and that was it. I was supposed to drive my mom's car back to school at the University of Minnesota-Morris on Sunday because I had so much stuff to bring back, and I would be back home Wednesday anyway for Thanksgiving break. Needless to say, I never made it back to school. My parents and I decided that because I wasn't feeling well, and because my first class Monday wasn't until 10:30, that I'd wake up early Monday morning and drive back then.

Dinner time came around on Sunday night, and I still wasn't hungry, so when my parents and brother sat down to dinner, I went upstairs and threw up – for the first time. I slept in our living room that night and was going to the bathroom to throw up almost every hour. By 2:30 in the morning, my throat was burning, and I was breathing very hard. In fact, I could hardly breathe at all. I finally decided I needed to go wake up my mom, so I slugged upstairs and woke her, and when she sat up, I took her place and layed down in her bed, telling her I felt like I was dying. What we didn't know then was that I wasn't lying.

My mom insisted I was being a wimp and just didn't want to go to class Monday, but she went downstairs, and I could hear her muffled voice on the phone as she called urgent care. As I was lying in my parents' bed, I told my dad that it was really sad, but the thought had gone through my head that I would rather be dead than be feeling what I was feeling. I told my dad that it felt like I was breathing so hard and fast, like my heart was going to burst through my chest. He told me that I was actually breathing very slowly.

When my mom returned, she announced that the only open after-hour clinic was in Apple Valley, but as soon as she had told the nurse on the phone my symptoms, the nurse told her to bring me into the emergency room right away, to Fairview University Medical Center. We stumbled downstairs and my mom helped me get on my shoes (which I didn't want to put on, I wanted to go in my socks) and a sweatshirt, grabbed the barf bucket just in case, and headed out to the car. By this time I was still conscious, but very groggy and not functioning very well, having a hard time paying attention or concentrating. This will be true up until around Tuesday night of that next week.

As soon as we got to the ER and entered the building, I found a wheel chair and sat down in it. A male doctor came out to ask me what's wrong. All I could do was mumble at him, but he knew right away what was wrong by the fruity smell of my breathe that comes with ketoacidosis. Before my mom could finish checking me in, they had me whisked away to the back and were getting my clothes off and a gown on. Two female nurses were doing this, and I remember one of them commenting on my tattoo and that she liked the colors, and her telling me that she had a big sun tattoo on her upper back. They stuck both my left wrist and the crook of my right elbow with needles so they could hook up IV's. A different female nurse was then called and she put a Foley catheter in me. They did a blood test on me, and the meter just read HI. For a diabetic, a normal blood sugar level would range between about 80-120. On the hospital meters, a HI reading means over 800.

I really had to defecate at this point, even though they told me I should go before the catheter goes in. So they brought in a commode and gave me a private moment. I hadn't wanted to use a commode, which is why I turned it down the first time, and now here I was using it anyway, with a catheter in. Would have been easier had I used it before, but I guess this is how we learn. I remember sitting on it for a long time, and the male doctor coming back to ask me if I was OK or if I was done, and I told him no. It soon began to sting very bad, and it suddenly got really loud in the ER, like an airplane was hovering overhead. Turns out they had to turn on the industrial strength fans to air out the smell.

While my mom was standing in the hallway waiting for me to finish, one of the ER doctors came over to talk to her. They sat in a little lounge-type room across from my bay and he asked her if I had ever been hospitalized for my diabetes before, and she said I had not. I'd been to the ER before, but never admitted. He told her they were going to admit me, and she said that was fine. He asked a bunch of questions and she was rambling off a bunch of answers but really didn't know what she was saying. She told the doctor that she was sorry that she was jumping from thought to thought, and he said "you're doing fine." He explained to her that I was in ketoacidosis and they would have to start IVs to get my blood sugars down (which they had already started).

After I was done, my mom came back in to join me as the nurses prepared to move me up to the CCU (critical care unit). I squeezed my mom's hand and told her "thank you for bringing me here. I love you." They had me hooked up to a portable EEG monitor to monitor my breathing, which was beeping away with every heartbeat. I made some comment to my mom about the irritating beeping, and she replied with "Krystin, it's measuring your heartbeat. If it stops making noise, it means you're dead. You WANT it to be making noise." In less than a minute, a male nurse came in and reached over me and pushed a button on the machine that made the beeping stop. The room immediately became quiet, and I opened my eyes wide and looked over at my mom. She had seen what the nurse had done, but I hadn't, since I was flat on my back and had my eyes closed. It was the only half humorous moment of the whole experience.

Up on the 4th floor, in the CCU, they hooked me up to my 2nd IV, as well as other machines to measure my vitals. At one point my mom asked the doctor how I was doing. He told her "she's in very critical condition right now. There is a chance we might lose her, but we're doing everything we can to make sure that doesn't happen." By 6:30 the next morning, my pulse was still over 150, and jagged lines were all over the screen of the EEG monitor.

I don't remember much about the proceeding day and a half. I just remember a lot of people coming in and out and asking me questions which were hard for me to answer because 1) I was so dehydrated and my mouth was so dry I was having troubles talking, and 2) I was still not able to fully concentrate or pay attention to anything. I never slept, because my short, heavy breathing hurt when I exhaled and kept me from sleeping, but my eyes were still closed most of the time. On Monday the 22nd my uncle Jeff came and visited, but I never really saw him. I heard him talking to my parents, as I could still hear all that was going on around me, but I did not interact at all. My best friend Christine also came to visit that day, because my dad had called and told her what happened. She had been sitting in a lecture that was about to start, but when she got the call, she informed her professor that she needed to leave; family emergency. I remember her showing up and giving her a hug, and maybe talking a little, but I do not remember her leaving because I drifted off on her.

Whenever the doctors or anyone would talk to me or ask me questions, I would reply to them in my head, but not out loud, although I thought I had answered out loud, so questions would have to be asked twice. I was SO thirsty, but I was not allowed to drink any liquids because my stomach could still not handle it. My mouth was so dry that my lips were bleeding, so they had little sponges on sticks that I could dip into a cup of water and swab my mouth with to wet it. I was so desperate for something to drink that I would dip the sponge in the water then stick it in my mouth and suck all the water out of it.

By Tuesday I was keeping my eyes open more and was able to talk more with my parents. My uncle Jeff visited me again, as did Christine. My blood sugar was finally coming down, and everything inside of my body was getting back under control. I was still far from ready to go home, however. My dad sent emails to my professors at Morris to let them know that I would not be returning for classes until after Thanksgiving. I was finally able to try drinking some water, and after that proved successful, my mom even went to the hospital cafeteria and got me some Crystal Light Raspberry Ice water. I had never tasted anything so good in my life. Refreshing is an understatement.

Soon after, I was put on a liquid diet, then the full liquid diet, then the moderate carb diet. I could only eat small amounts at a time. Even though I began to feel hunger again, my stomach got full very fast, after four days of not eating at all. I began small, with oatmeal, soups, yogurt, mashed potatoes; things that went down easy. It took a couple more days for me to move up to the solid food diet. Still no cheeseburgers for me, but instead of mashed potatoes I would order French fries. Instead of oatmeal I would order cereal and fresh fruit. I was making progress, getting stronger every day. It was even required that I get up and go for walks, to keep my legs strong. When I didn't have visitors, I watched TV, read, or napped. Mostly napped. Not much else to do in a hospital, is there?

I was released two days before Thanksgiving, after eight days and seven nights in the hospital. At the Thanksgiving table that year, I had never felt more thankful to be surrounded by family.

[As you read some of the following entries, in which Krystin complains about how poorly she does on tests even though she studies a great deal and attends all the classes, remember these sentences from the opening paragraph of this chapter: "My diabetes management got worse in college. I was no longer under the supervision of my parents or doctors, so I didn't feel as guilty about not doing my insulin." Among the side effects of high blood glucose levels (hyperglycemia) are headaches, trouble concentrating, blurred vision, and fatigue (weak, tired feeling), per WebMD and other reputable websites. At some point after we returned from Scotland, when Krystin was seeing physicians at the eating disorder programs, one of them was incredulous that Krystin had completed two years of college. He was amazed that anyone with such long-term, consistent hyperglycemia had been able to study enough to complete college classes. That she did so is a tribute to Krystin's tenacity in the face of her lack of control of her disease—and is also likely the explanation of why she did not do well in classes despite her hard work at being a student.]

October 6, 2003 Diary

Today is the day I begin my journal. It's only a month and a half into my freshman year of college and already there are problems. Mostly with my roommates. My mom said I'd feel much better if I wrote things down, so here goes. I got along with my roommates and enjoyed my classes. But now, I don't get along so well with my roommates and I'm nervous about how I'm going to do in 2 of my 4 classes. In Psych, we've already had 2 tests and I got 27/60 on both. Yikes, not good. I just don't feel like I'm college material. I did fine in high school [well, not really!] but college just isn't for me. And in my Solar System class I'm getting behind. I feel so overwhelmed. I get text [she meant "test"] anxiety so even after I studied for 8 hours when I sat down for the test it all leaves my mind. I have to get a C or better in Psychology for the credit to go towards my major so if I don't improve my test scores, I'll have to take it over.

Then there's the roommate issue. . . . So then there's the issue that's pissing me off the most: insulin. Yes, I know I'm not taking it like I should be but that's my problem and I wish they'd stop acting like my fucking mother. I get enough shit from my doctor/parents/friends, I don't need it from them. I came to college to get away from all the nagging and all I got was more. . . . So the meeting with the 4 of us (Lindsey, Ashley, Sara, and I) was horrible, it was basically a "let's bash on Krystin" meeting. I was very pissed how they went to Sara with their issues before coming to me, so I had to hear it from Sara and not from them. I actually started to cry during the meeting when they started telling me to do my insulin and what can they do to help. Nothing. I just wanted to leave, walk out.

Afterwards I called my dad and talked to him, and then again at 9 to talk to my mom. I thought I would feel better after talking to her but I only felt worse. She took Lindsey and Ashley's side just like Sara did. I cried again but kept it to myself. I think just had my first college breakdown. Sometimes you just need to cry. It helps I guess. They had a little birthday party in the lounge tonight for anyone with an October birthday and I missed it. Nobody came to tell me or get me. Makes me feel even sadder and unappreciated. Sam came in though and said he would've come and gotten me if he had known I was still in my room.

Speaking of Sam, I really like him. He's such a nice guy but very flirty, even if doesn't realize he's being flirty. But he has a girlfriend of 9 months, Alice. . . .

All the drama that's going on makes me want to scream. I don't adapt well to change, and this has been a lot of change. I need Chris right now, I miss her so bad. I saw her on Friday but only for about 10 minutes. And she's always distracted or busy when I call her cell or talk to her online. I don't want to lose her. I love her like a sister. So basically I need to toughen up and get serious about what I need to do with my school work and diabetes. I'm all out of thoughts for tonight.

November 18, 2003 Email
Krystin to dad:
Hi dad,

I just got back from a meeting with [a professor]. There was a review session yesterday at 4pm just to go over what we've been talking about in class and what's going on in the chapter, but I have my solar system lab from 3:30 to 5:30, so I missed it. So we set up a meeting and went over the stuff together – my own review session! It was good because we worked through what just *I* needed to work on. I think it helped a lot. We'll find out after my next test on Friday!

I think I'll stick with Spanish next semester. [She did, for one more semester, then switched to German in Fall Semester 2007 and took it for four semesters—and got 3 A's and 1 B+. She liked German.] I know it doesn't sound like too fun a semester to you, but it will be good for me because I will be able to get so much more help with Spanish than I would if I took it this summer. Because I know you and mom wouldn't be TOO much help! Admit it. (: You said as long as I think it will be an OK semester then that's OK with you. I think it will be a fine semester.

I'm so excited to come home for Thanksgiving. I'm hoping to come home Wednesday.... It's going to be a very full weekend, which unfortunately makes it go way too fast, but it will be fun. I'm most looking forward to getting our tree and decorating it and the house. I love getting into the Christmas spirit, it's my favorite time of year! [That was true all her life.]

November 24, 2003 Email
Krystin to mom, dad:
Hi mom and dad,

So, last night I went to the hospital in town. Don't worry, I'm not dying or anything, and it has nothing to do with diabetes! So let out a breath.... Last night Sara on my floor and I ordered Pizza Hut around 9:30, and it was good, and things were going fine, I was working on my paper, and around midnight my stomach started to not feel so well. I felt like I was going to throw up, and I kept going back and forth from the bathroom to the lounge (where I was working on my paper) but nothing was happening. I threw up a tiny, tiny bit, but not enough to make the feeling go away. So around 1am, since our health services was closed, I had John (a guy on my floor) drive me to the hospital in town, because if I was going to be sick, I didn't want it to be in the dorm. So we sat in one of the patient rooms and we did a blood test and my number read "hi" on the machine, but I had done my lantus and humalog [forms of insulin; "hi" probably means her blood glucose number was above 500] at dinner, so they gave me some more Humalog and gave me a shot in my arm for the nausea (which by the way, my whole left arm is super-sensitive and sore today), and drew blood from my arm – 4 tubes worth! So I was starting to feel a little better so we came back to the dorm about 2:15am, and I worked on my paper a little more then went to bed. I didn't actually finish my paper, but the doctor gave me a written note to give to [the professor], so I have until tomorrow to finish it! Today Keith comes out and tells me that a couple of his friends went to Pizza Hut last night and they got sick too – so it turns out it was food poisoning. Bleah. I'm much better today though....

Love you and talk to you soon,

November 25, 2003 Email
Krystin to dad:

There is no LD [learning disability] testing here. [One of her faculty members] gave me the name and e-mail of a girl, I think she's a senior maybe, who works in academic assistance that I should talk to about psych and getting tested, so I e-mailed her. She said they cannot test students, but she can set up a meeting with me and talk to me about study strategies and how to deal with test anxiety. So I can always do that, but as far as testing for a LD, that will have to be done somewhere else.

Remind me again when we are going to start decorating the house [for Christmas]. Thursday instead of Friday? I suppose I could get up in time to help with that. Then there's not going to be anything left to do on Friday but get our tree! We are still going to put the real tree in the living room right? I don't want the fake one in the living room, even though that's what mom wanted to do. It's not as pretty.

December 1, 2003 Email
Dad to Krystin:

We enjoyed having you at home this weekend, even if I did feel crappy most of it. . . .

Before you came home this weekend, Elliott told me out of the blue that he liked it when you came home because you were fun to be with and he liked doing things with you. . . .

December 4, 2003 Email
Krystin to mom:

Mom why are you so depressed? I hope it's mostly because of menopause and will go away eventually. If we are getting a puppy after we get back, can we try to find one before I go back to school. . . .

Mom to Krystin:

I am depressed because I am watching my beautiful little girl die a very slow and ugly death and there is not a damn thing I can do anymore to help her.

December 5, 2003 Email
flu shot
Krystin to dad:

THERE. I got my flu shot! See, I told you I would get it done! Now I can go to Cancun.

Dad to Krystin:

Thank you. Indeed, you may go to Cancun. (I would have felt very, very bad if I had had to make you stay home. I like your company and I think you'll have a great time.)

December 9, 2003 Email
Krystin to mom:

Dad asked me in an email today if I thought UMM was too hard for me. Did you get this email? I replied to him that I have thought about it. What I didn't tell him though, is that I feel like HE'D be ashamed to tell people I have to go to a different school because this one was too hard for me. After everyone knowing I'm at UMM, it doesn't look good to say I had to switch to, say for example, St. Cloud State (although don't really want to go there). I don't think dad would be very proud of me. I want to prove that I can handle it here, but really what if I can't? I like it here, and I like the people, but the work just may be too hard. I don't know. It's too late to transfer for spring semester, and that's fine, I wouldn't want to just pack up and leave now, but as for next year, I don't know. We can talk about it. We'll see after my finals and after I get my grades. . . .

Mom to Krystin:

No, dad didn't share that email with me. But rather than run from school to school, why don't you do what really needs to happen and just get that glucose into your brain so that you can think more clearly? Again, you're building that wall around you and then asking for help. It's gotta come from you, Krystin.

Love, mom

Krystin to dad:

I've thought about it. But like you said, where else would I go? And I wouldn't want you to be disappointed in me for not going to Morris. I'm not saying yes I want to go somewhere else, but I have thought about it.

December 9, 2003 Diary
I don't remember the last time I wrote—looks like when Molly was here, but I didn't write down a date. I think was the middle of October. Anyway, right now is a very stressful time at school. So again I'm writing because hopefully it will help. Next weekend I take my finals, and I'm not nearly ready. I have done shitty this semester, and I know it's because of my high blood sugars. My parents have gone back to nagging me about it, and I wish they'd stop. They're pushing, and the more they push, the more I pull back. I don't know why I can't pull myself together and just do it. I have motivation (doing well in school), and I have everything I need. I just can't seem to do it and there's no explanation for why. If I do bad in school, my dad will be disappointed in me. He's always cared about how well I do in school and I feel I have to do well for him. [Even though I told her repeatedly that I wanted her to do well for *her*, not me. She knew that and acknowledged my point at Remuda, four years later.] I got an e-mail from him today asking if I thought UMM was too hard for me and if I wanted to switch schools. I've thought about it. But again, it would look bad if I had to switch to a school and didn't have as good a reputation. I think my dad would be ashamed of me. [I wouldn't have been. But she didn't know that. I don't have any messages indicating I told her so.]

I'm not happy here. [To preview what's coming, she completely changed her mind on this later. She loved UM-Morris and missed it when she wasn't there.] I don't get along with my roommates at all—they are making college life miserable for me. I hate being in my room. I spend as little time as possible in there, and when I AM in there, I feel like I'm invading, and there's so much negative energy I hate it. . . .

Maybe I'm depressed or just really unhappy and stressed. I want to cry every day and have even thought about killing myself. Enough said. I'll write more as it comes to me. Just kidding I'm not done. It's now later at night though, and I just found out something at dinner. I guess Lindsey and Ashley are moving out! Down to 3C. But, a lot of people on my floor knew before I did. Even Steph, and she doesn't even live on this floor. Jeff said Sara was filling out the paperwork, so it sounds definite.

AHH! More news. OK so soon after I finished writing last time Lindsey came up to me and told me that they were moving and I had to sign a sheet agreeing to it, and whether I'll find a new roommate myself or have one assigned to me. I checked to have one assigned to me. They're moving after finals week. I can't wait. OK really now that's all.

December 12, 2003 Email
Happy Friday!
Krystin to dad:
Dad,

    I just finished my 6-page paper for Greek Myths. Actually, I just called mom's cell and left her a message to call me if she gets it before she goes to work, because I need some info from a book that's in my room for my paper, and then I realized I can go to Amazon. com and get the info. . . . So if you get this in the morning before you go to work and she's still there and hasn't called me, tell her not to! Otherwise no biggie, she'll just be my wake-up call. Anyway feels good to be done. That was my last assignment of the semester! Now all I have to do is get through finals, which actually shouldn't be too bad. Both psychology and solar system have study guides, so at least I know what to study.

    I'll be home Monday night. . . . I'll be home around midnight! Probably earlier though because it'll be so late there won't be much traffic and we shouldn't have any troubles. Maybe a potty stop. What are your plans for the weekend? Since it is a Friday night, you and mom could sit up and wait for me, but if you don't want to that's OK. My only option would be to come home Wednesday night or Friday night, and if I'm done with finals on Monday afternoon, I really don't want to hang around here for a couple of days. . . .

    The interaction with my roommates leaving was actually pretty civil. I already knew about them moving of course, so I wasn't surprised by it anything. . . . Then we went back to ignoring each other. So, nothing's changed. I'm just glad they're leaving. . . .

    Off to bed now – my eyes are starting to hurt! And droop. Happy Friday! No classes for me because it's a study day so I can sleep in a little and then get to studying! Love you, talk to you soon.

December 15, 2003 Email
new roommate
Krystin to dad:

    My final went alright. The one thing I didn't study was the essay questions, which he gave us 4 of and said one or two will be on the final. But when I sat down, I was surprised how much of the information just came back to me, which is the opposite of what usually happens – it all goes away! But like you said, maybe that's for multiple choice, maybe I am better at essay questions. So I think it was alright. That was worth 150 points and all the others were only worth 100. I was afraid I was going to walk in and he was going to say "well not matter how well you do on this test you're going to fail anyway." Luckily he didn't say that, so MAYBE I still have a chance. I asked mom though, what if I DO fail? I know [you] will be disappointed in me, but she said she will still let me come home and won't disown me or anything. It hasn't happened yet, but I need to know there are options if it does.

I'm going to take a nap now before I go to lunch and then my psychology final. Then only a few (ok, like 6) hours before I leave to come home. Love you and talk to you soon.

December 15, 2003 Email
Hello
Krystin to dad:

It's good to know that you won't kick me out of the house if I fail one class. I do plan on doing a lot better next semester. I know everyone says first semester is the hardest, and I'm one of those people that "they" use to prove it. . . .

December 17, 2003 Email
psych
Krystin to dad:

Ok, pretty sure I failed psychology too. I checked my score for the final, and I got 32 out of 80. Then I added up all my scores for the semester and divided it by the total number of points, and I only have 255 out of 498, so that's only 51%, and so far in all my schooling, 51% is an F. I still don't know what my solar system grade is. So, now what? How about I cry. I've reached the bottom in college already – does it start to go up from here?

Dad to Krystin:

This is a bump in the road of life. You'll get over the bump. We just need to help you figure out how. Don't cry. We'll help you get through this.

Love you.

January 14, 2004 Email
hello
Krystin to dad:

My classes are good. Spanish will be pretty easy, and the professor is nice. I forget his name at the moment. James is really funny. Geology is in the science auditorium, same as psychology last semester. It's a full class – around 250 students. I sit with one of the girls on my floor.... I think it's going to be a really fun and interesting class. Statistics, I think that will be my most challenging class. My professor has a strong accent and I can't understand everything he says, but not to the point that I'm going to fail because of it or anything....

Anthropology is in the same room as my astronomy class. Avi is in that class too, we sit next to each other.... My professor for that class has been teaching there since 1971 and has never used a whiteboard, always a chalk board or something, so he was amazed with the whiteboard and how easily it erased. He also thinks he's dyslexic. He's a pretty funny guy too, also kinda airy like my astronomy prof, but this time people actually laugh at his jokes because they're not really jokes, it's just him being him. That will also be a fun and interesting class I think. So overall I think it will be a good semester, definitely better than last. [Her GPA was 2.20 in the fall, 2.25 at the end of spring. So she was right, it was better in terms of academic performance—by a minute increment.]ser I had a tough load for being my first semester, with 4 classes and two labs (psych and solar system). I don't have any labs this semester, so I think that will make a difference too....

January 20, 2004 Diary

Wow so much to catch up on. I'll start with break. I didn't end up working at the U, so it was a relaxing break. We went to Cancun from Dec 20-27. It was fun, but I had bad stomach aches all week, so I felt uncomfortable a lot of the time. I didn't even really get to use much Spanish because everyone spoke English?! I did get kinda tan—on the last day we went snorkeling and I got burnt like a tomato! Oh well. And I was able to keep my tattoo hidden! We were there over Christmas but it didn't feel like Christmas because there was no snow and we weren't with family all that seasonal stuff. I did get a lot of souvenir-y stuff though!

So what next.... I found out all my final grades online. They were as follows:

College writing: B
Greek Myths: B
Psychology: D
Solar System: F

So that puts me on academic probation. My GPA is 1.67 or something like that, and I need at least a 2.0 to get off probation. This semester I'm taking Spanish, Geology, Statistics, and Anthropology. 16 credits. And as of today I also have a learning-to-learn class—2 credits so I have 18 credits. It's only half a semester long and no homework, so it will be easy. I'm thinking of taking Solar System again next fall, because if I get better grade, it will override the F and will improve my GPA. That would be a good thing.

So, next thing—I have no roommate/s! I was assigned one . . . but she's not coming to UMM this semester. So I have the whole room to myself! It's pretty nice. I like it—I have quietness, privacy, everything. I LOVE it. And if they haven't assigned me a new roomie by now, I don't [think] they will at all. I have a huge fridge now too! My dad's office got a new one so I got that one. It's so cool, now I don't have to put things in the floor fridge. My dad and Elliott brought it to me last weekend.

Pretty sure that's all for now. Later!

January 20, 2004 Email
two matters
Dad to Krystin:
Hi, Speed.

A couple of thoughts on two issues.

One: I trust you know that this is your most important semester in school ever. You don't want to be in a position where you cannot return to UMM because of grades. . . . If I were you, I would talk seriously about them with your academic advisor. Maybe you already have. (And I will say once more, you do not have to get good grades FOR ME! You need to get them for yourself. I assume you want to come back to UMM next year.)

Two: I would like to have you do an A1c when you are home for spring break. I want to know where you stand now. (And gee, it would be great if you work on it this semester so I can say, once we get the result, "that's really great, Krystin!" As I said in my letter that I sent but didn't send [I have no idea what I meant here], I wanted to work out an incentive plan; if you can think of one that would work—we never talked about it—let's discuss it. Maybe Saturday night if you come home?) [Presumably she was coming home for the long Martin Luther King weekend.]

Krystin to dad:
I have a meeting with my advisor today at 3:45. We will be discussing the matter of academic probation. I will let you know how it goes. When figure out what I need to do (or, how I need to do) this semester, I will work hard at it.

Also, I am working harder on my diabetes, so that should help me do better as well. I want you to know though that when I do an A1c during spring break, it might not be at what you are expecting, but know that I'm working on it.

February 17, 2004 Email
Krystin to mom:
GUESS WHAT . . . 55/60 on my anthropology quiz!!! I was so happy I wanted to jump up and down around the room screaming. Of course I didn't, I just put on a smile and it hasn't gone away since. That's the best I've done on any of my college tests so far. I should buy a magnet and stick it on my fridge. (:

February 18, 2004 Email
Hello
Krystin to dad:
Are we surprised that Vickie and the kitten are hissing at each other? [our new kitty, Bela] I'm not! Mom sent a digital picture of him but I couldn't really get a good idea of what he looks like because he was on the carpet in the living room. Is he all black? . . .

I'm so glad Genie is willing to teach me some cooking techniques. I'm really looking forward to it. So this summer then? I hope that that means if I learn some really good meals from her, you'll let me (try) to make them at home too for you guys?

February 24, 2004 Email
hello
Krystin to dad:
Hi dad,
Yes, I am still here. I'm really excited for tomorrow (Wednesday) because I'll find out my Spanish test score! I told you how my

professor said that everyone did really well and there were a lot of A's right? Hopefully that's me! But what I really want to know is my geology score, but I won't know that until Friday. Oh well, if I keep my mind off of it, maybe the time will go by faster. . . .

February 25, 2004 Email
99/100 on my spanish test!!!
Krystin to dad:

I actually originally got 94, but because everyone in the class did so well, our daily quiz turned into an option extra credit quiz, and the score would be added to your quiz score. It could only help you, so I figured, why not?? And I got 5 extra points, making my score 99/100!

Yay, go me!

Dad to Krystin:
GREAT!!!!

February 26, 2004 Email
test
Krystin to mom, dad:

Oh man, that anthropology test was so easy! And the nice thing about tests is that you can leave afterwards, and getting done with a test in 20 minutes for an hour and 40 minute class, gives me an extra hour and 20 minutes in my day! How nice. Now I can go to food service for lunch with Sara. Good deal.

February 26, 2004 Email
pop
Krystin to dad:
Hi dad,

So remember in Cancun how I had bad stomach aches all day? And how I've had stomach aches almost every day since? Well, we know part of the problem from when we were in Cancun, but I think I figured out the other half of why I got them – POP! I think my stomach decided it doesn't like [to] digest pop, maybe the carbonation or something. Because today, I didn't have any pop at all, and I haven't had any stomach aches, where before I've usually had a pop at least once a day. I can't say that's for sure because today is the first day I haven't had a pop, but I think I'll go a while without having pop and see if that really makes a difference. I guess I wouldn't mind not being able to drink pop, it's not good for you anyway! (Diet or not, studies have shown that pop makes you gas-y and carbonation is harder on your system.) I'll just have to drink water instead! And a juice once in a while if I do insulin with it. (:

February 27, 2004 Email
job
Krystin to dad:
   [I had asked what she was going to do about a summer job.] I don't know yet what I'm going to do. Why, do you have some ideas? I was going to ask you if you knew anybody else at the U that might be looking for a student worker during the summer. It not, then I don't know... I know there is no way that I'll work at Lunds [a nearby higher-end grocery store; she had been a carry-out person in the past] again, mostly because the hours there are bad, and because I hated it. I don't know what I'm going to do yet.

March 1, 2004 Email
test
Krystin to mom, dad:
   So, did you ever take a test and feel that you did really really well and then when you get it back, find out you didn't do as well as you thought? [I told her that indeed I had—and had the reverse phenomenon occur as well, receiving a better grade than I had expected (or thought I deserved).] That happened with my geology tests! I got 64/100, but with the curve it still ended up being a C. I need to get 70's on the next two tests (there are only two more) to get a B in the class. . . . C is good but I need to do better to stay here next year! Ok, so just wanted to let you know that. Talk to you both soon I'm sure. Love you.

March 4, 2004 Email
hello
Krystin to dad:
Hi dad,
   Please, please, please stop bugging me about stats! I know what I have to do, and I know the consequences of my actions. Don't worry about it, things will be fine. Just because I didn't do so well on the first test, doesn't mean I'm going to fail the course! It was one test, and there are lots more assignments worth of points that will make up for

it. If you asked me right now, I would tell you that the class is going well and I am doing fine. . . .

March 18, 2004 Email
Krystin to dad:
Hi dad,

My days back in reality are going well. . . . My Learning to Learn class is over now so I no longer have 4 classes in a row. I think that will make my Mondays, Wednesdays, and Fridays less stressful. And less stress on my back because I won't have to carry ALL my books.

How is Bela doing? I text messaged mom right after we left Sunday and told her that I miss him already! Oh yeah, and that I missed you guys too. I fell in love with his cute little kitty face the moment I saw him. I loved him right away, even if he did wake me up at 2 in the morning!

April 7, 2004 Email
Krystin to mom, dad:

I got all my classes! So, assuming I'm coming back next year, here are the classes I will have:

Intro to World History to 1500
The Solar System
Intro to Literature
Solar System Lab
First-Year Drawing

Yes, I'm actually taking a drawing class! It's required for generals anyway, so I might as well get it over with. Maybe this is one class Elliott can help ME with. Maybe I can just draw stick people. Haha yeah right . . . Off to read anthropology. [Elliott had been drawing since he was little. We hired private tutors (art students) at the University and at Macalester College for him and also put him in a few classes outside of regular school (with his enthusiastic consent). Krystin was referring here to his considerable training in art even by the time he was in his early teens. He graduated from Moorhead State University in 2016 with a BFA in drawing and painting.]

April 13, 2004 Email
Krystin to mom, dad:

So, I just thought I'd e-mail you and let you know I got a job for the rest of the year and possibly next year! Working at the post office – and I start tomorrow! I work MWF from 9:15 – 10:15 AM and then also for a half hour from 1:40 – 2:10. Yay! So it's only 4 and a half hours each week, but there isn't much school left and maybe it can be increased next year. And anyway, I need to be using my extra time to study! But yeah, go me I got a job! Now I have to worry about finding one this summer.

May 3, 2004 Email
Krystin to dad:

Well, I'm feeling a little better today. Sleeping for the past three days has really helped. Plus, today Keith gave me about 5 different kinds of medicines that he doesn't need because he's not sick . . .

I emailed my anthro professor today about me taking the final a couple days later. I told him I've been sick, so hopefully he'll believe me.

Did I tell you I got a 78/100 on my stats re-take? I studied from the test I took first time around, so it helped that some of the same questions were on the re-take! . . .

May 4, 2004 Email
GOOD NEWS!!
Mom to Krystin, cc Gary:

Well, I think this is good news. I went on the web to check your driver's license status and it says VALID. So I'm assuming the signed form from [the physician] got into the system? [At least in Minnesota, people with diabetes have to have a form signed by their physician in order to obtain a driver's license. Or at least some of them do.] We should be getting a letter in the mail soon stating this, but I think as long as it states VALID on the web, you're good to drive.

Krystin to mom, dad:

Yay about my license!! I was worried about that.

I have GOOD NEWS too! I get to take the anthropology final on Thursday! And, it will be all essay, which is good for me. No multiple choice or true/false, all essay And we get to use 150 words of notes for EACH essay, so this is also a good thing. I went to the review last night and talked to him and he said he always prepares a second, all-essay test for those who feel they are not ready when the final comes around. So, that's the plan.

July 18, 2004 Diary

    I have a lot of things to say and catch up on, so I may have to do this in increments, depending on how tired my hand gets. I suppose I should start with the end. The end of last school year. My first year of college at UMM. Second semester was a lot better. I got my ass in shape and did OK. My grades were as follows:

Spanish: B+ (or was it A-?)
Geology: C
Statistics: C (YAY!)
Anthropology: C

    I thought for sure I was going to fail stats. I am taking the Solar System class again this fall and Sam and Keith are in the class (and same lab with Sam) so I should do better!

    Next, summer job. I am working downtown at Bigsby's, not to be confused with Bixby's, the bagel place. There's my boss, Kris (40), Mike (34), who likes to tell me about his pregnant wife and his cats, Dan (33), Bernie and Ramon, whom I don't know how old they are. So I do the same thing every day. In at 10:30, set up, serve the lunch rush, lunch break at 1:30, clean up, leave at 3:30. I then either walk to my mom's office and wait for her, or ride home with my dad who picks me up. Oh, and I take the bus/light rail to work. My last day at work is August 26 and I go back to school on the 28th or 29th (I haven't decided yet).

July 19, 2004 Diary

    OK, so here's the big story and the drama of my life—my diabetes. My parents sat me down last Thursday and had a serious talk with me. They said they are very worried about how I'm not taking care of myself and how others have voiced concern, like family, and Chris. So there are 2 new house rules. (1) My dad is going to look at my log book every night and make [sure] there are 4 blood tests done and written down, and (2) no more juice in the house. Diet pop or water or whatever. OK, both rules are fair. I want to do better and I know I need the help. My dad made me another deal. I still owe him $225 from loans I took out last year, so he wants me to write him 3 $75 checks. IF, when I go back to school in August, I've done all my tests and insulin, he'll tear up the 3 checks. GREAT! But then when I go back to school will I fall back into the bad pattern? I don't want to be the kind of diabetic that always needs a motivation to do well. My parents say I have family and friends who love me and care about my health, and that should be motivation enough, but I guess it's not. My parents also want me to go on mild anti-depressants because that might help ME want to stay in a good pattern and do well. So we'll see I guess! I don't know how I feel about my diabetes. I sub-consciously just pretend it's not there. I can still save myself though and slow or stop the complications. I have to go to bed now. More later. Sweet dreams.

August 5, 2004 Diary

Payday! $433 right into checking. OK so it has been a month since I started my new diabetic routine. It's going fairly well. I had a doctor appt. with [physician] yesterday, and I was pretty nervous going in, but that also went fairly well. She was just glad I had data for her to look at. My A1C was 13.5 [remember, this is a terribly high number], but by Thanksgiving my mom thinks it will be down to 10. Let's cross our fingers. The only thing is that I'm gaining weight again. I was 119, now I'm up to almost 135. My tummy (gut) is showing it too. I try to wear bigger shirts but I look like I'm pregnant! I hate it. And I can't stop eating damn Reece's Pieces. But I've also started doing leg lifts. I've thought about bulimia, but I can't make myself throw up, and I love food too much to be anorexic. I see all these girls with flat stomachs and I wish that were me. Hate hate HATE.

Oh yeah, and my Vickie kitty is going to live with grandpa. For a trial month, but he'll probably end up keeping her. She's my kitty and I'm sad and I'll miss her. But I think she'll be happier. And Bela will be a better cat (dog to him). Now I just need to find a new place for Andy. [Vickie was our 17-year-old cat, who was having difficulty dealing with the addition of a kitten and a dog to the household. So we asked my dad, living in a senior high rise, if he would be willing to take her, where she could have a quiet life and sleep most of the time. He agreed to do so as a trial, and then kept her.]

August 14, 2004 Diary

Why can't I discipline myself enough to stop eating so much? And stop eating so much junk food. I hate the way my body looks, yet I can't do anything about it. I hate seeing thin girls everywhere. I hate looking at Maria. It's probably why guys don't like me, because I don't have a flat stomach, big boobs, and I have fucking red cheeks 24/7. I'm already 20 almost and I'm a virgin and have not had a real relationship. ALL my friends have. I really really like [ ] but he and [ ] have been together for so long, and I like [ ] and don't want to hurt her. I don't think [ ] likes me anyway. Only the loser guys do. Sometimes I think I'd be better off dead, but I can't do it. I don't really have anything in my life to be proud of, nothing really big accomplished. I work so hard on my social life and it hasn't gotten me anywhere. Maybe I should just concentrate on my studies and do well in college, and try to get a successful job. It's all I'd have going for me. Anyway, enough depressing thoughts for now.

August 21, 2004 Diary

Biggest news lately: my left arm is having problems. I've lost almost all strength in it, and parts of it are tingly. In the past 2 weeks I've been in for 2 MRIs and like 4 doctor appointments, and a trip to the emergency room. The conclusion? Absolutely nothing. I had an MRI on both the brain and neck, and they both came out normal. So next week I get to go in for an EMG on my left arm so maybe they can narrow it down to just the arm. My dad thinks it's a pinched nerve. He had surgery 12 years ago for a pinched nerve and had to wear a neck brace for 3 weeks. The neurologist didn't think I'd need surgery, thank god. My biggest fear is amputation. A lot of doctors think it is diabetes related. So I really need to get my blood sugar under very tight control. I'm trying! And I hate this. I can hardly do anything with my left arm. I can't pick up a lot of things and I can't bend it in certain ways. I can't even get my bra on normally! Not good news. The neurologist wants me to start taking steroids to strengthen the muscles back up. Oh good, I'll start feeling masculine, maybe even start growing some facial hair? Haha. Oh yeah and when I had the MRIs they made me take out my nose ring! The next night I couldn't get it back in myself to I made my mom shove it back in for me. But I wasn't going to let the hole close so anyway we'll see how it all turns out.

Chris now lives in an apartment on 23rd and Lyndale with Luke and this girl Katie that she works with at the Bell Museum. So now she's far away from me. My mouse is going to live with her when I go off to school. Anyway I'm going to go cry in the shower because my life is shit. Later.

p.s. All the times I've said Morris isn't for me, that's no longer true. I love it and can't wait to go back.

August 27, 2004 Diary

Tonight is my last night in MPLS, tomorrow morning my parents and I head back to Morris. I have had a very interesting past couple days. Wednesday was my last day of work. I got a card, signed by everyone. Bernie gave me a hug when he left. No surprise there. He was always trying to touch me in some way. I'm gonna miss them. But Kris said I could come back, so hopefully that means I can work there again over Christmas break and/or next summer.

Thursday I had probably one of the worst experiences of my life: an EMG. [I agree with her: I had one in 1992, also up and down my arm, and it was extremely painful.] The doctor stuck needles in my wrist and sent shocks through my hand for about 45 min., then took a longer needle and stuck it in different muscles up and down my arm for about an hour. Felt great. My eyes watered the whole time. My arm was sore for a long time after that. And the conclusion is that what's wrong with my arm is complications from diabetes and I need to keep my blood sugars under very tight control. My arm probably won't fully heal, but I can keep it from getting worse. No steroids or exercise can help. So it will probably feel like this forever. I cried about this later. I'm only 19 and already having complications from my diabetes. The neurologist wants me to have another EMG done in two weeks, which I can do at Morris supposedly. Oh joy.

So today I had one last appointment so they could tell me yup, my arm is still weak, you don't need steroids, but you need tighter blood sugar control. Then my parents and I went to grandpa's and had lunch and saw Vickie, then I went back to the U with my dad and I went to the bookstore and bought a t-shirt and sweatshirt. Then we picked up Chris at the Bell Museum, went home to get my mouse, and delivered it (the mouse) and Chris to her apartment on Lyndale and 23rd.

Anyway, that was my exciting 3 days. I am now off to sleep my last night at home until who knows when. Goodnight.

p.s. today we picked up my antidepressant which I will start taking tomorrow.

August 28, 2004 Diary
   This morning my parents and I got up nice and early and took off for Morris. They stayed for a little bit then left. I unpacked pretty much everything.

September 1, 2004 Diary
   So here I am done with my 3rd day of classes. It is going well so far.
   This weekend is Labor Day weekend, so we have Monday off, but I'm not going home. Too soon! Oh, I have another EMG scheduled at the hospital for 3 PM next Thursday, so I'll get to leave my art class early.

September 10, 2004 Email
Krystin to dad:
Hi dad,
   Yeah, it is too bad that mom missed the EMG, I actually feel bad because she feels bad for missing it, she was real disappointed. But it's not her fault, it's their fault for moving my appointment up 2 hours. I was really mad about that, because it means I had to miss my art class altogether. And it sounds like mom told you this one wasn't as bad as the first. The doctor only did a few shocks, none as strong and bad as the ones they did last time, and he only did 4 pokes with the long needle in my muscles. One was right in the middle of the palm of my hand, and that one really hurt, I needed a band-aid afterwards, but none made my eyes water like last time. He told us that there wasn't really anything big wrong, just one muscle is damaged that's connected to the wrist, and he didn't say anything as far as treatment or it being related to tighter blood sugars, even though we know that's probably what it is. . . .
   Umm, I will send you my blood sugar numbers when I have enough to send you. I admit I have been kinda slacking on it (not the insulin though) but I promise next week you will get numbers, k?

September 23, 2004 Email
Krystin to dad:
Wednesday numbers:

5:15 pm – 66
11:00pm – 215

I have adopted a cold, so my numbers might be funky the next couple days, since they tend to bounce when I'm sick, but I'll do my best to keep it leveled.

September 26, 2004 Email
BGs and stuff
Krystin to dad:

5:30 – 238
2:30 – 397
10:30 – 156

Hmm, I'm not sure about that high one, but I did a bunch of insulin. It came down a little by dinner, but I guess not too much, so I did more. I'll do another test soon and let you know what that one is.

Dad to Krystin:
From my point of view, there are TWO high numbers there, and one that's not great. Anything over 120 is too high as far as I (and your nerves) are concerned. But some [of] this may be the cold. Just be sure you are taking enough insulin. And do let me know the numbers later.

September 30, 2004 Diary
Last time I wrote I mentioned my 2nd EMG schedule. My mom drove out to Morris to be with me, but they moved my appointment from 3 to 1, so she missed it. She was disappointed. But it's not her fault. And this one only took about 10-15 minutes. The guy only did a few shocks, and only 4 pokes with the long needle—but one of the palm of my hand! That hurt like a bitch. But at least I got to see my mom, and got lunch at Pizza Ranch!

We found a new home for Andy [the dog]. A lady at my mom's office has a friend that took him. I think he'll be better off in a house where everyone loves him. I feel kinda bad for my mom, but she says she doesn't miss him. You know why? Because we got a new puppy already! Her name is Abby, she's a year old, and a springer spaniel mix. I saw her online and my mom sent me a digital camera picture and she looks adorable! I'm going home this weekend too so I'll get to meet her. It sounds like everyone likes her, so hopefully that means I will too. I'm pretty sure I will though.

September 30, 2004 Email
this weekend – final plans
Krystin to mom, dad:

I have some art that I'm bringing home for you. And I can't wait to show you my sketchbook and all the new stuff we've been working on. Can you believe I actually look forward to going to art class now?

October 10, 2004 Diary

OK so I'm talking to [ ] online and I just found out she lost her virginity this summer with a guy at Culver. Then had sex again at the beginning of the year with a guy she was seeing. And I have a feeling [ ] has had sex with [ ]. Am I going to be the last one of everyone I know to have sex? I think already am. . . . Everyone thinks I've had sex with [ ] but I haven't. I'm sick and tired of being a virgin! What is it about me that guys just don't like, or makes them not want to be with me! Anyway, I gotta get back to my lit. paper, I just wanted to write this short note. Later.

October 10, 2004 Email
Krystin to dad:

Ok, so I just got a lot accomplished. I e-mailed my astronomy prof. and told him I want to talk about my test grade and if I can make up points by doing extra work, and I e-mailed my history prof. asking him for help on our paper topic that's due October 20 and if he can meet with me outside of his normal office hours (since I have classes during them), and I e-mailed my advisor seeing why I got an e-mail saying that I'm still on academic probation (even though my cumulative GPA is over 2.0 and I got over a 2.0 last semester), and how to go about changing from a psychology major to an English major. Whew! Oh yeah and I also e-mailed my Lit. prof. about my paper and about the test on Friday. I'll let you know what they all say when I hear back. I hope my paper is ok! Thanks for going over it for me.

October 11, 2004 Email
almost final copy
Krystin to dad:

Ok, I have everything done with my paper except the conclusion. I was hoping you could help me with that. My professor said don't just sum up what I've written, it needs to be in the broader context, answer the question "so what?" Why does what I said matter? I guess I don't know how to do that. Also, do my quotes seem like they're placed OK?

And if the title is stupid, can you think of a better or more creative one? Thanks!! [She included the paper as an attachment.]

October xx, 2004 Email
stuff
Krystin to dad:

Thanks for the paper suggestions. I feel pretty good about this paper.

11:45 – 157. Guess I need more insulin!

October 13, 2004 Diary

So today I e-mailed my mom complaining about [ ] having the TV on all the time and how it drives me crazy, and she had a very funny response. She said to give her ['s] e-mail and she will e-mail her and tell her I've been diagnosed with supraradioabsorption syndrome and cannot be in a room with a TV or microwave for more than 2 hours a day or my brain will turn into a glowing green mass which will make me unable to bear children. I thought this was hilarious, but I told her not to do it.

Oh, by the way, I found [ ] and [ ] have not had sex, so I'm not alone!

October 25, 2004 Email
Krystin to dad:

B ON MY LIT PAPER!

He said it was very clearly written and I've clearly put time and effort into it. I know, why isn't it an A right? Well boo to you. I'm happy with my B. Ok talk to you later, love you!

~November 1, 2004 Email
Krystin to dad:

2:30 – 115

November 4, 2004 Diary

Bush is president for the next four years. FUCK

Yesterday was a very depressing day. It was Elliott's birthday too. So Tuesday I went to vote, and I really thought Kerry would win. We (people on my floor) stayed up really late watching the election returns too. I don't get it. How could so many people want to re-elect that asshole? Even after [all] that's happened in the last 4 years.

Anyway Saturday was my birthday. It was really boring because not a lot of people were here. So I slept in late then watched movies on TV all day. But with Tom 😊

My parents and Elliott came on Sunday. We went to the Pizza Ranch buffet, and I think mom ate them out of business. Ha ha. They brought all the animals too, so Bela and Jenny got to chill in my room! It was good to see them. Mom brought the dogs up for a while, but mostly they stayed out in the van.

November 10, 2004 Email
Dad to Krystin:

Hi, Speed. Have you just decided you're not going to keep up your end of the bargain by sending me the BG numbers? Come on, Speed, you have to do your part, too.

November 12, 2004 Diary

I've decided I have to let my heart go. I have to let [ ] go. I have to make myself realize he and I will never be. And it hurts. It really does. Because I really like him, but he just doesn't like me, and never will. I have to accept that. It's going to be hard though. I have to act it around him too. I have to let him know I'm over him without saying it. I wish my antidepressants were working. I want to cry. Sometimes I want to end my life. [ ] keeps walking into my room to talk to me, and it makes it so much harder. Last time I walked into his room though some girl from FC, the new girl that's been hanging out in his room lately, was standing all close and playing with his hair. And my heart hurt. That's why I have to give him up, because don't want to hurt anymore. Maybe if I were a more aggressive person it would work, but I'm not, and I can't try to be someone I'm not. I don't want [ ] to like a fake person anyway. Enough of this, it just makes me sad. Later—

November 12, 2004 Email
Dad to Krystin:

Hi, Speed. I assume you've either given up sending me your BG [blood glucose; we'd made a deal that she'd email me her numbers regularly] numbers (but are still doing them) or you have just quit doing tests (and insulin?) and have nothing to send me. I hope it's the former, because if it's the latter, you'll go straight down hill for the rest of the semester. I sure hope that doesn't happen.

~November 13, 2004 Email
Krystin to dad:
3:00 – 200
    Oops, time for insulin.
    Got my history paper back today. 14/15! He said it was very well written, I have a nice writing tone and good flow. He also said he is proud, I am doing much better lately (with the quizzes and stuff). This is good!

November 17, 2004 Email
Dad to Krystin:
    Hi, Speed. You forgot your BG#s again for me. I do my end of the bargain about 80% of the time; you do it about 20%. Come on, kid.

December 5, 2004 Diary
    Well it's been almost a month since I wrote last and a lot has happened. I'll start with my almost dying, but the short version because I'm putting the whole thing in a Word document on the computer. So, the weekend before Thanksgiving, I go home because my mom is going to let me take the car back to school because I have a lot of shit to bring back and I'd be home again on Wednesday for Thanksgiving break. I never make it back to school. Friday night Molly and I go to a party and get totally wasted. It was the beer Olympics after all. Saturday morning I wake up feeling shitty and I feel that way all through Sunday. And I don't do anything those 2 days either. But I still go out and about and do stuff. Sunday night comes along and my parents decide I should stay overnight and drive back Monday morning. OK. Dinner time I'm still not hungry so when the family sits down to eat, I go upstairs and throw up in the bathroom. I decide to sleep on the couch in the parlor, and I'm throwing up almost once every hour. By 2:30 AM my throat burns and I'm having trouble breathing. I go wake up my mom and convince her to bring me to the hospital. She brings me to the ER and turns out I went into ketoacidosis, and was within an hour or so of dying. The doctor told my mom there was a possibility I wouldn't make it. They hook me up to 2 IVs and keep me in the Intensive Care Unit until Wednesday night, running saline and liquids through me to flush out my body. I

finally start eating a little on Tuesday night, also when I come out of my coma-like state and start interacting. Wednesday night they move me to a normal hospital room so they can watch me without the IVs, and they finally let me out Thanksgiving morning. My mom was with me the whole time except at night when she went home to sleep. So I never made it back to school, but I'm caught up with all that I missed. 81/100 on my make-up Solar System test—yay! So anyway we were gonna have Mae and grandpa over Thanksgiving night for dinner, but it ended up just being the 4 of us, which was alright with me. Because I couldn't find a ride back to school, my mom ended up letting me take the car back, so I may have it until winter break!

Oh and I got the super single next semester! I'm so excited. Andrea and I get along alright, but I can't wait to have my own room. And I'll get to work at Bigsby's again over break, which is really good because I really need the money.

November 26, 2004 Email
[purposely out of chronological order; this is my summary of the events sent to a few friends earlier than Krystin's diary entry, but it seemed appropriate in this narrative to let her description come first]

Gary to a few friends:
[transmitting a few paragraphs already written for his 2005 annual holiday letter—because the 2004 letter had already gone out]

We had a quiet Thanksgiving 2004. On the Monday before Thanksgiving, we took Krystin into the ER at 3:00 a.m. She had been feeling under the weather since Saturday and even vomited a little Sunday night (when she was supposed to drive back to school at UM-Morris). We assumed it was a touch of the flu, pretty common at that point in the year. In the middle of the night she came and woke us up and said she felt very sick. We called urgent care; they said get her to the ER.

The ER people immediately put her in medical intensive care. They knew immediately what the problem was because she had a "fruity" smell to her breath (which we never detected): ketoacidosis. Ketoacidosis results from a high level of acid in the blood generated by cells burning fat as a result of astronomically high blood sugar levels and no insulin. Krystin was not coherent and barely conscious all day on Monday; they had her on two IV drips with insulin and various other liquids. All the numbers—pulse, blood pressure, respiration—were 75 to 200% above normal. Her blood sugar levels were in the 400s (normal for non-diabetics and diabetics taking insulin is in the 90-110 range)—but those were down from over 800 when she was admitted. They don't know how high the number was; their machine only registers "high" when the number exceeds 800. Pat asked the ICU doctor how Krystin was doing; the doctor told her that they were doing all they could but there was "a chance that she won't make it." (I only learned about this several days after the fact.)

So we spent Monday, Tuesday, and Wednesday of Thanksgiving week sitting by Krystin's bedside in ICU, watching monitor numbers and quizzing doctors and nurses.

By Tuesday she had reconnected with the world, although her monitor numbers were not yet normal. She told us that because she had felt lousy during the weekend, she had not eaten—and since she had not eaten, she hadn't taken any insulin. But not eating and not taking insulin does not mean low blood sugar numbers; the result is the opposite. The doctor (in his mid-30s, perhaps) told her (with Pat present) on Tuesday that "I consider myself young. But if I had had the level of acid in my blood that you did, I would not have survived." (I also only learned about this after the fact.) He said she made it only because she was young, otherwise healthy, and lucky. In retrospect, I am glad that we did not know at the time that we nearly lost our daughter, and only learned it when she was clearly on the mend.

Wednesday afternoon she was moved to a regular hospital ward for monitoring for 24 hours; Thanksgiving morning we got to bring her home, pretty much back to normal. Since our families were doing Thanksgiving dinners at other times during the weekend (due to the usual schedule conflicts with in-laws), we decided that we would have Thanksgiving dinner with only the four of us. And we all went to bed by about 8:30 that night—Pat and I because we were exhausted from 3 days in the hospital, Krystin from the ordeal, and Elliott because he had spent Wednesday night at a friend's birthday party.

This episode affected Pat (and Krystin) much more than me because I was basking in unintended ignorance. I did not understand the depth of the crisis until it had passed, and I do not find it easy to become retrospectively panicked. By the time I was fully apprised of things, the threat of death had disappeared.

It was interesting to learn that in ICU, there is one nurse per patient (or occasionally one nurse per two patients, if one is clearly recovering). We had a lot of time to talk with the nurses, with whom we were extremely impressed. This episode made me once again think about health-care coverage. I was extremely glad we have very good coverage; one of the nurses estimated that Krystin's hospital stay would cost between $50,000 and $75,000. We could not pay that without great financial maneuvering; what on earth would a family with no or inadequate coverage do???? I think we had to pay the $10 co-pay for the doctor visit.

So our Thanksgiving was small—and much closer than we normally are as a foursome—but we were thankful that we were still a family of four, not three.

December 1, 2004 Email
[also purposely out of chronological order, for the same reason]
Gary to a faculty colleague at Indiana U:

It was a surreal week—Monday morning the ICU doctor told my wife they were doing everything they could but "she [my daughter] might not make it." They released her from ICU on Weds and from the hospital on Thursday, so we had a quiet Thanksgiving dinner. Friday night she and her brother went out a movie! There was something dizzying in this sequence of events. But she's fine and now back at college. My wife and I are still kind of dazed.

December 6, 2004 Email
history
Krystin to mom, dad:

My history Professor, Randy, is pretty positive I'm going to be getting an A in the class! I went to talk to him today about a topic for our second paper, and he was looking at my points so far and said I'm doing really well. . . . He looked at me and I look like an A student, I don't look like a B student, I look like I strive to get all A's. I just smiled and said "I try." Haha, I wish were an A student! Oh well, good to know he sees me in that light.

December 28, 2004 Email
Grade
Krystin to dad:

'A' IN HISTORY! My first college A. Feels great. My term GPA AND cumulative GPA are now above 2.0.

January 3, 2005 Diary

I haven't written in a while so there is a lot of catching up to do. I probably won't get to it all tonight. Let's start with classes. Here are my grades:

Art: C- Lit.: B-
History: A Solar System: C

There's nothing I can do about my art grade, but I'm pissed about my Solar System grade. I'm going to talk to him because I got good scores on everything except the first two tests so I should have a B. Aargh. Did I mention I get my own room next semester? I got the super single.

Next, I'm working at Bigsby's again. Been there 2 weeks now and I have another 2. Bernie's last day was last week cause he moved, so Kris is in for the lunch hour. I think every day last week I was sent home early cause business was slow, but it's picking up this week. I hope so because I need all the money I can earn! So year, work is same as always.

Christmas was great. I got Harry Potter 3 DVD! And Spiderman 2. And Elliott got me a DVD player even though I already bought one when I was at school. Oops. From my parents I got socks, a clown mobile for my room, and an MP3 player! It's awesome. I put all my songs on it as soon as I got it.

Time to go to bed now. I've had a cold for over a week now and it's kept me up at night. But I will finish up writing tomorrow.

p.s. Also for Christmas from Chris I got a Mr. Potato Head! Neither of us had one as kids so it was awesome.

January 6, 2005 Diary

So there is still a lot to catch up on. I was home from work today and Tuesday because of my damn cold. I've had it for over a week now.

Anyway, I don't think I mentioned we don't have Abby anymore. After I was in the hospital my mom decided she didn't want to deal with Abby's peeing/pooping in the house anymore, so my dad [took] her back to the Humane Society. I don't think my mom is going to look for another dog for a couple years. Cody enjoys being an only dog though, more attention for him!

A couple weeks ago Maria and I dyed our hair, mine is a dark auburn color. And last weekend I got my hair cut—short. Still longer than my mom's, but shorter than ear length. I think I like it. Because diabetics hair gets dry and damaged easier and faster, most go short. So I did! I'm still trying to figure out a good style for it, but at least it's fast to dry and easy to deal with.

I bought a dwarf hamster from Petco! She's grey and white and fluffy. I like the name Miss Piggy, but mom just calls her stubbems. Oh well. She's coming back to school with me, I don't care what anyone says. I'm in my own room so it's not like anyone will easily know. I don't think KT will care anyway. I didn't want to ask Chris for my mouse back (well, her mouse now) so I just got a new one!

Elliott had bought cousin Adam a Blockbuster G.C. [gift card] for Christmas, but Adam told Holly he couldn't use it, so then we had this $55 G.C. for Blockbuster that couldn't be returned. Well, it ended up in my hands, so I bought a shit load of DVDs with it.

It was payday at work yesterday! After I deposited my $247 I find out I had 3, $33 overdraft fees on my account, so I was over $100 in the hole! So I really only have like $127 in my account now. This sucks. And I owe my parents money. I'm really going to have to cut down on spending this semester!

OH, I can't believe I forgot to mention New Years! That should've been first! I went over to Chris's apartment. Kate is gone in Guatemala so it was just the 2 of us. We decided that we didn't want to go anywhere, and she didn't want anyone over.

January 18, 2005 Diary

I'm back at school now, in my new room. My parents and I drove back here yesterday. My new room is so small, but I like it, it's cozy. And Miss Stubbems has made herself at home, enjoying the college life. I got her a running wheel and she has been running on it 24/7, it's driving me crazy! I think she only stops to poop and eat. Oh well she'll get tired of it eventually—I hope!

Today was the first day of classes too. I only had U.S. History and I have it with Mike. I went to the bookstore afterwards and got my books for all my classes—all 17 of them! And $415 worth.

Now I have to do more reading then go to bed. Goodnight.

January 27, 2005 Email
A few annoying matters
Dad to Krystin:
    A few annoying matters. . . .

2. I hope you are working hard on your blood sugar numbers. I meant what I said about not taking you to Europe this summer if your A1c is not below 10, which as you know means you better consistently have numbers in the 80-150 range. Even if I have purchased airline tickets for you, if your A1c is 10 or above on July 1, I will cancel the tickets.

3. I suppose you never bothered to talk to either your art or astronomy professor about your grades from last semester. That would be a shame, if it is true, because you could boost your GPA a fair amount with only a modest change in those grades.

Krystin to dad:
Just because I don't mention something to you doesn't mean it's not happening. You're not my secretary, I don't have to tell you everything.

Dad:
That's only partially true, because I'm still footing the bill for you in life and still have you as a dependent. . . . And it is my health care coverage that is picking up these horrendous expenses for you. But I'd hope you'd tell me about things you know I am concerned about without my having to prompt you. (Actually, I hope you'll do that even when you're NOT a dependent, just because I'm your dad and deeply, deeply concerned about your welfare—just as I am and always will be about Elliott's, too. It's normal for a parent who cares a lot about his kids.)

Krystin:
[She did contact her professors about her grades. "So there."]
My blood sugars are under control. You never ask me about them on the phone or in e-mail, so I don't tell. If you would ask me then I would tell you I'm doing fine. [I didn't really believe this at the time but there wasn't much I could do about it.]

February 9, 2005 Email
Krystin to dad:
The University of Edinburgh website says visiting students have to be in good standing at their current school with a GPA of at least 3.0. So, if it doesn't look like I can get in, because I don't have a GPA

of 3.0 even with the F from last year wiped off, I'm not going to bother applying. And then I'm not going to go.

Dad to Krystin:
We'd like you to come to Scotland with us whether or not you can go to school. We like your company—and you might even enjoy the weekends traveling around Scotland. Hey, you can see where the Loch Ness monster is supposed to live!

February 14, 2005 Email
Dad to Krystin:
K—
My dad says that Vickie is not doing well. We may have to put her down. Do you feel strongly that you want to be here when we do? (We would do it at our house, not my dad's place.) I will talk to him again to find out if she has gotten better, but if not, we should probably act fairly soon. I know this will be hard, but she's not in good shape.

Krystin to dad:
Mom told me that Vickie is not doing well. Now that I think about it, why did we give her to grandpa in the first place? . . . We knew his place was always smoky and that he never airs it out or opens any windows. We should've seen this coming. I know Vickie was old anyway and didn't have much time left, but she probably would've lived longer than she will now if she had been somewhere else, and she would've been happier. Now she'll die in pain. I don't want to be home when you put her down, it would be easier for me if I weren't there. You will let me know when you do it though.

February 17, 2005 Email
Krystin to dad:
Hi dad,
I decided I quite [dislike?] the whole college student thing. Too many times now have I sat down for a test and I do crappy on it, and I'd been to all the lectures, and done all the reading. I don't know how I did on the essay part of my history test yesterday, but I always get essay tests back saying "too broad" or "not enough information." I feel OK about my test, but I just have a feeling I'm not going to do very well on it. Maybe I should talk to him about it, and point out that I've been to every single lecture I had done ALL the reading. Maybe we

can talk through the book and lectures and I can somehow prove that I was there or something. I dunno, it would be nice if it could out that way, but if he made an exception for me, he'd have to make exceptions for everyone. I guess it wouldn't hurt to ask though. . . .

We didn't have U.S. history with Roland at all this week. He got called out of town for a family medical emergency, so no class Tuesday or today! I guess that's OK with me because I've had a lot of studying to do this week, and that just gives me more time for it. He assigns us so much reading for a week though. Like this week he wants us to read two documents from one book, and then 258 pages in another book. Mike on my floor, who is my class with me, and I complain to each other all the time about much reading we have for his class. It's actually pretty ridiculous how much he expects us to read in a week, like we don't have any other classes to do reading or studying for. He's a nice guy and all, and I like him, but he gives us too much reading!

February 22, 2005 Email
Krystin to dad:
81/100 on my test! I got 62/70 on the essay, and 19/30 on the IDs. Yay! So that's a B. Today at 4 is my anthropology test. Wish me luck! Love you.

March 2, 2005 Diary
WOW I haven't written in a while and I have too much to catch up on but I probably won't get to it all tonight because my hand gets tired. Anyway, biggest news ever: My dad got a job in SCOTLAND! It's only for 4 months, so fall semester of '05, but that doesn't matter, what matters is we're fucking moving to Edinburgh, Scotland for 4 months. Chris is coming too, and through Morris, obviously. So we won't actually be taking any courses over there. But we'll all travel on the weekends, travel around Europe, it will be so awesome! We are losing my mom's salary for 4 months though. So I'm going to try and find an extra job this summer besides Bigsby's so that I have lots of money and don't ever need to borrow from my parents. [That didn't quite work out; we "lent" her $1000 or $1500—I forget the amount—that never got repaid, as I sort of knew would happen.] Elliott is going too but he's not very excited about it at all because it will be his first year of high school and he doesn't want to leave all his friends. Whatever. I

think he'll end up having a good time anyway. I hope to meet a Scottish guy. 😊

Anyway, I'm really upset with [ ] lately. He never comes to world history class, or does the reading, and he got an A on our first test. It pisses me off, he doesn't deserve it. At least we get to do an extra credit 2-page essay, so I can hopefully raise my grade there. I got 16/32 on my American Gov't class, but found out another girl got 12/32, so it doesn't make feel as bad, but there's no extra credit. 63/100 on my anthro test, and there will be make-up essays, as there will be for world history, in which I got 116/200 on our test! Ick. Oh well I guess, what's done is done.

March 7, 2005 Email
Dad to Krystin:
  Mom tells me you're a little upset about a history test. Don't sweat it. Just keep working. You'll do fine.

Krystin to dad:
  Yes, I did bad on my history test, and my TA Charlie e-mailed him as well as I did about it, and he told Charlie that he does not allow re-takes or extra credit, but that I should study really hard for the next test and do really well on our final project. Well, OK, but even if I get A's on them both, I still have the F from the first test (is 116/200 an F? I think so. . .), then I'll still be at like a C for the course, and that's not what I want! I want a least a B in all my courses, that was my goal this semester. Especially if history is my major, I need to do well in this course. But I'm still going to go in and talk to him in person with my test, maybe we can work something out.
  I got my anthropology test back today. 63/100. Yay. Because it's the first test, he's allowing make-up tests in essay form on a certain part of the book that we were tested on, and our score on that essay he will add to our first score. So again, I'm aiming for at least 20 more points so I can be in the B range.
  And if I can't do anything about raising either test, I quit school. Just FYI. I hate working my butt off 24/7 and having nothing to show for it, I feel like I'm wasting my time. I don't know if mom told you the whole story, but one of the big reasons I'm so upset about my history test is because [ ] got an A on it, and he never comes to class.
. . .

Anyway, this is why I'm looking forward to Scotland . . . no tests for a semester, and nobody to compare those test scores to. . . .

Ok off to read now, although it's not doing me any good.

Dad to Krystin [on quitting school]:

No, you don't. Your father will be very angry if you tell him that's what you're going to do.

[On having nothing to show for it]: That, I have told you many times, is not true. The question I ask you, and I assume you are telling me the truth when you answer, is "are you learning anything?" You tell me yes. That is what is most important. If you are learning, then you will do just fine in the world once you are out of school (or at least out of classes where you have to take in-class tests) and can do things your own way. . . . But the most important thing is that you are learning. (And it's not even all the facts you're reading. It's the learning to learn that matters. You won't remember all the facts. You probably can't remember most of the facts from your freshman year. I certainly can't remember more than about 1% of what I learned in college. But I learned about a lot of stuff in general, and learned general principles about humans and life and science and belief and emotions and on and on. One of the most important things you learn from college is how to think about things, not that you know all about them. So long as you get grades sufficient to get you a degree, that is fine.)

March 21, 2005 Email
Dad to Krystin:

How'd your test go?

Krystin to dad:

My test went worse than it probably could have. I set up two weeks ago with disability services to take my tests there, and they said by the time I got back from break things would be all set up. Well I go in this morning and they say that they don't have anything for me as far as a test goes and that they didn't the form back from the professor, and then I'll have to go to class, get the test, and bring it back to take there. So I go to class right as he's handing out the tests, tell him what's going on, he said he never got the form, hands me a test and I have to go sit down in the classroom. So I have to take it in the classroom. I'm sure I did horrible because besides the text anxiety, I was irritated and not expecting to have to take it there. I went back to disability services

after the test and told them, and that I have the second part of the exam on Wednesday. I also e-mailed my professor on told him the situation. I expect to take the part on Wednesday in disability services, because I'm not going to take it if I have to take it in the classroom. It's not my fault they can't get their stuff together in a two-week period.
So yeah, that's how my test went.

March 25, 2005 Email
Krystin to mom, dad:
Hello,

    Sorry I haven't been in touch with you for a while. Don't worry. It's nothing to worry about, I've just been busy. I had my world history essay exam on Monday, the ID part of the exam on Wednesday, my U.S. history test yesterday, and I had to get a lot of information ready about the politics in Columbia for a group meeting today. It was a busy week. I don't know how my essay in world history went on Monday, I think it went OK though. I know the ID part Weds. went really well, I could fill all 10 IDs in with a unique statement, and I just feel good about it, probably because I finally got to take it in disability services. The U.S. history test, I'm not so sure about that. For the essay part I think it went well, and we also have to do IDs in that class, and he gives us 9 and we have to pick 6, and I know I might have messed up on at least 2 of them, but hopefully that's it.

    I've been kinda sad about Vickie lately, but only when I think about it, so I've been trying not to think about her, which I can avoid by keeping myself busy, which has been easy to do this week. [I had told her in an earlier message that we had to put Vickie down. The vet told us she was dying of old age.]

March 27, 2005 Email
Krystin to dad:
Hi dad,

    I have a favor to ask of you – and you probably saw this coming. I was wondering if, again, I could take out a little loan from you guys to last me through the end of the school year. Nothing big, especially compared to last year. Only $35. My tax refunds will be $65, so I was wondering if you or mom could put $100 in my bank account, and then I will write my tax refund check over to you, so it will only end up being $35 that I borrow from you guys. I have about $50 in my bank account right now, and I would just feel better knowing I had a little more, you know? Let me know if you are willing to do this.

Dad to Krystin:
OK. I'll do it Monday or Tuesday.

March 29, 2005 Diary

Last night [ ] and I were talking in the lounge. It was one of those talks where he was drunk, so I don't really know if I should seriously listen to what he says, but on the other hand he's really insightful and says some things might not say when he's sober. Anyway, we got to talking about Scotland next year and about Scottish boys, and I commented on how I would go home alone every night and Chris would be hooking up with the guys, and [ ] was like "you gotta wear those low-cut shirts. I'm tellin ya." Really [ ]? Is that what guys really want? Surely not all guys. I don't want to be one of those girls that can only get a guy by wearing tight clothes and acting like a bimbo. My mom says never to change myself for a guy, but who I am isn't working! When will I finally find a guy that will like me for me, and my personality? I know I'm not a size 2 jeans and I'm not gorgeous and I don't have big boobs, and I may not have the most exciting and outgoing personality, but I'm who I am and I want to find a guy that appreciates that. And I'm afraid that if I do find someone, he'll get pretty bored with me after a short period. I've never had a real relationship, although many people think I have. Many people think I've had sex and dated [ ]. I've lied to so many people. But I don't want the world to know I'm so unwanted. I get so lonely sometimes and just wish I had someone to sit down with and hold hands with. I see some people in relationships that you'd never think could find anyone, so what's wrong with me? Why can't I find someone? I'm going to die alone with my cats. Something to look forward to huh.

April 19, 2005 Email
Krystin to mom, dad:

I got 20/35 on my American government and politics test. So that's a 16/32 and a 20/35. What do you guys think I should do? Use my 'get out of jail free' card (AKA use my free withdrawal)?? [University policy permitted a student, once during their undergraduate career, withdraw from a course at any time without penalty. Other withdrawals, after the normal cancel/add period for the first week or so, require a passing grade or an F will be entered on the transcript. That one-time withdrawal permitted became known as the 'get out of jail free' card.] I e-mailed him with my situation and asked him what he thinks is best. I told him I really don't want to drop the class because I am enjoying it immensely, but I can't afford to have the low grade on my GPA, it might put me back on academic probation! I was just honest with him and told him the predicament I am in and what he thinks I should do. Hopefully I'll hear from him soon.

I took my anthro test yesterday in disability services – 6 essays! Boy was my hand tired. One main essay, worth 40 points that was 6 pages in my blue book, 4 essays on Fast Food Nation that are 10 points each and took up about 1 page each, and then another essay worth 20 points on two videos that we watched that took up about 2 pages. [Most who went to college, particularly those who majored in the social sciences, are familiar with the blue book: a stapled set of 5-6 pages, folded, with light blue covers, distributed at test periods in which to write essay responses to questions.] WHEW! Boy was my hand tired after that. Took me almost an hour and a half. I'm glad it's over though. I feel I did really well on the main essay, which wasn't the one I read for you in the living room, but mom it was the one you read in the van on Saturday. As for 4 on Fast Food Nation, I think I did pretty well on 3 of them but not so well on the last one. And the last essay on the two videos I also think went alright, maybe not as thorough as he's looking for, but had some good points in it. He is VERY slow at getting tests back, so I'm guessing we'll get them back by next Thursday at the earliest! Oh well.

I kinda miss Stubbems! I keep looking to the spot on my shelf where her cage used to be, and she's not there! Oh well. My room smells better now! Before it smelled like . . . well, hamster poopy. That's alright, I know she'll go to a home of someone who can give her more attention than I ever did.

April 20, 2005 Email
Krystin to dad:
Professor Thorson said that it still likely that I can pull off a C in the course. I don't think he will make any allowances for me, but when I went in to talk to him last week, he said he is always there to help students who need help, no question about it. So, maybe I'll go in and talk to him again before the final and see if he can give me any extra hints for the test. Wouldn't hurt! So I'll stay in and stick it out.

April 29, 2005 Diary
[indented text is that which she printed and pasted in from the online journal]

I haven't been writing in here in a while but I have been writing in my online journal, so I'm just going to print them out and tape them in here. So, here goes!

> Here it is Friday night, and I have no plans! I like it though, having no commitments and knowing I don't have to do anything or go anywhere. This past week was pretty uneventful. As is my life. Only one more week of classes left, then the week of finals, then I'll be done! Can you believe I'll be halfway through with this part of college? Then there's graduate school, but I'm not even going to think about that yet. I know I'm going, and hopefully to the twin cities campus, but for now I'll concentrate on getting through Morris! Yes, I will be home this summer, I'm not staying here in Mo-town. I'll be home working my ass off at two jobs so I can have lots of money for Scotland! I will write more later, time now to find some grub. Later.

May 1, 2005 Diary/Journal
Happy May Day!

> I just found out my grandpa died this morning. 82 years old. I don't know how to feel about this. I'm crying, yet I know he had been going downhill and it was his time, so why was I so surprised to hear the news? I guess when you're not expecting it, something like a death is a surprise no matter when you hear it. His funeral is next Thursday, so what do I do? Finals are the week after. Do I contact my professors and see if I can make some arrangements for my finals? My mom said she would come get me Wednesday evening if I wanted to come home for the funeral. I just have a lot of thinking to do. He was living in an assisted living apartment, [not quite right; he was in a self-sufficient apartment, but it was a seniors high rise] so it's not like he was alone or anything. And his cat, Bianca . . . my mom said they will leave her there for a while and just keep going over there to make sure she has food and water. My mom thinks it will be less stressful for her if we leave her there for a bit without him rather than just bring her back to the humane society. I never even got to say goodbye, I think that's the hardest part. I know his Alzheimer's was taking its toll,

sometimes he would call me by my cousin Katie's name, but that didn't matter. And I always used to roll my eyes and kinda giggle when he would do that, and now he's dead. I am going to go do something else now, I probably shouldn't be alone, although I hate when other people see me cry. . . . Later. [Her grandfather had Parkinson's, not Alzheimer's, and was in reasonably good physical shape and his mental faculties were fine, although it was clear they were just beginning to decline, but Krystin had an exaggerated view of the seriousness of his situation. He died while napping before his Sunday afternoon poker game.]

Today I spent 3 hours in the library with my Colombia project group working on our power point! It felt so good, we got so much done. I'm actually kinda looking forward to our presentation, which is on Wednesday. Our group has done so much research I think and it will be great. The only thing that worries me is that our professor is a Colombia fanatic, he even lived there for a while, so I hope he's not more critical of our group then [sic] he has been for the others. That wouldn't be fair of course, but I'm afraid subconsciously he's going to grade us harder just because he knows pretty much everything about Colombia and will notice any tiny mistakes. Oh well, all we can do is do our best!

I missed the Tinman Triathlon today! I had signed up to volunteer ya know, and I was supposed to be to RFC by 8 to get my free shirt, and then 8:30 were the meetings, and I was to be in the pool counting people's laps. I had my alarm set for 7:10, and I don't' even remember it going off! I wake up on my own and look at my phone to see how [much] time left I have to sleep before it goes off, and it says 8:50! Normally you'd think it's OK I can still make it, but no, the swimming is the first event of the triathlon so I had to be there right at 8:30, they stressed how important it was to be on time, and I wasn't. I really kicked myself, I was so disappointed. No free shirt for me! Melissa, who had volunteered to hand out water and such to the runners, said the shirts are really nice and soft. Dammit! Oh well. Next year I will volunteer again.

May 6, 2005 Diary/Journal
Alright, so I haven't written in a week. I ended up going home for my grandpa's funeral. My mom came and picked me up

Wednesday afternoon and we drove home, and Thursday was the funeral. It was definitely an experience that caused me a whole wave of different emotions. We had to be to the church by 9:30 Thursday morning, and when we got there my aunt and uncle Holly and John were already there (Holly is my dad's sister) and soon after we showed up, my other aunt and uncle Tracy and Joan showed up (Tracy is my dad's brother). The funeral ceremony didn't start until 11, but visiting started at 10, so between 10 and 11, I don't think I've said "thank you for coming" and given so many hugs so many times in my life. My dad told me I would have to be very social butterfly that day, and I was! After everyone was seated, we, the family (my mom and dad and aunts and uncles and cousins) walk in last and sit down, and the ceremony started. I knew that if I was there alone I wouldn't cry, because my aunt Joan and my mom are water faucets, I got a little teary-eyed too, especially when my mom reached over and held my hand. Also because it was then that it really sunk in that my grandpa was gone. Afterwards we had a light lunch in the church, then us immediate family members went over to the Fort Snelling cemetery. Because my grandpa is a WWII veteran, they did the 21-gun salute, shot three fire shots, and played the war tune that I don't know the name of off the top of my head. And during this time, my grandpa was in a gold box (he was cremated) on a table in front of us. That caused more tears from a few of us. We took some pictures of all of us together, then my parents and I went back to the church to get some of the flowers that were left there. I wanted some of them, so they let me have one of the small bouquets, and I brought it back here to school. I was going to drive back here Thursday early evening, but my [parents] decided if I want to, I could stay overnight and drive back today, which is what I did. I left about 10:45 this morning. I took a nap when I got back, then watched an extra credit video for my anthropology class while eating some Chinese food.

I am really glad I got to go home for the funeral, but now it's back to reality. I have finals next week that I really really need to get studying for, especially since for one of the finals I haven't read a book for yet! Yea, I need to get on that. I suppose I could've done some reading at home, but I just didn't feel like it.

Off to read I suppose. I'm still so tired though, and I know it's because of my high blood sugars, so I'll do some insulin and hope that I can wake up a bit and not fall asleep while reading. Later.

May 6, 2005 Email
Dad to Krystin:
I am very glad you came home for the funeral. You were a joy to have with me at events. I very much wanted you here.
Love you very much.

May 9, 2005 Diary/Journal
There's a famous saying: "You were born an original. Don't die a copy." I wonder how many people out there look at their lives thus far and say to themselves, "I really haven't been myself, I've been trying to be this person." I may not have been myself some of the years of my life, but my life in general has definitely not been a copy, I don't think anyone can have even come close to living the same life that I have. First of all, my life did a complete 180 once I started high school. Elementary and middle school were hell for me, I hated it and I didn't like the people and they probably didn't like me because I was different and not like them (I was a late bloomer), but once I got to high school, things completely changed. [Krystin wasn't consistent on this story. At other times she wrote that elementary school up until about 5th or 6th grade was fun and she liked it, and that version accords with my memory of her early school days.] I started meeting people that liked me for me, I guess you can say I found my niche. And college, even better! Then there's all the different experiences and situations I have found myself in over the years. I'm not going to go into them all because some of them I don't want to share, but let's just say my life has definitely been one big learning experience, and it's too bad that it had taken me until half way through high school that I began to like my life and myself. Anyway, I don't know what brought up this spurt of insightfulness, I just thought I'd share my thoughts. Later!

May 11, 2005 Email
Krystin to mom, dad:
2 down, 1 to go!

My procrastination kicked me in the ass yesterday, though. For my anthropology test that was at 8:30 this morning, we had to have this one book read, and my professor gives us a couple essay questions ahead of time and then picks one and puts it on the test ya know, so we can prepare for it. Well, as of yesterday afternoon, I still hadn't read the book (oops, guess I'd been focusing on my other classes a little too much the past couple weeks!). So last night around 10:30, I couldn't get anything done here in the dorm because with my computer and the people, there are too many distractions, so I headed over to the 24-hour study lab that's in the student center. I sat down to read and write out my essays—until 3 in the morning! I know that's late for you guys, but to us college students, 3 AM is nothing. I know, dad, you went to bed at 11 every night in college and woke up at 7 to do your studying. [I'm quite sure I did nothing of the sort.] Well when I got back at 3AM, I still wasn't done with the second question, so I just stayed up all night. It's easier to do than go to bed for a couple of hours, because then I'd really be tired if I had to force myself to get up, whereas if I just stayed up, my body doesn't know it was supposed to be sleeping! Uhh. . . yes? Ok maybe not. Anyway, end of story is that I just took my test and I think it went really well. I'm definitely not going to make a habit out of that though, it was a one-time big procrastination thing. No way else to explain it. Now I don't have my next test until Friday, so I am going to take a nap for a couple hours, or however, long, maybe 5, then get up and finish reading for my American government class, then possibly start studying, but tomorrow will be the big study day. Sound like a plan!

OH, I almost forgot . . . I FINALLY got my test back from my last anthro test. . . 89/100! On the syllabus it said the second test was out of 125, so when I looked at my score I was way disappointed and depressed for like 2 minutes, until I looked at his math and figured out it has to be out of 100. It just made the 4 short essay question out of 5 each instead of out of 10, so the test was only worth 100. So 89, that's a high B! Maybe even an A- depending on if there's a curve. Yay! And I feel good about the final, so I'm hoping to get a B- at least in the course! Same with U.S. history. I think that final went pretty good yesterday.

May 11, 2005 Diary/Journal

Don't you love finals? I hate my fucking computer and it hates me, although I need it so I can type up an essay for my anthropology final. Our professor gives us two essay questions in advance and says he will choose one to put on the test, so we can prepare for them and bring in a notecard with 100 words per essay to help us. Well, "fuck that" my computer says. My Microsoft word has been a bag of garden implements (P.C. term for hoe bag) for a while now and freezes for like 5 minutes after every letter that I type. So I give in and go to the 24-hour study lounge in the student center and do my reading and type up my essays there. Oh, I should mention that I haven't even read the book yet that the essays are based on. Each essay has to do with 3 chapters of the book. I'm there for 3 and a half hours and I only have one essay done! And it's already 3 AM. So I print it out and come back to my room. I'll just write out the second essay on the back of my printed-out first essay. Oh, but then I have to find a way to cut it all down to 100 words each and put it on a note card and hope that when I take my test, which is at 8:30 AM, or in 5 hours, however you want to look at it, that I remember all the shit I wrote for it! Damn. So I have 5 hours to write that second essay, and quick skim the remaining 3 chapters of the book that will be covered by multiple choice and true/false questions. What a fun time! At least when that's done, I don't have another final until Friday and I can just come back from my anthro. final and sleep for like half the day, then get up and start studying for my political science final that is on Friday. Then I'll be done for the year and HALFWAY DONE WITH MY UNDERGRADUATE DEGREE! Don't even get me started on graduate school. . . .

Today (Tuesday, although technically Wednesday because it is after midnight), I took my U.S. history final, which I think went alright. I've gotten B's on the last two tests, so I'm thinking even if I get a C on the final, I can still be a B in the course, at least a B-. Hopefully. Same this anthropology final, because I got, well, a D on the first test, and B+ or A- on the second test, so if I get a C on the final, then I can probably get a C in the course! Maybe a B- there too because have an extra credit paper to turn in. So my grades won't be so bad after all. . . HOPEFULLY.
Alright time to make some food, since I haven't eaten in forever, then back to work. Later.

May 17, 2005 Diary/Journal

Well it's 3:30 in the morning and I can't sleep, so I figured I'd update this, cause I have some updating info! It's finally summer, as of Friday the 13th I was home, although I know I'll miss Morris over the summer, because I love it there. I am currently on the hunt for a job, because I didn't get my job back at the cafe downtown that worked at last summer and over winter break. They lost a lot of customers due to the smoking ban, so things are really slow there and they didn't need me. Major bummer! And I really really need a job because I'm supposed to earn a lot of money this summer for when we go to Scotland (assuming we're going).

Today (Tuesday) I have a dentist appointment to get some cavities filled. Oh joy.

So, on Saturday when I was coming back from Famous Dave's, I got in a car accident! BUT, not my fault. I was just driving along, minding my own business, when a guy that a few cars ahead of me decided to pull a u-turn on one of the side streets, and apparently didn't see me and pulled right out into the passenger side of my car! And he hit me pretty hard too because it caused my car to spin around so that I'm facing the opposite direction of the way I was going, and I come less than an inch from hitting a van parked on the side of the street. Well, the damage to my car was pretty great: the whole blue panel (my car is blue) of the back passenger side door came completely off, so you can see the organs of the car door, and there is a huge dent around the door handle of the front passenger side door. Of course the first person I call is my house, and tell my parents they are going to have to come get me. Oh, and the only damage done to the guy's SUV is that his bumper was detached and was just hanging off the front of his vehicle. So my mom gets there, and we hadn't called any police yet so she does that, the squad car arrives like 20 minutes later and we get all the details figured out, etc. etc. The guy that hit me doesn't have car insurance, so he's in big trouble for that, plus that means he'll have to pay for the damages out of his pocket. Oh, and his license will be provoked [revoked] for a while because he was making an illegal u-turn. Nobody was hurt luckily, but it was just a lot to deal with, and now we have a loaner car until my mom's Saturn gets fixed at the Saturn dealer. My parents think they might decide the car is totaled and then we'll have to buy a new car, which my parents are not looking forward to. Plus our insurance will go up, even though it wasn't my fault. Anyway, my mom drove home the banged-up car, because it was still drivable, and I drove home our van that my mom drove to the scene in. Oh yeah, and both passenger side windows were completely blown in, so there are no windows on that side either. Good times huh? Great way to start out the summer. First full day back from school and I get in a car accident! My first one too. Oh well, that's pretty good for having my license for almost 5 years and having no accidents (or tickets, still haven't gotten any tickets, knock on wood!)

May 19, 2005 Email
Krystin to mom, dad:

C+ in anthropology. Pooey. I thought I could do better. I thought I WAS going to do better. I was expecting at least a B- or B. I could've done better. Guess I only did mediocre on the final. Oh well. So now my term GPA ended up being 2.5 or something, and my overall GPA is now 2.4. So at least I'm not back on academic probation! I didn't expect to be. Ok just wanted to let you know.

Love you both.

May 21, 2005 Diary [back to being hand-written]

I miss Morris already. My dad found out yesterday that Glasgow said "no," so we're not going to Scotland. Maybe to Oxford or Cambridge in the spring, but mostly likely next year. Bummer too, because I found out Morris assigned me a freshman roomie for next year. They assigned all of us juniors roomies. I can see this being a disaster already. I don't get along with roommates, plus I'll be 21 in October. So this really sucks. But maybe come August there will be enough open space to move the freshman. We'll see.

So, still no job. I have turned in applications to 5 or 6 different places downtown, now I just need to go back to them on Monday and talk to the person in charge (I have names). I REALLY need a job! I hate the searching and I hate not having money. I am working at Bigsby's for one week in June, though, while Kris has surgery. I really want a waitressing job so I can make mad money in tips. Plus I get bored just sitting around the house all day. No fun.

May 27, 2005 Diary

Still no job. All the restaurants downtown I applied at, all the positions at the U I applied for, all no-gos. This is really starting to get annoying, and I'm getting tired of looking. I hate not having money. I'm almost desperate enough to go apply at Target. Tomorrow I'm going out on the search again, hopefully I'll find something. I suppose I could deal with having like 3 OK jobs instead of one or two good jobs. We shall see. I just need an income! Besides making money for the school year, I owe my parents a lot.

My mom had her surgery Wednesday morning. All went well. We went and visited her that afternoon. Dad and I had to wait like an hour though for them to bring her to the recovery room because couldn't get her pain under control. But they finally brought her up. Then I went got Elliott and Chinese food and we all had dinner in mom's room, although she couldn't eat Chinese. She didn't want to anyway. Thursday I got up early and went in with my dad to visit her again. Then I dropped him off at work and got the van for the day to job hunt, but I only went to the Rail Station. I don't think they are hiring but we shall see. Tomorrow I will call Famous Dave's back too. Anyway, mom got to come today already, so she's mostly been living on the couch in the family room sleeping and watching movies. Bela enjoys it!

By the way, here were my 2nd semester grades:

Poli Sci: C
U.S. Hist: B   Term GPA 2.5
World Hist: B-   Cum GPA 2.4
Anthro: C+

June 7, 2005 Diary

I GOT A JOB!! After almost 4 weeks of searching, I finally got a job—and it's back at Bigsby's! Mike got offered a job at Target headquarters, where his father-in-law works (and manages), so he took it. It pays better, which is probably better for him now that he has a baby, and because his wife wants to stop working for awhile. So Friday is his last day at Bigsby's. Which means I'll be taking over the morning breakfast shift too, so I'll be working like 6 AM to 3 PM. LOTS OF MONEY! I'll have to get up at 5 AM but it will be worth it and it will be good for me. Kris is going to pay me more too. Yay! I thought I was never going to find a job. This, as my dad calls it, was purely dumb luck. No shit. I am so glad to finally have an income. I'm sure my parents are glad too, because means I can finally start paying them back the $550 I owe them. [I don't believe we ever received the money.]

July 16 [19], 2005 Diary/Journal

I found out a couple days ago that I'm going to Florence and Rome over our fall break in October! My parents will be in Tuscany for a week for a good friend's birthday, and then they're taking another week in Rome and asked me to join! Our fall break is only a Monday and a Tuesday off, so I'll miss 4 or 5 days of classes, but it will so be worth it, and I don't think my professors will protest or anything and tell me I can't go. If they do, I'm dropping the class. I have a lot of transfers too. I fly from here to Denver, to Paris, to Florence. I'll be meeting my parents in Florence, probably at the hotel, where we will stay for a couple days, and then take the train to Rome, where we'll stay for a few more days. It will be the most awesome trip ever, especially because I can drink, since their drinking age is only 18, and because my brother won't be along! And I just love the old architecture of European cities; it's not something you see a lot of around here anymore. As Eddie says, Europe is where the history comes from!

I guess the only reason I posted was to announce that. Not really much else to say. Tomorrow is payday, that's always exciting! I've been working really hard at not spending all my money over the summer, to save most of it for the school year, and I think I'm doing really well. Even though I'm getting bored with work and am really, really ready to go back to Morris, I am still enjoying it, and I'm finally starting to develop friendships with some of the regulars who come in for their coffee every day.

July 24, 2005 Diary/Journal

The trip to Rome is definite, my dad has bought the plane tickets. I'm not flying with them, because they will already have been over there in Tuscany for a week. I'm leaving the Wednesday before our school fall break. My flight is a Wednesday night. I fly to Denver, then to Paris, where I have an hour and a half lay-over (just enough time to go to the airport bar and get a glass of wine, because I can, of course!), then to Florence, where I will meet my parents. We will spend 2 days there, then take the train to Rome, where we will stay for 3 more days, then fly home. Monday and Tuesday we have off of school, but I think I'll miss Wednesday and Thursday of that week. I'm not too worried though; actually I'm not worried at all about missing class. I think my professors will be delighted that I have been granted this great travel opportunity and will make exceptions as far as if I miss any tests or anything. I'm so excited! This is my 21st birthday present from my parents, although it will still be a week and a half after we get back before I actually turn 21. Another thing to be excited about! I am going to go to the government center downtown this week (because I work downtown, very convenient) and see about renewing my license, since I will need a new one when I turn 21. I'll get to have a new picture taken and everything. Although my dad is not sure if they will do it this early since it's still 2 months before I turn 21, but I can get all the paperwork and picture taking and what not done now, and then maybe they can send it to me on my birthday? I don't know, I'll find out I guess!

Ummm . . . so yeah, we got a new dog too. Her name is Marla, she's 13 months old, a 40 pound springer spaniel mix. We got her on Thursday from a foster home, and so far she is perfect!

So this guy that comes into my work, I think I've mentioned him before, his name is Caleb, and we kinda have this flirty game going on. I wear a white apron, because I tend to make a mess of myself and don't want to get lots of stains on my clothes you know, so he comes in on Friday to get lunch and he comes up to me at the register and says "so if we go on a date, would you wear that apron?" Only if it turns you on, Caleb. No I didn't say that, I said "but of course, you wouldn't recognize me otherwise right?" We had a laugh and wished each other a good weekend, but I can't help but think, where is going with this? Is he actually considering asking me out? He's cute, and funny, but he's 30! That's a little too old for me, I don't go that old. I'll do like 22, but not 30. That would just be weird, right? Anyway, pretty sure it's just some fun at work to keep things interesting, which it definitely does! It's a good time, I can't help but smile to myself whenever I see him coming.

August 5, 2005 Diary

    Happy payday! $578, plus $40 my dad owed me, plus $20 from my tips, right into checking. And I still have almost $50 in my wallet. I'm making a shit load in tips. We started serving Caribou coffee at work on Monday, and it's going well, definitely bringing in more customers, to make up for the ones we lost over it. Today Caleb came in for his chicken breast sandwich—tomato only—and said to me "thanks dear, have a good weekend." Aww why does he have to be so damn nice and flirty AND smell good?? Oh well, just another guy I'll only have in my dreams. No Caleb, no Tom, no Mike, no Sam. No nobody, just me. Alone. Forever. With my 5 cats.

August 18, 2005 Diary
Step back from the ledge
Dry your tears
We need you down here
There's nothing up there for you
On that ledge
Where your feet touch the edge
But take a step back
And come back down
Here to us
And think this through
There's nothing up there for you on that ledge.
[I did a Google search in June 2018 using some of this language and nothing showed up, so this may have been original with Krystin.]

Few thoughts:
    3 days left of work. I don't feel appreciated or needed anymore, don't feel I will be missed. Chambray is better than me, as is everyone else. And everything is my fault. Mom tried to convince me I'm a beautiful person inside and out. I just feel depressed. More on this later.

August 31, 2005 Email
[I had invited one of Krystin's friends—one she chose—to join us in Scotland for spring semester. The friend emailed me, with a copy to Krystin, explaining that she could not come.]
Krystin to dad:

I am not surprised. I think I already knew she was going to say no. Now have to decide how badly I want to go. I have actually been thinking about this for a while, that if a friend wasn't coming along, would I still want to? Not just about a friend coming along though, but about where I am here at Morris and what I would be leaving and missing out on. I know this is a great, great opportunity, but there are people here I don't want to leave, classes that I want to take in the spring, I like where I'm living and just where I am in life here. I guess it's hard to explain, but I wanted to throw the idea out there that I want to stay here. I just have to weigh the pros and cons basically. I figure if I don't go, I can spend spring break there, take off a few extra days and make it a long break, and I can see Edinburgh and surrounding areas in that time. Anyway we can talk about it more later, this isn't definite of course.

Dad to Krystin:
I understand. You have to make a decision based on what's best for you. I still think that going to Edinburgh would be an experience more important than UMM this spring, but so would any study-abroad program. And as mom said last night, you might think about people around you there who you might ask.

The one who will miss you the most is Elliott. We would miss you, of course, but he'd rely on you to spend time with him when we couldn't.

September 3, 2005 Diary
I realized I haven't written since school started. I have now been here a week and a half. I should probably start with the Sunday before I moved back here, with my date with Mark! Alice, who works over at Thrivent, set us up on a date. Mark is 24 and works at Thrivent also. So that Sunday before I came here, we had our date. He picked me up at 6pm and went downtown. We went to The Brits Pub for dinner then saw 'Four Brothers' at the downtown theater. To me it didn't really feel like a date, I was very comfortable and conversation came very easily. After the movie he drove me home and walked me to my front door and we kissed! I didn't know how I felt about it. At first I wish hadn't but now I'm glad we did. Since being here at school we've talked online every day and we have another date set for a gopher hockey game in October. And I'm so excited about it! I just want things to

move too fast cause I've never been in a relationship before and just want to move slow.

So I've been drinking a lot so far this year. I can't wait till I'm 21 so I can go to the liquor store for myself and can drink in my room without worrying about being busted or anything. I will be able to drink when I'm in Italy over fall break though! Then when I turn 21 I can freely drink with Tom and Mike in their room, if Mike doesn't move up, and go to quarter taps at the bar with Tom!

September 7, 2005 Diary

Ahhh! I got an e-mail from my mom saying she put an order in at Bigsby's and Kris said Caleb says hi and wants to communicate!! I got so excited. I smiled so much and I still do whenever I think about it. It just makes me so happy. On my last day I wanted to ask him for his e-mail, or give him mine, but I didn't know if that would be weird or whatever, so I didn't, but now HE wants to communicate with ME! That's just so awesome. So my mom gave Kris my e-mail address and school mail address, so now I just have to wait to see what happens!

I was talking to Mark online today, as we do every day, and when he was saying goodbye, he called me beautiful. How do I reply to that? Say thanks? Well I do, and tell him to have a good night. I'm not used to people saying that to me.

October 2, 2005 Email
Krystin to mom, dad:

So part of my online course is a discussion board, where at the beginning of the week the professor posts a question, most of the time a few, and we post comments and responses to the questions throughout the week and add to what each other says and blah blah blah. One of the topics of each week is to discuss what each other wrote about in their brief essays, which are published early Monday morning on the web site for everyone to read. We all read each other's and then talk about them. One of the guys in the class, Paul, posted a comment about me just tonight (Sunday). Here is what he said:

"Just a comment on Krystin's responses. That I could only dream of writing her way. The topics blends into the writings and they show balance. For instance, the first essay, the one that we had to comment on all of the intro's. She touched on them all, while I got stuck and kind of mushed it all together. However, I'm sure that a lot of historians that were not that great writers actually made a difference in some part of their career."

Awww, how nice! One of those little things that may not seem like a big deal but just make your day, you know? That, plus here is what my professor said about my first essay:
"This is really very good, and it's doing just what I hoped would be done with these brief essays: you've identified the purpose of each author, what they intend to do, and drawn those together into a single account. Well done!"
That makes me feel so good about the course! To get praise from the professor and other students feels really good, it makes the course all worthwhile. I keep up really well with conversation and am really good at participation, and I know the professor likes it, because he will say in the public posts, in reply to some comments I made, about how I'm bringing up really good points and how he is impressed at my insight and good stuff like that. So, yay! I'm doing good. I didn't tell you guys the comments about my women in the middle ages paper, but she really liked my paper too and my use of quotes and how I developed a unique and interesting approach to the assignment, and my intriguing observations of the themes and use of symbols that she (the author of the topic) uses.
Proud of me? (:
Just wanted to let you both know all of this because it definitely makes me happy, especially when I get comments on my writing.
Love you!

October 7, 2005 Diary
Caleb emailed me finally and wanted me to come visit him in Eden Prairie last weekend to party at his place, but I was already going to St. Cloud that Saturday and had WAY too much homework to do, so I had to cancel on him. Too bad cause it would've been a good time and Caleb is fine as hell, but it also made me a little nervous and cautious cause I don't know that his intentions are. Either way it's a long ass drive there and gas prices are high! I do have my mom's car here though cause I'll be driving home this coming Wednesday for my flight to Italy on Thursday! I am SOOOooooo excited for Rome. Words don't even explain it.
So I posted on my Xanga a bit ago, complaining about my diabetes, and a day later I get an IM from Kristina and it made me

really happy to know she cares and that she's reading my Xanga, cause I write largely for her! [Kristina wrote that she missed Krystin, wants to stay connected, suggested a trip to Morris, and urged Krystin strongly to take care of her diabetes because many people care about her. Kristina could not be at Krystin's memorial event on October 29, 2017, but sent a large peace lily with a heartfelt card.] That would be awesome if she came to visit. I can't wait to show her everything and introduce her to everyone. Molly is planning on visiting too in mid November. Yay! I love visitors. We can party it up Morris style.

Classes going alright but I sleep a lot, am trying not to skip a lot. So, working on that too.

All caught up for the most part. I'll be better at writing down feelings as they occur. Later.

October 8, 2005 Diary
Out on a Limb

Alone at night, in my bed he comes to mind—
I reach out my heart to him and wonder what I'll find. . .
Fear reaches in at the mistakes I have made,
telling him how I feel too soon, but I could not hold it in any longer. . .
He is new in my life but love knows no time—
it can happen over years or the blink of an eye.
But to him who is so quiet, who shows me love but
says not a word . . . how am I to know
that what he feels is not the same.
So here I am, out on a limb—
one whose heart has been broken so many times
that I almost expect it, but for some reason still fear it,
As if some part of me still holds on to some hope
that he won't be like the others. . .
Afraid of love, or afraid of me and what I feel
So many run away at the first sign of this dreaded
emotion which is like elixir to a woman
but poison to a man. . .
He has shown himself to be different, so open
and accepting, but part of me still knows and fears
that in his hear he may be the same. . .
Out on a limb, waiting and watching for his every word

and reaction, wonder which things I have said or done
may be the mistake that ends it all.

[I do not know if this is original. It does not show up on a Google search. I sent it to a friend who's a published poet to ask his opinion about it, and I asked if he thought it original. He wrote back:

It certainly looks (and reads) like a poem to me. Original, as opposed to borrowed from another source? You say the first two lines aren't borrowed--I'd say the rest of it is even less likely to be someone else's, just because it seems fairly uneven. It looks like a first draft, not something that's been published and is in circulation in the world. Original, as in innovative and unique in the annals of literature? To be honest, I guess not so much. It resembles other relationship poems I've read over the years from poets in the high-school-through-college age range—some of my own included!

From what you've told me, I already know Krystin used her writing to help her process all that was going on her life. I take it that most of the rest of diary is prose? If so, I'd guess she was experimenting with poetic lines while still primarily writing to get her thoughts on paper, as opposed to writing with primarily artistic aims. Nonetheless, it's clear to me that she has a clear grasp of what she is saying and how she is saying it. Her sentences are varied and broken by ellipses and hesitations, yet their meanings are never confusing. If I was giving her feedback, I would have pointed that out as a strength. I also like the elixir/poison contrast. It's curious that she starts out with a couplet that rhymes and is roughly iambic in meter, but then drops that goal (it's slow going to compose that way!) and simply writes free verse.]

October 9, 2005 Diary
[Long entry about hurting because nothing is going to develop with Mike, she didn't know heartbreak before, "Oh my aching heart." Hard time putting emotions down on paper.]

October 10, 2005 Diary
[Email from Christine Lenzen printed and pasted into the diary; Chris's capitalization.]

heartache is hard. We'll have to talk about it more on wednesday when I see you. I'm glad you are coming weds – that's the only day of the week I would have been able to see you.

It takes a long time to get over someone. It takes even longer when you are friends, but ultimately being friends with someone after "rejection" – not that mike rejected you so to speak – makes you a stronger person and a stronger friend. and it will make him realize how great you are, not make him change his mind, how mature you are with your feelings. No one can control how they feel but we all have the ability to choose how we react to [a] situation.

just remember to breath. that is usually my hardest part.

I got this e-mail from Chris after e-mailing her the whole situation about Mike. What a great friend, she knows just what to say.

October 16, 2005 Diary
So much to catch up on! I'll start with last week. I decided to go home on Tuesday afternoon instead of Weds. evening. I had to get out of there. So I drove home right after my Europe's 20th Century class.

Wednesday I didn't do much. I slept in then Chris and I got together. We ate dinner at the Lake Street Garage then went to this tattoo/piercing place in St. Paul called Visual Addiction so a guy there could look at my foot tattoo. It's infected. He told me to go to the doctor and get an antibiotic, so Chris and I went to urgent care at Fairview Riverside and I got some huge fucking pills that I take twice a day for 7 days. Oh, but at Visual Addiction I got a new nose ring! It's a purple stud. I guess my silver ball was always sticking out cause when I got it pierced at Saint Sabrina's, they put it in wrong! So this one sits on my nose much better.

Thursday I was supposed to go downtown and renew my license and have lunch with Mark but I ended up sleeping instead. I got an e-mail from Kris saying Caleb was even in for lunch that day and they were expecting some drama. DAMN! I should've gone. Oh well. So I caught the 3:10 bus and got out to the airport, got all my flights and arrived safe at the hotel in Florence. I didn't sleep at all on the flight from Detroit to Paris, but I watched 'Bewitched' and 'March of the Penguins.' Both good! So when I got to the hotel, my parents were gone so I took a nap! When they got back we got ready for our 8pm dinner reservation, and slowly made our way to the restaurant. We were a little early so we sat and had a beer outside a little café. At our dinner I had veal! It was actually very good and I was starving. I would have it again though. All the food here is delicious. When we got back we got ready for bed. I was so tired, I put in my ear plugs and was out like a light. I haven't slept that well in ages!

Saturday we got up and had hotel breakfast, then headed off for our first walking tour. It was basically an introduction to Florence tour. OMG this city is so gorgeous. So much old architecture and SO MANY HOT GUYS. Damn are Italian boys fine as hell. I want to take their pictures but that would be awkward as hell. So I just look. After the tour we had lunch at an outside café. I had a beer and some real Italian pizza! So good. We had some time after lunch until our next tour, so my mom and I did some shopping! I got a Florence bracelet and coin purse, a t-shirt and sweatshirt that both say ITALIA on them, and a plain green zip-up long-sleeve shirt. Mom got another suitcase. Hehe. Much needed. We had our own private tour at 3, but I only made it about ¾ of the way through and was so tired I had to go back to the hotel for a nap. I felt bad leaving the tour but I was just so tired I wasn't enjoying it, and my dad could tell. So I took a short nap.

Then . . . my "date" with Pietro! He picked me up at the hotel at 6:15 on his motor scooter! He is damn fine too. I was surprised because I didn't know what to expect. He showed me a few of the Florence universities. Holy shit they are crazy fucking drivers here, just like in London. There aren't any lanes, and we were going like 60 MPH (literally!) down the streets. We went to a bar where I had a margarita, which they make strong as hell here, so I was feeling it a bit. He bummed me some cigarettes too. Then we went to his HUGE ass house on the hill that overlooks Florence, and got his car. We picked up 2 of his friends and pizza, then went to another friend's house where were 3 more people (so 7 of us total), one other girl. None of them speak much English except Pietro so I just sat there and listened to them talk, but was still fun. Had wine with pizza. I got very tired, so instead of going to the bar with them I had Pietro bring me back to the hotel, which is too bad cause I would've loved to stay out with them longer. He gave me a kiss on the cheek and a long hug goodbye. *SIGH* I am going to marry that guy. Hehe. We decided to stay in touch through e-mail, which I am excited about! I will visit him when I am in Scotland spring semester too. God he's fine. For a bit he even made me forget about Mike. Only until today though. . . . OH, and Pietro likes System of a Down! I love that. A huge plus. *SIGH* again.

October 18, 2005 Diary

I hate writing in pencil but it's all I have right now. I am sitting alone at a café in Rome near our hotel, having a tequila sunrise and a cigarette and a small snack of tomatoes and mozzarella. I like the alone time! Today we went on a tour from 8:30am to almost 3pm! With a lunch break. We covered a lot of ground. It was so much walking, but after we had a casual walk back to the hotel and I did some shopping in a store called 'Killer Loop.' An interesting note, the store was playing American rap music and they don't censor it! Pretty cool, but probably not for my mom. Then we got back to the hotel and I decided to go for a walk and here I am! Yesterday we took the train from Florence to here (Rome). Oh, Sunday night we called Pietro to see if he wanted to go out again with me but he was busy. Major bummer! I really like him, he makes me forget about Mike. But I still think about Mike too. Oh well. I can have 2 husbands!! Anyway today we visited the huge place that the pope used to flee to in times of emergency. It was pretty cool. We also sat on the Spanish Steps. Thursday is the Vatican. More later.

November 5, 2005 Diary

I see it's been a while since I updated. Obviously I'm not in Italy anymore. It was a great trip, although the last 3 nights I got almost no sleep cause my dad was coughing all night. He thinks he had bronchitis. Anyway, I was crabby the last 2 days and my parents hated it. My dad said I am never traveling with them again. Whatever. He says that every time. Maybe I don't wanna travel with them anymore anyway. After being here at college and away from them, I get tired of being with them 24/7 anyway. That's why I think it will be weird to be living with them again next semester in Scotland. That's why I'm glad Mike will be there so we can go off and travel a lot. I'm afraid though that I won't [have] enough money to do all that traveling, cause I've been spending money way too much here at school and won't make enough at Bigsby's in the 2 weeks I'm home for winter break. If I'm lucky, I'll go to Scotland with $1000. Yikes!

So October 30 was my 21st birthday! It was on a Sunday, when no bar or liquor store is open, so Saturday night at midnight Mike,

Alicia and I went to the Met. They are only open till 1, so in an hour I had 5 drinks (tequila sunrise), a shot, and a glass and a half of beer. I had such a good time, it was awesome. Got a good picture of me and Mike. And he has no idea how much I cherish it and how much it means to me. On Monday I tried to go to the liquor store, but because my license had expired and I hadn't renewed it yet, the guy couldn't accept it. I was so pissed. So on Tuesday I went to the license bureau in town and renewed it. So now I can use it until my new one comes in the mail, which will be in a few weeks probably. By the time I'm home for Thanksgiving.

I'm afraid I'm making myself sick again from diabetes. I have felt shitty lately and little nauseous some nights. I'm sure the drinking isn't helping either. I feel like I'm killing myself and doing nothing about it.

I am having problems dealing with my feelings for Mike. I think it's making me depressed. Even though he says he and Becky won't get back together, it hurts when he says he still loves her and I get jealous when he hangs out with her or talks about her all the time, which is always. And I think about him all the time too. I want to be around him always so that I know where he is and what he's doing, which sounds stalkerish, but I'm afraid he's getting tired of me or soon will. I dunno.

November 16, 2005 Email
Krystin to dad:

Do you have the book 'Guns, Germs, and Steel'? Would it be a book that I would like? I decided, that as a history major, and therefore being someone interested in history, I would like to start reading more books on history, other than just my text books. But I like books more that tell personal stories or that are novels, not just books that are like a documentary video, you know what I mean? . . . Maybe you have some good ones in the study? I feel like I am a bad history major, like I don't know enough. I don't want to read more books just for that reason though. I guess on the other hand then, I am a good history major, because I yearn to know more! It's kinda like, I wanna know everything, but where do I start? There's so much to know about history and I want to learn more. What kind of history? All kinds! European and American, and all time periods. Well, actually, I guess more the 19th and 20th century. [I don't believe Krystin ever read *Guns, Germs, and Steel*, but she did end up reading a considerable amount of British history as well as, for example, Hilary Mantel's Cromwell trilogy.]

November 29, 2005 Email
Hi dad,
 I wanted to e-mail you and let you know that I got my two papers back in my Europe's 20th century class today (the one with Marynel), and on one I got a B, and the other I got an A. And the one that I got a B on I thought would get like a D on because it was at the point where it was early in the morning, the morning it was due, so I printed it and said to myself well, this is how I'm turning it in and we'll see what happens. And I get a B on it! So I definitely work well under pressure. Maybe I should do all my papers the night before it's due?? Ok maybe not. I don't usually write my papers the night before. So yeah, I just wanted to let you know how I did.

December 11, 2005 Diary
 Once again, long time no update, I know. Umm, let's see, what to mention that would be of interest to people. Oh, biggest news: I've decided that I don't want to feel horrible anymore. And by horrible I mean as far as my diabetes goes, feeling constantly drained of energy and motivation to do anything, always being tired and putting no effort into my homework. As we know, this comes from high blood sugars, and I decided I don't want to feel this way anymore and I'm going to take control. I hope this time it works. So since Wednesday I've been doing all my insulin and have been feeling much better. Most of my reasoning behind this is also because I was talking to my mom on the phone earlier in the week and of course the conversation turned towards my health and she said how at Thanksgiving like everyone in my family kept telling my mom how awful I look, how thin I am how they can see it in my face that I'm not taking care of myself. And now that I think about it, one of my aunts was being kinda silent towards me, I think because she works in the health industry and she knows what's going on inside my body and what I'm doing to myself, so she of course wasn't very happy with me. And one of my other aunts, upon arrival, instead of giving me a hug she just looks at me and says "oh my god you're too skinny it's scary – almost Lindsay Lohan skinny!" Thanks aunt Holly. I did finally get a hug out of her, but that comment did kinda strike a nerve. So, I'm going to show them. By Christmas I am going to have gained weight (since I'm taking all my insulin now,

I'll start absorbing the nutrients in my food and will gain some weight), and will be feeling much better as well. I guess this makes it sound like I'm doing it for them, but really I'm doing it for me. I also figured out that if I continue on the road I was on, I only have 7 years left to live – at least according to the doctor here at health services who I had sign my driver form. He looked at me and was just like "you're not doing well. I've seen people with diabetes only 28 years old and on dialysis . . . that's where you're headed." Good times. I don't want to hear any more stories, I don't want to hear anyone else tell me how thin or bad I look, I don't want to hear anything else from anyone anymore related to how bad I'm doing, because I'm not going to give them reason to. And like I've said, I hope this lasts. I don't want it to be another case where it goes well for a while and then I fall back into my old pattern. Please don't let it happen.

On another note . . . my new burst of energy after only 3 days is starting to kick in. I spent like 4 hours on Friday afternoon/night writing one 4 page paper and another short essay (only 250 words). I was pretty proud of myself. And here it is Saturday night and I started working on my final paper for my Women in the Middle Ages class. I'm going to try to get my final papers done early so I can get everything done and in early so I don't have to worry about it next weekend when my parents come to get me on Sunday. Good story.

I am so excited for Christmas! I always get really excited at this time of year because Christmas is my favorite holiday ever, I don't think people realize, I really get into the holiday spirit. My mom e-mailed me asking what is on my Christmas list, and I actually can't think of anything that I want! Which is odd really. I want to tell her that it's not about presents, I'll just be happy to be home and with family sitting by the tree, the lights sparkling and twinkling in our eyes, the snow falling outside, listening to carols and having good conversation. Cheesy? Probably, but it's what I love best about Christmas. I don't have any money this year to spend on presents for other people, so I don't expect anything in return. Which wouldn't happen anyway because none of my friends have money either! Hehe. I have two (maybe three?) weeks at home before I'm gone for 4 months, so I want to spend as much time with friends, being happy and enjoying each other's company since it won't happen for 4 months after that.

[hand-written addition:] Now that I'm doing my insulin, I'm absorbing my food and I'm hungry all the time! I can tell I'm gaining weight too, my jeans are starting to fit snug. I also made the mistake of eating a lot of caramel corn in one sitting because I have had flatulent diarrhea the past day and it will last like 3 more days. Never making that mistake again!

Mom is going to give Marla back to the lady we got her from to find a new family because no one will take her when we go to Scotland and no one in the family likes her except mom. Yay! Mom is sad and I feel bad about it, but I'm glad Marla is going. She drives me crazy. And mom isn't going to look for another dog – ever. Cody is going to stay a single dog, thank god. And we will just be dogless when Cody dies.

I miss Bela a lot. My fat boy.

December 13, 2005 Diary

The caramel corn diarrhea is finally coming to an end.

Today I pretty much finalized both my directed studies for next semester.

I pulled an all-nighter with Bre last night, reading stuff for my final paper in my Women in the Middle Ages class and the reading assignment for my Europe's 20th Century class today. I went to bed at like 6:30 and woke up at 9. I thought for sure I wouldn't make it to class but I made myself go, and I'm proud of it.

I think my love feelings for Mike are finally starting to go away. Next semester is going to be so much better. I can't wait. We'll all get our own bedroom. We'll have broadband Internet, and my mom's office is giving her a brand new laptop for us. Good times.

Chapter 4

The College Years: Scotland and Treatment

January 9, 2006 Diary

So much to update on, it's almost been a month! Moved out of Morris on Sunday Dec. 18. Started working again at Bigsby's on Tuesday the 20th. Final grades:

Women in the Middle Ages: C
Europe's 20th Century: B
Lewis and Clark: A-

Not too shabby! I thought I would get all C's, so I did better than expected. The first week back at work Dan was gone on vacation, the 2nd week Ramon was gone, and the 3rd and last week Kris was gone. I got to work 2 morning shifts. All in all it was a good 3 weeks of working. My first check was $251 which I didn't get to deposit before leaving, and the next pay day is the 20th and Kris will directly deposit it into my bank account. Until then no VISA purchases!

Edinburgh: we're here! It's a beautiful city, our flat is pretty cool, we have to walk everywhere cause we're in a ritzy residential area. Yesterday we all walked to the grocery store, about 15 min. away, and a movie theater about 10 min. away. Our fridge/freezer is only a little bigger than a mini fridge, so we will have to go to the grocery store once a week cause it can only fit a week's worth of groceries at a time! All the outlets have switches, as well as the shower. We only get about 4-5 minutes of shower time each or we run out of hot water. And the toilet has a mind of its own. Sometimes it flushes, sometimes it doesn't.

Mike joins us this weekend. I miss him. And still like him.

January 16, 2006 Diary

Mike arrived at 7:30 Saturday morning but I did not see him cause he took a shower then went to sleep. He had taken a bus from London overnight, so I don't blame him. Yesterday was Mike's b-day, so we (he and I) went on a walking adventure. We tried to find the ocean but didn't, so we ended up seeing like 4 miles (at least) of suburban Edinburgh. Found a shopping mall though! Might go to London this weekend! Melissa is going to come on Wednesday and stay here, then Mike and I are trying to go to London with her on Thursday, until Monday. I'm excited! That would be awesome. Then we think we will take one big trip in February, that will last the month, and one in April that will last the month. Those will be Europe trips, and in between we'll do some traveling around the U.K. and Scotland, like to Wales, Glasgow, up north.

January 21, 2006 Diary

Last night Mike and I had a long talk, mostly about me, and I came to a few conclusions: A1. I need to be more confident, it's more appealing to guys. B2. I need to care less what people think about me and go out in public with my hair messed up. C3. My dad is self-centered and nobody can change that. D4. When a relationship is meant to happen with a guy, it will. But I don't like that I have to wait for it. OR, I have to stop pushing away opportunities for it to happen because I may have done so in the past and not even known it.

January 27, 2006 Diary

Got back from Stirling yesterday. It was pretty fun, I slept on a mattress in Melissa's room and Mike slept on a sofa in the public living area. 4 people, including Melissa, live in her flat. My legs fucking killed me all week long, and the computer lab at the U is up a big steep hill. They wanted to walk into town every day but I made us take a bus. On Tuesday we went to both the Stirling castle and the William Wallace monument, although we didn't go into either. Got great pictures though because both are up on hills. On Wednesday night we went to the William Wallace pub near Melissa's flat. We wanted hard cider but they were out! Major bummer. So I had 2 Bacardi Breezers instead. We came home yesterday and my parents and Elliott left today for St. Andrews. I was gonna go with them but I had too much work for Deane to get done by today, so I didn't go, and I didn't even get my work done. But anyway the Stirling trip was fun. Mike got a tattoo. I had to resist getting another one.

I asked my dad for a loan and he is going to give me $700 which I will repay this summer. I expect to have many hours in at Bigsby's, so it shouldn't be a problem. Now I will be able to do more things on our travels. Pietro is picking us up from the bus station in Florence. I'm so excited! He is really busy these days with studying and work but I hope to spend some time alone with him. I told Bre online that I'm going to jump all over that. Haha

January 31, 2006 Diary
    So here is our itinerary:

Feb 6	Pisa (for the day)
Feb 6 – Feb 9	Florence (Italy)
Feb 10 – Feb 13	Montpellier (France)
Feb 14 – Feb 17	Madrid (Spain)
Feb 17 – Feb 20	Barcelona (Spain)
Feb 21 – Feb 23	Geneva (Switzerland)
Feb 24 – Feb 27	Vienna
Feb 28 – Mar 3	Paris (France)

    I wanted to stop in London for the weekend on the way home and have Elliott join me, but parents won't let him. So instead I get to be on a bus for a day and a half cause there are no cheap flights from Paris to Glasgow or Edinburgh! Oh well, guess I'll get to see a lot of scenery! And get a lot of homework and word finds done. Mike won't be with me cause he'll stay and spend a week with Alexis, who is flying to Paris to then go to Germany for the week of spring break, then another week in Marseille with his friend Illy. Anyway, we will be in Barcelona over a weekend and Melissa wants to join us, so that would be fun! Maybe that's when we'll get our tattoos and/or piercings. Either then or with Pietro in Florence, we will have to see. I am going to get my next tattoo at some point, and it's going to be a star on my left right where my IV was when I was in the hospital November 2004. So it will have meaning.

February 9, 2006 Diary
    So here I am in Montpellier (France) in Rachel's apartment. I will start with our leaving Edinburgh though. We took the train to Glasgow. No problem. We walk up a hill to the bus station to find out it's a train we take to the Prestwick airport, so we walk back to the train station to find out it's a different train station we go to. So we get to the right station and have a little while to kill so we go to a bar in the station and I have a hard cider. Yum. We get to the airport and settle in for a long night. OH, but on the train to Glasgow there were 2 girls that sat next to us who were piss drunk who had just come from rugby game. There were so hilarious, they were sticking food on the window to make faces. I got a little sleep at the airport but not much. I got a lot of word finds done! Our flight went fine, we got into Pisa on time. We took a city bus to the Leaning Tower, got the typical tourist picture of me holding it up, then walked back to the bus station.

The bus ride to Florence took an hour. Pietro picked us up from the central train station and took us to his house. Mike and I laid down to take a nap and ended up sleeping until noon the next day! We were so tired. But that next day we went into the city and walked around all day. Saw the Duomo again, ate some gelato, froze our butts off, and were late meeting Pietro at our pickup spot. But we went back and had a delicious Italian dinner at his house with his parents then went out to have a drink with one of his friends whom I met when I was there in October. I had like a pint and a half of beer and was tipsy! A sign that I haven't drank much in a while! But we had some really good conversation and learned a lot of interesting stuff about Italian culture and the current political system. I slept great that night. We had our bus out of Florence the next day at 5:15 but Pietro had to bring us into the city at like 1 or 1:30, so we sat in the McDonald's across the street from the train station for like 3 hours. It was a good time. Our bus to Montpellier left at 5:05 pm, and we arrived here at 4:10 in the morning. The bus stopped every hour and a half-ish for bathroom breaks for 10 minutes, and one break for 45 minutes for dinner. I only slept a couple hours on the bus. I wish it had been lighter out because I bet there was a lot of pretty scenery going through the mountains. The walk from the parking lot to Rachel's apartment is really short, but we got a little lost. It was 5 am by the time we found her place but we weren't sure if it was hers because her name wasn't on the door buzzer thing, so Mike just pushed a button with American names on it and luckily it was hers! We sat and talked to her till like 6:30 then decided we were all tired and went to sleep, Mike and me in the living room. We got up at 12:30 and went and had lunch at the student café at the university. I had a taco salad and it was delicious. Rachel's friend Tara joined us. Rachel had a class after that, so Mike and I slowly made our way back to by where Rachel lives. I spent half an hour in an Internet café but couldn't deal with the French keyboard so I gave up.

 I e-mailed Deane and told her I couldn't deal with all the reading questions and didn't want it bogging me down while I travel and could we work something out, and she e-mailed back and said OK I don't have to do the questions, she understands. She'll just base my grade on the 6 tests. Whew. I am behind on the reading anyway, and I have a paper to write now for Roland that is due early next week, so I have to do all that. So I think I'll get started on that paper tonight.

February 18, 2006 Diary

I'm in Barcelona right now, but I'll go back to Madrid. We were there for 3 days, and it was awesome. Such a great city.

So we got into Barcelona last night around 8pm and went right to the Eurolines office to reserve our bus spot to Geneva on Monday. I think the guy was new because he was trying to tell us there was no bus to Geneva. Ahh. Then another guy came over and said yes, don't worry, there is a bus, and to come back Monday morning to reserve our spot. So we'll do that. Then we took the metro to where our hostel is but walked around for like 45 minutes trying to find it, to find out we had passed it in the beginning.

I split off and took the metro to Port Olimpic and saw the ocean and the beach, watched some people play sand volleyball. Then I went to the Arc de Triomphe and took some pictures, walked down to the zoo and took a picture outside of that, then went to the grocery store and got soup and applesauce for dinner. After eating in the hostel I went to an Internet place to vent online, and am now in the hostel writing in here. Mike went out with some people from the hostel but I didn't want to. I'm going to go to bed early, I have a big day planned tomorrow. I'm getting up at 10:30 again and am leaving when I'm ready, with or without Mike.

February 22, 2006 Diary

Currently in Geneva, Switzerland. An interesting city indeed, but beautiful as all others have been as well. We got in yesterday at like 7:30 am. The bus ride was great, only 15-20 people on it, so I took up the whole back row (5 seats) to sleep, which was great. Our bus had troubles at one point and we had to stop and sit for like an hour while it was being fixed. We couldn't check into our hostel room until 3pm, so we put our stuff in a locker and went out exploring. We were able to get into our room around 2:30, so we did and at 3 I laid down for a nap and slept till like 8:15! I've been sleep deprived on this trip, so it felt good.

Today I had my alarm set for 10:45 but just turned it off and kept sleeping until around 12:30 when the maid came in to clean! I showered and ate lunch and Mike and I walked to the Red Cross museum. It was really cool, it tells of how the Red Cross got started and how they helped during wars and stuff. We walked back to the hostel after that and I took another nap.

I've been telling people who [how?] Geneva really upholds the reputation of Swiss banking. Banks are fucking everywhere! And because the city is so rich, everything is as expensive as all hell. So I've been good not to spend a lot of money here. I already have to cut down our second trip because I won't have enough money to go to as many cities as this trip. So it's looking like it will be Amsterdam, Berlin, Prague, and Krakow. Maybe Hamburg.

My mom and I are going to Dublin! March 7-10. I'm really excited for Ireland, it will be awesome. Then in April Tracy and Joan are visiting Edinburgh and we will all take a trip to Copenhagen, Denmark. Yay again! I love all this traveling I'm getting to do, although I see now how it is exhausting. I really like it here, but I know I will be glad to be home in Minnesota in May and back to normal and not living out of a suitcase! And work, oh work, bringing in the dough! And to have my kitties back! The best part of all. And to see Chris and the rest of my friends, and to drive again! There, that was my nostalgia for the day.

February 25, 2006 Diary

Just finished our second day in Vienna. We arrived yesterday at 6am and pretty much didn't do anything all day. We booked our bus tickets to Paris then went to our hostel. They were able to get us into a room right away so we went right up and laid down to take a nap! Slept for like 6 hours.

March 3, 2006 Diary

Sitting in the Paris Beauvais airport waiting for my flight to Glasgow, which was supposed to be a 2:30 but has been delayed to 6:00! Oh joy. Anyway, Paris was pretty cool. Our first day here was the most productive. But let me start with our hotel. Oh, lordy what a disaster. It was a hotel, not a hostel, so we had our own room, but they messed it up. We were supposed to have a 2-bedroom for $97, but we got a 1-bedroom for $100.40. We were gonna argue but figured it would be too much of a hassle, so we didn't. Mike and I just shared the double bed with his feet at my head and vice-versa. It was a tiny ass room too. But we dealt with it.

So, the first day, we did a lot of fucking walking, basically in a big circle through Paris. We walked to the Arc de Triomphe, then to the Eiffel Tower which I went up to the top of but Mike did not. Amazing views, too. Then we walked through town and made our way to the river, walked by the Orsay museum, the Louvre, and Notre Dame. Took lots of pictures! We made our way back up to the hostel and about halfway back it started to fuckin blizzard! Biggest snowflakes I have ever seen in my life. And even though we were freezing, we had a good time catching snowflakes in our mouths.

The 2nd day we had kebab lunch and then were going to do the Louvre. Mike was gonna walk and I was gonna take the metro. We met back at the hotel at like 9:30 pm and neither of us had gone! Mike got lost and just walked around all day, and I went to the grocery store after lunch then went back to the hotel and went back to sleep! Kinda funny. We didn't even go out that night cause Mike was too exhausted. No shit.

Yesterday we did make it to the Louvre. 8.50€ and I was only in there for like 45 minutes. Mike and I ended up splitting up, and after I saw the Mona Lisa, I was ready to go! I feel bad leaving so soon, but at least I can say I was there. Got a picture with the pyramid too, of course. I went back to the hotel and took another nap, then later after Mike got back we went and had Chinese dinner. Yum! Then around 9pm we left and walked to the Moulin Rouge! A little disappointing, not what I thought it would be, but still cool to have been at. We listened to the movie soundtrack when we got back. We were going to walk back, but while we were sitting in a bar so I could have a beer it started raining, to we took the metro back instead. Chilled out, went to bed.

Got up early today to go to the train station to get to the airport. Found out we needed to take the metro to a bus station. So we did that, and that's where Mike and I said goodbye. I took the 45 min. bus to the airport, and here I am waiting for 3 or 4 hours for my flight. Good times.

So now that the trip is pretty much over, looking back on it I had a good time, even though it was freezing from Geneva on. Lots of good memories though! More reflection later. Au revoir.

~*March 3, 2006 Email [hand-written]*
Krystin to [diabetic nurse educator and endocrinologist]:
I need help. I have come to terms with this fact, and am willing to work with you to get the help that I need. We (my family and I) are in Scotland until May, but if there is someone I could work with online, like through e-mail, until can meet in person, I would like help in looking into something like that. I know that it seems like we have

exhausted all options, but I know that is because in the past I have resisted and pushed against any and all help, whereas now I would like to work with, instead of against, any help. And I am hoping that you can help me find options; I am ready to find options. Where is a good place for me to begin? That is, aside from my parents, who are willing to help as well. Hope to be in touch soon.
Krystin Engstrand

March 16, 2006 Diary

Last Tuesday through Friday I was in Dublin with my mom. Then over the weekend with mom, dad, and Elliott. Dublin was awesome. I could easily live there. The people are so nice, and my mom and I went to pubs for a drink (or two, or three. . .) at least twice a day. Hard cider has become my drink of choice. We went on a Viking Splash tour, saw St. Patrick's Cathedral and the Guinness Brewery, and of course did some shopping! It was a good trip, I enjoyed the bonding time with my mom.

Had a long talk (like 3 hours) with my mom the other night at the Golf Tavern about my diabetes. I've finally decided to really take control and take care of it, and even seek professional help. I never realized how much I've been hurting people around me, friends and family, and how they can't stand to look at me. Even cousin Peter said something to his mom when we saw them at Christmas. And he's a 16 year old boy! If Peter said something, then that's really a sign that I need to do something. So I'm going to, and for real this time. Not just for my family, for me as well, obviously. I want to have a healthy future. I want to be able to have kids. Even if it means gaining all that weight back. I'm really trying hard to do all my insulin. I want people to tell me I look good instead of how skinny and bad I look. So there.

I have everything planned out for my next trip, which I leave for on Monday. I will fly into Brussels, which we will be for 2 days, then to Amsterdam for 4 days, Berlin for 4 days, Warsaw for 3 days, then I'll go to Paris where my family will be. I'll spend a day with them then fly home to Edinburgh a day before them so I can get laundry done, because 2 days after that we are going to Copenhagen for 5 days! Whew. A busy and traveled girl I will be. It will be fun though. Convinced my dad to increase my loan, so I will now owe him $1500. Oh well. That's what this summer will be for. I'll be registering for classes for next fall while in Berlin, and I'll be doing hopefully 19 credits, plus I'm hoping a 1 or 2 credit directed study for Marynel. We shall see.

I'm really falling behind on my work for Deane. Like a month behind. I have a test that's a month overdue and a paper that's 3 weeks overdue. Oops. And I don't know why I keep putting it off, for some reason I can't muster up the motivation to do it.

April 19, 2006 Diary

Brussels – flew into Brussels on Monday, March 20, and met Mike at our hostel. He was already there. It was nice to see him again after a couple weeks away. We actually didn't do much in Brussels because there wasn't much to do, which surprised me considering it is the capital of Belgium. We mostly walked around the town, looking at stuff.

Amsterdam – Awesome. I loved it so much. We were there 4 days and I wish we had been longer. My only regret is that I didn't make it to the Anne Frank house. Or the Van Gogh museum. But we did go to the Red Light District, which was very interesting, and I got high 3 of the 4 days we were there! And one night Mike had shrooms and really liked it, but I was too cautious and scared to, so I didn't. I mostly loved it because it's such a beautiful and lively city, with lots of canals and cool old architecture. Old buildings yet a modern style to it. Everyone in Amsterdam spoke English, so we didn't have any language problems. This was probably my favorite city of all.

Berlin – also awesome. Our hostel was located in apparently a very trendy part of town, lots of bars and clubs, about 2 miles from Alexanderplatz. We came here 4 days as well, maybe 5, I don't remember. We did a LOT of walking, but we also ended up doing a lot of stuff on our own. We had planned to go on a tour of Sachsenhausen concentration camp, but when we were on the U-bahn going to the tour meeting point, I had forgot to validate my ticket so the guy made me get off, while Mike stayed on, and I missed the tour. Turns out Mike did too, but he went to the camp anyway and took the self audio tour. After missing the tour I walked down Unter den Linden, to Alexanderplatz and I went up into the TV tower. It was cool, got some good views! The day or two before, when Mike and I walked the town, we saw Bebelplatz, site of the 1933 book burning, and Checkpoint Charlie, and went into the Topography of Terror, which is located at the site where there is some of the last remnants of the Berlin Wall, and tells the story of WWII and the Jews and the concentration camps and the Nuremberg trials afterwards. It was very good and education, but sad. Oh, we also hung out at the Brandenburg Gate for a while! On our last day, our bus didn't leave until 11pm. So I went on a Fat Tire Bike Tour. It was a lot of fun. We saw some of the things Mike and I had already seen, but also new stuff, like the Victory Tower and the last remaining guard tower from when the Wall was up, and the hotel that Michael Jackson hung his baby over the railing from! And we had hot tea over the site where Hitler's bunker is! That was cool. The only bad thing is that it was raining for most of the tour. But we rode through the Tier Garden and had lunch at the Bier Garden. Our group was small—only 8, including myself and our guide. Oh, we also saw the Reichstag building, and the small section of the Wall that was artistically painted. It was a really good tour. And our hostel had free Internet, so that was a plus! I got all registered for my classes next fall. 19 credits! I'm not taking the creative writing class, but an Intro to Fiction. And hopefully a 1 or 2 credit directed study for Marynel. But anyway yeah, Berlin was awesome, I loved it, love the city, everything about it.

Warsaw – were there 3 days, I spent 2 of them sick in bed coughing and sleeping. But I did get out to see a bit of the city. I wish I had seen more of the city, but I was just too sick and tired.

[The following part of the diary is largely redundant in light of the long essay Krystin later prepared, but I've included it because there are bits and pieces not in the essay. The essay also has some life history that appears elsewhere.]

Paris – oh boy, where to begin with this. Long story short: I got ketoacidosis again and after my 25 hour bus ride from Warsaw I went straight to the hospital. I didn't make it to meet my parents and Elliott. I had been throwing up the whole bus ride, and when I got to the Paris bus station, I layed down on a bench to die, because that surely would've happened if a guy hadn't come over and asked me if I needed a doctor. So off to the hospital I went, where I spent 3 days in the CCU and 3 in a recovery room. Not fun at all, obviously. My parents visited every day, but I found out later that they were considering not coming because they were so angry. They were going to fly back to Edinburgh and let me figure things out on my own. I'm glad they didn't. We missed our flights back to Edinburgh, so we took a Eurolines bus to London, then a train from London up to Edinburgh. We missed our weekend trip around NW Scotland. I feel bad about that. We got back early Tuesday morning. The hospital staff spoke very broken English, if any at all, and I didn't know French, and my mom had only taken 3 years back in high school, so it was a very interesting experience. So was getting my catheter out after they moved me to my recovery room, because it was stuck! They had to call in a specialist and he had to take a needle and poke my bladder from the outside through the wall of my bladder to pop the water bubble that was keeping the catheter in. It worked, but only after poking me like 12-15 times! OMG that hurt so bad. I never want to have kids. But I had TV 2 of 3 days, so I watched music videos or read all day, when my parents weren't visiting. I was so happy to get out, I am not going to let this happen ever again. I found out though that I have 'diabulimia,' which is diabetics not doing their insulin to keep their weight down. So I have an eating disorder. I have many appointments when we get back to Mpls in May, so we will figure out a plan that works me so that this doesn't happen again, because it's basically a suicide attempt, although that was not what I was trying to do. So again I almost died, scared the shit out of my family and friends, but am doing better. I feel better, and I can tell I'm gaining weight back.

[Beginning of essay; diary resumes several pages later]

From Warsaw to Paris: A Tale of Survival

If you are curious what hell feels like, let me tell you: It's a 26-hour bus ride from Warsaw to Paris, during which you are back-and-forth between your seat and the bus bathroom, defecating or vomiting because all your internal organs are shutting down and are ridding themselves of anything that may be blocking their path from actually exiting the body themselves. And when everything is empty, you're still dry heaving because your stomach is still convinced there's something in there, maybe some bit of tomato peel from your sandwich the day before. Whatever it is, even if nonexistent, is coming out! I'm going to die here in this cubby hole of a bathroom, I kept thinking to myself. Not quite.

This is the story of how I would almost die.

I should preface my tale with this forethought: Don't get the impression that I take death lightly. It's not like I wake up and think, "Today would be a good day to scare the living daylight out of my family and friends." Quite the contrary; but let's face it, there is no way to sugar-coat it: I almost died.

I have had type 1 (insulin dependent) diabetes since shortly after my fourth birthday in 1988, and since my teen years, I have not been very good at taking care of myself. If there were a Diabetics Anonymous group for people with diabetes who fail to make peace with and acknowledge their illness, I would be the head honcho; a fact that I am not proud of.

Let's go back to spring of 2006, when I embarked on a journey around the European Union, visiting 13 countries in four months. My family was living in Scotland that spring because my father was on sabbatical from the University of Minnesota, to do research on higher education at the University of Edinburgh. While he was busy working every day, I stayed busy by traveling around Europe. Since I was a young woman, my parents did not feel comfortable with me traveling alone, so I was permitted to invite a friend to live with us, and travel with me. Mike, a friend of mine from college, agreed to come to Scotland and join in all the adventures that I had planned. Although Edinburgh was our home base, we were away travelling on the continent more than we were in Scotland.

At this point in my travels I had gone into a downward spiral of not taking my insulin, which had been a frequent occurrence in my diabetes management for the previous six years or so. In fact, by April of that year it had been around three months since I'd taken a single dose of insulin. And a blood test? I don't think I even packed my blood glucose meter when we moved to Scotland. I am not at all proud of this fact. I only mention it to give an idea of how bad things had gotten. Friends, family, doctors, and even I myself were surprised that I made it that long with no insulin without going into hyperglycemic shock.

My declining health was becoming more and more apparent not only in my lethargic behavior, but also my physical appearance. I was down around 105 pounds (at 5 feet, 4 inches tall). When the body does not have insulin to break down the foods that are consumed, the body does not absorb any of the nutrients. It's kind of like putting dough through a noodle maker: it comes out in a different shape and form, but everything that you started with is still there. I was eating all the time, but my body was still starving. Starving for insulin, starving for nutrients. But I didn't care. I was having the time of my life traveling around Europe with Mike, seeing the sites, having a blast, and experiencing cultural things that were once-in-a-lifetime opportunities. I wasn't going to let something like taking a shot of insulin waste my precious time.

In early April, on the last leg of one of my trips with Mike, I found myself on a 26-hour bus ride from Warsaw, Poland to Paris, France, going into diabetic ketoacidosis. Also known as DKA, it is a medical emergency which results in the body not having a sufficient amount of insulin, causing the body to start burning fat and muscle. This produces ketones (acid) that enter the bloodstream and essentially poison the body. Think industrial-strength glue; you know, the kind that melts plastic. Symptoms of DKA include vomiting, dehydration, deep gasping breathing, confusion and disorientation, fatigue, and decreased consciousness. If not treated quickly, DKA progressively worsens until the body starts shutting down and every function ceases, resulting in death. For some people with diabetes, DKA can occur after a short period of time of mismanagement, around a week or two; for others, a month or more. It occurs quicker for diabetics who have had much better, tighter control over their diabetes, so as soon as their blood sugars start to get out of control, their body reacts quickly. For me, I had not been taking care of my diabetes for years, which means my body had become accustomed to always having high blood sugars, and it was going to take a lot to finally sound the alarm. Since I had not taken insulin even once in three months, that meant that my body had slowly been building up acidic ketones and spilling them over into my bloodstream, and it was finally starting to take its toll.

Mike and I had been in Warsaw for four days, which included a weekend. Monday morning I was going to hop on the bus and take it to Paris, where I would meet my family, while Mike continued on traveling through Eastern Europe. The whole weekend prior to me leaving Warsaw I stayed in bed in our hostel. I felt too weak and tired to do anything, including eat, which was strange for me considering I was otherwise eating all the time. Looking back at the pictures that Mike took during our travels, many of them that are of me are of me eating. I knew why I was hungry all the time, but I kept justifying all my eating by telling myself I was just enjoying all the authentic cuisine of each country. Although Mike and I were both on a budget, any money that didn't go toward our hostels or museum entrance fees went toward food. When I finished one meal or snack, I was already thinking about what and when I would eat next. I wasn't eating large quantities in one sitting, but rather constantly eating small things here and there between meals. I was enticed by the aroma of almost every street food vendor we passed. Piadas and gelato in Italy. Churros and castanyas (roasted chestnuts) in Spain. Crepes and fresh French fries in France. Bratwurst and shashlik in Germany. Even McDonald's (where we dined often, unfortunately), became appealing to me; up until the weekend we were in Warsaw, when my appetite disappeared completely.

Of course it would be the morning that I was about to hop on a bus alone that my body would start to shut down. I knew when I woke up that morning that something was wrong. That thought of "uh oh, I know this feeling," came to mind. The acidic ketones had started poisoning my body, and once DKA starts, there's no stopping it without medical attention. I had no other choice, however, but to get on the bus; my family was expecting me in Paris, after all. It was a stupid decision on my part to leave Mike, especially without telling him what was going on, and there were no guarantees that I was going to make it to Paris. All I kept thinking was that if I could just make it to Paris and to my family, everything would be OK, and they would take care of me from there.

After spending almost every hour of every day with Mike for the past month, there were many times, as is natural when two people spend that much time together, when I wanted to smack him. I was ready for a break. But what I didn't realize was that I would soon need him more than ever, and he wouldn't be there. I had been so unworried about anything happening because I had decided that no matter what happened to me, the medics could make it all better. That may be true in the continental U.S. and in most major Western European cities. Not necessarily true when travelling on a bus through the mountains of Poland with a dozen or so other travelers who speak very little English, and a bus driver who speaks even less. I was just thankful that the tiny bus bathroom was open for passenger use; Mike and I had been on a couple buses where the driver had locked the door, I assume so that he didn't have to deal with cleaning and emptying the bathroom out at the end of the journey.

I spent a lot of time in that bus bathroom, which was smaller than the smallest broom closet you can think of. I'm surprised my stomach didn't give up on trying to get rid of everything in it and just hurl itself up through my esophagus and into the toilet. I knew right away after my first trip to the bathroom what was going on: Ketoacidosis again (the first time it occurred was in fall of 2005, [Krystin misremembered; it was 2004] and the first of my two brushes with death).

I wasn't always a "bad" diabetic. Up through middle school, my parents did most of the work for me at home. When it was time to do a blood test or take an insulin injection, they got my monitor and syringe ready and all I had to do was be there to do it. At school, I went to the nurse every day before lunch to do a blood test and take insulin. Both at home and at school, therefore, I had someone holding me accountable and monitoring all my blood tests and my injections. High school is where everything changed.

Eventually this self-talk became not just an idea in my head, but a lifestyle. Everyone around me saw my health declining. I saw it and felt it, too, but I continued to ignore it, telling myself that if I didn't acknowledge my failing health, it might not be true. Nobody ever told me to my face how unhealthy I looked. I would find out later from my mother that a cousin or an aunt would inquire if I had been sick lately. They could see it in my face, in my eyes that no longer shined, in the bubbliness that no longer existed in my personality. I let the illness begin to define me: I was no longer Krystin, but Krystin the Bad Diabetic. Even if no one said it out loud, I assumed they were all thinking it. Over the years, after high school and into college, even with all the emotional pain it caused my family and friends to watch me struggle to be healthy, I let diabetes win. I no longer cared about the illness, or myself. I had somehow convinced myself that it wasn't worth taking care of; that I wasn't worth taking care of. Perhaps I had been on that leash for too long, been under the care of my parents and my doctors for too long, and I had become too comfortable being taken care of. Even though I was enjoying the freedom of no longer being on my parents' ball and chain, if you will, I had no idea the damage I was doing to my body by not taking my insulin, and how within a couple years, the consequences would confront me in a way that could not be ignored.

Imagine being a passenger on a bus with ten to fifteen other strangers, most of them who don't speak your language, and you know you're dying. Do you try to explain to them what's happening to you and that you need medical help, or will that only create too much confusion? I was not willing to put in the effort to find out. Now put yourself in the shoes of one of those strangers sitting near me. You see a young American woman curled up in her seat almost the entire bus ride, stirring only to rush to the bathroom every half hour, the color even more drained from her face than it was the last time you saw her pass. Is she swaying because of the moving bus? Why does she have to go to the bathroom so often; does she get motion sickness easily? At first I noticed the strange, curious glances from the other passengers near to me, but I was declining so fast that eventually I didn't care. All I was worried about was that the bathroom would be occupied the next time I went, and that the unfortunate gentleman sitting in the seat nearest the bathroom would end up with my stomach on his lap.

About halfway through the trip, the bus stopped at a large station just off the highway that had a convenience shop and restaurant. The stop lasted one hour, to give people time to eat and the bus drivers a rest, so everyone was required to exit the bus, and the door was locked. I was already quite disoriented, so I just followed everyone else inside. I just wanted to lie down. I found a chair in a hallway near the bathroom and sat on that, waiting and watching until I saw people heading back to the bus, where my presumed deathbed was waiting for me. There was only one bathroom nearby, and I was occupying it for the majority of our stop. Come to think of it, I don't actually think it was a public restroom. I think it was a janitor's bathroom; it was stocked with mops and cleaning supplies and was beyond dirty. Didn't matter though, at least it had a toilet. When we all returned to the bus, I curled back up in my seat, closed my eyes, and focused on my breathing. Only six more hours to Paris.

I was convinced that my final resting place would be right there on that bus, and the poor unfortunate Polish bus driver would find me after he arrived at his final destination. I say this now, but at the time I actually wasn't too worried about him. I was more worried about how my parents were going to be notified. All anybody would find on me that would be of any help was my Minnesota driver's license. Would my family go back to Edinburgh without me and hope that I somehow made my way back there? Would they finish up their time in Scotland and go back to Minnesota in May and hope that I had somehow mistakenly gotten on the wrong bus and ended up back in the U.S.? (I know, I know, you can't get back to the U.S. by bus). In between my thoughts of "just end this pain and let me die," these questions remained on my mind. However, the closer I got to Paris, and the more my thought process deteriorated, the more my thoughts were consumed with just wanting the pain to go away.

As you can probably infer, I didn't die on that bus, but I didn't make it to meet my family either. By the time I arrived in Paris, I was in a bad condition and hardly conscious. I was suffering from every symptom of DKA, and with little left as far as hope for survival. The daylight was almost blinding; I didn't want to open my eyes. When I did, all I could see were black and white spots floating in front of me. I was having a hard time breathing. I was still curled up in my seat, and although I knew it was the Paris stop, I didn't sit up until the bus driver finally came through and made his final announcement that we were in Paris. It took a lot of effort to get off the bus and get into the bus station. I knew that the bus station was on the very edge of the city and it was a long subway ride to the city center where the Louvre is located, which is where I was to meet my family. When I walked into the bus station, I noticed an empty bench nearby, walked over to it, propped my suitcase up against it, set my backpack on the floor beside it, and laid right down on it. If the bus wasn't going to be my death bed, surely this would be. Sad to say, I didn't really care by this point. It was only a matter of time now, probably less than half an hour, before all this suffering would end. Before I would end.

This is the story of how I survived.

They say that right before you die, your life flashes before your eyes. I experienced not flashbacks of the life I've lived, but rather flash forwards, of what it might be like if I didn't make it off that bench. My mother, crying at my funeral. My brother, becoming an only child. Mike, with the unforgiving guilt weighing on his heart for years to come when he thought of me dying alone. What about all those things I had yet to do in life? Finish school. Write a book. Fall in love. As these images started to fade into a haze, they seemed to matter less and less. I stopped struggling to regulate my breathing. I accepted that this was the end. I was ready to let go.

Then, instead of that white light that people say they see, my savior arrived. I must have clearly looked like death in human form, because a figure suddenly appeared next to me. A male voice asked me, "Miss, do you need a doctor?" I never saw his face. I don't know if he was skinny or fat, what color his eyes were, if he had any facial hair, ugly or handsome, short or stout, had a handle and a spout. My eyes were closed and I was struggling to breathe. I just nodded and managed to mumble "just don't make me move." No sooner had he left my side, than a woman appeared at my side, asking me the exact same question. I gave her the same mumble jumble, and off she went as well. I have no idea how much time passed; it could have been five minutes, it could have been twenty. Before I knew it, French paramedics were lifting me off the bench and onto one of those cots they use to carry injured soccer players off the field. Except this one had wheels, so really it felt like a stroller for grown-ups. I can only imagine how this must have looked to everyone else in the bus station. Had I just come from Amsterdam and OD'd on marijuana? Was I some boozehound who just spent a bus ride drinking a whole bottle of rum? Did I get in some fight out in the parking lot over which café in Paris had the best crepes? Who knows. All I knew was that I was being whisked away to safety, and that I owed my life to one good citizen whom I would never see again. To this day, I still think about him once in a while and quietly thank him for saving my life.

I don't remember the ride to the hospital. I don't know if the sirens were on, and I don't remember exiting the ambulance and entering the hospital; that whole transfer is a bit hazy. All I remember are the paramedics saying my name and telling me to look at them. "Don't close your eyes Krystin, stay awake Krystin." Easy for them to say. They had no idea how hard it was for me to keep my eyes open. Before I knew it, though, two IVs had been inserted in each of my arms; one with insulin and another with potassium fluids. And when did that Foley catheter get put in? Wow, they were good. I wasn't allowed anything to drink, and wouldn't be for at least a day, even though I was thirsty beyond parched, and my mouth was drier than the Sahara Desert. All I was given were damn ice chips. They did bring me a wet sponge once in a while so that I could wet my lips, which were cracked and bloody. Forget my lips, I just sucked all the water out of it in an attempt to quench my unbearable thirst. I admit that I was quite wrong in thinking that France was still all medieval in technology when it came to hospital care. I was imagining a doctor walking in with a stethoscope around his neck and saying "I'm not sure what this is for, they just arrived in the recent shipment from Madagascar, but I can sure tell you where it doesn't go." I know this is ignorant thinking on my part. Of course France is a first world country, and has the best health care in the world, to my pleasant surprise and great relief. I was overly impressed with how attentive and knowledgeable all the doctors and nurses were.

My parents showed up a little after 8 PM that night. While I was still at the bus station and that nice lady who called the ambulance was waiting for the paramedics to arrive, she was trying to get as much information out of me as possible. Such as, who am I and what the hell is wrong with me. I did have, in my backpack, a notebook with a single street address on one of the pages: the address of the small flat my parents had rented for the week and a half they were in Paris. No telephone number, of course, and they never did ask me for either of my parents e-mail addresses, which in hindsight, would have been the easiest way to contact them. In fact, soon after I didn't show up at the Louvre (our meeting place), my parents had assumed that, like in the U.S., buses can't always be relied on, and I must have been delayed. My mom did e-mail Mike, however, and ask him if he'd heard from me and if I'd gotten out of Warsaw OK. (I found out later that he replied quickly, and as far as he knew I did make it out of Warsaw, but he had not heard from me either). No worries, though, I'd show up. Or not.

As it turns out, one of the hospital staff members had a friend who lived near the flat my family was staying in. He called his friend, explained what had happened, and had his friend write it all in a note. This friend then went to the flat and left the note taped on the door, notifying Monsieur and Madame Engstrand that their daughter was in the hospital, including, naturally, the address of the hospital. All in French. Of course. When my family returned that evening and found the note taped to the door, they were deeply worried about what it could be saying. My mother took French in high school, but that was millennia ago. She proceeded to hastily walk up and down the street, asking anyone she passed, "Parlez-vous Anglais?" She finally found two men, who were walking their dog, who did indeed speak English. They translated for her: Mademoiselle Engstrand was in the hospital. They also helped her with the address and directed her in the general direction of the hospital. A 45-minute taxi ride later, voila, they appear, after having utterly confused their taxi driver by handing him a note that essentially said 'your daughter is in so-and-so hospital.' It took them a few minutes, many hand gestures, and lots of reassuring that it wasn't his daughter who was in the hospital, but theirs. I had no idea, of course, whether or not my parents had even gotten the note. That didn't stop me, however, from asking my nurse every ten minutes when my parents were going to show up. Ten minutes felt like hours, and the hours until their arrival felt like a day.

My mother was not initially planning on coming to see me. She knew right away what this was all about, and was slightly more than pissed at me about it. She figured I was a big girl, I could figure this out on my own and find my way back to Edinburgh when I was released. My father, the more cool-headed at the moment, kept my mother calm and convinced her that they should still go and figure out what's going on and what they should do. They had already been in Paris for a few days, and we still had another whole week there before returning to Scotland. Even though at this point none of us knew how long I was going to be held up in the hospital, lucky for me I had already been to Paris with Mike a month earlier. It sure would have been a bummer to tell people I'd been to Paris once but spent the whole time staring at the white walls of a hospital room the entire time.

When they arrived at the hospital, my mother was still peeved at me, and was planning on telling me so. However, as she has told me this in more recent years, that when she walked into my ER bay and saw me hooked up to all those machines and still in critical condition, she broke down and started crying. She knew right then that she could never leave her little girl. As soon as I saw them walk in, a flood of relief washed over me. Something inside me was telling me 'it's OK now, they're here. Everything will be alright.' It was as if all my thoughts and worries dispersed into the air like a bunch of balloons being released into the sky. If I was going to die, it was alright now, because at least I had seen my parents one last time. My mother came over and hugged me and kissed me as she whispered "I love you." The only thing I could manage to mumble to her was, "don't tell anyone about this yet." Yeah, right, like that was going to happen. Pretty sure by the next day my entire family, including that weird 3rd cousin twice removed from California, knew.

My family moved out of their flat in the city and into one closer to the hospital, which, like the bus station I arrived at, was on the outskirts of the city. They visited me every day as I regained my health and strength. I remained in the hospital for six days. I would've stayed longer for the sole purpose of enjoying the delectable meals that I was provided. In the States, a hospital meal consists of reheated, sometimes unidentifiable protein and vegetable selections. In Paris: Foie gras with mustard seeds and green onions in duck jus, accompanied with a bisque soup, for example. Perhaps I exaggerate on the exceptionality of the menu, but that's the way I like to remember it.

Not speaking a lick of French made it hard to order my food for the next day, which I had to do on a daily basis. The young man who came in every day to go over my food choices and take my meal order for the next day spoke English well enough; a couple years prior, he had spent six months traveling around the western part of the United

States. He thought it would be fun, however, to make someone who knows absolutely no French, use those nonexistent French skills to order their menu. They probably don't get many foreign patients, so I'm sure he takes advantage of playing this "game" of his whenever he gets the opportunity. Can you guess what it was I ordered when my mother and I scanned the menu and ordered 'petit moo-moo?' That's right: veal. Instead of using proper French, we compromised by using animal sounds and our fingers to make cow ears on our heads. It's the best we could do. Nonetheless, he had a great sense of humor and was fun to talk to. His daily visits gave me something to look forward to, and were the best part of my otherwise boring days, which I spent either watching French MTV, or napping.

The day before I was to be discharged, the nurses told me I should get out of bed and walk around, since lying in bed for the past five days was not good for my leg muscles. I was allowed to leave my floor, so my mother and I took the elevator to the ground floor and walked around the outskirts of the courtyard in the center of the hospital grounds. I must admit, it was nothing like our modern, ugly hospitals that look like they were designed by prison architects. This hospital could have easily been someone's summer palace back in the 1600s. Peaked roofs, long hallways with tall ceilings and floor-to-ceiling windows with artfully carved Neoclassical window sills. It was one of the most beautiful buildings I'd been in in Europe, probably hundreds of years old, and here were patients left and right walking around with the backs of their hospital gowns hanging open. Kind of disrupts the beauty of it all.

I was discharged the next Monday. We returned to Edinburgh, where we finished out our time there, returning home to the States in early May. After having been on the brink of death, literally, for the second time, I made a vow that I would never let that happen again. It has not been easy, and although I have not returned to the hospital with DKA, there have been other instances, such as a bad kidney infection, and finding out in August 2012 that I'll need a kidney transplant due to diabetic kidney failure. Not to mention the cataract surgery and numerous laser treatments on the nerves in my eyes, to prevent further damage and future blindness. These have been reminders that I can't afford to play Russian Roulette with my insulin anymore. As one of my uncles puts it, I'm still teetering on the tightrope, and not doing much to keep from falling. Like a recovering alcoholic or drug addict, diabetes is an everyday struggle to maintain the balance. Sometimes it's easier, and sometimes it's harder to juggle, and after the damage I've already done to my body, one little slip could mean falling, with no net below to catch me. Alcoholics use alcohol, drug addicts use drugs, and I use insulin (or lack thereof) as my weapon of choice. No matter what the weapon, they all have the same ultimate result: self-destruction.

I don't fear death; I fear the things that I'm going to miss if I die too young. I still have many aspirations and dreams. I can't achieve anything from the grave. I will not let the thought 'I can't do the right thing for the rest of my life, the hill is too steep' keep me from living my life. Even though I'm still climbing that hill on a daily basis, I'm taking it one day at a time instead of looking at the rest of my life. I do the best I can, but I don't expect perfection, because there's no such thing as a perfect diabetic. Sure, the finger pricks and the insulin injections may be painful, but the pain is temporary. Losing my eyesight, a kidney, or a foot is even more painful, and lasts forever. I will proceed to build on small victories, because as that same uncle said to me once, "the war is won in victories in small battles on a daily basis." It hasn't been easy, but with a little help and optimism, I CAN win the war, one small battle victory at a time.

[End of essay, back to the diary entry for April 19, 2006]

That same day we got home, Elliott and I went to Princes Street to a music store and I bought 3 CDs and some headphones, and on the way walking back to the flat I tripped and fell and sprained my middle finger on my left hand! It hurt so bad, and overnight it swelled up to 3 times its size. And here it is a week later and it's still swollen and very sore. I hope there isn't more wrong with it. Hopefully it's just taking a long time to heal, like my dad said it might.

Copenhagen – Wonderful. Probably one of our best family trips. Hardly any arguing or fighting. The city reminds me a lot of Amsterdam, with canals and row houses and bikes and such. One evening we went into Tivoli, the huge amusement park-type place, and ate dinner there then Elliott and I rode rides for a couple hours. And got cotton candy twice! Hehe. Earlier that day we had gone into the Glyptotek Museum and seen cool mummy stuff, and some art, and walked down the main pedestrian shopping street, although nothing was open. The next day we walked to the other side of town and saw the Little Mermaid statue, then walked back to the hotel, eating dinner at a restaurant along one of the canals. On Saturday, more walking, first to a flea market that turned out to be a bunch of crap, then to a church which I didn't climb to the top of, and to Christiania, the hippy community of Copenhagen. A very interesting place. Lots of cool art and graffiti on the buildings, dogs walking around everywhere, and a little open market where all the places mostly just sell pipes, bowls, pleces [?], lighters, and other paraphernalia. Cool, but I wouldn't wanna live there, it's a little sketchy. Had dinner that night at Pasta Basta, where my food was very late and it was like 100° in there and I started dripping sweat and had to go outside. Sunday my parents and I took a day trip to Malmo, Sweden. Because it was Easter nothing was open, so we spent a couple hours walking around (it's not very big), had a beer at a bar in a popular courtyard, and then took the train back to Copenhagen, only about a 35 min. ride. Went to a Chinese buffet for dinner, went back to the hotel and watched 'Madagascar,' then went to bed! And Monday morning we flew home here to Edinburgh, and have been here since. It was a good trip, but maybe a little stressful considering what had all just been through. But I got a Danish and Swedish flag, and a Copenhagen sweatshirt, and a couple other souvenir things. Now it's time to get some work done for Roland.

April 25, 2006 Diary

Yesterday we walked up Arthur's Seat, AKA Dumbo [our nickname for it], and today my knees and ankles are killing me. On Sunday we drove to St. Andrews, the birthplace of golf! That was pretty cool. Then we drove back along the coast.

Today was shopping day! We walked up to Princes Street and quick walked through the National Gallery of Scotland, which have been to before with Mike. But then we walked to the Royal Mile, stopped in St. Giles church, had lunch at a pub, then went shopping! By the time we got back here to the flat, my ankles hurt so bad and my knees. My parents have already agreed to buy me a new pair of tennis shoes, thank god, but I may have to wait until Vienna, which isn't until Thursday, and I can't even guarantee we'll go shoe shopping the day we get there! Hopefully tomorrow I can find some decent shoes, when we go on our 2nd road trip to Stirling and Loch Lomond. We shall see.

My mom and I talked and it sounds like I may have to give up working at Bigsby's this summer, depending on what my eating disorder assessment comes out to. I have no idea what kind of commitment I'm going to have to make, and I know Kris will have to do what is best for Bigsby's, which mean hiring someone else. But I hope this is not the case. I will see what Kris says.

April 30, 2006 Diary

Luckily I got new shoes in Stirling before we came here, so my feet feel much better. Although my legs get sore in the mornings and wake me up all early and make it hard to sleep. And my finger still isn't healing any. I think I did more than just jam it, I think it's sprained, maybe even broken. But now I won't find out until after we get home to Mpls. They may have to re-break it and tie it up so that it heals properly. How fun.

May 3, 2006 Diary

So here I am at the end of my journal, a 3½ year adventure, and I don't quite know how to end it. Do I end it with just another normal entry, or with a reflection on the last few years, and how I've changed, etc., etc.? I have another journal after this, so I have chosen neither. A normal entry would make it seem like I'm leaving you hanging, with that "what next?' feeling, but a summary and conclusion would make it seem like my life ended there, and I don't want to do that either. I have definitely noticed a change in myself, and in my writing, but being that I experienced it all and that I will probably be the only one to ever read this, I am not going to go into all that. This journal has seen the good times and the bad, the love and the hate, the loneliness, sadness, confusion, and happiness. I will end it at that, for I know I have a whole new journal ahead of me, waiting for experiences to come. With that I cheer you adieu. Cheers.

Krystin Engstrand
May 8, 2006 Diary

So begins the next chunk of the journey that is my life; and what a perfect time to start a new journal. I have been living in Edinburgh, Scotland the last 4½ months with my family, and on Thursday we fly home to Minnesota. A lot of what I write in here will be related to events that I have written about in my other journal, so this is merely an extension, a continuation. But I am not going to dwell on an introduction or anything, so, moving on with life. . .

This past weekend we took a driving trip to NW Scotland, Inverness and the Isle of Skye. Inverness is on Loch Ness, so I was keeping an eye out for Nessie, but did not find her. Bummer. The Isle of Skye was beautiful. Saw some Highland cows, aka heelan coos, and many, many sheep. And some more countryside and mountains. It was a good trip.

I have decided that this summer I would like to go to an inpatient treatment house for a couple of months. That is, if my health insurance covers it. I found out that Maria went to one in Arizona for 42 days in Feb-Mar. I hope it helped her, because she was looking unhealthily thin too. So I'm going to skinny camp to be fattened up.

The Rope ED
[Eating Disorder; this (final) entry in her life narrative "The Rope" summarizes the summer and fall of 2006]

Soon after returning to the States, I had frequent appointments with my endocrinologist, to make sure that I was staying on top of things with my diabetes. New to the medical field at this time was something called diabulimia, an eating disorder named for diabetics who abuse their insulin to keep their weight down. Instead of purging or restricting food intake, diabetics inject less insulin than is required, so that the body does not fully absorb everything that is being consumed. That way, most of the nutrients exit the body, keeping the person thin.

My doctor must have just been introduced to that idea, because she began asking me if I was not doing my insulin so that I could stay thin. I told her no over and over, but she didn't believe me, and quickly became convinced that I was, and had been, suffering from diabulimia since high school. She even convinced my parents that that was my problem. At one of my appointments, I made the mistake of being honest. I told her that I liked being thin and it made me like my appearance better, but I wasn't doing it on purpose. It was more like a side effect that was welcomed but not intentional. Being thin just happened to come with the habit (of not doing my insulin). I wasn't doing my insulin because I hate needles, and I hate the hassle of doing it. End of story.

My doctor still recommended that I try an inpatient program for people with eating disorders, so that I could start getting help from professionals, while also having meals and my diabetes needs monitored, in an attempt to get my diabetes under better control while I gain back much-needed weight at the same time. They referred me to Methodist Hospital in St. Louis Park, MN. They had a whole floor just for people suffering from eating disorders. We had gotten home from Scotland in May, and by the end of the month I was already admitted to Methodist; for the first time.

The summer of 2006 was a rough one for me. Over a 3-4 month period, I was in and out of Methodist 5 times. My average stay was only a week. The problem with the program is that it is not long-term. It is short-term, mainly to get patients stabilized, eating three meals and three snacks a day. I say "patients" because there were both men and women there, anywhere from age 10 to 50. The rooms were like normal hospital rooms, but without all the monitors and tubes everywhere. We slept in hospital beds, but most patients brought a blanket or pillow from home to make it more personal. Most of the rooms were doubles, but there were a few single rooms, in case there were an odd number of males, or if someone was sick. A male and female were never put together as roommates, for obvious reasons.

The days were spent in groups, from group therapy to stretching to music therapy to individual therapy to body image group to educational groups. All very helpful – if you have an eating disorder. I would sit through the groups and listen, and participate, but I was never on the same emotional level as the other patients. I didn't understand them, and as a diabetic, they didn't understand me. I just couldn't relate to them. At meals, I didn't understand why a girl wouldn't eat her sandwich, and instead just sit there and stare at her plate. I was hungry all the time and was usually the first one to finish my meal. Many times I wanted to look at the other patients and say "if you're not going to finish that, can I have it?"

My stays were so short because as soon as they got my blood sugar levels under control, and I was eating all my meals and snacks, there was no reason to keep me anymore. My shortest stay was only three days. Some patients can be there three or four weeks before being discharged. The other problem with the program is that after getting patients stabilized and eating, they discharge them and send them right back into the environment they were in before. Every time I was admitted back, I would see girls I had seen there before. During one of my stays there was a young girl there, probably around age 9 or 10. One evening, during visiting hours, I was sitting in a room with my parents, and she was sitting with her parents not far away. We overheard her say to her parents, "I like it here. It's like being at camp." Oh dear.

After being discharged, I would return home, and take good care of my diabetes. For a short period of time. The motivation and determination from my previous stay at Methodist would wear off, and I'd fall right back into my old habits. After three unsuccessful stays at Methodist, my doctor announced that I needed something more long-term. A residential program. My parents and I had already decided at this point that I would not return to school that fall. I would take the semester off so that I could focus on taking care of my health. Especially if I was going to be in a residential program, that would overlap with when school started.

My doctor recommended the Ana Westin House, located in Chaska, MN., about 45 minutes from Minneapolis. A girls-only program, in a nice suburban house in a nice suburban cul-de-sac. There are only 8 girls there at a time, so it's more personal and homey. There are always nurses there, but they wear their street clothes and not scrubs. Everything is still supervised, everyone eats meals and snacks together, and the groups that the girls attend are almost exactly the same as the ones at Methodist Hospital. Breakfast at 7:30, group therapy, morning snack, art therapy, acupuncture, lunch, process group, individual therapy, afternoon snack, menu planning, nutrition group, dinner, optional yoga or family and friends time. Each day of the week is slightly different to allow for all the different groups to attend.

The Ana Westin House is a 4-month program. Some girls "graduate" earlier, but most are there for the full 4 months. I moved into the house in August, but only made it about 2 months, due to other circumstances. At one point during my stay I had to return to Methodist Hospital for a very short period of time, due to not being able to eat. Over the previous couple months, I had begun to lose all appetite completely. I was never hungry, and even felt sick sitting down to meals, which I was unable to finish. I was sent back to Methodist in the hopes that they might be able to help there, in a way that the staff at the Ana Westin House couldn't, but I was only in the hospital for a few days before returning to the house.

My not being able to eat continued. I felt so full all the time, and I believed that it was because I was also constipated and hadn't used the bathroom to poop in over a week. One night at the dinner table, when one of the staff members was encouraging me to eat, I got so irritated and upset that tears formed in my eyes, and I stated "nothing more can go in until something comes out." The girls probably thought

I meant throwing up, but I knew I needed something to come out the other end. Some of the girls put down their forks and gave a disgusted face, but I didn't care. I meant what I said.

After another few weeks or a month of not making progress at the Ana Westin House, the doctors and staff there decided that I needed to return, once again, to Methodist Hospital, this time for a bit longer. Even there, I was throwing up after meals and feeling nauseous all the time. I was feeling hopeless, not understanding what was going on with me and why they couldn't find and fix the problem. It's a hospital for Christ's sake, why couldn't they make me better? Since I wasn't able to eat most of my meals, each meal and was accompanied by half a glass of Boost, and each snack was accompanied by TwoCal, another high-calorie, high-nutrients supplement.

By then is was October, and nearing my birthday. I had been at Methodist for almost two weeks, and had been moved from the eating disorder floor down to one of the regular medical floors. A feeding tube was placed in my nose that ran down into my stomach, so they could give me a 24-hour slow delivery of nutritional fluids. I was officially discharged from the Ana Westin House, so that they could make room for another girl. They aren't making money from an empty bed. All my stuff had been boxed up, and one evening my dad drove out to pick it up. So I never completed that program, but that didn't matter to me, since I found the whole thing pointless anyway.

On my birthday, I was allowed a one-day pass to leave the hospital. My parents had planned a birthday party for me at our home, with friends and family and family friends. There was food and cake, but I wasn't supposed to eat any, but that didn't matter because I wasn't hungry for any of it. I enjoyed spending those few hours with friends and family, even if I had a tube hanging out of my nose. A few of my close friends were there, and even my boss from the café I had been working at both over that summer (in-between all my Methodist Hospital stays), and the previous summer before. I didn't quit working at the café, and I wasn't let go or fired, but when it was decided that I was going to go to the Ana Westin House, my boss and I had a mutual understanding that I was done working there.

After being discharged from Methodist in early November, and having failed at the Ana Westin House program, my endocrinologist told my parents that something better needed to be done. She said a residential, long-term, more structured and dedicated program would work best for me. I'm not sure why, since Ana Westin was a residential long-term program, but apparently that wasn't good enough. I started looking online and doing research of other programs, almost all of which were out of state. They all had pros and cons, but I ended up choosing Remuda Ranch, located in Wickenburg, Arizona, 65 miles northwest of Phoenix.

I began the application process, having my endocrinologist submit the application and referral to the program, and to my insurance company (which ended up paying the entire bill; not one penny out of my pocket). I was given high priority status because of my poor health due to my diabetes. The Tuesday after Thanksgiving, a representative from Remuda called me to tell me that my application had been accepted and my health insurance had been approved for coverage. "So we'll see you on Thursday," she said out of nowhere. As in, two days from then. They wanted me in two days! Waste no time, I suppose. There was an opening available, and like with the Ana Westin House, they aren't making money on an empty bed. My mom wanted to accompany me out there, so she booked two tickets to Phoenix for Thursday, December 30, 2006.

We were picked up at the airport by a woman who was to drive us to Wickenburg. It was about an hour-long ride, and at one point my mom had to tell our rather chatty driver that she would prefer to spend the last half hour talking to and focusing on me, which was the whole reason she came with me in the first place. Upon arrival in Wickenburg, we weren't brought right to the ranch, but to the office located in town, where I was checked in. Then my mom and I were brought to the ranch, where she had to say goodbye before being driven back to Phoenix. She was not allowed to enter the lodge, for privacy purposes of the other girls. It was an emotional goodbye, but we both believed I needed to be there to get healthy again.

The ranch is in a desert setting, on an actual ranch, hence the name. I had never been on a real live ranch before, so amongst my nervousness was also excitement to know I'd be living amongst sandy hills, mountains, and cacti for the next two months. It was the winter months, so there were no risks of snakes, or waking up to scorpions in my shoes or bed. I chose Remuda for one specific reason: horses. Included in the treatment program is equine therapy, where patients are assigned a horse for their entire stay. She takes care of the horse, brushes and cleans the horse, and, of course, rides it; not only in the small corral located near the stables, but also on group trail walks.

Remuda is a 5-building campus with a main lodge. The main lodge is separated to have two sides, each with a dining area and a living room. Instead of having all 46 girls in one big group, it's split into three. Each group is named after a type of horse. The side I was on was called 'Paint,' and the group on the other side of the lodge was called 'Appaloosa.' The third group, 'Palomino,' had their own separate building away from the main lodge and houses. Each group also had their own set of therapists, and went to support groups with their own group members. We ate with our group, relaxed with our group, and got to be a family. I did not get to live with a roommate in one of the houses. Since I have diabetes, I had to live in the 4-bed room that's located in the main lodge, so that if I have any diabetes-related problems during the night, nursing staff is right there to help out. One other woman in my room was also diabetic, although she was in the Appaloosa group. The two others had to do feeding tubes at night, which is why they had to room in the main lounge. One was in my group, the other was also in 'Paint.'

The program on the ranch is only two months long. The second half, if the patient wishes to continue, is called the Life Program. Located in a cul-de-sac in Chandler, a suburb of Phoenix, it consists of six houses, two of which are designated for girls under the age of 18.

July 31, 2006 Diary

I have a lot of writing to do. It may take me a few entries. I'll start with coming home. We did. Got my kitties that same night, it was very nice. That was a Thursday. I started back at work that next Monday. It was so nice to be back at work. The next day, Tuesday, I had an assessment at Methodist Hospital in St. Louis Park. They admitted me to inpatient—that day! So I went home to pack up stuff and called Kris to tell her I wouldn't be able to work for awhile. I was at Methodist at 4pm that day, and was there for a little over a week. There was a lot to get used to there. To start off with, we get up anywhere between 5:45 – 6:30 am to take vitals and weights and shower. Breakfast at 7:30. No going back to your room until 9:30pm to get ready for bed. Groups throughout the day, and any time in between is spent in dayroom. I will put the schedule on the next page. The weekends are really boring—everything is in the morning and the rest of the day is visiting hours. Then there are all the rules to get used to. No standing, always sit. Observed bathroom for at least the first 48-72 hours, until they can trust you aren't going to throw up or do jumping jacks when they aren't looking. No problem for me. Dinner must be finished in 30 min., snacks in 15 min., or you get a liquid replacement (Boost). Hands above the table at all time. No talking about food or E.D. at any time. Bedtime at 10:30 pm. I hated it. Especially the first couple days. But it got easier, and gained some weight back.

When I left, I still couldn't work for a while, because I then started the partial day program, from 11am - 7pm Mon-Fri. After a little bit though, I decided to work the morning shift to give Chambray a break. So I worked from 6-10 then took the bus to Methodist, and home afterwards, so I wouldn't get home until around 8:15 pm. It began to be too much, so after a week and a half I stopped working. Partial is a 4-6 week program, but I only made about 3½ weeks in. I started feeling sick, missed a week of partial, had terrible stomach aches all day every day, wasn't hungry, and I was losing weight again. One night I decided to go to urgent care, and they put me in the hospital for 3 day with mild ketoacidosis.

I got out of the hospital on a Wednesday and went back to Methodist that next Monday. At least that time I knew the routine. I was there for a week, got out just in time for the 4th of July, which was on a Tuesday. I went back to work that Wednesday, working 11am – 4pm, because Tammy had started working the morning shift. Between then and about a week and a half ago, I had been working on and off. I was still having stomach aches all day and my vitals were high. I felt horrible. I had no appetite ever, was hardly eating anything all day long. My weight kept dropping.

Then a couple weeks ago I went and bought "fat bars" (460 cal./bar) at GNC and ate one, and my stomach ache went away! Funny how a little food can do that. It hurt so bad because it was starving, but I couldn't eat because it hurt so bad. But I have been able to eat more lately and my stomach aches are pretty much gone.

But I am still not gaining weight back. I am currently sitting around 100, and I hate it. I WANT to gain weight back. I hate having no energy or stamina, being tired all the time, not enjoying the things I like, being antisocial, not enjoying eating, always being lightheaded. . . it all sucks. Now my family and doctors want me to go back to Methodist for a while, and figure out what to do from there.

Because I'm not going back to Morris. Nobody supports me going back. My whole family. My mom is mostly convinced that I am going to crash and burn again. Or that I will sleep through half the semester and will do bad in my classes and it will have been a waste of money.

And the sad thing is that I can't even convince myself that I will do well in Morris. I want more than anything to go back and prove everyone wrong, but I can't even prove it to myself. My parents think I should go to the Anna Westin residential house in Chaska for a few months, but I know for sure I don't want to do that. No way.

August 6, 2006 Diary

I have not cried in many nights, but I did a couple times about a week ago. I cried over my future, and where it's going and what I'm going to do. It's definite that I'm not going back to Morris. I told Mike that they should look for another roomie. I can't do it, I can't go . . . as much as I would absolutely love to. But I would cry about it, and the fact that there are more negative aspects than positive in my life right now. And it's put me in a funk that even customers at work have noticed. I'm not going back to school, I'm not making enough money, I haven't seen hardly any friends all summer, everyone wants me to back to Methodist, my parents want me to go to the Anna Westin house, I'm always tired and don't have any energy, I can't keep my weight up, I have body aches all over. . . . I could go on. I'm afraid that this has made me depressed. I feel I've become unreliable to everyone and am the kind of person no one wants to be around.

I still have to take the step of withdrawing from my fall classes and e-mailing Roland and Marynel, and that is my hardest step. After admitting to myself that it's best I stay home this fall. But do I stay home all year or just the semester? Dad thinks I should change my enrollment to the TC campus. Perhaps. But I want Morris. I want to see my school friends again, take those classes, go to parties, be social, have fun, graduate, live happily ever after. So why can't I just do what I need to do with my diabetes and be able to have what I want? Why can't I even convince myself that I can do it? I told my dad that maybe I'm one of those people that won't ever be able to take care of themselves and will need to live in an assisted living place my whole life. He e-mailed me later and said he hopes I do not feel that is true; I think I scared him because he himself is afraid it might be true. I don't want it to be, but . . .

And I would cry because I hurt inside and the world could care less and I don't want to live anymore. Not this life.

May 19, 2006 Diary
[the entries for 5/19 through 5/22 were written at the Methodist Hospital eating disorder program]
Do I belong here?

I have been asking myself that the past few days. My case, although an eating disorder, is a little different than the other girls. I don't vomit, binge, restrict, over-exercise, etc. I don't connect with the other girls as well and they don't connect with me. I wish there was a program strictly for diabetics.

Locked bathrooms and showers with the door open. I don't need that.

3 meals and 3 snacks a day, but the amount of food does not fill me up. Today I got my bracelet saying I don't need observed bathroom or showers. It's pretty boring around here. Lots of word find puzzles. Always need to sit down, no standing.

Girls at the table cry over their food. It's too much, they don't want to eat it, can't finish it. I don't have enough food. Observed insulin shots. So all that is getting done. Up at 5:45 am is shit. No naps.

Visiting hours are not long enough. I wish my parents could stay longer. I want to go home and be normal. But I never will be.

I'm hungry. All the time.

Haven't had a B.M. since I got here 3 days ago. Maybe I will now that they don't have to observe my bathroom usage. I feel bloated because of it.

Cody misses his cookies and I miss him. I want my kitties and to see Chris.

My lantus is only 28 units, 2 units of Humalog per carb choice, and no correcting high numbers. A mistake.

Sick of seeing girls cry and complain. Going to do the partial program when I get out.

Following rules so I can leave!

May 20, 2006 Diary
I miss Chris. I need her.

Starting to gain weight and it scares me a little. My stomach is bloated-looking and my pants are fitting tighter; had to ask mom to bring me more t-shirts and pants/sweats when come to visit tomorrow. I want to be happy with my meal plan and follow it and not slip again, but I hate the feeling of a healthy stomach cause I look pregnant and have to suck it in.

Will keep an exercise routine and do it with my mom so we can motivate each other. I hope I can stick to it when I go back to school in August.

Finally had a B.M. today!

I miss my chex and cheez-its. And pop tarts and skittles. Everything I can't have here.

I don't seem to be making friends with other girls as fast and easily as they all do with other. No surprise there. I don't think Sarah likes me that much.

Am I surprised that no one has come to visit me except my parents? Not really. But I did get 3 cards in the mail the other day. From Deb, Coby, and grandma and grandpa. That was nice. Called Chris last night but she didn't answer. Will try again later.

Today was fine but boring. Started therapy for my finger, they woke me up from a nap to go to it.

I want to go back to work. I hate that I only had one day back and then had to leave to come here. I need the money. I want the money. I hope my parents keep their promise to pay me what I'm losing by coming here and not working. That was part of the bargain.

Mom e-mailed Mike to tell him I am here. I asked her to. Dad e-mailed Roland and Marynel to get my summer assignments.

Been thinking about my plan for when I leave and how I am going to try 100% to follow it and do good. But I will need help.

I can take responsibility of my diabetes. I can do it. I am worth it. Cried for first time here today. People love me and want to see me be healthy. I need to remember this always and keep telling myself that.

Suzanne said in group yesterday that things would be easier for her family if she just slipped off the earth, aka died. And that scared me, because I remember having thoughts like that. It's hard to convince myself that this is not true and that I'm worth it. Positive thoughts.

I want a DQ heath blizzard. But I need to make it a special treat once in a while.

I hope to go shopping with mom at the end of the summer for clothes that will fit the healthier me who will be at a weight I can be happy with. Kohls and H&M, here I come!

Monday I do meal group at lunch.

Overall a good day. Happy, optimistic road.

May 21, 2006 Diary

Pretty good day today. Parents visited, but not until 3:30, which was snack time, so I had less than an hour with them. Saddened & disappointed me a little bit. They are my only visitors, so I wish they would stay longer, but I know they get bored and have other things to do.

May 22, 2006 Diary

Great news! I had my family therapy session today and found out I get to go home on Thurs! Tomorrow I'll have cafeteria experience at dinner, so Mom and Elliott will come eat with me. Then on Wednesday I get a 5-hour pass, from 5-10 pm. Either Chris or Jeff (uncle) will come get me, and Chris will come over for dinner. Then I will get to drive the car back here so that when they discharge me on Thursday, which should be around 11am, I can drive home. I am so excited. Not just to leave but also to work on my plan, which I am very optimistic about it working.

Had meal group today, so those of us in adult group got to go down to the cafeteria with one of the dietitians and the O.T. lady, and we all eat down there together. I had a salad and cheeseburger and Special K bar for dessert. Delicious.

Yesterday I did 'select-a-tray,' so I went down to the cafeteria with my nurse, picked out my lunch, and brought it back up to eat with everyone.

Next Tuesday I'll start the partial program. 11am – 7pm. And I have to take the bus. Thanks Mom. But the program will be good for me because I'll continue to get help while still living at home.

Tomorrow I start modified stretching. I don't want. Too lazy.

Apparently I'm not doing meal planning right cause they keep taking food away from my meals so I get less than I am expecting.

When I leave here on Thursday I am driving through Arby's for lunch. Market Fresh sandwich. With side of insulin.

Pretty good mood today overall.

More finger therapy.

p.s. Found $14 in one of my jeans pockets 😊

[As Krystin explains shortly, after a summer and fall of programs, she and we and her physician agreed she should go to Remuda Ranch in Arizona in late 2006.]

December 3, 2006 Letter
Krystin to Christine:
Dear Chris,

    I fear that I am ruining my parents' marriage. I fear that too many factors are going to come together to make my mom leave my dad. And I fear that she has already made up her mind. If only I had been a different daughter, if I had done things differently, my mom wouldn't be so unhappy. If only dad knew how to show emotion. I have been feeling a lot of guilt that it is all my fault. How is it not? My mom even said, all I have to do is say the word and she knows who she would pick. My heart would be broken if anything happened between my parents, because my dad loves her and needs her so much, even if he doesn't show it, but I don't think my mom needs him anymore. But she does need me, more than anything, and that makes me feel guilty too. I guess I have a lot of talking to do about this with the therapist here.

    Things here are going well. All the staff and the girls are so nice and so welcoming, and jump right into being friends. Even though this is treatment, I think I'm going to have a good time. I am currently sleeping in a room in the main lodge that has a couch that folds into a bed. It's pretty ghetto, but all the new girls have to do it. Thursday and Friday was busy meeting the doctors and staff, but the weekends are very low-key so we just hang out and relax and watch movies. And I nap since I get up at 5:30 am. Bleah. But I get to go to bed at 9 pm, so that nice. And we have to wear shoes all the time because of scorpions. They even get into the buildings, but I haven't seen any yet. That's good.

    I miss you lots. Help take of my mom K? She's a wreck.

    I will write more when I'm more into programming and have more to say. I hope to hear from you soon!

    Love you always, Krystin

December 14, 2006 Letter
Krystin to Christine:
Dear Chris,

    Thank you so much for your letter, it made me excited to see mail from you. I am glad that your show opening went well. I really wish I could've been there. Do you think you could send me some pictures from it? I would really like to see some!

I still don't know how I feel about the situation with my parents. My mom still wants to keep it a secret. Why? Why would she need to keep it so secret if nothing is going on? I understand if it's because she doesn't want to hurt my dad. But she has said herself, he's not a dumb guy, he must know something is going on. So wouldn't it hurt him more that she's not talking to him about it? I'd think so. I don't really see any good excuse. And even if it's not my fault, I only made it worse. If you can come up with one, let me know.

Things here are going pretty well. I'm still having some struggles with the meals but overall I'm having a good time. It still feels like camp. I have gotten sick and thrown up at dinner twice since being here (NOT intentionally), so that scares me. I really hope it is not starting all over again. My mind is too powerful and I need to learn to control it. I'm trying to learn some mediation techniques.

I started riding my horse this week. His name is Sunny. When my family comes for family week we put on a rodeo. So I'm teaching him to go around barrels and cones and stuff. It's fun. Good story.

I hope all is going well with you. Keep staying in touch. And good luck with finals! Love you lots.
Krystin

Tuesday July 10, 2007 Diary
[her first entry since August 2006; she used this July entry to introduce the following entries, which began in January 2007]

Wow it has been a long time since I wrote. Last time I wrote I was in and out of Methodist hospital and the Anna Westin house in Chaska. Eventually my parents and I decided I needed something more long term, so we looked into Remuda Ranch in Arizona, and I decided to go. I knew it would be the best option for me.

January 20, 2007 Diary
This be my Remuda Journal. Although I have been here 7 weeks already, I decided just now that this experience needs a journal all its own. And quite an experience it has been. I got here on November 30, 2006, and today there is no one here anymore that was here when I first got here. I finished my family week last week, and it was a disaster. My mom told me that after almost 25 years of marriage, she is leaving my dad. I tried to leave the Lazy Fox premises. I just wanted to go back to the Ranch. I didn't want to go through with my Truth in Love. But Darren challenged me to. He made me. So I did, as hard as

it was to keep my mind on the point at hand. I don't know where she will go. She and dad have decided that they will stay together in the house for a while. My dad is going to try to keep the house, but it will cost a lot. And he wants to remarry at some point, but not for a while because it will take him a long time to get over mom. He doesn't want to be single the rest of his life. Elliott is depressed. I am depressed. I'm sad, angry, uncertain, guilty, and more all at the same time. And I don't how to fix myself, how to let myself heal. I've been physically barfy sick for the last week and a half.

[Krystin's progress was reversed after we left, after the announcement about the end of the marriage. To jump ahead in the story, I can relate that by a few years later, Pat and I had a good relationship, and she with Kathy, and the two kids saw both Pat and me regularly and were happy with their relationship with their parents. Both the kids continued to live with me but saw their mother frequently. She only lives about six blocks away.]

They have now set requirements for my meals for me to be able to go out and smoke. As of today, I have to finish 90%. Starting Monday it will be 100%, yesterday was only 75%. This isn't fair at all. I shouldn't be punished in this way. I'm not trying to not finish my meals. I really am struggling. I don't like that they're threatening to not let me smoke as a motivation to finish. A cigarette is like one thing that I need so bad to calm down and I only get it if I eat ALL my food. It pisses me off. Really. And if I can't finish, I don't get supplement either. It has to be solid foods. And it frustrates me because it frustrates and triggers other girls. I think some of them even dislike me because of it. Jessica J. doesn't like me very much, or Maddie. But then there are girls who it doesn't bother and have shown support and said they are here if I need it. So that helps some, but me being a worrier, I care more about the girls who don't like me, and I get all self conscious around them. But people keep telling me to focus on myself, this is my recovery, not theirs. But still . . .

I've really been thinking about the whole Christianity part of being here. Everything is Christian-based and I have to go to chapel every day, but I just don't think I'm going to pick up the faith and religion. I've been open-minded about it all, but just don't think that after 22 years of skepticism I'm going to change. I mean, I don't want to sound like my dad saying that I need to see proof or a study, but I don't think it's physically possible for there to be a god or heaven. If god wanted people to be happy and prosperous, why is there so much war and poverty and chaos in this world? Surely even a god wouldn't feel that someone should be punished, who may be a perfectly nice person, be the victim of arson and having their house burn down. And if Christianity is against homosexuality, why aren't gays dropping dead left and right? I just don't understand it all. And I'm not going to pray to the dust bunnies under my bed. So there you go.

I leave Sunday and I have a lot of work to do by then if I want to do the LIFE program, which I do, but right now do not qualify. I want to go and see RJ! I miss her so much. Plus the structured meals and programs yet still a little freedom and outing time I will really like. So I will see how this week goes.

January 21, 2007 Diary

Starting off the day already pissed. The nurse Dianne told me I can't smoke after breakfast because I had an EQ1 and not an EQ2 at HS snack last night. This is bullshit. She's trying to tell me that each meal affects if I can go out after the NEXT meal. Oh no, that's not how it works. Each meal determines whether or not I go out after THAT meal. I am so incredibly mad at her right now. This isn't fair at all. At least I had a snack last night. So what's my motivation to complete 90% of my breakfast? To go out after lunch? No, lunch determines whether I go out after lunch. ARGH! I can't wait to get to LIFE where we can smoke any time. I'm an adult and they shouldn't be treating me this way. If I want to go have a smoke, I'm gonna go have a smoke. At least I'm fucking eating anything at all. *sigh* But, I'm not gonna beat a dead horse over this, so moving on.

It's really sad when I can look at girls here and know that when they leave they will just return to their eating disorder. Like Sheree when she left, who was doing sprints up to the main lodge every morning. And Amanda, who disliked it here so much she tried to leave. And my roommate Megan, who paces like crazy just so she can be moving. It's sad really. Then I think of myself. What about me? Surely I don't want to be one of those girls. What do other people think about my future when they look at me? Hmm. If only I didn't have diabetes, that would solve all my problems. I don't know how much I trust myself yet, and I leave a week from today. That's all for now.

January 22, 2007 Diary

Today is an OK day. I ate all my breakfast and went out for a smoke. I only had 2 cigs in my box, so I smoked them both figuring the night staff just forgot to refill mine. Then I find out I don't have any left for after lunch. I didn't finish lunch because I couldn't go out for a smoke anyway. Then after lunch Barbara Ann told me that I did have some left, that they were in Sam's bag. Dammit. I have 6 left, so I called my mom and asked her to overnight some more.

Had a meeting with Darren this afternoon. Because things are going better, I will get to go to LIFE next Monday when I am discharged from here, and will probably be there for 30 days, maybe longer if I need it. But I won't get to spend a few days with my mom first, which bums me out. I really wanted those few days of freedom.

I really blew it today with sneaking CDs in. Rachel M. sent us all a package, and in it was a box of Kleenex. Well I read the letter from her out loud, and it told Sarah to open the Kleenex box carefully from the left end. Shit. Gary was standing right there, so of course he knew that something was in the box. So he made Sarah open it, and sure enough, come Q-tips and 6 CDs, all of which were confiscated. And we won't get the CDs even if they are approved because they were smuggled in and that's against the rules. I feel horrible that I blew it. They might have had a chance of getting away with it. I'm such an idiot.

January 23, 2007 Diary

I talked to my mom last night. See, I don't like talking to her as much lately because all she does is cry now. All the time. I understand she's upset but it's getting annoying really. And she tells me things that she's told me before that she doesn't remember telling me. I think [she] is hoping that I will cry with her. And whenever I call I know we'll just talk about what is going on. Dad will tell me that everything will be OK and not to worry about him, and mom will tell me how [she] just can't live with him anymore and needs to leave. I know, I know. I'm ready to move on (finally) and talk about other things.

I got back on green status today! So I got to go riding at equine. Sunny was a good boy. Since this was my last time in the arena, I did a victory lap. And I cantered! It was pretty exciting. I got some pictures with him too. I'm really gonna miss him. We've bonded.

This morning at breakfast I didn't eat ½ a bagel, so Diane put the requirement back on that I need to finish 100% to go out to smoke. ARGH! This pisses me off so much. There are gonna be days when I can't finish, it's one meal. We all have those days, get over it! But tomorrow at staffing they will reassess and see if I still need it.

Got a letter and $10 today from grandpa Stephens. Since I leave next Monday, I'm keeping the money, not turning it in. And tomorrow I will write them back because it's been a while since I have.

January 24, 2007 Diary

I am out of cigarettes as of breakfast this morning and the ones my mom sent overnight yesterday did not come today. I am both sad and mad over this. Although it will be good to show Diane that I don't need cigarettes as a motivation to finish. In your face Diane. We almost lost all smoking privileges today. Some MHTs found smoked cigarettes down by the bunkhouse. They announced that if nobody turns them in by dinner, no more smoking. Turns out it was Jan and Jen W. Makes me angry that they would do that—plus that they were careless to leave the butts on the ground.

I just hope my cigarettes come tomorrow.

January 25, 2007 Diary

Today in home group I was kinda attacked. When we were in the main lodge and it was time to go to group, people were just then going to the bathroom, when they'd had 20 minutes to do so. I made comment, sarcastically, to Barbara Ann, that maybe we would be on time to group if people would learn to go to the bathroom earlier. I said it because I know it really ticks her off when people do that. Well Lyndsey heard and got offended and told me in group that it was very hypocritical of me because there are many times when smokers are waiting for me to finish a meal to go out and smoke. Then Jennifer J. brought up a comment I made last week about her getting off the couch and to the med window on time, and how the nurses are always coming looking for me to do or take something, which is a lie because I've been very good lately with all that. But whatever, I don't care, I leave Monday. So fuck them.

January 27, 2007 Diary

I haven't written in a couple days so there is quite a bit new, and I hope this pen doesn't run out on me.

Yesterday was my last equine and I had to say goodbye to Sunny and it was very sad. It was rushed too because Jen J. wanted to get back to take a nap before lunch. Sad day.

I finally got the package from Mike! It was an adorable stuffed animal dog with a Morris beanie hat on. Of course we can't have stuffed animals so I couldn't keep it, they put it in my luggage. BUT, I got my luggage today to start packing, so he will sleep with me the next couple of nights. And I will get to have him at LIFE.

Talked to my mom, and she has started looking at houses. One she really likes is a block and a half down 46th Ave, on 38th St. How awkward would that be for my dad to have to drive by her house every day to and from work. No thank you, I say. And as much as I hate all this, it would be pretty convenient to walk between the two houses. I will probably spend more time, though, at home with dad, because that is my home and I promised dad I would never leave him. They already figured out who gets what for the most part. She's not interested in most of the stuff, but she gets the living room furniture and some other stuff. And Cody of course. The kitties stay.

Had to say goodbye to Susan last night and that was really hard. She almost cried and so did I, almost. I am going to miss her so so much.

Found out that IF health insurance approves it, I could be at LIFE for 60 days, not 30. I'm OK with that, although I miss Bela like crazy.

OK I'm tired now. Goodnight.

February 12, 2007 Letter
Krystin to Christine:
Dear Chris

Did I tell you I am going to the Remuda Life program? Well, I've been here for 2 weeks now. It's been going really well and I really like it. I know a lot of girls here from the ranch, so it made the transition a lot easier. We have a LOT more freedom, which is great, but for some girls it gives the more opportunities to use their eating disorder, like exercising and binge eating and purging, and I see a lot of that going on, and that's sad and frustrating when one of my housemates is eating half of the stuff in the fridge in the middle of the night. But the one who was doing that is gone now. There are 7 girls per house, and 7 houses, but only 6 are in use. We have most of the same groups here as at the ranch. I don't have to stay on the cul-de-sac anymore, I can walk to nearby places, and we can smoke whenever we want, as long as it's not during a group time. We go out quite a bit, to Target once a week and the library on Saturdays to use the internet, and we have a TV with cable. It's pretty sweet. So even if you don't write letters, you better say hello on Facebook! I'm doing alright on the eating part, but it could be better, and I hope it gets better soon! Overall though I'm doing great and my mood has greatly improved, so I'm feeling really good too. Oh, and I left a message online for Mike telling him that I still like him. I'll keep ya updated on that. The weather has been beautiful and sunny. I'm working on my tan daily. 😊

Love you much, I'll write again soon! Krystin

April 2007 Facebook
waiting patiently to register for class this summer
feeling like she's freeloading off her father, because that's the impression he gives her.

May 2007 Facebook
bored out of her mind
still bored out of her mind
finally starting working! In rocket dogs, of course
working her ass off taking caps off water bottles used by the research mice

[In the summer of 2007 Krystin began taking classes at the University of Minnesota, Twin Cities campus. She transferred from the Morris campus to the Twin Cities because she had been gone from Morris since fall semester 2005; in the meantime, her cohort of friends at Morris had graduated or left, so it made little sense for her to return there.]

Chapter 5

The College Years: University of Minnesota Twin Cities

June 2007 Facebook
starting her class this week - how exciting!

Diary [undated, but next in sequence in the pages]
    I did end up going to the LIFE program, for 60 days. Saying goodbye to everyone at the ranch was hard, mostly with nurse Susan. I still miss her like crazy. When I got to the LIFE program in Chandler, Rachel, my favorite person in the world, was there, and it was so great to see her again. Soon after, Crystal came too. Both of them went home before me though, and that was real sad. Crystal and Rachel and I tried to get together this summer at Crystal's in Seattle, but it didn't work out. Overall I liked the LIFE program, but not my therapist, James. What a dud. Jess was my dietician and she was hard on me but it was for the best. After 60 days they recommended another 30 days, but I declined. I really needed to come home, especially to be there when my mom moves. Jess says I was running away from recovery, and I got mad at her for that. Although I didn't even gain any weight while I was there, I actually lost weight. But I got horribly sick for about 3 weeks, and towards the end I got my period back!!! But it gave me the most awful cramps ever. I was nauseous and throwing up like my last week, even on the flight home. Surprise surprise, though, within a couple weeks I started feeling better, AND, my appetite by now has fully come back! I am hungry all the time again, and eating lots, but I'm still not gaining weight, which is frustrating. And I'm afraid that I'm slipping back into old habits again. I'm not doing blood tests, and I'm missing shots. But when I got home I found out my A1C is 6.5! That's pretty exciting! However, I also have diabetic retinopathy, so I've begun doing eye laser treatment for the nerve damage. For 2 months after I got home I did absolutely nothing. I sat around all day, although I was searching for a job. At the end of May I finally got a job at the U in the animal research department. I assemble mouse cages. It's hard work, but it's money, and I really like the people I work with, like Jess and Andre, and Febrece from Paris. And now I am halfway through my summa course, History of the Holocaust, which I am really enjoying, and I got an A- on my first paper! So class is T-Th from 9:05 – 1:10, and I work on M, W, F from 8 – 3:30.

Mom has been in her house since I got back, about 6 blocks away on 43rd Ave., and she got 2 kittens! Lena and Ella. I love them

July 2007 Facebook
back to the real world
studying for her final exam until Thursday

August 2007 Facebook
done with her class!! Free time! (other than work, of course)

Monday August 2007 [no date] Diary
    I finished my summer course, and I got a 'B' as a final grade! I am very happy with that. I took the final in a room by myself in the Social Sciences building. But I am going to go to the Disabilities Services office and register to take my tests there, and then I will scope out my options.
    Since my class is over, I am working 5 days a week, and it sucks, I hate this job, I can't wait to be done. Assembling mice cages all day is so boring! And Jess is in a mouse room now so she's not even in assembly with me. I'm supposed to work till 3:30 but Jess and I totally leave early every day. I feel guilty sometimes about it but I would otherwise be sitting there for half an hour by myself doing nothing. But I am done Aug 31.
    I have an appointment with [physician] coming up in a few weeks and am going to talk to her about the ilet (sp?) [islet] cell transplant so that I don't have to do insulin any more. I will have to take like 50 pills a day to keep them working, but I would take that any day over doing shots. I think that no matter how much treatment I go through, I will never be able to do all my shots, because I hate them! And I can't get over that. And I can't live at Remuda my whole life. So I need to start looking at other options, and I don't think the inhaler insulin is ready for me yet. I feel I am a lost cause if I have to keep doing shots my whole life, and I don't want to end up in the hospital again.

September 2007 Facebook
sitting in class or in Coffman union, Mon.-Fri.

October 2007 Facebook
missing the safeness and security of AZ
is 23 and very thankful I don't have to spend my birthday this year with a tube up my nose

December 2007 Facebook
is studying for finals
is done with finals!!
May 2008 Facebook
the stress is taking over!
Now only finals to get through...
is doing last minute preparations for the British history final tonight!
One final down, 2 more to go!
Two finals down, one to go!
is DONE!

June 2008 Facebook
last day of May session class!

June 17, 2008 Email
Krystin to dad, mom:
'A' IN SOCIOLOGY! (:

September 2008 Facebook
is kinda looking forward to class starting again tomorrow, and kinda not..

November 10, 2008 Email (meanwhile, the reality of life)
Gary to therapist and Krystin physician:
    I'm trying to figure out what to do. ([the physician]: FYI, Krystin and I met with [the therapist] last week, primarily about her lack of diabetes care and what role I could play in it. The short answer is "none" because basically every time I say anything, it just irritates her. We also learned that after her last A1c, when it had not dropped below 14, she has sort of given up. So she's essentially committing suicide faster and there seems not to be much I can do about it.)
    One of my conclusions, harsh though it is, is a matter of self-defense: I want to tell her that unless she gets the A1c below 10 by May 31, she has to move out. I do not want to see her disintegrate medically, and if she's going to stay on that path, she can do it out of my view (since there's nothing I can do about it, apparently). I don't want to have to watch, so she has to leave.
    Have you an opinion?

Physician to Gary, therapist:

I'd wondered how she was doing. She has resisted our efforts in this clinic to help her repeatedly. She doesn't bring her meter to visits or drop it off between them so we can work aggressively with her to adjust her insulin, but then often when seen she was not even applying the algorithm she had in the first place and we'd want that in place so we could have a base to work from with reasonable changes. I've tried to get her to go back to [a psychiatrist] (who'd wanted to see her again and had questions about whether or not the eating DO [disorder] was active again). I have to say it is a very difficult situation and it's not so much about the disease itself, it's a psychological issue. In the past when she had applied the algorithm things did dramatically improve. We need your help, [the therapist], and it would be good to re-involve [the psychiatrist] (but the problem is getting Krystin to follow through on anything). As to whether or not kicking her out is the best idea, I'd tend to think not but that is a question for you, [the therapist], and I defer to your opinion on how we can engage Krystin to start self-managing.

Physician to Krystin's nurse/educator:

Do you see anything to add about the psych aspects of this situation?

Nurse/educator to physician:

Her eating disorder is still very much alive and well. Unfortunately she left the Methodist program before really making any progress, and was pulled from the AZ program, although they wanted to keep her there longer. Gary could make it a requirement that in order to live with him, she must attend the program at Methodist again. Until her eating disorder is dealt with, (and hopefully he knows that it can take a long time) she is simply not going to change. That is my opinion! Feel free to forward this to him if you would like. [I was never convinced that Krystin had an eating disorder. She had a diabetes management disorder. See also the 11/26/08 physician email.]

Physician to Gary:

Another vote that it's the psychological part of things . . . another opinion that the eating DO has not been fully treated. And the suggestion that Krystin must attend the Methodist program again if she wants to continue living with you.

Gary to physician, cc to therapist:

I'm not opposed to this. Are we talking about the live-in program or an outpatient program? The live-in program there was a complete failure for her; the AZ program was successful. (I wouldn't say she was "pulled" from the AZ program; she was determined to leave, and with everything else going on in her life [this was when Pat and I were in the midst of the divorce proceeding while Krystin was in Arizona, and we arranged for Pat to move out before Krystin returned to Minneapolis], I did not oppose it. Her mother did.) I'd like to hear from [the therapist] about this, too.

I could also insist that she see [the psychiatrist] and see a therapist. [The therapist] has been pushing that for awhile (as have I), also without much success.

Physician to Gary, cc to therapist:

Would she be willing to go back to the AZ program?

Gary to physician, cc to therapist:

Would [the health care provider] pay for it again?

Physician to Gary, cc to therapist:

I don't know but if she is willing it would be worth checking. But could start with the local outpatient Methodist program if she's willing to do that.

Therapist to Gary, physician:

Last week in our family meeting when Krystin endorsed [I believe "endorsed" is therapist lingo for "reported"] noncompliance, hopelessness and SI; she also endorsed continued high sensitivity to noise and tactile which keeps her in a constant state of irritation. She stated that this sensitivity interferes with her compliance and contributes to her depression. I referred her to PRC [I don't know what PRC is, but OT's is surely occupational therapists.] who have OT's who assess and treat sensory integration difficulties. I believe that this is a missing piece that has not been addressed previously. I have only had Krystin in family meetings, but Gary described some addition developmental issues around not wanting to be held as a baby and child which some Asperger-like qualities. This is not a specialty area of mine, but I believe an important piece to look at.

The other idea I had was for Krystin to be referred to an outpatient treatment program that has an onsite nurse that could help her monitor her diabetes during the day and then check her reading in the morning. If she fails at this outpatient program then you would look at a more restrictive inpatient setting. A team meeting including [the psychiatrist and the physician] may also be an important piece to clarify the urgency of the matter. How impaired is she, does she need a case manager? As I stated to Gary and Krystin in the family meeting, aftercare is so crucial. Certainly a missing piece. I will call Krystin this week and see if she was able to schedule with PRC. Since we are both part of the University, I am taking the liberty to coordinate services with [the psychiatrist and the physician]. It turns out that Krystin no-showed an appt with [the psychiatrist] in the past 2 weeks. At least she made one?? It will be good to tell Krystin that we are coordinating care, once again b/c it is life-threatening.

Gary to therapist, physician, psychiatrist:
OK, I have too much information. If the first step is a team meeting, I'm all for it. . . .

Each of the options that has been suggested sound fine to me—I'm willing to go with whatever works. (Except AZ, if that one can be avoided; I am sure Krystin would be happier if she can stay here and finish her college degree this spring semester—I suspect taking her out of school at this point would cost more in distress than could be offset by any medical gains.)

Physician to Gary, therapist:
The problem I have with an in home nurse is that they may not have the expertise/sensitivity to all of the issues here. I like the idea of group/team meeting and I can come to Psychiatry for the meeting. I also like the idea of Krystin getting back into the outpatient Methodist program. If that ends up needing to inpatient, maybe the AZ program would be the best option because that was a positive experience before.

November 25, 2008 Email
Gary to physician, therapist, psychiatrist:
 One long paragraph from an email Krystin sent to me after our meeting this morning, and forwarded with her permission. She was speaking frankly to me, which I appreciate (and told her so).

Krystin to dad:
 I went and looked at the website for the Emily Program day program. It looks nice and all, but it is specifically for eating disorders, even though [the psychiatrist] thought they dealt with other stuff as well, but it doesn't look like they do, and I just don't need all those eating disorder groups, even though [the physician] is still convinced I do. It has nothing to do with eating, it has to do with putting in the time and doing my shots and getting over the needle phobia. I don't know what other types of day programs are out there, though, and there probably isn't one for my specific need, so I may have to settle with an eating disorder program, although in any evaluation meeting THEY might decide it's not right for me when I answer "no" to all their eating-related questions! I mean, I don't barf, take laxatives, refrain from eating, have problems eating in front of others, have eating rituals, etc. etc. IT'S THE DAMN SHOTS I HATE DOING!! So, guess I have to do a little more research into programs, or get help from [the physician and the therapist] on finding one. I don't look forward to it, but I know it's what I need. I think one of my other biggest fears, which I didn't bring up this morning, is not working. I've realized that I have a fear of not having money. Not really a phobia, but a fear. I don't like the idea of not working and not having any money. No, I'm not buying clothes now and there isn't really anything I HAVE to buy and have, but life in general has expenses, going out with friends and such, and if I'm not working, I'm not making money. Plus I have bills to pay. I just don't like the idea of not having any incoming money.

Physician to Gary, psychiatrist, therapist:
 Hi (and please send this to Krystin, too, because this is for you, Krystin, and for continuing our group conversation that began yesterday),
 First, it seems like yesterday was really good. I am so happy that you're thinking about things and really, deep down inside you are the one who really knows what's going on, what all of the roadblocks and

motivations really are, so the more you take the time to think this all through, the better.

I'm not convinced you have an eating disorder. I have not been sure what the exact problem(s) was/were and was one of the things to consider. But from a pragmatic standpoint, as you allude to in your note and as was brought up in the meeting yesterday, the structure of those kinds of programs is what you need. They do seem to get results for you, and it's really the results part that is important. That's why I think they are part of the answer. They may be the best thing we have for dealing with this part of the problem.

On other parts of this, I contacted [the nurse/educator] so we can get you back in to look at all of the meter options, take a look at the arm testing, and also address the possibility of going back to the pump to help deal with the shots issue.

Thanks for the follow up, follow through, and honesty.

December 2, 2008 Email
[responding to a query from me about Krystin seeing her]
Physician to Gary:

No, not necessary to see me to look at different testing options.

Please tell Krystin to be sure to bring meter with when she sees [the nurse/educator] (and to try to follow through with testing before meals and bedtime in the interim with her old meter for now as well as apply her insulin algorithm) so that meter can be downloaded at the visit with [the nurse/educator]. . . . It actually is good if the visits with [the nurse] and me are staggered to that overall, the frequency of visits to our clinic is greater . . . that will hopefully give Krystin more reinforcements to follow through on recommendations, more support.

December 5, 2008 Email
Gary to physician, therapist, psychiatrist:
From a long-time friend of Krystin [Nicole] who works here at the U as a department administrator. I told her she should not back off.

Hi Gary!

I had lunch with Krystin today and we got to talking about how she's been doing and she mentioned she hasn't been doing her #s or taking insulin throughout the day (just in the morning). She said you knew about this because of the appointment you had together last week. I was pushing her pretty hard to start doing her #s and insulin again so she could get into the range to be eligible for the study and be healthy. I also recommended she see a therapist on a regular basis and possible give the pump a try again since she HATES needles. She said she's looking for another day program to get into to get back on track. I hope I didn't push too much, but I worry about her and want to make sure she's o.k. I can't begin to know all the details of the situation, but I want to help in whatever way I can. If that's to back off, I will do so. Just let me know.

Physician to Gary:
    Thanks for this follow up—she knows what she needs to do and is thinking about the options, but hopefully she will follow through.

Gary to physician:
    True, but she's known that for 10 years.

Physician to Gary:
    Yes, but you have to keep hoping that it will click at some point and turn into behavior change.

November 2008 Facebook
is working on typing up my Mpls. field study all evening . . . blah it's going to be a loooooong night of homework and studying. . . .

December 2008 Facebook
is done with college lecture courses for-ev-er!! (at least until grad school . . .)
is beginning to feel the stress and tiredsomeness of studying for finals. And yes I realize tiredsomeness is probably not a word
1 final down, 2 to go! Then no more finals EVER!
is done with the Crusades, now on to studying the American criminal justice system and the geography of the Twin Cities!

March 2009 Facebook
is rearranging the outline for my thesis paper
is lunching and thesising

April 2009 Facebook
has 12 pages of thesis paper written and needs 25 by Tuesday. Crap.

May 2009 Facebook
The thesis paper is printed and stapled. There's no going back now. Graduation, here I come!
is DONE WITH COLLEGE

Krystin graduated from the University on May 16, 2009, from the College of Liberal Arts on the Twin Cities campus with a B.A. in History. Her graduating GPA was 2.755, a C+/B-. There was an evolution in the grades she earned. Her term (semester) GPAs at Morris were 2.2, 2.25, 2.60, 2.5, and 2.89. Her directed study while in Europe and summer 2007 GPAs were both 3.0. When she resumed studying on the Twin Cities campus, her GPAs were 2.8, 3.3, 3.6, 2.4, and 4.0. When she was living at home (with me), where she was more conscientious about her diabetes care and didn't have the distraction of partying in the dorm, her grades improved noticeably. She received outstanding comments on her senior paper, on the Sobibor concentration camp in Nazi Germany.

Chapter 6

An Interim Year After College

May 20, 2009 Diary
[only this page and date was written on in the journal]
　　Here begins my post-graduation journal. I thought the cover/theme of this was fitting [a collage of air mail labels], considering all I want to do this summer is travel, and my dad promised me a trip to Germany, but none of that is going to happen! Anywhere in Europe is too expensive. My dad promised me a graduation trip back in high school, but whatever. Now I have no idea what I'm doing with my life. I applied for a summer job at Yellowstone but haven't heard from them yet. I also applied to Glacier Park but didn't even hear from them that they got my application. I recently applied to a secretarial/clerical position at the UMPD, so we'll see. All I know is that I need to find a job with health care by the end of October cause I go off dad's insurance when I turn 25. For now I'm stuck at the bookstore with my shitty hours and pay. I can stay there through September, but really hope I can find something before then. I'm going to cancel my parking contract in the Northstar lot, which is $65 a month, and park in the $3.75-a-day lot when I work. Such a better deal. What I thinking?? I got my graduation check from grandpa last week. $1000! That will help a bit with my VISA bills. Also with my trip to visit Rachel in Michigan this summer, if I go.

July 2009 Facebook
I had an epiphany and have decided what I want to do with my life. Yay for life ambitions! [Several wrote to ask "doing what?"]
Krystin: I'm going to write. Travel and write. But first I have to work for a couple years to save up the money to travel! [Krystin did write at length about her travels in future years. This was a goal she enunciated frequently during her life.]

September 2009 Facebook
"I remember back—" "Something really boring happened great story ok bye"

January 30, 2010 Facebook
Working at the bookstore today for the last time. Tis a bittersweet day!

Early February 2010 Blog
[Krystin made six entries to a blog she titled Thoughts, Exposed]
One Complaint After Another

    This is not another blog about the writer's (my) daily activities. I will not write about the time spent with my cat, or the book that I read, or the things I found on my floor while cleaning my room. This is meant to be my space to complain about things in life and to contemplate the problems of the world. It's a "why?" blog. There are so many questions that have gone unanswered, that I hope to answer with my own opinions, or provide an answer to said questions with sought-out research. Some will be funny, some will be serious, some will be downright ridiculous. Either way, I hope you enjoy! So on that note, let's jump right in. . . .

February 17, 2010 Blog

    It's not just my brother. It's every male in the universe who does it (that is, every male who plays video games): when one thing goes wrong, they believe that they can make it all better by throwing the controller across the room and yelling profanely at the TV screen. I'm waiting for the day when the TV speaks back and says "I'm sorry you messed up that play. Even though it was you, good sir, the one holding the controller, who led your character astray or pushed the wrong combination of buttons and did not complete the KO, I will make everything better and go back and give you the slaying-the-dragon points and achievement." This would solve a lot of frustrations and further anger, but I won't hold my breath for the day this happens.

    Many years ago, my now 19-year-old brother got so angry that he picked up one of his shoes, threw it across the room, and (accidentally) hit a framed picture on the wall. It broke the glass and the picture fell off the wall. He no longer throws shoes, but he does still yell and throw his controller on the ground. From 3 rooms away I can even hear him hitting the controller and swearing under his breath (at least he thinks it's under his breath – if I can hear it from 3 rooms away, however, it certainly isn't). I am irritated on almost a daily basis by having to listen to this. You can hear him from any room on the first floor of the house, and I don't want to have to always isolate myself in my bedroom upstairs just to avoid listening to his grumbles and stomping and tantrums and throwing and etc. etc. Whenever I happen to be nearby when he starts to get out of control, I always say "yeah, 'cuz that'll make it all better," to which he replies with an aggressive "shut up."

[Fortunately, as Elliott matured, he no longer exhibited this behavior. Krystin was, however, accurate in her description and story.]

I have found that males, even grown men, do the same thing with sports games on TV. When their team of choice makes a great play, they shout in happiness and high-five each other; but when a bad play is made, they shout even LOUDER and yell at the TV as if the referee can actually hear them.

Again, why do they do this??

My theory is that it all has to do with testosterone. In some way, I think the yelling actually makes them feel better, let's them get out their rage. Women would never do this! By nature we are much more patient and don't feel the need to express our rage through physical activity (for the most part). Do males realize how ridiculous they look and sound when they yell at the TV? Surely they must realize that the game, or the ref, or the player can't actually hear them. As everyone always says: IT'S JUST A GAME. The world will not explode, your life will not end, your house will not be repossessed if you do not pass that one level the first time, or if your favorite team makes a bad play. Get over it. Males tend to disregard common sense and reality when caught up in a game (be it sports or video). Their first instinct when something goes wrong is to hit something. It's in their nature and probably won't ever change. It's just too bad the rest of us have to deal with it.

March 2, 2010 Facebook
During the Walk for Diabetes, the Minnesota chapter of the Diabetes Research Foundation alone raised $1.9 million for research for a cure! That's one step closer to my freedom!!

March 4, 2010 Blog
Why . . . do bad things happen to good people?

I'm going to approach this topic cautiously, because I don't want to offend or insult anyone. I want to mention right away that I have no religious affiliation. I am an atheist and a skeptic, but I am not against religion. I respect people for what they believe and I feel that people can believe what they want. Just because I don't believe in a higher being, doesn't mean other people can't; I'm not selfish or narcissistic at all in that way. Many people I know base much of their life on their faith, and for that I have admiration and the utmost respect. But that's not for me.

That being said, why DO bad things happen to good people? I'm thinking specifically here about recent natural disasters: the earthquakes in Haiti and Chile. Or even 9/11. If we go back in history, the 1995 or 96 earthquake in Pakistan; the Holocaust; WWI. I could name endless possibilities. My question then, more specifically for those people of faith, is why would God let these things happen? If he is the almighty being, why have all these horrible events taken place?

Some people say it's to bring people together. So to bring people together, hundreds of thousands of people need to die? Surely there must be a better way to unite people. Others say it's to keep us humble. Again I ask: 200,000 people in Haiti had to die just so we can appreciate our lives and the things and people that we have in our lives? Why did hundreds of thousands of people in Haiti need to die for that? What did they do to deserve this? Why did your God feel it was necessary? Some people say "well it doesn't work that way, God doesn't control everything like that." No, maybe not, but that doesn't seem like a good enough explanation for me. For many, many years, skeptics all over the world have been asking the question "Why?" If there really is a God, then why did this or that happen?

I'm open to explanations.

March 6, 2010 Blog
Can cats have Down Syndrome?

This is Ella, my baby who we adopted from my mom. . . . For example: She takes forever to jump up onto something. If I'm on the couch and she comes over, I'll call her name and pat my lap for her to come up. She'll sit there for sometimes over a minute just staring, not blinking, almost contemplating the move. Then she'll finally jump up (maybe) and lay down next to me but not on my lap. And when she jumps down from things, she more falls than jumps. Most cats use their back feet as leverage against whatever they're sitting on to jump onto the floor. Ella will use her front feet to jump but then her back legs just go splaying out behind her and she does almost a belly-flop onto the floor, with a loud thud. When my dad throws treats to the other 2 cats, she sits there and watches the treats fly by; only if one lands in front of her will she eat it. Of course she thinks this is all normal. [Ella got into the treats game later; she chased them into the kitchen, which she knew was her spot at which to get treats.]

I actually looked this up and yes, cats CAN have Down Syndrome, or something similar. In humans, Down Syndrome is a birth defect where all or part of a third copy of chromosome 21 occurs (this is the reason for the condition's usual medical name: trisomy 21). Cats only have 19 chromosomes, so the condition is not exactly the same, but the traits can be similar.

Vet and President of the Albury RSPCA Branch Dr Arthur Fruaenfelder says "Down Syndrome is a very rare condition among cats. Down Syndrome is a deficiency in the development of the lower brain and what you have got is basically incoordination. One way to consider Down Syndrome, is that you have got a spinal cord it comes up into the back of the brain and then it gets relayed all through the brain and the messages go back. What is happening here is that 'relayed box' is not working properly." Pretty sure this is Ella.

But we still love her all the same!

April 11, 2010 Facebook Miguel Haggar is with Krystin Engstrand.

Krystin: Haha, I look very mischievous. . . .

May 17, 2010 Facebook
I just submitted my application to teach English abroad! Crossing my fingers now for a phone interview!

> Marissa Forrest: when would you have the interview?
> Krystin: I had the initial one today! If I accept the job, I would interview with the people at the actual school in Korea.
> Marissa Forrest: wow that is AWESOME news!! :)
> Krystin: Yeah! And I wouldn't leave till the end of July, so I could still come to the BASH!

[Big Annual Stephens Happening, Pat's annual family gathering. We were amazed and impressed at Krystin's courage in taking a teaching job alone in a country and culture that are very different from the one she grew up in, and in teaching, of all things, which she had averred many times that she did not want to do. Krystin eventually went to South Korea in July 2010 and returned to Minneapolis at the end of August 2011. She wrote a blog while there, posted on Facebook, and exchanged many emails with me. Her writings from and about South Korea totaled over 250 pages. What follows in the next chapter are excerpts from her writing that highlight her experiences both teaching and traveling, but about 80% of the material has been omitted. Krystin had a wonderful experience in South Korea but it was a discrete part of her life disconnected from the main story lines. Kathy, Elliott, Kathy's son Spencer, and I visited Krystin in South Korea in the summer of 2011 and all five of us went to Japan on that same trip.]

May 25, 2010 Email
[This is the point in the story when Krystin's email messages with me start to be included. I had saved messages going back to May 2010; there were many earlier messages but I no longer had them. I had paper copies of some of them from earlier years, which I have quoted.]
Dad to Krystin:
   Have you thought seriously about why Asia rather than Europe? What's the reason for the preference? There's nothing wrong with it, but I'd like to be reassured that you've given this serious thought and know why you want Asia rather than Europe.

Krystin to dad:
   Because I've wanted to visit an Asian country for as long as I've understood the concept of travel. I want to experience their culture and learn all about it. I know that I won't understand any signs or pretty much anything, but I didn't when I was traveling around with Mike, either. [When she and Miguel Haggar ("Mike") were traveling in Europe when we lived in Scotland—and Krystin ended up in ICU in Paris.] Yes European languages use alphabetical letters like we do and not symbols, but just because I could read a word doesn't mean I knew what it meant. Thousands of people have been doing this for years, and the programs know how hard it can be for people, which is why they set up huge networks before you go, so you have people to go to if you need anything, and you get to know the people you'll be working with during the week of orientation before you actually start teaching. Erin already has 3 friends over there teaching, some of them for the 2nd time, and she said that most people over there speak English

anyway (minus children, which is why they're learning it), especially in the bigger cities, which I would be working in. Remember this is my adventure and my decision, and I want Korea.
Dad to Krystin:
    OK, just so you've thought about it.

May 21, 2010 Facebook
[A photo posted on Facebook by Katie Engstrand Volker, Krystin's cousin, taken at Katie's home outside Almena, Wisconsin.]

May 31, 2010 Email
Thomas Cromwell
Krystin to dad:
    This is the Cromwell I was talking about:
http://en.wikipedia.org/wiki/Thomas_Cromwell,_1st_Earl_of_Essex

Dad to Krystin:
    Sounds like he did quite a bit of good for the English government.

Krystin to me:

But he was also a huge jerk when it came to the common people. He was a selfish man who was probably wealthier than the king because he took thousands of pounds in bribes from men who wanted to buy the property of the abbeys that had been destroyed when Henry separated from the Catholic church. He sent people left and right to the gallows or to be beheaded or burned for treason (which he would make up), if he thought that someone was getting in the way of his visions for the church of England. He's pretty much to blame for Anne Boleyn's death, because he stood nearby why men physically tortured guys into admitting they had committed adultery with her, when they didn't really; only so that they could use it as an excuse to get rid of Anne. He constantly tried to persuade Henry to run the government in a way that pleased himself and that would benefit him more. Yes he may have done some good, but I think Wikipedia is leaving out quite a bit! I'm just saying. This is my opinion. (:

June 3, 2010 Email
Eyes
Krystin to dad:

My eye exam went fine. I picked a pair of glasses off the clearance rack, and they were only $85, but I forgot that's just for the frame. With the lenses, I ended up paying $260. Uuuuuuugh. :(I think I can't afford my contacts now. I have an appointment to go in on Monday for a contact fitting, because the doctor said I could order a different brand of contacts that would be cheaper than the ones I have now, but still, they're going to be a lot, and the fitting is $50 too. And then I have to go renew my passport, and get the criminal background check? I don't know where I'm going to come up with the money for all this, I just don't have it. I'm getting $100 this week from unemployment, and some from Prostaff on Friday for working the games last weekend, and then I have some in my checking account, but not enough for all these things. Why is life so expensive?? I'm not sure what I'm going to do. :(Bummer.

Dad to Krystin

You have a couple of options.

You can borrow money from me. (I will help you out some with this. Find out how much your lenses will cost.)

You can take some of your bond money from Grampa Stephens.

June 21, 2010 Email
Krystin to dad:
Hello!

I went and renewed my passport today. . . . Ouch. I'm not sure how it added up to that because my receipt is itemized, but of course I don't understand all the state lingo. I thought it was going to be $130; $70 to renew and $60 to expedite, but surprise surprise, of course not. Ugh. Guess I'll be going to Korea broke. I'll live on nothing but rice and water for a month. And I haven't even picked up my contacts yet, those will be another hard hit. Like I said before, this Korea thing better be worth it, because it's making me bankrupt before I even get there! :/ But now I just wait for my visa issuance number, which Sally said will take about a week or 10 days, then when I get that and my passport, I can go to Chicago and get my visa, and I should also have my plane ticket in 2 or 3 weeks too. So it's all coming together!

Thursday night I'm having some bookstore people over for a small goodbye gathering. A good handful of people can't come, so we're going to do another thing later in July as well (we're thinking bowling). So that will be fun.

Not much else here going on. You would hate to see the dining room table right now. It's completely covered with stuff that I have to pack. But it's a good way for me to visualize what all I have to pack that isn't clothes. This is going to be tough. I may need both you AND mom to send me a package after I get there. Which would really help save weight in my suitcase. Actually, I'm attaching a picture so you can see. Don't have a hissy fit, it will all be cleared off by the time you get home. (: [Kathy and I were traveling in Sweden and Denmark at the time.]

Chapter 7

Teaching and Traveling in South Korea

[Krystin's blog while she was in South Korea, when transformed into an MS Word document, is over 250 pages. This chapter thus provides only brief highlights from her time there.]

Korea Rough Draft
[Krystin began this in March, 2011]
     Helen Keller once said, "Life is either a daring adventure or nothing." Some people define adventure as a road trip, or trying an exotic food. For me, being a 25 year old, still-living-at-home, unemployed college grad, I needed a life changing adventure. One to keep me from falling into that depressed state that inevitably seems to happen to those who can't find a job in the "real world" in over a year after graduation. What better way than to uproot oneself from all things familiar and plant myself down on the other side of the world, to do something I said I never wanted to do: teach. Not only that, but teach to my least favorite of people: children.

June 1, 2010 Diary
[There are only a couple of entries in that book. Krystin evidently decided to switch to a blog]
     This journey actually begins about 3 weeks ago.
     I was having dinner with Dan [a friend, college classmate?], because he was going to leave the next week for South Korea, where he's going to teach English. He was telling me about the trip, and at one point he said "you know you could do this too." I had never thought about it before as an option for ME. When I got home that night I really started thinking about it. I asked Dan what program he's doing it through, and I looked it up. The idea of it started becoming more appealing as I read more about it. The benefits are great, and the timing could never be better. I'm having such a hard time finding a full-time job, why not take a break from trying to enter Corporate America and do something that would not only look good on a resume, but also be a once-in-a-lifetime experience?
     The next day I submitted my application. Within 15 minutes, Sally [ ] from Education Adventure called. Before I knew it I was sending back an official application with pictures and a cover letter and

resume. Sally and I exchanged many emails over the next couple of days. My parents got hesitant over the fact that they couldn't find anything to legitimize this program, but that got straightened out. Other than that, they both think it's a great opportunity.

June 7, 2010 Diary

I got the job! Oh how nervous I was all weekend, and all day today, knowing that today would be the day I found out. So I wonder what's made Mr. Lee choose me over the others. For a minute I imagined how they must feel, those who were not picked. What will they do now?

So now I scramble to get everything in order.

June 24, 2010 Blog
Pre-travel Thoughts
Current Mood: anxious

Although I am very excited about this trip, I am also feeling quite nervous. There are a lot of questions that I am hoping to get answered before I go. One of my biggest concerns is about getting all my medical supplies there. I will be carrying half of my pump supplies in my check-in bag, and ALL my insulin (yes, a year's worth) in my carry-on backpack.

I don't think there is any way to prepare myself mentally 100% for this. It's just not possible, no matter how much I read up on the culture and no matter how many meals of stir-fry or kimchi I eat. The only part of culture shock that I'm worried about is the shock it will have on my digestive system, and as awkward as it is to talk about, you better believe I'm packing LOTS of Metamucil to help me through those first couple weeks! I didn't have any culture shock when I was traveling around Europe in 2006, but that doesn't surprise me too much. I did, however, surprisingly or not, experience some unfortunate culture shock when I was in Cancun in 2003; and Cancun is basically considered an extension of Texas, one of the most "Americanized" cities of Mexico. Korea is going to be like arriving on Mars. I was told not to think about the culture shock too much, don't allow my mind to become worried and obsessed about it, and that will help.

June 25, 2010 Facebook

I find it interesting that I'm going to Korea to teach. What have I told everyone my whole life I'm not going to do as a career? Teach. Hmm.

July 20, 2010 Email
Itinerary for ENGSTRAND KRYSTIN.STEPHENS.HERMANSON
Krystin to mom, dad:

Well, here it is. Bright and early Tuesday morning I take off. Lots of layovers! I can't believe I leave next week already. I really thought I had another couple weeks. Oh well, it's not like I'm moving for forever, so anyone who I don't get to say goodbye to (which is pretty much all my friends), it's not like I'll never see them again. Just not for over a year! But this isn't the middle ages and I can easily keep in touch with everyone, so that makes me feel a little bit better about it. Unfortunately, it means I have less time now to spend with you guys before I go. :(

July 21, 2010 Email
MADE IT.
Krystin to dad:

I'm here!

I MADE IT! I'm in the hotel now, and exhausted and going to go to bed right about now. I can tell you more about stuff when we Skype (soon?), but I was put on a 2-hour bus ride from the airport to Cheonan, where I was picked up and brought right to the school, where I observed Sarah's (the one who I'm replacing) classes for 3 hours until they finished at 9:10. Didn't even get to eat dinner really, haven't eaten since the plane, but I'm so exhausted and I'm going to get fed bfast, lunch and going out with some of the teachers for dinner tomorrow night. But wanted to send you a quick note and let you know I arrived safe and sound and with all my luggage! Miss you and love you.

July 28, 2010 Blog
S.L.P. [the initials of the school where Krystin taught]
Current Mood: excited

The first few days I was here, I shadowed all of Sarah's classes, since I will be taking over all of them. The kids are very curious, which is understandable considering they don't see many foreigners in Cheonan except the English teachers. They want to touch my arms and my nose ring, and point at my freckles all over my arms and face and ask "what?" and "why?" They absolutely LOVE to ask questions, especially my age.

The kids have very short attention spans. They don't like to stay in their seats, want to draw on the whiteboard, crawl under the desks, fight with each other, and talk in high-pitched, squeaky voices. What on earth have I gotten myself into here?? Chaos. Lots of chaos with these kids. By the time I'm done with this in a year, I'm going to be the most patient person in this universe since the beginning of time. Either that or I'll need to be put into a room with padded walls.

July 31, 2010 Facebook
Seoul was awesome: found a foreign food market (got me some pop tarts and Kraft mac & cheese!), a Canadian pub, and stayed until 3am at a sketchy underground dance club where old creepy Korean dudes hit on you and offer gum. Good times indeed!

August 1, 2010 Blog
Busan 7/28-7/29

I've only been here a week and a half, and already I've been on two travel adventures! This was only possible because the past week was a school vacation, so we had the whole week off. On Wednesday Tessa and I went to Busan and stayed overnight. It is home to one of the most popular and famous beaches of S. Korea, Haeundae Beach. On any given sunny and hot day, you can find half a million people there. This is what Tessa and I mainly went to see, but unfortunately that day it was overcast (although still hot and humid), so there weren't very many people there.

On Thursday we went to the Beomeosa Buddhist temple. It was originally built in 678, but was destroyed during the Japanese invasion in 1592. It was renovated in 1713, and the name means "fish of the Buddhist scripture temple." It is Busan's most famous temple, and when at it, you feel very far away from the civilization of the large city. It was amazing walking around. Most of you know that I have no religious affiliation, but being there was pretty cool; you can still feel the spiritual vibe, since although we didn't see any monks, there are still natives who come here and pray on a daily basis, so it's a very quiet and peaceful place.

August 4, 2010 Blog
Culture: Here and There

Naturally, while being here I have been introduced to many new cultural beliefs and traditions, and have already learned many new things. For example, nobody here gets tattoos or piercings. I may have mentioned this before. Whereas in America, everyone gets tattoos; even the upper-class, rich, prissy blonde girls get a butterfly or heart tattoo on their shoulder or ankle. Here it's considered "bad blood." Only the lowlifes and gangsters get them (tattoos and numerous piercings). It was quite amusing when Tessa and I were in Seoul last weekend, to notice all the stares that we'd get, mostly from old ladies on the subway. One lady in particular was quite upset with our public display of lowlife-ness. We were sitting on the subway and this lady was just staring us down, not even being discreet about it. I stared back a lot, but even when she would make eye contact with me, she wouldn't look away. She had no shame in her staring. When we finally got off the subway, as we were walking out of the train I turned and gave her a little wave. She just kept staring, no change in expression.

August 7, 2010 Blog
The First Week

Yesterday I finished up my first week of teaching. I went to bed last night around 1 or 1:30am, and slept in today until 3pm. 3PM! I think I was so exhausted from the first week and all my concerns about making a good impression on my students and impressing the school director, that it all caught up with me. It sure felt good to sleep in, though! I think the first week went fine, about as good as it can for someone who has never taught before and had a very little idea of what to expect.

August 15, 2010 Blog
More observations

I have now been here 3 and a half weeks. It's hard to believe that on Wednesday I will have been here a month already! For those of you who told me my time here would go fast, you're right. I am having a wonderful time though. Towards the end of the teaching week I start to get irritated with a lot of my students' behavior, and especially when Friday finally comes I'm so glad it's the weekend. On the other hand, it's already been rewarding, even if in little ways.

August 21, 2010 Blog
Update

I just finished my third week of teaching, and I've now been in Korea for almost a month. My feelings about teaching and about being here in South Korea in general are very different. As far as the teaching goes, I am still unsure about how I feel. Like I said earlier, there are some things that make it really rewarding, and other things that make me think this sucks.

Unfortunately it's the times that I get irritated with my classes that seem to overshadow the small rewards. Three of my classes are still very hard to control.

As far as the whole being here in South Korea experience, it's been amazing. I am thoroughly enjoying being in Korea and experiencing the culture. My stomach is still getting used to the change, even after a month, but hopefully things will eventually . . . hmmm, now to word it . . . normalize?

August 30, 2010 Blog
Class Changes

I have come to the realization, mostly because it's what a lot of the other English teachers who have been here a long time already have said, is that what we foreign teachers do is actually not that important. Tessa calls us glorified babysitters. It's actually the Korean teachers who teach them 95% of the important stuff. We are there as a marketing tool and to keep the kids happy. Frank, our boss and the owner/director of the school, is most concerned with us keeping the kids happy. Parents will want to send their kids to SLP because it has native English-speaking teachers who know the language through-and-through, and we are supposed to keep them happy so that they stay, so Frank can keep making money. What we teach them apparently isn't that important. I don't agree with this 100%, because there are some classes that don't have any Korean teachers, they are only taught by us foreign teachers, so obviously what we teach them is what they're learning and absorbing, so what we teach them is pretty important because it's all they're getting! But most children also go to more than 1 academy. A lot of students will go to their regular school, then come to SLP, then go to another academy after that, and even usually one on the weekends. It's intense. Kids pretty much get no childhood or social life here. Learning English is so important to parents and they really push their kids to learn it, because English is becoming the common language of the world, especially in international business. If their kids can speak fluent English, they are more likely to be successful, and being successful here is at the top of the list of things to be in life.

September 4, 2010 Blog
Food

I decided I should dedicate a post specifically to my eating experience here. It has definitely been interesting. Koreans use many different vegetables, spices/herbs, sauces, and other unidentifiable food products that we don't use in the U.S., and they make food combinations that many times make me turn up my nose. I'm hesitant to try so many things because I don't know what's in it, and it looks and smells bad besides.

September 10, 2010 Blog
Maria
Current Mood: sad

As some of you already know, I lost a close and dear friend, Maria, on Thursday morning (your Wednesday night). I got a message from Maria's sister, Leila, on Tuesday morning, telling me that Maria tried to commit suicide on Friday and was in the hospital on life support and unlikely to make it. If she did pull through, she would be a vegetable on life support for the rest of her life. Still, her mom prayed for a miracle. I don't know if they finally came to the realization that she wasn't going to make it, or whether she went on her own, but I found out Thursday morning that she was no longer with us. Some of you may never have heard of Maria before, some of you have met her, some of you know her well. To me, she was one of my best friends. I knew that she has been unhappy and struggling with a number of issues for quite a few years now, but I didn't realize how unhappy she was. I don't think she got the proper therapy or medication for her depression, because it seemed like every time we'd start hanging out again, it was worse. But I knew there was nothing I could say or do, it was way beyond anything a friend could help with.

This hits very close to home for both my parents and me. For me, being the one in the hospital (and twice, for that matter), and for my parents having to watch me be in critical care and not knowing if I'm going to make it.

September 12, 2010 Blog
Eulogy

Maria's memorial service will be October 3. Christine, my best friend who I love so dearly, told me she would read something for me, if I'd like, at the service. I cannot have asked for a better friend.

(Excerpt) My heart is heavy with the loss of a dear friend, and I am saddened that I cannot be here today to celebrate Maria's life, but I believe that all the love that fills up this room from those in attendance today makes up for my absence. We will all mourn the loss of Maria, but after all the grieving and mourning is over, I know that I will look back on my friendship with Maria with happiness. She is now happy and free, wherever she may be.

September 12, 2010 message to friend

I'm really loving being here. The whole living in South Korea thing has been amazing. I love my apartment, which isn't much bigger than the efficiency apartment you had over by Uptown, but that's ok because I don't really need any more space than that anyway. I have my own bathroom and a small kitchenette with a stove, so it's all good. I could use a bigger fridge, but I won't get picky. I'm already lucky that the school provides housing for us. All I have to pay are the gas and electric bills each month. I think I can handle that.

The teaching part, eh, that's going alright. There are 2 things I've been telling people for years now: I don't like kids, and I never want to teach. Yet here I am. Most of the kids drive me crazy, because they don't listen to me and just want to talk in Korean to their friends all class long, which is not allowed. And we're not allowed to speak any Korean to them, so it's not like I could learn how to say "be quiet" or anything in Korean, because I would get in trouble if my boss or a parent found out. So about half the class time (which is 40 minutes long) is teaching, the other half is class management and shouting at the kids. I teach kids ranging from 1st grade up to 6th grade. The younger kids are restless and have no attention span, and the older kids want to gab with their friends or play games. But, there are rewarding parts to it as well, like with the very very beginners, when I can see their English improving from week to week. My mom always says you can do anything for a year, so I'll stick it out and I'll come home a better person because of it. I think. I hope. . . .

But all in all I'm having a good time. Not even homesick! I Skype with my dad often, so I think that helps. I miss my cats like crazy, though, and just little things about living in America that I can't get or do here. I mean, I'm waaaaay out of my bubble being here, so there have been a lot of things to get used to! I don't have a dryer, so I have to hang-dry all my clothes, and I don't have a dishwasher, so I have to wash all my dishes after I eat. My clothes are stiff and my dishes are still crusty the next time I eat, but I'm not dead from it, so I guess I can't complain! It sure will be nice to come home to a nice meal out of the oven though.

September 26, 2010 Blog
Thailand

A/C pretty much doesn't exist on Samui. It's such a poor country and having A/C basically doubles the electric bill, so nobody can afford it. Some offices and businesses do, and the nicer resorts and hotels do. So all week I was a hot, sweaty mess.

Tuesday morning Tessa and I headed over to the gaudy tourist trap that is Big Buddha. Don't get me wrong, it is still a place of worship and importance for the locals, but it sure is a sight to see.

Last but not least, it was time for me to ride an elephant!

October 2, 2010 Blog
Cheonan update

Fall has arrived in Korea! We left a hot, humid Cheonan on the 18th of September to go to the sweltering heat of Thailand. We left the sweltering heat of Thailand and came home to a cool Cheonan. I, of course, am enjoying it, because it's like fall in Minneapolis, minus all the colorful leaves on the trees (because they are lacking in trees around here). I can finally walk outside and not automatically be in a sweat.

I signed up for the foreign teacher (and Frank) fishing trip on the 24th of October (a Sunday). Every year Frank takes his foreign teachers out on a day-long sea fishing trip. I absolutely hate eating fish, and the smell of it makes me want to vomit, but I'm going to be social and because it will be a fun adventure anyway, I think. I believe the lunch menu includes raw fish, so I will be packing my backpack with a back-up lunch.

October 31, 2010 Facebook
I couldn't have asked for a better Korean birthday. Thanks for all the birthday wishes and to all my SLPers for a fabulous night!!

November 4, 2010 Blog
Fishing Trip

We all sat around the edge of the boat as we traveled about 30 minutes out to the good fishing spot. When we got there, we were all given our "fishing rod," which was a roll of thick twine with a weird contraption on the end that had the squid bait and a weight on it. We would drop it into the water and let it fall all the way down until it hit the bottom. Then we would sit and tug it up and down until we felt something bite and pull.

We did this for like 3 or so hours. In the entire time we did this, I caught one fish and one octopus. Apparently octopi like to eat squid, even though they aren't that much bigger than squid. But they bite, and actually almost everyone caught an octopus. One of the bus drivers caught a baby octopus, and he handed it to the other bus driver, who popped it in his mouth and ate it! Alive. The whole thing. It was disgusting. I think I tasted a little bit of my breakfast in my mouth. For them it's probably a delicious treat, but I was just so shocked and it was so unexpected that above all else I was disgusted.

If you know me at all, you know that I absolutely, positively, utterly, entirely hate fish. I knew this was part of the trip, and I told everyone before the trip that there was no way I was going to eat raw fish - I don't even eat it cooked! But everyone kept badgering me to just do it, just one, so I decided FINE, I'll try it, but if I barf on someone's shoes I'm not responsible for it. Jenny told me to pretend it's like spaghetti. Yeah, right. Here's how it went:

Nope. Not for me. Not even CLOSE to spaghetti. But I did it! Krystin: 1, Raw fishie: 0. All the fish heads had gone into a big pot, which was then filled with water, boiled, and had about 12 packages of ramen added to it. I would've eaten some, being that I enjoy ramen, but those 6 fish heads floating in there kind of deterred me from it.

November 8, 2010 Blog
DMZ

Yesterday was our adventure to the infamous DMZ. For anyone who doesn't know, the DMZ (demilitarized zone) is a buffer zone that runs along the border of North and South Korea, and was established in 1953 after the armistice agreement was signed. It's 160 miles long, 2.5 miles wide, and is considered the most heavily militarized border in the world.

We were picked up in Itaewon. It was about a 45 minute drive out of the inner city. You can tell when you are getting close to the border and the DMZ line, because along the highway you start seeing barbed wire along the highway. Then you see barbed wire and every half mile a guard station. Then you see barbed wire, a guard station, and a guard or two with guns at them. This is serious stuff. A couple different times we had to stop at checkpoints where our passports had to be checked. Any time we were at a checkpoint or around military personnel, no pictures were allowed.

We went to the Third Infiltration Tunnel. The tunnel is only 27 miles from Seoul, and was discovered in October 1978. After the Korean War, when the armistice agreement was signed in 1953 and the DMZ was established, the N. Koreans started secretly building underground tunnels under the border, in a plan to launch a sneak attack on Seoul. It's size is about 6 feet wide and 6 feet tall, and built so that 30,000 men with light artillery can move through it within an hour. Obviously no attack occurred, because when it was discovered, all the N. Koreans fled back. Only four tunnels have been discovered so far, but there are believed to be upwards of 10 more. South Korean soldiers regularly drill within the DMZ in the hopes of finding more.

November 29, 2010 Blog
No bombs, No worries!

There have been a lot of inquiries about how things are going over here with the whole North Korea issue. Everything is business as usual. I'm sure you've all read up on it now so I don't need to explain what happened. North Korea dropped a bunch of bombshells on a small South Korean island, Yeonpyeong. As you probably know, 2 South Korean soldiers were killed, and 18 others wounded. Although this was one of the most serious clashes between the two sides in decades, no one seemed to be too worried about it the next day. There was shock and some fear the day of, but everyone really kept their cool, and it's not even a topic of conversation anymore. If my Korean co-workers and boss aren't worried, I'm not worried.

People are more worried about the kimchi shortage. I'm not joking; there really is a kimchi shortage, and people are freaking out about it. Let me explain, and bear with me, I know kimchi isn't the most exciting of topics, but it's a good story, I promise. Here's how it works: kimchi is fermented cabbage, and is the most popular side dish/household food in Korea. It's like pickles in the U.S. Cabbage is harvested in the autumn and then sits, fermenting, all winter long. Two summers ago, for some reason people weren't eating as much kimchi as usual, so last autumn, not as much cabbage was harvested as usual. That means this summer there was not as much kimchi, yet people were back to eating their normal 10 servings a day (I exaggerate, of course... but not by much. Maybe 8 servings a day). Kimchi is served as a side dish with EVERY meal, in every restaurant. I think you can even get it at McDonald's. . . . Anyway, because they didn't make enough kimchi last spring when it was done fermenting, now by the end of the summer the kimchi supply in Korea is running low. It is literally called the 'Kimchi Crisis.' It's a supply and demand thing, that's for sure. It has become SO expensive to buy in grocery stores, and some restaurants have stopped serving it as a side dish; or if they do, they tag on a nice little fee for it. Now I haven't been to any restaurants that don't serve it, but at the grocery stores, for a bag of it that's probably about a gallon and a half, it's a little over $10. For fermented cabbage. That's how bad it's gotten! There you have it. It's a crisis that's unfortunate to Koreans, but quite humorous to those of us who don't give a damn. (Although, I've come to realize in the last couple weeks that I DO actually like kimchi - just not the kimchi that our school cook makes. She probably buys cheap, rotting cabbage).

On to Thanksgiving.   I worked.   I worked Friday, too. Thanksgiving is not celebrated in Korea (obviously, since it started with the Native Americans and the British). Korea has Cheusok, which was back in September. That's their Thanksgiving equivalent, when they spend time with family and eat lots of food and do traditional Korean stuff. However, we did have a potluck Thanksgiving at Tessa's apartment on Saturday night, since we had to work Thursday and Friday. Everyone was to bring a food dish, so let me draw a picture for you of the very, very random assortment of foods we had: spaghetti, pizza, curry with rice, a mandarin orange salad, Stove Top stuffing, deviled eggs, pickles, crackers with tuna and cheese on it, ddeokbokki (which I brought), and some other things that I can't remember. It was quite a feast, plenty of food for everyone. Which is good, considering there were 16 of us in Tessa's apartment. Imagine trying to fit 16 people in a room a little smaller than a dorm room. She has a lofted apartment, so her bed is upstairs, but for the evening she put the ladder up. We were squashed, but cozy. Lots of food, lots of beer, good company, and good conversation. It was a good time. It was the best we could do being away from our families on the other side of the world with no access to our normal Thanksgiving foods (except the pickles, which Jenny got at the Costco here, and the stuffing, which Emily's friend Joe, who was visiting from his Air Force base down South, brought). Turkey does not exist in Korea.

That's all for the time being. More thoughts on happenings at school soon to come. Bye for now!

November 22, 2010 Email
when you get back
Dad to Krystin:

At some point you need to think about what you're going to do when you get back home. (You probably already have.)

In one of my conversations with Richelle [my therapist following my divorce from Pat] last spring, she talked with me about a parent's responsibility for their children's individuation (the technical term) or "launching" (the lay term). What it basically means is that at some point parents have a responsibility to kick their kids out--to make sure they get out on their own, get "launched." She suggested that I talk with you about setting a date when you would move out, like maybe January 1 (this was in March or April). I was going to talk with you about that, but then the Korean opportunity came along, so it was moot at that point.

But it will come up again. Surely you don't want to come home and plan on staying with me forever. One thing you should do, next spring, is start looking for jobs (on the web). You've now lived by yourself for several months, and it seems to agree with you, so that wouldn't be bad.

No, I am not going to put you out on the street. But I will be disappointed if you don't look actively and vigorously for a job, and of course I will help any way I can. But you really do need to get out of daddy's house and on your own.

Does this make sense? Love you.

Krystin to dad:

I have thought about this quite often. Believe me, I love you and all, but I've been ready to live on my own for a few years now. The only reason I've still been at home is because I couldn't afford to move out! So don't worry, you don't need to worry that I'm going to try and live at home until I'm 35. When I can afford to move out, I will. I just hope you'll let me stay until I can afford to move!

December 15, 2010 Blog
Everywhere a thought, thought

It's a week and a half until I leave for Singapore and I can't wait. Even though there is no snow here, it is bone-chilling cold. My heater is selective and sometimes it works and sometimes it doesn't. It goes on and off and on and off and on and off every couple minutes, which is not at all effective in heating my apartment.

Here is my sad little Christmas tree that I got in the clearance section of Lotte Mart last weekend. It's not as good as the real thing, but it'll do while I'm here:

January 4, 2011 Blog
Singapore: a city-country

    I have returned from my week-long trip to warm, amazing Singapore.

    One of our stops was at Merlion Park. The Merlion is the national tourism symbol of Singapore. As you may have guessed, it's half lion, half mermaid. In the park is a big statue fountain of the Merlion.

    On Tuesday we went to the Singapore zoo. I love zoos, and never tire of them. Many people say that once you've seen a zoo you've seen them all, but for some reason this zoo was different.

Our evenings in Singapore were pretty much the same. We would go eat dinner, then have a drink or two at a bar. Food and alcohol in Singapore are very, VERY expensive. You can spend easily $20-$30 on one meal (per person!!). I found hard cider, but it would be between $14-$16 for a pint. Ouch. I only had it a couple times on the trip. We ate a lot of Western food while we were there, too. We ate dinner one night at Chili's, lunch one day at Hooters (we did it for the boys), and a place called Lena's another day for lunch, where we had pizza and burgers (I had corn on the cob, chicken skewers, and pizza). On our last day, Emily and I had Thai food in Chinatown. Chinatown was also fabulous. It's a labyrinth of side streets of souvenir and trinket shop after shop after shop. Emily and I were in shopping heaven, although we were both on a budget.

January 14, 2011 Blog

My next heating bill will be through the roof. It's cold here. Like, almost Minnesota cold. No below zero temps, but close. And damn icy on those streets. Korea isn't big on sidewalks, so you can find everyone walking down the middle of the street where it may or may not be less slippery from where the cars drive. We're all bundled up in our coats, hats, scarves, and gloves!

It has been brought to my attention that I have not really mentioned anything in a while about the teaching aspect of this whole adventure and how it's going. All I can say is, it's going fine. It's getting easier, this whole teaching thing. I don't feel like I need as much preparation time and I did the first couple months. I'm no pro, of course. I still look at all my lesson plans for my classes that day to see what I'm teaching, but I feel more comfortable in the classroom and with teaching. That doesn't mean I like it. I still don't like teaching, but I don't hate it either. I can still confirm that it's not a career I want to pursue when I get home, and I'm not going to renew my contract for another year, but as a year-long experience, it's alright.

There are parts of the job that put a smile on my face, though. For example, earlier in the week when I was in my SEC1 class, my smartest class, I don't remember what we were talking about, but one of the girls (the smartest in the class), Stella, said she wanted to live in the U.S.A. When I asked here where, without hesitation she said "by your house." AWWWW. Or like when I come into school and kinder is just getting done with classes or with lunch, and if they see me in the hall, students run down the hall yelling "hello Krystin teacher!"

Current students, past students, and ones that I'm pretty sure I've never taught before. The kinder kids are the most adorable, and they absolutely adore their teachers. They are also very touchy-feely, so they run up and hug me and hold my hand and put their hands on my butt (which, honestly, they don't realize that they're doing it. It just happens to be at the same height as their flailing arms).

January 28, 2011 Blog
Long awaited and way overdue

Last weekend was an interesting yet fun weekend. One of our Korean friends, Daria (that's her English nickname) rented a cabin at a little cabin resort in Daechon, which is about an hour north of here, for Saturday night. 9 of us went. Daria is the only one who drove, so 4 people went in her car, and the other 5 of us took the train, and we met up at the cabin. It was SUCH an adorable place, and such beautiful surroundings.

January 30, 2011 Blog
A couple more things . . .

As I pass my 6 month mark here in Korea, I've really started feeling nostalgic for the conveniences of home. A dryer. A washing machine. An oven. Foods that I love and miss. Going into a grocery store and being able to read the labels. I once bought what I thought was a bottle of lotion, only to realize, as I'm spreading it all over my arm, that it was body wash. At least I didn't buy a stick of "chap stick" and discover it was actually a glue stick. I really shouldn't let myself miss all these things terribly, as I still have 7 months to go here!

February 8, 2011 Blog
On Saturday a group of us took a day trip to Seoul. I saw some areas of Seoul that I had not seen before, wandering through some markets, had a delicious dinner at a Mexican restaurant (at a restaurant that is an American chain called 'On the Border,' so it was Mexican like at home), and ended the night at a British pub where I got a hard cider. Plus we went to the foreign food market, where I found applesauce cups!! I was so freaking excited, like a kid in a candy store. I haven't had applesauce for six and a half months and I've been craving it and missing it like you wouldn't believe. So of course I bought a pack. The first one I opened when I got home I dropped on the floor and it spilled all over. Figures. Luckily I have 5 more.

February 10, 2011 Facebook
My daddy is coming to visit in July!! Not 100% sure yet, but... my daddy MAY be coming to visit in July!!

> Kathy: And what am I, chopped liver? That's ok, I'll get over it. Somehow. :-P
> Krystin: lol Kathy of course I would be excited to see the rest of you!

March 27, 2011 Blog
Long awaited, round 2

A couple weekends ago a group of us went to Seoul, and I picked up the painting that I had won at an art auction two weeks prior to that. It's not a small painting, so it was a challenge to take it on the subway and then on the train back to Cheonan and in the taxi to my apartment (with 3 other people in the taxi), but I made it. It's called 'Kiss,' and here it is!

When we were in Seoul I had my first experience in a jjimjilbang, which is where we stayed overnight. A jjimjilbang is a large gender-segregated bathhouse, with pools, hot tubs, showers, saunas, massages, eating areas, sleeping rooms, and common rooms to hang out in. There are sleeping rooms that are for women only and men only, and co-ed rooms (for couples, or if you don't care). The showers, pools, and hot tubs are segregated because they are nude areas. No bathing suits allowed! The locker rooms are of course men and women only, but so are the bathing areas. When you first get there, you take off your shoes and put them in a locker for which you get a key. Then women go up the stairs to the left, men to the right. There you go to the locker room where your key also opens a locker in there. You put all your stuff in your locker, and either so in your birthday suit to the showers and then to the bathing areas (you have to shower before going into one of their public pools or hot tubs), or you put on the outfit that they give you when you check in. Since I'm not big on public nudity (I don't have a problem with other people doing it, I'm just not comfortable doing it), I sported the trendy getup and wandered around the place. By trendy, this is what I mean:

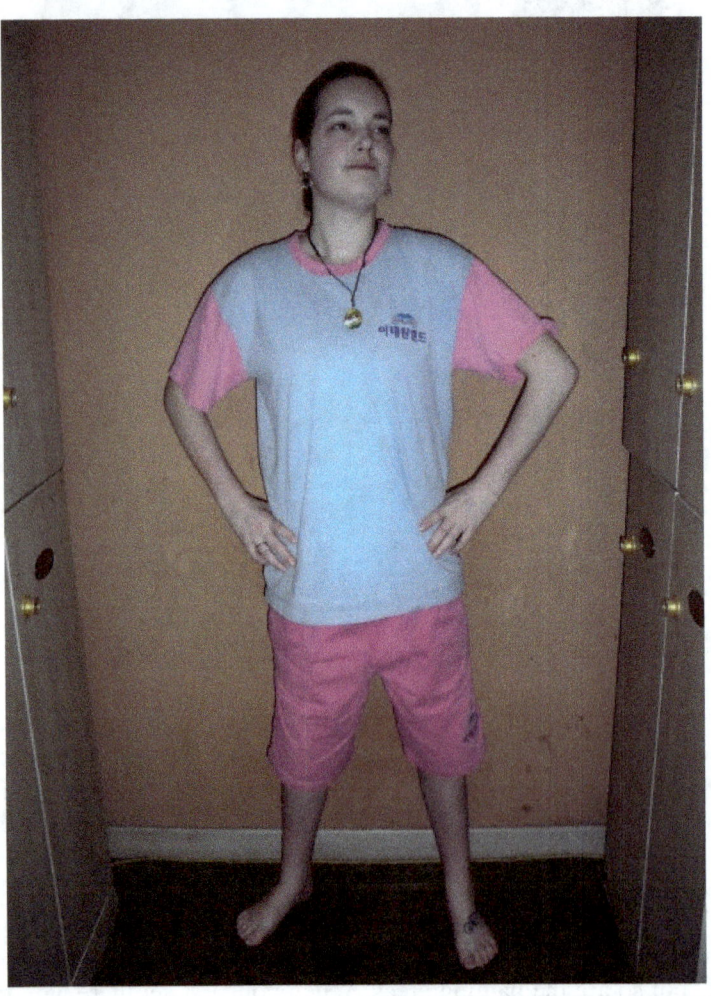

This particular jjimjilbang was HUGE. It has 5 floors, including a cafeteria and a common room where you can sit or lay on a mat and watch the big screen TV. The sleeping arrangement was probably the most interesting part. We slept in a women-only room, which was a long room that had cubbyholes on both sides of the room. Not just one level, but two; there were short ladders that you used to climb up into one of the second level cubbyholes. There was no standing in these, of course, so even the second level cubbyholes weren't any higher than shoulder-height. You grab a thin mat and pick a cubby that isn't occupied, and crawl right in. One person per cubby, of course. The pillows were the size and shape of a brick, and not much softer. Since you are in the shorts and t-shirt they require you to wear, and because it's still cold outside, the place was incredibly hot. It was probably some of the most uncomfortable and restless sleep I've ever had. I got maybe a total of 3 or 4 hours of sleep, and that's collectively, not all at once. It's fine for one night, and very cheap, less than $8 a night, but not something I'd want to do all the time.

April 6, 2011 Blog
We meet again
Spring has arrived! In general I feel my mood has greatly improved. I think I'm finally getting out of that winter funk, and the lovely spring weather is brightening my disposition. It was so nice this weekend that we had a rooftop potluck party on the roof of the building that some of my co-workers live in. It was in the high 50s, so what better excuse to be outside and enjoy the sun and beautiful weather. Everyone brought great food. Aaron brought Salad, Emily made tuna salad and rolls, Tessa made deviled eggs, Reuven brought chicken, Julie brought fruit, we had lots of veggies and healthy food, chips, cookies, and of course beer! I hadn't had a salad in 8 months, so that was probably the most satisfying thing of all. It was a good crowd, too.

April 19, 2011 Blog
A compilation of tidbits.
This weekend was amazing. I went to Seoul to see a cherry blossom festival there, and I wasn't at all disappointed. [After a couple of events] we hopped on the metro and went to the Han River for the cherry blossom festival there. Oh my was it beautiful. There is a park

area that runs for a mile or more along the river, which is also lined with cherry blossom trees.

May 13, 2011 Blog
Festivals

    We had last Thursday and Friday off of work. Thursday was Children's Day, which is a national holiday to honor children, I guess. That day, a large group of us went down to Hampyeong, which is a city that's a 3-hour train ride down south. Every year, hundreds of thousands of butterflies migrate there, so naturally, as Korea does, they turned it into a festival! It couldn't have been a more perfect day. We had gorgeous weather, and there was tons of stuff to see at the festival. We walked through a couple different greenhouses, one with cacti and one with lots of green plants and flowers. There was a small section of tents dedicated to cows and farming. They had lots of baby farm animals, and a few cows. I got to milk a cow! My first time milking a cow, too. It was exciting, and I have to admit, different from what I thought it'd be like. I got a pretty good stream of milk, though, so I must be a natural. :)

It was a great day. Great company, great weather, beautiful scenery. Like I said, it couldn't have been any better. It was being at an event like this on a gorgeous spring day, that I had to take a minute to take it all, and really enjoy the experience and being here in Korea and letting myself have the time of my life, and getting to experience these things that most people don't get to experience. What an amazing day!

On Saturday Jenny, Josh and I went to Seoul for the annual Buddhist and lotus lantern festival. Jenny and I went to Bongeunsa temple, which is a beautiful temple smack dab in the middle of the city. It's funny, though, when you're in the temple, aside from the skyscrapers sticking up behind the trees, you'd never know you're in the middle of a bustling city. It's so serene and quiet. I love the temples here in Korea. They're so beautiful and full of color.

At the top of the temple. It's such odd sense, my mind not knowing how to take in the picture. The beautiful nature and historical temple, and then all these skyscrapers shooting up into the sky in the background. Yet I still really like this photo. The two scenes definitely clash.

A small pond at the temple with fish and lotus lanterns in it. Fishy face!

May 18, 2011 Blog
As promised, I'm back again soon

One of the kinder students has seem to have taken an attachment to me. Julia, who I teach science special class to on Fridays, comes into the teacher's room almost every day after kinder is finished, while she waits to go to her bus, which comes last. It's so cute; of all the teachers she could choose to visit with, every day, without fail, she comes bouncing in to where I sit. Today Heather had special class with them, and she must have gotten some stickers either from Heather or she brought them from home, and Heather told me later that as soon as the bell rang to end class, she bolted out the door to come to the teacher's room to give me her two stickers. I was teaching a special class in a different class, so when Julia didn't find me in the teacher's room, she went around the classrooms until she found me! Which she did, because as I was cleaning up the room that I had finished teaching art with, in came Julia, and she gave me two stickers. Whenever she sees me for the first time each day, she shouts "KRYSTIN TEACHER!" and her face lights up and she gives me a big bear hug around my waist (since that's all the taller she is). It's moments like this that make this so rewarding. Julia has become one of my favorites, and maybe it's because I give her attention that she likes me so much. I have a feeling these kids don't get enough attention and love from their parents at home. I'm going to miss her.

On a somewhat similar topic (family), I have realized in the past couple months how lucky I am to have such a wonderful, close family. This thought came to me a while back. Normally I Skype with my dad every weekend. There have been a couple weekends when I've just been so busy and/or exhausted that we don't get a chance to talk, and maybe I won't get to sending a quick e-mail either saying sorry to have missed our chat. That Monday, I may get an e-mail from him, just short and sweet, asking how everything is and if I'm alright, and be in touch when I get a chance. I think this is something that I take for granted. So many people have distanced relationships with their parents. They can go for weeks, months, even years without talking. I go for 2 or 3 days, and he worries. Maybe it has something to do with me being on the other side of the world and he just wants to make sure everything is still alright, but even if I wasn't here, I'm still lucky to have such a great relationship with both my parents. When I hear people say "I don't really talk to my parents much" or even "I hate my parents," I think, wow, I can't even imagine. So, thanks mom and dad for being so great. Love you both!

June 7, 2011 Blog
Weekend at the beach

Today (Monday) was South Korea's Memorial Day, so we didn't have to work. On Saturday a large group of us went to Daecheon, which is out on the west coast, about an hour and a half away. They are famous for their huge beach there. We stayed in a small condo right off the beach, which consisted of a living room with a small kitchenette, with an open double-doorway separating it from an empty room in which you spread out blankets and pillows on the floor to sleep.

It was really cloudy on Saturday when we got there, but we still spent quite a bit of time at the beach. I even stuck my feet in the water! So I have now officially been in the Yellow Sea. Sunday it was VERY foggy most of the day - so foggy that we couldn't even see the sea while sitting 20 feet away. It cleared up late afternoon, though, and then it became a sunny, beautiful day. We pretty much spent all afternoon on the beach.

One huge difference that I have noticed over the past 10 months between Korean food habits and American food habits, is that they don't have nearly the wide variety of foods that we have in America. In restaurants, and in our homes, we cook and eat foods from every cuisine. American, Mexican, Chinese, Italian, French, Greek, Japanese, etc. etc. Here, they ONLY eat Korean food! They eat a lot of noodle soups, vegetable, seafood, kimchi, and rice. I ask my students what they eat for breakfast, lunch, and dinner, and ALL their responses are the same for all 3 meals: kimchi and rice. Except for dinner they usually also get fish and/or soup. Maybe once in a while their mom will make something with beef or pork. Seriously, these people don't know what they're missing out on! Maybe those in Seoul get a wider variety of foods if they go out to restaurants, but in their homes, their recipe boxes must be pretty bare. Koreans do love eating out at pizza and fried chicken places; every block will have either a pizza place or a fried chicken place on it. I can't wait to eat all my favorite kinds of foods when I get home. Oh how I miss chicken chow mein and enchiladas!

June 15, 2011 Blog
Let the countdown begin
   It hit me recently how little time I have left here. As of today (Wednesday), I have 50 working days left. I don't count the weekends, only the week days. In a little less than a month and a half, my dad, Kathy, Elliott, and Spencer will arrive. They will be here in Cheonan for a week, which I'm sure will fly by, and then it's my summer vacation, when we will all go to Japan for a week. After I return from vacation, I only have 3 weeks left! I feel there are still so many things I want to do and not enough weekends left.
   I find it interesting that even when we're completely out of our element, we still fall into a comfortable routine. One of the TV shows that I watch airs on Monday nights at home, which means I can watch it online Tuesday night here. I have fallen into this routine for the past couple months of almost every Tuesday stopping by this little Korean take-out place on my way home from work and getting dokkpokki (look it up - it's basically thick, short, rice noodles cooked in red pepper paste). Then I plop down in front of my computer to watch my show while eating my dinner. I go to that little restaurant probably twice a week. I used to go more, but I have cut back. The two ladies who work there have become my new BFF (best friends forever), even

though we don't understand each others' language. They try to talk to me, but I just have to shrug and say "mulayo" (I don't know). They are so friendly, and I'm going to miss that place when I leave. I've been tempted to have a Korean write a note for me asking if I can have their dokkpokki recipe, but I don't think I will. They might not be able to give it to me anyway.

On a similar note, it's also interesting how you start to fit in with the neighborhood after a while. There is another small restaurant on the first floor of our building that some of us go to usually once a week during one of our longer breaks. The owner knows by now that when I order dokkpokki, I don't want the fish in it. I don't even have to say it, but I can (sorta) understand when he yells back to the cook our order, not to put fish in the dokkpokki. He usually stands by the large window at the front of the store when he's not busy, and if we happen to walk by when he's standing there watching the world pass, we smile at each other and wave. It's little things like that that make me feel happy here, that make me feel a little sense of belonging.

Everyone has been feeling pretty stressed at work lately. Everyone, and I do mean everyone, has been feeling like we don't get enough praise. All we hear is the bad stuff. What we're doing wrong, and not even from Frank, but from our Korean co-teachers. Really it's not that often, only sometimes a co-teacher will say "I talked to so-and-so's mom, and she was wondering about this and that." Even though it's only once in a while a parent complains, that still need to be balanced out with some praise. Am I right or am I right? The other problem is, we all feel as if Frank is unhappy with our teaching styles, yet we never hear anything about it. Instead of telling us what he doesn't like or making suggestions of what we could do differently or better, he continues to be unhappy with us for months and months. How can we be better teachers if we don't know what we're doing wrong? I've been meaning to sit down with Frank or Summer for about a month now and find out how I can improve as a teacher, because although I'm working my butt off and trying my hardest, I was informed a while ago by a co-teacher that Frank doesn't think I'm a good teacher anymore. Do I know WHY? Of course not. None of us do. I know this is only a temporary job, and I only have 2 and a half teaching months left, but I want those to be good months, and I want to leave SLP on a positive note, and I want Frank to have a good impression of me and be able to look back on me in the future and say "she was a good teacher, she worked really hard." Unfortunately, our hard work goes unappreciated around here.

June 16, 2011 Blog
A few more things

    Last night some co-workers and I went out for dinner, and I pointed out that today begins my 50 day teaching day countdown. I brought it up because Jenny, who's contract ends at the same time, was sitting there. Aaron made some comment like "You can't wait to leave here." I said no, that's not completely true. I guess I took it in a negative way, thinking he thought I hated being here and couldn't wait to go home. When I gave him a quizzical look, he then said "all you talk about is going home to your cats." Ah. Yes. This is true. How sad is it that the only reason people think I can't wait to go home is to see my cats?? Honestly, if I had my Bela or Ella here with me in Korea, I could probably easily stay longer. Extend another year. But I miss my cats too much, I'm not gonna lie. In 50 years I really am going to be that creepy cat lady on the block. OK, so it's not just my cats. I've realized since being here that I like, and miss, the American way of life. I miss driving to a bar or restaurant to meet a friend for American style food. I miss the conveniences of America. I miss the appliances. I miss my friends. I'm also a traveler. I want to see the world. I want to travel to every and all countries and spend weeks seeing the world, but then I want to come home. Living in Scotland for 4 and a half months was alright, maybe because the UK is similar enough in lifestyle that I didn't miss my life in America too much. Or I just wasn't away long enough. Obviously I'm going to want to go back to the culture and lifestyle I grew up in. Many people can move to a new country and adapt to their new lifestyle after a certain amount of time, but I think I can't. I think I will always miss America if I'm away long enough. Don't get me wrong, I have completely enjoyed this experience and I wouldn't take it back for the world, but I'm ready to come home. Maybe if I do this teaching thing again, one of my kitties will come with. I hear cats don't have to sit in incubation very long. . . . Start packing your kitty bags, Ella!

June 28, 2011 Blog
Happy 11 months in Korea to me!

    I've discovered how much or how little I know about history (American or elsewhere) while teaching. I'm actually learning a lot, too, from some of the topics I cover in classes. Did you know that people didn't start eating tomatoes until the 1800s, because they thought they were poisonous? Or that people fart, on average, 14 times a day? Or even that I must be destined to be a writer, because right-handed people use the left side of their brain more, which controls speech, language, writing, logic, math, and science. OK, so I blew it in math and science class, but I'm logical, and great at writing, so there you have it. I guess the bit about tomatoes and farting isn't exactly history, more like useless information, but admittedly, I am learning history, too. Especially a lot of Korean history, which I knew absolutely none of before coming here.

I'm also learning a ton of synonyms and ways to explain the meaning of something. I know a lot of synonyms for words, but students are really testing my ability to conjure one up right on the spot. I've also never had to explain the meaning of a word or phrase so often. Numerous times a day a student asks me, "Teacher, what does this mean?" Oh ummm, shit- I mean, look it up in your phone dictionary. I mean, well, you see... For being good with words, and wanting to be a writer, I'm really NOT good with words!

July 25, 2011 Facebook
My family arrived safe and sound! 5 days until Japan.

August 7, 2011 Facebook
Vacation in Japan was fabulous, but I'm glad to be back in Korea. Feels like home!

Diary
[only about Japan, no date, but after the trip]
Afterthoughts

Japan is not exactly what I expected it to be. I guess I'm not sure quite what I was expecting, but it's so much more modern that I thought it would be. Of course it is; this is 21st century, after all. I think I had more an idea of what I wanted it to be like. Aside from Tokyo, there was a lot of Japanese architecture, which I absolutely loved. I was glad to see that still existed. It's strange to see the old Japanese-style houses and roofs tucked amongst the brick and concrete and glass structures. There is very little of this in Tokyo, however. Apart from signs and stores being in Japanese, I felt like I was walking through any major city of the U.S. However, when you do come upon a structure of long ago, you can't help but stop and take a picture. I love old architecture, which is probably why I also love Europe. The U.S. just doesn't have anything old. I also think I like Japanese architecture specifically. All the old temples and shrines amaze me. The idea that something has been around for hundreds of years or more, for some reason I can't grasp my mind around it (in a good way). It awes me, I suppose.

Tokyo is that land of black slacks and crispy white dress shirts. As tourists, there were many times when we felt like the black sheep in a herd of white sheep. Tokyo is a very business-y city. And big. Another concrete jungle of the world. It was a pleasant change to go to a temple and get away from the concrete and blacktops and be surrounded by trees. There were even women walking around in traditional kimonos. Most of the time, you would have no idea you were in the middle of a giant city populated by millions of people. I wish the U.S. had a longer history and beautiful things like in Asia. I wish we could've seen the gorgeous, serene mountains like in the movies, but we never had that opportunity. I guess it's a reason I'll have to go back to Japan.

I love the bowing custom of Japan and I'm going to miss it when I go back home to the U.S. Even the Koreans don't really do it. The Japanese bow for everything, even in this modern day and age, and I love how polite it makes everything feel. It makes a person feel acknowledged and appreciated, which is something people don't get enough of at home (or in Korea, for that matter). On the other hand, Koreans show their respect with their hand motions (putting their hand on their elbow or forearm when giving or receiving). But I could definitely get used to the bowing thing.

August 12, 2011 Blog
Japan

So I suppose you want to know all about Japan, eh? I apologize it has taken me a few days to post about it. As great as vacations are, they can also be exhausting. I got back Sunday night, and every night so far this week I've come home from work and crashed. Almost everything we did in Japan was outside, in the sweltering heat, and I'm just not made to be in that kind of humidity for long periods of time, so it really took it out of me. I guess it took 3 nights of getting 10 -11 hours of sleep for me to finally feel refreshed again!

That being said, aside from the heat, Japan was amazing. I can imagine that it would be even more amazing and wonderful in the fall, when it's not so hot, or in the spring, when it's not so hot AND the cherry blossoms are in bloom. It was a weird feeling, being in Japan, and I'm not sure how to explain it. It was a different feeling from being in Korea, or other parts of Europe when I traveled around. Japan has so much history, and it's own unique reputation, and so much hype. All week I kept looking at Elliott and saying "dude, we're in Japan." When people ask me where did I go, and what did I do, I almost feel like that part doesn't matter, I was in JAPAN! It was great to experience it with my dad, Elliott, Kathy, and Spencer. Since I hadn't seen them in a year, I think we were all on great terms all week and we got along well and just enjoyed each others' company. Of course there were the occasional sighs and irritations, but that mostly occurred when we were standing around in the heat trying to figure out what to do.

We stayed in Fukuoka for one night, so we didn't really do anything there.

Sunday we headed to Hiroshima. We all stayed in the same hotel, since we were only going to be there for one night. We pretty much devoted our one day there to visiting the site where the A-bomb was dropped, which was only 2 blocks from our hotel.

Monday, before going to Kyoto, we spent the day on Miyajima Island, which is an island right off the coast of Hiroshima, and considered part of Hiroshima. On the island, its main attraction is Itsukushima Shrine, which is a Shinto shrine. It also has a huge orange gateway in the waters, which is the symbol of Miyajima. On the island live hundreds of free-roaming deer. Inevitably, with all the tourism on the island, the deer are pretty domesticated.

After the island we headed for Kyoto on the fast bullet train, called the Shinkansen. We spent 4 nights in Kyoto. During our days in Kyoto, we saw many things. on Tuesday, we saw the silver temple, went on the Philosopher's walk, and went to a traditional handcraft museum, where we saw the tools and techniques that people used hundreds of years ago to make pretty much everything.

We spent one day in Nara, a town just outside of Tokyo that was the capital of Japan from 710-784. Nara is home to Todaiji temple, which is one of the most famous and historically significant temples in Japan. It was constructed in 752 as the head temple of all provincial Buddhist temples, which is why the capital was moved from Nara: to lower the temple's influence on governmental affairs. It houses Japan's largest bronze Buddha, and is also the world's largest wooden building.

On our last full day in Kyoto, we visited the golden pavilion and Nijo castle. The golden pavilion, or Kinkakuji, is a zen temple, whose top 2 floors are completely covered in gold leaf. It was the inspiration for the silver temple (a few decades later), which we had visited a couple days earlier. It was torched in 1950 by an angry monk. It was rebuilt within 5 years, and was re-gilded in 1987 at a huge cost. It sure is a beauty to look at!

Nijo castle was built in 1603, and used as the residence of Tokugawa Ieyasu, the first shogun of the Edo Period (1603-1867). Shortly after the fall of the Tokugawa shogunate in 1867, the castle was donated to the city and opened up to the public as a historic site.

On Friday we pretty much headed to Tokyo right away. The only thing we did that first day in Tokyo was check out some department stores, because we were told that walking through a department store in Japan in a cultural experience. I found the department stores were exactly the same as department stores in the U.S., except they sell some different things that we don't.

Saturday was my only full day in Tokyo, since I departed for the airport Sunday morning. So we decided the best way to see the best of Tokyo is to take a day-long bus tour. Kathy and Spencer went off to do something together, so my dad, Elliott, and I went on the tour. Next was Meiji shrine, which is a shrine dedicated to the deified spirits of Emperor Meiji. It's located in a densely forested park in the middle of the city. Next, on to the Imperial Palace East Garden. The palace buildings no longer exist, but we could see the gardens, which offered a lot of scenic beauty, as well as some great contrast between the concrete jungle and a quiet, peaceful garden.

Now it's back to the grind. Another week at work has already passed, which means I only have a little over 2 weeks left of teaching. It's hard to believe. I shall end with a picture that was taken of Elliott and me in a shop in a shopping mall right around the corner from our hotel in Kyoto. Enjoy!

August 18, 2011 Blog
Oh hey, long time no see

2 weeks and counting! As I'm sure many of you are wondering, I return home Labor Day weekend. I'm not sure if I'll be home that Thursday or Friday yet. I can't even believe how quickly the end is approaching. I can say out loud "only 2 weeks," but my brain hasn't really grasped the idea yet. I think as soon as my replacement gets here and I start training him/her, that's when it'll sink in.

I've been thinking lately, did you ever think of me as the kind of person who would uproot themself and do something like move to the other side of the world to teach English? I feel I've always been a "safe" and boring person. I realized recently that I kind of surprised myself with this whole adventure. Did I surprise you? I don't think me being here and doing this is something anyone expected. People keep telling me how brave I am for doing this. It seems to be something that a lot of recent college grads are doing, so is it really something that's so courageous anymore? I know that not everyone has the guts to do it, or the opportunity. I suppose there are a lot of factors that contribute to ending up in South Korea. You have to have a college degree, not have a job, and have pretty much no commitments at home. Such was my life before coming here. As I'm sure I've mentioned to many of you, I may be back in Korea after the New Year if I can't find a job at home. I guess this goes to show that I DO in fact have a wild, adventurous side!

I already miss my co-workers, and I haven't even left yet. I think it's more the idea of leaving the people I've shared a year of my life with. I hope to stay in touch with most of them, and if I'm lucky, our paths will cross again someday.

August 30, 2011 Facebook
Can't believe my last day of work has arrived. Time to say my goodbyes to all my fabulous co-workers and students. See you soon, America!

August 31, 2011 Facebook
Homeward bound. It's been real, Korea. I'll miss you, but not the smell of kimchi permeating your every nook and cranny.

August 31, 2011 Blog
Final Thoughts

Well, this may be my last post while I'm here in Korea. I feel like I should give some eloquent speech, but that's not my style, so I'll do my best.

We had our work farewell/welcome party on Friday night. It was a farewell to Heather, Jenny, and me.

I know the big questions here is, will I miss Korea? The answer is yes and no. There are certainly things that I will miss and things that I won't. I won't miss not having a dryer or washing machine. I won't miss the smelly streets. I won't miss the old ladies pushing me aside in the aisles of the grocery store. I won't miss SLP the school, but I will miss my co-workers. I'll miss a lot of my students. I know I always say that I don't like kids, and that's true, but some of them did grow on me. Even though I was always telling students to get out of the teacher's room, or to be quiet, or whatever, I still cared, and I hope they know that. I think the hardest thing for me this whole year was to remember that they're just kids. I fret that in the back of my mind I always expected them to act mature, like adults. But they're not adults. They're just kids, and they want to play and have a good time, and I think I frequently forgot that. I know that on my last day, I will give all my students a hug, I will tell them good luck, and that I will miss them. And maybe give them a cookie as well.

The impression of Korea that I have leaving here is extremely different from what I expected when I first got here.

Chapter 8

An Interim Year Between Korea and Transplant

September 1, 2011 Facebook
Back on American soil!

September 6, 2011 Facebook Jessica Leigh to Krystin Engstrand
Hey Krystin! Just wanted to let you know that Robbie almost broke down in tears when he realized you weren't going to be there today for Art class!!! The kids were talking about having Amy and Robbie was like "No! Krystin teacher!!!" and then he said "Two art teachers!" -- he was grasping at straws...I thought he was going to break down when I said you were at your house in the US, but he kept it together. I told him that he could draw a picture for you and we could mail it to you...hope you are doing great! love ya!

September 19, 2011 Email
Stuff
Krystin to dad:
[I had written to her earlier about the excessive amount of clothing she owned]

OK, I lied; I didn't get all my stuff out of the hallway. Sorry. I promise, promise, promise that I will get it done tomorrow (Tuesday - which it will be by the time you read this). I don't know why I'm procrastinating so much on this. I just need to get it done!

Oh, and I've been meaning to talk to you about something ever since you sent me the e-mail about buying clothes. Yes, I bought a lot of clothes while I was in Korea. I did so because I could, and because it was cheap. Clothes are a lot cheaper in Korea, and were especially cheap in Thailand, which is where I did a lot of shopping also. I could afford it, though. I was making enough that I could send money home every month to pay my loan bill, and buy myself food and pay my utilities bill. I know that I didn't *need* more clothes exactly, and yes, I would've come home with a lot more money if I hadn't gone shopping a lot, but the way I see it is that I got lots of souvenirs that I can wear, and when people ask me "oh that's such a nice dress, where did you get it?" I can say "oh, Singapore!" or "oh, South Korea!" Can YOU say that about any of your clothes?? (Never mind your DMZ shirt). I haven't bought any more clothes since I've been home, don't worry, and going through all my drawers and such since I got home has made me realize that I don't need to buy more clothes for a very long time.

Just thought you should know, because I feel like I need to defend myself and my shopping choices.

Love you.

September 20, 2011 Facebook
The Marines have banned soldiers from farting out loud in Afghanistan because it's offensive to the natives, but actual bombs are still OK?? (Of course silent farts are still allowed, under the "Don't Ask, Don't Smell" policy).

September 21, 2011 Facebook
Teaching abroad round 2: Ukraine! Application: sent.

September 22, 2011 Email
Possible job
Krystin to dad, mom:
I sent my resume and a cover letter to a woman about another English teaching job that could start in January. In the Ukraine!

September 28, 2011 Email
jobs
dad to Krystin:
As I said last night, and I meant it, going back to S Korea means again delaying your departure from the house and "growing up." I don't think that's a great idea. LY [I *very* strongly discouraged Krystin from going back to South Korea for a second year of teaching, both because she needed to get a real job and get on with her life and because she needed better medical care than she'd get there. She wasn't happy about my view, but she didn't go.]

December 13, 2011 Facebook
All I want for Christmas is health insurance. Unless anyone just happens to have an extra bottle of insulin sitting around . . .

December 17, 2011 Facebook
This year I have volunteered to make the Christmas turkey, and it shall be the best, most awesomely delicious turkey ever. Challenge accepted!

December 23, 2011 Facebook
Today is my day to shine-- Time to stuff and cook my 21 pound baby! My turkey baby, that is.

December 23, 2011 Facebook
My turkey baby is done, carved, and ready to be nommed. Damn I did good; sometimes I even amaze myself.

December 24, 2011 Facebook
What a wonderful day!

December 28, 2011 Facebook
You WILL see me published in 2012, and that's a promise.

January 3, 2012 Facebook
Job and grad school, or back to Korea? Decisions, decisions . . .

> *Krystin*: Plan: Get part-time job. Be resourceful and save, save, save. Take GRE [Graduate Record Examination, required for admission by many graduate schools and programs]. Go back to Korea in late spring/early summer and have a blast. Take grad school courses online while doing so. Ready . . . go!

January 10, 2012 Email
Gary to Kathy:
　　FYI. I sent this this morning. There has been no easy way to bring this up, and even Pat commented one time that Krystin pays more attention when something's first presented in writing. She won't react well, but I just don't think I have/had much choice. She's not doing a DAMN THING that I can see to get a job or get going.

---------- Forwarded message ----------
Gary to Krystin:
Krystin,
　　My therapist Richelle told me, at the end of my sessions with her (when the discussions were focusing more on you kids than on me), that parents have a responsibility to "launch" their children, get them going independently in life, and that I needed to do that with you. I am failing in doing so. It is past the time when you should be out on your

own. You need to focus your efforts on getting a job and moving towards an independent life in your own place. (How many of your friends--your age--still live with mom and/or dad?) The job market is tight, yes, and you may have to work more than one job to make ends meet, but you are a smart young woman and I am confident that you can figure it out.

You will always be warmly welcome to visit 4020, of course, but "home" needs to be somewhere else. In order for you to have a goal, I am setting May 1, 2012 as a "move out by" date. I suppose you could say that I'm "kicking you out," but it's something I believe I have to do. When I promised you two, nearly five years ago, that I would not boot you out, I confess that I had no idea you'd still be in the house five years later. (I will not permit Elliott to stay home as long as you have stayed, but I suspect he's going to move out on his own initiative after college.)

I have seen no visible movement on your part towards getting a job or becoming independent; you have declined to apply for a dozen or more jobs at the University where I could have helped you out. (I have concluded you really don't want to work at the University, which is fine, but I'm going to quit looking for jobs for you.) You should be applying for 5-6 jobs per day--and should be in touch with a temp agency, which often provides a foot in the door to an employer. You have to get going because you will need to be able to afford a place to live beginning May 1.

And BTW, Kathy has nothing to do with this nor have I consulted her about it. I have been thinking about this for a considerable while. Your mother didn't have anything to do with my starting to think about this, but I have discussed my thoughts with her and she agrees with me.

I want you to know that I am not angry or upset with you in any way; I am just making a straightforward statement to you. I have dawdled on sending this for some time because I keep hoping you're going to tell me you've gotten a job and are planning to move forward. But that seems not to be happening, alas.

LY

Kathy to Gary:

Oh boy. I was actually thinking about this the other day and wondering if it was going to come up again. You'll have to let me know if you get any kind of response. [I do not believe I ever did, at least not in writing. We may have had a conversation.]

January 11, 2012 Email
Talk & cover letter
Krystin to dad:
    I have written a cover letter that I would like you to look at. It's a generic one that will be tweaked for each job that I apply for. It was this daunting task of writing a decent cover letter that I think has kept me from applying to a lot of jobs, but now that it's done, I feel I can get the ball rolling faster.

January 16, 2012 Facebook
The ONLY good thing about going to the ER is that mentioning I have diabetes always gets me to the top of the list.

> *Krystin*: Feels like there's been a knife in my side for the past week, causing excruciating pain, and now nausea. :/
> *Krystin*: Had a CT scan done, there was some kidney blockage issue, but no worries, nothing a few good meds can't fix. I'm on the mend!

January 21, 2012 Facebook
Would have been nice if they had discovered that kidney infection the first time in the ER. Thursday night's round 2 resulted in being admitted. IV fluids and antibiotics in full swing. Hopefully home on Sunday!

January 22, 2012 Facebook
They asked me if I want to go home today, and of course I said yes, but secretly I want to stay. I strangely enjoy being here and being fed and taken care of . . .

January 22, 2012 Facebook
This trip to the hospital has been like taking a car to the mechanic. I go in for one thing and they find 4 more problems! Oye.

January 23, 2012 Facebook
After 4 days of being poked and prodded, I'm home!! =)

January 25, 2012 Facebook
The cute tech guy at the hospital who did the ultrasound told me I had to put my arm above my head so it was easier for him to work. The heavy pain killers I'd been given washed all discretion out the window; I asked him if he often got girls to put their arms above their head. O.o

January 26, 2012 Email
thinking about jobs
Dad to Krystin:

I know you're looking for a short-term job so you can go to S Korea in the fall, but I think your health is fragile enough now (and will remain so if you don't get that A1c down drastically) that you should put S Korea on the back burner and try for a U job (or at some outfit that has very good health coverage). I forgot about the pre-existing conditions requirement that some places have--that could be a big problem for you. The U [University of Minnesota] does not have any such clause--you're hired, you're covered. And as I said, the U's cost for employees is a lot lower than employee costs in private-sector organizations.

Something to think about, anyway. I wish you'd get your name in for the CEHD job. [College of Education and Human Development. I must have referred a position opening to her.]

Dad

FB Krystin Engstrand
January 27, 2012 · Minneapolis ·
Congrats to my dad and Kathy on their marriage today!!!

January 27, 2012 Email
Krystin to dad, mom:

Are we related?? [Elliott and Krystin, taken at Murray's restaurant in downtown Minneapolis, at the family celebratory dinner after Kathy and I were married late on a Friday afternoon.]

February 10, 2012 Facebook
Oh, hello $23,000 hospital bill. You are not welcome here.

February 21, 2012 Email
interview
Dad to Krystin:
   Good luck with the interview.
   But Krystin, I'd still like you to rethink this. You've now essentially wasted the last 6 months doing nothing productive for your life/career or society because you want to go back to S Korea. Moreover, you're going to do nothing productive for your life/career for the NEXT six months as well (other than hold some meaningless grunt job at low wages). Going to S Korea will do nothing for your life/career. You've done that already--the first time was a wonderful learning and life experience; the second time is a waste of time because you aren't going into teaching (here or there).
   Meantime, you've still got no health insurance, haven't had your eyes or teeth dealt with in a long time, and aren't on the road to any kind of career. Lindsey has just applied for a job in Kathy's office,

Chris is advancing her education and artistic career, and you're doing zip to get along/advance.

I continue to believe firmly that your plan is a bad idea and that you should abandon it so you can start doing something real--and getting on the path to writing, if you still want to do that. (And BTW, one of my high-school classmates is the chair of English at Metro State, which might not be a bad place to look for schooling if the U turns out not to work.)

But what you're doing now is wasting time and your life through the summer of 2013. How is it you can think this is a good idea?

Love you.

Krystin to dad:

Then I guess I'll stop wasting my life, if it's what makes you happy. Since what would make me happy apparently doesn't matter. It's not always about what is best for someone. Sometimes what is best is not the same as what makes someone happy. Doing what other people want you to do because it's "what's best" can only make a person depressed. Good for Chris and Lindsey. I'm not them. I'm just saying. Easy for you to say that I should continue my education when you're not the one who has to pay for it anymore.

Dad to Krystin:

You nailed it right here: "Sometimes what is best is not the same as what makes someone happy." I agree completely. What is best for you (right now) is apparently not what will make you happy. I am arguing that what you need to do is what is best for you now (get a real job, go to school), because in the longer run it is what will make you happier (later). Much happier. Right now you are dawdling and killing time and getting nowhere.

(I was not happy about going back to graduate school when you were little, but it had become clear I needed to do that because it was best for me (and you and E and mom). So I did.)

Dad

February 21, 2012 Facebook
Apparently I've reached that point in life where I need to do things in life that make other people happy. Sorry Korea, dad thinks I need to get a "real" job, and we can't disappoint dad. Pfffff.

February 22, 2012 Facebook
I'd rather have a life of "oh wells" than a life of "what ifs."

February 23, 2012 Email
your comment
Dad to Krystin (bcc Kathy):

As I told you all along when you were growing up, you did not need to get good grades for ME. You needed to get them for Krystin.

And now, as I talk with you about S Korea, it is not because I need you to make me happy. From a very personal standpoint, it doesn't matter to me if you go to S Korea or not. What I am suggesting to you is that it is not in KRYSTIN'S best interests for her to go to S Korea. And your friends are wrong, as are you: It is not always wise to do what makes you happy. I would be happier if I didn't go into work every day until 10:00 and left at 2:00. But that would not be wise. Going to S Korea might make you happier but it certainly is not wise. I don't think it is, your mother does not think it is, nor do several other adults I know who know you think it is. You are squandering two years of your life.

I think you owe me an apology, on Facebook, for your cheap shot on Facebook.

February 23, 2012 Email
My thoughts – FWIW ["for what it's worth"]
Kathy to Krystin (bcc Gary)

I've been thinking a lot about you and your plans lately, and I have a couple things I need to say. I'm not your mother and I have no plans to lecture you. I do think, however, that I need to be honest with you about what I've been thinking recently, even though you haven't asked my opinion.

You know your dad (and your mom, too) are concerned about the life choices you've been making. I'm certain you know that they both love you and want the best for you. I'm also certain you know that you are the best one to decide what is best for yourself. Apparently you've determined that going back to Korea and possibly (though not aggressively) finding some kind of temporary employment until then is what is best for you.

I don't understand your reasons for making those decisions, and maybe if I did, I wouldn't be as disappointed about them as I am. But the fact is, I've gotten to know you over the past few years and I've come to really like you. I think you have a great personality and a wonderful writing style. I have the idea that if you put your mind to something, you can make it work. I know you have a goal of being a writer and I think that's a good goal to have. What I don't understand, tho, is your lack of (or at least this is the way it appears to me) any drive to pursue that goal.

To be blatantly honest, it appears to me that you're doing everything you can think of to avoid pursuing what you say is your dream. If there's a reason for it, I don't know what it could be. I agree with your dad, in that going back to Korea is not a good idea. I wish you would either reconsider or help us to understand why you're not pursuing what it is you say you want to do in life.

We both want you to be happy and we're both ready and willing to help you make the leap to the next big thing but (speaking for myself, now), I don't think a job in a restaurant or another year in Korea is the next big thing. To me those seem like fun or easy things to do while avoiding the responsibilities of life.

OK, now I'm starting to sound like a lecture, so I'll stop. If you'd like to help me understand why you've chosen the course in life that you have, I'm all ears. Or if you'd prefer that I mind my own business, just say the word. I'd just like to help if I can.

February 24, 2012 Email
thank you
Dad to Krystin (bcc Kathy)
    for the additional comment on Facebook. I appreciate it.

February 27, 2012 Email
Job
Krystin to dad:
    176821 [The number of a University of Minnesota job posting.]
    It's not glorious, but I'm certainly qualified. Would this be a position, however, that provides benefits, do you think?

Dad to Krystin:
    It's 100% time so it would include benefits, yes.
    I'll look to see if there are any others that might fit.

March 5, 2012 Emails
writing
Dad to Krystin:
 I hope you're working on job applications as diligently as you are your other writing.
 At this point in your life, the job applications MUST come first.

March 9, 2012 Facebook
 I went to an online thesaurus and looked up 'ninjas.' it told me ninjas could not be found. Well played, ninjas. Well played.

March 12, 2012 Facebook
 My story is published online!! Check out my story on the We Are Diabetes website. Thanks Asha for giving me this opportunity and taking a chance on me! I hope others can learn from my mistakes. I'm so excited to share this with everyone. =)

wearediabetes.org
We Are Survivors - Krystin: It's never too late. - We Are Diabetes
http://www.wearediabetes.org/articles/71/we-are-survivors-krystin-its-never-too-late [This is the link that worked as of July, 2018.]

March 12, 2012 Email
My story is online!
Krystin to [a number of family members, including aunts, uncles, and parents]:
Hey everyone,
 My story has been published! My friend Asha, who I've known since middle school, is the founder of a website called We Are Diabetes. The site has been up less than a year, but it has already been recognized nationally as a resource site for people with diabetics. It has stories, forums, and other resources. She agreed to put my story up her website, and it's up!
 She cropped out some parts since it was so long, so if you would like to read the full version, let me know. I'm very excited to share this with others. I hope you like it!
Love, Krystin

March 14, 2012 Email
Favor, again
Krystin to dad:

    Ok, I've waited until the last minute to ask you this, but I have a huge favor to ask. I hate, hate, hate asking for money, but once again I'm kinda in a desperate situation. I have a bill coming up and I don't have enough to cover all of it. I need about $120. I get paid by Jeff and Randy next week after they get back, but that will be past my bill due date. I know I already owe you money from helping me out last month, but until I get a job and/or my tax refund I don't know what else to do. Please don't give me a lecture about needing to find a job, I already know that, and as you know I've been more active about applying to jobs. I don't qualify for unemployment, and the other option I can think of is going to the bank and declaring bankruptcy, which I really don't want to do. :/ But if I have to, I will. Ugh. And no, I have not been spending money on shopping or other indulgences. I've been very tight with my money for the past couple months.

Dad to Krystin:
    OK.
    But I do expect to be paid back the $200 once you receive a paycheck. Like $100 from each of the first two checks.

Krystin to dad:
    Of course.

March 23, 2012 Facebook
FINALLY, a job interview at the U (University of MN, for you out of towners)!! Fingers crossed they see how awesome I am and want to hire me. Time to dazzle.

March 29, 2012 Facebook
Apple was considering making an iPod for kids, but apparently the name 'iTouch Kids' didn't sit too well.

April 6, 2012 Facebook
I've had an insulin pump for over 3 years now, and people still ask me what it is and how it works. Of course I don't mind explaining, but for those of you who may still be curious, here you go.

medicinenet.com
Insulin Pump for Diabetes Information - MedicineNet

April 12, 2012 Facebook
All this applying, waiting, interviews, waiting, and rejection is depressing and exhausting. I need a vacation from unemployment!

April 16, 2012 Facebook
I tried to be funny at my doctor appointment today. She asked me if I watch what I eat. I told her "yup, I do every time I eat. I watch it as it leaves the plate and goes into my mouth." She was not amused, which left me awkwardly laughing alone at my own joke.

April 19, 2012 Facebook
Finally decided to do what's best for ME, and this time I'm sticking with it. Late summer/early fall 2012, look out Korea, I'm coming back to ya!

April 20, 2012 Facebook
[my guess is that this Facebook post was put up after the email exchange that follows]
Ugh, the worst feeling in the world is having someone disappointed in you. Especially when it's family.

April 20, 2012 Email
Emails
SPA [Sponsored Projects Administration, the grants-management unit of the University of Minnesota]
Krystin to dad:
 Ok, so you can be as irritated with me as you like, but I want you to know why I turned them down. I did not want a position that was only 6 months and that did not offer benefits. I figured telling them I was accepting another position sounded more polite than saying I wasn't interested in the job. I'm sorry I lied to you, but I did not want to tell you because I was afraid this would happen. However, it happened anyway, and I'm sorry you had to find out this way. I'm sorry it made you almost look stupid. I know we have discussed that right now I need to take anything that I'm offered. so I have no excuse for this. Obviously I'm going to keep applying for jobs. Go ahead, give me your lecture about how you're disappointed; I deserve it.

Dad to Krystin:
Here's the email message to you that I have been deciding whether or not to send:

So your email to me that you had received a message from SPA that you were not chosen was simply a lie. You were asked to come in and turned them down. Do you have any idea how angry I am about this? Not only did you not take an opportunity to be considered for a good job, after I put in a word for you, you lied about it to me.

If that's your approach, then get yourself to S Korea fast, because I'm not particularly keen on having you around the house. I am disgusted. And you may not plan on returning to the house when you come back to the U.S.

There is one lame explanation I could offer to Pamela. [Associate Vice President and director of SPA, and a friend of mine. She told me that they had offered Krystin a position but that Krystin had turned me down. I was not happy.] *That you had decided to go to S Korea, so turned them down, but now are having second thoughts. But I'm not going to tell her that unless you commit to taking a job if it's offered-- and forget going back to S Korea, at least for now.*

So what do you want to do?

Krystin to dad:
Well either way you're disgusted with me, so I could choose to take an interview here and have you still be disgusted with me and not want me around, or I can go back to Korea and have you even MORE angry with me and not even want me in the house. It's a lose-lose situation for me. Obviously the biggest issue is that I lied to you, and it's going to take a lot for you to forgive me. Well, actually at this point is appears you're never going to forgive me for this. I made a mistake, that's all I can say. I'm sorry I betrayed your trust. You could tell Pamela that I was planning to go back to Korea but that it didn't work out, and if they call me for an interview, I'll take it. Like we discussed last night, I'm still going to pursue things with Korea, but I'm also going to keep applying for jobs here, and if I get offered one, I'll put Korea on hold. That's the best I can do.

Dad to Krystin:
I accept your apology. You made a mistake. I will not forget but I will forgive. Just don't do it again. If you pursue this and other jobs while also considering S Korea, I'm glad to have you around. I trust

you understand that it's because I love you and want to see the best for you that I get so upset. If I didn't care, I wouldn't get angry. I do not get upset about people or things I don't give a rip about.

You should know that I STILL think going back to S Korea is no gain for you. It's not a new experience and I don't think it adds much to your resume. And as I've said before, it simply postpones you getting a good job--and one that allows you to live away from me/the house and would allow you perhaps time to write as well as go back to grad school.

Do you wish me to email Pamela, saying essentially what you said in your last message to me? But if you are interviewed, and accept a job, then you simply CANNOT walk out of it in a couple of months because you want to go to S Korea. If it's a temp job (which you should have thought of), and it doesn't lead to a permanent job, it's at least giving you the opportunity to earn some money for six months, pay your bills, pay me back, and perhaps even save some.

Krystin to dad:
Yes, you can e-mail her. It's technically not completely lying to her about S. Korea, since that WAS my plan. And I promise to be honest with you from here on out.

Dad to Krystin:
OK. Thank you.

Dad to Krystin:
P.S. You could have told me that you have really concluded you do not want to do anything except return to S Korea, and I would have accepted that as an explanation for why you turned SPA down, and I still would have accepted your apology about lying to me.

I want it to be clear to both of us that YOU decided to go ahead and be considered for the job at SPA. Yes, I have strongly encouraged you, but this was ultimately your call. I did not HAVE to email Pamela--it could simply have been left that you'd taken another job (S Korea) and no one would think anything more about it.

Right?

Krystin to dad:
I'm glad to hear that now, but I did not know that before. I honestly was afraid to tell you how I felt about going back to S. Korea, which

is why I asked you about it last night. I realized that I finally needed to be honest and let you know that going back is really what I want to do. At the time, I made a quick, rash decision to tell SPA that I had accepted another position with the intention of telling you my wanting to pursue Korea again, and then I chickened out talking to you about it right away, and instead lied about it, because I was afraid of how you would react, and have you disappointed in me. And having you disappointed in me is one of the things I hate most. It's been a battle in my head for a while between getting a job here and going back to Korea. I WANT to go back to Korea, but I know that getting a job here and settling down and continuing to work on my writing is BETTER.

The only thing I fear is if I get a job here, yes I'll have an income and it will allow me to get out of the house, but will I be happy? Will it only make me more depressed? Will I spend every day at work thinking "I could be in Korea right now"? I don't completely see teaching in Korea as postponing adulthood and being worthless on a resume. I think I gain a lot of knowledge, life experience that can be useful in a workplace, and further enhance my office skills. No, it's not a new experience, but it also helped me grow as a person, I gained more confidence and independence, and I learned a lot about myself, kind of like a self-discovery experience. A second year would only double all that, and I feel it would make me feel better as a better, and more happy with myself and who I am. I realized that doing something that affects the lives of others (In this case, teaching English, being able to look at the students' progress after a time and be able to say "I did that. They are better English speakers because of me") is what makes me feel worthwhile as a person, like I'm making a difference, like I'm not just another person who is born and dies without doing anything with their lives. Yes, I could have my writing, but no matter how much I write and write and write, it's never guaranteed that I'm going to get published. Perhaps someday, but that could take years. In the meantime, being in Korea is what keeps me going, keeps me motivated, and keeps me happy. Seeing all those smiling kids every day, eager to see me, and being able to praise them and be proud of them, and myself, when they succeed. Do you understand where I'm coming from?

Sorry this has turned into me blabbing. I guess the Pandora's Box of my mind has been opened. I know I'm already 27 and I can't delay getting a full-time permanent job for much longer. But what happens if I get offered a job both from Korea and the U at the same time??

Then I'm back in the same position and battling which one to take, based on what I WANT to do and what I SHOULD do. :/

Dad to Krystin:

One of the characteristics that distinguishes children from adults is that children mostly do what they WANT to do, not what they SHOULD do. Adults, on the other hand, at least those with a more fully-developed sense of responsibility, will usually do what they SHOULD do rather than what they WANT to do (if there is a conflict between them).

But see the comments below, inserted in your text. [The italicized text interspersed in her message is my responses.]

On Fri, Apr 20, 2012 at 10:20 AM, Krystin Engstrand wrote:

The only thing I fear is if I get a job here, yes I'll have an income and it will allow me to get out of the house, but will I be happy? Will it only make me more depressed? Will I spend every day at work thinking "I could be in Korea right now"? I don't completely see teaching in Korea as postponing adulthood and being worthless on a resume.

My view is a little different. The first time you did it is a great addition to your resume, absolutely no doubt about that. The second time, from a hiring standpoint, doesn't mean much. But I do think you're postponing adulthood.

I think I gain a lot of knowledge, life experience that can be useful in a workplace, and further enhance my office skills. No, it's not a new experience, but it also helped me grow as a person. I gained more confidence and independence, and I learned a lot about myself, kind of like a self-discovery experience. A second year would only double all that,

This is where we may not agree. I'm frankly not sure you have that much more to learn with this experience. You don't give yourself enough credit: You learned much while there for a year, and in fact probably learned about 90% of what there is to be learned with that kind of experience. Maybe there are a few additional matters you can learn around the margins, but I doubt it's much that will be important to your life.

and I feel it would make me feel better as a better, and more happy with myself and who I am. I realized that doing something that affects the lives of others (In this case, teaching English, being able to look at the students' progress after a time and be able to say "I did that.

They are better English speakers because of me") is what makes me feel worthwhile as a person, like I'm making a difference, like I'm not just another person who is born and dies without doing anything with their lives.

I don't dismiss this as a trivial point at all. It's very important. But then my question is: Why don't you return to the U, get the postgraduate degree in teaching, and become a teacher here? You can certainly have just as much of an impact on people's lives here as you can in Korea. (There is clear research in education about the tremendous impact teachers can have on students.) Making a difference is something that's always been important to me, too, and in my own little way, I do that quite a bit at the University.

Yes, I could have my writing, but no matter how much I write and write and write, it's never guaranteed that I'm going to get published. Perhaps someday, but that could take years.

Often does. You should not give up.

In the meantime, being in Korea is what keeps me going, keeps me motivated, and keeps me happy. Seeing all those smiling kids every day, eager to see me, and being able to praise them and be proud of them, and myself, when they succeed. Do you understand where I'm coming from?

Yes, but you're bringing an altogether new perspective on your teaching into this. You've never spoken like this about the teaching experience. In fact, you have generally indicated that you liked everything about Korea EXCEPT the teaching. This is a rather new perspective.

Krystin to dad:
We can talk about this more at some point.
I have an interview with SPA on Wednesday. Yes, for real this time. I also have an e-mail back from Sally already about a position in Gwangju.

Dad to Krystin:
Still a temp job? If so, as I wrote before, it could be the best of all worlds: you can work 6 months, save some, pay debts, and see how it goes. If the temp job led to an offer of a permanent job, then you'd have to decide what to do. If you liked SPA, you could stay. If not, and no other interesting job appeared, you could go to Korea.

As for making a difference, I think that's true of many jobs at the U.

April 25, 2012 Facebook
I am FINALLY a working member of society!! Today I accepted a job at the University. This puts Korea on hold, but only for a little bit, as this is only a 6-month position (but with promotion potential). Happy Krystin!! =)

Email
finance matters
Dad to Krystin 4/26/12
OK, so here's the plan as I understand it.
I've now lent you $1200, so you'll give me $200 per check for 6 checks. (I'm willing to wait until you receive your second paycheck-- the first one might be only partial because you won't be there a full pay period, and you'd be able to get a little money in your checking account without having to pay me immediately.) If you want to write me 6 post-dated checks, that would be fine. LY

Facebook May 1, 2012
Ahhh the joys of a new job. So. much. information. Brain . . . overload.

May 4, 2012 Email
Another favor
Krystin to dad:
Ich habe eine kleine probleme. I went to Super America this morning to get some cash to pay for my parking and lunch today, and discovered I have a -$22 balance. Apparently one of my bill pays that I had set up to make automatic deductions from my bank account started last month, even though I thought I had signed up for it to start this month. So now I'm in a bit of a pickle, because it means I have NO money to last me until my first paycheck. Or for parking or lunch today, even though I still parked in the lot because I have nowhere else to park. So, I may need to take out one more I.O.U. before I get paid. Here's what I propose: The check I get from Jeff and Randy will be $335. You could write me a check for that much, and then when I get it from them, I can write the whole thing over to you. Or, if that is too much right now, then maybe another one for $200 and I can make you out another dated check and put it in the envelope with the others. (I

prefer the first option, but I understand if you don't want to do that). Yes, I know this means I was not keeping a close enough eye on my finances. I obviously didn't realize the automatic deduction was going to start LAST month. Now I know. [I seem not to have responded. Presumably I gave her some money.]

May 8, 2012 Email
Story
Krystin to dad:

I sent [an English professor friend] an e-mail and asked him if he's had a chance to look at my story, and if he thinks it would be good to use as one of my writing samples when applying to the creative writing program. We'll see what he has to say!

May 30, 2012 Email
checks, etc
dad to Krystin:

I will cash the first of the $200 checks you gave me. I assume that's OK.

Would you like to give me some amount of money out of each of your checks for saving? To help prevent you from spending it? Or do you think you can (or should) discipline yourself to start setting aside money? (Obviously, that will be easier once all my $200 checks are cashed.) Either way is fine with me, but I'm glad to help if you wish.

June 8, 2012 Email
Fw: Re: Story submission
Krystin to dad, Kathy:

I had e-mailed this diabetes magazine about publishing my story (as you can see in my original e-mail), and this is what I got back. They're interested in my story!! Now I just have to find a way to separate it into smaller stories. This is very exciting!! My first publishing opportunity. :)

From: Diabetes Health Managing Editor <editor@diabeteshealth.com>
Subject: Re: Story submission
To: "Krystin Engstrand" <kengstrand227@yahoo.com>
Date: Friday, June 8, 2012, 4:58 AM

How about breaking the 6000 words into 6 stories and make it a series. Are you submitting this pro bono?

On Jun 7, 2012, at 11:45 AM, Krystin Engstrand wrote:

Hello,
I am writing to ask you about submitting a story to your magazine. I have written a memoir-type story about being in a hospital in Paris with ketoacidosis (and the 26-hour bus ride from Warsaw that brought me to Paris) back in 2006. I read the submission guidelines on your website, and my story doesn't fit 100% in the guidelines. My story is a bit longer, almost 6,000 words, but I could cut it down drastically if need be. It is a personal story about strength and survival, and I am wondering if that is something your magazine is interested in publishing. I hope to be in touch soon to discuss this. Thanks for your consideration.

June 27, 2012 Email
coins
Dad to Krystin:
Krystin,
 I still think you should look at other U jobs, at least until you're told you have a permanent job with SPA.

Krystin to dad:
 Supervisor David has already been mentioning getting me hired full time when the new fiscal year starts. I can keep an eye on the U employment site, but sounds like I'll get to stay here at SPA.

Dad to Krystin:
 If you get hired for real, that obviously would be wonderful! (Or I hope you think that--that SPA is a good place for a day job while you work on writing.) But it does no harm to keep an eye on the position postings. (Maybe the bookstores will hire you as assistant director.)
 Have you given any thought to a date when you'd like to move to your own place? I guess my thought has sort of been after the New Year--maybe Feb 1 or something like that? Would that give you enough time to get rid of, or at least pay down, debts and save a little? (I'm not kicking you out, I'm just assuming you WANT to get out, as we've talked about before.)

July 18, 2012 Email
Earrings
Krystin to dad:
   Hahahaha, I JUST now realized, through closer examination, that my earrings are penguins! :)
Dad to Krystin:
   Yep! That was on purpose, of course!
   Which reminds me: Have you made an appointment for the eyes?

Krystin to dad:
   Yes, I have. I have to do the laser treatments before the cataract surgery, and the first opening for the laser treatment wasn't until Aug. 23, so that's when I'm going in for part 1! See, I can be a responsible adult sometimes. :)

Dad to Krystin:
   I have no doubt that you can be—are—a responsible adult! You could not have lived in S Korea by yourself if you were not. I just think sometimes you let adulthood slip a little from time to time because you live with Dad and he'll take care of things :-)
   Glad to know you've got the scheduling going. Do NOT want to see your vision deteriorate!

July 30, 2012 Email
moving
Dad to Krystin 7/30/12
   Have you given any thought to when you'd plan on moving to an apartment? One thought I've had is perhaps February 1--that should give you enough time to save whatever you need. (Remember that in most cases, you need two months' rent up front--the first month's rent plus a security deposit usually equal to a month's rent).
   Does this sound about right, or did you have something else in mind?

Krystin to dad:
   Oh, yeah, sorry, I thought I had replied to you the first time when you brought this up. Feb. 1 sounds like a good goal. I've already started putting some of each paycheck into savings, so by February I should definitely have enough for whatever is owed up-front. I'm really

hoping I can find an efficiency apartment that's cheap, but still in a good neighborhood!

August 10, 2012 Facebook
After close to 10 years, I'm finally no longer a "bad" diabetic. All my hard work lately has paid off, and my doctors are proud of me. I'M proud of me, and that's the best feeling in the world. Life is good again. :)

August 14, 2012 Email
how doin?
Dad to Krystin:
　How you doing, and how'd the test go?

Krystin to dad:
　Doing fine. . . . The test was fine, but boring. I had to sit there for 2 hours and blow up a small balloon-like bag every 20 minutes. I guess they are testing to see if I'm lactose-intolerant. Seems like they could figure that out from a shorter test, but I'm not a doctor, so what do I know?? See you tonight.

Dad to Krystin:
　Glad to hear you're OK. Lactose-intolerant? Wow, that would be a shock! After all these years of drinking milk and eating cheese.

Krystin to dad:
　Yes, but it would also explain why I've had stomach issues for years. Mom said even when I was little I complained about my stomach not feeling well. It sure would suck though if I were. :(

Dad to Krystin:
　Well, at least we'd know the source of the problem and you could deal with it. Milk might be out; I bet that you could eat modest amounts of cheese--and I think there's something you can take to deal with the intolerance. I assume if that's the medical conclusion, you'll get advice from the docs on what you can and should not do.

August 15, 2012 Facebook
Shots in my eyeballs?? Ummmm no thanks.

>Miguel Haggar: my Grandma has that done every few months . . .
>Krystin: I'd have to go in once a month for a year. :/ It wouldn't be so bad if I could look away, but considering it's my EYES, I can't really do that!
>Lindsey Kasch: What kind of shot? sounds awful :(
>Krystin: I'm not sure exactly. Something to make my vision better, and not get worse from my diabetes.

August 16, 2012 Facebook
Apparently my stomach digests at a snail's pace, which has been causing a lot of nausea. The doc prescribed me a med to relieve the nausea (but it only works for people 1/3 of the time). What's one of the side effects? Nausea. A little counter-productive, don't you think?

Part II

Paying the Consequences: The Downhill Slide

Prologue to Part II

Blog
This mask I wear
May 21st, 2015 at 4:57 PM

    Recently, an acquaintance and facebook friend said something to me that really made me think. He said that he notices I say things on facebook about a procedure I'll need to have, or give an update on something I learned at the doctor, and stuff like that, and it will seem like it scares me, but I'll insert humor into it, as if to downplay the severity of the issue and to perhaps make those around me, who I love and care about, feel more "at ease". He said that when he really began to understand what I was writing, and what I went through from hour to hour every single day, it taught him what it is to have humility, and showed him that attitude is one of the most important things while dealing with illness. He said I don't always have to be the one who makes everyone "at ease", nor do I always have to hold my head up and say "Everything is OK with me today." It's OK to take a sick day once in a while; it's OK to want to do nothing at all but rest; it's OK to cry; it's OK to not act fine when I know I'm not.

    I admit that I DO do this. Everyone I know, friends, family, doctors, have been telling me for the past 3 years how strong I am, how resilient I am, how inspirational, determined, and positive I am. I'm not sure why I feel the need to appear so strong and brave in front of people. I'm really not. I mean, maybe I am, because I don't know how else anyone would get through all that I've been through without being strong and brave, but I guess that's not how I see it. I see it as doing what I have to do to survive. I don't want to say I see it as punishment for not taking care of my health for so many years, but as all this IS my fault, I look at it as dealing with the cards I've been dealt. The dealer has been waiting to deal them to me for a long time, and I've finally arrived at the table. Nothing to do but accept the hand, right? I don't have any other options, so might as well go with it. I'm just playing the game of life, and each card in my hand has a different ailment on it. A different consequence for my actions long ago.

    One of my favorite quotes is, "The mystery of human existence lies not just in staying alive, but in finding something to live for." - Fyodor Dostoyevsky.

    Not only am I dealing with all this with a brave face, I'm doing it for a reason. Because I have something to live for. I haven't been able to [enjoy] doing anything really enjoyable for a few years now, and my list keeps growing of things that I want to do when I'm finally "healthy" and have enough energy and stamina to do them. I want to do outdoor activities like biking and rock climbing. I want to travel more. I want to participate in more volunteer activities like with the Humane Society, and the National Kidney Foundation (which I've actually already started getting involved in). I want to really get back into my writing and actually complete something. And this is all just the short list. I have SO many things to live for.

So what does me not trying to be Superwoman in public look like? Good question. I don't know. I don't know if I would know HOW to not always put on a brave face in public. I feel like it would just be me with a pained look on my face and complaining all the time, and nobody wants to be around someone like that. I do cry, believe me. It's when I'm at home. That's when I allow myself to be vulnerable. That's when I allow myself to feel all feelings, to think about all my experiences over the past few years. I let it overwhelm me, and I let myself cry. I let myself hate my current life, and hate what I'm going through. I allow myself to feel the physical and emotional pain. I let it hurt.

But I DON'T let it get my spirit down. For too long I tried push down my vulnerability and sadness and emotional hurt, and it took its toll. That's how I ended up in the hospital with depression back in December. When I was at the infusion clinic prior to being admitted, I was talking to my nurse, and I knew I couldn't hold it in anymore; I couldn't be strong ALL the time anymore, not even when I was alone, which I had been trying to do. I cried, and told my nurse I didn't want to go home. I told my family how I was feeling, and I told my close friends how I was feeling. I felt a little better almost immediately after doing so. It was like a big weight had been lifted, like I was finally sharing all my pain with others, and not trying to carry all the weight around by myself. My shoulders broke, and I admitted defeat; that I needed help.

I still put on my strong face at work, and when I'm out. It's not that I don't want people to see me cry, or to see me vulnerable. Perhaps it's that I don't want the pity, or the sympathy. I know that people don't really know what to say or do for me, because there isn't anything anyone can say or do. I don't want other people to feel helpless, and I don't want people to get tired of me and have this negative impression of me. Like, "There she goes again, complaining about something else, as always." I smile through the hurt and say I'm fine because it's the easiest thing to do. If I didn't have to worry about a job, and paying bills, and all the other obligations in life, I would spend every day at home in sweatpants, watching TV or movies, reading, and sleeping a lot. (OK, that is what I do in the evenings and most of the weekends, I admit; but not during the work week). But that's not realistic. That's not how life works. Even with all my ailments, I still need to hold down my job, I still need to pay bills, and I still need to make a living and have some sort of a social life. THAT'S how I survive. When my alarm goes off in the mornings, and after pushing snooze twice, then exhaling a deep sigh, THAT'S how I'm able to get myself up out of bed, and dressed, and out the door. Because I have to. Because I have things to live for. Is it wearing down my body? Maybe.

My brain is tired now, so I'll end it here. Bye for now.

Chapter 9

Journey to Transplant

August 20, 2012 Facebook
Who has an extra kidney they'd like to give me?? Apparently I'm going to need a transplant in the next couple years. Figures that just as I'm finally starting to take care of myself, my organs are starting to fail. fml :(

> Krystin: One of the good things that will come out of this is that they will do a pancreas transplant at the same time, so I won't have to do insulin anymore. It's just unfortunate that it takes kidney failure for them to also do a pancreas transplant.

August 21, 2012 Facebook
I've started a blog for this whole procedure. There's not much to it yet, but over time there will be!
krystine227.livejournal.com
From One Organ To the Next

Blog
Welcome, one and all
    Welcome to my blog! I hope you are here because you want to come along with me, either from near or far, on this transplant journey that I am embarking on. The purpose of this journal will be to document all the steps of this procedure. I will be completely open about everything that happens, as well as my feelings and reactions along the way. I will not hold anything back, so be prepared for raw, detailed information. I believe this will not only help me keep things in perspective, but will also help you, as the reader, feel like you are right next to me holding my hand throughout all the ups and downs,

whether you live just down the street or on the other side of the country. Thanks for following along. We'll get through this together!

Step 1: Let the journey begin
August 21

Yesterday, during an appointment at the nephrology (kidney) clinic, I was told that I am going to need a kidney transplant in about the next 2 years. I knew this day was coming, but I didn't realize it would come so soon. All throughout my teenage and college years, I kept telling myself, "I'm still young, I have time, I can turn it around." Well, here I am almost 28 years old, and although I have turned it around the past 6 or so months, it's too little too late. The damage is done to my kidneys, and once they start to fail, no matter how well I take care of my health from here on out, I can't bring them back. My kidney functions are currently working at 21% and are spilling a lot of protein in my urine. Neither of those are good things. I don't think anyone's kidney functions at 100%, but certainly not 21%. Those whose are, get a transplant. My options were transplant, or dialysis. My decision was easy. Hands down, no question, no hesitation, I'll go with the transplant. No way in hell am I going to sit for 3-4 hours, 3 days a week doing dialysis. I know a lot of people have to, but if I have other options, I'd rather not, thankyouverymuch. You know how I feel about needles . . .

Today I called and registered for the donor program at the U of M. I would not rather have this procedure done anywhere else except the U. I grew up around the University, all my doctors have been here for years, and I trust them completely with their medical care. I know I am in good hands. The wait time for a kidney can be 3-5 years, since they have to wait for someone to die, AND the kidney has to be a match. So the wait could be long. However, the wait is significantly shorter if you have a willing, living donor who is a match. You would not believe how much support I have gotten from people telling me they'll get tested. I feel so loved, and I can't even express how truly grateful and thankful I am to have so many amazing people in my life who are willing to get tested to give up an organ for me. It's a nasty procedure, and I don't imagine it will be easy for a donor, either. In the meantime, however, my months will be filled with information sessions and meeting with the transplant surgeon and learning all about what is going to happen. Like I said, this is hopefully still a couple years down the road, but lots needs to be done along the way to prepare for it. Getting registered with the donor program was the first step, and that is done.

Believe it or not, there is an upside to this. Aside from getting a new, healthy kidney and being better off with that, I'm also going to get a new pancreas! Yes, that means I will no longer be diabetic and won't have to do insulin anymore. Apparently the University has been doing pancreas transplants since 1973, but not just for any and all diabetics, which is why this hasn't been an option for me in the past. The pancreas transplant goes along with the kidney transplant, so only diabetics who have kidney failure can get the double transplant. I will be needing to take lots of anti-rejection drugs, probably for the rest of my life, but I will take that over shots any day, and the doctor told me yesterday that patients who get the kidney transplant have shown improvements in their health and have continued to live happy, healthy lives with no issues. This is good news.

So, how am I feel about all this so far? I'm surprisingly (or not) fine about it all. I didn't have any extreme reactions when they told me I'd need the transplant, because I kinda knew this day was coming. Admittedly, I didn't know it was coming so soon, like I mentioned before, but I knew it would come eventually. I brought this on myself, so I can't be too surprised. After not taking care of my diabetes for 10 or so years, what did I expect? But I trust our medical system and I know they'll take good care of me, and I'm just thankful and lucky that I'm living during a time when these options are available to me. 50 or so years ago I would've been S.O.L. I'm not letting this damper my spirits, and I'm not feeling down about it. I'm not happy, of course, but I'm not depressed either. I'm just . . . fine.

Here is a link from WebMD that gives a pretty good overview of a kidney transplant: http://www.webmd.com/a-to-z-guides/kidney-transplant-20666

And here is a picture, for your entertainment, of what a kidney transplant looks like:

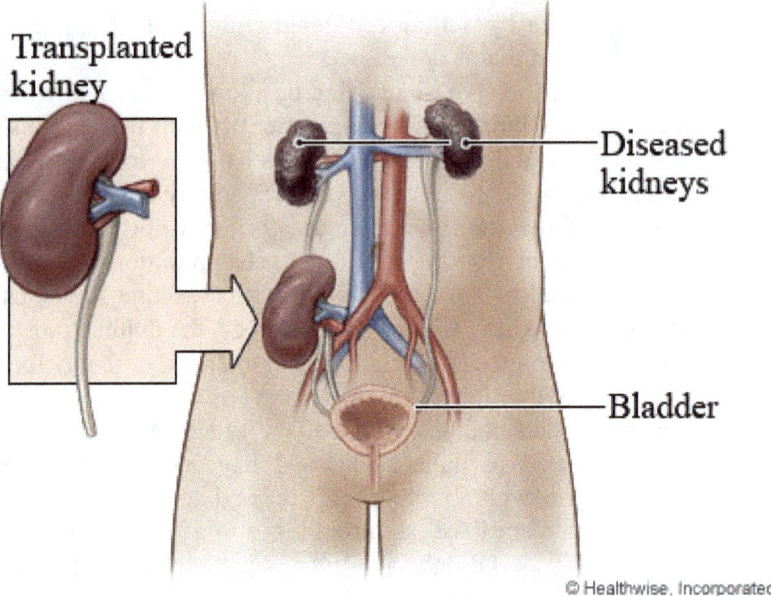

Later this week I will be getting a packet of information in the mail, and next week I have a kidney ultrasound scheduled. If I learn before then, I'll be sure to share it. Until then, keep on keeping on.

August 23, 2012 Email
Dad to Krystin, Elliott:
K&E,
It has been suggested (not by Kathy) that I am too involved in you guys' decision-making in your lives--that I should step back and just let you handle things as the adults you are.

You should tell me if you think that's true. It's of course hard for me to know--parents don't have any good way to make comparisons. If there are times when you want to say "I can handle this myself, dad," that's fine. I start with the assumption that if I can help you, I should--but perhaps I should start with the assumption that you'll ask for my help if you want it and otherwise stay out of your decisions.

Krystin to dad:
I know with us still living under your roof, it's hard not to be involved in our decision making, especially if it affects how much longer we stay in the house, or if we're doing anything to move on and

move up. To be honest, the only time I felt pressure from you recently about decision making was about whether or not to go back to Korea. The ONLY reason I didn't end up going back, the only thing keeping me from going, was you. I don't mean that in an accusatory way or to make you feel guilty. I'm just saying that is the only time (since I've returned from Korea) I've felt you were maybe too involved in my decision making. I know that you only had my best interest at heart, and I'm happy now with my job and I know working here at the U has given me lots of benefits and whatnot, but Korea does still pull at my heart, and I will want to go back.

Other than that, I can't think of anything else off the top of my head. I don't mind you being involved in my life, and I haven't really had any other big decisions I've had to make anyway, so for now, I don't think it's a problem. Obviously I can't speak for Elliott, but that's my take.

Love you.

Dad to Krystin:

Thanks. It helps me to know that. And as I wrote, you can say bug off if you think I seem to be controlling. (As for Korea, I know. I knew at the time that I was being more opinionated with you than I am other times, and you COULD have gone anyway, but that was also the case where I felt the strongest—and that you weren't looking far enough down the road. And of course you can go back, although it might be awhile before you could go back with a JOB over there.)

LY

August 27, 2012 Blog
So much info!

This morning I had an appointment with radiology for a kidney/bladder ultrasound. Since we have a kidney on both sides of our stomach area, and the bladder is more in the frontal region, by the time we were finished, I had that warm gel stuff all over my stomach and sides. Pleasant. At least I got a nice clean towel to wipe it all off before pulling my shirt back down. We didn't go over any results today; I assume that will be done at my next nephrology (kidney clinic) appointment, which isn't for another couple months I think. I'm not sure what it is they were looking for, since we already know I have kidney failure. Maybe they just want to see how much of a raisin my kidney has become. I could see the screen from my lying position, but of course I have no idea what I'm looking at to begin with, so the image meant nothing to me. Is it bad that the technicians face was scrunched up in a frown while looking at the screen??

This afternoon I called a lady from the Transplant scheduling office to make some appointments in the upcoming months. For a day in September, I'll take a whole day off of work; sounds like I'll have a whole day of appointments, just going from one to the other. I don't know exactly what they'll be at this time, but I'm going to get an itinerary and information in the mail with my schedule. Then I'll have another half day of appointments in October. So, things are moving along. Even though my kidneys have about 2 years of life left in them, at this rate (assuming I can find a donor), this may be happening a lot sooner rather than later!

I spent this weekend reading a lot of the information that I got in the mail. It was a folder full of information about both the pancreas and kidney transplant. I learned so much! I mean, I guess unless you've had the transplant yourself or know someone close to you who has, you probably don't know a lot about it either, unless you spend your free time googling transplant information. The kidney/pancreas transplants may or may not be done at the same time. The impression I get from the information is that the pancreas is from a human donor, not from a pig, as I had originally thought it was, since pig pancreases most closely resemble human pancreases. Apparently a living donor can donate part of their pancreas and give it to the patient. No, that does not mean the donor becomes diabetic. My dad is not sure, but he contemplated out loud whether or not part of a pancreas can grow back. Thus, is you have half a pancreas, the other half will form and you'll have a whole, functional pancreas again. But this may be stem cell research that is yet to be developed. If I don't get it from a living donor, then, like with the kidney, I'm on a waiting list for a pancreas from a deceased donor. This is why I may end up having two surgeries, since no one can guarantee that they'll have both a kidney AND pancreas ready for me at the same time.

The kidney, obviously, I will get from a human donor as well. No animal kidney transplants (yet). I was reading about all the medications that I'll have to take daily, for the rest of my life after the procedure, and their estimated costs. I could have to pay $1600 or so a month for all the medications; I'm hoping insurance will cover a huge chunk of most of those. Another reason I'm so glad to be working at the U and have amazing health insurance. :/ I was most interested in reading about recovery after the transplant. I'll for sure be taking an anti-rejection med three times a day for the rest of my life. For the first month after, I'll have to go in for blood tests three times a week. During the time I'm still in the hospital after the surgery, if my body does not seem to be taking to the new organ right away, I may need some dialysis to get things moving. Fabulous. Dialysis is exactly what I was trying to avoid by choosing transplant! This is less likely if I get the organ from a living donor, though, because there is less time between transferring the kidney/pancreas from one body to the next. Naturally, that makes sense.

With any transplant, there is the possibility that my body will reject one or both of the organs, but we'll hope that doesn't happen.

In the meantime, I googled foods that are good for kidney function, in an attempt to slow down my kidney failure. I was quite pleasantly surprised to find so many of the fruits that I love on the list! Raspberries, strawberries, red grapes, apples, and cranberries, as well as red bell peppers, garlic, cauliflower, and onions. All things I love! There were others, of course, but I only noted down the things I like. Apparently things high in sodium, protein, and phosphorus are also good. I went to the grocery store over the weekend and stocked up on lots of fruits and veggies. This is a good idea anyway for a healthy lifestyle. I feel so good and proud of myself sitting at my desk at work eating my carrots and assorted fruits! Go me. :)

I'm still feeling good about the procedure, but a little nervous about how much time I'll have to take off of work afterwards. I'll probably have to spend 7-10 days in the hospital after the procedure, and then people have told me probably 2-3 more weeks after that recovering at home before returning to work. Yikes! I did find out, however, that after I've depleted all my sick/vacation/comp time, Kathy can donate vacation time to me. I'm probably going to use up most of my sick and vacation time with all the appointments I have to go to leading up to the surgery, so I'm very very thankful she is able (and willing) to donate to me! She is pretty much going to be my hero and savior. Thanks, Kathy!! They said that for a couple weeks I won't feel like doing much of anything because my energy will be low. Understandable, that was no surprise to read. What WAS really surprising was that it usually takes anywhere between 3-6 MONTHS to fully recover! I hope they don't expect me to take that much time off work. Luckily my job is not high-stress or high-energy, so I think

I'll be OK to go back to work after a few weeks, as long as I start out taking it easy.

That's all I got for now. When I know more, so will you!

August 30, 2012 Blog
Evaluation, Concerns

I got my schedule for my all-day evaluation stuff coming up at the end of September. Here is what my schedule is going to look like that day:

    8:00am - Review evaluation process & daily schedule
    Continue - Blood tests
    Continue - Chest X-ray
    9:00-11:00am - Pre-transplant class (my mom will be joining me for this one)
    11:00am - Appt. with the transplant nephrologist
    1:00pm - Pulmonary function tests
    2:45pm - Appt. with transplant surgeon
    With Dr. appt. - Meet with transplant coordinator
    TBD - Meet with study coordinator
    After last appt. - Check out with transplant nurse

I then have another half-day of more tests and appointments in October. After that, my entire transplant team will meet and decide if I am eligible for the transplant surgery. If I am, I will then be put on the donor waiting list. I watched an information video last night, and it really looks like if I get a kidney from a living donor, that would be much better. It has a much higher success rate of surviving in my body, and the wait time would be shortened, like by years. The surgery could happen as soon as both people are considered a match. This would also mean I probably wouldn't have to go on dialysis, whereas if I wait for an organ from a deceased donor, that could be 5 or so years, and I may have to start dialysis before then. Ick. This is NOT me putting pressure on anyone to get tested, so if you're reading this, please don't suddenly feel like you should go get tested. It is completely voluntary. Actually, if you're considering it, don't do anything yet. I haven't even gone through my evaluation stuff yet, so it will be a couple months before any action would need to be taken to find a donor. I'll remind everyone again at that time. :)

Right now my biggest concerns about this surgery are regarding my lifestyle afterwards. I'm worried about how much time I'll have to take off of work. Will I be able to work part-time for a month or so? Will they fire me because of this? I certainly hope not, but you never know. In the 4 months I've been here, I've gotten the impression that they are very supportive in anything going on in your life and taking time off will be no problem. However, I'm still on a 6-month hire, and have not been hired on permanently yet. I have not put the word out there yet about this transplant, because I'm afraid it will affect whether or not they hire me on permanently, and that would be coming up soon.

My other concern is about all the medications I'll have to take after, especially the anti-rejection med, which needs to be taken 3 times a day. What if something happens that prevents me from being able to take one of them? Will missing one dose make my body reject the new kidney? That's my biggest fear. I'm sure missing one dose isn't a big deal, as long as it doesn't happen often. Luckily my schedule is pretty routine, but you never know what activity or unscheduled event may be thrown my way!

That's all for now. More later!

August 31, 2012 Facebook
Full of happiness today! Not only is it Friday, but lots of good things going on recently and coming up. Enjoy the weekend, friends!

September 5, 2012 Email
pancreas transplant
Dad to Krystin:
Krystin,

I've been in touch with a faculty member in the Med School who studies diabetes and pancreas transplants and has patients in both.

1. The long-term survival rate for kidney transplant patients is very good. There also appears to be no effect on mortality rates (age of death) of kidney donors.

2. The news about the pancreas transplants is not so positive. "When you give part of a pancreas, the chance it will work in the recipient in 5-10 years is 50-80%." There is also a significant risk of diabetes for the pancreas donor, she said.

So the kidney news is fine, but you may have to keep on living with diabetes until a better cure is found. I would certainly not ask any living donor to donate part of his/her pancreas and run a substantial risk of getting diabetes.

Krystin to dad:
    Good to know. I will print this and put it will the information and stuff that I'll be bringing to my evaluation day, and bring it up with them. Obviously in the end it's my choice which transplants to go through with or not, so this is something good to discuss with them. Thanks for inquiring!
Dad to Krystin:
    You're welcome. The info about the pancreas transplants was disappointing--both for long-term survival of the transplant and the potential effect on the donor. Rats. But at least the kidney transplant info is very encouraging.

September 11, 2012 Facebook
Why yes, I am actually spending my down time at work looking into what it would take (educationally) to become a forensic anthropologist. Another bachelor's degree before grad school . . .

September 14, 2012 Facebook
I just had a chat with my supervisor and was offered my job as a permanent position, I filled out my grad school application to submit for a Masters in Liberal Studies here at the U, AND it's Friday. Who's a happy camper? This girl. =)

September 17, 2012 Blog
I'm back!
    I apologize that it has been so long since I posted last. Mostly it's because I don't really have much to post about. Nothing more has happened, and my evaluation day is next Monday, which is when I will find out, well, everything. I was advised that for any surgery, a person should always seek out a second opinion. Therefore, I called the Mayo Clinic down in Rochester and am going to set up an appointment to have an evaluation done there, as well. If I have the transplant done at Mayo, that would be fine with me too. I don't really care WHERE I have it done. Well, as long as it's not in some back-alley clinic and performed by a man named Slick Willie or Wokie Bill or something like that. I do not have any evaluations set up with them like I do here at the U, but a couple Fridays a month, some of their

doctors come up to a clinic here at the Mall of America. I have an appointment on Oct. 5 to go get checked out by one of their nephrologists when he comes to town. Then, depending on how that goes, I may go down to Rochester for the full evaluation. If I do, that's a 3-day process. It's 3 days of testing! Which probably means lots of poking and prodding. Ugh.

So right now I'm just waiting. I am already getting anxious, even though this procedure could be a year and a half or two years away still. I just want to get it over with. Now that I know how much better it will improve my health and how much better I'll feel, I don't want to wait. I want to do it tomorrow! I have been doing a lot of reading about kidney transplants, and a lot of the lifestyle changes I have to make afterwards make me nervous, especially with all the medications I'm going to have to take. I'm afraid I'm going to do something wrong and end up back in the hospital.

I may just do the kidney transplant and skip the pancreas transplant, at least for now. The success rate just doesn't make it look like a good idea. I don't WANT to be diabetic anymore, but I'd rather have a procedure done to cure me of it that has a better than 50-80% success rate. I especially don't want any donor to run the risk of getting diabetes. So many people in my life growing up have said "if I could take the diabetes for you, I would." No, no, no, don't ever make that offer! I mean, I appreciate it, but I would not wish diabetes on anyone. I'm a tough girl and can deal with it (and take care of it) until something successful comes along. Having the kidney transplant will actually be good motivation to keep tight control of my diabetes, because I don't want anything going wrong with my new kidney!

A lot of people have been asking about my feelings, but I'm just not sure how to express them. I'm not scared to have this done. I'm ready. And I'm anxious, not in a bad way, but in a good way, because I know how much this is going to help me. Like I said, I want to just do it tomorrow and have it done with so I can be healthy again!

Other than that, life goes on as usual. Trying to eat more fruits and veggies, since they're good for kidney function. The next time I post will probably be next week, after my evaluations. I'm sure I'll be flooded with information and will have lots to share and update you on. Until then, ciao.

September 26, 2012 Blog
Evaluation Day

Monday was my all-day evaluation day at the U. It went well, and I got a lot of information. It wasn't overwhelming or anything, though. The first thing they did in the morning was all the blood work - they drew 15 tubes of blood!! I almost had a minor anxiety attack - you know how I am with needles. The lab tech had to tell me a couple times to relax my fist and breathe. She did a very good job, but I was glad when it was over. I also had a chest scan, and a pulmonary function test, which tested my lung functions (so the anesthesiologist would know how much anesthesia to give me during surgery). The lady told me I had very good lungs. Oh good, at least I know one organ in my body is working right! I also met with my nephrologist again, and the transplant surgeon. My mom came for a 2-hour pre-transplant class. I found out that for someone who is waiting for either a kidney or a pancreas (not together), the wait time on a donor waiting list can be anywhere between 3-6 years, but for those who are waiting for a kidney/pancreas transplant together (like me), the wait time is only 6 months to a year. This is because those who are in need of BOTH a kidney and pancreas are diabetics who are having more problems than those waiting for just one or the other, so we get moved to the top of the list. This isn't to say that those who are waiting for just a kidney or pancreas aren't important and aren't also having health problems, it just means I'm having a few more.

This means, once I get on the waiting list, I could have a kidney and pancreas from a deceased donor any time in the next year. however, as I've mentioned before, the success rate of organs from a deceased donor are lower than those received from a living donor. This is why, although I will still be put on the waiting list obviously, I'm trying to find a living donor. Not for a pancreas, but for a kidney. If someone is willing to donate a kidney, that's already a lot. I'm not going to also ask if they'll give me part of their pancreas. So I'm only looking for a kidney from a living donor, and will stay on the list for a pancreas, which means it could be a number of years until I get one, but at least in the meantime I'd have a healthy, functioning kidney. Unless I can find a different living donor who would donate part of their pancreas. The pancreas donation just means they shave off a small part of the donor's pancreas and transplant it in mine, and my body adopts it and starts using it to make insulin, and the anti-rejection drugs I'd be taking would keep my body from rejecting it.

I've been told that I can start looking for a donor. Since this is a big, big life decision, I do not feel comfortable asking someone straight out if they'll get tested to see if they're a match for me. This is completely voluntary. There are many things to consider before agreeing to be tested. "Getting tested" just means getting some blood work done, because the donor needs to be both a blood type and tissue type match. Here is some helpful information:

-- I'm blood type O. I can ONLY match with another person who is blood type O. If you are not blood type O (either positive or negative), although I appreciate your consideration, you would not be chosen.

-- You wouldn't even need to go to a clinic. The Donor Program sends you a bunch of information, as well as a home kit (if you request it) for you to swab the inside of your mouth and send it back to them. Or you can go into your local clinic and have blood drawn.

-- Everything is covered under my insurance, so you wouldn't need to pay for anything - including the transplant!

-- Donors need to be between the ages 16-65 and in relatively good health.

That being said, if you are interested in getting information about donation, or are even considering seeing if you are a match, you can call the Donor Program at 612-672-7270 and tell them you are (possibly) interested in kidney donation to me (Krystin Engstrand). It is completely confidential, and I never find out if you've called or even gotten tested.

Please, please, please spread the word. I have already put this information on Facebook, so some of you already have this information. A lot of people don't even think about or consider kidney donation if they don't already know someone who needs one - it's just not something we think about on a daily basis! So please get the word out that you know someone who is in need of a kidney. The more people who know, the sooner and more likely it is that I will find a living donor. I really, really appreciate any help you can provide!

As far as how I'm feeling, I have very mixed feelings after my evaluation day. I still just want to get this over and done with so that I can start feeling good and healthy again. As my kidney functions have decreased, I've been feeling more and more tired. I'm tired ALL the time, and just want to sleep. On the weekends I take numerous naps, and during the week while I'm at work, by the afternoon I'm yawning so big that it hurts my jaw, and sometimes my eyes are so heavy I have to get up and walk around to keep from falling asleep. Admittedly, that's probably also because it's been slow at work, so I don't have a whole lot to do. When it's busy I stay awake easily, but when I have nothing to do, then my body just gets tired. So with all that, I'm anxious to have this transplant done. It almost excites me, in a way.

It also makes me nervous. I've really begun to realize what a big deal this is, and what kinds of complications there are and will be in the future if I don't do everything I need to do after the transplant. I have every bit of faith in myself that I'll be able to take all my meds. What worries me the most is how much time I'll have to take off of work. I'll need to take off at least 2 weeks for sure. Some people have taken off 6. I can't afford to take off that much time! I'm scared that SPA is going to regret hiring me. Not even a year into employment and I already need to take a month off? That doesn't look good. I know it's not like I'm just taking off a month to go sit on a beach, it's for a legitimate health reason, but still. I'd feel bad for leaving my 2 counterparts to do everything that would normally be split up between the 3 of us. Then if one of them needs a day off, that would leave only 1 of them here to cover everything. I know I need to not think about these things and do what I need to do for me to be healthy again. I also know that my office and my supervisors are so supportive, and will do anything to help accommodate for my absence.

That's all I got for now. More to come as I find out more, but it might be a week or so before I post again. Bye for now!

October 3, 2012 Email
blood type
Krystin to dad:
Mom and I are the same blood type. Too bad she hasn't said anything about being a possible donor. Hmm.

October 5, 2012 Blog
Through the darkness there is optimism
It's time for that post where I need to complain for a minute, so bear with me.
I'm tired. All the time. All I want to do is sleep. It's hard getting out of bed in the morning, and my body is always achy, and it seems

like simple, everyday things take effort. I get dizzy and disoriented if I stand up too fast. I don't have the energy to do hardly anything. I'm able to go to work, and get by, but by the time I get home in the evenings, I'm exhausted and just want to take a nap. It is apparent that since my kidney infection back in February, my kidney functions have been declining quite quickly, which makes the body very tired. I just thought my hemoglobin levels were low and I wasn't getting enough iron, but now I know that's not true. I'm tired for reasons I can't control. I hope I find a donor soon, because I can't imagine feeling like this for the next 6 months to a year. Icky. It just feels like everything in me is failing all at once. :(

On a more positive note, I'm really looking forward to see what kind of person I am after the transplant, as a non-diabetic. I've only known life with diabetes. I can't wait for the freedom, to not have to do blood tests, or count carbs, or change my insulin pump at 3 a.m. because I forgot to add more insulin before going to bed. Presumably I'll even have enough energy again to start exercising, which I have had zero motivation to for, well, many years. I'll have more brain juice to work on my writing. I'll an all-around happier person.

So, even though I feel like crap, I'm really trying my best to stay positive, because I know it will get better. I just have to keep on keeping on until then. Bye for now, and happy Friday!

October 7, 2012 Facebook
Another long night in the ER. Don't worry, nothing too serious, but I sure do wish my body would stop failing on me.

October 11, 2012 Email
a1c
Krystin to dad, mom:
    My a1c is down to 7.5!!!!! Am I awesome or am I awesome?? :) :) :)

Dad to Krystin:
    that is just great!!!!

Gary to Kathy [Krystin's message forwarded to Kathy]:
    Too bad she didn't do this 10 years ago.

Kathy to Gary:

Yup. Do you think she has any concept of how people (like her family) are basically mad at her for neglecting her responsibilities to her health for so long?

Gary to Kathy:

Yes. She knows her mother is. I am--but what's the point, now? What was that I was saying about spilt milk? I can continue to be mad and make her feel bad or I can just move on and help her to whatever extent I'm able.

Krystin to dad:

Thanks! I couldn't believe it when she told me. It feels sooooo good to have gotten it down into the 7 range. Proof that I'm finally doing something right.

My appts. went fine. I met with the dietitian and social worker, had an EKG and echo-something done, and met with the cardiologist. The cardiologist told me I have a strong heart! They did another ultrasound of my heart, and it was so cool, I got to see my heart beating, from different angles.

Yes, I'm drinking water, don't worry! Even if I don't feel thirsty, I'm drinking it. See you tonight.

October 14, 2012 Facebook

Apparently my kidneys are failing at a faster rate than my kidney-protecting meds can keep up. If ever in your life you've thought to yourself "hmm, I think I'd like to donate a kidney someday," now's a great time! Just sayin. :)

October 14, 2012 Blog
Hospital & Evaluation pt. 2

As most of you already know, last week I was admitted into the ER for extreme dehydration. Since last Thursday, I had been feeling very fatigued, tired, dizzy and lightheaded when I stood up, and all the muscles in my body ached whenever I did anything. Getting out of bed and getting dressed was an effort. Sunday night I called urgent care and talked to a nurse and told her my symptoms. She said because I'm diabetic and having kidney failure, I need to go to the ER. So I went to Fairview University. The last time I was a patient there was in November of 2005 when I went into DKA and was in CCU for a week. Luckily this time was different, and not so critical. The blood and urine labs they did showed elevated levels of magnesium (whatever that means) and very very low levels of electrolytes. They hooked me up to an IV and started giving me fluids. I was brought up to a room about 2:30 in the morning. For the next 2 days I got somewhere around 15 large bags of fluids. You'd think I'd then be peeing every half hour, but I actually only went to the bathroom once during my whole stay. That's how dehydrated I was. I had absolutely no idea that I was so dehydrated. I guess I hadn't noticed that I hadn't been drinking enough water during the previous week. They did an ultrasound of my heart, and it showed my heart pumping and working very hard to get blood flowing through my body, since it didn't have any fluids to help it. That explains the headache, fatigue, and achy muscles. By Tuesday morning the doctors said my levels were much better and I should be able to go home that night. I was discharged Tuesday night. Unfortunately, this also gave my kidneys another hit. Great.

I have been very good about keeping up my water intake since then. I'm not going to make that mistake again. Even if I don't feel thirsty, I make myself drink water. I have a water bottle at work, and I fill it up in the morning and make sure it's finished by lunchtime. Then after lunch, I fill it up again and make sure it's finished by the time I go home. I am also surrounded by awesome co-workers who check in on me and ask if I'm drinking my water. :)

Thursday was the second half of my transplant evaluation process. I met with the social worker, nutritionist, and cardiologist. I also had an echocardiogram done, which is basically another heart ultrasound, so I got to see my heart twice in one week! Before I saw it at the hospital, I had never seen an ultrasound of my heart before. It was pretty cool. The cardiologist told me, when looking at the photos, that I have a very strong heart. I thought, awesome. That's because I have lots of love in it to give! My whole transplant team (social worker, cardiologist, nurse coordinator, nephrologist, nutritionist) will meet on Wednesday of this week and make a decision about putting me on the donor list. I asked at one point how often people aren't approved to be put on the list, and it sounds like it very rarely happens. Basically anyone who is very elderly or someone who has a serious heart condition isn't put on the list. I don't fit either of those categories, so I'm not too worried.

I feel like my kidneys are failing faster than my medications can keep up with protecting them. I'm still so tired all the time, and have lost almost all motivation to do anything in the evenings or on the weekends. I just want to stay home and rest. I know this isn't something you hear very often, but I'm considering talking to my nephrologist about starting dialysis. There's a new system now where I can do dialysis at home, at nighttime while I sleep, so it wouldn't affect my work schedule. A catheter is placed in the stomach, and I hook up to the machine at night. And by morning I'm feeling refreshed and energized and ready for the day. For those of you who don't know what dialysis is, it's hooking up to a machine that takes my blood out, cleans out all the bad stuff in it, and puts it back in. It does what my kidneys can't. I know it doesn't sound pleasant, but I don't want to feel like this while I wait for a kidney to become available.

I really, really don't want to push people into considering donation, but I'm almost to the point of desperation. I just want to do this! I'm so eager for the transplant. I've said it before and I'll say it again, please please please, spread the word! I would literally owe someone my life.

That's all for now. I will hear from my transplant coordinator late this week after they meet, so I'll be sure to update you with the verdict!

October 14, 2012 Facebook
Christine Hinz Lenzen shared a photo.
My good friend Krystin has been in my life since I was 2 years old and needs a kidney transplant. If you have type 'O' blood please consider getting yourself tested for donation. You could literally save her life.

Christine Hinz Lenzen: do you think our matching outfits were made from bed sheets?

Krystin: Awww you're gonna make me cry! And yes, it does look that way, doesn't it? This is one of my FAV pics of us!

October 18, 2012 Email
A couple things
Krystin to Dad:

I'm having dinner with mom tonight and looking at a bunch of stuff that she wants to give me for when I get an apartment. I'm going right from work, so I won't be home until later.

I talked to David today. Of course he was very understanding. He said don't even worry about things on this (work) end. He was quite surprised when I told him I would be out for probably 2 weeks. He said "Only 2 weeks?" So, he's ready for me to be out longer if need be. I did tell him I was going to start transitioning back into work as soon as I felt well enough to. He said that he would donate hours to me. I reminded him that that can only be done once I've passed my 6 month probation, and that if I get a donor before then, I'll just take time w/o pay. He shook his head and said "oh no, you won't have to do that. I'll make sure of it."

See you tonight.

Dad to Krystin:
Wow. That's certainly a positive response. Great!

October 22, 2012 Email
dialysis
Dad to Krystin, Kathy:
Krystin,

I just talked to Mary briefly; it turns out she has a good friend who has some disease that causes renal failure, so she has to be on dialysis. She's doing the home dialysis now (just started), and it does not require another person to come and do it--you do it yourself (after training, of course). And yep, it's done at night.

So you definitely should ask your docs about this possibility (and whether health insurance will pay for it--but I can't imagine it wouldn't).

Krystin to dad:

I have a renal appt. next Monday, so I will definitely be bringing it up. They probably don't hear people say very often that they WANT to go on dialysis, but I really really want to stop feeling so crappy and tired all the time. And I really like this home dialysis thing. So, we'll see what they say!

October 26, 2012 Email
doc?
Dad to Krystin:
So what happened this morning?

Krystin to dad:

Well they did labs and a urine sample, and I saw Dr. Ibrahim. He thinks I had yet ANOTHER UTI. I'm not sure why I keep getting them, and not even knowing. But this time, unlike at the hospital, he prescribed me an antibiotic that I'll take for a week. They also gave me two liters of IV fluids. I go in to work about noon. I'm glad I remembered to bring my book.

I did talk to him about home dialysis, and he wasn't against the idea. However, I would need to get this thing put into my arm, a permanent fistula I think it's called. That takes approx. 2 months, after insertion, before it can be used for dialysis, so the soonest I'd be able to start is in 2 months. Something about the body healing around it and "accepting" the fistula into the vein. Dr. Ibrahim said, however, that he doesn't think I need it quite yet. My kidney functions are down to 15%, but he said dialysis only raises kidney function by 5%, and there isn't much difference in how I feel between 15-20%. If I were at a 0, then yes, raising functions up to 5% would make me feel better, but it wouldn't be beneficial yet. But, we're getting the ball rolling on getting the fistula inserted, so if 2 months down the road I do need to start dialysis, I'll be ready. Does that make sense? As far as the nausea and vomiting, Dr. Ibrahim said that is most likely gastro related, so that's something I'll need to keep working with Dr. Soltis on in GI. So in the meantime, I guess put up with it and just be really careful what I eat.

That's all I know for now. See you tonight.

October 26, 2012 Blog
The roller coaster continues

Ok, I've finally got some updates for you! I got a call from my transplant coordinator on Thursday evening, and I talked to her for a bit about some things.

First, the transplant team met last week, and everyone gave a thumbs-up on getting me on the transplant list. However, my blood has a large number of antibodies. Antibodies are basically a protein produced by the B cells that is used by the immune system to identify and neutralize foreign objects, like bacteria and viruses. Or in the case of transplant patients, new organs to which the immune system is saying "hey, you're not mine." Antibodies would attack a new organ. My blood is 48% antibodies, which means that transplant isn't impossible, it just makes it harder to find a match, because it means the possibility is even higher for me that my body will reject it. So anyone who gets tested has to be pretty much 95% exact match or higher. Sheesh.

She was also worried about a test I had done recently in my primary care clinic. It showed very small traces of some cells in my cervix that can cause cervical cancer. Nothing to worry about, they're not even active, but it's something they can't take a chance on, so as a pre-transplant patient, I'll need to get the HPV shots. I think it's a series of 3 shots over the next 6 months. Who knows where the cells came from, I don't even know if it's genetic . . . but it's a risk factor. Yay, yet another way my body is failing.

Other than that, the ball continues rolling. I've been put on the transplant list, but still on hold (so not moving up or down the list), because my coordinator, Mary Beth, is still getting everything figured out with insurance. When it all goes through, the hold will be taken off and I'll officially be "waiting!"

In the meantime, I've been having a lot of nausea and unexplained vomiting lately. I had mentioned a bit ago that I had connected it with dairy, and had cut dairy products out of my diet. That is still true, that dairy makes me sick, but lately it's been happening for no apparent reason at all, when I haven't even eaten anything dairy. So then I thought it was when I ate too big a meal at one time, and my stomach was just saying "woahhh, too much, too much, you get it back," but the last couple days even that hasn't been the case. So this morning I went and saw my nephrologist, and they did some more blood lab work/urine test. My nephrologist, Dr. Ibrahim, said he thinks I have another UTI (urinary tract infection), which is what I had in the hospital when I was there 2 weeks ago, too! Maybe it just never went away. At least he gave me an antibiotic this time. They also gave me 2 more liters of IV fluids. I just can't seem to keep up with my fluid intake! I have a 32-oz. water bottle at my desk at work, and I go through 2 of those every day at work. Then whatever I drink at home in the evenings. I feel like I'm drinking ALL the time, but it just isn't enough. I think because my kidneys can't do a thorough job of cleaning out my system, my body requires more water (and cranberry juice, apparently) to help wash out the bad stuff. I was joking on Facebook that the docs should just insert a permanent IV catheter in my arm and I can just push around a mobile IV pole with me everywhere. Sounds like a good solution to me. So overall, he doesn't think my nausea and vomiting is related to kidney failure, but with my gastro issues, which is completely separate, and which I'm working with a GI doctor on.

    I also talked to Dr. Ibrahim about home dialysis options. I told him I was, well, sick and tired of being sick and tired all the time, and that if I did home dialysis, that would help me feel better until the transplant, and since it's at home and done during the night, I would still have my work days. A thing called a fistula is inserted somewhere on my arm. A fistula is like a passageway between two blood vessels that do not normally connect. It is put in doing same-day surgery, no anesthesia needed or anything, and it will allow for easier blood transfer in and out during dialysis. Then at home, I would put two different needles into the fistula at night: one to take the blood out, and one to put it back in after it has been cleaned in the machine. I would wake up feeling rejuvenated and rested. If you want more information about it, I found this website that is pretty good:http://homedialysis.org/types/modality/what_is_nhhd

    Dr. Ibrahim didn't think I was at the point of needing dialysis yet, though. My kidney functions have dropped to 15%, and dialysis raises kidney functions by 5%. That would bring me up to 20% function. There isn't really much of a difference in how I feel physically between 15 and 20%. If my kidney functions are 0, then yeah, increasing it 5% would make a difference, but right now he doesn't think it's necessary. We still planned on having me make an appointment to get things rolling on getting a fistula put in, because once it's put in, you have to wait approximately 2 months before actually starting dialysis. I guess the body needs to adjust to these two blood vessels now being connected and whatnot. So even though I don't need dialysis quite yet, if I do a few months or so down the line, I'll be ready. In the meantime, I guess I have to put up with the fatigue.

So on almost a daily basis, I'm tired, achy, fatigued, nauseous, and sometimes barfing my stomach up through my esophagus. Or so it feels. I guess this post contained more bad news than good. . . .

I'm trying really hard not to let it affect my mood, but I'm not going to lie, it is a bit depressing. Some days are easier, and some are harder, than others. I keep telling people I'm fine, I keep a smile on my face, and I get through each day. But I'm getting to the point where I can't keep this mask on much longer. I honestly want to stay in bed all day, scream into my pillow once in a while, and wish this were all over and I was the new, healthy, happy Krystin that I will be.

OK, I'll stop complaining. That's all I know for now, anyway. Hopefully next post will bring more positive news and I'll have an update on where I am with getting all this official. Bye for now.

October 29, 2012 Facebook
I wish there was a rollover plan for all the childhood naps I refused to take.

November 2, 2012 Facebook
Got a call from my coordinator telling me that my insurance went through, and I am OFFICIALLY on the transplant list!! Wooohooo, what a great start to the weekend. :)

November 12, 2012 Email
Dad to Krystin:
Krystin,

I am not indifferent to your feeling lousy but I don't sense I can do anything, although I sure wish I could help you. I hope the docs can today.

(Probably late August 2012) Email
[this isn't out of order; keep reading]
Gary to his friend Scott [in response to a request about how Krystin was doing]

Krystin, as you perhaps know, has had diabetes since she was 4 years old. For the last 15 years, she's tried to pretend she doesn't have it or just ignored it. She's twice ended up in the ER on the verge of death from not taking insulin (once in Paris, where we ended up staying a week, but maybe you read that story in one of my long Xmas letters).

Anyway, in the last few months, she's FINALLY assumed adult responsibility and done a marvelous job of getting her blood sugars under control. Her reward, so to speak, has been that she's been diagnosed as needing a kidney transplant. She told me, when she called me in my office to tell me, that "it's my own fault." She's correct; the years of neglect have taken a terrible toll on her body, and the kidney is one of the first organs to show it. So now, at age 27, she needs a transplant. There is much I can say to you about this, but not in an email.

Fortunately, Krystin is treating this as an adventure, she's upbeat about it, she's started a blog about it (this is a kid whose aspiration is to be a great creative non-fiction writer), and she's going to begin going through all the necessary tests in the next month and more. Unfortunately, the waiting list for cadaver donors (love that phrase) is 3-5 years; she needs the transplant in the next couple of years, the docs say. Four of her Facebook friends immediately volunteered to be tested for a match.

This prospect, of course, raises extremely difficult questions in the family (that we haven't even begun to talk about). Her brother is the most logical donor--and the literature says that--but I'm wary about having TWO health-impaired children. I can think about being a donor. So could her mother, although I haven't (and won't) talk to her about that possibility. The troubling aspect of asking her brother, in particular--and I don't know if Krystin understands this—is that the transplant extends life about 10 years, on average. Do I or Elliott or her mother give up a kidney so Krystin can live to be 38 rather than 28? These questions have arisen in my mind but I despair at being able to reach a satisfactory answer that is ethically and morally "right." I'm having lunch tomorrow with a retired faculty friend who taught genetics to every medical and dental student at the U for 30 years, who's thought a lot about these kinds of questions. When I talked to him on the phone about the diagnosis for Krystin, his first reaction was "oh, there are very difficult questions you'll have to face."

What we can hope for is that stem-cell research, or some other advances in medicine, will make it possible sometime in the near future for her to have an organ implanted that is grown from her own cells, thus avoiding the need for a donor and lifetime of anti-rejection drugs. This is a microcosmic example of why I detest G W Bush, who put the brakes on stem cell research. Had there been 8 more years of research, the treatments would likely be considerably advanced.

That's probably more than you wanted to know. I am deeply troubled by the myriad implications and questions that this diagnosis elicits and I already know that I have no easy way to address them.

Scott to Gary

Oh dear, I'm really sorry, for her and the whole family. I'm glad she's upbeat and tackling it as a writing project. Maybe she could get a book out of it. But that 10 year projection is pretty grim and obviously one of the last things a parent would want to hear about their child.

Yes, I do remember the early diagnosis, the storminess and denial, and the story about Paris. I guess I'd been assuming that she'd become more self-managing in her 20's. But my own experience with my 20-something sons is that their minds are not always on taking care of the basics. It's clear from what you've written that this hit you like a ton of bricks. Glad to hear that you're finding people to talk about it with who have some background and potentially helpful perspectives to share.

Thanks for the detail, really. I wish I had something insightful or even helpful by way of reply but I'm not sure what to say. At least it's not something that needs to get figured out immediately, that's good, right? Will she have to go on dialysis while waiting for a transplant?

November 13, 2012 Blog
Complaints, and more complaints

I know it has been a while since I posted last, but that's because there isn't much new to report on. Now that I'm officially on the donor wait list (insurance went through fine), it's just a waiting game. It's kind of exciting on one hand, having to keep my phone on me at all times, knowing that I could get a call any time, any time, telling me they have some organs for me. On the other hand, I know it won't be any time soon, and the waiting is getting really hard. I'm getting anxious for this to happen. I just want it to be over. I'm not anxious in a scared kind of way, but in an excited way.

As far as how I'm feeling physically, I feel pretty shitty almost every day. Sometimes I feel fine, and am able to function normally at work, but I'm always tired. Other times I'm nauseous, other times achy, other times fatigued . . . you get the picture? I could go on. It's always something; if it's not one thing, it's something else. I don't know what it's like to feel good anymore. What do people do when they feel consistently crappy for long periods of time?

I often wonder if I'm putting up with more than the average person would put up with. I wonder if the average person walked in my shoes for a day and felt all the things (physically) that I go through, would they say "oh that's nothing, you're just being a wimp complaining about it," or would they say "OMG, how do you get out of bed every morning?" I guess it differs with people's pain tolerances. I have a very low pain tolerance, but I don't like to complain about it. There's not much that can be done about it anyway. Sure, I would love to spend all day in bed sleeping and not having to do anything, but that's not productive, and it doesn't earn me a salary. I still need to work. As much as it's a struggle some days to get up, with an achy body and dizziness, I just can't stay in bed all day.

Emotionally, it's been a roller coaster. I don't know how much I can say here without people worrying too much. However, I want to be as honest as possible and not hold anything back, so here goes. I'm not going to lie - this is depressing me out quite a bit. Not the transplant stuff, but my stomach issues. I thought it was just a lactose intolerance, but it has gotten so worse that it has pretty much become a food intolerance. I can't eat large meals, and it seems like the smallest of things will set my stomach off. For the past couple weeks I've been throwing up almost on a daily basis. There's no pattern, no certain time of day, and no connection to any particular food. It can be within an hour of eating, or 5 hours later. A person shouldn't have to live like this. It's miserable, and it's making it hard for me to keep my weight up. Not to mention it's causing more low blood sugars.

I had an appointment today with my GI doctor, and he has scheduled me for an endoscopy (where they put the tub with the tiny camera on the end down your throat to see if there's any blockage). This will be the third time in my life I've had an endoscopy. The sedative that they give me to make me able to swallow the tube makes me feel fantastic afterwards. I'm not saying I'm looking forward to it, so I do enjoy the loopy after-effects. That's scheduled for next week. In the meantime, I'm supposed to double my dose of the medication from Canada that I'm taking. It hasn't been helping at all, obviously, and the doc is quite surprised, since it helps pretty much everyone else he's put on it. I'm already taking 2 tablets three times a day, so I'm upping it to 4 tablets three times a day. This stuff better start working!

Thanksgiving dinner just won't be the same if I can't indulge in all my favorite T-giving foods.

I don't mean to make this post a complete downer. I wish I had some more uplifting news to give, but right now I don't. For those of who you are not on Facebook, you probably don't know that an acquaintance of mine from high school, Crystal, is the same blood type as me, and has gone through all the steps to get tested to see if she's a match. She has sent in the paperwork, gotten the blood work done, and did her own home science experiment, swabbing the inside of her mouth for DNA and sending it in. She and I even share the same birthday, so that's gotta be a good sign! Fingers crossed while we wait. Trust me, as soon as I find out something, I'll be sure to let you know!

That's all for now. I hope everyone finds themselves in good health and is looking forward to Thanksgiving coming up next week!

November 29, 2012 Blog
Surgery and Eyes (but not surgery ON my eyes)
A few things to report on this time around!

First, I'm having surgery on Tuesday to get the fistula put in my arm in case I need to go on dialysis. I have decided NOT to do the home night system, but instead do the in-clinic option, if they have evening hours. I could go a couple days a week after work, and one day on the weekend. I decided not to do the home system because it requires 6-8 weeks of training before I can get it at home, and the fistula, once put in my arm, can't be used for 2 months after the surgery, for my body to get used to it. And with the home system, I have to have a partner help me with it every night, which means my dad or Kathy will have to help me, and that's not really going to work if I'm trying to get my own apartment sometime after the New Year.

So even though I'm not doing the home system, I still need to get the fistula put in my arm. I'm going in on Monday to get some vein mapping and imaging done, so they can figure out which arm to put it in. Then I go in on Tuesday at 11:30 a.m. to have the surgery. I will be given general anesthesia, and Kathy will drive me home after, since I can't really go back to work after that. I may not even be able to go back to work on Wednesday, but I'm going to play it by ear and see how I feel. I'm not too nervous or worried about the surgery. I've been in the hospital so many times and have had so many tests and pokes and prods done on me, this just feels like yet another procedure. No biggie. And it means if my kidney takes another nose-dive, I'll be all ready to go on dialysis if need be.

For a little arm surgery, there sure are a lot of restrictions beforehand! My surgery is at 11:30 a.m., but I'm not supposed to have any food after midnight. I talked to the lady on the phone and told her that could be a problem with my diabetes, that I could go too low, and she said how about 8 hours before, so I can eat something before 6 a.m. Even though I'm to be at the hospital at 11:30, I think there's a lot of prep, so the surgery won't actually start until around 1, I'm guessing. So I'll be setting my alarm for 5:30 so I can get up and eat a light breakfast. I will also have to reduce my bolus rate in my pump, knowing that I won't be getting any food for a while. Wouldn't want to go low during surgery! I also can't take any of my medications that morning. I guess they don't want anything in my system when they give me anesthesia. This will be my first surgery. I know it's weird to say this, but it's kinda exciting!

Second, I had an eye appointment on Tuesday morning. My vision has improved slightly since my last visit at the end of August, but I have a new problem now. When I look at small things, like print, I have a hard time reading. My eyes are not able to focus together on the words; I see them double, side-by-side. Apparently there's a misalignment of my eyes. Not sure how that happened. If I close one eye and try to read with one eye, then it's fine, which is what I've been doing a lot of the time lately, both on the computer and with books. If I try to read with both eyes together, I really have to strain them, and that gives me a headache. I've been wearing my glasses lately so that if I have a hard time reading something, I can just take off my glasses and hold the document or book right up an inch from my face. Then I can read it just fine!

Also, the cataract that is developing in my right eye has made my vision in that eye a little blurry. On top of that, there's a lot of liquid build-up behind my pupils, which is also causing the slightly blurry vision. There is a way to fix that, however. To get shots in my eyeball. Pleasant, huh? Did that send a shiver down your back like it did mine? I thought we were going to start the shots at the next visit, but oh no, my eye doctor decided we were going to start them that day. So, they put numbing drops in my right eye, squirted a whole bunch of this cold gel stuff on my eye, and put a little circular thing in to keep my eye from closing. Then he had me look up and to my left, told me to keep very still, and poked the syringe in my eye. Not in the pupil, but in the white part to the right of the pupil. Yes, I felt it, and yes, it was very uncomfortable. I wouldn't say it was painful, but it certainly hurt. It was like a tiny pinch. The poke only took about a second and a half, but my eye was sore almost the rest of the day. I have to go in and do this once a month, for a year. Joy.

The upside to it, is that those who have had it done have reported an improvement in their vision. At least that's something to look forward to. I'll have to have this done in both eyes, but for now we're starting with the right eye, since that one has more fluid build-up than the left eye. And if all goes well with the right eye, we'll start on the left eye in a couple months-ish. At some point I will also have to have cataract surgery, but the doctor wants to get the fluid and swelling behind my eyes all cleared up first, otherwise the cataract surgery would be pointless. One of my biggest fears in life is going blind, so whatever they need to do to prevent that from happening, I'm all in.

My mood these days. Well, it's been better this week. I haven't had any throwing up, or hardly any nausea in at least 3 days now. It's sad that it's little things like this that make a day good or bad, but in my condition, I'll take what I can get. I feel like it has kept my spirits up, at least. Today I'm feeling tired, and yesterday I was tired a bit in the afternoon (I had to take a nap when I got home), but Monday and Tuesday I was quite pleasantly surprised that I didn't feel tired at all, all day.

Still no word on whether or not Crystal is a donor match. It's been a couple weeks now, so I'm hoping they get the results soon. I'm so anxious to find out! If she's not a match, it will be a major bummer, but either way, I am still so thankful for everything she has done and gone through to see if she's a match.

That's all for now. Life goes on, albeit uneventful and unexciting. Until next time! Ciao.

December 4, 2012 Blog
Thoughts, fears, confessions

I decided now is a good time for another post, since I have a lot of emotions going on in my head that I think would be helpful to get out. My eyes leaked a little yesterday for the first time since this all started. It has become very overwhelming, and although I have always considered myself a tough girl, everyone has their limits, and I think I found mine. Just like with Superman, I think all this transplant business is becoming my kryptonite. Also for the first time last night,

I said to myself "I don't wanna do this anymore." I don't want to have the fistula surgery, I don't want to do dialysis, I don't want to be a transplant patient. Like I said, the weight of all of this is suddenly all coming down on me at once.

Yesterday I had an appointment to get the vein mapping done of my arm, so the surgeon can decide where to put the fistula. Normally they like to put it in the wrist area, connecting one of the larger arteries to a vein. This location gives dialysis nurses easy access to the line they will use for dialysis. The surgeons look for any arteries that are 2cm in diameter or bigger. Those are the best ones to use. ALL of my arteries, in both arms, are smaller than 2cm in diameter. This makes it more difficult to find a good location for the fistula. They decided that they will put it in the upper, inside part of my left arm (since I'm right-handed). The arteries and veins there are still small, but it seems to be the best option. However, because the vein they want to use is deeper in the arm, they will need to make several incisions, pull the vein up, then stitch me up. Then, in 2-3 weeks, after that has healed and the body has gotten used to the vein being in its new location, they will go in AGAIN and connect it to the main artery that goes down my arm. So I will have to go in for surgery again in a few weeks.

I am not liking this for a couple reasons. The first is the incisions. I will have 2-4 incision scars on the upper part of my arm for the rest of my life. I am already self-conscious about my appearance, now there's one more thing to be self-conscious about. Who wants to be with/date/marry someone with ugly scars on their arm? Yes, I am ashamed to admit, this thought crossed my mind. I know the whole saying "if someone doesn't love you for all of you, flaws and all, then they aren't the right one for you," but how can someone get to know me and love me if they see my scars for the first time and say "eww, I don't want to be seen with you like that in public, see ya." I know, I know, that's not the kind of person I want to be with anyway, because beauty is only skin deep, but it's think like this that I think of. Or just being out in public in a tank top in the summer and having these scars visible. Not something I am thrilled about. And the fistula is permanent; even if I don't end up needing dialysis, unless I am really having troubles with it, it will just stay in forever. Just in case something doesn't work out with my new kidney and I end up needing to go on dialysis for any reason in the future, then it will be there and ready. If I DO need to start dialysis before I get a transplant, all the poking at the fistula sight will also cause bruising and possible swelling. ICK.

The second is that it's a two-step process. Where do they think I am able to get all this time off work? After today, I won't have any hours left to take off, even for doctor appointments, and since I'm still on my 6-month "probation" period, nobody can donate hours to me yet. I will have to take time without pay, which doesn't excite me, but it's my only option.

Speaking of work, that is one of my other concerns, and one that has been weighing heavily on my mind since this all began. I fear that my work is going to start regretting hiring me. Admittedly, I didn't know about the transplant yet when they hired me, but I don't want them to think I deceived them and waited until after I was hired on permanently to tell them about it. I fear they are going to wish they had hired someone more dependable, who didn't take so much time off to go to appointments. I'm a good, hard worker, always have been, and always put 110% into my work, but I really feel like all this leaving to go to appointments and shit is not looking good for me. I know my health comes first and I need to take care of ME, but I really really really don't want all this to affect my relations with my managers at work, and they're going to start frowning at all my absences.

Let's just hope a transplant option comes through before I need to start any dialysis.

Today I go in for the surgery on my arm. I have to be to the hospital at 11:30, and surgery is at 1:30. I will be given general anesthesia, so at least I don't have to be awake for any of it. The procedure will last approximately 2-3 hours, which I don't understand why. All they're doing is making a few small cuts in my arm, pulling up a vein, and stitching me back together. What part of that takes so long?? I rode in with my dad and Kathy today because I can't drive myself home afterwards, obviously. It's outpatient, so I don't need to spend the night. I will get a ride home either from my mom or my dad and Kathy.

I also have not been able to eat anything since last night. I can't have any food 8 hours prior to operation, because they can't risk the chance that the anesthesia may cause the stomach to reflux, and they don't want any food stuff getting caught in my throat while I'm under. Understandable, but I'm huuuuuuungry! And with my diabetes, not eating runs the risk of my blood sugar getting low. I turned the basal rate on my insulin pump down so that I'm only getting 50% insulin instead of my normal dose, so I should be alright. And the surgeon said that if I start to go low during surgery, they can give me some sugar fluids through my IV.

One of the things I forgot to ask about yesterday is about the location of the fistula. Being on the inside of my upper arm, won't it rub against me all the time?? That can't be good for its healing. I plan to return to work tomorrow (Wednesday), and they are giving me pain meds, so hopefully all goes well. Luckily my job is not strenuous in the least bit and I just sit at a computer all day (mostly). If I had a manual labor job, then it would be another story, but considering my job is pretty laid-back, I will just play it by ear and see how I feel tomorrow morning.

SO, all that being said, where do we stand? I'm overwhelmed, honestly a little depressed, and feeling like my spirits are down. Now more than ever and I kicking myself in the ass for not taking care of my diabetes better for the last 10 or so years. If I had, I wouldn't be in this position. Hindsight is indeed a bitch, as the saying goes, and I'm learning that and living that the hard way. I always told myself throughout high school and college "I'll be fine, I have time to turn it around, nothing will happen to me," because at the time nothing WAS happening to me. Organ failure is a slow process, so although it didn't seem like anything was wrong at the time, it has begun, and now it's in full swing and my kidneys are on the fast-track to complete failure. I wish I had had someone then, who was going through this same stuff at the time, to slap me in the face and say HEY! This is serious. That whole "I wish I knew then, what I know now" idea.

BUT, what's in the past is in the past, I can't go back, I can't change any of it, and the only way to get through it is to keep a positive attitude and use all the resources and support around me that I have. When I feel alone, I have to be sure to talk to someone. Everyone I know, friends, co-workers, and family, have all said that they are here for me if I need it, and I need not forget that. On the other hand, it's hard to reach out when my brain is telling me "but they just don't understand what you're going through." Easy for everyone else to tell me to stay strong. Don't get me wrong, I truly, honestly appreciate the encouragement, and I need the reminders and support once in a while, so please, don't stop giving it. Even if it doesn't seem appreciated, it is, more than you'll ever know.

I think that's all for now. I should get some work done before I have to head over to the hospital. I will post again post-surgery, even with some pictures! Bye for now.

December 5, 2012 Blog
Surgery

Well, yesterday was the surgery on my arm. All went about as well as could go. I got to the hospital at 11:30, but brought back to the pre-op room until 12:45. Apparently all the pre-op rooms were occupied. My mom pointed out that even though my surgery wasn't scheduled to start until 1:30, they would want me there early in case another surgery gets done quickly and they're able to call me back early. That way I'd already be there and they wouldn't have to wait for me. That wasn't the case, obviously, but I can understand that reasoning. When I did finally go back, it was all the usual pre-op routine. Change into a gown, check my vitals, get blood work done, give a urine sample, go over a bunch of questions, and get the IV line in and started. They did a blood sugar, and my blood sugar was 55, so they gave me some sugar water in my IV line, since I wasn't allowed to drink or eat anything before surgery. I finally got wheeled down to the operating room around 2:00. On the way, they gave me a relaxant in my IV. Love that stuff! Once on the operating table, they put these cool things around the bottom half of my legs that alternate squeezing my legs, to keep blood flowing during surgery. They also put an oxygen mask on me, which, after given anesthesia to put me to sleep, they would use to pump something through to keep me asleep. I don't even remember them giving me the anesthesia. I don't even know if they told me they were giving it to me now, or if I was told to count back from 10. Next thing I know, I'm waking up in the recovery room.

They didn't end up putting the fistula in the upper, inner part of my arm as I had said before. It's right above the crook of my elbow, on the inside. Still on the left arm, though. I guess they decided that was a better location. And they only had to make one incision, so I don't need to go back for surgery round 2 at all. Whew. Here is what it looks like:

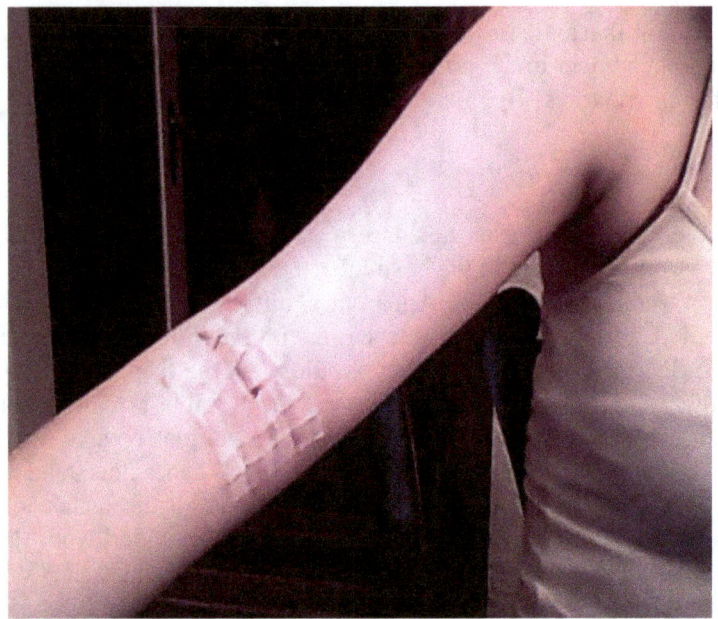

The surgery took 3 and a half hours, so it was about 5:30 when I was brought to the post-op room, and a little after 6 when I woke up. Naturally, I was pretty groggy, and my arm hurt pretty bad, so they gave me some painkillers through my IV. After 5 minutes, it wasn't feeling any better, so they gave me some more. After another 5 minutes, the rest of me was feeling great, but the pain in my arm had only gone down a little, so they gave me another half dose. After that, it finally began feeling better. Since I had taken my insulin pump off for surgery, my blood sugar was 248 when they did a blood test in the post-op room, so they also gave me a couple units of insulin through my IV. My mouth was incredibly dry from the anesthesia, so I got some ice chips to suck on, too. Around 7, when I was pretty much fully awake and the pain in my arm subdued, I was brought down to the recovery room, which is just a big room with a bunch of little cubes. There they gave me some apple juice, saltine crackers, got help getting dressed, and went over my discharge instructions with me. I was also given a prescription of Percocet, for the pain, which I have been taking, 1 pill every 4 hours. At 8:00 I was put in a wheelchair and wheeled down to the main entrance of the hospital, where my mom picked me up. I was very wobbly on my feet, so when we got home my mom helped me into the house and onto the couch. My dad and Kathy had been at a University event, and got home shortly after I did.

Since I hadn't eaten all day, aside from the crackers, I had a little leftover Chinese food from a couple nights earlier, talked with my dad and Kathy about how everything went for a bit, and by 9 I could hardly keep my eyes open anymore. My eyes were so heavy. I grabbed my bottle of Percocet, went upstairs, plopped down in bed, set the alarms for midnight, 4am, and 8am (to take my pill), and fell right asleep.

I was going to play it by ear as to whether or not I went to work today, and I didn't end up going. Probably a very good decision. My arm hasn't been in any pain all day, but I was incredibly tired and spent most of the day sleeping. I fully plan on going to work tomorrow, though, and I hope that I don't fall asleep on my keyboard. Of course if I'm just too tired and can't stay awake, I know my office will be understanding if I need to leave early. I'll just see how it goes.

The bandage on my arm stays on for 7 days, after which I go back in for a check-up and they see how it's doing. I'm not sure if they put another bandage on it again or just leave it. In the meantime, I can't get it wet at all, which will make showering interesting. I may need to wash my hair in the sink and do sponge baths to wash the rest of me. Not too thrilled of that idea, but I have to follow directions, so I'm not going to risk anything. Another option I came up with is to wrap my arm with a plastic bag, like a bread bag, and just stand to one side in the shower. I'll let you know how that goes.

I realized recently that in the past 4 months, I have seen more of the inside of me than most people see in their whole lives. I've seen an ultrasound of my heart, stomach, bladder, spleen, and kidney, as well as an ultrasound of the veins in my neck and all down both of my arms. I've had both a colonoscopy and endoscopy, so I've seen both down and up the inside. This has all been like my own Discovery Channel special! It's been fascinating though to see all these things.

Well, it's 9:30 now, and even though I've slept most of the day, I'm pooped, so I'm off to bed. Ciao for now.

December 8, 2012 Facebook
No matter what may come, I won't surrender.

December 17, 2012 Blog
Last Week

Last week was a pretty eventful week for me. I've been meaning to write about it sooner, but I've been having some eye issues and had not been able to see the computer screen very well, so did not have much motivation to stare at a computer and try to write a post.

I'll start with that. I noticed last weekend that my vision had really started going downhill. I had dozens of black floaters in both my eyes, blocking my line of sight. I could see around them, but it was like a dozen or more little black streaks going across my vision. On top of that, my vision was blurry. So last Monday they fit me in last minute. That was the day we had that big snow storm the night before, so a lot of people must've cancelled their appointments. I could hardly see anything. I could make out shapes, but nothing was in focus. Luckily I know the U campus like the back of my hand, so I could navigate through the tunnel system with no problems. Of course I rode in with my dad and Kathy, since there was no way I could drive. I actually ended up riding in with them most of the week.

I saw my usual eye doctor, Dr. Terry. He had some photos of my eyes taken so we could look at them together (not that I could see the photos). Turns out there was hemorrhaging in both my eyes, which means they are bleeding on the inside. That was all the floaters I was seeing, and what was also causing the blurriness. There is no immediate solution to this. The best and quickest option was to do those shots in my eyeballs again, and for me to stay vertical at all times. So, he gave me a shot in both my eyes (which, even after an extra dose of numbing drops this time, still hurt), and for the past week I've been sleeping in our recliner chair in the living room, so that my head can stay elevated. This is so that gravity can work faster on draining the blood on the inside of my eyes (no, this does not mean there has been blood dripping OUT of my eyes - it's all on the inside). As of today, almost all the floaters are gone, and most of the blurriness has gone away. I'm finally able to do computer work again (hence me finally posting).

Finding this out last Monday seems to be the straw that broke the camel's back for me. I was fine all the way back to my office, but as soon as I called my dad to let him know what I found out, the flood doors of my eyes opened and I totally lost it. I wasn't even in the privacy of my own cube. The phone at my desk doesn't work, so I was sitting up at the front desk. The whole conversation with my dad I had my head in my hand, sobbing. I don't know what anyone walking past thought, but I didn't care. Only a handful of people in my office know about my transplant. It's not something I'm hiding or ashamed of or anything, but it's also not something I sent out a SPA-wide e-mail announcing.

My biggest fear right then wasn't about the health of my eyes or my body, but about my work. I was so worried to tell my supervisor that I couldn't see anything and would have to take a few (unpaid) days off work, since I wouldn't see anything to work. I even said to my dad on the phone, "I might as well quit, because at this rate I'm going to get fired anyway." I have not had a good track record, as far as attendance, since I've started. And now with my eyes going to hell, I'd have to take even more time off. And unpaid, since I used all my remaining sick/vacation time the week before, for my surgery. He said no, don't plan on taking any time off yet. If I felt physically well enough to be there, he would find something for me to do that utilized my brain but that didn't require me to be reading things or working on the computer. So he started asking around, and that afternoon I was helping out with other projects. Menial, tedious tasks and projects, but stuff that needed to be done nonetheless, and it kept me at work, so I didn't have to take any time off. I am so appreciative of this, since, let's be honest, nobody likes to take time off from work unpaid.

By Thursday I had started to see improvements, and was even able to drive myself to work. I went in a bit early, so that I could leave a little early while it was still a little light out. I didn't trust myself driving at night yet, but during the day was fine. On Thursday I even started doing some computer work again. It was slow going, and frequently I just had to remove my glasses and put my face up an inch from the screen to read it, but at least I was able to do stuff. Same with Friday. Even though it was slow going, I got a lot done. Today, no problem. Whew.

On Wednesday I go to a clinic in Edina that specializes in retinal surgery and other eye issues, so I look forward to see what they have to say about my eyes.

A week and a half ago I took a visit to the ER. It actually wasn't last week, it was the Thursday before. I was worried about my surgery incisions, because my whole arm, from wrist to shoulder almost, even my hand, was very swollen. The underside of my arm was even a little blue and purple. I still could not bend it or straighten it very well, and was still taking my Percocet numerous time a day. This was over a week after surgery, so I didn't know if that was normal. I went in around 9 p.m. and got home at almost 3 a.m. In that whole time, the only thing they did was do another ultrasound on my arm, to make sure there weren't any clogs, which may be causing swelling. Everything was normal. The swelling can last up to 2 weeks or so after surgery. Tomorrow will be 2 weeks, and it's still a little swollen and stiff, and I still can't totally straighten my arm, but bending it is getting much easier. I finally have my post-surgery follow-up appointment today, so they'll take a look at it and make sure it's looking good. All the surgical strips they put on the incisions after the surgery have fallen off, on their own, which is fine. It means the incisions were ready for them to come off. The incisions look good; no redness or anything, so they seem to be healing well. I'll keep you posted on what the docs say today.

    All this has made me a roller coaster of emotions. I feel like the whole ordeal with my eyes last week was my tipping point, and ever since then I've felt almost bipolar. My day can be going fine, and I'll be in a good, normal mood, then all of a sudden I'll notice I'm feeling sad, defeated, and depressed. Yesterday I was in the car listening to the radio, and they were talking about a program they do called 'Christmas Wish,' where they give a whole bunch of free stuff to a family in need. One little blip they played was for a family that has a son who is on his 2nd kidney transplant. That made me tear up. Then I was listening to Christmas music on another station and "All I Want for Christmas" came on. The main chorus line is "All I want for Christmas is you," and I was singing along in my head with "All I want for Christmas is a kidney." That made me tear up. Then last night I was taking a shower and had Andrea (pronounced Ahn-dray-uh) Bocelli playing, and his amazing, passionate singing made me tear up. The smallest things can set me off! I think it's just because of how overwhelming this all has become.

    There are times when I just want to give up, when sometimes I think this isn't worth waiting for and living through; like I can't take all this feeling miserable ALL the time. Does that mean I'm actually going to hurt myself in any way? No no no no. Don't get me wrong. There are so many things I have left to do in life, so many things to look forward to, some way still to leave my mark on the world. All I'm saying is that some days it's hard to deal with and I'm tired of waiting and just want it to be over and done with. Not knowing how much longer I'll have to wait is stressful, but I try not to think about the wait. I try to think about one day and a time, and just getting through today successfully. It's a rocky road, but like I've said in the past, I'm a tough girl (I do take after my mother in this respect), and I won't let it keep me down (too much). I'll keep plugging along.

I am very lucky to have such supportive co-workers. One of my co-workers, one of our grant administrators, Anjeanette, has been my own personal nurse and therapist for the last couple weeks. She has helped me take care of and re-wrap my incision site, and been a supportive shoulder to cry on (literally). She even came with me to talk to my supervisor last Monday, for moral support, when I told him about my eyes. That really helped to have her there with me, knowing someone was there with me who had my back and was on my side. That's not to say that my supervisor isn't on my side. Oh no, he definitely is. He was also been very, very supportive and accommodating through all this. Everyone has been. One of my biggest worries is that people around here would start to look down on me with how often I was gone, but I'm starting to realize that's not true. Like Anjeanette has pointed out, it's not like I'm gone just be gone. It's all been for medical reasons. As someone who has always had very high personal standards for my work performance, accepting this has been a challenge. But I'm working on, and every day I'm beginning to realize more and more how lucky I am to work in such a great place.

Alright, I think that's all I got for now. Back to work, since I can finally do some. I hope you all had a good weekend and have a good pre-holiday week!

December 20, 2012 Blog
More pokes in my eye

Yesterday I had an eye appointment at Vitreo Retinal Surgery in Edina. As with all major health issues, it was highly suggested that I get a second opinion on my eye issues, and this clinic, and specific doctor, was recommended to me by the son-in-law of a long-time family friend. The doctor who I saw, Dr. Bennett, is one of the best ophthalmologists in the Twin Cities (maybe even the state?). Even though I've been going to the eye clinic at the U for many years, I recently learned that ophthalmology is not the U's strongest field, and that I should actually steer clear of the U when it comes to ophthalmology. So I went to Vitreo.

They did the usual exam, where I had to read the letters on the wall covering each eye, and they took some photos and did some eye scans. The usual routine. Then Dr. Bennett came in, and we brought my mom in, too (she drove me, because they said I would need a driver), so that he could talk to us both at the same time. Also because I think it's always good to have a second pair of ears along. And eyes (HAHA). He said he's going to be very straightforward and frank with me. No sugar coating it. My eyes are not good. I have cataracts growing in both eyes, and have a lot of diabetic neuropathy damage. If we did nothing to my eyes, eventually I would go blind. Good news is, something CAN be done. He said my vision will never be better than it is today, but we can prevent it from getting worse. It will take a number of procedures, though.

First, I'll continue getting the shots in my eyeballs, of this stuff called Avastin. That will be done once a month, which was the same as at the U, so that doesn't change. I will also continue getting laser treatments. The laser treatments I was getting at the U were apparently very weak treatments and didn't do much for my eyes. They didn't go deep into the eye, and couldn't get past the cataracts. The lasers that Dr. Bennett would use go deep into the eyes, and CAN get past the cataracts. Each eye will need probably 3 treatments, and he'll only do one eye at a time, so a total of 6 treatments. Those will be done about every 2-3 weeks, along with the Avastin shots once a month (but they won't be done at the same appointment). At some point within the next 7-12 months, I will need cataract surgery, which didn't come as a surprise. Dr. Terry at the U told me that a long time ago. But that will come after all the laser treatments are done and the Avastin has done most of its work. His last resort, if need be after cataract surgery, is retinal surgery. I'm not sure what that entails, or what exactly the point of that is, but Dr. Bennett wants to avoid that, so it sounds like that's only an option if everything else isn't working.

Are we having fun yet??

He said he will be honest with me, that it's going to be a tough year, and nothing about this is going to be comfortable, but in the end it will be better for my eyes. He told me that he's had patients who were younger than me, and whose eyes were worse, and today they are in grad school and happily married and sending him baby pictures. Well, ok then, good to know. . . . He didn't mention if they were blind or not, but I'm going to go ahead and assume that it's a happy story and that they're not; otherwise he wouldn't be telling me that, right??

He said that he could start the laser treatment as soon as that day. He left the room, and my mom and I talked it over, and decided yes, I'll do the first treatment then. Since we were already there, why postpone it? Might as well start it as soon as I can. So they put in the numbing drop and gave those a few minutes to set in. Then Dr. Bennett gave me two shots of novocaine, both around my upper cheek/lower eyelid area. They felt like a very painful pinch. After a few more minutes, he gave me another, bigger shot, in the same area. Even though it was a shot, it did not feel like a needle going into my skin. It felt like someone was pressing down on my eye, forcefully, trying to push my eye into the back of my skull. That was not pleasant at all. It was downright painful and more than uncomfortable. Even after he was finished, it still hurt, even with the novocaine. What that shot did was to basically disable my eye. After the solution completely set in, I couldn't even open my eyelid. When he held it open, he told me to look up, down, left, and right. My left eye was moving in those directions as directed, but my right eye was dead, completely unmoving (is that a word?).

The laser treatment only lasted about 15 minutes, and after all the shots, I didn't feel a thing. I could still feel the soreness from the shots, but not the laser. He only did my right eye this time. Afterwards, they taped a patch over my eye, which I only had to leave on until bedtime. Even on the car ride home, I could tell the numbing stuff was starting to wear off, and the headache behind my eye was growing. When I got home, I took two of my Percocet that I had left over from my surgery. It took the edge off, but was still sore. This morning I took 2 more Percocet, and even by lunch time it had done nothing. It hurts a lot today, like there's a migraine in my eyeball. I may need to go home from work early, because besides hurting every time I move my eye, it's making me feel nauseous. Now I understand what Dr. Bennett meant when he said this was not going to be pleasant. It certainly isn't. I've only had this done once and I already dread the next session. :/

My next appointment is January 6, which is when he'll do laser on my left eye. I can't wait. And by can't wait I mean can we please slow down time so that it never happens? Just one more form of torture that I have to put up with.

I may not post again now until after Christmas, and probably even after New Years, so I hope everyone has a wonderful holiday with friends and family! Try to stay warm if you're here in the Midwest, and I'll see you all in 2013!

December 26, 2012 Facebook
How long after Christmas is it OK to leave Christmas decorations up in your work cube?? If you tell me March or April, that would be OK with me. :)

December 27, 2012 Facebook
Pending a final blood test, I'm getting a kidney!!! Ya'll could give me all the riches in the world, but nothing compares to what I'll be getting from the wonderful Crystal. Merry Christmas to me indeed!!

December 27, 2012 Facebook
Crystal Lescault to Krystin Engstrand
Well guess what little lady???! The transplant nurse says my blood is "relatively antibody free and we are a pretty good match!" Ahhhhhhhh!!!!!!!!!!!! So, I gotta go for some more standard testing (and I think you do too) but if all that looks good then we are a go! Keep your fingers crossed but it looks good :)

> Krystin: omg omg OMG! This is exactly what I needed to hear today. I probably shouldn't have read this at work, cuz I almost started crying. That would be so fantastically, fabulously amazing and I can't even express how grateful I am to you. I'm so, so happy that things are looking good!! =) =)
> Crystal Lescault: My words to the nurse, "holy s*it, really??!" Hahaaa. I was pretty excited, and so was she. Now take care of yourself, as will I. We need to be in good health for this to work. I'll let you know when my big testing day is, in the next few weeks I think.
> I had a good feeling about this from the beginning . . . yay :)
> Krystin: It's the October 30 birthday luck!
> Krystin: I called my coordinator today to ask if I should go in for more blood work, and she said not yet for me, that you aren't yet in the system as "fully approved," and to sit tight until you hear more. Your coordinator will let you know when you are fully approved, but my coordinator said if you don't hear anything by the end of this week, maybe try calling again early next week to see what the status is!
> Crystal Lescault: They have to schedule me for a full day evaluation, blood tests, scans, fun stuff to make sure I'm in good

health, okay for a surgery etc. I'm currently playing phone tag with the scheduler but ill let you know when I'm set up for that :)

Krystin: Oh wow! I didn't realize you had to do all that. Do you have a job that's pretty supportive in you taking a day off to do that stuff??

Crystal Lescault: Um, no . . . Lol. I just started at my job but I don't work Wednesdays (I nanny that day) so I'm trying to work that out. I guess they usually do these appointments on Fridays but they are going to try to work me in on a Wednesday.

Krystin: I'll keep my fingers crossed they can! You rock. :)

Crystal Lescault: The first available appt is February 6th so I snapped it up!

Krystin: Woohoo!

December 31, 2012 Blog
Great news!

For those of you who are on facebook, you already know this, but for those of you who aren't, I found out some good news last week - my friend Crystal is a match!! I'm sure you remember me saying how she did all the necessary blood work about a month ago to see if she is a match for me. We hadn't heard anything in a long time, so she called the clinic to find out what's up. The nurse told her that we will both have to go in for some more blood work, but that so far everything is looking really good! She has very little antibodies in her blood, which is a good thing - it means the new kidney won't fight so hard against it's new (my) body, which is also especially good because my blood has a LOT of antibodies in it.

I called my transplant team here at the U to find out what the next step is, like if/when I need to come in for more blood work. I actually don't need to do anything yet. Marilyn (the coordinator who is just covering for my coordinator, Mary Beth, who is on vacation until Wednesday), said that she doesn't see Crystal as fully approved in the system yet. When she is fully approved, her coordinator will let her know as well as my transplant team, and then Mary Beth will contact me. At that point, that's when we go in for the final blood work. So in the meantime I sit tight.

As I've been telling people, I can't imagine that they would find something in a final blood test to make us incompatible that they didn't find in all the previous testing. I asked Marilyn how often it happens that they find something in the final blood tests that make the donor and recipient not compatible, and she said it does happen, but the odds are very very small. She said in her 17 years of doing this, she's only seen in happen 3 or 4 times. I like those odds. Well, I don't like that it happens at all, but if it has to, I like only 3 or 4 times in a 17-year period.

I also asked about surgery scheduling, and how long usually after the donor is approved do they schedule surgery. Marilyn said about a month. They like to have time to educate the donor and recipient about the surgery and post-care and all that. So at the earliest it would be early February, but probably closer to late February, which is completely fine with me, if that's fine with Crystal! I'm pretty much leaving the surgery date up to her, since I'm ready to take the time off from work any time. I don't know what her work schedule is like, so I'm pretty much leaving it open for her. As long as it's not November of 2014!

I am feeling very good about this. I still feel like crap every day, but it has greatly lifted my spirits. I have had so many things go wrong lately with nothing going right, that I was getting so down and depressed and overwhelmed with it all, and I really needed to hear some positive news. This finally puts the light at the end of the tunnel. I don't know how close or far I am to it, but I can see it! Last week on Thursday and Friday I was so happy at work, nothing ruined my day. Crystal had told me the news via Facebook, and when I read it, I was sitting at my desk at work. I couldn't help but shed a few tears of joy. I couldn't believe it! My luck had finally turned around. I am proof that you really do need to hit rock bottom before you can start getting better. Everything does need to go wrong before it can go right. I still feel exhausted physically, but a little less so emotionally now. This gets me through the days with a smile on my face and hope in my heart.

It's going to be a great start to the New Year

UPDATE, as of about an hour after posting this: Crystal informed me that she will need to go in for a day of tests and evaluations to make sure she is healthy for surgery and whatnot (like I had to do). She has it scheduled for Feb. 6. Woohoo!

January 3, 2013 Blog
Eye update

Yesterday was my second appointment at the new clinic I'm going to. The agenda was to have the 2nd laser treatment done (which I was dreading), but there is now a slight change of plans. They did the usual exam and eye scan, and it turns out the cataracts in both my eyes are getting worse. Even though the laser that Dr. Bennett uses is used to laser through/around cataracts, mine have gotten too bad for him to be able to work around. In case you don't know what a cataract is (I certainly didn't at first), it's basically a cloudy area in the lens of the eye that affects vision, making vision look cloudy or blurry. Although I am experiencing blurriness in the right eye, I'm not in the left eye. However, that does not mean that the cataract isn't there. It just might not be right in my line of sight. Some people with cataracts don't even know they have them.

For "normal" people, cataracts can take years to develop, but for me especially, he said (meaning patients with diabetes and kidney failure), development can happen really fast, which seems to be happening. Just in the 2 weeks since I was there last, he's seen a lot more development of them. He wants me to have cataract surgery before he continues the laser treatment, and since they don't do cataract surgery in that clinic, he's going to call me with a recommendation for a good cataract surgeon. I will then meet for a consult and discuss surgery options. Dr. Bennett would really like this to be done before my transplant. He said that after cataract surgery, I may not even need to wear my contacts or glasses at all, only reading glasses. I'm a little skeptical about that. I don't think he realizes how blind I actually am without my contacts/glasses. I just don't believe that having cataract surgery will fix my vision to the point that I don't need corrective lenses at all, especially since my almost blindness is due to many many years of bad diabetes management. So I'll believe it when I see it (no pun intended).

In the meantime, we're going to continue with the shots once a month, so he did that yesterday instead. Although shots in the eyeballs are not fun, it was much more pleasant at this clinic than it was at the U. At the U, I got numbing drops in my eyes, and that was all. I could still feel the shots; painful, I would even call it. At Vitreo, they put numbing drops in, but then Dr. Bennett also gave me a little shot in each eye of Novocain. That shot I felt a little bit, but it was only like a pinch, it wasn't painful at all. Then the Avastin shots I didn't feel at all. And he was so quick, it was over and done with in less than a second. Much more bearable. It makes me not dread the future ones as much. I did have quite the headache last night afterwards and pretty much went right to bed when I got home, and my eyes are a little sore today, but it's nothing I can't handle.

That's all I got for now. Happy New Year to you all!

January 7, 2013 Blog
Happy New Year!

I hope everyone had a good Holiday season and the New Year finds everyone happy and healthy! The Christmas tree finally came down this past weekend, and all the decorations boxed up until next year. We've now entered into the drab, grey, boring part of winter. Blah. But I have something to look forward to (hopefully) in the next few months, so no seasonal affective disorder for this gal! (Not that I ever get it, anyway).

Just a brief update this time. I have been doing pretty well these days as far as my spirits go. My stomach, however, is not doing too well again. There was about a two-week period where I had no "getting sick" incidents at all, and then the last couple weeks it has started up again. Almost on a daily basis. I have decided I must have a food intolerance, since I can't pinpoint any specific thing that makes my stomach upset. Apparently that is common with renal failure, and then with the gastro issues on top of it, nothing is safe. I have to eat very small amounts at one time, and hope for the best. And there's no telling if/when something will make me sick. If it does, it's not even necessarily right away. It can be an hour later, or 8 hours later. And once I start to feel nauseous, there's no stopping it. Nothing I take makes it go away (I've tried Maalox, as well as a couple other things meant to settle upset stomachs). I just have to wait it out and let it works its way out (literally). Of course I feel significantly better afterwards, but it means I've just lost all the nutrients I had consumed. I can tell that I'm losing weight because of it and I'm sure this doesn't help with my energy level (of which there is none).

My right eye has become really blurry again. I'm sure it's the cataract that's doing that. Dr. Bennett's office called me on Friday with a recommendation for a cataract surgeon, so I will be calling her today to set up a consultation visit. I would like this cataract surgery to be done soon as well so I can get back to seeing properly. I think tonight I may try sleeping on the chair in the living room again to keep my head vertical, and see that makes a difference. Here's crossing my fingers to an improvement tomorrow.

I'm really looking forward to this all being over. Like I've said before, I'm crossing my fingers that this transplant solves a lot of other little problems. Soon . . .

If you are wondering how my fistula is doing these days, you're in luck! Here is a photo to curb your curiosity:

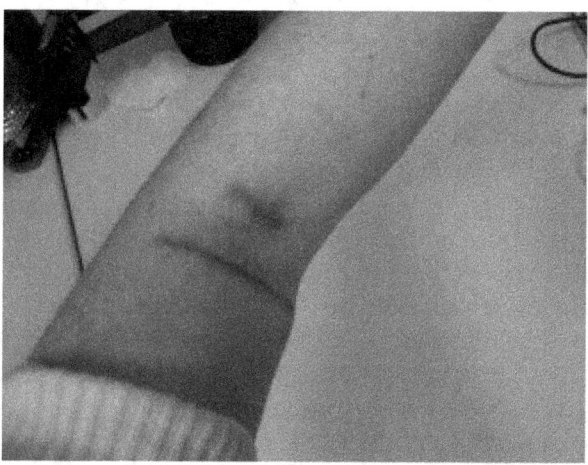

Verdict from the docs is that it's looking good and healing great! Pretty much all the swelling has gone down, and I have full motion of my arm back. Presumably the incision scars will continue to fade over time, and I'm hoping that even the small bulge that remains under the bigger incision will get even smaller, too. I told my mom about a week ago that now it just looks like I got a couple bad cat scratches, and she said, "it looks like more than just a cat scratch." OK, she's probably right.

That's all for now. It's Monday so I think I'm going to treat myself to some Chipotle for lunch. Yum yum. Bye for now.

January 9, 2013 Blog
Better vision is on the way

Lucky you, I'm back so soon!

I had the appointment this morning with the cataract surgeon, [whose office is located at 50th & France. Which, I have to say, always makes me feel like I need to get all dolled up and fancy when I go to that neighborhood. It's like THE ritzy part of Edina. I have this impression that the people who live in the area are the hoity-toity people of the Twin Cities. Pulling up in my Saturn sure makes me stick out like a sore thumb amongst the BMWs and Mercedes. OK, so there aren't really BMWs and Mercedes everywhere, but there should be.

Anyway, the appointment went exactly as I expected. [The surgeon] dilated my eyes and did an exam, and verified that yup, I need cataract surgery in both my eyes. We are going to do one eye at a time, and start with the right eye, since that one is worse. Then about a week later she'll do the left eye. What happens in cataract surgery is she will go in, remove the optical lens that has the cataract on it, and replace it with a new one, which will actually have my contact prescription built into it, so I won't have to wear contacts anymore! Well, she said I may still need contacts, but if I do, a much weaker prescription than I have now. I will always need reading glasses after that, but that's OK. Guess I'm starting to turn into an old cat lady at a young age. A funny thing [the surgeon] said was "the cataracts that have developed on your eyes are ones that are more common in young people and are different from those that develop on older people, so don't feel like you're being put into the old folks category." Oh good, because, you know, I was so worried about that. :) Looks like I need to start looking for some cute reading glasses!

The surgery will be done at Fairview Southdale hospital (date currently not scheduled). Prior to the surgery, I'll need to go to my primary care clinic and get a pre-op physical. I assume that's to make sure that I'm healthy enough to handle surgery. Well, "healthy" by the eye clinic standards, since I'm not really healthy in any way these days. I will also have to go into the clinic in Edina to get a retinal measuring before the surgery, so [the surgeon] knows what size lens to put into my eye. I'm hoping that all this can be done in the next month so I can hurry up and see better!

Although the surgery procedure only lasts about 15 minutes, I will be there about 3 hours. My mom will be taking me, since obviously I will not be able to drive myself home after. I felt bad about her having to take such a chunk out of her work day to just sit there and wait for me for hours, but she said she can bring her laptop and work on work stuff in the waiting room. Oh, good. Maybe bring some sudoku, too. [The surgeon] said I will be able to use my eye right away afterwards and won't need an eye patch. I will have prescription eye-drops that I'll need to use for about a month afterwards.

One of my co-workers pointed out that I'm becoming the bionic woman. New kidney, new pancreas, new eyes . . . what next?? In a decade half of my body parts will be replacements! Whatever keeps me going, I guess. I still have so many things I want to do, there's no time for my body to fail! I feel like for being so young still, I sure have gone through a lot of big life events, all of which are (negatively) health related. I need a vacation.

Back to work. My eyes are finally losing their dilation from this morning, so hopefully I can finally get some computer work done. Bye for now.

January 17, 2013 Blog
Cataract surgery schedule

Next Tuesday (the 22nd) I will have my first cataract surgery, on my right eye. The week after that, Tues. the 29th, I will have the second surgery, on my left eye. I would do them both at the same time if I could, but that is not an option. Probably a good thing, anyway. However, these surgeries are taking me away from work a lot. On Tuesday of this week I went into the clinic so they could do a scan of my lenses (the natural ones in my eyeball, not my contacts) so that [the surgeon] knows what size lens to put in when she does the surgery. Next week I need to be at the hospital at 11:30, and the Tuesday after that, at noon (and out from the work the rest of the day, of course). Then for both surgeries, the morning after (Weds.) I need to go in to the clinic in the morning for a follow-up. Those days I should get to work hopefully by 10. Still, all these hours add up. I don't have enough sick/vacation time for all this! On the mornings that I can get my butt up out of bed an hour early, I've been going in to work an hour early, to make up the time gone (which also means I don't have to take an hour of sick/vacation time here and there).

I've also started asking around to see if anyone at work has some extra projects or work they need help with that I can come in on the weekends and work on, to earn some comp time. That's time and a half! So even if I only go in for 2 hours, for example, that's 3 hours comp time. Even that would help greatly. It sounds like, from my supervisors, that a couple people have some things for me. I figure this also looks good on my part, that I want to put in the extra time to make up for being gone.

I had to go to the pharmacy the other day, too, to pick up some eye drops. There are 3 different drops, 2 of which I'll have to start on Saturday, so before the surgery. Then I'll continue with all 3 of them for about a month after the surgery. 6 tiny bottles of eye drops knocked me out $160. OUCH. When the pharmacist gave me my total, I gasped with shock and said "and that's WITH insurance??" She said yup, without insurance I'd be paying somewhere between $600-$800. Dang. I need to move back to Korea where prescriptions are less than $10 no matter what it is. Sheeeesh.

I'm not too nervous about the procedure. The only thing I'm nervous about is that they're cutting my eye open, and it's not like I can look away or close my eyes and not watch. I will be given many numbing drops and some nice sedative, so hopefully I'll just get to lay there and watch the pretty color light show that goes on in my head. Ideally I'd like to fall asleep, but I doubt that's going to happen, and I doubt even more that I'd be able to convince them to give me general anesthesia to make me sleep. I will be going to work that morning, so that I can at least get in a few hours of work before going to the hospital, so staying up all night so that I'm super tired probably isn't a good idea. I know I won't feel anything at all, but I still have this paranoia that something will go horribly wrong and they'll make the first cut in my eye and I'll feel this horrible, unbearable pain; because that's just how my luck in life goes. [The surgeon] said that it's up to me how much sedative I get, so I'll tell them to just keep pumping it into me until I feel completely relaxed and ready to go. Sounds like a good plan to me.

Other than that, I'm doing fine. Making it through every day, but extremely tired. By 3 in the afternoon I just want to take a nap. For the last week or so I've been seriously considering sitting down with my supervisor and seeing if there's any way I could work 75% time until after my surgery and my health is back to normal. I just get SO tired in the afternoons, I feel useless around here. The only thing that makes me uneasy about doing that is that I'm still on my 6 month probation at work, which means they can let me go at any time, for any reason, without explanation. I know there is a 99.99999% chance of that NOT happening, and that my supervisor would be understanding and help me work something out, but again, like I said, with my luck in life . .

My brother has been sick for the past 3-4 days, and yesterday I thought maybe I was starting to come down with it, so I left work at 4, went straight home, put on my sweatpants and sweatshirt, turned on my heating pad, crawled into bed, and slept until I got up this morning. I feel very rested today, but 3:00 is rolling around and I'm already starting to feel tired again. Ugh, stupid kidneys! Making me a bad employee. I have this fear that everyone else at work sees it as laziness, when really it's a legitimate health problem that is draining my energy. Which is maybe why it would be better for me to work 75% time. At least that way I can be productive while I'm here, and then go home and rest before the exhaustion sets in. Now I just have to get up the courage to talk to my supervisor about it. I feel like this is just one more exception that I'm asking for, and at some point it's going to be asking too much. *Sigh.

That's all for now. Next post will probably be after my first eye surgery. So until then, stay well and carry on, everyone.

January 24, 2013 Blog
Cataract Surgery: Round 1

It has now been a couple days since my first cataract surgery, which was on Tuesday. I'll admit, I let my nerves get the best of me way more than I needed to. Both my aunt and uncle have had cataract surgery recently, so on Monday night I called and talked to my aunt, just to get some reassurance about the procedure. Turns out, it was easier than a piece of cake. I got to the hospital at a little after 11:30, in the eye care center. They brought me back to my own little alcove, where they did the usual vitals and going over my medical info and such. Then the nurse started giving me eye drops. 4 different drops, 3 times each. Then she put in the IV. As always, that part freaked me out and I got all clammy and hyperventilated a little, but once it was in I breathed a big sigh of relief. Hate that part. Then around 1 they wheeled the hospital chair I was sitting in right into the operating room. We had to wait a little bit for [the surgeon] to come, but they started giving me the anesthetic eye drops and get my head adjusted and all ready for surgery.

I'm not sure at what point [the surgeon] came in, or when they started giving me sedative, but I know we were talking about my kidney transplant and about Crystal being a match. When she actually started the procedure is also a bit hazy. I was aware that she was near me and doing something, but I just saw a bunch of pretty colors (like looking through a kaleidoscope), and I felt absolutely nothing. [The surgeon] told me later that I was talking to her during the procedure, but that my speech was slurred, so she could tell the sedative was working. Even though I was very comfortable and felt nothing, I think next time I'm going to ask for a tiny bit more sedative, because I DO remember that my stomach was still clenched and I felt tense most of the time.

The procedure was over in no time, though. I guess it took about 20 minutes, but it seemed like she had only just started when she said "alright, you're all done." They put a clear plastic cover over my eye and wheeled me back to my alcove to recover.

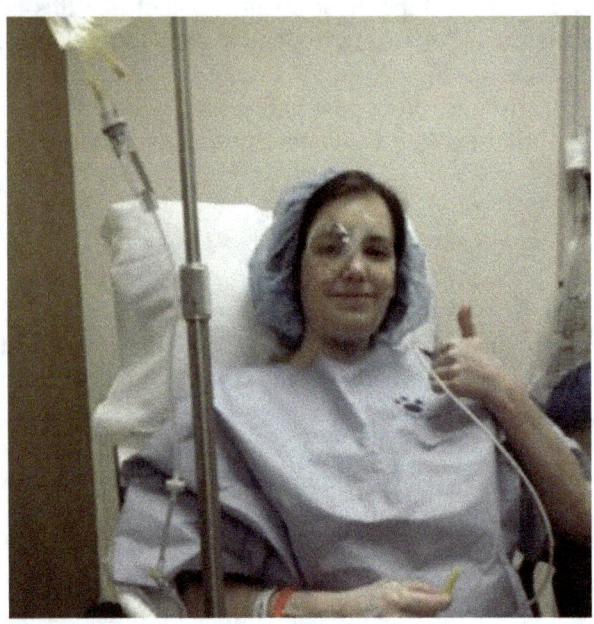

My mom joined me, and we sat there while they fed me toast with peanut butter and jelly on it, with cranberry juice. Having not eaten since the night before, toast never tasted so good. Maybe the lingering sedatives had an effect on my taste buds, too. We went over discharge and after-care instructions, and the nurse had me sit in a wheelchair and she wheeled me to the exit, where my mom's car was waiting. I felt completely normal, as if nothing had just been done. No pain or soreness, no grogginess, no side effects at all. I could even already tell the difference with my eye. I felt so normal, that my mom and I drove through McDonald's (I was in the mood for some greasy food) and went to Saver's. Then I was ready to go home for a nap, which is what I did.

It was probably one of the easiest procedures I've ever had done. The hour of prep work before the actual surgery is more tedious than the actual procedure! OK, not tedious, because it is all necessary, but more nerve wracking for me, since it involved getting the IV put in.

Everyone told me beforehand not to worry, that it's so easy and there's nothing to worry about. Everyone was right, so go ahead and say "I told you so." Next week will be even better now that I know what to expect. I know that it's the unknown that is a big part of what made me so nervous. I had no idea what to expect and of course I pictured the doctor cutting up my eye with an X-acto knife while I just lay there watching, not being able to look away since it's my eye she's working on. Nope, nothing like that. Aside from the IV, I actually look FORWARD to the procedure next week! Especially if I'm going to get extra sedative. I like that stuff. :)

2 days later and I'm so happy with the results. Everything in my right eye is so much clearer, crisper, sharper. I need reading glasses to read, and always will, but even reading on a computer (or book, or whatever) with my reading glasses is so much easier than with just my contacts. I should've gotten reading glasses ages ago! So currently I have one contact in my left eye, but not in my right eye, since the new lens that was put in my right eye actually has a prescription in it. So after both eyes are done, I won't need to wear contacts at all anymore. Just the glasses for reading. That will be nice! Bummer that I just paid $130 for a 6 pack of contacts back in December. . . . Maybe I can see if I can return the un-opened ones for some kind of refund? Unlikely, but worth the try, right?

Some of my co-workers were surprised that I was back at work on Wednesday. They thought I would take the day off to recover, but there isn't any recovery. Even the next day there wasn't any pain in my eye. I haven't had to take anything for pain or discomfort. My only job now is to keep putting in my eye drops. I have 3 different drops, 1 of which I have to put in 4 times a day for a month, but the other 2 are only twice a day, until they're gone. They gave me a little schedule of when I should give each one, with a little box to check it off. That is very helpful, especially since this Saturday I have to start the drops in my left eye for the procedure next Tuesday. The stinking eye drops cost $160! Did I mention that before?

My follow-up appointment Wednesday morning was very quick. I think I was in [the surgeon's] office all of 10 minutes. She looked at my eye with one of those magnifying machine things and told me everything looked great and there were no signs of infection or problems. She expects it to heal very nicely. Yay! I love when things go right. Fingers crossed it all goes as smoothly with the left eye. As long as her hand doesn't slip and she jabs her incision knife up into my brain, there should be no problem. I'm not at all as nervous about it anymore (except the IV part). Before Tuesday, my left eye was my good eye, and I would use it to read the computer screen because through my right eye everything was so blurry. Now, my left eye seems blurry compared to my right eye!

In case you're wondering, my eyesight will not change now, ever. The artificial lens that was put into my eye cannot be affected by my diabetes or anything else, because it is artificial. It may adjust a tiny bit over time, but I will never get cataracts again, and never have to wear contacts again. I feel much more comfortable driving at night now, too, with my sharper vision. I really look forward to a month from now when both eyes are done and healed up. It will be amazing.

That's all for now. Our furnace at home broke and we need a new one, so we will have no heat tonight. Just thinking about it makes me cold, so I better get back to work and get my mind off it. More later, I'm sure. Bye for now.

January 28, 2013 Blog
Oh for Heaven's Sake

I have come to realize that as a transplant patient, a check-up is never just a check-up. At least not when you're me. I had my 6-week fistula surgery check-up today, and found out that it is not "maturing" as they had hoped. Apparently there are vein branches that are branching off of the main artery that my fistula is in, and they are hogging all the blood that should be going to the fistula to mature it. How do they fix that? Another surgery. They have to go in the upper part of my arm and tie off a couple veins. This means they will put a small band around them so that they stop stealing all my blood. This won't affect my blood flow at all in my arm, since there are plenty of other veins for the blood to flow through. But these specific ones are affecting the maturation of my fistula. When will this surgery be? Why delay - how about Wednesday! Yes, this Wednesday. I need to have an ultrasound done on my arm again so they can do some more vein mapping and figure out exactly which veins, and where, they need to band. That will be done tomorrow morning (Tuesday). Then my mom will pick me up and I'll go for my 2nd cataract surgery. Wednesday morning I'll have my post-op follow-up at the eye clinic to make sure the eye surgery went fine, then race back to the U to have the surgery done on my arm, since the surgeon isn't available after 12pm. Are we having fun yet??

Seriously, it's just one thing after another. I'm not bummed or feeling down or anything about it, though. At this point, I'm just going along with it like it's no big deal, like "yeah OK, let's do this." No biggie. For this surgery on my arm, they will be making at least 2, probably 3 small incisions on the upper part of my arm, which means I will now have 5 incision scars on my arm. I no longer think of them as ugly marks that will be on my skin forever. Now I think of them as battle wounds. All chapters in my best-selling autobiography, when I write it. :) Every new development of this whole process is just another writing opportunity. At least for the surgery I'll get general anesthesia, so I'll be feeling good after! That's the best part. Is it sad that every time I'm told I have to have this or that procedure done, the first thing I think is, "oh yay, that means I get fun drugs"?? Hmm.

OH, and interesting side note - I did find out something good at my appointment today. Based on my most recent blood tests, which were done within the last couple weeks, my kidney functions have gone UP! Last time it was tested, back in October, it was at 15% functioning, and now it's at 18%! Must be all that cranberry juice I'm drinking. The doctor said "whatever you're doing, keep doing it."

You're probably wondering why I'm going through all this fistula surgery stuff if Crystal is most likely going to work as a donor. Even if she is fully approved, and I don't need to go on dialysis before the transplant, it's still all precautionary. Just in CASE I need dialysis in the future for some reason, I will have a fistula that is matured and ready to use. The fistula will never be removed from my arm. Even if it is never used in my life, it will always be there. I guess I understand that. Better that it's there and never need it than suddenly have kidney problems 10 or 15 years from now and not have it, and need immediate dialysis. If that happens, they'd have to put a catheter through the heart, since there wouldn't be time to insert a fistula and wait for it to mature. Yikes! I'll take the fistula now, thank you very much.

I can't eat anymore now until after my surgery tomorrow, so I'm going to bed. It's SO hard not to eat or drink anything in the morning. It seems like whenever I'm having a procedure done where I'm not supposed to have eaten after midnight the night before, the procedure is always scheduled for late morning or early afternoon. Why can't they do these things first thing in the morning, so I don't have to sit and deal with my hunger for hours?? I think they do that to me on purpose. They're secretly testing my willpower. Well let me tell you, it's a nasty joke and I don't like it!

That's all for now. I probably won't post again tomorrow after my eye surgery, but will at some point later this week so I can update you on both eye surgery tomorrow and fistula surgery on Wednesday. Ta-ta for now.

January 31, 2013 Blog
Surgeries, Round 2

Well, the last 2 days have certainly been eventful. Hardly any time to stop and think. Tuesday morning, I went in to work early (rode in with my dad and Kathy) since I knew I was going to be leaving early. The guy who covers our front desk was out sick, so I covered the front desk until I had to leave. I started logging in proposals at 7:45, which is when I got up there, and didn't stop until I had to leave at 10:15. There was a deadline coming up for submitting proposals to us, so they were coming in non-stop. I actually didn't mind it, because it made the time go by fast, and kept my mind busy from thinking about how hungry I was, since I wasn't allowed to eat anything after midnight the night before. At 10:15, I grabbed my coat and was out of there, off to my ultrasound appointment at 10:30.

That appointment was uneventful. Exactly how you would expect an ultrasound to go. Put on a robe, and lay there while she squirts warm gel all over my arm and maneuvers the ultrasound wand thing up and down my arm, mapping out the veins for my surgery the next day. I get out of there right at 11:40, to find my mom ready and waiting to pick me up to head out to Fairview Southdale hospital for my 2nd cataract surgery.

One of my uncles also had cataract surgery, and his 2nd surgery happened to be at the same hospital, on the same day, around the same time! He was already back being prepped for surgery when I got there, but I got to see my aunt for a little bit. After they called me back to start prepping me, she even came back with my mom to keep me company before I went into surgery. Even though my surgery was supposed to start at 1:30, they didn't get me back there until 2:20 or so. Apparently there was a complication with the person in front of me, and they must have needed the expertise of more than one surgeon, because even my uncle was late going in. His surgery was supposed to be at 1, and he only went back about 10 minutes before I did (he had a different surgeon). I asked for an extra dose of sedative this time, and they definitely gave it to me. I don't recall feeling any tension this time, or clenching in my stomach. I did see the pretty colors again, but it's a pretty hazy memory. I don't remember Dr. Meiusi coming into the room, when she started the procedure, when it ended, or being wheeled back to my room to recover. It's all a pretty hazy blur. That's good, though. On the way home, we drove through McDonald's and my mom bought me a happy meal. I went home, ate, worked on some crafts while watching some Netflix, took a little nap, got up and ate 2nd dinner with my dad and Kathy, then went to bed shortly after, since I had another big day the next day.

Wednesday morning was my post-op follow-up appointment with [the surgeon]. I was scheduled for my fistula surgery at 10, and had to be to the hospital at the U at 8, but I told them I had an eye appointment at 8:45 and would get there as soon as I could. My dad and I left the house a little early, so we got to the eye clinic early. I was very impressed that they even got me in early! [The surgeon] took a look at my eye, told me it was looking great, and that she would see me in 3 weeks for my 3-week follow-up. I was out of there at 8:45, which is when the appointment was scheduled to start! Woohoo. Off to the hospital we went.

I checked in at the hospital at the U at the admissions desk and went up to the surgery clinic to wait. I waited about 15 minutes before they called me back, which is surprising considering I was supposed to be there at 8, and didn't actually get there until 9:15. You'd think they would rush me back right away. Back in my pre-op room, all the usual stuff. Going over all kinds of info, getting me into the surgery gown, and getting the IV in for the anesthesia. Even though the surgery was supposed to start at 10, I don't think I went back to the surgery room until at least 10:30. When they were wheeling me back to surgery, they gave me a little sedative through my IV. I was quite alright with that. After that, I don't remember anything until waking up in recovery. I don't know if they told me they were administering the anesthesia now or not, who knows. Usually when they tell me that, I like to start counting backwards to see how far I can get, but I don't remember that. I guess before I was even given the anesthesia, they put a breathing tube down my throat, which is what the sedative was for. They like to give patients who have gastroparesis issues, like I do, breathing tubes, in case anything happens during surgery. I don't even remember seeing my surgeon, Dr. Kandaswamy, at all.

When I woke up in the post-op room, it was about 2pm. I could tell that there had been a tube down my throat, because my throat felt dry and sore. I think I was in post-op for about half an hour before being brought back to a recovery room. Naturally, after just waking up from anesthesia, I was still very sleepy and groggy, so the nurse in recovery turned off the light, pulled shut my curtain, and let me sleep, I think for hours. When I finally reached the point that I could keep my eyes open, I was given some saltine crackers and apple juice. I had to take my pump off for surgery, so when the nurse brought me all my belongings and I could start getting dressed, I looked at my pump and it was a little after 5pm. I was so glad that she had just left me alone to sleep, but I knew my mom was probably wondering what happened to me, since she was the one picking me up. I didn't get Percocet for the pain this time, since the procedure was much less invasive than when they put the fistula in. I didn't even feel any pain or discomfort at all! While getting dressed, I finally snuck a peek at my arm:

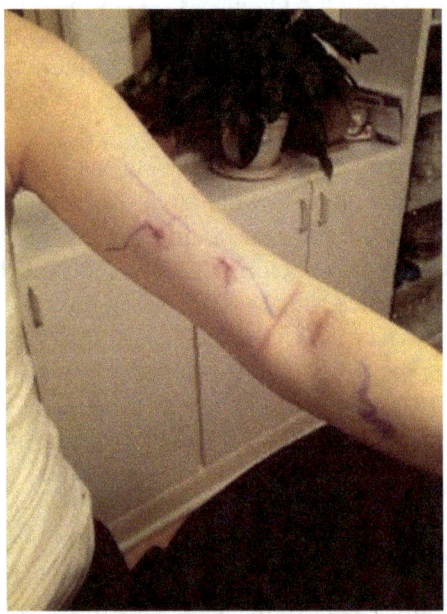

I was given Tylenol with Codeine in it to take for pain, as needed. In the past 24 hours, I've only taken it once. I took one as soon as I got home, just in case there would be any pain once all the anesthesia wore off. I was also given regular Tylenol, which I have to take once every day now. 325mg, which I guess is a lot. It's to keep my blood thin enough to run through the vein and get to my fistula. I got a much better understanding of what they had to do. Since the main vein going to my fistula had branched off, blood was going to my fistula still, but also going off into the other veins that were branching out, so my fistula wasn't getting all the blood it needed to grow and "mature." You can see by the pen marks the 2 veins that they tied up. A good analogy that my mom used is that blood veins are like a river. When one way is blocked, it will just find another way to go. This way, by blocking the path to those other veins that were branching off the main vein, all the blood will flow down to my fistula and help it grow. Make sense? It didn't to me after my appointment on Monday, but it does now that they explained it in "dumb" people terms.

So there you have it. As I've been saying, I'm ready to be done with surgeries now until the BIG surgery day. No surgeries for 28 years, then in the last 2 months it's bam bam bam bam, one surgery after another. Whew! Good thing I have such a strong soul, and I know that this will all be over soon enough (assuming all goes well with Crystal's evaluations next week).

On the bright side, now that I've had both the cataract surgeries, I can see great! It's amazing to finally have both my eyes seeing the same strength, have no blurriness, no floaters. Just clear, sharp vision. I've even found some reading glasses that are cute and don't make me look and feel like I'm 85 years old. Good times.

I went back to work today, even though it's the day after surgery. Surprisingly or not, I managed to stay awake and alert all day, but now I'm ready for a nap. Good thing it's almost time to go home anyway. So there you have it. Surgeries done, and now just waiting again. Bye for now!

February 1, 2013 Facebook
Are you KIDDING me?? I just got a phone call telling me I have to go in to the hospital again next week for yet another short procedure on my arm. FML. If you're having a bad day, walk a mile in my shoes and then try telling me again how bad your day is. If you've got a roof over your head, food in your stomach, and all working organs, then SMILE, you've got it good. Just sayin.' I WILL stay strong, keep calm, and carry on.

February 8, 2013 Blog
Rough week
This week has been a rough week. Let's start at the beginning.

I found out last Friday that I had to go back to the hospital this past Monday for one more procedure on my arm. Nothing invasive, no more big cuts or anything, but it was something that was going to take me out of work the whole day. You can imagine how thrilled I was to send that e-mail out to my co-workers. Typical Krystin, out yet another day. I think by now they just expect it. Anyway, I had to be at the hospital at 11am for a 12:30 procedure. What they were doing is called a fistulagram. It's where they put colored dye in my blood stream and watch it as it flows through my arm, making sure that the blood is getting where it's supposed to be and that the surgery they did last week is working. I'm pretty sure it's working, but I was given LOTS of sedation, so I was out of it for pretty much the whole procedure. I don't think I slept, because I don't remember dreaming, but I know I dozed in and out. I think I was even snoring in my daze, because sometimes I startled myself with a snort. I didn't feel anything, except some pressure on my arm when the doctor said "OK Krystin, you're going to feel me pressing down on your arm now." I think he did that 3 times. I don't know what for, but whatever.

Even though things seem to be working fine as far as blood flow, they did have to make two tiny injections. They injected into a vein in my arm, in two different places, a tiny balloon that they then slightly inflate. The balloon is smaller than the tip of a pen, and with all the sedation, I didn't even feel it going in. I don't even remember them telling me they were going to inject them now (although I knew before the procedure started that they were going to have to do that). Like I said, I was pretty out of it, but feeling good. I love sedation!

Tuesday I was fine, but by the evening I wasn't feeling so hot. I think I ended up going to bed at 8, without dinner. My stomach was queasy and I didn't think eating anything would sit well. Of course that means I kept getting low during the night, so was constantly up to drink some apple juice or eat an applesauce cup. That would raise my blood sugar temporarily, but a couple hours later I would wake up low, again. Process repeat, all night long. When I get low, I get really hot, so I sweat. When my blood sugar goes back to normal range, my sweat dries and I'm freezing. So it was also a lot of covers on - covers off, heating pad on, heating pad off. I slept very little.

I still felt so icky Wednesday morning, still nauseated, and so extremely exhausted (I pushed my snooze button I think 6 or 7 times), I knew I had to stay home. I stayed home that day, but again, didn't eat anything, and played the high/low game with my blood sugars. I slept

ALL day. Even that evening I still wasn't up for eating, even though my mom brought me chicken noodle soup and lots of fruit. Once again I went to bed without dinner. I've been cat sitting all week, so I'm sure the cats enjoyed the extra time having me there; Kenny kitty likes to sleep on my face, or next to me on my heating pad, if I'm not already laying on it.

Thursday morning I woke up feeling a little better, at least well enough to go to work. I felt weak, since I hadn't eaten much the past couple days, but I made it through the whole work day, munching here and there on veggies, fruit, and crackers. Unfortunately, the OK feeling didn't last long, and I felt ickier as the day went on. I had tomato basil soup for lunch, from a can, and although there were NO dairy products in the ingredients, my stomach rejected it, and I was regretting that all evening. I even had to pull over on the way home and quickly pull out a plastic Target bag, because I knew I wouldn't make it to the house. No fun. It's moments like this when I think to myself, "just kill me now." I felt horrible again, and couldn't wait to get home and lay down for a nap. Which I did. Again, no dinner.

So here it is, Friday morning, and I was able to get up and come in to work early to make up some of the time I've been gone. I'm feeling alright so far, no nausea, although a little lightheaded since again, no food in my stomach. I'm going to take it easy today. I have an eye appointment in Edina this morning to get the next round of shots in my eyeballs, but other than that, hopefully it's not too busy at work, and tonight I will relax and enjoy it finally being the weekend and making it through this shitty week.

I know it's not the flu that I have, because I don't have flu-like symptoms. No headaches or congestion, no fever, or anything like that. I do worry, however, that it might be an infection. One of the incision sights on my arm does hurt, and increased exhaustion, nausea, and vomiting are all signs of an infection. I didn't want to go in to get it checked out last night, because I knew the only place open would be the ER, and it seems like every time I have to go to the ER, they admit me, and I really want to avoid that. So today I may just stop over at the transplant clinic on the way back from my eye appointment and see if there is someone available to take a look at my arm. Again, hopefully they don't say they want to admit me for X number of days while they give me fluids and antibiotics. But, like I said, with my luck in life, anything is possible . . .

I'm really worrying lately about work, and all my being gone. I've been coming in early a lot, and have come in the past couple weekends, to earn comp time, to show that I'm willing to make up the time being gone. But I still feel like this all looks bad for my work reputation. I fear that people have just begun accepting that I'm a worker who is gone a lot, which, before all this transplant stuff, wasn't true. I want to prove that I'm a dedicated, reliable, hard worker, but all these appointments are making that hard to do. It's not even the managers or director who I'm worried about, either. It's my supervisor. I don't know why it's so important to me what he thinks of me and how he sees me as a worker, but it is. I just don't want him to have reasons to regret hiring me.

On the up-side, it sounds like all of Crystal's tests and evals on Wednesday went well, and hopefully by next week we should hear something! Let's keep our fingers and toes and everything in between crossed that the docs liked what they saw and fully approve her as a donor. I would be one happy Krystin.

That's all for now. I hope everyone has a good weekend!

February 13, 2013 Facebook
Crystal Lescault to Krystin Engstrand
Well . . . we're 99% a go. They are just waiting on the fellow to do a second review on my CT. There is a chance that could change things but its slim. I wasn't sure if I should wait until I heard about that to tell you but in the words of my coordinator "it all looks pretty good" . . . so, I thought you'd like to know that. If that's fine then we're looking at June-ish for surgery. Hope you can hold out till then. My kidney is all yours girl :) Crazy!

> Krystin: AHHH omg that's so exciting! That guy better hurry his butt up and review it. :) If we're a go, I hope time flies and June gets here fast!
> Krystin: Did they say June, or is that when it works for you to take some recovery time off work? Obviously I'm ready to go whenever. The sooner the better! :)
> Crystal Lescault: I would much rather get moving along sooner too but because I just started this job I'm going to have to give them a lot of notice. That, and I need to save vacation time. Since my job is pretty physical and involves lifting the kiddos I'll need

to be off for 6 weeks after. Hope you can hold out, it'll be great recovery weather by then :)

Krystin: Ah yes, I thought that was probably why, since I knew you were new at your job. Makes sense! No worries, I will do my best to hold out until then. I'm a tough cookie, I can make it! Yes, it will be the perfect time to lounge outside while recovering. :) (p.s. WOW, I didn't know you would need that much recovery time, too!)

Crystal Lescault: If I had a desk job it'd be different but I do a lot of lifting/chasing/running at work. Autistic children are . . . active. Haha. I think it'll be worth the wait though so hold on!

Krystin: Another couple months is no sweat. :) your health and well being after surgery is just as important!

February 18, 2013 Blog
Just a little update

Not much new to report on, but it has been a while since I've posted, so I figured I'd stop in and post a little something for you.

As you all know, Crystal went in for her tests and evaluations on the 6th. We still don't have a definite answer as to whether she's fully approved or not, but it's looking good. The only thing that still needs to happen is they want to do a 2nd review of her CT scan. So, we're 99% a go! I suppose, like anything when it comes to the health field, that review could change things, but it sounds like the chances are small of that happening. It has now been almost 2 weeks, though, since her appointments. How long does it take to review a CT scan?? I'm getting anxious waiting to find out! When/if Crystal is approved, we can schedule surgery. At this point, it's looking like surgery would be some time in June. Crystal works with autistic children and has a very demanding job, that requires lots of bending/lifting/energy/etc., so she will need lots of time off to recover after surgery. She is still fairly new at her job, so June is the earliest that she would be able to take off 5-6 weeks. I know that seems like a long time away, but her health and recovery after surgery is JUST as important, so we need to make sure she has enough vacation/sick time built up to make a proper recovery!

As for me, I can hold out until then. Just getting surgery scheduled and on my calendar is the next big step right now, and knowing that it's been scheduled and that the end is in sight will be enough to get me through to June. I have been debating contacting the transplant clinic and seeing if I can start doing some dialysis in the meantime. I think they will say no, because my kidney functions are not low enough yet that dialysis will make a difference in how I feel, but I'm convinced otherwise. I'd at least like to try it out once and see how I feel. Maybe they can do a trial run? Obviously I don't want to take up the time and resources that could be used for someone who needs is more, but if they can fit me in, why not? I'm just pulling at all strings here as far as what could make me feel better and help me get through each day with enough energy and stamina. I'm just SO exhausted by the end of each day, and my job isn't even that strenuous! Just being up and out is tiresome for my body. Seriously, all I want to do is sleep, all the time. That's pretty much all I do on the weekends now.

About a week and a half ago, I had one of my monthly eye appointments to get my eyeball shots. Before I get the big shot, [the doctor] gives me a small shot of numbing stuff. This last time, when he gave me the numbing shot, he nicked a small blood vein in my eye. Ever since then, there has been internal bleeding in my eye, which has made my eye blood-shot red. It just started out on the right side of my eye, since that's where he gave the shot, but it has slowly migrated and now covers my whole eye. It looks really creepy. Here is a picture, to give you an idea:

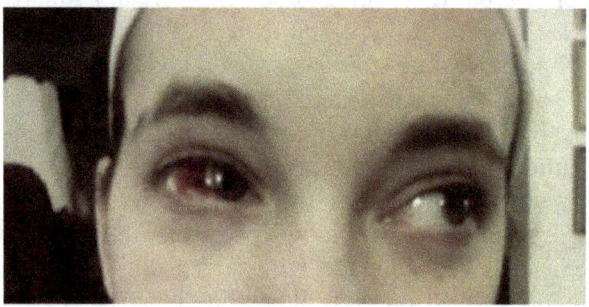

Isn't it gross?? My brother said I look like a wraith. One of my co-workers says I look half zombie. No matter what I look like, it's just plain creepy. People don't know how to look at me when they're talking to me. Co-workers have asked what happened, which is much better, because then I can explain it. That's better than not explaining it at all and just having people give me weird looks all the time. Apparently it can take up to 2 or so weeks for the eye to re-absorb all the blood. This Friday will be 2 weeks, and it doesn't seem to be getting any better. Other people are telling me it's starting to look better; more pink than red, but I don't see it when I look in the mirror. I just see creepy eye! I certainly hope this doesn't happen a lot when I have to get the shots. I really don't want to spend a year (which is how long I have to do these shots on a monthly basis) looking like a zombie!

That's all I got for now. Let's all cross our fingers for good news this week!

February 18, 2013 Facebook
I realized recently that I have been complaining a lot on facebook, which is not in my character. I vowed I wouldn't do that, because I hate when others constantly use facebook as a pity party. So, time for me to build a bridge and get over it. I am NOT a whiner. A glass of WINE, on the other hand, I could be OK with. :)

February 19, 2013 Facebook
Crystal Lescault to Krystin Engstrand
FULLY APPROVED!!!!!!! My kidney (not sure which one yet . . . haha) officially belongs to you my friend. Surgery is being scheduled :)

> Krystin: AHHHH I'M DOING A HAPPY DANCE!!!! And tears of joy are threatening to come. You are absolutely amazing and are my favorite person in the world. Words can't even express my joy and gratitude for you and your kidney!! :) :) :)
> Crystal Lescault: I'll take good care of it! Now that I'm approved they should be able to give you more info if you have questions. I plan to call tomorrow and see if I can get a date for surgery, or at least an idea, so I can tell my job. But what did I tell you?? I knew it...I just knew :)
> Krystin: I still can't believe it. What are the odds that we were brought together like this and everything worked out?? It truly is a miracle!!

February 25, 2013 Blog
Current Mood: tired
Gotta take the good with the bad

Well, good news and scary news. I'll start with the scary news, so that we can end on a positive note.

I had a very new and scary experience last week that has never happened to me before. It happened both on Wednesday and Friday morning. I "woke up" around 5 a.m., and was completely paralyzed on my right side. I couldn't really lift my right arm or leg. All my muscles were just limp. Even lifting my head was a challenge. I had lost all speech, anything I tried to say just came out as a slurred noise. On Monday I woke up on the floor. I was cat-sitting at a townhouse in St. Paul all week, and slept on the couch close to the fireplace to keep warm. I couldn't get anywhere except by rolling, because I couldn't stand, and if I tried to call, my arms couldn't support my weight. Also during this time my mind is not clear, I can't think, so I can't make any kind of decisions or do anything. My vision also blacks out, so I don't really see any of my surroundings. All I can do is wait it out, which I didn't know on Wednesday since it was the first time this has ever happened to me. I was still partly sleeping when it began, so this was happening while I was still dreaming. I was aware that something wasn't right, and that I needed help, but I couldn't get my brain to wake up and focus.

I knew I had to get to my phone. I was able to drag myself around on the floor using my left arm, but would have to stop every few feet and just lay down, because I got so disoriented and dizzy, and had to reorient myself and figure out where I was, and where I was trying to go. A few times I would "come to" and realize I had been dragging myself in the completely wrong direction of my phone. I would turn myself around, get a few feet, then have to lay flat on the floor again to rest. Eventually I got to my phone, which was in the kitchen, on the center island, charging. I called my mom's number numerous times, but she didn't answer. I knew it was before she wakes up, and she turns her volume off during the night so as not to be disturbed by all the incoming notifications. I had a really hard time dialing, and had to keep pushing the end button and starting over. I kept hitting the wrong numbers. I finally dialed my house number right, and Kathy answered the phone. I think I woke her up. I asked for my dad, and when he got on the phone, all I could say was "help me, I can't move." Luckily my speech had come back, so at least I could form words. By this time it was past 6:30 I think, so the whole seizure (or whatever it is) had gone on for about an hour and a half. Only now had I finally got back speech, a clear mind, and the ability to drag myself around the main floor of the townhouse.

We still couldn't get a hold of my mom, so my dad actually drove over to her house, knocked on her door, and asked for the address of the townhouse I was at. I had been able to drag myself to the front door and unlock the deadbolt, so my dad could come in. When he got there, I was still laying on the floor, but not all the feeling had completely returned to my legs. He helped me stand up, and I tried walking a little bit to get the blood flowing in my legs. I was still pretty shaky and wobbly, but at least I was on the move again. He made sure that I was OK, said he was going to go home and shower and finish getting ready for work, and would swing back by and pick me up and bring me in to work. I was still scared about what had happened, and extremely tired, so I didn't end up going to work that day.

I did call my endocrinology clinic here at the U that afternoon and asked if my endocrinologist had any openings/cancellations that day, and luckily, she did! So I went in and saw her that afternoon. That's when she said it's probably low blood sugar seizures. She said to make sure I always have my meter, my phone, and glucose tabs/juice/whatever near my bed every night. Also if it happened again to call 911. Easy for her to say! When it happens, I can't do anything at all. By the time it has passed, then it's pointless, because I'm back to normal. Of course I also wasn't thinking about a blood test, so I didn't do one right away, so I don't even know what my blood sugar was right then. I didn't feel ANY of the other symptoms of a low blood sugar. And when I get low in my sleep, my body has ALWAYS woken me up, and I'm able to treat it before it gets too low. Which is what makes me think it's not low blood sugar related. All I know is that I was scared to death, and never wanted it to happen again.

But it did, Friday morning. Same time, same symptoms.

On Friday I was able to stay on the couch and didn't let myself roll onto the floor, but that was actually probably a mistake. Friday was even scarier than Wednesday, because on Friday I woke up coughing and choking. I couldn't swallow, and since I was on my back, I was choking on my spit. I could feel my mouth making spit bubbles, and the drooling down the side of my face. But I couldn't move myself! When I was able to form words, I laid there for who knows how long, yelling "help" out loud. I don't know what the purpose of that was, like I thought maybe someone in one of the neighboring townhouses would hear me? Even if they did and called 911, all the doors were locked and they wouldn't be able to get in without a locksmith.

Even on Friday, though, when it happened again, I was convinced I was going to die there. It was one of the scariest things I've ever experienced in my life, even more than DKA when I was in Paris. Maybe that's because I was alone at the townhouse, and I was afraid I was going to die there alone and nobody would know for a long time. I was scared because no one was there to just sit with me and keep a hand on me and tell me that it's OK, it will pass, it will get better. Even now, still thinking about it, makes me shudder and almost want to cry. Both times it happens, I DID cry, because I just wanted my mom there. I remember mumbling to myself (or maybe it was in my head, who knows), "I just want my mom. Where are you, mom?"

When it did happen again on Friday morning, though, I called the endo clinic and talked to my endocrinologist's nurse and told her it happened again. She consulted with my endocrinologist, called me back, and told me to go to the ER. She said it sounds like something bigger than just low blood sugars. I agreed, and said I would be in that evening. So Friday night my mom brought me to the ER at the hospital here at the U. They actually got me back pretty quickly when I wrote on the sign-in in sheet "recurring diabetic seizures resulting in paralysis." They did the usual strength tests of my limbs and the whole smiling bit to see if it was a stroke. Negative on that one. Then they did an MRI to see if it's brain related. Nope. My brain is normal, too (well, as normal as it can be for our family). :) So they discharged me with no answers as to what it could be, but with instructions to follow up with the neurology/seizure clinic here at the U. Oh, and I have a bladder infection, so I have an antibiotic for that. Of course I have an infection. Doesn't it seem like I always do these days??

So, so far the medical field is just as mystified as I am as to what happened and what caused them. All I know is that if it never happens again, that is quite alright with me. At least now I'm back at my dad's house, so if it happens again, there is a good chance that someone else will be home. My dad is supposed to call 911 if it happens again, in the hopes that they can get there quickly and see it while it's in progress, maybe do some blood work right then and see all the symptoms and everything. Fingers crossed it doesn't get to that, though. Well actually, it's kinda bittersweet. Of course I don't want it to happen again because the experience is scary and horrible, but on the other hand, I do just so that the medics can witness it. All I can do is wait and see what happens. In the meantime, you better believe I'm making an appointment to get into the neurology clinic!

OK, now for the good news. Crystal is FULLY APPROVED as a donor!!! I actually found this out on Tuesday of last week, so I've known for almost a week, but with the seizure things going on, I got caught up in that and didn't have time to share the good news on here, for those of you who aren't on Facebook (of course I posted it on Facebook right away). This means that surgery can now be scheduled! Like I've mentioned before, it won't be until June, but it will feel so, so, SO good to have a date written down. Now to just wrap myself up in bubble wrap and keep myself safe and healthy until then. We don't have a set date yet, but I will be sure to let you know when it's set!

That's all the news I got for now. I know my good news was only one paragraph long, but it's enough good news to make everything else not matter as much. It's keeping me happy, keeping me on cloud 9. I'll be sure to let you all know when I find out more. Bye for now!

February 27, 2013 Email
recup time
Dad to Krystin (cc to Pat, Kathy):
Krystin,

I happened to run into [a friend in the Medical School] over lunch; he's a Medical School Associate Dean (and faculty member in something that has to with transplants or endo or something—I'm not sure what his medical specialty is). He told me that one of the AHC staff just had a kidney transplant last week. Was in the hospital for 3 days and out up and about in two weeks. He said you feel sort of lousy about eating the first week, but after that it's all up hill. ([He] himself, about two years ago, had a heart transplant.)

Krystin to Dad:
Every person is different.

Krystin to Dad:
I won't be out of the hospital in 3 days. I have to stay there for 5-7, depending on how I'm doing. I don't know what his circumstances were and why he was up and about so soon after, but EVERYONE in the transplant office has said 4-6 weeks of recovery. Like I said, I'm going to take 3 weeks off for sure, and see how I'm doing after that. Crystal plans to take 6 weeks off, and she's not the one receiving the new kidney. Like I said, recovery time is different for everyone. I'm not going to push it.

Dad to Krystin:

I'm not suggesting you should. I just passed along that bit of information.

March 8, 2013 Email
warm comments from dad
Dad to Krystin:
Krystin,

I have told you this over the last couple of months, in bits and pieces, but I want to tell you in writing as well as orally.

When I came home from work one day last January and told you about my lunch conversation with Andy, who had related that he had been struck down with the flu from roughly Christmas to mid-January and constantly fatigued that entire period, you responded something like "welcome to my world every day."

I have been appalled ever since you told me that because I think I would have been in bed ever since. I think you are heroic to get up and go to work every day and just get from one bedtime to the next. Combined with the eye treatments, and the occasional pain they cause, and the dietary problems you've had, I am simply astonished at how well you manage to lead a life. I cannot tell you how much I admire you for your perseverance and determination. So even though I occasionally grouse at you about leaving clothes and shoes and stuff all around the house (you really ARE messy!), you should know that I cannot say enough positive about your stamina, your commitment to doing your job well, and getting to the surgery in June. I have said as much to a number of my friends and colleagues.

If you want to berate yourself for sleeping too much, that's up to you. Under the circumstances, I certainly will not.

We must race to June!

Love you.

Krystin to dad:

Thanks, dad. I have been meaning to get back to you on this for a while. I really appreciate it. One of the things I'll be talking with Nancy [Krystin's therapist] about is how I can express verbally and in writing how I feel these days, but nobody REALLY understands. But your warm comments offer me the support and recognition that you understand that even though you can't feel what I'm going through, you know that I'm having a hard time. I appreciate that a lot, so again, thank you. Like you said, let's just hope the next couple months go by fast and June hurries up and gets here!

Love you.

March 20, 2013 Blog
We have a date!

It has been a while, so I have a few updates for you.

Most of you know this already, but in case you don't - we have a date for surgery! Mark your calendars for JUNE 4! It is still tentative, because when I talked to my transplant coordinator a few weeks ago and gave her that date, the schedules weren't out yet for June, but she penciled it in to get it on the schedule as soon as they are available. SO, unless something needs to change for some reason, that's the plan! The 4th is a Tuesday, but Crystal and I would need to be at the hospital Monday evening, so they have time to prep us, since surgery is at 5AM Tuesday morning. Since both Crystal and I will need to stay in the hospital for a while after surgery to recover (5-7 days, I believe), I think it would be awesome if they put us in the same room together! These days patients rarely get their own room, so I'd much rather be with Crystal than spend a week next to someone I don't know. Crystal and I could bond over recovery. :)

So now it's just the waiting period. Mentally, it helps a lot having a surgery date set. Physically, I'm tired every single day. It really is a struggle to get up every day and go to work, but I'm still doing it. Everyone is amazed that I'm still working full-time, and will be all the way up to surgery (at least that's my plan, for now). Every morning my body aches, I always push my snooze button at least once (sometimes up to 3 or 4 times), and my appetite has greatly decreased, but I'm still plugging along.

I decided to start seeing a therapist, as well. I can write on my blog, and talk to friends and family, but none of it is the same as talking to a professional who has education, training, and experience in therapy and psychiatry. Her name is Nancy, and although I've only met with her once so far, I really like her. I think we will get on greatly. I feel like I'm pretty open on here and don't hold much back as far as what I'm thinking, but from her I can get feedback, and she can work with me on our goals. Our main goal right now is to help me de-stress, since that is a big issue for me right now, and is (most likely) causing a chunk of my fatigue. Stress or not, kidney failure causes fatigue and exhaustion, but at least if we can cut down on my stress, it will make life a little easier for me until surgery. Our goal is to get my heart and my head on the same page. I know in my heart that I need not worry so much about work and what all my co-workers think of me and me being gone so much, since it's for a legitimate reason, but my brain keeps saying that I need to keep proving that I'm a good worker, that I'm reliable/dependable, and that I'm really doing my best. I know my supervisor and managers like me and are happy with me, and are more than supportive of everything I'm going through and me being gone for appointments, but there's still that little voice in my head that says "don't make them regret hiring you, don't let them wish they had hired someone who could be there more." So getting my head and heart to work together, and cut down on my stress, is what we'll be working on. Last week, my first visit with her, was mostly just the usual intake process: getting to know each other a bit, giving her my background and my story/situation, and deciding what we're going to work on and how we're going to do that. We'll start working on those techniques when I see her this week.

It was interesting, when I was sitting with her last week, I had mentioned how all I want to do these days is sleep. If I didn't have to worry about money, I would love to just take the next 2 and a half months off until surgery and stay home and sleep and relax, and not have any work obligations or places to go, things to do. She asked me, "so what if you did take off work until surgery?" It was an interesting proposal. What if I did? Hmmm. Well, I'd probably lose my job, for one. Of course I don't know that for sure, but I'm pretty sure of it. Taking off 2 and a half months before surgery, plus a month after surgery to recover, that makes me gone from my job for a good chunk of time (at least 3 and a half months, for those of you who are bad at math). What employer wants to keep someone employed who is going to be gone for a quarter of the year?? Maybe if I were higher up, like a grant administrator or manager, it would MAYBE be possible, but as a lowly support staff employee, I'm easily replaceable. Again, maybe this is one of those things that my brain is convincing me of even though it isn't true, but I'm afraid to even bring it up with my supervisor, "hey, what if I took off a month before surgery as well as a month after?" So that's not even 2 and a half months, only a month before surgery, which means I would only need to be working for another month and a half. 6 weeks seems doable, but for some reason 10-11 weeks to work until surgery seems like forever! Ugh, how am I going to make it??

You're probably wondering if I can just start doing dialysis to help me feel better. Basically, no. My kidney functions aren't low enough yet. Apparently they need to be at or close to 0% functioning before they do dialysis, and I think I'm still somewhere between 15-18%. They say if I did dialysis now, I wouldn't notice a difference in my energy level (or well-being in general), but I dunno about that. I'm convinced I would. But I guess they're the doctors, they know what they're talking about, right? I have an appointment with Dr. Ibrahim (my nephrologist) at the end of the month, so you bet I'll be asking him about it. I also am going to ask him about lactose intolerance, and if he's seen it before where patients with kidney failure develop lactose intolerance, and if so, if it goes away after transplant. I certainly hope so, because I really, reeeeeeeally don't want to have to avoid butter, and CHEESE, for the rest of my life! I mean, how is life worth living if you can't eat cheese and butter?? And drink milk?? (I'm kidding of course, but it sure would suck).

I'm still doing the laser treatments AND shots in my eyes. The shots I only get every 4-6 weeks, the laser treatments [the physician] is trying to do every couple weeks. The last treatment left me with a black eye from the numbing shot he gives me in my upper cheek bone. It looked like I had been punched in the eye. Even now, 2 weeks later, you can still see a little bit of bruising under my eye. That was my left eye; next week is my next appointment, and he'll be doing laser on my right eye. He said we have at least 2 more treatments on each eye to do, but we'll keep doing the shots. After a few months he'll slowly start to wean off the shots, so within a year I won't be needing them at all. These appointments I dread more than anything these days. The laser treatment I don't feel at all, but the two different numbing shots I get beforehand are excruciating, and by evening time, once the numbing has worn off, I have a killer headache that lasts all through the entire next day. I have Tylenol that's coated with Codeine, and that helps a little, IF I remember to take it before the pain gets too bad. After the last treatment, I went home and went right to bed. The pain was so bad, my eye stung from the shot (he did both the laser AND the shots), and I had a migraine. I even had to leave work early the next day because everything was just making it worse. Doesn't that just make you look forward to the next visit?? NOT. It's a good thing my mom is taking me to these appointments and keeping me accountable for going (I have to have a driver to drive me home), because if it were up to me, I would never go. I would keep rescheduling, and rescheduling, and rescheduling. It's just so horrible. Another thing that I just have to be strong and put up with. *sigh*

On the whole, my mood is teetering back and forth, and I find myself extremely, easily irritable these days. Yes, more so than normal. Most of the time I want to be alone/left alone, and just sleep or do my work. I literally have no social life. I get up (grudgingly), go to work, come home, take a nap or hang around, eat some dinner, go to bed. Repeat that, day after day, and that's my life. I spend 80% of the weekend sleeping, the other 20% awake, lounging about and wishing I was sleeping. The only reason I get up on the weekends is because I know I need to eat something, or my blood sugar will get too low. That's why it's a good thing I'm still living at my dad's house. He comes and tells me I need to get up and eat something. I know that if I were living in an apartment by myself, I would never get out of bed. This is why I'm not looking for an apartment until after my transplant and I'm all recovered and have the strength and energy to live on my own. That's just not an option right now.

Alright, I'll stop complaining for now and end it here. I'm keeping my chin up and trying to stay positive! Some days that's easier than others, but I'm going to keep on keeping on. Bye for now!

April 3, 2013 Blog
Some updates

Last week I had an appointment with my nephrologist, Dr. Ibrahim. We were talking about how I'm feeling these days, and where I stand as far as a transplant. I told him that Crystal was fully approved and we even have surgery scheduled already, for June 4. He looked at me and said "oh, that soon?" Ummm, excuse me?? What do you mean that SOON? I asked him what he meant, and he said they don't usually do transplant surgery until the recipient is at or around 0% functioning. Although my kidney functions had increased in February from 15% (back in December) to 19%, they have decreased slightly again, down to 17% functioning. At least it's staying relatively stable in the high teens. When I explained to him how tired, achy, fatigued, exhausted, and just generally crappy I've been feeling, he said that although some of that is natural for someone with kidney failure, but he doesn't think it's all related to kidney failure. He asked if I would be willing to postpone surgery if we could figure out what is making me feel so bad, and get me feeling better. I said "I guess," but my plan is to keep the June 4 date. Ultimately, as the patient, it's up to me (and Crystal, of course), and I don't want to wait longer. He may be able to get me feeling a little better temporarily, but not to how much better I'll be feeling with a new kidney. Also the longer I wait, the more likely I may become to needing dialysis. No thank you very much.

In the meantime, he stopped two of my medications that he thinks may be adding to my fatigue, and put me on two new ones: sodium bicarbonate (which my dad thinks is just baking soda in pill form), and something with calcium in its name. Both my calcium and vitamin D levels are low (understandably, since I'm not eating dairy), which he also thinks may be adding to my fatigue (not to mention my lack of iron intake, but I'm trying to eat more iron-rich foods, too - spinach salad with lunch every day!). So we're going to try all this, and I have a follow-up appointment at the end of the month, when they'll do more lab work and see where I'm at.

I'm also cutting down my work hours at work starting next week. Instead of starting at 8:45, I'll start at 10:45, so I'll get a couple hours more of sleep in the mornings. They need me here in the afternoons until closing time, so that's why I'm starting later instead of leaving earlier, as I had mentioned earlier as a possibility. It's not the mornings when I have the hardest time, though; it's that last stretch of the afternoon, after being up and about and at work all day. I'm thinking, though, that since I'll be up two hours later, I won't start to feel so exhausted until later in the day, and by then it will be time to go home. So everything will just be shifted a couple hours later. I think it will work out. I'll know by the end of the week probably if it is helping. If not . . . hmmm, well then I won't know what the next step is. Maybe working while I eat lunch and then taking "lunch" break to take a nap?? For the next couple months, I'll make it work. I can't believe it's only 2 months away! Last time I checked, it was 3 and a half months away, so the time is flying by. I hope the next couple months go by just as fast! I think once I'm working fewer hours, it will (go by fast).

Aside from the physical fatigue, my mood remains optimistic and positive, for the most part. There are always days, or parts of days, when I feel like giving up, and saying "I don't want to do this anymore. I just want it to be over." I hate the way I feel, and everything I do feels like a daunting task, even if it's just walking from my bedroom down to the first floor. I get up every day and shower, dress, and go to work, but only because I tell myself I have to. People don't believe me when I say that if I could, I would spend the next 2 months in bed. I'm not exaggerating. If I could actually just stay in bed and sleep, not have to get up and eat, or work, or do anything for the next 2 months, I seriously would.

Sometimes I swear I feel bipolar. Even though, like I said, I feel positive most of the time, there are roller coasters and mood swings, where I can be sitting at work and think "huh, I feel pretty good right now," and then an hour later I can be thinking "I just want to go to sleep. Is it time to go home yet?" At the end of the work day, I can be feeling like I actually have a little energy, and like I don't need to go right home and take a nap, but then something about that car ride home, in that short amount of time, when I get home I'm ready to curl up under my blankets and take a nap. The first thing I do when I get home every day is change into sweatpants and a sweatshirt! Getting out of my work clothes and into comfy, baggy clothes is one of the best feelings ever these days.

Something I like to do these days is plan all these trips I want to take in the future. Kind of like it gives me something to look forward to. I have a list of the top 4 countries I want to visit next, and they are (in order): Vietnam, India, Greece, and Russia. Just for fun, I have looked at airfare to Vietnam and picked out which hostels I would stay in. I want Vietnam to be my next big international trip. I want to fly into Ho Chi Minh City (Saigon), spend a few days or so there, rent a moped and ride it from Saigon to Hoi An, which is a little over 500 miles. I would make a stop in Nha Trang along the way, which has some of the best things to see and do in Vietnam. I would then spend a few days in Hoi An, before making my way up to Hanoi, which is about another 600 miles (a little less), with frequent stops along the way, since it can't all be done in one day on a moped! I would spend some time in Hanoi before flying home. In all I would make it a 2-week trip. If I'm going to travel back to Asia, it's not worth it to make it anything LESS than that! SO, who wants to go??

I think that I always need something in life to look forward to. Specifically, a trip. All I want to do in life is travel and see the world, and write about it, and planning trips make me happy. All the possibilities, practically the whole world at my fingertips to see, and I want to go EVERYWHERE. Traveling is what makes me happy, and for now, even if it's only planning for the very distant future, I'll take it.

I have an eye appointment on Friday for another laser treatment, and I'm dreading it. I hate these laser treatments, absolutely hate them. With today's technology, I'm surprised there isn't a way to make it more bearable. It's not the laser treatment that I find so unbearable - it's the numbing shots before that make me cringe and give me a mild combination panic/anxiety attack. First the small shot right under the skin in my lower eyelid, then the bigger one that goes in straight towards the back of my head, underneath my eyeball. *shiver* I don't know how many more of these I can take!

That's all I got for now, although I'm sure I forgot something. Happy Wednesday to everyone. Take care, and by for now!

April 19, 2013 Blog
A few updates, but not much

Sorry it has been a while since I posted last, as always seems to be the case. There really isn't much to post about these days, since I'm just waiting until June! Crystal and I are still set for our June 4 date. My transplant coordinator, Mary Beth, said she will call me by the end of the month to confirm it (I think they only put the surgery schedules out a month in advance), and if I don't hear from her by the end of the month, to call her and make sure we are on the schedule for CERTAIN. She even thinks she knows who our surgeon will be: Dr. Kandaswamy, who also did the surgery to put the fistula in my arm. He is a good guy, I like him, and I know he will take good care of Crystal and me. I am happy to have a surgeon do the transplant who I have met and had as a surgeon before. There's something comforting about it.

This is the end of my second week with my later work hours. I think it's going better for me, but sometimes it's hard to tell. On the days that I feel somewhat rested when I wake up in the morning 2 hours later, it's no problem making it to 5:00 at work. However, there have still been some days where I just don't want to get out of bed (but I do), and I'm dragging all day long. I still take a nap many evenings when I get home, but at least overall it has been easier to get through the work day. The day certainly goes by faster when I'm here 2 fewer hours. So I guess it's hard to say whether I'm feeling a little better because of the fewer work hours, or because of the 2 medications Dr. Ibrahim put me on a few weeks ago (the calcium/vitamin D, and sodium bicarbonate). Perhaps all of the above? I was really impressed last weekend when, for the first weekend in many months, I didn't sleep all weekend! Both Saturday and Sunday I got up before 10. On Sunday, I went to brunch with a couple friends, then went to Michael's (the craft store), and in the evening went to dinner with my mom and Elliott. I only took a short nap on Sunday afternoon before dinner. And for all those things, I actually felt like I had the energy to do them (otherwise, trust me, I wouldn't have done them). I even got some of my arts and crafts project done. I hope this weekend can be the same. It felt good to get up and out and be social. Kind of like a glimpse of what life will be like again after surgery (when I'm all recovered, of course). =)

The sessions with my therapist are going well. We are STILL discovering new things we want to work on each time I visit. That's not to say I have a lot of problems, but the few issues we are going to focus on, we have discovered, link together and are connected in ways. Even if we haven't really started "solving" anything yet, she has really helped me track my own thought pattern and make realizations about things that I hadn't realized before, which makes her, in my opinion, really good at her job! I think I've said that before. I guess I don't want to say we're necessarily going to SOLVE anything, since that's not what a therapist does. The word solve also has the connotation that there's a problem, and I'm sure therapists will tell you nothing is a PROBLEM, even if that's what we, as patients, call our issues. It's more like we have thoughts, behaviors, emotions, etc. that just need a little support and reassurance once in a while, with a little advice thrown in.

I have been feeling really grateful and thankful lately. I was telling Nancy (my therapist) this week that Crystal is literally saving my life (along with today's technological health advances). If I had been in this position about 65 years ago (I believe the first successful kidney transplant in a human was 1950), I would be dead. Crystal is giving me a 2nd chance at life, if you will, and you better believe that I'm going to take advantage of it. I have been feeling so sick and unhealthy for so long, there are so many things I haven't been able to do that I want to do, and my bucket list could be a novel. There are SO many things I want to see and experience in life. After I'm all recovered, it's like I can FINALLY start living my life. Of course, I could've lived my life to its fullest and been healthy all this time, but as we all know, I struggled with my diabetes for many years and never really took on the responsibility of taking care of myself. So here I am now, getting this 2nd opportunity.

I learned some interesting facts from Wikipedia today: Diabetes is the most common cause of kidney transplantation, accounting for approximately 25% of kidney transplantations in the U.S. The majority of kidney transplant recipients are on dialysis at the time of transplantation. However, individuals with chronic kidney failure who have a living donor available more undergo pre-emptive transplantation before dialysis is needed - like me! Also, in 2006, 47% of kidney donations came from living donors. That means that now, 7 years later, that number could (hopefully) be even higher! How amazing is that? How amazing are PEOPLE who donate?? Also from Wikipedia, here is some interesting information about kidney-pancreas transplants:

> *Occasionally, the kidney is transplanted together with the pancreas. This is done in patients with diabetes mellitus type 1, in whom the diabetes is due to destruction of the beta cells of the pancreas and in whom the diabetes has caused renal failure (diabetic nephropathy). This is almost always a deceased donor transplant. Only a few living donor (partial) pancreas transplants have been done. For individuals with diabetes and renal failure, the advantages of earlier transplant from a living donor (if available) are far superior to the risks of continued dialysis until a combined kidney and pancreas are available from a deceased donor.[citation needed] A patient can either receive a living kidney followed by a donor pancreas at a later date (PAK, or pancreas-after-kidney) or a combined kidney-pancreas from a donor (SKP, simultaneous kidney-pancreas).*
>
> *Transplanting just the islet cells from the pancreas is still in the experimental stage, but shows promise. This involves taking a deceased donor pancreas, breaking it down, and extracting the islet cells that make insulin. The cells are then injected through a catheter into the recipient and they generally lodge in the liver. The recipient still needs to take immunosuppressants to avoid rejection, but no surgery is required. Most people need two or three such injections, and many are not completely insulin-free.*

Alright, off to another laser eye treatment. At MOST, 2 more treatments, but hopefully we are done with the right eye, which would mean only 1 more on the left eye! Then no more EVER; or at least for a long, long time. I'll still need to keep doing the shots once a month, but only for another few (or 6 or so) months, then those we'll start tapering off of, too. And the shots aren't even a big deal, those I don't mind. It's these damn laser treatments. *shiver* I could complain about them all day long, if you haven't gotten that impression by now. So I'll stop. At least by the end of June I'll have healthy eyes and a healthy kidney! It's a win-win. :)

I hope everyone has a great weekend, and for those you fellow Minnesotans, stay warm! Keep your heads up, spring is supposedly right around the corner. . . . Bye for now.

April 24, 2013 Blog
I feel so loved!

I called the employee benefits office yesterday to find out if the paperwork from everyone who donated vacation hours to me had been processed. It had been over 2 weeks since everyone sent in their forms, and I hadn't seen the donated hours reflected in my vacation "bank" when I checked online through the employee self-service website. SOME of the donated hours had been put into my vacation bank, to get me up to 80 hours. The lady who is tracking it (Megan) said that she will keep an eye on it, and as I use the hours and as I need more, she'll keep processing and putting in more of the donated hours. I asked her if it was possible to know how many donated hours I have, so I can know going into my surgery about how many days are covered for my recovery, and I found out it's a little over 250 hours!! I currently have about 32 days' worth of vacation that I can use, which is 6 weeks, which should be plenty for my recovery. I definitely don't plan to be out from work for more than 6 weeks. I know that there's always the possibility that something could go wrong and I could end up back in the hospital, but knock on wood, let's hope that doesn't happen. Things have gone so well so far, and I've had so much luck, let's hope it continues after surgery. I know I'll have a lot of appointments to go to, even when I start back at work, but those won't require me to be gone for whole days at a time (I assume/hope). I am so grateful that I have such amazing, supportive, and generous co-workers (and Kathy, who also donated a big chunk of those hours). Right now I really couldn't ask for better co-workers. Love my job!

I got great news at my eye appointment last Friday - I may be all done with the laser treatments! My next appointment is in 2 and a half weeks, at which time he'll look at my eyes and decide from there what to do, but that we're most likely done with the laser. We'll still do the shots, but he wants to start weaning me off those, too, so that he can see what effects the laser treatments are having on my eyes. If we keep doing the shots once a month, it's hard for him to tell if my eyes are maintaining good health because of the shots, or the laser. I don't know how often he's going to want to do the shots; maybe once every 2 months instead of once a month? He said there is still the possibility that I'll need eye surgery, but that's the last resort, and what they try to avoid. They'll only do that if it looks like neither the laser OR the shots are doing their job. It sounds like even when people get the laser treatments, there's still a 50/50 chance that they'll need eye surgery down the road. My mom made a good point after my appointment- so then with those high odds, why don't they just do the surgery in the beginning instead of putting patients through all the pain and torture of the laser treatments?? A good question indeed. There must be more risks and dangers involved with eye surgery that makes them keep that as a last option. I'll be sure to ask. So when I have my appointment in a couple weeks, I'll find out what the game plan is for the upcoming months.

    I think I had mentioned something before about how cool it would be if Crystal and I were roomies at the hospital during our recovery after the surgery, for however many days we have to stay there. My mom (who worked in the transplant division here at the U many, many years ago) said she doesn't think we'd be put in a room together, because the post-op recovery is different for the donor and the recipient, so we would probably be in different recovery wards. Lame! Crystal has a friend who works for Fairview, and said that she would do some investigating. She (the friend) said that sometimes you can put in a request to be roomed together, so she'd see if there's anything she could do to help make that happen. Yay! I hope Crystal and I can be roomies. I really don't want to be stuck in the hospital for 5 or however many days with someone random who just, possibly, went through their own life-changing operation. I want to share that recovery time with Crystal! Mostly so if/when I'm in pain, I can joke with her about how her kidney is not being nice to me. :p

    I seem to be having some kind of hormonal or endocrine problem lately, and this happens every once in a while, and it drives me nuts. I start sweating for no apparent reason whatsoever. I can be doing nothing, feeling completely comfortable, neither hot nor cold, and just start sweating down the back and side of my neck. Sometimes I even get these chills, where I get so cold that I'm shivering, and at the same time I'm sweating. It's like my body's attempt at regulating my internal body temp when I'm cold is to start sweating, but it doesn't work! My body can't seem to regulate itself, and nothing stops the sweating once it starts, except sleep. For some reason, when I'm sleeping, my body is able to figure things out and get all regulated, then when I wake up (like in the mornings), it has stopped. But in the meantime, during the day and in the evenings, once it starts, I get so uncomfortable. I can feel it dripping down my neck, and the combination of feeling cold yet sweating is just awful. I get all self-conscious about it, I feel gross and icky, and it's especially irritating knowing there's nothing I can do to make it stop. It makes falling asleep at night hard, and it's bothersome when I'm at work. I've talked to different doctors about it, and none of them know what's going on or why it's happening. What the heck? I'm hoping this is just one of those things that with a new kidney will work itself out and not be a problem anymore.

That's all for now. 6 weeks and counting until surgery!!

P.S. I talked to my coordinator, Mary Beth, this afternoon. I wanted to find out how close a match Crystal is to me, because even though I do not anticipate getting a call from the national donor program, it is always a possibility. If they call, they are able to tell me how close a match their organs are, so I wanted to have something to compare it with. I have 8 antigens in my body, and out of those 8, Crystal has 7 of the same, and we match on 2 of them. An antigen is a substance in the body that triggers the production of antibodies. Antibodies are proteins in the immune system that are used to identify foreign/harmful objects (like a new organ). The immune system will try to destroy any antigen that is recognized as foreign or potentially harmful to the body. I know, it's confusing. My advice is to do what I did and go read about it on Wikipedia. Very informative!

Since Crystal was obviously approved for donation, this means that the other antigens that we don't match on aren't as important. Or at least it's something that the anti-rejection drugs that I'll be on after transplant will be able to cover. Even though this is all good information to know, I have already decided that even if the program calls me in the next 6 weeks and tells me they have a kidney and pancreas for me, I am going to stay with donation from Crystal. As Mary Beth pointed out, success after a transplant is higher from a living donor, and if I'm offered a kidney/pancreas from a deceased donor, I don't know who that person was, what kind of health they were in, what their background is, etc. etc. So DON'T WORRY Crystal, there's no way I'm backing out of your donation!! Besides, how could we be post-op roomies if you aren't there?? :)

April 30, 2013 Blog
Appointment

Had an appointment yesterday with Dr. Ibrahim, my nephrologist. I really like him and am so glad he is my doctor. When he came into the room, I was reading my book (The Ice Princess, by Camilla Lackberg), and when I put the bookmark in and closed it, he took it from me, looked at the cover, handed it back, and said "is this about you?" I chuckled and told him no, it's a Swedish murder mystery. Apparently he really likes Swedish murder mysteries, because we then spent a couple minutes talking about different Swedish authors, all of whom I've heard of because I've seen books by those authors lying around the house, since my dad also enjoys reading Swedish crime novels. He gave me recommendations and told me one series even have a few movies made that are available on Netflix. At one point he left for a while because my blood lab results weren't back yet, and I wanted to know what they were. When he came back, he told me about a woman who he had just seen who was back for her 6th liver transplant, and how she is one of the sweetest women ever, and her body just keeps rejecting every new liver. How unfortunate and sad for her. This is what I love about Dr. Ibrahim, though. He always makes each visit personal, and talks about things aside from just medical issues. It makes me feel like not just a patient, but also, in a way, a friend.

It was quite a productive appointment. At my last appointment with him a month ago, I stopped 3 of my medications, but yesterday I was put on 3 new ones. One is a shot that I have to get once a week, for my hemoglobin level. Just as a quick reminder, is the iron-containing metalloprotein (protein that contains a metal) in the red blood cells. Hemoglobin in the blood carries oxygen from the lungs to the rest of the body, where it releases the oxygen to burn nutrients to provide energy. When your hemoglobin levels are low, well, as you can probably figure out, it means you don't have a lot of oxygen going to the rest of the body to burn nutrients, so energy levels are really low. For the average adult, hemoglobin levels range from 12-15 (I'm not sure of the units associated with hemoglobin). Mine is around 10 or so. My maternal grandma has chronic low hemoglobin levels, around 8 pretty much all the time. This is probably a big part of the reason I'm so tired all the time and have no energy. So once a week I'll go in for a shot of Aranesp, which is a man-made form of the protein erythropoietin (yeah, don't ask me what THAT is). Aranesp stimulates bone marrow to make more red blood cells, and having more red blood cells raises hemoglobin levels. This shot is not a prescription that I fill at the pharmacy and take home and do; I have to go in to the clinic once a week and have it given to me.

One of the pills he put me on is a high-dose vitamin D tablet, called Ergocalciferol. It's 5,000 units (mg?) of vitamin D, and I only take it once a week. Even though when I was in a month ago he put me on a calcium/vitamin D combo supplement, my blood labs yesterday still showed low levels of vitamin D. So now, not only am I taking this once-a-week high-dosage vitamin D pill, I'm also doubling the calcium/vitamin D med that I've been taking for a month already; so I'll be taking 2 of those every day instead of 1. Next time I'm in for blood labs, my vitamin D levels better be through the roof! I think I just need to use this as an excuse to spend more time in the sun. Can I use that one at work?? "Excuse me, I have to go sit outside for an hour, my vitamin D levels are low today." =)

And last but not least, the third med he put me on is called Phoslo, or Calcium Acetate. It's a phosphate binder that is given to patients with end stage renal disease, like I have. I have to take it with meals, which allows it to combine with dietary phosphate in order for the body to eliminate it without absorbing it. Eliminating phosphate is good, because absorbing too much of it leads to high levels of phosphate in the blood, which results in an electrolyte disturbance. My phosphate levels are higher than Dr. Ibrahim would like them to be, so I'm taking this med to help eliminate it from my body and lower my phosphate levels. This doesn't necessarily cause fatigue or tiredness, it's just something that he wants to keep monitoring because my phosphate levels are elevated.

Still with me? Aren't we learning a lot today!? So basically, between the shots of Aranesp and the high-dose vitamin D pill I'm taking, hopefully I'll start to notice even more of an improvement in the next couple weeks. You know how at the end of any appointment they give you a print-off of any upcoming appointments, as well as a list of your current medications? My medication list now goes on to 2 pages. Yikes! It will be interesting to see, after my transplant, what all I stay on and what they take me off of. Depending on what they keep me on, combined with all the anti-rejection meds I'll have to take, I could be taking a dozen or more pills a day! Just call me a walking pharmacy . . .

I also asked Dr. Ibrahim why, when I was in last month, he asked if I would consider postponing transplant surgery if he could get me feeling better. He said there are a couple reasons. The first is this: Take person A, whose kidney functions are at 0%. Take Krystin, whose kidney functions are currently at 17%. Give us both a new kidney, which gives the recipient (me, or person A) 50% kidney functions again. Test our kidney functions 6 months or a year later, and person A's functions will be at 50%, as expected. Where will Krystin's functions be at? Not 67%. 50%. When I get a transplant, my body pretty much disowns the old, failing kidneys. They shrivel up like raisins and "die." So my body doesn't function with both the new kidney and any remaining functions left in my failing kidneys. My body takes on the new kidney as its only kidney. So why have the transplant when my current kidney is still functioning at 17%, since it would still only be 50% kidney functions after transplant anyway?

The second reason is they don't like to subject people to all those nasty anti-rejection medications before it's necessary. If he can get me feeling better, while also continuing to avoid dialysis, why not postpone transplant and save me a couple years (or however long) from having to take all those meds? His reasoning makes sense, and I understand what he's saying, but I'm still sticking with our June 4 surgery date. I still stand by my argument that I could still get a call from the National Donor Program any day. Even though I have Crystal, what if I didn't? What if I didn't have a donor, and the program called me? I'm supposed to say "No thanks, my doctor thinks he can get me feeling better, so I'm going to pass this time but keep me at the top of the list just in case. OK thanks!" I don't think so. Due to the high level of antibodies in my blood (remember, those things in the white blood cells that fight off foreign objects), finding a match for me is difficult. So I'll take the transplant while I can!

You may be asking, "well if Crystal is a match now, won't she still be a match in a couple years?" Yes, most likely, but who knows where the 2 of us will be in a couple years! Right now the timing is good for both of us, we've worked it out with our jobs, our friends, our families. . . . We've both pretty much planned the next couple months of our lives around this June 4 surgery. I don't care if I have to act like a stubborn child, kicking and screaming. I WANT my June 4 surgery, and that's THAT! ;)

I have to go in and see his dietitian. He says he can see in my face that I feel better, but from the way my body looks, he doesn't think I'm eating, and says I'm too skinny. I assured him that I AM eating, and am trying to gain weight, but not being able to dairy (things like cheese, butter, and cream, which have a lot of calories) combined with my stomach issues, makes it really hard to absorb all the nutrients I'm eating and gain weight. The problem is that I eat a LOT of fruits and veggies throughout the day, and although they are very healthy, they don't add up to a lot of calories. I need to eat more fatty foods. In the long run, no, eating lots of fatty foods is not a healthy lifestyle, but for the short term, I need to gain weight, so I'm going to be very picky about HOW I gain it. Last night when I went to the grocery store I bought bratwurst and bacon. I LOVE BACON. Then when I see the dietitian, she will discuss with me what kinds of things to eat that will get me to my daily calorie goal and, as Dr. Ibrahim put it, "put some beef on my body."

I had a dream the other night that it was surgery day. I was at the U, but it wasn't really the U; at least not how I know it. I was in my surgery gown, and in a hospital bed. The nurse was going to roll me up to the surgery room, but it took us FOREVER to get there. We went through so many different buildings, down so many long hallways, and it seemed like we were never going to get to surgery. I was panicking because we were SO late. Surgery was supposed to be at 5am, and it was already almost 2 in the afternoon. Crystal was already in the surgery room, because her nurse was quicker about getting her there than mine was. I was also panicking because I didn't have my phone and couldn't update my facebook status before going into surgery. We finally got to where we needed to be, and I was rolled into the surgery room, but that's where the dream ended. Strange. As Kathy joked, I wonder what Freud would have to say about that dream??

That's all for now. Other than that, I'm feeling pretty good and am counting down the days until surgery. 5 weeks away!! =) Bye for now.
May 1, 2013 Blog
What to expect when you're expecting . . . an organ donation!

I've learned a lot of information the past couple days about what to expect when I go to the hospital for my transplant surgery, about before, during, and after surgery, and I want to share it with you, as it's all very interesting.

Before my surgery:

Crystal and I will have to go in for some blood work 3 weeks prior to surgery, for another cross-match of our blood, to make sure we are still compatible. This will also be done the night before surgery, and I believe again the morning of. Just to make SURE they didn't miss anything! I will get information in the mail telling me when to be at the hospital and where to go. Even though surgery is Tuesday morning, Crystal and I will have to be at the hospital Monday afternoon some time. Once admitted, I will be assigned to a patient room. Family and friends are welcome to visit me during this time! This will be in the pre-op area, so it most likely be the same room that I'll be in during recovery. I'm not sure if Crystal and I will be together during pre-op, but I can always ask when I get there! This is when I will put on a hospital gown, as well. Different members of the transplant team will stop by to talk with me, the surgeon should stop by to walk me through the surgery process. and the anesthesiologist will stop by to discuss how I will be put to sleep for the surgery.

I could be given various tests during my pre-op time, which may include: blood samples, a chest X-ray, an EKG, a bath with special disinfectant soap (oh yay!), and an IV will be put in. For many transplant patients, they start giving you anti-rejection meds the day before, to start getting them into your system. This is mostly what will be done Monday. My guess is that I won't be able to eat or drink anything after dinner. Hate that part.

Surgery:
Friends and family, if they want, can wait in the waiting room while I'm in surgery. I don't ask anyone to, and I don't expect it, since surgery will take about 4 hours, and is scheduled to start at the butt-crack of dawn. And I don't imagine hospital waiting rooms have very good coffee, OR decent TV options. When surgery is over, a nurse will let any waiting visitors know how surgery went. After I am given anesthesia and am in a nice, comfortably, dreamy sleep, the surgery team may insert several more IVs, so that they can monitor me and my fluids, medicine, and drugs during and after surgery. They will also insert a Foley catheter, if they didn't already do that prior to surgery. I will be connected to a heart monitor machine, and an endotracheal tube will be inserted into my mouth or nose and into my windpipe, to control my breathing. A nasogastric (or stomach) tube will probably also be inserted in my mouth or nose and down into my stomach to keep my stomach empty during surgery. Don't want any messes on the surgery table! Some of these tubes and IVs will be removed after surgery, but some of them will stay in for a few days, like the catheter.

The surgeon will make an incision that is about 8 inches long, in my lower abdomen. The donor kidney will then be placed in the small pocket under my pelvic bone, on either the left or right side. The surgeon will connect the main blood vessels going to my leg, to the blood vessels on the donor kidney. The surgeon will also connect my bladder to the donor's kidney ureter, which allows my new kidney to make urine. Donor kidneys typically start working right away, but some may take hours, days, or even WEEKS to start making urine! After all those connections are made, the surgeon will close up the incision. My own defective kidneys will not be removed during surgery. They stay in there like little raisins just hanging out.

After surgery

After the operation, I will be brought into the surgery recovery room. This unit is specially staffed and equipped to take care of post-surgical patients. I will likely only stay in the recovery area until the anesthesia wears off, so about an hour or two. As I wake up, a nurse may ask me to breath into a spirometer, which is a tube device that tests and improves lung functions. This is also a very critical time to let the nurse know if I am in pain or experiencing any nausea.

After the nausea wears off, I will be taken to a "step-down" unit, which is for patients who are stable but still need continuous monitoring. The nurses and doctors will be watching me closely here, to make sure my new kidney is working properly! I will still have many tubes in me in various places. I may even have a central line in my neck, which is a thin tube that is inserted into a vein and threaded toward the heart. It is used to measure the pressure in my vein and collecting fluids. I may also have a line in the artery of my wrist, which is used to take blood and measure my blood pressure, but will probably be removed after 24 hours. I will probably also have electrode patches on my chest, which are attached to a heart monitor. Those usually stay in place a day or two, until they are sure that my heart is recovering from surgery. The Foley catheter will stay in my bladder for at least a few days, since it will be almost impossible for me to get up and go to the bathroom right away. Fine with me; as strange as it may sound, I actually LIKE having a catheter in. I can go potty whenever I need/want, right from the comfort of my bed! And I don't even have to deal with the urine; nurses will check the urine bag (that hangs off the side/end of my bed) numerous times daily, to see if my new kidney is producing urine yet. Ahh, such is the life. I will likely have a surgical drain in my lower abdomen. This flexible, plastic tube helps remove any excess fluid or blood into a container. And the last but not least addition to the wonderful hospital attire are special socks or compression sleeves on my legs, to keep the blood flowing and prevent blood clots.

Many patients say they feel little or no pain after surgery, but some say they feel quite a bit of pain. Most likely (HOPEFULLY) I will be given a patient-controlled pump that allows me to give myself pain medicine through one of my IVs. This is my favorite part. The key is to control my pain while avoiding any side effects from pain meds, such as confusion and mood swings. And so, how would they be able to tell the difference from me normally?? Within 24 hours, a nurse will help me sit up and take a short walk. Every day I'm in the hospital, the walks will get longer. The sooner I move around, the quicker I recover.

I should be able to start drinking fluids within 24 hours of surgery. Once I'm able to digest clear liquids, I be given some solid foods. However, I will be getting all the fluids and nutrients I need through my IVs, so I probably won't even feel hungry. It's very common for transplant patients to feel little or no hunger for a few days, or even a week, after surgery. This idea does not excite me, considering eating is one of my favorite things to do ever.

Many tests will be performed during the first few days, to see how well my new kidney is functioning. These tests may include blood and urine analyses, ultrasounds of the new kidney, and biopsies. For a short while after surgery, I'll be getting my anti-rejection meds through my IV, but soon after surgery the nurse will bring me the pills to take at the right time. They will also start educating me on the different meds I'll be taking, and when to take them.

The rest of the hospital stay

I can stay in the hospital anywhere from 4-7 days. For younger people, it is generally a shorter period of time since we heal faster, but of course the recovery period is different for everyone, and it's always possible there could be complications that affect my recovery stay, so it's impossible to say exactly how long I'll be there. I may stay in the step-down unit the entire time, but likely, after a couple days, I will be moved to a room on the transplant unit. I will be eating solid foods, and taking longer and more frequent walks. Eventually, the catheter and many of the IVs will be removed. I will be discharged from the hospital when I have recovered enough to eat, walk without assistance, and move my bowels (go poop, to put it bluntly).

Even after I return home, I will need to return to the transplant clinic often for blood work. For the first month or two, I will need to go in three days a week, so they can make sure my new kidney is functioning properly and the anti-rejection meds are doing their job. I will not be allowed to drive for the first couple weeks after surgery, so my dad, mom, and Kathy will take turns bringing me to the clinic and back home again those three days a week.

That's all I know for now. You now know as much as I do about the transplant process! Wasn't that fun? That is how a typical transplant goes, but of course anything could change at any time, so I won't know EXACTLY how it goes until it's happening! I will be bringing my computer to the hospital with me, so I'll be able to update you on things while I'm there. Maybe not for the first day or so, but eventually. If you come visit me, though, then you won't have to wait to read this; I can just tell you in person! :) As soon as I'm able to inform people what room I'm in, I'll be sure to do that, or have someone post it.

I hope you enjoyed reading this very informative entry. Bye for now!

[Comments on the foregoing blog post:]
Christine Hinz Lenzen: Are they still planning on a pancreas transplant too?
Krystin: Yes, but not from a living donor (unless someone else wants to see if they are a match and donate!). I will be moved to the pancreas-only donor wait list, so hopefully in 3-5 years I'll get a new pancreas, too!
Christine Hinz Lenzen: How come they won't do that without the kidney transplant?
Krystin: Like why didn't I had a pancreas transplant 10 years ago? They don't do pancreas transplants in diabetics unless that person ALSO has kidney failure. Apparently just having diabetes is manageable, but once kidney failure is involved, then it's more urgent to also get the pancreas transplanted. Makes sense. . . . I guess?
Christine Hinz Lenzen: i guess . . .
Krystin: Right? Considering a pancreas transplant years ago could've prevented me from needing a kidney transplant today.

Christine Hinz Lenzen: out of curiosity, is this something that would have happened despite previous poor management of your diabetes?

Christine Hinz Lenzen: and just so you know, although I don't comment often, I do keep up with your posts. I will be in town the first weekend of June and hope to see you before the surgery.

Krystin: No, if I had taken better care of my diabetes, I most likely would not be needing a kidney transplant. Believe me, I've been kicking myself in the ass about it the last year. Alas, what's done is done, and now I'm not looking back, but looking instead at the bright, amazing future this will allow me to have!

Christine Hinz Lenzen: That's good. And we are still young, your body has more resilience for getting better and healing now than it would in ten, twenty years.

Krystin: Exactly! That's a good way to look at it. If this were inevitably going to happen, better now than later, when there's a greater chance of rejection and complications. I like the way you think. :)

Crystal Lescault: Hopefully my kidneys are behaving, I've been taking good care of them. You know, no contact sports or anything crazy. Lol. I feel like I'm the carrier of precious cargo :)

May 8, 2013 Blog
Give me your bloooooood!

Alright, SO, a few new updates for you.

Last week I had an appointment with my nephrologist, Dr. Ibrahim. (Are you learning everyone's names yet?) I think I mentioned that in my last post, about getting the high-dose Vitamin D prescription to take once a day, and those shots I was going to start getting once a week to bring up my hemoglobin level. I actually talked to one of Dr. Ibrahim's nurses later in the week, and they changed the game plan a little. Apparently, I have no iron in my body. His nurse said that, based on my lab work from that week, my iron levels are pretty much depleted. Which would explain a good part of the reason why I'm so tired all the time. So instead of doing the shots once a week, I'm going to start doing blood infusion therapy. 5 sessions over a week and a half period, and they last about an hour and a half each session. They are going to pump me full of iron! And then the shots for my hemoglobin will only be once every 4 weeks. I had my first blood infusion on Monday, another this morning, then the others are Friday,

Sunday, and Tuesday of next week. Then they'll do lab work again and see where my levels are at. It's through an IV, so I have to get an IV put in my hand every time I go in. It took them FOUR tries this morning to finally find a vein. I think I almost passed out from hyperventilating. On Friday I'm tempted to ask her if they can just wrap it up and keep it in since I'm just coming back again on Sunday. My hand is already bruised; I'm sure it's not looking forward to getting poked again in 2 days.

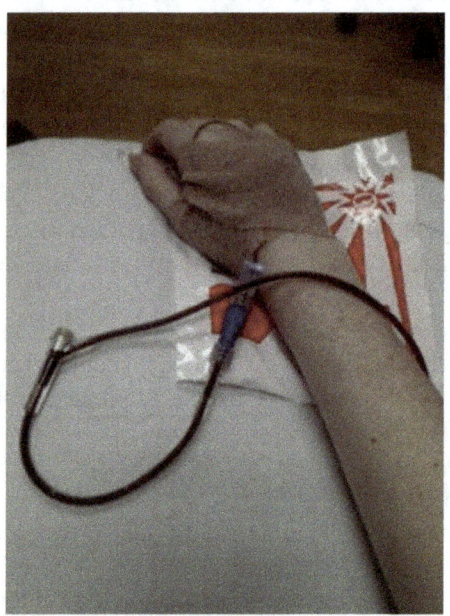

I'm not always sure what I should say on here and what I should keep between my therapist and me, but I said from the beginning that I was going to be open and honest, because I have nothing to hide in this process. That being said here goes; just please don't judge me by what I'm about to say. I've decided to go against medical advice and go ahead with the surgery on June 4. Last week when I saw the surgeon, he told that me that both he and my nephrologist, Dr. Ibrahim, are in agreement that I should hold off on the surgery and wait for an offer from the National Donor Program for a kidney/pancreas transplant, or until I would need to go on dialysis (in which case Crystal would still be my donor); whichever came first. According to blood work that was one back in January, I do have one antibody against Crystal, that will fight against the new kidney. That antibody didn't show up in my recent blood work last week, but as the surgeon, Dr. Kandaswamy, said, that doesn't mean it won't come back, and it could come back with a fury. This puts me at higher risk for rejection. It means I will need closer monitoring after surgery. Dr. Kandaswamy said that if I had already been on dialysis for the last 6 months and had no other option, he would say hands-down let's go forward with surgery. But since I'm not on dialysis, and I still have some kidney functions left, let's wait and see how things play out. He wants to see 2 or 3 more blood tests without that antibody showing up. I believe his exact words were, "I'll do the surgery if it's what you really want, but I don't like the looks of it right now."

I know what you're going to say. I should wait. If all the doctors are saying wait, and considering I still have some kidney functions and I'm not on dialysis, why not wait? Here's the thing. I can't wait. I just can't do it. It's easy for everyone else to say wait, but everyone else isn't me; they aren't living my life, walking in my shoes everyday. They don't know how I feel, what this feels like. Having that date set in June is what's been keeping me strong, keeping me going every day, getting me up out of bed. If you take away that date and give me an indefinite day that this could happen, I don't know how I'd make it. Dr. Kandaswamy said that it could still be another year before I got a call from the donor program. I just can't wait that long. I'm willing to take the risks involved to do the surgery with Crystal on June 4. And yes, there is the possibility that my body could reject it, but there's also the possibility that it could ACCEPT it. We have had so much luck on our side so far, and I don't want to jinx it or anything, but I feel good about it. I thought so long and hard about it Monday night after my appointment, and got so stressed out about it, I literally made myself sick. I got a migraine and felt sick to my stomach. This was one of the biggest decisions I've ever had to make in my life.

I am the ONLY one who can make this decision, and I'm making it for me, and me only. I'm not making the decision based on what will make others happy. I'm making it based on what will make ME happy, and this is what will make me happy. Too many times in my life I have gone against my own wishes and done what other people wanted me to do. I know when it comes to help and listening to the medical professionals, it's a bit of a different situation, but I don't want to live the rest of my life thinking "I should have just done the surgery on June 4." So, end of discussion. :)

I think I need a day at the spa. Or a good massage. Maybe some yoga. I will be glad when this is all over. Until then, I'm going to eat lots of spinach every day. Bye for now!

May 8, 2013 Email
E

Krystin to dad:
I have a message to Mary Beth to give me a call, and I'm going to ask her if it's even possible for Crystal to donate both kidney/pancreas. If not, what about asking Elliott to get tested for pancreas donation? I know he wants to keep both his kidneys, which is fair enough, but what about pancreas? He's not losing it, and he won't get diabetes from it, since they only shave off part. If he's the same blood type as me, like I've said before, as my sibling he is the best possible match. Just something to think about. I haven't mentioned this to him yet. [I seem not to have responded and nothing ever came of it.]

May 14, 2013 Facebook
Krystin Engstrand is feeling inspired.
Fall 2013 I will be a student again!! Taking a creative writing class here at the U - the first step in the grad school creative writing program, and the first step in finally following my dream!

May 14, 2013 Email
what class?
Dad to Krystin

Krystin to dad:
Topics in Creative Writing: First Person Singular.

Dad to Krystin:
This sounds wonderful. I'm delighted you're doing this.

May 17, 2013 Blog
The plan - revised
I finally got my letter in the mail from the transplant clinic, with all my info regarding surgery! Every day for the past week and a half I get all excited to check the mail when I get home from work, to see if I've gotten the letter yet, and yesterday it finally came. The plan is a little different than what I had laid out before, as far as the schedule. I

won't be staying overnight at the hospital Monday night. Everything I need to do the day prior to surgery I do in the transplant clinic, as an outpatient. I need to be at the clinic at 7am Monday morning of the 3rd. Then it's a day full of blood tests, an EKG, chest X-ray, and meeting with numerous staff, such as the transplant information services, nursing staff, the transplant surgeon (Dr. Kandaswamy), my nephrologist (Dr. Ibrahim), and my coordinator (Mary Beth), complete pre-op admission paperwork, complete pre-op teaching, and watch a video about preparing for transplant surgery. Crystal has to do all the same things, so maybe we will get to go some of them together. We will get a breakfast break, and are encouraged to eat a generous breakfast, since lunch will be light, and after 2 PM we can only have clear liquids for the rest of the day. This is the part I'm not looking forward to the most. I HATE not being able to eat. I'll probably just make myself go to bed super early, so that I don't have to think about eating. And I'll have to keep some Sprite on hand in case my blood sugar gets low. I will probably want to go to bed early anyway, since I have to check in at the hospital at 5:30 Tuesday morning! I'll have to make sure my light lunch on Monday is a good one, because it's the last solid food I'll be eating for a few days. After surgery, I'll be getting nutrients and stuff through my IV, and won't be ready to eat solid foods yet anyway. I wonder if the cafeteria has steak and potatoes . . .

    I can't believe it is only a little over 2 weeks away. I keep telling myself, and everyone (who will listen), how fast the time has gone by. I swear just yesterday is was 3 months until surgery, and I thought I was never going to make it until June 4. Now it's only 2 weeks away, and it's no sweat to make it until then. The excitement and anticipation is giving me the energy boost I need every day to make it to surgery. I think about the surgery all the time; even when I'm laying in bed at night, it's all I think about. I think about everything I've gone through up to this point, and how the next couple weeks will go. I imagine what it will be like after surgery, being in the hospital for those 4-6 days, and what I'll do with my time when I'm home recovering. I try to picture what my body will be feeling, how my mood will be, how the meds will affect me, etc. etc. I think about pretty much anything that can be thought of in relation to surgery. But in a good way; I'm not nervous at all, and I'm not scared. I'm ready.

    On Tuesday I finished my iron infusions. They drew blood to test my hemoglobin levels, as well. At the end of April, before I started the infusions, my hemoglobin was 9.9. Anything under 12 is considered anemic, and their goal was to get me to at least 10.5 (adults run anywhere between 12-17). When they drew my blood on Tuesday, I was only up to 10.3, which means the infusions did not raise my hemoglobin level as much as they had hoped. Kind of gives you an idea of how low my iron levels are if after 5 infusions I'm still not where they want me to be. So, I'll go back in for the shot of Aranesp, which is the stuff that increases red blood cell levels and is used to treat anemia. Then they'll do another blood test in a couple weeks and see where I'm at. However, a couple weeks will bring me right up to surgery, so hopefully after that I won't need any more of the shots, because with the new kidney, ideally my hemoglobin won't be an issue anymore (at least, hopefully, I won't be anemic anymore). There's a lot of "hopefully" that come with this transplant! Even though the infusions didn't raise my hemoglobin a lot, I do feel better from them. I don't feel as tired, and if I have an errand to run or need to do something, I have no problem doing it. My body doesn't ache like it used to, and I don't feel as dizzy/light headed as I sometimes would. I'm also trying to do better at drinking plenty of fluids, so I'm sure that helps, too. One of my co-workers helped me find this soy protein powder that is made for vegans, so it doesn't have any dairy in it at all (no condensed milk or anything, like a lot of those powders do). So no, I'm not a vegan, I just got it to avoid the dairy. I have been using that to make a protein shake every day, so at least I know I'm getting my protein in. I can even use the powder and put it in cookies or muffins or anything that you can bake. Love that part. Any excuse to eat cookies is fine by me. Oh who am I kidding- any excuse just to EAT is fine by me. :D

    I feel like there was something else I was going to write about, but now I can't remember what it was, so I'll end it here. Which means just a short update for you this time. Happy Friday to all, and have a good weekend!

Chapter 10

Kidney Transplant

May 23, 2013 Blog
My mind never rests

I can't believe how close surgery is. A little under 2 weeks already. After tomorrow, only 1 week of work left! And tomorrow I start cat sitting, which will go up through the Sunday before surgery, so that will make the time go by so fast! I love the kitties that I cat sit for, so the time with them always goes by fast. That's good though, because I'm getting so anxious and so excited. It almost feels like the big day is teasing me: it's so close, just dangling there in front of my face, but still just out of reach. Like dangling candy in front of a toddler.

I've been reading a bit about Prednisone, and I am not learning good things. Prednisone is an immunosuppressant, which I'll have to be on after surgery. It suppresses the immune system, which helps prevent my body from rejecting my new kidney, but that means it also puts me at higher risk for infections and getting sick. It also has a lot of nasty side effects. Here are the major ones (only a few):

- Increased blood sugar for diabetics
- Difficulty controlling emotion (I've heard there can be some crazy wicked mood swings)
- Difficulty in maintaining train of thought
- Immunosuppression
- Weight gain (I'm not worried about this - I could use a little weight gain)
- Facial swelling (like I said before, my face will look like the Michelin tire man!)
- Depression, mania, psychosis, or other psychiatric symptoms
- Unusual fatigue or weakness
- Mental confusion / indecisiveness / anxiety / nervousness
- Blurred vision / cataracts / glaucoma
- Abdominal pain and/or bloating
- Peptic ulcer
- Infections
- Painful hips or shoulders
- Steroid-induced osteoporosis
- Stretch marks

- Osteonecrosis (cellular death of bone components due to interruption of the blood supply. No blood = bone tissue dies, bone collapses.)
- Insomnia
- Severe joint pain
- Black stool / diarrhea
- Mouth sores or dry mouth
- Hepatic steatosis (AKA fatty liver disease)

As one of my co-workers pointed out, my body will be going through so many changes, I may not even know what is being caused by the Prednisone and what isn't.

I've inevitably begun pondering all the "what ifs" in my mind. What if my body rejects the kidney. What if I have to take off even more time from work because I'm re-admitted to the hospital? What if I have a lot of appointments to go to that take me away from work, and I don't have enough vacation/sick hours to cover it? What if my job starts realizing that they need to replace me with someone who is more reliable and can be there full-time every day? (That's my biggest "what if" fear). I know I really need to try to not let these questions bother me, because there's nothing I can do about it. I just have to take it one day at a time and see what happens. Worrying too much about the future is not healthy and only adds more stress, which I really don't need right now. I know I'm probably stressing out about work for nothing, but it's kinda hard not to. Isn't it natural that anyone going through this would worry about their job security? This surgery is a big deal, and is going to require a lot from me. I know that after I return to work, it's not just going to be all fine and dandy and I'll be able start back at 100%. I'm going to have a lot of appointments, and often, that are going to take me out of work sometimes, even if I schedule them first thing in the morning or late afternoon. I just hope everyone at work is still as supportive of that as they have been so far.

Don't Google 'kidney donor scars.' It's not pretty. I imagine my scar will be similar looking. I myself am not really worried about scars, since I don't wear bathing suits very often (and if I do, it's not a skimpy bikini), but I hope Crystal is OK with having a nice battle scar. I'm considering getting some kind of tattoo near/around the scar, to kind of commemorate it. Nothing gaudy, and I haven't even begun to think what I'd get, but it's an idea that I've been considering. Obviously I wouldn't do it for a while, to give the scar time to heal. But maybe in a year or two. We'll see.

I have been having a hard time keeping my weight up lately. It seems like half the things I eat upset my stomach now. I hardly ever feel hungry, and when I do eat, I get full really fast. If I eat too much, I get sick (and by get sick I mean throw up; just so there isn't any confusion). If I eat tomatoes, I get sick. If I sit and stare at the wall, I get sick. I no longer know what is good and what is bad to eat. Lactose is still on the no-go list, but it seems like anything else is fair game now too, to make me sick. I love eating; it's one of my favorite things to do, so I hate living in fear that anything I eat could upset my stomach. I would be surprised if I even get 1,000 calories in most days.

I have decided that while I'm at the hospital after surgery, I'm going to tell them I want to talk to a gastroenterologist (digestive system doctor), because this is just downright ridiculous. Since I'll be there and not going anywhere, that's the perfect time for them to run whatever tests they need to help figure out what is going on with my stomach. I know I have diabetic gastroparesis, which, as I'm sure I've mentioned before, is a medical condition that results in food remaining in the stomach for a longer time than normal. Instead of the stomach contracting to move food down into the small intestine for digestion, the damaged nerves don't contract, so food moves very slowly through the digestive tract, or not at all. When it doesn't move through at all, since it can't keep moving it downward, it sends it back up. Apparently this can happen to people with diabetes who have had many years of high blood sugars, like I have. High blood sugars damage the nerves. Most of the treatments for gastroparesis are medications. I've tried a couple different meds so far, even one that I had to get from Canada, but they didn't seem to help. I must have a very severe case. I'm not sure what they could do to fix this problem, but I certainly hope there's something, because this literally affects my everyday life, not to mention other things. The acid from throwing up is not good for my esophagus, and it's damaging my teeth (wearing away at the enamel). I've been crossing my fingers that the kidney transplant will cure it, but the more I think about it, the more I realize it probably won't. This is a completely separate issue. Kidney transplant may (hopefully) cure my lactose intolerance and be able to process dairy again, but I don't think it's going to improve the gastroparesis any. *sigh* All I can do it ask while I'm at the hospital.

My dad is sick; he thinks he may have pneumonia. Great. I can NOT be getting sick right now. If I do, they'll postpone surgery! At work I made a cup of hot tea and added a packet of that Airborne powder. I'll also be buying and drinking lots of orange juice. Good thing I start cat sitting tomorrow, so I can get out of the house. Gotta stay healthy!

Alright, I think that's all I got on my mind for now. 12 days to go!! Bye for now.

June 4, 2013 Facebook
Krystin Engstrand is with Crystal Lescault.
Kidney day is HERE!! Please send lots of positive vibes to Crystal and me today, for a safe and successful surgery. I will be out of commission for awhile, but will give you updates as I come out of my drug-induced fog. Check back here for updates on my room information if you are planning to visit. See you on the other side!

June 4, 2013 Facebook Crystal Lescault
OR nurse says kidney is out of Crystal in transport to Krystin Engstrand. Crystal should be done in surgery in 30.

June 4, 2013 Facebook
Krystin Engstrand is with Crystal Lescault at University of Minnesota Health.

June 5, 2013 Facebook Crystal Lescault
I had my nurse call Krystin Engstrand's nurse and it sounds like she is doing good. The kidney seems to be working, yay! I just got some morphine and am hoping that will help me relax and sleep. Night all!

June 5, 2013 Facebook
Crystal Lescault to Krystin Engstrand
Are you okay? Feeling good?

> Krystin: Yup, I get to eat food today, so just waiting for my breakfast! How are you feeling? When I woke up after surgery yesterday I was in the most excruciating pain ever. I was bawling. But they got it under control and it has been very manageable since.
> Crystal Lescault: I had a reaction to the pain meds I got in recovery and my heart rate went a little crazy. They told me today would be painful & they weren't lying. But I'm feeling okay. You are lucky to get food! I get liquids still.

Krystin: Have you been up out of bed yet? I'll be moving up to the 7th floor today, so one of these days when they take me on a walk I'll come visit! That sucks about your reaction to the pain meds. Did they get it under control quickly?

June 6, 2013 Facebook
Surgery went great and I'm in recovery! Possibly going home Friday [June 7] already, but that seems too early. In the meantime, come visit me

June 7, 2013 Facebook
Crystal Lescault to Krystin Engstrand
How are you feeling?? You were at class I think when I left but my Mom sent "hugs", haha. Hope you finally had success in the bathroom area ;) I'm doing good, no more throwing up so far!
Krystin: Yeah I was bummed that I missed saying goodbye! I almost fell asleep in that class, too. Lol. Still no luck in the bathroom. Am staying another night and getting my 2nd enema shortly. Woohoo! Haha. So glad to hear you are keeping things down!

June 8, 2013 Blog
The big day!

Oh, where to begin! How about starting off with the transplant being a great success! My body is taking to it great, and is producing lots of urine, which s wonderful considering that's what the kidney does. It also means it is successfully flushing everything out of my body that it needs to flush. The doctors and surgeon are very happy with the how everything is looking thus far.

On Monday before surgery, when I was in the clinic for all the pre-op tests and exams, my coordinator put me on a 24-hour pancreas donor watch, which means they would try to find me a matching pancreas by surgery Tuesday morning. The chances of that happening were about 1%, but the idea was pretty exciting. That way they could transplant both organs in one surgery. They didn't find one, but the surgeon said that since I have been on the National Donor List since November, he thinks I will get a pancreas by the end of the year. Woohoo! Apparently I don't lose my place on the list when I'm moved from kidney-pancreas to just the pancreas list. So that's good news! I'm also still keeping the pancreatic islet cell transplant as an option, but that is still up for review by the FDA. When it's approved though,

I'll be first in line! And they like doing the islet cell transplant on patients who have had a kidney transplant, so I got one leg up there.

Alright, On to surgery day. I had to be at the hospital by 6:30am. I was brought back into a pre-op bay and changed into a lovely hospital gown. At least it was purple, my favorite color. Crystal was in the bay right across from me, so we could wave at each other. A little after 7 my mom showed up and joined me in my bay, and shortly after that my dad also joined me, so I was with both my parents during pre-op. they got an IV started and got me all prepped. They took me back to surgery around 8:45, only 15 minutes after they had brought Crystal back. I thought it would be longer, but we had different surgeons, so she had hers, who opened her up and got the kidney out, and I had mine, who opened me up and got the kidney in and connected. While I was under anesthesia, they also inserted a Foley catheter and an IV pick in my neck.

The whole surgery took about 4 hours, I think. Here is my beautiful incision:

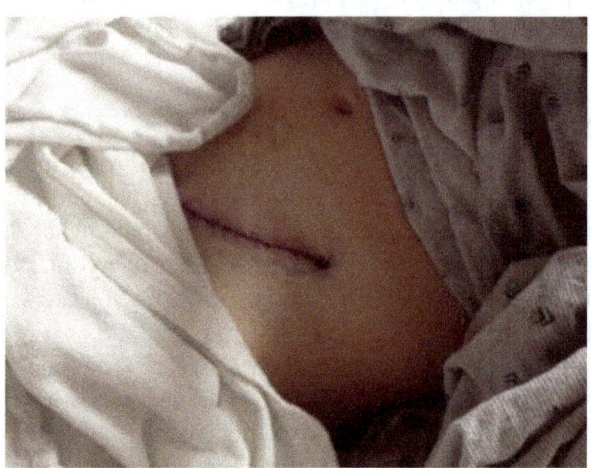

They also put a stent in with the transplant, which I'll have to go in for another surgery in 4-6 weeks to have it removed. A stent is a mesh 'tube' that is inserted into a natural passage in the body to prevent or counteract a disease-induced flow constriction. In simpler words, it keeps my blood flowing to my new kidney to help it heal properly. It's also used to hold that natural passage open to allow access for surgery. I don't think the surgery to remove it is inpatient. I'll be put under general anesthesia, but I'm pretty sure I'll go home the same day.

When I woke up in recovery, I was in the most excruciating pain I've ever been in. I was sobbing and couldn't breathe. They were scrambling to get it under control. Apparently what they had already given me wasn't working. Whatever they eventually gave me worked, and even made me fall back asleep. When I woke up again, I was in a room on the recovery floor. I don't remember who was there with me. Probably my mom? I don't remember much from that first day. I know my dad stopped by at some point after work, and Chris and her mom stopped by in the evening. They had my pain under control by then, so I was comfortable. I didn't have the high, loopy feeling that I usually get from the IV pain killers, which is kinda disappointing, since I was looking forward to that a little bit. . . . Oh well. I only got IV pain killers that first day. Since then I've been taking Percocet, orally. My pain has actually been very minimal. I didn't take any Percocet all day Friday. When I woke up this morning, though, I had quite a bit of pain in my incision. I've been taking Percocet, but it hasn't fully eased the pain, since now I'm just chasing the pain and not preventing it.

I have not been able to poop since the surgery. They had me eating solid foods starting Wednesday morning, so I've been eating full, regular meals since then, and nothing is moving through! In the last day and a half I've had 2 suppositories and 3 enemas, and they've done nothing. I am so incredibly bloated and uncomfortable, and my stomach looks like I'm pregnant. All the food I've been eating is just sitting there! But the steroids I'm on are making me ravenous, so I'm hungry ALL the time. I won't be on the steroids forever, but I like that I have a good appetite again so I can finally start gaining some weight back. When I weighed in on Tuesday morning, I was 112 pounds. Today I'm 136. Whew! I know that's mostly water weight though. A lot of it will go away, but I'm going to try and maintain most of it. Most people want to lose weight, while I actually want to GAIN! The docs think that once I get home and am in the comfort of my house, it will be easier to go poop. It's also normal for patients to be constipated for 3-5 days after surgery, from the hard narcotics, so I'm on schedule. Any time now things will open up and I will finally get some relief. TMI? Sorry. :)

I found out I don't have to be on Prednisone! I was on it for the first few days, but I won't be taking it from here on out. It's not part of the transplant regimen here. I was glad to hear that, since that was the med I was worried about the most. I have plenty of other meds to take, and the pharmacy gave me one of those pill compartments will numerous slots for each day. It's huge. At breakfast alone I take like 9 or 10 pills. Sheesh. But half of my meds I only take for the first 3 months, so after that there will be fewer to take. And one of the transplant educators gave me a few co-pay cards that will cover 3 of my meds for close to a year, so at the most, I shouldn't be paying more than $50 a month for all my medications. Good deal! That I can handle.

I signed up for home health care. Since I can't drive for 2 weeks, my dad or Kathy or my mom were going to have to alternate bringing me into the clinic 3 days a work to have blood labs done, but now a home care nurse will come to my house and draw my blood and bring it back to the lab for processing. This will be really convenient, and less of a hassle for those who would've had to drive me. I do have to go to the infusion clinic tomorrow at 7am to get blood work done, and to have my 5th and final round of steroids through an IV. It will take about 4 hours for the steroid drip, but then I'll be done with the steroids. So another early morning! But at least tonight I get to sleep in my own bed, which is going to feel so great. I am going to have a LOT of doctor appointments in the next couple months, but at least in a couple weeks I'll be able to drive myself to those.

OH, best news ever - I think my lactose intolerance went away!! I had a side of mac and cheese with my lunch today, after having some cheese on my breakfast sandwich this morning, and neither one presented a problem. No barfing! So we decided to really test the limits and ordered pizza for dinner when I got home. Again, no barfing. Woohoo!! I am so, so, SO excited if it's gone. If any of the cheese today was going to make me sick, it would have done so a long time ago. This makes me incredibly happy. Pizza had never tasted so good. Life is grand again. :) I was really impressed with the food at the hospital, too. For being hospital food, it wasn't too bad. Now, admittedly, I'm not very hard to please when it comes to food, but considering I've spent a lot of time in hospitals in my life, I know good hospital food from bad hospital food. The only other hospital food I've had that was better was in Paris, but that's probably not surprising. I think I ordered the Montreal grilled pork chop twice a day while I was there (at the U; not Paris).

Alright, I think that's all for now. Even though the transplant is over, this is not the end of my blog. There is still lots to come! I will still keep you updated on how everything proceeds, at least over the next few months, if not longer. So, this isn't the last of me yet. I'm off to enjoy the comforts of my bed and get a decent night sleep, finally. Good night, and goodbye for now!

June 23, 2013 Facebook
Krystin Engstrand is feeling energized.
I'm feeling fantastic these days! I'm already feeling the benefits of the new kidney. I can't wait to live life to its fullest. Look out people, the new and improved Krystin is ready to take the world head-on!!

June 24, 2013 Blog
A little bump that turned into a big bump

My second post since transplant, and it doesn't bring good news. Last Sunday night, for Father's Day, we went to the Nicollet Island Inn for dinner. Unfortunately, I didn't get to enjoy any of the what looked like an amazingly delicious meal. I threw up at home right before we left, on the way to the restaurant, and again during the meal. No dinner for me.

On Monday morning I woke up feeling lightheaded and dizzy when I stood up. The home health care nurse came around 9, and I told her how I was feeling. She said to make sure I drink plenty of fluids during the day so I don't get dehydrated. After she left, I spent the entire rest of the day on the couch. I couldn't even sit up without feeling like I was going to pass out. By 3pm I decided to call my coordinator. I told her what was going on, and she said to go into the ER. Sounded like I needed some fluids. So I text my dad and he comes home to bring me over to the U hospital.

My coordinator called ahead to let them know I was coming, so I got in right away. The usual drill: vitals, blood draw, insert an IV. Blood work shows that I have a UTI (urinary tract infection). They want to admit me overnight to give me antibiotics and for observation. Ok fine. I wasn't expecting to be admitted, but I could handle one night. Well, 4 days later I was still there.

On top of a UTI, one of my anti-rejections meds has a side effect of nausea and vomiting, and I suffered from that side effect. So they switched me to a different one, and put me on an IV antibiotic for the infection. All day Tuesday I was throwing up. Nothing stayed down. I didn't even eat any dinner. Starting about 3am Wednesday morning, I started feeling nauseous. I felt nauseous ALL day, literally. Wednesday morning they took out the stent that was in my kidney, which was just a short operation. I didn't even get anesthesia, just heavily sedated. At least the sedation gave me some relief from the nausea for a little while, but it came back within a couple hours. They decided to take the stent out early because it may be what caused the infection, so it was a precautionary to make it not happen again. However, if that doesn't cause another UTI, I'm sure something else will, because I tend to get them a lot.

I didn't eat all day Wednesday. The sedation had a very lingering effect, so I was groggy and out of it most of the day. I think I opened my eyes maybe 5 times all day. Thursday was a much better day. I didn't have any nausea when I woke up. I didn't any breakfast, but I had some lunch. I was on a clear fluids diet, so I only had jello and yogurt and juice. Same with dinner, but I added some cream of mushroom soup and pudding.

I was starting to become very restless. I took about 6 or 7 walks around the entire 7th floor. I took another one at 3am when it was storming, and a couple more Friday morning. With my new kidney, and with feeling significantly better, I have all this energy and can't just sit around in a hospital bed the whole time. Even at night, sleeping was restless. It probably didn't help that my roomie had her TV on 24/7, even throughout the whole night. I just wanted to get out and be able to get back to life and not just sit around. I've got important Krystin shit to do! =)

Finally, early Friday afternoon, I was discharged. I was feeling 100% better, and more than ready to be discharged and blow that Popsicle stand.

My roomie, whose name is Sarah, was just a kidney donor earlier this week. She donated to a friend, who was in a room nearby. I met her recipient, Connie, one day when she came to visit Sarah. I told Sarah at one [point] that what she did will forever make her Connie's hero, and that no words or gifts can ever express how truly thankful we, the recipients, are in our hearts. So Crystal, if I haven't already said thank you enough, I'll keep saying it over and over. THANK YOU!! You will forever be my hero. No lie.

So the good news is that it was nothing kidney related. The new kidney is still doing great, and functions are right where they should be. The reason they sent me home after transplant with the anti-rejection med that was making me nauseous and vomiting was because they hadn't been in my system long enough for the side effects to start showing. Also, I think the steroids I was on for those first 5 days after was masking any side effects. It was just making me ravenous!

Recovery is otherwise going very well. I have very little pain these days, and haven't had to take any Percocet in probably a week. I'm feeling energized and can't stand just sitting around. I still take a nap every afternoon, but I emailed my office and told them I'll be ready to start back on Monday July 1st. Not full-time, but 12:30-5 on M,T,TH,F, so I'll have Wednesday to recoup and rest. I'll still have lots of appointments, and I'll still need to go into the clinic to have labs drawn 3 days a week. But since the pain is essentially gone, I'm going to start back and see how it goes. I'm excited and ready to go back! I've said many times, I love my job. =)

Alright, that's all I got for now. I hope you are all well. Bye for now!

June 13, 2013 Facebook
Krystin Engstrand is feeling ecstatic.
3 weeks of recovery down, 3 weeks to go (for the average 6 week recovery period). Which means 3 weeks until Wild Onion time. This girl is finally going dancing again!!

July 2, 2013 Facebook
Crystal Lescault is feeling happy.
Official one month Kidney anniversary Krystin Engstrand!! Exhausted myself at work yesterday so today I get to pay for it...on the couch. Someday I'll learn not to push so hard. Someday. Haha. Hope that kidney is still treating you well :) Cheers to one month, hopeful there will be many more!

> Krystin: Yay! And it's still working perfectly! I was also banished to my couch for the rest of the week. Guess we gotta look at the silver lining- yay for afternoon nap time again!

July 3, 2013 Blog
Patience is not my virtue
Have no fear, I'm back with another post!

The past week has been very interesting. I went into the ER last Thursday, because all day long I had been dizzy again, so the point that it was hard just to sit up from a lying position. I thought I was dehydrated again, so I went to the hospital around 8pm. It only took 2 tries before they got the IV in (my record is 7), they drew some blood, and started saline fluids. The doctor came in almost an hour and a half later and told me that my blood work came back all good, and I'm not dehydrated. My electrolytes are good, and my hemoglobin level is good, so it's not anything I'm doing wrong. I'm getting enough fluids and salt, but for some reason my blood pressure is still running low all the time. They let me go, and I got home at almost midnight. I felt better the next day, but over the weekend the dizziness returned.

I went to work on Monday. My plan all along had been to return to work on July 1. I felt Monday morning that I was OK to go in. I worked from 12:30 to 5, and I actually made it all the way to 5! I even stayed busy all day, since there was quite a bit to help catch up on. When I got home a little after 5, I realized how utterly exhausted I was. I didn't get my afternoon nap, which I still have been taking. I had called my coordinator during the day because I thought maybe one of my medications was making me so dizzy. A couple of them do actually have a side effect of dizziness. She didn't think that was causing it, but she said she would talk to Dr. Ibrahim and get back to me. She did call me back, but it was after 5, when I was in my car driving home. I don't answer my phone while I'm driving, and with my music on, I didn't hear it anyway. She also called the house and left a message with my dad. Both she and Dr. Ibrahim agreed that I should not be back at work. They were actually very surprised to hear that I had started back already. They were concerned that I was going to get too dizzy and fall and hurt myself, so I was forbidden to work, and banished back to my couch. I was also started on a medication to help raise blood pressure. Turns out even though I'm getting enough water and salt (salt helps raise BP), it's all staying in my legs and not going to the rest of my body. How rude and selfish of my legs to hog it all! I'm not sure how that's happening, but that's what's happening. This new medication can take up to 2 months to take full effect, but I'm hoping that by next Monday I will already start to feel an effect and the dizziness has subsided enough that I can try returning to work again. Fingers crossed. I know I can't rush it, and I need to be patient, so I'm working really hard on listening to my body and taking it easy. But I'm getting so restless!

Here is my one-month anniversary photo:

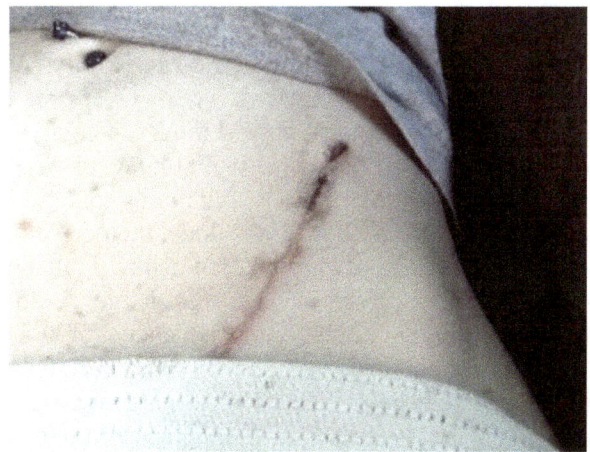

Everyone (in the medical field) keeps saying it looks good and is healing great, so I'll take it! A lot of the durabond glue has come off, there's still just a little left at the top, near the biggest scab. Oh yeah, at the top there it's still pretty scabby, but that's normal, and it will come off when it's ready. My fistula is also healing quite nicely. It's still red, but the scar lines are slowly fading. I still feel a little self-conscious about it when I'm out and about in a tank or dress, or anything with short sleeves. I have this idea in my head that people think I'm a "cutter," that I cut those into my skin. Which of course isn't true, but it's the kind of thing that goes through my head. I also know that the scars are in the wrong location for a cutter, but still.

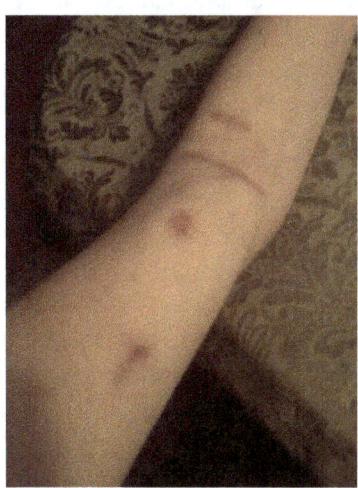

The home health care nurse only comes twice a week now; no longer 3 days a week. Next month, I'll go down to only one a week! Then a month after that, once every two weeks. Over time it will get less and less that I need to get labs done. I think I'm going to have the home care nurse come until I start work at 8:45 again. When I'm not working, or not starting until 12:30 or so, I'm not going to drive into the clinic at 8:30 just to have some labs done, then drive home until it's time to go BACK to the U for work. If I had to do that, there's no way I'd be able to fall back asleep once I got home. As long as this home care is an option, I'm going to take advantage of it. Then when I start work at 845 again, I can just stop in before work. The labs have to be done before 9am, because I take my morning meds at 9, and they need to draw blood before I take my meds, since they can alter the results.

Other than that, I'm feeling well. I'm still tired most of the time, and can't really run any errands without feeling fatigued halfway through, so most of the time if I'm out anywhere, I don't even finish whatever it was I went out for. Just another reminder to take it easy.

For those of you who are wondering (which is probably most of you who aren't able to keep up with her on facebook), Crystal is doing well! She has noticed a difference in how she feels, like something feels "off" with her body, but she knows that's just her body adjusting to only having one kidney now. She also started back at work on Monday, a half day, but like me, was out again by Tuesday because she was just too exhausted. A lot of people forget that recovery for the donor is just as hard, even harder, than it is for the recipient. Her body also has a lot of adjusting to do. She was still having quite a bit of pain, but recently got a new pain med, so it is better managed now. Don't worry, she doesn't have any regrets about donating; it's just going to take time for both of our bodies to heal and get back to a "normal" state.

On a completely different note - I bought a car last week!! My Saturn had gone into the auto shop early in the week, and turns out it needed about $1400 worth of work. It's a '98, and well on its way out anyway. My dad and I decided that for an old car that needed that much work, it wasn't worth the investment, because we don't even know how much longer it will last anyway. So my mom, who absolutely loves used car shopping, helped me find the perfect car fit for me. We found a 2002 Honda Civic EX coupe at the Honda dealership in Richfield/Bloomington. It's black, and it's perfect. I love

love love it, especially considering I bought it ALL on my own. My very first car purchase! I feel like such a big girl now. :) My mom and I are going to try to sell the Saturn on CraigsList or CarSoup.com. I'll advertise it for probably $1,000, as a car that needs work but is great for someone who wants to buy it and work on it. So it would be good for someone who works on cars, obviously.

My mom and brother are at the family reunion out east at Virginia Beach this week, but when they return, my mom is going to continue the apartment hunt with me. I had a move-out date of August 1, but by the time she gets back and we get looking again, it's going to be close to mid-July, and there may not be any availabilities starting August 1. I also need to keep in mind that I still need more recovery time than I expected, and still need some help around the house, so I may need to push my date back. I have a feeling that if I moved right now, I would never eat and never bathe, because it's being around my dad and Kathy that help me to get up and eat, since Kathy cooks dinner most nights, and give me the motivation to get up out of bed and take care of myself. If I lived alone right now, I'd just be a hermit and would slowly waste away. We don't want that! I am excited about looking at apartments, though, for when I AM ready to move. It WILL be some time this fall!

That's all I got. I hope everyone finds themselves well and in good health and spirit. Bye for now!

July 10, 2013 Blog
Some tidbits, some fun stuff

I was incredibly bored the other day, so I took a picture of my right arm and put black stars in all the places that I have marks and bruises from where I've gotten blood drawn or had IVs put in. Here is the result:

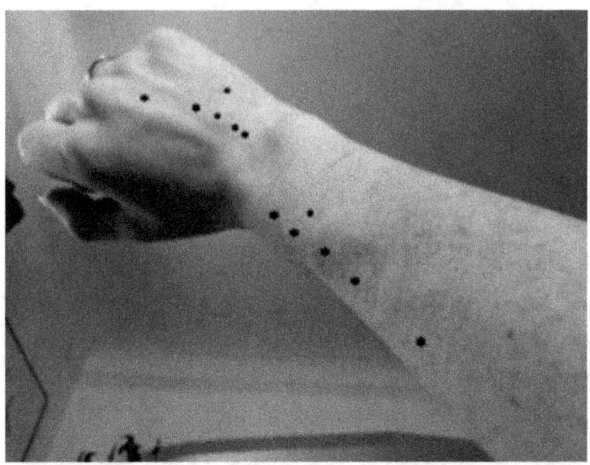

There are only 12 here, but when I counted again later, I actually counted 15. And that's just in the last few weeks! Some of them have been used more than once, too. We can't ever use my left arm, because of my fistula. I've never really understood why blood can't be drawn from there, or IVs put in there, but I have to believe the docs when they say it can't be done. So my poor right arm/hand is sore and bruised. It seriously looks like I've been abused. Pouty face. :(

I found out a couple interesting things this week. On Monday I went into the infusion clinic (known as SIPC, or specialty infusion and procedure center), for some blood tests. I had to be there at 7am. They took blood before I took my morning meds (which I took at 8), then they drew blood +2, +3, and +4 hours after taking them. This is so that they can see how my meds affect me over a 4 hour period, to see if any fine tuning needs to be done. So I was sitting in the clinic for 5 hours, but I had my book and iPad, so I was good to go. What they did was put an IV in my arm that they used to get blood at the designated times, so it wasn't like they kept poking me every hour or anything. I also got a liter of fluids, just for the hell of it. I don't think any of my meds will be adjusted, though. My nurse from that day called me later that afternoon and told me that all my labs look perfect, so for now, they'll stay the same. All transplant patients have to go through that half-day of testing. You can see why it's important, though.

I had an appointment with Dr. Ibrahim later that afternoon, but since he knew I was in clinic that morning, he stopped by to see me while I was already there, so I didn't have to go home then come back that afternoon just for an appointment with him. What a guy.

Anyway, I learned why I'm so dizzy all the time when I'm up. I'm getting enough fluids and salt, but it's all staying in my legs. Because of my diabetes and nerve damage, the nerves in my legs aren't able to properly pump all the fluids and salt up into my bloodstream. So basically my legs are hogging all the nutrients. A little rude of them, I think. So I got these special knee-high leggings that I have to wear at home. They're made out of a really thick material, and they're really tight, and are supposed to help increase circulation.

I also got put on a sodium medication, to help give me an extra sodium boost. I'm already supposed to be putting salt on almost everything I eat, since salt help raise blood pressure, but I really don't like salt that much! I like salty foods, like chips and pizza and popcorn and Asian food, but as far as giving things extra salt, I'm not really a fan. I'm ALSO on a blood pressure medication, to help raise my blood pressure. So between the stockings and the meds, we'll see if we can get my blood pressure up so that I'm not so dizzy all the time. Literally, if I go just from one room to the next, I can feel my body getting flushed with warmth and my head starts spinning and I need to sit down and take a break. Sure does make daily life difficult. Unfortunately, the blood pressure med can take up to 2 months to take full effect, but I'm hoping I start to notice a difference a lot sooner than that. I've already been on it a week, but don't feel any different yet. I am NOT the patient type.

I've also been told not to go back to work yet. I was going to start back Monday July 1, and I did go that day for 4 and a half hours, but was told after that not to, and on Monday morning Dr. Ibrahim said not to go this week, either. They are afraid that with my low blood pressure, I could fall and hurt myself. So my vacation has lasted 2 weeks longer than I had planned, but I know it's for the best. All I have to do is sit up from a lying position to know that I shouldn't be at work yet. I feel guilty not being there, because they have been short-staffed ever since I left, but I know I have to listen to my body (and the docs) and trust them, and be patient. Dr. Ibrahim has been doing this for many years; he knows what he's talking about.

Here are my scars, day 1 and 33.

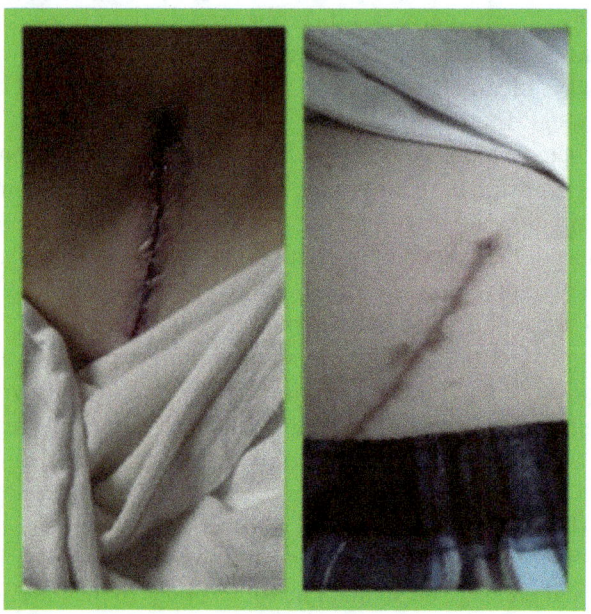

Alright, that's all I got. Gonna spend the rest of the week/weekend resting up and hoping this medication starts to kick in and I don't feel so lousy by next week. I'm ready to get back to work! By for now.

July 15, 2013 Facebook
Krystin Engstrand is feeling wonderful.
Returning to work round 3: success! AND it's the 6 week mark, so I'm so close to being fully healed! And I found out today I will soon be active on the pancreas waiting list. 'twas a great day!!

July 17, 2013 Facebook
Krystin Engstrand is feeling ecstatic.
Signing a lease for an apartment!! Come September 1, I'll be living in my very own studio apartment in Highland Park! Can't waittttt! [In St. Paul, just across the river from Kathy and me (and Pat), about 2 miles away.]

July 29, 2013 Blog
Where does the time go??

It has been a few weeks I think since I posted last. Nothing too exciting to report on, except . . .

I got my official letter telling me I'm active on the pancreas donor waiting list!! So that's pretty exciting. Since I'll be waiting for a deceased donor, who knows how long the wait will be. It could be anywhere from tomorrow to a year from now. My surgeon Dr. Kandaswamy thinks I'll have one by the end of the year, which would be pretty awesome. I'm not holding my breath, because I know pancreases are harder than kidneys to get, but if I DID get one before the end of the year, then New Years this year will definitely be extra special. Two new organs, a new car, and a new apartment all in one year. What a great 2013 it has been! I've only known life as a diabetic, and I can't believe that sometime within the next year, I will no longer have diabetes (or at least have to take very small amounts of insulin if I still need to. But fingers crossed that won't be the case). I know what it's like to have a working kidney, because up until about a year and a half ago, mine worked; but I don't know what it's like to have a working pancreas, and I can't even begin to imagine what it's going to be like. I know that I look forward to the freedom from blood pricks and insulin shots, wearing a pump and having to change it every few days. It will be amazing.

Even with the excitement of a new pancreas, I've started feeling frustrated again, like before transplant, but this is for a different reason. Kinda. It's been almost 8 weeks, and I'm still not feeling a more energetic life. I know that the diabetes causes healing to occur slower, but I thought by now I would feel at least SOME of the benefits of the new kidney. I've been having these blood pressure issues for a little over a month now. Almost every morning I wake up feeling dizzy and still tired. The dizziness and lightheadedness (is that a word?) cause a headache when I'm not lying down. Most of the time I get up, am able to walk to another room, but then need to lay down for a couple minutes to let the pounding in my head subside. It's frustrating, because it's keeping me from going out and living my life. My social life is still pretty non-existent because I don't have the energy or the high enough blood pressure level to do anything. I feel pretty lame spending my evenings and weekends lounging around at home almost 2 months after surgery. There are some good days when I don't feel dizzy, and I feel really happy, and I'm able to run errands and such, but those days are few and far between. I've been wearing those stockings that help get blood pumping through my legs, and I've been taking the medication to help raise blood pressure, but none of them seem to be making a difference. Dr. Ibrahim said this will pass, but I'm not patient enough to wait!

I fear that I made all these promises and said all these things I was going to do post-transplant and how I was going to be this new, amazing Krystin, but that they will end up being empty promises. Like I just said, I know this will pass, but I'm only thinking in the present, not in the future. I don't want to let myself down, or other people, by not living up to these new expectations that I set for myself. What if I can't do it? What if I'm the same lazy, unchanged person as before, but now with a functioning kidney? My hemoglobin level is great; it's over 12! Which means I should have energy back; unfortunately, the low blood pressure trumps that, and just makes me need to lay down all the time. I'm able to go to work, because I don't go in until the afternoon, so when I get up feeling dizzy, I have a few hours to drink lots of water and get some food in, so by the time I have to go to work I'm feeling mostly better.

On top of that, my diabetic gastroparesis is keeping me from being able to gain weight. I still can't get my weight over 110 pounds, and I want to get into the 120s. Everything I eat just goes right through me; I don't feel like I'm absorbing hardly any of it. Same with fluids; my body is so happy to have a new, working kidney, that it gets over excited, and gets rid of all fluids I drink, just because it can. It's like it's saying "HEY, we have a working kidney now, let's use it to its full extent and get rid of everything!!" Which I'm sitting here saying "NO, slow down, we need to keep some of those fluids!!" Eventually my body will realize that the kidney is here to stay, it's a permanent thing, and it will calm down. This is also what Dr. Ibrahim told me. But it means in the meantime, that's adding to my low blood pressure issues, because it's making me dehydrated and not able to retain most of the water I drink. Ugh, hurry up and figure this shit out, body!

Can you see why I'd be frustrated? I'm almost tempted to ask Dr. Ibrahim to temporarily up my antidepressant dosage, just to get me through this period until things get better. I'm not saying I'm feeling more depressed, I'm just saying the situation in general is depressing. That does NOT mean, in ANY way, that I'm not thankful and grateful to have the new kidney. I could never, ever be more thankful for anything in my life. I just wish it were a couple months from now and everything was all good and happy and working together. Come on body, you can do it!! It just needs a little encouragement. :)

OK, enough depressing news.

This week I'm trying to get to work by noon. Luckily I have enough donated vacation time that I can ease back into work slowly. Everyone here is still so nice and helpful, telling me if I need anything, or need help doing anything, to just let them know. I love my co-workers, and my job. :D

In other good news, I got an apartment! It's a studio apartment in the Highland Park area in St. Paul, so right across the Ford Bridge, by the old Ford plant. It's called the Yorkshire Grove Apartments, on Yorkshire Ave (obviously), which veers off of Cleveland Ave. I absolutely love Highland, and am so glad that I got a place there. I love the atmosphere of Highland, and there are so many shops and places to eat, and it's very friendly and safe. I move in September 1. I am renting a UHaul truck the morning of the 1st, will be loading up my room at my dad's (with the help of Elliott and one of his friends, whom I'm recruiting), then driving over to the apartment (less than 2 miles away), where my mom and Elliott will then help me unload. I only have the truck from 8 AM - 4 PM, so we'll have to work fast. But with a bunch of us doing it, we'll get it done in no time. I am BEYOND excited for this move. Aside from living in Korea, this is my first apartment. My mind is also more than anticipating the mood. It seems like everything everyone does at home irritates me or gets on my nerves. At 28, I need my own place. It hasn't been an option really before this, with first not having a job after graduation, then going to Korea, then not having a job when I got back, and then when I got a job, I started having my kidney failure, and the timing just hasn't been good. But now, finally, the time has come, and I will get my FREEDOM! (No offense dad and Kathy; it's been fun, but it's time for me to leave. I know they are ready for me to be gone, too. As much as they love me)

That's all I got. For those of you here in the Twin Cities, I hope you enjoyed the cooler weather this weekend. I personally liked it, even if it felt like we were back in April. Hope everyone is well. Today is a "I'm feeling good" day, so let's hope there are more of those on the way. Bye for now!

August 4, 2013 Blog
Not a happy post

This will not be a happy post, but I need to have my pity party, so please bear with me.

On Friday I got a call from Dr. Kandaswamy's (my surgeon) fellow, telling me that they had a pancreas offer for me. A local young man in his 20s was in an accident, and his pancreas was a pretty good match. I said I was definitely interested. I emailed my office to let them know that I would be out of work again for a while, and I posted all over Facebook that I was getting a pancreas. I was so excited I could hardly contain my excitement. My heart was beating so fast. I called my mom with the news, packed a backpack, and she had me at the hospital within an hour. I was admitted to my favorite unit, 7A. I was flying high, endorphins speeding through my whole body. Nothing could get me down. A new pancreas! Potentially no more diabetes; no more finger pricks, no more insulin pump, and total freedom from the illness I've struggled with almost my entire life. They started an IV, took some blood, and I settled in for the night. The plan was for a morning surgery, around 10 or so.

The fellow, whose name is Elliot, came to my room around 2 in the morning to introduce himself. I wasn't sleeping, I was wide awake with anticipation. He introduced himself and went over the procedure. The surgery would last about 5 and a half hours, with another hour or so beforehand getting me all prepped and ready. They would put a tube through my nose and down my throat once I was out, which they would use for a couple days afterward through which they would give me my meds until I switched to pills. He told me was on his way to another local hospital, where the donor had died, to have a look at the pancreas. He bid me farewell and said he'd see me in a few hours.

I didn't sleep all night. At 6am a nurse came in and told me that Elliot was on the phone at the nurse's desk and was momentarily going to be transferred to my room phone. I knew right then and there that that couldn't be a good thing. I answered the phone, and he told me that he had looked at the pancreas, and unfortunately it wasn't going to work out. I felt the first tear roll down my cheek. He said that it just didn't look good, it was too damaged and wouldn't be a good idea to put it in me. He said "we are trying to help you, not hurt you. We want to put a good pancreas in you." He continued talking, but I didn't hear much of what he was saying. I had already checked out of the conversation. He apologized, I told him understood, and he said hopefully he'll see me again soon. A nurse had been standing in the room for support, because she already knew his reason for calling. After I hung up, I dropped the phone by my side, covered my eyes with my hand, and started crying. The nurse came over, not saying anything, and just put her hand on my shoulder. She said she was so sorry, and repeated what Elliot had said on the phone, that another one will come along, and I don't want them giving me a bad pancreas.

I let myself get too excited. I have never felt such heartbreak in my life. I feel like my heart has been ripped from my chest. I felt a big, dark cloud descend over me Saturday morning, and it still hasn't gone away. Now I just feel depressed and hopeless, even though I know another, better pancreas will come along. Right now my brain can't comprehend that, and all I can see is the present, still a diabetic without a new pancreas, the disappointment and anger taking over. I've slept pretty much since I got home from the hospital Saturday morning. Right now nothing else matters, all I can do is live in my misery and sadness and tears. I knew that with a deceased donor there was the possibility that it wouldn't work out, but I convinced myself that it would. That I would be in recovery right now with a new pancreas getting to work and settling into my body. That I would be on my way to diabetic freedom and a life I've always dreamed of.

Even in my despair, I keep reminding myself that a family has lost their son, brother, grandchild. I have been thinking about that family a lot. I hope some of his other organs were good enough for donation to another person who is in need of a liver, kidney, etc. I have to be thankful that I still have my life, and thankful that people like that young man are donors, so that I have this opportunity to live a longer and better life. Same with Crystal, and other people who choose to be living donors.

I'm in a funk now, and don't know how I'm going to get myself out of it. I just need to be sad for a little bit. I'll be ok. I actually don't want people at work to be real sympathetic and sorry for me, because I know once they start expressing their condolences, it will just make me want to cry. This lost opportunity is all I can think about, and weighs heavily on my mind, but I'm trying to stay positive. Fingers crossed I get another call soon.

August 17, 2013 Facebook
Crystal Lescault is feeling happy with Krystin Engstrand.
Awww, I feel so loved today! Thank you Krystin DrDoolittle Engstrand!!!!! Perfect timing too, the last few days have been a little tough ;) Oh, and the cherry blossom body spray reminds me soooo much of Korea in the springtime! THANK YOU!

Krystin: It's the LEAST I can do! In the future I'm not even going to tell you, boxes will just appear at your door.

August 29, 2013 Blog
WBC deficiency

No news can be good news, but no news can also mean I just don't have any news. Well, I do have a little news, but it's not very exciting. I'll share it with you anyway.

Last week (it was Tuesday) I went to get my labs drawn, as usual. I got a very urgent call from my coordinator in the late morning hours, telling me I had NO white blood cells. Remember, the white blood cells are the ones that fight off illness, infections, etc. The normal range of white blood cells, in people, is, on average, 4-10 (or 4,000 - 10,000 white blood cells per microliter). Last week my count was at .5. Not good. That meant I was susceptible to anything and everything. If anyone even sniffled around me (and not from allergies), I could catch it ("it" being a bug, if that's what they had) and get sick. I had to go into the clinic THAT afternoon and get an injection that would help stimulate my bone marrow into making more white blood cells. It's a 3-shot procedure, so I had to go back in on Wednesday and Thursday to get another round of the shot. I forget the name of the stuff they were giving me. Then on Weds. and Thurs. they also drew blood to see if it was helping. My labs on Thursday showed that it wasn't helping at ALL, not even a tiny blip of a raise. On Friday I went in just to get my regular post-transplant labs done, which means all 3 doses of whatever they had given me were in my system. Still no raise in white blood cell count. Pat (my coordinator) called again and said I had to go in for an infusion (so, via IV) of a stronger medication. I decided to go in over my lunch hour to have it done, since it was only supposed to be a 30-minute procedure. I get there at 1, but they don't get the medication started until a little after 2!! That lasted 30 minutes for the drip, then 10 minutes to flush it, so by the time I got back to my office, it was slightly after 3. A 30-minute procedure that ended up taking over 2 hours. I should've known better than to think I would be in and out in less than an hour. HA!

The infusion that they gave me is a long-lasting anti-rejection med for my kidney. They stopped one of my oral anti-rejection meds, thinking that was having an effect on my WBC (white blood cell count, in case you couldn't figure that out), so the infusion I got would be a slow-releasing one, so I would have that in my system to cover for me not taking one of my oral meds. I think it was also supposed to help stimulate production of WBCs. I was instructed to stay away from crowds and busy places. No theaters, no game stadiums, no shopping malls . . . and no state fair, which was a real bummer, because I was supposed to go yesterday for the internet cat video festival. Bummer. I went in again on Monday for my regular labs, and, good news! My WBC count is up to 3.9. Still not quite within the average range, but pretty damn close. I go in for labs again tomorrow, so I'll find out if it's gone up even more. I was looking online at my other lab results from Monday, and I noticed that my Creatinine level was down. Creatinine is a phosphate in the muscles that is removed from the blood mainly by the kidneys via filtration. There is little or no reabsorption of Creatinine, so if the filtration in the kidneys deficient, Creatinine blood levels rise. That was not a very clear explanation, but basically the higher the creatinine levels, the higher kidney failure you have. The lower the creatinine level in your blood, the better your kidneys are working. So you want a really low creatinine level! The average range is 0.5 - 1.0. Before my transplant, my level was almost up to 4. After transplant, and just last week, my level was at .56! The best it has been since transplant. That means my new kidney is working fabulously!! However, my Monday labs showed my creatinine level was up at 0.76.

My Prograf level was down. Prograf is one of my immunosuppressant/ anti-rejection drugs. The average range for that should be between 5-15 for the first few months after transplant. My level on Monday was 6.7, which was in the range, but was down from over 10 last week. I emailed Dr. Ibrahim yesterday to ask if I should be worried about that, but he said no, everything looks really good. I guess as long as it's within the range, it's alright. It just worried me that it took such a dive. But, okey dokey then, I won't worry.

I have been feeling SO MUCH better lately! I feel like I'm finally getting back to "normal." I've been working my regular work hours the last 2 weeks, and I haven't had any drops in my blood pressure when I sit/stand up. So aside from my lack of WBCs lately, things are going very well. I'm starting to feel more energetic, but I need to work on getting my stamina up. So I get up and out and do things, but not for very long. I don't even take naps very often any more. I still sleep in on the weekends, but I figure that's just my body getting used to working full days again, and catching up on the extra sleep I'm not getting during the week anymore. At least that's how I'm going to justify it. :)

No more calls yet for a pancreas offer, but that's OK. I have a lot going on the next couple weeks, so if any offer were to come, if it could wait a little bit, that would be great. This weekend I move into my apartment! I am so, so, SO excited. Aside from my 13 months in Korea, this is the first time I'll be living on my own, in my own place. I don't really count living in a college dorm living on my own. This is an apartment, that I'M paying for, that is all my own to decorate and furnish as I please. It's only in Highland, so I'm not moving very far from either my mom or dad's house, but I don't mind. I've known for a long time that I've wanted to live in Highland, and now I will be!

With rent, bills, loans, gas, groceries, internet, etc. etc., I have to be VERY frugal with my monies, but I have already figured out about how much I owe, in total, to different things each month, so I have a pretty good idea of how much "extra" funds I'll left over for me. Not much, but maybe I can go to a movie once a month . . .

That's all I got. My life still isn't very exciting. I mostly read in the evenings. I'm reading a British series about a young woman in London who is a detective/investigator. There are I think 10 books in the series so far, and I'm on book 5. That's what I do with most of my free time: read! I'm stimulating my mind. :) Now that I'm starting to feel better, though, I hope to get out and be more active and catch up with some friends who I haven't seen in a while.

Hope everyone is well. Bye for now!

September 1, 2013 Facebook
Krystin Engstrand is at Highland Park, Saint Paul.
Moved to Highland Park, Saint Paul

My first apartment!

September 4, 2013 Email
so how things going?
Dad to Krystin:

Between the cat-sitting and getting your apartment organized, how things going? You going to be ready to move in and live there? Need anything from me?

Krystin to dad:

Things are going good! Jeff and Randy actually come back today, not tomorrow, like I thought. So I scrambled to get all my things together and in my car this morning. All my refrigerables (yes, I made that up) I brought into work in a Cub bag and am storing them in one of the fridges here, so I can bring that to my apartment tonight. Which means that tonight will be my first night in my apartment! Mom is coming over for dinner and to help me hang some more stuff. Exciting!

At this point, I don't think I need anything, but I'll let you know if I do. :)

Love you.

Chapter 11

Kitties and Hospital Visits

September 11, 2013 Facebook
This little lady was on stray hold when I called last week, but nobody has picked her up, so I'm going to meet her today! Fingers crossed that we bond, and that she comes home with me!! [A kitten at the local Animal Humane Society. Pat and Kathy and I did *not* believe this was a good idea, for medical reasons as well as because we didn't think she'd have the energy to take care of them.]

September 12, 2013 Facebook
Meet Gabi, my new 5 month old baby girl!

September 16, 2013 Facebook
Krystin Engstrand is feeling accomplished.
This year I have been fortunate to get a new kidney, a new car, a new apartment, and now two new kitties to greet me when I get home. And the year isn't even over yet! Life is good.

October 28, 2013 Blog
Adventure - Part 1

    Surprise! I'm back from the dead. I'm sorry to have left you all hanging for so long. I can't believe I let it go this long without posting. I may even have lost some readers who thought I gave up on this. My bad. But oh no, things are far from over. I realized recently that I need to get this down on paper (or, type it out on the intrawebs) before I start to forget, because I recently had a pretty significant stint in the hospital. So let's see what I still remember . . .

    The first week of October, I woke up one morning with a sore throat. It was dry, and a little hard to swallow. I figured it was from sleeping with my mouth open all night, which I've started doing more often. All that week it got sorer, and became harder and harder to swallow. Like, painful. Not just when I'd swallow, but even just to breathe it hurt. My nose was a little congested, so I again figured it was a cold. That Friday evening I went to urgent care and had my throat looked at. The doctor there said it looks red and swollen, and that I probably have a virus, in which case all there is to do is wait it out. Like a cold, there is no cure. He said take it easy, give my throat some TLC, and let it run its course. I spent my Saturday in the normal way (being lazy and doing nothing), but Sunday it really hit.

I didn't get out of bed all day. Literally. I woke up feeling dizzy and light-headed, and as the day went on it only got worse. And in the afternoon I started throwing up. If I even sat up in bed, I started seeing spots and I felt like I was going to pass out. I tried drinking water, but it wouldn't stay down. At 5:00 pm I finally decided this was not normal, and I needed help. I need to go to the hospital. I called my mom's cell and told her I needed help, but that I couldn't get out of bed. She had no way to get to me without being able to get into my building and into my apartment. But if I tried getting out of bed, I would blackout and fall on the floor. Try to get to my door to unlock it, and then get to the main door to let her in? Not gonna happen. Even talking made me throw up. Halfway through our conversation I had to tell her to hold on, so that I could lean over the side of my bed to the trash that I had dragged beside my bed (earlier in the day, when I was still able to get out of bed, if I crawled). She told me the only other option was to call the fire department and they would come and have to get into the building, and then break my door to get in it. I said fine, if that's what it takes. I just need to get to the ER ASAP. She said she would call 911 and meet the paramedics at my apartment. We hung up and I leaned back onto my pillows to wait.

About 5-10 minutes later, I got a call from the dispatcher. She told me the paramedics were almost there, and was there any way possible I could unlock my apartment door for them. I said nope, there's no getting out of this bed. She said I really, really needed to try, because otherwise they would have to break my door down. Oh dear. She said she would stay on the line with me, and I could take as long as I needed. I sighed a heavy sigh, said OK, and slid myself down onto the floor to shuffle, on my elbows and knees, to my door. Along the way, my cats are in my face and walking in between my arms and legs and getting in all kinds of the way. The little buggers. I finally made it to my door, reached up and unlocked it, scooted back so I was off the front entrance tile, and collapsed onto the carpet, telling the woman on the phone that I did it. She asked if I was OK hanging up with her now, since the paramedics had arrived, and I said yes. As I was laying there waiting, I could hear the paramedics in the hall. My mom thinks they ran the buzzer to the other apartments until someone let them in. I'm in apartment 102, and I could hear them across the hall knocking on the door to 101. "Fire department. Did you call 911?" I heard a faint woman's voice saying no, sorry. I'm laying there on my floor shouting "over here!" When they finally figure out that it's my apartment they want, they come right in to help.

I'm laying there in my front entrance wearing a U of M t-shirt and my silky, bright blue boxer from Australia, that have yellow crossing signs all over them, with different animals from all over Australia in the crossing signs. How embarrassing. We go through the whole "what's going on?" business, in the middle of which I start throwing up on my floor, because they've been making me talk too much. One of the paramedics quickly grabs a barf bag from her bag and hands it to me. Once we've got all that settled, they are ready to get me on my way. My mom has shown up by then, and is waiting outside. They tell her she should pull her car around and bring me to the ER. They said it will save money on an ambulance ride, etc. etc. She leaves to go pull her car around, and they start getting me up to get me outside. I tell them I can't walk, and they said that's fine, they'll support me. One guy lifts me up and is supporting me under both arms, but I still have to move my feet back and forth. We make it down the 10 stairs to the entryway, and the next thing I know I'm already laying on my side on the gurney outside. Turns out I passed out in the paramedic's arms. I told them not to put me upright! One of my neighbors, the guy Jim who lives above me, was standing in the doorway, watching. My mom thinks he's the one who came down and let them into the building. Now I was really regretting those boxers. I think I had remembered them wrapping me in a blanket before we left my apartment, though, so perhaps I had nothing to worry about. Mostly was worried because I didn't have any underwear on underneath my boxers. . . . Geez, next time I'll better prepare for my trip to the ER! After the passing out incident, the paramedics told my mom they were going to take me to the hospital instead. She was very relieved at that news.

They hoisted me up into the ambulance, but before we went anywhere (read: before the ride got bumpy), they wanted to get an IV inserted. One guy tried 2 times and couldn't get it, so a different guy tried, and he got it, so they started some IV fluids, and started off for the hospital. It had taken so many tries because I was SO dehydrated, so none of my veins were popping up for them. The fluids started making me so incredibly cold, I was shaking like crazy and couldn't stop. They brought me to the U, which, as you know, is my home away from home. I told them that's where I wanted to go. The nice thing about arriving in my limo is that there's no waiting at the door, I get VIP treatment and roll right into my VIP ER bay. They know how to treat me well. Again with the doctor we went through all the usual routine stuff, and he said he thinks I should be admitted overnight, just to make sure, as both a diabetic AND transplant patient, that nothing else is wrong. I'm there for a couple nights; I get out that Tuesday, 10/8, with a diagnosis of viral pharyngitis, which basically means swollen throat glands (tonsils?).

Think it's over? Think again.

I return to work that Wednesday, even though my throat still hurt, both to talk and swallow. The rest of the week, my voice gets worse and worse. By Friday I hardly have a voice at all, I have to force myself to swallow, since it hurt so bad, and because it was so swollen, I could hardly open my mouth to eat. I had gotten a chicken sandwich for lunch that Friday and had to smoosh it down so that it could fit in my mouth. When I got home that evening (we are now at Friday 10/11), almost like a light switch, suddenly my left ear starts aching my jaw hurts really bad. Around 9:00 pm I go back to urgent care. There's a different doctor working, and she does a mouth swab and has blood drawn for some labs. No strep, no mono, no laryngitis. She looks in my ear and tells me I have a mild ear infection. That explains the ear ache. She looks in my throat and says it's very inflamed, very red, and it's possible that I could have an abscess behind my tonsil. If so, it would need to be drained. That's not something an urgent care office can deal with, so she tells me to go to the ER. Sigh. I had only just been discharged a few days ago! But I knew it was the same issue. So I go home, pack up my hospital bag (because I KNEW I was going to be admitted - I always am). Here we go again. I've already texted my mom, and she's going to pick up my kitties and keep them at her house until I return home. She had done that the weekend before, as well.

When I get to the ER, there's NO ONE in the waiting room. No waiting at all! The triage nurse took me right back. WIN.

OK, I just realized that some of this I've been typing in past tense, as I should be, and some in present tense, which is incorrect, but I'm too lazy to go back and fix it, so you'll have to deal with it. Don't judge me. At least I've realized my mistake. :)

Anyway, this time they take things a little more serious. The doctor called in the ENT guy (ears, nose, throat), and he came and also looked at my throat, and stuck his finger in the back of my throat to feel around. Gag. He told me there was an abscess back there, behind my left tonsil, and that it would need to be drained, even though it was small. The docs didn't find this the previous weekend when I was in urgent care/the hospital because it hadn't formed yet, so aside from the redness and swelling, there was nothing for them to find. But during the week it broke the surface and grew, so now there was something for the ENT guy to work with.

Let me tell you about one of the most painful experiences of my life. Looking back at my life, I kid you not: this was almost the most pain I've ever been in, without being under anesthesia (aside from waking up after my kidney transplant with no pain meds running through my veins). Patients should NOT be awake for the draining of a throat abscess, let me tell you. First, the guy gave me numbing shots in the back of my throat. That meant sticking a needle into the back of my throat and giving 5-7 shots in a small area. That was painful. Worse than a bee sting. I was clenching my fists. Then he took a small scalpel to slice open the abscess. Cringing? Don't worry, I was so numbed up I didn't feel that. But then he uses a bronchus clamp (which looks like small scissors only the ends are not sharp, they are bent at a 90 degree angle to the stems) to spread open the small incision he made. Oh. My. God. The horror, the pain. That hurt like nothing I'd ever felt. I was shaking from head to toe, crying, and whimpering. My ER nurse was standing there the whole time with her hand on my hand and telling me how good I'm doing, just a little more, almost done, etc. When he's finally done, I take a big sigh and wipe my eyes. I told them I never want to go through something like that again. The ENT tech said he got some puss out, and a little bit of fluid, which he took a sample of and sent to the lab for analysis. The doc started me on an IV antibiotic for both the ear infection and to make sure the incision in my throat didn't get infected. She also gave me a dose of steroids to help heal the incision faster, AND some morphine for the pain. Suddenly I was feeling good and didn't really care what was going on.

I was admitted, of course, so that I could be monitored for a while, while on the IV antibiotics, to make sure that my ear infection and incision were healing properly. Especially, like I've mentioned before, since I'm a diabetic and transplant patient, they like to keep an extra cautious eye on me. Too many things could go wrong.

That's the end of part 1. I shall return soon with part 2, all about my inpatient stay. More good stories are to come, I promise. Bye for just a short while!

October 30, 2013 Blog
Adventure - Part 2

Where were we? Oh yes, my inpatient stay . . .

It must have been a busy night for admits, because I had to wait a while until they had a bed for me on one of the admit floor. Luckily I had my book and my bag of candy corn, so I was content to wait as long as I needed. I was brought to the 7th floor, but not to my favorite unit 7A. I was brought to 7C, which felt foreign, cold, not right. . . . The evening was uneventful, as I just kept munching on my candy corn and reading my book.

Saturday late morning I was brought over to 7A. I felt so much better being over, so much more at home. Perhaps it's because that's the transplant unit, so I knew they'd take good care of my kidney and me. It's gotten to the point that most of the nurses recognize me now. They'll either walk into the room and say "hey, I've had you as a patient before" or "hey, you're back!" Yup, I'm back. For the 5th, 6th, 7th time. . . . I've been joking that I need to order my own fitted hospital gown, with my name embroidered on it, cat print all over, and button up the front or side, so there's no flap in the back to worry about flying open and exposing my toosh. Is this even possible? I'm going to google it.

I spent the next 3 days reading my book, eating my candy corn, playing around on my iPad, and resting. I felt fine, and was bored out of my mind, but they had to keep me there. On Monday morning, the doctors decided they wanted to do a CT scan, to make sure that the antibiotics were working and nothing more was growing behind my tonsil. For a CT scan, you have to have not eaten for some number of hours. I wish they had decided to do this scan BEFORE I had eaten breakfast. That means I had to sit and wait until about 5pm before they finally brought me down for the scan. I hadn't been able to drink any fluids or eat lunch or any snack all days, so I was irritated, crabby, and hungry. I had also been told by the docs that if the CT scan showed an abscess still growing, they would have to cut and drain it again. I told them there was no way I was going to go through that again awake. They would either have to put me under, or punch me in the face and knock em out before doing it again. I kid you not, that's exactly what I told them. Dr. Kandaswamy, who was the one who I spoke with, said that it would be no problem to give me anesthesia. So why didn't the ENT guy who that the first time?? If Homeland Security wants a new scare tactic, that would be it. Pretend they're draining a tonsil abscess.

For the CT scan, they have to give me an IV contrast fluid, which enhances the structures or fluids in the body. It's so that on their screens, my bone structures and fluids (like blood) become more apparent, so they can better see anything abnormal. They did a scan of my neck, so that they could see if there was any abnormality, like an abscess, still behind my tonsil. The contrast makes you feel really warm, and gives you a sensation down below as if you're peeing your pants. It was a real quick test, only 5 minutes, then I was brought up to my room, where I immediately ordered dinner! Whew.

The test came back normal; nothing more was growing behind my tonsil, even though it was still swollen and sore. That meant I just had to let the antibiotics do its job. It was looking good that I would get to go home the next day. And, good news, I did! When the docs came on their rounds, they said everything looked good, and they felt comfortable sending me home on an oral antibiotic. A new food menu had come out the night before, and I wanted to try some of the new food on the menu, so I called my dad and told him he could come pick me up at 12:30, AFTER lunch. Why pass up a free lunch, anyway?? I did already have the whole menu pretty much memorized, and I've been there so much, new items on the menu is something to get excited about as a frequent patient. :) My dad picked me up, brought me to my apartment, I ran over to my mom's to pick up my kitties (she had been cat sitting them for me), then went home and took a long, uninterrupted nap. I returned to work the next day.

One of the times that Dr. Kandaswamy had come to talk to me, he told me that weekend before, when I was there in the hospital (read Part 1 blog entry), he was going to call me with a pancreas offer. But since I was in the hospital with a viral infection, he knew it wasn't a good time for an organ transplant (being sick and all), so he didn't call. DAMN!! I really wish he hadn't told me that. I wish I didn't know what I missed out on. It was hard enough being told the first time that a pancreas wasn't going to work out, and it was almost as disappointing the second time. BUT, it has been pointed out to me by numerous people that I have now had 2 potential offers within only a couple months. That means pancreases are coming in, and I'm at the top of the list. I have to keep reminding myself of this. The first weekend I was in the hospital, I was put on hold on the list for a month, so that everything could clear up and I can get fully healthy again, and then I'd be reactivated. I haven't lost my sport, just put on hold. I should be reactivated in just a couple more weeks. I'm really hoping for another (successful) offer before Christmas. That would make this the best New Year's ever!

Today is Crystal's and my birthday! Tomorrow I go in for my gastric pacer surgery. I have to be to the hospital at 7:30 for a 9:30 procedure, the surgery will take about 2 and a half hours, and I should expect to be in the hospital about 3 days. So at least I'll only miss tomorrow and Friday of work, since I then have the weekend to recover. Recovery can take up to 2 weeks, but that's for a full recovery, and does not mean that I can't go back to work. This is not considered a major surgery, I don't think, so I plan to go back to work on Monday. I have literally NO sick or vacation time left, so I'm racking up hours that I've been gone that I'll have to find a way to cover. Over time!

I think that's about it for me. The last few weeks have been hectic, but after this week's procedure, things should calm back down. Although, easier said than done, since these medical emergencies can't be predicted. So I should rather say, I PLAN on things settling back down. We'll see how that goes. :)

Bye for now!

November 7, 2013 Facebook
The last couple days have been very painful. This morning I went to the clinic almost in tears from the pain. They're changing my pain med from Percocet to Dilaudid. Yaaay, now we're talking. I'm getting the good stuff!

November 14, 2013 Facebook
Sitting in this hospital bed in so much pain really makes me look at my life and wonder what I did to deserve this. This isn't a pity party, I'm just bitching out loud here. Thank you and goodbye.

November 16, 2013 Facebook
All this has inspired me to become a nurse. Yes, become a nurse and take the night shifts so I can stand in patients' rooms and excessively push buttons on their IV pumps while they try to sleep.

November 16, 2013 Facebook
After already being here 5 days, they finally compiled a list of everything that's wrong with me:
- Mono
- Cytomegalovirus
- Esophagitis
- Slight pneumonia
- Another virus I don't remember

Probably at LEAST 3 more days here on a shit ton of meds and lots of monitoring. I still have no voice, but today am finally able to eat mushy foods, the first time I've really eaten since LAST weekend. But hey we're having fun right??

> Krystin: I figure that the last year has been my body's getting back at me for all the things I did to it over the last 25 or so years. So, I probably deserve it.

November 18, 2013 Facebook
This setback will keep me on hold on the pancreas donor wait list for 3 more months. Doc said to call him mid-February to reactivate. I told him I'm calling him on Valentine's Day then. I don't need no man, I need me a pancreas!!

November 18, 2013 Facebook
Shit, I got a real reality check today in my conference with my medical team. They told me I am very lucky for my youth and for calling an ambulance when I did, because if an older person had come into the hospital with 4 bad infections and being as sick as I was, they most likely wouldn't have survived.

November 20, 2013 Blog
Gastric Pacemaker
    This is old news, since I just spent 8 days in the hospital, but I'll get to that later. Right now I need to catch up, so let's go back a little.
. . .
    Two and a half weeks ago I had my gastric pacemaker surgery. The surgery was scheduled for 9:30, so I had to be at the hospital at 7:30. It was on Thursday, Halloween. I was upset that I was going to miss the Halloween party at work; people could wear their costumes, and there would be a pizza lunch at lunch time. The surgery was

originally scheduled for 12:30, which meant I was going to go in for a little bit in the morning, and then head over to the hospital late morning. Then it was changed to 7:30 (I would have had to be there at 5:30!!), then finally to 9:30. Since I was going to miss the Halloween festivities to work, I wore my costume to the hospital! I wore my full-body yellow tiger outfit. I took a picture of me sitting in the waiting room of the surgery floor.

It's kinda blurry because it's a cell phone photo, but you get the idea. I got lots of stares, but I didn't care, because I needed SOME of my Halloween! Even if I only got to wear it for an hour. It made me feel better. I did get some compliments, too, and a little girl got really excited when she saw me. So it was worth it. :)

In my pre-op bay, I went through all the usual stuff. Checking in, seeing all the people who would be in with me during surgery, changing into my enormous purple surgery gown, getting my IV put in, yada yada yada. I've probably explained this many times already, so I'll spare you the details. As I was being pushed into the surgery room, they gave me some sedative, which made me calm and happy and carefree. I remember laying on the surgery table staring up at the ceiling and all the bright lights, and next thing, I'm waking up in recovery. Isn't that how it always goes?

They took very good care of me in recovery. This time they remembered to give me plenty of painkillers before I woke up, so when I woke up, I was comfortable and not in pain. I was there for probably an hour, dozing in and out. When they decided I was awake and steady enough to be brought to the recovery floor, they unhooked me from my IV and rolled me away. The pain killers wore off instantly. By the time I was wheeled into my room on the recovery floor, I was in such pain. Worse than when I had my abscess behind my tonsil drained (although cutting an abscess and having incisions in your abdomen is a very different kind of pain). I was hyperventilating, sobbing, and shaking all over. The shaking and hard breathing only made it hurt more. Of course the order for more painkillers wasn't in the system yet, so there was nothing my nurse could do about it. I thought I was going to pass out from the pain. I even started holding my breath, since breathing was what was making it hurt even more, like a sharp, stabbing, burning pain in my abdomen. I imagine that if you were actually stabbed in the stomach with a knife, this is what it would feel like. I eventually figured out that if I slowed my breathing, and took long, slow, deep breaths, it didn't hurt as much. At least I would be able to handle it until I finally got some pain killers flowing through my IV.

My mom arrived shortly after. I didn't talk to her much, I just focused on my breathing. FINALLY my nurse came in with pain killers and quickly administered it to me through my IV. I felt much better, although naturally, like right after any surgery, there was still some pain. But it was dulled a lot now. Since that first day is pretty hazy, coming out of the anesthesia and all, I don't remember if I spent the night in that room, or if I was brought up to unit 7A that evening. It was either that evening or the next morning. I'm pretty sure it was that evening. Oh yeah, and here is what my incisions look like:

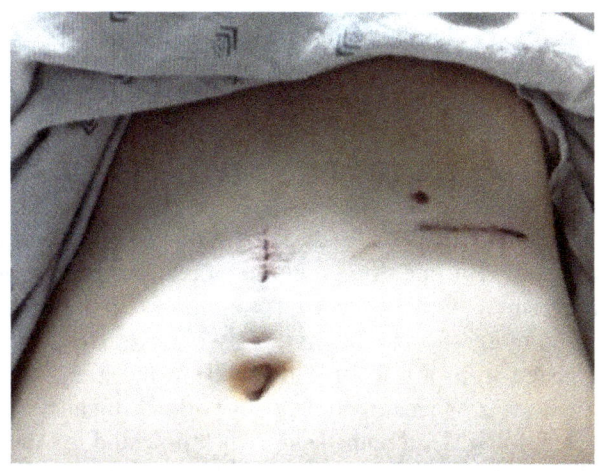

The vertical one above my belly button is where he made an incision to blow air into my stomach. There's another smaller incision up and to the left of that one, but it must be hidden by the shadow of my gown. Those two incisions were made so that Dr. Kandaswamy could blow air into my stomach, which would inflate it and give him more working room. The bigger, horizontal incision you see is where my stomach and the pacemaker are. I guess the pacemaker looks like a squid. That incision is so swollen that it looks and feels like there's a half-baseball on my abdomen. It's cool and creepy at the same time.

Since this was an abdomen surgery, getting in and out of bed, walking, and just moving around at all was painful. I took my pain killer whenever it was time again to take it, and although it helped, the pain was always there. After a couple days I started walking around the 7th floor a few times a day (7th floor houses units 7A, B, C, and D). 7A, as you've probably figured out by now, is the solid organ transplant unit, which is why I always end up there. I was SO itchy, I don't know what from, that after the first day I actually stopped wearing the gown and put on my leggings and t-shirt. A couple nurses pointed out that it could be from the gown and sheets, which are so starched and dry, that that could be what was making me so itchy. They also gave me Ativan through my IV, to help stop the itching. I was also constantly putting on baby lotion that they give you. It was a temporary relief, all of that, but I just kept getting itchy again. Must be a hospital thing!

Normally a patient would be in the hospital about 2-3 days after this kind of surgery. I was there 5. Of course. One issue was that we couldn't find good pain management. I was still in a lot of pain even with the IV pain killers. After the 2nd day the nurses actually stopped the IV pain killers and switched to oral, because a patient can't go home until off IV pain killers for 24 hours.

Even a week after surgery, I was in so much pain that I had to go back to the clinic. I had been taking the Percocet, but it wasn't helping at all. Not even to take the edge off. I got in to work a little after 8, and left a little before 9. I had done nothing since getting to work except sit and stare at my computer screen, trying not to think about the pain and having no motivation to do anything work-related. On top of that I was exhausted from a horrible night's sleep the night before, so I could hardly keep my eyes open. My co-worker Anjeanette told me I should go, but do NOT go home - go to the clinic and tell them what's going on. I knew that was a good idea, and I knew that if I went home first, I would not leave again to go to the clinic. The result of the visit is that I got a new prescription for a different pain killer. I was switched from Percocet to Dilaudid, which is a strong painkiller. My coordinator had to get the prescription hand-signed by the doctor, and then she personally walked over to the pharmacy and handed it to them. A prescription for a narcotic drug like that cannot be faxed. They also gave me a Tylenol with caffeine in it, I took a little rest in the clinic, and when I woke up I was already feeling much better. I returned to work about 10:45, and around 2 went and picked up my Dilaudid. It helped MUCH better, and I only had to take it for a few more days before the pain finally subsided.

I still have a small lump on my side where the pacer is. I'm not sure if that's still just swelling, or if it'll be like that forever. It's almost like half a baseball stuck on my side; I can almost grab it! When I lay on my side, I feel the pressure of it. It's not painful, just kinda annoying, like I'm laying on something. Which, I suppose, I am.

Even though I've had it for 3 weeks now, it's been hard to tell how well it's working since I've been having other health issues in the meantime. But that's another story. . . . Bye for now!

November 20, 2013 Facebook
Krystin Engstrand is feeling fresh and clean.
After 8 days in the hospital, the long, hot shower I just took is the best I've felt in a long time!

November 27, 2013 Facebook
All I want for Christmas this year is my ambulance bills paid. $1652, I pay 20% of that = $330 x 2 separate ambulance rides (so 2 bills) = $660 out of my pocket. Yikessssss. I think I'll be paying that off for the next year and a half.

November 27, 2013 Blog
Infections galore

As most of you already know, a week ago yesterday (Tuesday) I was discharged from the hospital, AGAIN, after an 8 day stay.

It all started the morning of Monday, 11/11. I wasn't feeling well Sunday night when I went to bed, which was about 7:30. I thought it was just blood pressure issues again and that it would be fine in the morning, and as long as I remembered to drink water throughout the night. I drank a big glass of water and went to bed. That's when I started throwing up. The water I drank didn't stay down. This lasted all night. Every time I threw up, my mouth and throat would be so dry and I would be so thirsty, I would drink more water, even though I knew it wasn't going to stay down. By 7:30 Monday morning, I knew something wasn't right and that I needed to go to the hospital. I was already feeling like death. I texted my mom and told her I needed to go to the hospital. When I didn't hear back from her within 10 or so minutes, I called 911 and said I needed an ambulance. Even talking made me throw up, so a couple times I had to take a break from talking to the dispatcher to lean over my bed into the garbage can. She dispatched an ambulance to come get me. I was able to unlock my front door and meet the paramedics at the front of my building, although I had to sit down on the front step for a minute because I was so dizzy and out of breath. At least this time I had sweatpants and a sweatshirt on, and not silky blue boxers with Australian animal crossing signs on them.

At the hospital they did a blood sugar, and my reading was over what their advanced test machines could read, which means it was over 800. All it read on the machine was 'HI.' We checked my insulin pump site and discovered that the little canula (the small, short tube that goes under my skin) had actually come out, and I didn't even realize it, so all the insulin I had been giving myself the night before never got to me. That would explain part of the problem. They hooked me up to an insulin IV drip, as well as saline fluids, since I was so dehydrated. I was admitted pretty quickly, starting out on the 6th floor, but only for the day - by the evening I was moved up to 7A, my home away from home.

I hadn't been able to call into work that morning to let them know I wasn't going to make it in. I THOUGHT about work, but it wasn't my first priority to contact someone. I figured I could explain later. My co-worker Anjeanette became worried when I didn't show up, with no call and no email. She decided to email my dad to see if he knew where I was. He and Kathy had just gotten off a plane from Georgia, so he had no idea, but said he would find out. My mom had been in a meeting that morning, so she didn't see my text message until later in the morning. My dad and Elliott even went over to my apartment to see if I was there, since they have a 2nd set of keys. Finally, between all of them, they figured out I was at the hospital. I don't know if it's because they called, or if I finally texted them. But they knew where I was, and knew I was safe. I know everyone was really worried and feared the worst for a minute there. That evening my mom went over to my apartment and got my kitties, and once again kept them at her house while I was detained.

For the first 2 days I didn't drink anything (I couldn't keep even water down), for the first 4 days I didn't eat anything (hurt too much to swallow, and had no appetite), and for 7 days I had no voice. It took about 3 days to figure this all out, but when all the blood work was done, when all the samples were taken, when all the Xrays and MRIs were looked over, and all the exams completed, here is what they concluded that I all had. Don't worry, I'll explain them in a minute:

EBV (Epstein-Barr virus)
CMV (Cytomegalovirus)
Esophagitis (inflamed esophagus)
Mild pneumonia
Hyperglycemia (high blood sugar)

EBV, or Epstein-Barr virus, caused me to get mono, as it does. It's not true that you can only get mono from kissing - you can also get it from contact with the airborne virus, OR if it's transferred to you through blood during an organ transplant. Crystal never had mono, because she has the antibody for it in her blood. We all have the potential to get mono, but most people develop an immunity (an antibody) to it in their younger years (teens). So if exposed to it, their body can fight it off. The virus was in Crystal's blood, but because she has antibodies to it, she won't get it. I never developed that antibody, so when the virus was exposed to me, I had no antibodies to fight it off. Yes, it's been almost 6 months since transplant, but my immune system had been able to keep it at bay up until this point. Does this make sense? It's confusing, and I'm not sure I completely understand, but this is the best I can do as far as an explanation. Basically all you need to know is one of the viruses I got was mono. Due to that, I had a sore throat, night fevers for a couple nights, and swollen lymph glands. Mono can take a LONG time to fully recover from, and unfortunately the EBV virus remains dormant in my blood for the rest of my life. There is no treatment for it; I just have to let it run its course. It makes me tired, makes my bones ache, and my body gets exhausted quickly. But each day I feel an improvement!

CMV, or Cytomegalovirus, is part of the herpes family, so it's frequently associated with the salivary glands. In healthy people, CMV can go unnoticed, but it can be life threatening for the immunosuppressed, like me. From the first lab draws they did when I arrived, the doc told me that I came in with almost nothing as far as an immune system, which is why all these viruses just jumped right in and took hold. Not only were my immunosuppressants for my kidney lowering my immune system, but so do high blood sugars. Anyway, CMV stays in the body for a long time, just like mono.

While I was in the hospital, they put in a picc line (peripherally inserted central catheter), which is like an IV, but is more long-term. It's inserted into a peripheral vein in the arm, and advanced through increasingly larger veins, towards the heart, until the tip rests in a large vein near my heart. Here is what it looks like once inserted:

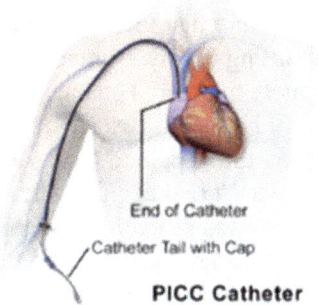

I have a double, which means I have two catheter tails on mine. A radiologist came to put it in, and he used an ultrasound machine to find the vein. He also numbed the area, so when he put the catheter in, I didn't even feel it. Nor did I feel the catheter and he wound it up through my vein. Only the little pinch from the numbing shot, and that's it. Easy peasy. They wanted a double for me because they were giving me insulin, saline fluids, and an antibiotic, and they aren't all necessarily compatible with each other, so they needed to be in separate lines. Plus, if I only had one, they could only do one at a time. Also, blood can be drawn from it, so they didn't have to keep poking me every time they wanted labs drawn. I admit, that part is convenient.

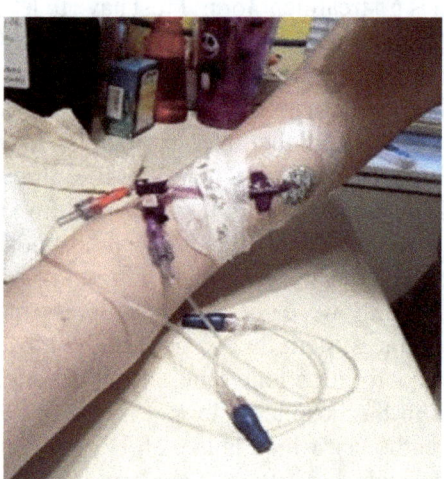

SO, back to the CMV. Through my picc line they started giving me an antibiotic called Ganciclovir. It's pretty much the best, and only treatment for CMV. They didn't want to give me an oral medication because I was having such a hard time swallowing anything, and because they wanted to be sure that the antibiotic was going right into my system, instead of sitting in my stomach and maybe/maybe not getting absorbed in a timely manner. The bag of antibiotic ran over an hour, and I got it every 12 hours (so twice a day, for those of you bad at math). For some reason they decided 5 was a good hour, which is fine when it's 5pm, but I wasn't real excited when they came in at 5am to hook me up. Just like I wasn't excited when they came in every HOUR to check my blood sugar, for the first 5 days. Finally over the weekend they let me put my own pump back on, so then we only tested before meals, and once in the night. When I'm on their insulin drip, they have to test me every hour to see if they need to adjust it. Ugh, how annoying.

The esophagitis is pretty self-explanatory. It's basically just an inflamed esophagus. Forms of infectious esophagitis are typically seen in immunosuppressed people (surprise, surprise), and include, that's right, CMV! I had to have an endoscopy done, and they did find some fungal growth down in my esophagus. That is being treated with oral medication. So I got the esophagitis from the CMV, but my throat was also inflamed and hurting because of all my throwing up throughout the night on Sunday and into Monday. The upside is that I got my own room at the hospital (good 'ole unit 7A), because at first they thought I might be contagious, and because I was coughing too much, it would have been really inconsiderate to put me with a roommate. I was even seen by a physician from the Infectious Diseases clinic while I was there.

One night the docs ordered for me a nebulizer, which is like an inhaler:

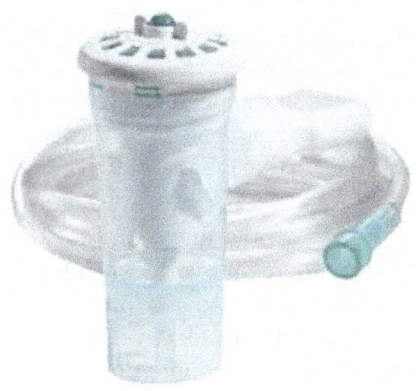

I didn't have the long tube and face mask, mine had a little tube coming out of it that I put in my mouth to inhale, but this is what it looked like. The medicine they ordered for it was Albuterol, which is mainly used for people with asthma, but they wanted me to use it to help open up my lungs so that my breathing wasn't so ecstatic. I did NOT like it at all, no no no. It made me shake like a Tickle-me-Elmo. For almost 5 straight hours, and my heart rate was in the high 130s. Finally my nurse gave me an Ativan (which is usually used to treat anxiety disorders). It helped stop the shaking, and eventually my heart rate returned to normal. But during that time, I felt like my heart was going to burst right out of my chest. I just laid there in bed staring at my ceiling, not able to do anything else. It was horrible. I never want to take that stuff again!

I rested most of the time during that whole week. By the weekend, I was finally starting to feel an improvement and was staying awake all day. During one of my mom's visits, she brought me a bunch of movies, so Sunday-Tuesday I watched probably 2 movies a day. Late in the week I also started ordering food off the menu, but only soft, mushy food that I could gum and that would be easy to swallow. Oatmeal, applesauce, soup, winter squash (whipped). I wasn't eating very much, and because my esophagus was still inflamed and swollen, it hurt in my chest to swallow. It felt like the food was getting stuck halfway down my throat. Kinda like heartburn, but in the throat. I would eat a few bites then have to take a break for 5 minutes while the pain went away. Eating was slow going, but at least I was getting some calories in. By Sunday or so I was ordering regular food, and was even getting my appetite back. I was still on the mechanical diet (like for people had jaw surgery, for example), so they were still mashing my food or cutting it up into little pieces for me. I ordered the meatloaf, and when it came it looked like canned soft cat food. But it went down fine. Almost every meal, except breakfast, I ordered the meatloaf and bread dressing (same as stuffing), both with gravy. I actually liked it; for being hospital food, it's not that bad. And it gave me calories and protein. It's the only thing on the menu that looked good to me, for some reason. They also ordered me a Boost shake with each meal, so I was getting extra calories and nutrients there.

I was finally discharged on Tuesday, 11/19. I was still pretty weak, but I had been going for walks a couple times a day around the unit, so I knew I would be able to get around my apartment. My labs all looked good, *I* was looking and feeling better, and they were sending me home with my picc line and an antibiotic to give myself twice a day, so there really was no other reason to keep me. Tuesday morning I went to a little class where I learned how to take care of my picc line at home and how to administer my antibiotic (they were sending me home with Ganciclovir, which they had been giving me all along already). It's a lot of busy steps, keeping it all clean and sterile and flushing it and whatnot, but it's easy. When it's not in use, I wrap the extensions around my arm and use an arm bandage to hold it in place. Even under a cardigan, it's hardly noticeable, only a little bulge.

My cats like trying to play with the extensions when they're hanging down, but I'm really good at keeping them away.

The day I was discharged, my mom picked me up and brought me to her house, where my car was. I drove my car to my apartment, and she followed a few hours later with my kitties and some containers of homemade soup that she made me so that I'd have some food until I was able to get to the store. The next evening I went to my dad's for dinner and picked up some groceries that they had gotten for me on their way home that day, so I had a fridge full of staple foods to last me through the week.

I didn't go back to work that week. I took Weds.-Fri. off. However, one of my work duties I can do from home, so I did spend time each day working. On Friday I even worked on and off for 6 hours! I figured if I'm going to be just sitting at home, I might as well be productive. Plus, that's fewer hours I'd have to use sick/vacation time on. I was still too weak and tired to actually go into the office, but I was fine sitting at my computer, knowing I could go lie down whenever I wanted. I know my supervisor was really happy that I was helping out from home. I already felt guilty leaving them one man down for 2 weeks, so it's the least I could do. Before I left the hospital they set up home health care, so during the week a nurse came to my apartment to draw my labs and make sure my picc line was doing good. I love them coming to me, and me not having to drive into the clinic!

I started back at work this week. It has gone really well. I made the whole 8 hour day on Monday, yesterday I had to leave at 3:30 because I was feeling really tired and fatigued, and today I feel really good again. The home health care nurse came to my work on Monday and drew my labs and changed the dressing on my picc line. Talk about service! There's still a lot of recovery left, but at least I'm feeling better and seeing an improvement with each day. I even get my picc line removed today! Which means I'll be switching to an oral med twice a day instead of Ganciclovir via my picc line twice a day. I'm so happy to be rid of the picc line, especially right before Thanksgiving. I'm very thankful that I'm feeling well enough to go to dinner tomorrow night, too. I was worried last week that I'd be too tired still, but that is not the case. My appetite has also returned 100%, so I'm back to eating my normal diet, and can fully enjoy all the delicious food tomorrow! That's the best part of all.

Well, I think that about concludes this episode. I hope everyone has a great Thanksgiving and enjoy your time with family. It may be awhile until my next post, unless something unexpected happens again, which, with my luck, is always possible, but we'll keep our fingers crossed and stay positive that all will continue on the up and up. Bye for now!

November 28, 2013 Facebook
Today I am so thankful for pretty much everything and everyone in my life. Despite the little setbacks, I am so lucky to be where I am in life. Cherish this day with your family. Happy Thanksgiving!!

December 9, 2013 Facebook
Just a routine check-up, and I come out needing a gallbladder ultrasound and potentially gallbladder removal surgery. Oh, ok then. O.o

December 9, 2013 Facebook
Dr. Ibrahim: Did your previous labs still show traces of CMV or EBV? Me: No, but now I have abc, nbc, bbc, mtv, kmsp. . . . 1 more point in the bank for Krystin's humor. Sometimes I amaze myself with how witty I am.

December 13, 2013 Blog
Revelations

I had a very enlightening session with my therapist last night, and I really want to share it with you, because I had so many realizations, and we came up with so many things we want to work on in the future. I said from the beginning of this that I was going to be open and honest with you, and I'm keeping my promise. You may wonder why I'm sharing information from a therapist session, thinking that's supposed to be confidential and just between my therapist and me, but it helped me, and I hope it helps you, realize how so many things in my past has led to where I am today, as far as my health. I'm not even sure where to start, so bear with me if this become scattered. Let's start back in elementary school . . .

6th grade was a really bad year for me. Then, I was still in elementary school, because my elementary school went up to 6th grade. Kindergarten - 5th grade were great, as far as I can remember. I had lots of friends, I was an extrovert, a social butterfly, unlimited self esteem and total confidence in myself and everything I did. Then in 6th grade everything changed. I became your classic example of a victim of bullying. It's hard to imagine that in 6th grade there would be such a thing as the cool and popular kids, but there were. They teased me, made fun of me, made jokes at my expense. I was a very late bloomer in life, so even in 6th grade I still didn't brush my hair, I had dorky glasses, I wore the same clothes for probably 3 or so days in a row. It was really easy to target in on me as the one to bully. During that year, the person I was disappeared, and I became more of an introvert, withdrawn, self conscious, and no self esteem or confidence anything. I was afraid that anything I said or did I would be judged for or made fun of for. Since a handful of my 6th grade classmates ended up going to the same middle school, that teasing and bullying followed me. 7th and 8th grade were the worst years of my life. Suddenly new classmates who hadn't even gone to elementary school with me were teasing me. I did anything and everything to avoid attention being drawn to me.

In high school everything changed again. At this point in my life my endocrinologist told my parents that they had to back off and let me take the reins with my diabetes. They had been controlling it and helping me with it ever since I had been diagnosed at age 4, but now as a teenager, my doctor said I was old enough to take care of it myself. Suddenly I found myself with all this new freedom that I had never had or experienced before when it came to my diabetes. Although the bullying had stopped (on a side note, I actually really enjoyed high school), it had already done its permanent damage. I stopped going to the nurse before lunch to do my blood test and insulin. I had gotten an insulin pump at one point, but I hated it, and despised it, because it would always beep in class, or depending what I was wearing, I couldn't hide it well enough. It drew that negative attention that I worked so hard to avoid. So when I would get to school, I would just take it off and put it in my locker for the day. If no one saw it or hear it, if I didn't have to leave class early to go to the nurse's office, then no one would know I was "different." I would be normal just like everyone else.

4 years of high school. 4 years is a long time; plenty long enough for a habit to development that became impossible to break. Even when I went off to college, the habit continued. No blood tests, no insulin shots. In college, nobody cares if you have diabetes. All my friends knew, and they didn't like me any less. I didn't get teased for it, they didn't look at me all disgusted like I had some contagious virus. Unlike in middle school and even a lot of people in high school, by

college MOST people know what diabetes is and understand the basics of it. Nobody cared that I had diabetes. But after 4 years of ignoring it and living like I didn't have the illness, it had become a lifestyle. One that I didn't even try to break, because it wasn't even at the front of my mind as something that I NEEDED to break. I always told myself "it won't happen to me," as far as diabetic complications. Or "I'm still young, I have plenty of time to turn it around." Or even "If anything happens to me, medics can save me." Yes, that last part has been true so far, but there have been too many times where I have come within an inch of them not being able to save me. At least half a dozen times. So, our big revelation last night in my session was that even though I'm an adult now, young Krystin is still in control of my diabetes.

My therapist (Nancy) and I concluded that in future sessions we need to work on getting in touch with 6th grade Krystin, and convince her that the dangers of the past are gone, the danger is over. The reason I'm so compliant with my transplant medications is because I had the transplant as an adult, so the more responsible, older Krystin is taking care of the transplant, while the defiant high school Krystin is still taking care of (or not taking care of) my diabetes. Which is why Nancy and I need to get in touch with the younger Krystins and get them to let go and let the NOW Krystin take over. Does that make sense? I know to some of you it may sound like a bunch of hocus pocus stuff, but it's not like Nancy and I are going to be doing weird hypnotic treatments or anything. It'll just be talking through it and working things out. One thing she wanted me to try to do before our next session is to try and get in touch with 6th grade Krystin. Try to imagine that 6th grade Krystin and today Krystin are face-to face. What would she say to me? What would I say to her? It's going to be an interesting experiment, especially since I've never tried something like that before. But I know I NEED to stop younger Krystin from staying in control of my diabetes care, or everything I've gone through in the last year will have been a waste.

This is going to take a while, but it's something I'm willing to work on. Something I WANT to work on. Something I NEED to work on.

On a different note, I had an ultrasound of my abdomen this morning. For about the past month, whenever I eat a meal, within half an hour or so I get an almost excruciating pain on my right side, right under where my ribs end. It feels like someone is inside whatever organ is there, with a knife, and has stabbed me. It's not a throbbing pain, but a constant pain. Sometimes paralyzing, so that I can't even move without feeling like I'm going to die. When it happens, I just go lie down and don't move and wait for it to pass. It can last up to an hour or more. On Monday I asked my surgeon what is there, and he said the gallbladder. He ordered an ultrasound, to see if there are gall stones in it. If that comes up negative, I'll have another test done to see if I have gallbladder disease. Either way, if there's something wrong with it, it will need to be removed. This morning during the ultrasound, the tech had me take a deep breath and pushed in with her little ultrasound device, to get a deeper, better picture. One of the places she put pressure on I felt a slight pain. I said "there, where you're pushing, what's there?" She said it's the liver! So it could be either the gall bladder OR the liver. If there's something wrong with my liver, well, you know, that can't just be removed, that would need a transplant. *Sigh* I will call my coordinator on Monday morning to find out the preliminary results, and then I have an appointment Monday afternoon with Dr. Kandaswamy (my surgeon), to go over results and decide what the next step is.

So, what it basically comes down to, no matter how many degrees of separation there are, is that my body is failing me at 28/29 years old because I was bullied in 6-8 grade. Isn't life fun? :-/

I will post again on Monday or Tuesday with what I find out. It will be a short post, but I don't want to leave you waiting in the dark. I try my best to keep my fans up to date! :-)

Bye for now. Happy Friday, and have a good weekend!

December 20, 2013 Facebook
My endocrinologist (diabetes doctor) doesn't want me to go for the pancreas transplant. Apparently the lifespan of a transplanted pancreas is only like 5 years? I'm still young; all those transplants every 5 years could be really damaging for my body. Definitely gave me something to think about. . . .

December 26, 2013 Blog
No hospital holiday for me!

I hope this post finds everyone well and happy. Merry belated Christmas, I hope everyone had a wonderful holiday with friends and/or family. Christmas is my absolute favorite time of year, and this year it couldn't have gone better for me, I am SO happy with the way all my holiday plans turned out. We had our Xmas gathering with my dad's side of the family on Saturday, the 21st. My cousin Adam and his wife Jackie were in town from Texas, with their two kids, Caleb, who will be 3 in March, and their newborn baby girl, Sofia, who is 9 weeks old (born mid-October). I hadn't seen Adam and Jackie in a couple years, and I had never met their kids, so it was really exciting to meet the kids and see my cousins. I also got to see my cousin Beth, who I only see once, MAYBE twice a year, her husband Tim, and their daughter Sarah, who is a year and a half I think. I hadn't seen Sarah since she was just a baby, last year at Thanksgiving I think, so again, it was really nice to see all of them, too. We had delicious lasagna for dinner, which my aunt Holly made, and an even more delicious desert of Oreo/marshmallow/mint cake that my cousin Katie made. YUM! So it was a great night and I felt very grateful to be able to be there and join in the festivities. Even though we aren't of any religious denomination, Christmas is a magical time for me, my favorite time of year (like I said before), and the more family I get to see, the better it is.

    My dad and Kathy couldn't join us for our big family dinner because they, and Spence (Kathy's son) went to Nebraska to visit Kathy's mom and uncle, but they did return early evening of Christmas eve, so we did our little family Xmas (dad, Kathy, Spence, Elliott, and me) that evening. I was very proud of the presents I got for everyone, and super happy and excited about the presents I got. I got everything on my list that I really wanted! I went home a happy girl.

    Elliott and I did our little Christmas dinner with my mom on Sunday night, the 22nd. I gave her the 2014 calendar that I made (but it was from both Elliott and me - he helped pay) on Shutterfly, a website where you can make personalized items, like calendars, pillows, coffee mugs, mouse pads, etc. etc. So each month had 4 pictures, either of Elliott, me, Elliott/me, Elliott/mom/me, Elliott/mom, mom/me, etc. You get the picture (no pun intended). I spent a long time making it and finding all the pictures from over the years, so a lot of love went into it! But she liked it (I think?), and it's something that's sentimental, and personal, that you can't buy in a store. *I* was certainly proud of it. :) We'll do the bigger Xmas gathering with my mom's side of the family this weekend, in Owatonna.

    OK, enough Christmas stuff, and on to other news . . .

    I am very conflicted right now about a pancreas transplant. Last week when I saw my endocrinologist, Dr. Saaed, he told me that he doesn't want me to have a pancreas transplant. He said the lifespan of a transplanted pancreas is only about 5 years, give or a take a year or so. At my young age, why would I put my body through a new, major surgery every 5 or so years for the rest of my life? In the next couple years, insulin pumps will be made that have the blood glucose sensor built into them, so I will hardly need to do anything except change my pump site every few days, and reload the insulin cartridge when it runs out. The pump would be able to sense what my blood sugar is, give me insulin if needed, and suspend itself if I'm getting too low. It would be like having an electronic pancreas that I wear. This is all what Dr. Saaed was saying.

I understand what he's getting at, but do you know how long I've been waiting for this? The idea of having a working pancreas, of not having to take insulin, not having anything (like a pump) connected to me, being able to have the freedom that "normal" people have. To BE "normal." Anyone who knows me at all knows that this is what I've been living for, what I've been waiting for, what I want most in life. And now he's telling me he doesn't think it's a good idea? Of course, it's my decision in the end, but he has given me something else to think about and consider. It's like he's raining on my parade; is the needle that popped my dream bubble. You get the picture? I don't WANT to stay diabetic and keep wearing my pump. I HATE my pump! I wear it because it's better than doing shots every single time I eat, and because I know it's giving me that constant insulin drip every hour. I HATE my diabetes. I just want it to be gone so that I can live my grown-up life and get young Krystin out of my head and live my life and do all the things that I said I wanted to do when I got my pancreas transplant (after I'm all recovered, of course; which I know will take a while). Recovery will be long, and I know I'll still need to do blood tests and even still some insulin after transplant, but after a full recovery, when the pancreas is doing everything it needs to do, successfully (knock on wood), I can finally live the life I've always wanted. The life I've dreamed of for at LEAST 15 years now. Why can't I just have that and be happy? Why did Dr. Saaed have to say those things? I know he is just looking out for me and was giving me his honest opinion and wants the best for me, but in my mind it was a dream crusher. I still like him a lot as a doctor, and will continue to see him weekly, but I think next time I see him, which is next week, I'll have to discuss this further with him. I will also definitely be discussing this with Nancy (my therapist). *Sigh

On another note, I had a scan of my gallbladder Monday morning. The test came back negative, which means there's nothing wrong with my gallbladder. It's working fine. Which means we're back at step one, not knowing what is causing the pain. I suppose it could still be my liver; we haven't completely ruled that out yet. I'm not sure what the next step/test will be. Dr. Kandaswamy is out of the country through next week I believe . . . or maybe it was just through this week. Anyway, I'll make an appointment with him to discuss what our other options are to figuring out this pain I get when I eat meals. If I can't get an appointment with Dr. Kandaswamy soon by calling the clinic, I'll call his nurse and see if she can fit me in somewhere. Dr. Kandaswamy has said he will over-book to fit me in. What an awesome guy. And I'm such a lovable patient. ;)

Hmm, other than that, not much is up. No big plans for New Years made, so I may just stay home and celebrate with my kitties and watch a movie. Truthfully, though, I'm OK with that. I still don't have all my energy back, so the idea of being out and partying all night sounds like a lot of work and really exhausting. At least for this year. I don't make New Year's resolutions, but my goal for 2014 is to really get serious about my writing and, aside from my taking care of my health, to make it a top priority for me. I keep making all these empty promises to people about my writing that I haven't been able to fill. Admittedly, I've had a few things get in the way this past year, but in 2014 I'm going to be more determined forever. My book won't write itself! Besides, I need to start writing before I forget it.

In case I don't write again before New Year's, I hope everyone enjoys whatever festivities you may be participating in, and ring in the new year with a bang! IF you can stay awake until then. ;) HAPPY 2014! Bye for now.

December 29, 2013 Facebook
Krystin Engstrand is at University of Minnesota Health.
Was only admitted for only one night, with a G.I. virus. It goes away quickly, and no more barfing for me today, so home tonight!

January 1, 2014 Blog
Happy 2014!

As most of you know (or maybe you don't?), last weekend I spent one night, less than 24 hours, at my home away from home, the hospital. It had started last Friday, when out of the blue I woke up Friday morning and threw up. I felt fine after, and went to work. Saturday morning I woke up feeling dizzy and lightheaded, but attributed that to me probably not having drank enough water the day before. My mom and Elliott and I drove down to Owatonna for our family gathering with my mom's side of the family. I brought a large bottle of water and some dry cereal to eat/drink in the car, thinking my stomach just needed some nutrients and water. I felt relatively fine when we got there, and I ate lunch readily at lunch time. After lunch, however, I started feeling nauseous, so I went into the back room and hung out in a big comfy chair, hoping it would pass. Around 2pm, I threw up again.

My aunt asked me if I wanted to go to the urgent care clinic that was just 2 miles down the road from their house. I decided that was probably a good idea. My mom brought me, they did blood work and took a urine sample, and the doctor deduced that I was feeling icky due to dehydration. I figured that was the problem, so I promised to drink lots of water, and headed out. By that time it was time to head home, so when my mom picked me up from the clinic, we hopped on the highway and headed home.

She dropped me off at my apartment somewhere between 7:30 and 8, I think. Around 9, I threw up again. And at 9:30. I texted my mom, but she had just gotten in the bathtub, so I called my dad and told him I needed to go to the hospital, and he agreed to take me. I brought a plastic bag along for the ride, just in case. Good thing, too, because I threw up numerous times on the way to the ER. From that point on, I began throwing up about once an hour, until the early hours of the morning.

Let me tell you, it was NOT dehydration. Turns out I had a 24-48 hour G.I. virus. I guess it's been going around? The doc said it works its way through the body on its own within a couple days, and then people are back to normal. So, for people who don't go to the hospital or to see a doctor, they're just sitting at home for a day/day and a half barfing their guts out thinking they're dying? How awful. I went to the ER because I go there when ANYTHING is off, but I imagine many people don't. On Sunday I wasn't feeling nauseous anymore (I had been from about noon on Saturday until about 2am Sunday morning - that's 14 hours of constant nausea), and at lunchtime I was even able to eat some food, and keep it down! Both indications that the virus was working it's way out. My dad picked me up and brought me home mid-afternoon.

Yes, I went to work on Monday. I was feeling much better, and was ready to get up when my alarm went off. However, that was short-lived. I got a stomach ache around 10am, and by 3:30pm it still hadn't gone away. My co-worker Anjeanette even said I looked very flushed, and felt warm, even though internally I felt cold. So I went home. I took a nice nap snuggled up in my electric blanket, and felt much better by dinner time. 4am Tuesday morning, I woke up and threw up. But interestingly, or not, afterward, when I crawled back in bed, I felt perfectly fine, and in a few hours when my alarm went off, I was ready to get up.

I haven't had any problems since. So there were a couple lingering symptoms, but now I'm pretty sure it's all out of my symptom. So I've said this before, and I'll say it again, if there's something going around, there's a pretty good chance I'll catch it! I seriously need a human bubble to live in.

Moving on . . .

It took me a lot of back-and-forth internal debating about whether or not to do this, but I finally decided to start up a fund for myself to help pay my medical bills. I do NOT find it easy to ask people for money, even if it's for a good cause, so it's even harder for me to ask for money for myself. But I have gotten to the point where it has become too overwhelming to deal with on my own. Between doctor appointment co-pays, medication co-pays (those stupid little blood test strips are expensive, and not covered by health insurance!), my now 2 ambulance bills, home care nursing co-pays, pump supplies, and bills for post-cataract surgery follow-up visits from the eye clinic that is NOT covered by insurance, it all adds up to, well, a lot, and I'm having a hard time keeping up. Hell, not even keeping up yet, I'm still CATCHING up. I decided that I was going to reach out to the world and cross my fingers for help. No amount is too small, and if you can't help, please share my story, and maybe even the link to my page. I have also listed the link to this blog on my fundraising page. Perhaps I've been getting sick too much and so easily lately because I'm so stressed about all these medical bills. I feel genuinely horrible for people who have no health insurance at all, and/or no amazing friend and family network like I do. Anyway, that's my spiel. Know that there is NO pressure, no obligation, and no matter what, I will still love you all the same.

That's all I got for now. I wish a very Happy New Year to everyone, and I can't wait to see what 2014 has to bring!

January 12, 2014 Email
Pancreas transplant vs. stem cell study
Krystin to Dr. Elizabeth Seaquist, U of Minnesota:

Hi Dr. Seaquist,
 I am diabetic, had a kidney transplant in June 2013, and am now facing a possible pancreas transplant. My father, Gary Engstrand, suggested I contact you. I am conflicted about whether or not to have the transplant. My endocrinologist, Dr. Saaed, does not recommend I have the pancreas transplant, saying the lifespan of a transplanted pancreas is, on average, only 5 years. Is this true? Obviously as a 29 year-old I don't want to be facing a new transplant every 5 or so years. He would prefer I stay on the pump, and get one that has the blood sugar sensor in it, so that it would pretty much do all the work for me. Well, I'm sure I don't have to tell you how they work! I have been diabetic for 25 years, and have hated it and struggled with it since my middle school years. For over a decade I have wanted nothing more than to be rid of this illness. I have been waiting for a cure, or for a stem cell transplant study that I can join. I see that there are now studies for diabetics who have had a kidney transplant, and as the head of Decade of Discovery, I thought you might be able to help me or give me some insights into options for me. I do NOT want to stay on the pump for the rest of my life. My kidney transplant was due to diabetic kidney failure, I've already had to have cataract surgery in both eyes, and I have nerve pain in my feet often. So you can see why I'm anxious to have a transplant of some kind.
 Thank you so much for taking the time to read this, and for any help you might be able to offer. If you or someone from the project would like to reach me by phone, I am at 612-799-0555. I hope to be in touch soon. - Krystin Engstrand

Krystin to dad:
 I got a response from Betsy. This is what she said. Good advice, but she didn't really give me an opinion on what to do!

On Thursday, January 16, 2014, Elizabeth Seaquist wrote:
Hello Krystin --
  Having diabetes is such a struggle! I can well understand how exciting pancreas transplant looks. It is wonderful when someone can come off insulin, stop checking their blood sugars,

and eat and exercise without thinking about their sugars. Unfortunately, this doesn't work for everyone. Dr. Saeed is correct that they generally last for around 5 years. Of course there is a range from not working at all even at the start to having it work for ten years or more. The challenge in having it done is knowing if for you it is worth the risks of having surgery to face whatever outcome is in store for you. I think a kidney transplant is much different because we know that people with renal failure feel better and live longer with a kidney transplant than with going on dialysis and that the transplant generally lasts many years. I am very excited about the new pump and glucose sensors. I know there is lots of work being done to develop the artificial pancreas and am hopeful that we will actually have something that works by itself in a few years.

   Hope this information helps!
Betsy Seaquist

January 17, 2014 Blog
To pancreas, or not to pancreas?
  I am so conflicted right now, I don't know what to do, and it's stressing me out. My endocrinologist (diabetes doctor), Dr. Saeed, told me a couple weeks ago that he doesn't think I should have the pancreas transplant, saying that the lifespan of a transplanted pancreas is only 5 or so years. With me being young still, why put the body through another transplant so often? He thinks I should stay diabetic, on an insulin pump that has a blood glucose meter. I understood his reasoning, but I didn't like it. Then last week I had an appointment with Dr. Kandaswamy (my surgeon) and told him about what Dr. Saeed said. Dr. Kandaswamy said that half of pancreas transplants only make it to around 5 years, but the other half make it longer. He knows a patient who is in his 26th or 27th year with his transplanted pancreas. Some people have told me that of course Dr. Kandaswamy wants me to have the transplant, because he just wants to do surgery. But he's not paid on commission. He gets his yearly salary whether or not he performs my transplant. He has done all my surgeries so far, and I've gotten to know him well over the past year and a half, and I do believe he truly cares about me and my well being. He's not just a faceless surgeon wanting to get paid.
  Dr. Kandaswamy pointed out the 2 biggest risks of transplants. One is the surgery itself, and the 2nd is the anti-rejection/immuno-

suppressant meds, and how they will react with the new organ and with the body. The medications after a pancreas transplant are the same as after a kidney transplant, so I've already been on them for 7 and a half months. My body is already used to them, and I didn't suffer any side effects. So really the only risk then is the surgery, which is a risk for ANY major surgery. So Dr. Kandaswamy thinks I should go for it. He did say, however, that if I get a call with an offer, I should make sure it's in 'excellent' condition. The physician who calls will be able to tell what condition the pancreas is in, and they rank an organ from 'fair' to 'good' to 'excellent.' Obviously 'poor' organs they don't call people with. They base the rank on the health and condition of the organ, along with how well it is a match to me. So he says I should go for it, but only take an 'excellent' pancreas. And since I already have a transplanted kidney, the success of a new pancreas is higher, since it's not my first transplant, and they would be putting a new pancreas into a body with a healthy, working kidney, instead of a patient who has two failing kidneys. Does that make sense?

I've been working on a pros and cons list, and I would like to share it. Here is what I have so far:

Pros
The transplant is successful = no more diabetes = diabetes freedom
No more blood tests
No more shots/insulin pump
Will halt further diabetes complications
If successful, with help keep my new kidney healthy
Body has already adapted to the medications
Happier Krystin

Cons
The surgery
The pancreas could reject

I mean, I'm not too worried about the surgery, because I trust my team, I know how my body handles anesthesia, and I'm a tough cookie. I'm confident I'd make it through. That only leaves rejection of the pancreas. So what if it rejects? As with the kidney, at least I'd know I tried. The doctors didn't want me to take Crystal's kidney either, but I went against medical advice and I did it, knowing that I had to try.

This is the same case. I need to try. If my body rejects it, then I'll take a break and won't reenlist on the donor list. I'll go back on the pump, on one with the blood glucose monitoring. And I'd be OK with that, because I would know that I tried, I gave it a shot. Yes it might reject, but what if it DOESN'T? What if my body ACCEPTS it? People always look at the negative, and say "what if it doesn't work? What if it rejects? Then what?" Well what if it works, huh? Let's be optimistic and look on the bright side here. I know it's a risk, but I've always thought of myself as more of an optimist than a pessimist, just like I was with the kidney, so I like to hope that there's a chance it will work, especially if I accept an 'excellent' pancreas.

I did get an outside opinion. I emailed a woman named Betsy Seaquist, who is not only an endocrinologist here at the U of M, but also the head of Decade of Discovery, which is an initiative whose goal is to find a cure for diabetes.

Anyway, I emailed Dr. Seaquist to see what she has to say about pancreas transplants vs. staying on the pump vs. joining a pancreatic stem cell transplant research study. She responded and said she understands how much of a struggle it is to have diabetes, and how exciting a pancreas transplant looks. She is very excited about the new pumps with glucose monitoring, there is lots of work being done to develop an artificial pancreas, and she hopes they will have something that works by itself in a few years. As far as a pancreas transplant, she said the biggest challenge is if, for me, it is worth the risks of having the surgery to face whatever outcome is in store for me. So basically I need to take my pros and cons list and decide if it's worth the risk.

The way I see it, like I said before, I can have the transplant, and IF it rejects, then there will be other options besides having another transplant. You will probably say that it seems as if my mind is already made up. That's true. Even with all this back-and-forth, the pros and cons, the stress, and the opinions and advice from other people, I've probably known all along, in my heart, that I'm going to get the transplant. Just like with the kidney. It's just something I have to do, and if you don't understand or don't think it's a good idea, that's OK. I don't want to not get the transplant and then regret it the rest of my life, having that "what if?" always in the back of my mind. I'm just not patient enough to wait for something more successful to come along. This is what I need to do for me, now.

OK, now that I got all that off my chest, time for lunch. I see Dr. Saeed again this afternoon, and will discuss my decision with him.

Even if he disagrees with me, I hope he understands, because in 2 weeks I'll be reactivated on the national donor waiting list. I'll keep you posted!

Bye for now.

January 27, 2014 Email
CMV/pancreas
Krystin to mom, dad:

OK, so my labs from Friday show that the CMV virus is back. Not full-blown, not anything that we need to worry about, just very, very slightly. Which sucks considering that my labs for the past month came out negative for CMV. I don't need to do home infusion or anything again, just start taking Valcyte again (which I took for about 4 months post-transplant, and for a month after I went off the IV home infusion antibiotic). This also means that I can't be reactivated on the pancreas waiting list yet. I don't know how long my system has to be clean of CMV and EBV, but I know it's at least a month, maybe a month and a half. I see Dr. Young, the lady who works in the infection disease clinic (dad you remember her from the hospital) next week, so I'll see what she says about it. Fingers crossed no picc line again!!

So, speaking of pancreas waiting list, I want you to know that I am going to go forward with it. I will only accept a pancreas that is in 'excellent' condition, but nevertheless, I'm going for it, even if it's against my endocrinologist's advice. Like with the kidney, I need to do this. I know the success rate and lifespan of a transplanted pancreas is not as high as a kidney, but I need to try. And if it rejects right away or 5 years down the line, I will be OK, because I will know that I tried. I would then go back on the pump (hopefully by then they will have released the pumps with the continuous glucose monitoring, where the pump delivers insulin for my, based on my BG, without me having to do anything - like wearing a bionic pancreas on my belt). If you don't support my decision to do this, that's OK, because it's my decision to make. I just want your understanding as to why I need to do this.

OK, enough serious talk. Love you both!

Dad to Krystin:
It's your call. I wasn't going to argue with you either way.

Krystin to dad:
Good, thank you. :-)

January 29, 2014 Email
Nickeled and Dimed
Krystin to mom, dad:

I split all my bills between the 2 paychecks a month that I get, depending on their due dates. After everything is paid, whatever is left over is for me, for gas, groceries, kitty food, etc. I have done NO pleasure shopping for a long time (not even clothes!!). After paying off the rest of this month's bills from the most recent paycheck, and the automatic deduction yesterday for my car loan from Affinity Plus, I have $2.49 to last me until next paycheck (next Wednesday). This is what it's like most months.

I hope my kitties don't mind starving. Or myself.

I don't wanna be an adult anymore. :(

January 31, 2014 Email
endo appt
Dad to Krystin bcc Kathy:

Sure, I would be glad to come with you next Friday (you mean Feb 7, I assume) to your endo appointment. But I'm curious to know why you think you need me along.

Krystin to dad:

Dr. Saeed asked who in my close circle of friends and family would be willing to be part of my support system again, at least for a little bit. Even though I'm 29 and not a kid anymore, he thinks it's a good idea to have people help keep me on track. I said you probably would be, so he asked if you could come in. So I said I'd ask you! Fri. 2/7, 2:00, PWB 6th floor clinic.

Dad to Krystin:

OK, but there's only a limited amount I'm prepared to do. Remember, I've been in this system for a long time, without great success.

Krystin to dad:

I know, and I understand. The problem before was that I didn't WANT the help. Now I'm in a different boat, and I'm ready to reach out for help. I discussed it with Nancy last night at my appointment, and I told her that I kinda feel silly asking for help, like I'm a kid again, but she pointed out that when it comes to one's health, you are never too old to ask for help, especially when it can be beneficial. And I believe this time around it can be beneficial. Well, we can discuss it more on Friday at my appointment!

February 17, 2014 Blog
Goodbye gallbladder, you're outta here!

Well, I'm back. I know there was a big gap in time since my last post, but that's because, as is always my excuse, there was nothing of interest to write about. Now, however, there is!

On Friday (Valentine's Day!) I had my gallbladder removal surgery. It was a last-minute opening in the OR schedule. I got a call at work on Thursday, around lunch time, from a triage nurse, telling me that they had me on the schedule for surgery tomorrow morning. Oh! Of course I took it, because who knows how much longer I'd have to wait to get scheduled, and with the pain I'd been having, I wanted to get it done as soon as possible. I sent out an email to my co-workers letting them that I would be gone the next day for surgery. They were all very supportive and wished me luck and a speedy recovery. My supervisor, who had been out Tuesday-Thursday due to illness, was returning to work on Friday, and in his reply, he joked about just because he's returning to work doesn't mean I have to go into the hospital. Ha! Funny guy.

So bright and early Friday morning - actually, not really bright and early; I didn't have to get up any earlier than I do any other weekday - I headed over to my dad's house, and rode in with him to the U. He dropped me off at the hospital about 8:30, I checked in with admissions, and went up to the surgery department to wait. My surgery wasn't scheduled until 11, but of course they like people to be there 2 hours early. I don't know why, operation never starts on time anyway. I wasn't brought back into the operating room until 11:30 or a little after. At least my pre-op bay had a TV, so I turned on the Olympics and watched some figure skating while I waited. When they brought me back into the OR, I was put under pretty quickly. They never tell me when they're going to start delivering the anesthesia, so I may have been in the middle of a sentence, talking to the nurses, when they did. I think they like to have a good time and just cut off patients mid-sentence. Gotta make the job fun somehow!

If you don't know much or anything about the gallbladder, its job is to collect bile that is produced by the liver, and is released by the gallbladder when you eat, to help absorb and breakdown fat. When the gallbladder is removed, the bile has nowhere to collect, so instead it drains, constantly, directly out of the liver and into the intestine. Over time, the body adjusts, and becomes better at digesting fatty foods. For some people, the liver never slows down between meals, which apparently can cause diarrhea on a daily basis. I was told to expect loose stools for about a month, but after that, the body adjusts. For people whose bodies don't adjust, they have to take a medication, but I'm hoping I'm not one of those people. With my medical luck, though, I probably will be. But results vary from person to person, so the next month or so will tell!

Here's how a laparoscopic cholecystectomy (bladder removal surgery) works: Numerous small incisions (I have 5) are made on the abdomen, in which are inserted small tubes with a camera and surgical instruments are placed. The camera illuminates the surgical field, and the surgeon (Dr. Kandaswamy) can watch it on a screen next to the operating table, and use that video feed to manipulate the instruments through the operating ports. My abdomen is inflated with air to create a working space, and when the gallbladder is identified, it is removed through one of the ports. After being clipped away from everything it's attached to and all the important surgical stuff is completed inside my abdomen. That stuff is too technical for me! The incisions are really small, between 5-10 mm in diameter, so I have no idea how they can pull an organ out of one of those incisions, but I guess the gallbladder is really small, so it works out! I was closed up using the Dermabond glue stuff.

I woke up in the recovery bay in terrible pain. This happened after both my gastric pacer and kidney transplant surgeries. I told the anesthesiologist about this before this surgery, and she said they would do their best, but it's hard to judge how much painkillers to give a patient before they wake up, because we aren't awake to tell them how much pain we're in. I told her that I require a little extra than most people (so does my mom; I take after her in that respect), and she said she would let the nursing staff in recovery know that, but they must have forgotten. Or something. So I woke up crying and hyperventilating, and I heard them moving around quickly to get me more painkillers. First dose: did nothing. Second dose: still in pain. My nurse asked me if I was feeling any better, and I shook my head no, so he gave me a THIRD dose. I finally started to feel the pain dull, and I may have drifted off for a little bit longer, but I don't think I feel asleep really, it was more of being in a haze. After a while I fully woke up and was aware of my surroundings and talking with my nurse. It was a little after 3pm. The surgery only takes an hour at the most, so I had been in recovery for a couple hours.

Most patients who have a cholecystectomy go home that day, but as a transplant patient, they wanted to keep me overnight. I was expecting to go up to unit 7A, as I always do, but I went to 6D instead, which is the recovery unit. I didn't complain, of course (I didn't really care), but I thought, awww, I won't get to see my favorite nurses! Now whenever I go onto 7A, the nurses just smile and say "Hey Krystin, you're back!" Oh well, I'll get to see them again after my pancreas transplant!

As always, once I was up on the observation floor, I wanted to see what it looked like, so I took a picture to share with you all.

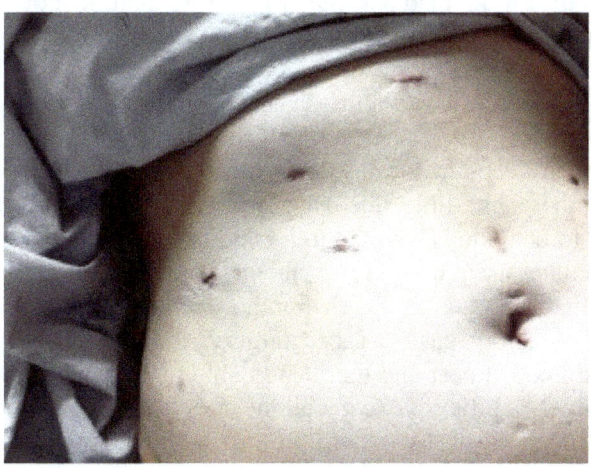

The scar right above my belly button is actually from when I had the gastric pacer put in. The 5th incision, which you can't really see in the picture, is right IN my belly button, at the bottom. The little hole you see right above my belly button is where my belly button ring goes, but of course I had to take that out for surgery. I put it right back in when I was in my room on the observation floor. It was really quiet on that unit. I had a room all to myself, except for a couple hours I had a roommate who had had a heart transplant a while ago, and was just in to have a tune-up and needed to be on observation for a couple hours, then go home. I spent most of the time watching the Olympics, or Animal Planet. I ate a regular dinner that night, and breakfast and lunch on Saturday, so I was back to my usual diet the evening of surgery! The nurses didn't even bother me much, so for being a hospital stay, this one was pretty decent.

Surprisingly, I didn't have a lot of pain in my abdomen from the incisions. Only a little soreness. Most of my pain was actually in my shoulders, and still is. I've been telling people that I imagine this is what it feels like to be shot in the shoulder. The painkillers don't help with that pain; I just have to wait until it passes. When they blow up my stomach with air during surgery, afterwards it all floats up the body, and ends up in the shoulders, so it causes a lot of pressure. It hurts.

One of the requirements for being discharged is eating and drinking normally (check), and urinating on my own. That one I was having trouble with. I didn't urinate all day Friday after the surgery, and when they did a bladder scan around midnight, it showed I had a LOT of pee in my bladder. So they had to straight cath me, which means they stick a tube, you know, in me, that goes up into my bladder and releases all the urine into a bag that's attached to the tube. It's different from a foley catheter in that the foleys are more long-term, that a patient keeps in for days, or even a week or more, whereas a straight cath is a one-time, one-use procedure. It's not comfortable, but it needed to be done. They had to do that to me twice, but luckily by late afternoon on Saturday, I was able to produce a little urine on my own, so that was good enough for the docs to discharge me. This happened after my gastric pacer surgery, too. I had to be straight cathed I think 3 times, and then I was able to go on my own. It just takes my body a little time to get all the anesthesia and narcotics from the painkillers out of my system. So my dad picked me up around 5 and brought me back to my apartment. I was so excited to get back to my kitties, and they were happy to see me! As soon as I got home I threw up, but then I felt better and haven't had any nausea or vomiting since. Random.

I read on Wikipedia that about 600,000 cholecystectomies are done each year. I guess our bodies haven't yet figured out that we really don't need the gallbladder any more, and doesn't need to develop it in the womb! I guess that's still a long ways off in evolution, if ever.

I don't really have any dietary restrictions now as far as what I can't eat, I just need to monitor my intake of fatty foods in one sitting, and it's advised to eat 6 smaller meals a day instead of 3 bigger meals, at least for a while, while my body adjusts and I learn what it can/can't handle. I don't have to take any extra medications, so that's nice. I'm really crossing my fingers that this solves the pain I've been having. If it doesn't, then none of us are sure what the next step would be. Let's hope it doesn't come to that.

So today I returned to work, even though I'm still having a lot of pain in my shoulders. I figured it was better to be at work and be productive while in discomfort than be sitting at home bored and in discomfort, with nothing to do but focus on the pain. And you know me, thinking I'm Superwoman (again taking after my mother), so if I feel like I can go in to work, I do. Luckily today it's pretty quiet around the office because there's a big symposium going on, so a lot of our staff is out, which, as you can tell, has given me some free time to write this!

But OK, I should find something work-related to do now. I don't think I have anything more of interest to say anyway. I hope you all had a better Valentine's Day than I did, and (for those of you living here in MN) are looking forward to some 40 degree weather tomorrow!

Bye for now.

March 7, 2014 Blog
Babopsy
(If any of you have seen the movie My Big Fat Greek Wedding, you'll understand that subject title)

I called my coordinator yesterday for my weekly check-in call, and got some bad news. She said my antibody level, for the antibody I have against my kidney, has greatly increased. Remember how before transplant, I had an antibody against Crystal's kidney, but not a significant amount. That's why the docs suggested I wait for a better match, but I went with it anyway.

The blood test that they do to measure such things after a transplant is called a PRA test. Percent Reactive Antibody. I'm going to try to explain this without being too technical or confusing. PRA is the amount of HLA antibody present in a patient's blood. HLA is Human Leukocyte Antigens, and when two people share the same HLA, they are said to be a "match", meaning our tissues are immunologically compatible with each other = unlikely to fight against each other. HLA are proteins that are located on the surface of the white blood cells and other tissues in the body. This is very important to measure when finding a donor, since the white blood cells are the ones that attack anything foreign (like a new organ!).

I'm not exactly sure how this specific antibody is measured, but it's measured per liter of blood. Prior to transplant, a crossmatch test was done, using my blood and Crystal's white blood cells, to determine whether or not I had an antibody against Crystal. Remember that? I had a slight antibody against such-and-such antigen, as I mentioned just above, but not enough to NOT do the transplant. My antibody level for this particular antibody against Crystal's kidney was between 300-500 (blood units?) per liter. It is now somewhere around 3,300, which means my body has developed an antibody to Crystal's HLA type. Yikes.

Still with me here?

Sometimes a patient can have an antibody that mimics HLA antibody. This means that it is not harmful, but it is difficult to determine the cause of the antibody production. Why did my body suddenly start producing this antibody against the kidney? Even something like strep throat can cause antibody production. Remember back in November when I was hospitalized with all those ridiculous viruses and infections that just helped themselves to my immune system? They may be partly to blame, if not all. Therefore, a biopsy is going to be done on my kidney to see if the antibodies are starting to do harm to my kidney. Even though my creatinine level is GREAT, and has been since transplant, that could suddenly change if these antibodies suddenly launch a war inside me.

So what could be done to help prevent future rejection?

I don't know. That is something I will discuss with them in the clinic on Tuesday when I go in for the biopsy. Possibly increase my immune-suppressant medication, but that would put me back at rock bottom as far as having an immune system goes, and I'm not sure if they want me to be THAT immunosuppressed again right before another transplant.

Pat (coordinator) gave me a run-down on how the procedure will be done. It will be at SIPC (specialty infusion and procedure clinic) at the U. The same clinic I had to go to every day for a week after my transplant to get those 5-hour long IV drips of steroids. And many times since for different infusions and whatnot. It is going to be done next Tuesday, 3/11. I have to be to the clinic at 7am. Ugh. They will do some blood labs, then feed me breakfast while they wait for the results. When they are ready to get started, they will use an ultrasound machine to figure out exactly where they need to insert the device into my abdomen to snip some samples from my kidney. They will then numb the area with Lidocaine or Novocaine. Pat said this is the part that is more uncomfortable (read: PAINFUL). Once they've numbed the area sufficiently, they will use their little snipping device, along with the ultrasound device, to stab me and take their samples. Sounds lovely, eh? Pat said that since I'm thin, it won't be a very difficult procedure, because they don't have much muscle and tissue to go through to get to the kidney. Also, since the transplanted kidney was not connected to the nervous system when it was transplanted, I won't feel any snipping they do.

I will need to stay in the clinic until mid-afternoon, on bed rest, so they can monitor me and make sure there isn't any internal bleeding or other complications from the procedure. I will definitely be bringing along a book and my iPad. I will probably even take a nap. Or two. They have plenty of different beverages and munchies at my disposal, so it won't be so bad. I am absolutely going to tell them beforehand, however, that they will need to give me some kind of sedative or relaxant before they get started, otherwise I will cry and be tense and freaking out the whole time. Some Valium would be nice. They don't put patients under anesthesia for this type of procedure, but I am definitely going to need a little something-something to calm me down.

Yes, I am still active on the pancreas waiting list. This antibody against the kidney does not affect finding a match for a pancreas, because a potential pancreas may not even have this particular antigen that my kidney has. It will be a completely separate cross matching test.

That's all I got. Not looking forward to this biopsy, but who would? The way I see it, it's just another procedure. Another thing I have to do. Bring it on! I will post again post-procedure and let you know how it went, and what the preliminary findings are.

Bye for now.
March 14, 2014 Blog
And the verdict is . . .

Before I get into how the biopsy went, I want to share some information that I received from my coordinator. I asked her about the antibody test they did, and what my levels were. The blood test that they do is actually called a DSA test, or Donor Specific Antibody test. They look at a certain antibody, B18. B cells are part of the immune system. Our bodies make millions of different types of B cells every day, that circulate in the blood and act as "immune surveillance." They do not produce antibodies until they become fully activated. It's activated when it comes in contact [with] an antigen that is NOT native to your body. Remember, antigens and antibodies work together to provoke an immune system response to anything foreign. Anyway, Pat gave me my levels over the past several months, as they have monitored it:

   6/3/13 (day before surgery)
   Class I: no DSA to Crystal
   Class II: no DSA to Crystal

   7/5/13 (one months after transplant
   Class I: DSA to Crystal: B18 = 511
   Class II: no DSA to Crystal

   7/16/13
   Class I: DSA to Crystal: B18 = 544
   Class II: no DSA to Crystal

   8/2/13 (2 months after transplant)
   Class I: DSA to Crystal: B18 = 511
   Class II: no DSA to Crystal
   8/26
   Class I: DSA to Crystal: B18 = 504 (yay, going down!)
   Class II: no DSA to Crystal

   10/3/13 (4 months after transplant)
   Class I: DSA to Crystal: B18 = 570
   Class II: no DSA to Crystal

   12/4/13 (6 months after transplant)
   Class I: DSA to Crystal: B18 = 680
   Class II: no DSA to Crystal

Now time to worry. Not only has my B18 gone up, but it also has made many, many friends, including some Class II buddies . . .

   2/28/14 (almost 9 months after transplant)
   Class I: DSA to Crystal: B18 = 3346; B62 = 2802; Cw5 = 727

Class II: DSA to Crystal: DR4 = 582; DQA1 = 2111

HOWEVER, just because the antibody levels are through the roof, does not necessarily mean that they are doing any damage. That is why the biopsy had to be done: to make sure that they aren't affecting my kidney, which can be determined by taking a few samples of kidney tissue.

I arrived at the clinic at 7 in the morning. The first thing they did was draw blood and take vital signs. Then I was to sit around and wait for my lab results to come back, and then until Dr. Sprong (who does the procedure) comes along to do it. There were about 4 biopsies being done, so who knew when it would be my turn. After they drew my blood, I was given a breakfast tray of cereal and milk, yogurt, a banana, and a bagel with cream cheese. I didn't eat the bagel, but I did bring a pop tart with me in my bag, so I made that as well. I putzed around on my iPad and ate my breakfast while waiting.

I talked to my nurse about getting something to help me relax, and after talking to Dr. Sprong, they agreed I could have some Ativan. However, after doing my vitals, it was decided that my blood pressure was too low to give me Ativan. Since Ativan helps people relax, it lowers blood pressure, and if they gave it to me, I would bottom out. So I had to get an IV put in and they started giving me a liter of fluids to raise my blood pressure.

Dr. Sprong came in to talk to me about the procedure, and seeing how nervous I was, he asked me if I wanted to go first and get it done with. He even said that he would do the procedure himself, instead of his Fellow. I agreed to both, and he somehow convinced me to do the procedure without getting any Ativan, since it would still be a while if we waited. I was convinced very reluctantly, but agreed nonetheless. I just wanted it done and over with so I didn't have to sit and wait and think about it anymore. So at 8:45, we began.

The ultrasound tech came in and did an ultrasound of my kidney and used a marker to mark where Dr. Sprong should insert the biopsy needle. Then Dr. Sprong came in and prepped the area, putting sterile towels around my abdomen, and cleaning the area. I was warned ahead of time that it was the numbing shot that was the most uncomfortable, like getting a shot of Novocaine at the dentist. You know, when they stick that huge needle into your gums. When I had my transplant last June, once I was put under anesthesia, I was given a nerve block in the region of my abdomen where they were performing the surgery. A nerve block blocks pain impulses through a nerve. I'm pretty sure I was given a neurolytic block, which is the same thing, but it can last for weeks, months, or even indefinitely, whereas just a regular nerve block only lasts a couple days or so. Today, the area around my transplant incision is still numb! So when Dr. Sprong gave me the numbing shot yesterday, I never even felt it.

After a few minutes, he began the biopsy procedure. The ultrasound tech guy was still there, to tell Dr. Sprong exactly where to insert the needle, at what angle, how far into me he would have to go, etc. He kept the ultrasound device on my stomach the whole time, so that Dr. Sprong could look at the screen on the computer and see where he needle was, and when he was in the kidney tissue. Here is what the biopsy needle looks like:

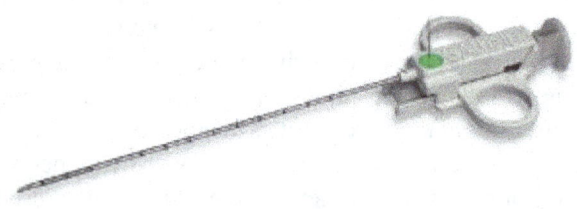

Don't worry, the whole needle doesn't go into me. Since I'm thin, and the kidney isn't too deep, only about an inch and half of it had to go in. When he pushes down on that button thing on the top, it makes a loud clicking sound, like a staple gun. It's really loud. That's the sound of it snipping a piece of tissue. He took 3 samples, and I didn't feel anything at all. I hardly even felt any pressure. If I didn't already know what was going on, I never would've known that someone was down there sticking me with huge needles. It took Dr. Sprong less than 10 minutes for the whole procedure, and he talked to me the whole time. He told me when he was going to push the button, but otherwise he talked to me about hockey, and travelling, and where I grew up in south Minneapolis. He was good at keeping me distracted, although I was still very tense. When it was all over, I breathed a huge sigh of relief. Of course, when the nurse took my vital signs afterwards, it sure had gone up a lot. It was about 9:15 when it was all done. No stitches or anything are needed; a band-aid was put on the hole.

After the procedure, the nurse had to stand there for 10 minutes and hold pressure on my kidney, to help prevent bleeding. Then I had to lie there on my back for an hour. It went by pretty fast. After that hour, I could sit up and get more comfortable, but I still had to stay in the clinic for another few hours. Around noon I was given a lunch tray of a turkey sandwich, a fruit cup, a cup of a cold vegetable pasta, milk, and Lorna Doone cookies. I also helped myself to the snack drawer. Again, I spent the afternoon putzing around on my iPad as well as reading my book.

Dr. Ibrahim (nephrologist) came to visit me about 3. I had an appointment scheduled with him that day anyway, so instead of me going over to the transplant clinic, which was right next door, he just came over to see me. It was just a check-up, since I hadn't seen him in a few months. We discussed switching from Prograf to that other anti-rejection med that stimulates hair growth, but he wants to hold off. He took me off 2 of my current meds and switched me to 1 med that does both of what the other 2 meds did. He wants to see if that switch slows down my current hair loss, and if that doesn't make a difference, then we can revisit switching. *Sigh* I just want my hair back! We also discussed why I'm so freaking tired and lethargic all the time. During the week, I go to work during the day, and go right home afterwards. That's it. On the weekends, I sleep pretty much all of Saturday, and hang around my apartment all of Sunday, maybe going to the grocery store if I really need to. Any errands, and any outings with anyone, all seem so hard, and like such a chore, so I avoid them all together. Dr. Ibrahim agreed that for someone my age, this should not be happening. So he's having me do this 24-hour urine collection. I was sent home with a big jug, and a hat to put on my toilet seat to pee into (and then transfer it into the jug). Then I'll bring it in to the lab, and they'll do the test Dr. Ibrahim ordered. I forget what it's called. He doesn't think it's any of my meds, so we're testing for something else. If that test comes up negative for whatever he's looking for, then we'll try something else.

After his visit, I got to go home. My post-procedure urine sample showed that there was no internal bleeding or blood clot, my blood pressure had gone up, and my hemoglobin level was good, so I was free to go. It was about 3:30pm when I left the clinic. The day actually went by pretty fast. When I got home, I put on sweatpants and a sweatshirt, made some chips and nacho cheese, and plopped down on my couch to watch some Harry Potter, while 2 kitties napped nearby.

I got a call early evening from Dr. Sprong's Fellow. She said she had the preliminary results from the biopsy, and . . . no issues with the kidney! The antibodies are keeping to themselves. It will still be monitored closely, but at least for now they aren't damaging my kidney. Whew. I don't think further study of the tissue samples will indicate anything different, so we can all breathe a sigh of relief. For now, at least.

Today I am back at work and feeling good. The liter of fluids they gave me yesterday, as well as the pitcher of water they made me drink before leaving really helped. I realized that may be part of the reason why I'm so exhausted all the time. I know I'm not drinking anywhere near the 2 liters a day that I should be drinking, and I'm sure (actually, I'm POSITIVE) that's putting strain on my kidney, and making me tired. If I can keep up on my water intake, I know I'll start feeling better.

That's all for now. I don't know when the next time I post will be, but I don't have anything in the near future worthy of writing about. Unless you want to hear about my dentist appointment next week, but I doubt it. I'd get bored just writing about it, so I'll save you from that one. I hope everyone is enjoying the warmer weather we're finally having!

Bye for now.

March 18, 2014 Facebook
I think I figured out why I love cats so much. Pretty sure I'm supposed to be one, complete with 9 lives. I want to do so much - travel around the world and write books, be an EMT, be a forensic anthropologist, be a transplant nurse, be a spokesperson for the American Diabetes Association, and volunteer for numerous charities - too much to fit into one little life!

March 23, 2014 Facebook
Krystin Engstrand is feeling strong.
This weekend I made one of the hardest decisions in my life. I turned down my first pancreas offer, because it was not an 'excellent' match. That was rough, but I know it's for the best. Better luck next time.

March 24, 2014 Facebook
These days I feel like I am barely functioning as a human being. After so many surgeries, procedures, illnesses, and other ailments crammed into such a short period of time, my body is exhausted. Everything is so hard to do and feels like such a chore, and my body always aches, even with just getting out of bed in the morning. Luckily my spirits

are still high, so I'm not letting it get me down. But I'm ready for this whole "feeling good" thing to take effect any day now!!

March 24, 2014 Facebook
My kidney doc says I need to stop being a hermit and be more social. That could be why I'm so tired all the time. My body has gotten used to going to work and sleeping, and nothing else, so now all my body wants to do is sleep. Getting out could make me feel better and more energetic. SO, who wants to make plans?? (And DON'T let me cancel.)

March 25, 2014 Facebook
Well, the rest of this week is going to be fun. Tomorrow to the eye doc to get the next round of shots in my eyeballs, and Thursday to the dentist to get a cavity filled. Yay! (said no one ever).

March 31, 2014 Email
FB posts
Dad to Krystin:
    Krystin, a neutral observer looking at your recent FB posts might conclude that you aren't a competent adult and you need to be in a supervised care facility. You hint that you can't manage your money and you indicate you can't manage a decent diet. The latter in particular shouldn't be different from managing your insulin: you do what you need to. Stop at Lunds x2 per week and get small amounts of good food and prepare it. You just have to start preparing meals for yourself.

Krystin to dad:
    I've been trying to tell you I need extra help. Maybe I DO need a supervised care facility. It's easy to say "go to the grocery store and buy healthy food and cook it." Yes, I know that. I know what I need to do. It's DOING it that I can't do. I literally do not have the energy to do it. My body is too weak to run errands. I force myself to go to work because I can't lose my job, but I have to get up earlier these days because it takes me longer to get ready. I have to keep sitting down to catch my breath, let my blood pressure return to normal, and for my body to stop aching. That's how hard it is. Everything I do, I have to take breaks. The reason I'm able to go to work is because I know that all I have to do is get there. Then most of the day I'm just sitting,

working on the computer. My body can handle that. Then at the end of the day, all I have to do is get home, and there is my couch. By then, I'm completely exhausted from the day and just want to sleep. I know what I need to do, but to do it, I need to feel better. But to feel better, I need to do it, and I can't do it without feeling better. It's a vicious cycle. I have discussed this with coordinator Pat and Dr. Ibrahim, and we are figuring something out.

Dad to Krystin:
As long as you're working on figuring something out, that's good.
I'm not sure, however, I'd make myself look incompetent with FB posts. There are some things better kept to yourself and your medical folks (and perhaps your parents, where you think it's appropriate).

Dad to Krystin:
I wonder if there are places to live for people who face various kinds of disabilities/difficulties. We know about senior living places, but you want one that's for anybody, not old folks. An apartment, but has meals, etc.
The problem with such places (at least for seniors) is that they are more expensive than you can afford. The senior places tend to run about $2K per month MINIMUM.

Krystin to dad:
I talked to coordinator Pat. Both she and Dr. Ibrahim think it's depression. I've been on an antidepressant for years, and Dr. Ibrahim even doubled my dose last week (although I know it takes a couple weeks at the earliest to have new effects). I don't FEEL depressed. My mood has been stable, I don't have any thoughts about hurting myself, I don't feel down about life (I actually have a lot of things I'm looking forward to and want to do), but they are pretty sure that's it. I told Pat that, and she's going to talk to Dr. I again and get back to me. In the meantime, I dunno. Deal with it I guess? I don't want to "deal with this" on my own for even another day, but whatever I have to do, I'll manage. This is just frustrating. :-/

April 14, 2014 Blog
So far so good
So, it has been a little over a month since I posted last, but that's because I really don't have much to update you on. I haven't had any

procedures or major illnesses or reasons to go to the hospital (yay!), so it's mostly just been me going along with my daily business.

As far as a pancreas goes, I got one call a couple weeks ago that I was strong enough to turn down (it wasn't an 'excellent' match; only 'good'), and a few weeks ago my name came up on the list, but Dr. Kandaswamy (surgeon) passed it up and didn't even call me (he told me this at my appointment with him last week). It must have been one of his fellows who looked at the one when I was called, and not Dr. Kandaswamy, because I'm guessing if Dr. K had looked at the pancreas first, I wouldn't have been called then, either. I like the idea of Dr. K looking at the pancreas first, because if HE says to give me a call, then I feel more confident about any decision I make to say yes. At least look at the bright side: I've only been active on the list again for less than 2 months, and my name has already come up twice! So perhaps it won't be long until a perfect match comes along. *Fingers crossed.

Last Friday I had my regular appointment with Dr. Saaed (endocrinologist, aka diabetes doc). We did an A1c blood test. For those of you unfamiliar with what an A1c test is, it's a simple test that only requires a poke of the finger and a few drops of blood. Put simply, it measures the average concentration of glucose in my blood over a prolonged period of time. Diabetics usually get their A1c level tested every 3 months. The higher the concentration of glucose in the blood, the higher the A1c level will be (which is bad). The ideal range for diabetics is in the low 7 range for an A1c. A non-diabetic would probably average around 6.5. Here is a handy-dandy chart to help give you an idea:

A1C Level	Average self-test glucose numbers (plasma)
12	345
11	310
10	275
9	240
8	205
7	170
6	135

As you can see, and like I said before, the higher the blood sugars run, the higher the A1c level will be. Back when I was in high school, I think around junior year, my A1c level was 17. Yikes. If a 12 means blood sugars are running consistently at 345, imagine what my blood sugars were running at consistently to result in an A1c of 17. Over 600. All the time. Not good at all. But, I have a kidney transplant to remind me of that.

Anyway, right after my kidney transplant, my A1c was around 12. However, after my transplant, that's when I realized how truly important it was to take care of my diabetes, so that I didn't lose my new kidney. I started seeing Dr. Saeed on a weekly basis. Over the next few months we did a lot of adjusting to my insulin, but it was very helpful to see him weekly. As a way to really help me get all 4 blood tests in each day, we even came up with a plan that I would text my dad my blood sugar number, so that he knew I did it. My dad knew my blood test schedule, which was the same every day: 8:30, noon, 5:30, and 9. If it got to be too long after that time and I hadn't texted him a number, he would text me and ask what it was. If I had done it but just forgot to tell him, I would respond and tell him what it was. If I had forgot to do the test altogether, I did the test right then and texted him the result. It worked really well. It was a great way to help hold me accountable for getting all my tests in. If I can see what my blood sugars are, I can better control them, by giving myself extra insulin to bring down a high number, and to help Dr. Saeed and me figure out how much insulin my pump should be giving me during the day, and at night while I sleep.

Slowly, my numbers began getting better and better. There were still high ones, don't get me wrong, but they weren't ALL high anymore. And by "high" I mean anything over 250. Ideally, blood sugars should run between 80-120, but for now, for me, we are happy with numbers under 200. When we did an A1c test in December of last year, it was down from 12 to 10.1! Almost 2 whole points. When we tested it again in February, it had come down to 9.2. Progress! And just last week, so beginning of April, we did it again, and . . . 8.3!!! I was so so happy, and Dr. Saeed was so proud of me. We decided to spread our appointments out to every 2 weeks, and try that for a while, and if things continue to improve, we can spread it out to once a month. He says if I keep up the good work, in a couple months when we test my A1c again, it will be down in the 7 range. Yay! Then all I'll need to do is maintain. Dr. Saeed said "once you get there, then you don't have to do anything else." I jokingly said, "I don't have to do diabetes anymore??" We laughed, both knowing that he meant maintain, not stop doing everything completely. Haha. Maybe you had to be there?

I am feeling very happy now. It feels really good to see results. I still get frustrated when I see a high number on my test machine, especially knowing that I had done everything right at the previous test/meal, but then I see my A1c number coming down and I know that on the whole I am doing a great job. Go me! I am still texting my dad, when I remember to. I don't text him all my numbers, but I am still getting all my tests in. I still have some high numbers, but there will always be high numbers. Even for the perfect diabetic (of which I'm pretty sure doesn't even exist), sometimes the body does stuff in there that can't be controlled, and a high number will pop up, and that's OK. My kidney is happy, I'm happy, my doctors are happy - we're all happy! And that hasn't happened in a very, very long time.

That's all I got. Bye for now! Current Mood: jubilant

Chapter 12

Hospital Visits and Another Transplant

April 24, 2014 Facebook
I decided today that I need to stop looking back at my mistakes and start looking forward. When I'm having a procedure, hospitalized, or getting a shot in my eyeballs, instead of telling myself "You brought this on yourself Krystin, this is your fault, you deserve this pain," I'm going to tell myself "I'm doing this so that I can get better. I'm doing this so that I can finish my book. So that I can do all those volunteer things I want to do. So I can travel the world. So I can become a spokesperson for young, struggling diabetics." No more beating myself up for my past. Time to move forward!

April 30, 2014 Blog
The good, the bad, and the teeth
 I have a few updates for you this time. I'll start with the bad, so that it can only get better from there.
 I have to have another biopsy of my kidney this Friday. Once again, I have to be at the specialty clinic at 7am, and will be there until mid-afternoon. I am doing this because my Creatinine level has been increasing over the last month. Creatinine measures how hard my kidney is working. I'm not sure how it's measured, but the range for transplant patients is .50-1.04. Since transplant, mine has always been in the .60 range. Over the last month, it has slowly been creeping up. 2 weeks ago when I had my labs drawn, it was 1.06. Only slightly elevated, but something to closely monitor. Today when I had my labs drawn, it was up to 1.24. Almost double what I have been running since transplant. Which means my kidney is working very hard in there, and we don't know why. So we're gonna go in and try and find out. We don't want the kidney working this hard, because it could OVER work itself, and that would be like kidney suicide. We don't need my kidney dying because it was trying to be too awesome at its job. We will need to find a way to tell it to CALM DOWN, it was already doing a great job, it doesn't have to further prove itself to anyone. At least this time I know what to expect, and I know that I won't feel a thing, so I'm not nervous. Actually, I'm more anxious to find out what's going on. Fingers crossed it's not too bad.

The good news: Remember when I had the first biopsy, because I had all those thousands of antibodies that were making us nervous, but turns out they were just hanging out in there having a big family reunion? Well my latest labs show that the party has ended! I no longer have any stage 2 antibodies, and the stage 1 antibodies that I had that were in the 3,000 range, has dropped down to the 1,000 range. So, that's good. Which is why we need to do anyone biopsy. Since this time we know it's not the antibodies throwing a rager in there, what IS it?

The next bit, which I also think of as good news: I'm getting new teeth. Yes, you heard that right. I'm getting crowns put on all my upper teeth. Over the years, between the diabetes, the gastroparesis (which was causing me to throw up almost every day, if you remember), and a number of other health issues, my teeth have pretty much deteriorated. Due to all the throwing up I did (having that gastric pacer put in my stomach has pretty much ceased that problem), the enamel is completely gone on the inside of my upper teeth, they are so discolored and eroded, and have been worn down into stubs. I have almost no teeth left on top; except my molars in back, those are doing alright, but will still need crowns. The plan to fix all this is very extensive, and will take months, but the end result will be amazing. The first step is gum lengthening. This is where they will go in (my mouth) and cut the gums so that they can pull/raise them up, so that more of my teeth are exposed. Luckily, I have long teeth with deep roots, so they can pull the gums up without exposing any roots, which made the dental surgeon think that over time my gums have just grown down over my teeth. They need to expose more teeth because they can't put crowns on them the way they are. My teeth are currently too short, so there's not enough tooth to attach a crown TO. They would just fall off.

After that procedure, it will need a few weeks to heal. Hello applesauce diet. Once my gums have healed, the dentistry lab will create a temporary, test insert that I can pop on and off my teeth. It will not be individual crowns that are put on each tooth - they will make one long composite to fit over 16 teeth, which is how many I have on top. So they will make a pretend one that I will wear for at least a month. To make room in my mouth for more tooth, my jaw will need to be very, very slightly opened up. Wearing the temporary insert, we will be able to tell if my jaw gets adjusted to it and can handle it. If I have constant headaches and jaw pain, we know that it won't work. If, after a month or so, everything is good and I like the way it looks and feels, the lab will make the permanent composite, which will be surgically inserted over my current teeth and attached to them and my gums. Voila, new teeth.

You're probably wondering how much this will all cost me, aren't you? Well, for everything I mentioned, then including the time and labor, it's a menial [she probably meant something like "measly"] $26,000. My dental insurance has a deductible of $1500. So what we did was submit everything to my health insurance instead, hoping that health insurance will cover it. Especially all these teeth issues are due to medical issues. If my health insurance denies it, I can appeal it with a note from my doctor saying that this needs to be done because of health issues, and they should reconsider. This really DOES need to be done, if not now then some point in my life, because, especially with my enamel gone, my teeth will only continue to get worse. So this needs to be done sooner rather than later. The surgeon I talked to says that if insurance denies it completely, we can do it in stages, we don't have to do it all at once. Well, the gum lengthening alone will be $500. I just have to see what insurance decides first. I have a tentative appointment set up for May 22 for the gum lengthening procedure. Insurance has another couple weeks to decide if they'll cover it. The procedure sounds scary, but they do it all under Novocaine. No knocking me out or anything. Go home same day. I'll have a special diet to follow, but only until I feel comfortable enough to move back to a normal diet.

This is very exciting for me. I have been very self-conscious about my teeth for many years, and I knew that they were being ruined from all my health issues. I don't know why it took me so long to take action to get them fixed. Well, at least I'm doing something now, right?

Last week when I was sitting with my therapist, we were talking about how I feel about needles and what I can do to help calm myself down when I have to go in for a procedure where I know I'll have to get an IV, or any kind of needle poked into me. She asked me what I do right now, or what's going through my head. We used the example of when I have to have dental work done and they have to stick a needle in my gums to give me Novocaine. I told her that I just keep telling myself, in my head, "This is your fault Krystin. You brought this on yourself. You deserve this pain." She was appalled that that's how I get through it. She asked me what would happen if I DIDN'T tell myself that. Good question. I told her then I would probably think the same thing I thought before I learned of my kidney failure. In years past I used to clench and ask myself, "why is this happening to me? What did I do to deserve this pain?" So I just swapped one negative justification for another.

Here's the thing about why I tell myself what I do, now. All the time I was growing up, my friends, family, and doctors would constantly remind me that I needed to take better care of my diabetes, or I would face complications down the road. I would always say yeah yeah, I know. I have plenty of time to turn things around prevent complications. I'll be fine, it won't happen to me. Oh look, it has. Neuropathy in my feet, retinopathy in my eyes, digestive problems, damaged teeth, kidney failure and transplant, and now soon to receive a pancreas transplant. I keep waiting for everyone to tell me "I told you so." Nobody has said it out loud, but I'm convinced it's what everyone is thinking. Which is why I keep telling myself this is my fault. I deserve this, I brought it on myself. I mean, if you think about it, that's all true. And everyone knows it. So why won't anyone say it? I TOLD YOU SO KRYSTIN. I tell myself, and I tell other people, that this is all my fault, so that everyone can see that I know I made a mistake. So that if I say it out loud, they don't have to. I made a mistake. A BIG mistake. A mistake that I drew out for over a decade. And now I'm facing the consequences and the complications, just like they all said.

BUT, I have decided that I need to stop that train of thought. It's not healthy. I need to stop looking back at my mistakes, and start looking forward. I should not scold myself, but be proud of myself for being so active in my health and doing everything I can to make it better. Obviously I've learned from my mistakes, and now I'm saying OK, well that happened, so what can I do now to make it better, or to prevent it from getting worse? I had a kidney transplant. I'm getting shots in my eyeballs to prevent further nerve damage that could make me go blind. I'm having all that dental work done so I don't lose all my teeth by age 35. I'm eating healthier so that I can regain my strength and stamina. I'm doing all these things not because I have to, and not because it's punishment for my mistakes. I'm doing it so that I can LIVE again. So that I can get back into my writing and finish my book. So that I can be a spokesperson for the American Diabetes Association and/or The National Kidney Foundation. So that I can travel more of the world. So I can go back to school and get my Masters degree. So that I can be active and go biking and kayaking and wall climbing and

Zumba. So that I can be the ME that I want to be. I have so many things I want to do, so many places I want to go. I hate sitting in my apartment all the time and sleeping, but I just don't have the energy to do anything else. Yet. I will get there. I WILL. I have such a zest for life, I get so excited just thinking about all the things I want to do. I just have to keep working hard, and keep positive.

So now, when I'm sitting in that chair at the eye doctor, and he's coming at me with that numbing needle, I will tell myself "you deserve this Krystin. You deserve this TREATMENT. It's not a punishment. It's so that you can SEE the world." I don't mean to sound like a motivational speaker, but in a way, I am my own motivational speaker. So, no more looking back. Here's to the future.

That's all I got. Today marks 2 years at my job. Woohoo! I can't believe how quickly the time here has passed. But in a good way. Bye for now!

May 5, 2014 Email
Rejection
Krystin to mom, dad:

The rejection in my kidney is called B1 cellular rejection. It's not because of anything I did or didn't do over the last 11 months. It's because I've been so immunosuppressed, especially back in November when I had all those viruses. That, plus diabetes is a natural immunosuppressant as well. So I just need to be extra monitored. So this is NOT my fault, and it's not because of my cats (which some people were questioning). Coordinator Pat came to see me and she said she has a patient who is 20 years into their transplant, and they experienced the same kind of rejection in their first year, and are now doing just fine. I will start Prednisone today, along with Valcyte, so I'll be super immunosuppressed again, but the Prednisone will crush this rejection. I will need to stay far away from sick people, which I do anyway. Then in 6 weeks they'll do another biopsy and see where we're at.

So that's the plan.

May 5, 2014 Email
Hospital
Krystin to dad, mom:

I'm being admitted to the hospital for just a day, to go an IV insulin drip. These steroids have made my blood sugars go out of control (reading HI, which means over 600) even though I've been taking tons of insulin. This is normal and I was warned this would happen. So they'll help get it under control. Will keep you updated as I know more.

May 9, 2014 Blog Written Tuesday 5/6:
Some bad, some good

    What better way to pass the time while sitting in a hospital bed than to update my blog. I got here yesterday afternoon, and thought I was only going to be here for 24 hours, but here I am on my second night. I should have known. Changes in plans are always very likely when it comes to me. Friday I had my 2nd kidney biopsy. This time it was because my Creatinine level had been increasing over the past month. This means my kidney has been working very hard in there. That first biopsy back in March was because I had all those thousands of antibodies in there. Those are all essentially gone now, so that's not the problem this time. That's the good news: no more antibodies partying it up in there and being a potential threat! The downside is that now we didn't know why it's been working so hard. The procedure was the same as the first one. No pain, just a lot of anxiety and tension knowing that a device was in my abdomen, snipping pieces of my kidney. It's amazing what they can find out, though, from just a couple samples of tissue the size of fish poop.

    The doc called me later that evening with the preliminary results. My kidney is showing cell rejection, which means my immune system is starting to reject the kidney. BUT, that doesn't mean total rejection, don't worry. He said that I would need 3 days of IV steroid infusions, then would start on oral Prednisone. I am also starting back on Valcyte, which is another immunosuppressant. So between the infusions and the Prednisone and the Valcyte, I'm going to be very immunosuppressed, but I'm gonna kick this rejection in the buttocks. My coordinator Pat said she has a patient who is 20 years into his kidney transplant, and he had the same kind of cell rejection within his first year, and now he's doing great. So I'm not out of the woods, but the odds are on my side, especially since we caught this early. Pat said it is VERY important to stay away from sick people and heavily crowded places! Again. Didn't I have to do that one time before, too? Saturday and Sunday I went into the infusion clinic at the U for my whopping dose of steroids. On Saturday it took 3 different nurses 6 tries to get an IV in. They never believe me when I say I'm a hard poke! The last nurse finally got it - in my pointer finger. Ouch, ouch,

ouch. At least the infusion only lasted half an hour. On Sunday I stopped in the hospital first and had the IV team put in an IV. Got it first try, no problem. And not in my hand. That one I left in overnight, so I already had it in for my 3rd and final infusion Monday morning. I was going to go right to work from the clinic, but does anything ever go the way it's planned with me and doctors? The steroids made my blood sugars skyrocket, like over 600, and I couldn't get them down, even with all the insulin I was doing.

So my diabetes doc decided to have me admitted to a hospital floor for 24 hours, on an insulin IV drip, to get my blood sugars under control. I said fine, I kinda had an inkling that would happen. I got to go home first, to get some stuff and make sure my kitties had everything they need. Around 1 I went back to the hospital and up to my favorite unit, 7A. The steroids make me so hungry, so I ordered a late lunch right away. Good thing I still had that IV in, so I didn't have to get poked again! Between my book, my iPad, and texting on my phone, I kept myself occupied. I got very little sleep, because they had to test my blood sugar level every hour, and my roomie has her tv on all the time, day and night, even when she's sleeping. You better believe that tonight I'm gonna complain to her nurse. Plus she moans in her sleep. I have never in my life gotten a quiet, low maintenance roomie. Why can't they all just be like me??

My blood sugars came down and were perfect all through the night. I couldn't see any reason why I wouldn't be able to go home. HA! My diabetes doc then decided to keep me here another day/night. I started Prednisone this morning (another steroid), and he wants to monitor me and make sure it doesn't make my blood sugars spike again, like the infusions did. Not part of my game plan, but again, nothing surprises me these days. I don't let it rain on my parade. I put on my rain boots and go jumping in the puddles! I know this is for the best. No way in hell am I going to make rejection easy for this kidney. If I have to take Prednisone and get all puffy like a marshmallow, then that's what I'll do. So, back to reading my book and watching my eaglet baby prepare to fly on the Berry College eagle cam. And maybe take a nap. And dinner just arrived! Winning. Bye for now!

May 8, 2014 Blog

I am still in the hospital this morning, but the plan is to discharge me today. At least that's what the docs all said yesterday. Yesterday morning I was moved off the IV insulin drip and onto my own insulin pump. I don't know why they didn't do that on Tuesday, but whatever. Since my blood sugars were still jumping around a little, I had to stay another day so they could see how my blood sugars do on my pump, and find a good setting to send me home with, so that I don't have to come back in a day or so with high blood sugars again. Makes sense, but I was very frustrated when they told me I had to stay again. I am so bored, and my roommate is probably one of the most annoying I've ever had. She moans and groans in her sleep with every breath, and her tv is on ALL the time, as well as her overhead light. Yup, even when she's sleeping. She must have caught on yesterday to my frustration, because last night she turned the tv volume down. And turned her light off for about half the night. Yesterday late morning I wrote this reminder on my patient board:

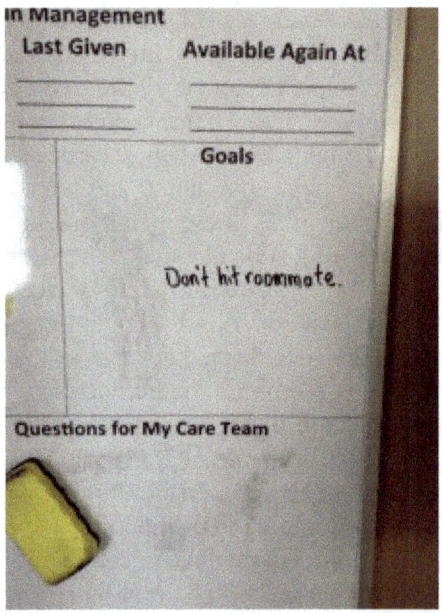

It was only up there for a little bit, before my nurse saw it and erased it. She did laugh though. She has been my day nurse every day, so she understands how I feel. My roommate never saw the note, so I didn't have to sleep with one eye open. I've gotten a lot of reading done and looked at a lot of kitty pictures online. I am beyond ready to go home. I'm going to take a long, quiet nap and then get my kitties from my mom's house. Now it's time for my cinnamon roll breakfast.

May 9, 2014 Blog

I'm back at work today and feeling great. I was discharged yesterday shortly after lunch. I was so glad to see my kitties and bring them home. This morning I had an appointment with my endocrinologist (diabetes doc) and things are looking good. We're going to stay in touch over the weekend and next week, and adjust my insulin doses as needed, as I take lower doses of Prednisone.

So that was my adventure for the week. I'm glad it's over. I feel much less irritable and like hitting people now that I'm out of the hospital. I'm pretty sure it was my roommate and lack of sleep because of her that was making me so moody. I felt like a new, happy person today! I hope everyone has a good weekend. Bye for now.

May 9, 2014 Facebook

So. Much. ENERGY. I know it's due to the Prednisone, but I feel AMAZING.

May 19, 2014 Facebook

I learned today that I "get" to be on Prednisone indefinitely, which means you're just going to have to love me as the pudgy-faced Krystin that I am.
{^-^}

May 28, 2014 Facebook

Dr. Ibrahim said that to prevent the Prednisone making my face real pudgy, I need to maintain a healthy lifestyle through diet and being active. He obviously doesn't know that I am the founder of the Minnesota chapter of Advocates for Laziness. Looks like pudgy face it is.

June 9, 2014 Facebook

Even though I will never stop writing, and will publish a number of books at some point, after thinking about it for a long time I decided that I would like to be a kidney transplant coordinator. I've been there, done that, seen it all. I would be good at it, and it would feel very fulfilling for me. I feel the job calling to me!

June 10, 2014 Facebook
Since I already have my bachelor's degree in a non-nursing field (history), I don't have to start over and get another undergrad degree! I can go right into the Master of Nursing program. Woo!

June 10, 2014 Email
nursing?
Dad to Krystin:
    You're going to go back to school to be an RN? My goodness, that will mean taking a lot of basic science courses! And what do your friends at SPA think of that, since you're saying you're bailing out on them? :-)

Krystin to dad:
    I'm not bailing out on them any time soon! I know it's a lot of science, and I was thinking about it last night, and I would just have to keep thinking about the end goal. How much it will be worth it when I'm helping others to save their life. I love working for SPA, but I've been drawn to the medical field my whole life. Since I can remember I've always told people that if I had my dream job (aside from writing), I would be an EMT. Or a nurse in the ICU/CCU. And if I can get in here and start taking nursing classes, I get a huge tuition break. Working in the medical field, like I said, is something that I've wanted ever since I was little, but in high school I turned away from it when I learned how much science is required. But that dream hasn't died! I think I'm finally ready to face it!

Dad to Krystin:
    You should certainly go for it if you think you can. But even with the tuition break for employees, it will be expensive--you still get to pay 25%. And you have to get admitted to SON.
    That's going to be a lot of biology and chemistry. . . .
    I dunno. GA [Grant Administrator in SPA] and up sounds like a more plausible path. Maybe keep working on your SPA career while you contemplate, or even pursue, nursing/a medical field?

June 19, 2014 Facebook
So. Tired. Can hardly keep my eyes open at work. I sure will be glad to be off the 2nd immunosuppressant by the middle of next week, so that EBV virus that's peeking its head around the corner can get

punched in the face, back into hiding. I want my energy back! Come out, come out, wherever you are. . . .

June 30, 2014 Text
Gary to Pat: You heard from K at all today? I emailed, called, and texted, nothing. I have a question for her.
Pat: I've not. I emailed her earlier too but no reply.
Dad to Krystin: Ok. I've been worried about you, and contacted Anjeanette, too. You OK?
Krystin: Am home. Been throwing up this morning.
Dad: Oh, great. Hope you feel better.
Gary to Pat: Have now heard. She sick, but in touch.
Pat: She threw up at my house last night after her party but I assumed it was the cake. She said it was too rich.
Gary: Still throwing up, it seems.
Pat: That's never good.

July 1, 2014 Text
Krystin to dad: I don't [feel better]. May need go hospital. Still puking.
Krystin: I need help.
Krystin: Need go to ER.
Dad: Need me pick you up?
Krystin: Blacked out and fell down when stood up. Still can't hold anything down.
Krystin: Yes. And need you to come in to help me.
Dad: I was just getting ready to leave. Will be over shortly.
Gary to Pat, Kathy: Have K at ER. Very weak.
Kathy: You going to stay there with her for a while?
Gary: Don't know yet. Probably a bit.
(later) Dad to Krystin: How you?
Krystin: Much better. Just got up to unit 6B. Had lots of saline and insulin drip.
Dad: I come by for a bit.
(later) Dad: Bored yet? Staying on 6B?
Krystin: As far as I know, I'm staying here. Just got dinner. Broth, jello, and Crystal Light. Also just FINALLY got my magic mouthwash.
Dad: Sounds appetizing :-(Feeling better?
Krystin: Yes, feeling much better. If you are going to stop by tomorrow morning, might you be able to bring me some pump

supplies from my apt? I grabbed my supply bag this morning, but didn't check to see if supplies were in it! Well, they aren't, and I'll need them tomorrow. I can tell you where they are.

July 8, 2014 Blog
Meh

Last week I was in the hospital overnight (Tues.-Weds.) with an early stage of DKA (diabetic ketoacidosis). I'm sure most of you know what that is by now, but if not, here's a very brief summary of DKA: Insulin breaks down the sugars in the blood. Without enough insulin, the body cannot absorb glucose (sugar), and starts burning fatty acids and producing ketones, which is acidic. This, therefore, turns the blood acidic, and starts poisoning the body. Slowly, organs start shutting down, and, if not treated, can be fatal. The doctors say I was in the early stages of DKA, but I think I was in the middle. I had already experienced the vomiting (24 straight hours of it, which is the body trying to rid the stomach of anything in it before shutting it down) by the time I got to the hospital Tuesday morning. I only threw up twice in the ER, and there wasn't even much, er, substance to it. I had extreme thirst, dehydration, and deep breathing (it felt like I was forcing myself to inhale and exhale). If I had reached the end stage, my speech would be mumbled, I would be seeing black spots if I opened my eyes, and all I would want to do is sleep, which indicates the body shutting down and going into a coma.

I could talk, but didn't want to. I couldn't walk on my own. Before going to the hospital, my dad had to come into my apartment and help me out to the van. Even in that short distance, I had to stop 3 times to sit down and rest, because I felt like I was going to pass out. Once at the ER, I had him go in and get a wheelchair, bring it back out to the van, and wheel me in. The ONLY good thing about DKA? It's so imperative to get insulin and fluids started via IV that there's no waiting. My dad checked me in and they brought me back right away. Since I was so dehydrated, it was SO hard to get an IV started. The nurse had to start a tiny one in my hand, and then once I was got a little hydrated, they inserted a larger, more comfortable one in my lower wrist. My body was shaking, and I still felt nauseous, so they gave me a dose of my favorite pain-killer, Dilaudid, which immediately makes the nausea go away and the shaking stop. It also made me sleepy and relaxed, so even though I didn't go to sleep, I was able to close my eyes and rest for a little bit. I was in the ER for a couple hours I think, before being brought up to unit 6B, which is the floor that transplant patients go to for a day right after transplant before going up to 7A for recovery. It's like the in-between unit. I was there for a day after kidney transplant, but that day is pretty hazy, so I don't really remember it. Luckily things stabilized quickly and I only had to stay overnight.

    I should have gone to the hospital Sunday night, when I threw up the first time. I thought maybe it was something I ate. This was supported by the fact that one of my co-workers, who had the same dinner I did Sunday night, went home from work early on Monday after getting sick. So I was convinced I just had food poisoning and had to let it run its course. I don't know much about food poisoning, but by Tuesday morning, when I was STILL throwing up 24 hours after it started, I knew it wasn't just food poisoning. That's when I texted my dad and told him I needed help, and needed to go to the ER. Luckily he hadn't left for work yet, and came and picked me up.

    While in the hospital, I became very disappointed in myself, and even felt a little depressed and discouraged. This is the first time that my spirit has cracked a little. I have been so strong through all of this over the past year, through one procedure and hospitalization after another, but even the Great Wall of China is not without cracks. I'm not sure why this particular hospital stint has made me feel discouraged. Maybe it's because I was doing so well. I had been working so hard with my endocrinologist, and had even gone 2 weeks at work without any days off. Then I fall off the bandwagon with my blood sugar testing for a little while, and this happens. After being in the hospital with DKA in Paris in spring of 2006, I promised myself I would never let it happen again, which is one of the main reasons I went on the insulin pump. Well, I slipped, and it happened again. And you could say "I let it" happen because I know how it happened. It's my fault. I didn't do what I know I'm supposed to do. I wasn't monitoring my blood sugar levels close enough to know that they were running high. What did I expect? If I had tested my blood sugar that Sunday night and seen that it was high, and covered it with insulin, I probably could've avoided the whole situation.

    I had an image of everyone I know just shaking their heads and saying "well, it was only a matter of time."

    I had a jumble of thoughts while I was in the hospital, the main one being that I fear this is all I'm going to be known for in life: hospitalizations. Have I already done too much damage to my body, that one ailment after another is what I'm destined for until the day I die? How can I accomplish anything in life if I keep having these setbacks? It seems like things just start to get better, and then my body says "just kidding" and has a good laugh at me and finds something to go wrong. In 4 generations, will they be saying "Oh yeah, aunt Krystin, she was the one with health issues her whole life. Never accomplished much, dear thing, because she couldn't take care of herself well enough." That's not who I am. I fear that these health issues are defining me, that they are becoming ME, becoming who I AM. Krystin the sick one. Krystin who can't take care of herself. Not Krystin the author, Krystin the world traveler, Krystin the volunteer and animal rescuer, Krystin the transplant coordinator. Who am I? I don't even know anymore.

There are so many things I want to do, so many things I want to BE, and even though I'm only 29, I already feel like I'm running out of time.

I realize that some of the things that have happened are out of my control. Back in November when I had all those viruses, that wasn't my fault. It's because I was so immunosuppressed. That I couldn't help. But other hospitalizations I could've prevented, if only I'd eaten better, drank enough water each day, monitored my blood sugars better, etc. etc.

After my great performance review at work, I felt a lot better about how much I've been out of work, knowing that I work hard when I'm there, and that people recognize and acknowledge that, and appreciate everything I do. They don't notice when I'm gone. They notice when I'm there, and how hard I work and what good, efficient work I do. Nobody has gone to my supervisor and asked why I'm gone all the time. They go to him and ask if I'm available to help with this or that, or take on this or that new task. I felt very complimented, and happy after hearing all this from my supervisor. It's like I had a whole new wave of confidence in my performance.

Now, my confidence about work is wavering again. I once again feel like I'm letting my co-workers down. Do I even deserve a job? Everyone keeps telling me not to worry about it, but everything has a limit, and how close am I to that limit at work before they throw up their hands and say "we can't do this anymore" and decide to replace me with someone who doesn't have chronic health issues? My supervisor keeps saying "we want to get you better." Yeah, so I can finally start being at work on a regular basis. I'm convinced that if I went back in time to the day I interviewed for the job, if I had been able to predict the future and told them "oh by the way, I'll be having a kidney transplant next year, and will be in and out of the office a LOT for numerous health reasons, so don't plan to rely on me too much," I never would've been hired.

Even after pancreas transplant, that will require a lot of recovery and appointments too, just like after kidney transplant. Will I have another year just like the last, with more hospitalizations? Will it be years before I can prove to my office that I'm the reliable, dependable worker that I know I am? When absences aren't automatically expected of me. I certainly can't move up the ladder during all this. My next goal at work is to be a grant administrator, but if things continue like this for another number of years, I'd never get hired into a GA position. It's a depressing thought.

Admittedly, when I'm out for extended periods of time, I do stay in touch and keep up on work email, and work on work stuff from home. Pretty much everything we do here in my office is time sensitive, so when I'm out, I do my best to stay caught up and get things done by submission time or deadline time, instead of relying on other co-workers to cover my work, which should definitely show my office that I'm committed to my job.

I'm sorry this was not a happy post. I needed to get this all out, because it's what's heaviest on my mind these days. I just want it all to be over. I am still happy in life, do not worry about that. I still have dreams and goals. I have not lost that, I just don't feel as optimistic about it as I used to, but I believe this is only temporary. I will get my spirit back.

That's all I got for now. I will find out this week if I finally get to be reactivated on the pancreas waiting list. I've been on hold now for a couple months, since my kidney rejection situation. Let's hope this time's the charm and it's the LAST time I'll have to be reactivated. Fingers crossed I get a pancreas by fall!

Bye for now.

July 9, 2014 Text
Krystin to dad: 309 BG this morn. Oops.
Dad: Oops is right. Hope you get it fixed!
Krystin: 148 at lunch. Btw, I'm sending you BGs again, k?

July 9, 2014 Facebook
These days, when people have a colonoscopy, you know it's recorded so it can be reviewed later by the docs. Can you ask to get a copy of it? Maybe it's just me, but I think it would be interesting to watch your very own Discovery Channel special...

July 13, 2014 Facebook
When I have the "I feel good today" days, I really cherish them. Today, I feel good! The optimist in me knows that eventually, most days will be feel good days. If you feel good today, too, make it worth it! I know I am! ^_^

July 17, 2014 Text
Krystin to dad: BG 111 this morn! Woohoo! Yesterday very consistent: 150, 151, 168, 139. :-)
Dad: Great!

July 21, 2014 Emails
EBV
Krystin to dad, Kathy:
From Wikipedia:
Most people become infected with EBV and gain adaptive immunity. In the United States, about half of all five-year-old children and 90 to 95 percent of adults have evidence of previous infection. [8]Infants become susceptible to EBV as soon as maternal antibody protection disappears. Many children become infected with EBV, and these infections usually cause no symptoms or are indistinguishable from the other mild, brief illnesses of childhood. In the United States and other developed countries, many people are not infected with EBV in their childhood years. When infection with EBV occurs during adolescence, it causes infectious mononucleosis 35 to 50 percent of the time.

Also, to answer a question you (dad) asked me in a text: mono is caused by the EBV virus. So EBV is like the mother virus, and mono (along with other sub-infectious diseases) are children of EBV. Hmm, I wonder if that means I could get other kinds of infections since I have the EBV virus. I also wonder if that means I can't kiss anyone for the rest of my life without warning them that they might get mono. Guess that's something to ask Dr. Young. Maybe if it's not active, it's not transmittable (is that the right word?). Transferable? Maybe that's the word I'm thinking of.

No word yet from coordinator Pat, but it's only 9:30, so I'll give her a bit longer to let me know about the infusion.

p.s. Let's assume that when I say 'Pat' you know that means coordinator Pat. Obviously if it were mom, I'd say mom. :)

Krystin to dad, Kathy:
Another little bit I just read:
Symptoms most often disappear after about 2–3 weeks. However, fatigue and a general feeling of being unwell (malaise) may sometimes last for months. Fatigue lasts more than one month in an estimated 9–22% of cases. In cases where fatigue lingers, it generally passes spontaneously within 2 years.

Oh, good. 2 years. Fantastic.

Dad to Krystin:
So what exactly are you getting for treatment? Your mother mentioned chemo in an email to me--is that what you're getting?

Krystin to dad:
Yes, the infusion that I'll be getting is a chemo medicine. But I'm only getting one dose. Since I don't have cancer, only one dose is needed to knock out the lymph nodes that are producing EBV. So then maybe I WON'T feel lingering fatigue after it's knocked out. Fingers crossed.

Dad to Krystin:
I think your mother is a little concerned about chemo, so would you keep her posted as well?

Krystin to dad:
Yes, I have been keeping in touch with her, too.
Krystin to dad, pat, Kathy:
OK, I don't think Pat has heard back from insurance yet, but I did get some more information from her. A lot of the medications they use to treat many conditions are also used to treat cancer, so this is normal for transplant patients (well, who are dealing with EBV of course). There are inherent risks with any medication such as this. I will require

premedication with IV Benadryl and steroids, and I will need a driver that day. I should plan to be in the clinic 5-6 hours, because sometimes they have to run it in really slow. I told her I'm allergic to Benadryl, but that the last time I had it was when I was 2, so maybe I've outgrown it? I joked and said well, if that's what they HAVE to give me, at least I'll be in a clinic and near a hospital! I'm really hoping this happens this week. If I'm getting some steroids along with it, maybe that means I'll feel good for a couple days after . . .

Krystin to all 3:
I sure will be glad when this is all over. I'm exhausted, not just physically, but emotionally, too! :-/

Pat to all 3:
OK it's fine to trust your doctors and all but tell them AGAIN AND AGAIN about your Benadryl allergy. No, I don't think it's something you grow out of. And this time it's not being ingested and filtered through your stomach. Nope. . . they're doin it straight line into your bloodstream. Maybe it's ok but man oh man I'd sure be staying on top of that one.

Krystin to all 3:
Update: the reason the docs want to give me this medication is not listed among the labeled uses for the drug, meaning insurance didn't initially agree to cover it. Dr. Ibrahim and/or Young are in the midst of writing a letter of "medical necessity" to get the insurance company to consider paying for it. It's not cheap, and there's a 50/50 chance that the insurance company will not authorize payment for it. At that point, someone will talk to be about what it might cost out-of-pocket, at which point I would then either decide to go with it or say no way. If insurance doesn't pay for it, and I can't afford it, then we go back to the drawing board. So I'm pretty positive, now, that this won't be happening in the next couple days. I may not be going to the BASH this weekend . . .

Dad to Krystin:
Ugh. I trust you'll keep us all posted.
LY

Krystin to dad:

Absolutely. I did ask Pat if I could go into SIPC for an infusion of steroids/fluids to get me through until then. I know it's a long shot, since there isn't a legitimate medical reason for just feeling crummy and not being a very functional human these days, but I'll see what she says.

July 22, 2014 Email
Gary to all 3
Krystin,

I agree completely with your mother. Be VERY wary of the benadryl. You have to be emphatic about this. You freaked out psychologically when you had it when you were little and you were hallucinating.

Krystin to dad:

I know, I told Pat, too, that I'm allergic. They are VERY thorough in the clinics and at the hospital. They all look at my chart, I always get an allergy bracelet, and before anything is done, a doctor/nurse always asks me if I have any allergies. So don't worry, I'm not going to sit back and let them inject me with anything before making sure it's not Benadryl!

Dad to Krystin:

Good. You should let your mother and Kathy know that as well. (Kathy expressed concern to me last night.)

Your one message seemed to suggest you were sort of nonchalant about it.

Krystin to all 3:

I didn't mean to be nonchalant in my email about them giving me Benadryl before my infusion. I know I joked about being near the hospital and all, but I wouldn't actually sit back and let them give it to me. Especially, as mom pointed out, it's not like I'm taking an oral dose like when I was young. This would be going right into my veins. I have told Pat that I'm allergic, and it's in my chart, which all nurses and doctors look at. They are very thorough and very adamant about knowing your allergies before doing anything. Even when I just get labs drawn, the lab techs ask me if I prefer tape or that stretchy coband stuff over the bandage. So no worries, they are all looking out for me (patients). Perhaps they could try giving me just a tiny dose and seeing if I react to it. But I doubt they would even be willing to take that risk. I'm sure there are other alternatives to Benadryl they could use!

Krystin to all 3:
    I couldn't find a very precise number, but looks like one dose of Rituxan could cost anywhere between $2,500 - $10,000 out of pocket, if insurance doesn't cover it. Yikes. F**king pharmaceutical companies.

Dad to Krystin:
    yikes.

Pat to all 3:
    Again, find out the "what ifs" if you didn't have that infusion. If the percent of benefit is small, it might not be worth pursuing.
    If insurance won't cover it, the next step is to talk to the pharmaceutical company (companies) directly. Many times they have financial help for patients who can't afford their drugs. I can help you with that part. Or Pat the Coordinator. She's maybe done this before.

Krystin to all 3:
    Pat isn't sure what the back-up plan would be. I don't think there is one right now. I got a more narrow number for cost. She said it runs between $6000-$9000. Even if the infusion is 100% effective, I can't afford to take out a loan for it, even if that's what a pharmaceutical company would offer (or some kind of monthly payment plan). I can't afford even one more monthly expense, unless I can only pay like $20 a month, in which case I'd be paying that off until I die.
    Also, I do need to see a hematologist before a letter of medical necessity can be written. Ugh. So Amy, who I think is my transplant social worker, is going to call me today. Well, this could take weeks, then. Who knows when hematology will be able to fit me in, then the letter needs to be written and submitted to insurance, then we have to wait for insurance to decide. UGH! What the hell, so I'm just supposed to sit here and wait while the virus gets stronger and stronger and does potential damage to my kidney? I even asked Pat if I could get an infusion of steroids in the meantime, but that doesn't sound like something that is a possibility right now. Great. I can't believe that in this day and age, when someone has a serious virus, we have to go

through all this nonsense before being able to do something. I hate America. I'm moving to Denmark.

Gary to all 3:
Surely Pat or Amy recognize that there is some need for alacrity here. And you should say so.

Krystin to all 3:
Surely. I also just emailed Dr. Ibrahim expressing my frustrations and asking if there's ANYTHING that can be done in the meantime, like a steroids infusion, since he would have to be the one to order it. We'll see what he says. Maybe I'll take a bus up to Canada . . .

Krystin to all 3:
My transplant social worker, Amy, called hematology today, and the docs decided I may not need to be seen in clinic - they can do it doc to doc. Hematology will then talk with Dr. Young and hopefully the letter of medical necessity will be ready to act on by tomorrow AM. Yay! Also, Dr. Ibrahim said steroid infusions are out of the question, because they actually make the virus worse. I had the infusions of steroids back in May for the rejection, not to treat EBV.
That's all I got for now. Hopefully more news tomorrow AM.

July 23, 2014 Email
Dad to Krystin:
I take it no news.

Krystin to dad:
The hematologists don't need to see me, and will write up the letter. Dunno if they have done that yet. Then they will give it to Pat and she'll submit it to insurance. So, not sure where in this process we are, and I don't wanna ask Pat because I've been bugging her enough.

July 24, 2014 Email
Dentist
Krystin to dad, Pat, Kathy:
OK, so you know all that dental work that I need done that is going to cost $26,000? Medical insurance won't cover it, even if I have a medical necessity letter. Of course this is one of those things that won't be covered, no matter what. Figures. I had an appointment in

Woodbury this morning, with the guy who would do the procedure, and I told him about insurance. He said there is another option, for a fraction of the price. Of course porcelain crowns last the longest, like 20+ years, they are just too expensive. So he said he could do resin crowns, which last about 5-10 years, but would only cost $4,250. Umm, yes please. Even though they won't last as long, in 5-10 years I'll be more financially stable, I'll have paid of my Wells Fargo loan, my car loan, and maybe even my then I'll have moved up at work and making more money (I better be after 5-10 years!). So I'd be more willing to take out a larger medical loan then. Plus, by then I'd already have the gum lengthening procedure done, and we wouldn't need to do the temporary crown because I'd already have, in my mouth, how we want the new, porcelain, permanent crown. I have the appointment for my gum lengthening procedure on Sept. 18 - mom's birthday! That's the earliest they could get me in. Then it will take a month to heal, then the Woodbury guy will start putting on the resin crowns, and that will take 4 separate appointments. So yeah. That's the new plan.

July 26, 2014 Facebook
Insurance came through for me, and I get my infusion on Monday!! You've probably never seen someone so excited to get a chemo drug. . . . Hasta la vista EBV, you've caused enough trouble, and it's time to go.

July 28, 2014 Facebook
I was given a TON of IV steroids today after my reaction to the Rituxan. I'd had an anaphylactic reaction, which is one of the most severe allergic reaction (hence the EpiPen). Now my blood sugars are through the roof (steroids do that). Taking lots of insulin and praying to the Flying Spaghetti Monster that they don't want to admit me to the hospital on an insulin drip again! Keep your fingers and toes crossed . . .

August 1, 2014 Text
Krystin to dad: Coordinator said to go to ER, so that's where I am.
Dad: Jeez. Keep me updated. You feel OK?
Krystin: Yeah, feel fine. Just hungry! They're going to talk to GI and kidney docs and see what they wanna do. Like I called it at lunch, probably an endoscopy, but it's Friday afternoon so may not be able

to. They will probably see if I can eat/drink, so they can see in person what happens. That's all I know for now.
Dad: Let me know. . . .
Krystin: Being admitted overnight. I get to run home first though. GI will do endoscopy tomorrow.
Dad: Great. Good luck. Keep me posted.

August 2, 2014 Text
Krystin to dad: Going for endoscopy now.
(later) Krystin: It was unsuccessful. They couldn't even get a baby camera down. So I have to sit here until Monday without eating or drinking anything. I am not happy.
Dad: Ugh. I am sorry. What happens Monday?
Krystin A different procedure in the OR.
Dad: Great. Can mom run over to see your cats? We leaving shortly for WI.
Krystin: Maybe. I am telling the docs that I don't want to stay here the whole time. I can sit here all day not eating, or I can be at home with my cats and not eating.
Dad: Aren't they worried you won't get nutrition and liquid? Or can you get small amounts down?
Krystin: Can't get anything down. Which is why I don't know why they're waiting until Monday. I am so angry right now.
Dad: What's up? You on IV?
Krystin: Just IV saline. Not nutrition or anything. Doc put me on liquid diet. Was able to get down and keep down broth, jello, and juice. That may be good enough to let me discharge.
As long as I can keep something down if need be if I get low, and I can.
Krystin: I agreed to stay overnight again. If I can get down some breakfast tomorrow, they will discharge me in the morning.
Dad: That sounds better than staying whole weekend!

August 2, 2014 Facebook
I am so angry right now, I hate everyone and everything. Why are they waiting until Monday to deal with this whole not being able to eat or drink anything issue? Especially as a diabetic, you'd think this would be a little more urgent. I haven't eaten since Thursday, and now they expect me to go 2 more days without food? I'm starving and I'm

crabby. Fuck this. I can't stop crying and I just want food, my kitties, and a nap.

August 6, 2014 Emails
Endoscopy yesterday
Krystin to dad, Pat, Kathy:
   I've attached an image of what the doc did yesterday during my endoscopy, and the result of it. The left image shows what my esophagus looked like pre-endoscopy, as he's putting the wire down. The middle image is him dilating my esophagus with a "balloon." The right image is him all finished. Dilated to 15mm, which he said is close to what a normal esophagus should be at. Looking at the pre-endoscopy photo, it's no wonder I couldn't eat or drink anything! And this is after the first endoscopy they tried to do on Saturday, so imagine how my esophagus looked on Friday when I went into the ER. O.o

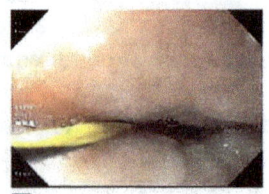 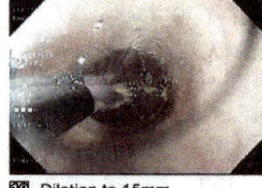 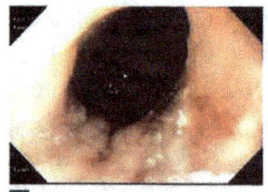

9 Wire in the esophagus   10 Dilation to 15mm   11 Post dilation

Pat to all 3:
   Yes but did he say WHY it closed up?

Krystin to all 3:
   He said reflux, so basically the gastroparesis and the lactose intolerance that I had for a while there, both of which were causing me to throw up so much. So he told me to double my Protonix, which is what I'm taking to treat erosion and ulceration of the esophagus that's caused by reflux. He said it's likely that I'll have to go back in 3-4 weeks for them to dilate it again. I asked him if this was something I'm going to have to be doing for the rest of my life, and he said NO, if it is a continuing problem, they go in and put permanent stents in to hold it open, so that it can't narrow.
   So I think even if I hadn't gotten that Rituxan infusion last week, this would've needed to be done. I think it's just a coincidence that I

happened to have that reaction AND my esophagus closing both in the same week. I guess we'll never know.

August 7, 2014 Facebook
I've been trying to find a good way to say how happy I am that I can finally swallow normally now, but I can't seem to find good wording without making it sound dirty. So we'll just leave it at that.

August 14, 2014 Facebook
Well gosh darn, that high school math finally paid off. I had to use the Pythagorean theorem yesterday to solve a work prob—oh wait, what am I saying? No, no I didn't.

> Leila: This made me giggle, I was wondering what kind of work problem required the use of the Pythagorean theorem!!
> Krystin: $x = -b +/- sqrt\ b2-4ac/2a$! Oh wait shit, that's the quadratic equation. . . .
> Annie: A squared + b squared = c squared?
> Krystin: Yeah! I've never used either of them since 10th grade math. Ever. Sometimes I sing the quadratic equation song to my cats, though.

August 17, 2014 Facebook
I am very impressed with how well everyone keeps their cool in Lord of the Rings. Through all 3 books/movies, I just keep waiting for someone to say "Well, shit. We're all f**ked, guys."

August 17-18, 2014 Text
Krystin to dad: Great, can't swallow anything again.
(later) Krystin: Hmm, well now I can swallow, so I'm gonna hold off on calling the coordinator on call. If I can stay hydrated on my own, then no inpatient for me!
(later) Dad: Still swallowing, I hope!
Krystin: Yes, but the difficulty of it changes by the hour it seems. Sometimes it's fine, sometimes it feels like I'm going to gag. Annoying.
Dad: Sorry. You have any appts to see any doc?
Krystin: Just had my pre-op physical this morning. Procedure next Monday, so just have to make it through the week. Will take it easy.

August 19, 2014 Facebook
This is the procedure I'm having done on Thursday. It's not invasive, and I don't think any cuts are being made, but it will finally let me get back to eating normally!

> en.wikipedia.org
> Esophageal stent - Wikipedia, the free encyclopedia
> *An esophageal stent is a stent (tube) placed in the esophagus to keep a blocked area open so the patient can swallow soft food and liquids. Esophageal stents may be self-expandable metallic stents, or made of plastic, or silicone, and may be used in the treatment of esophageal cancer.*

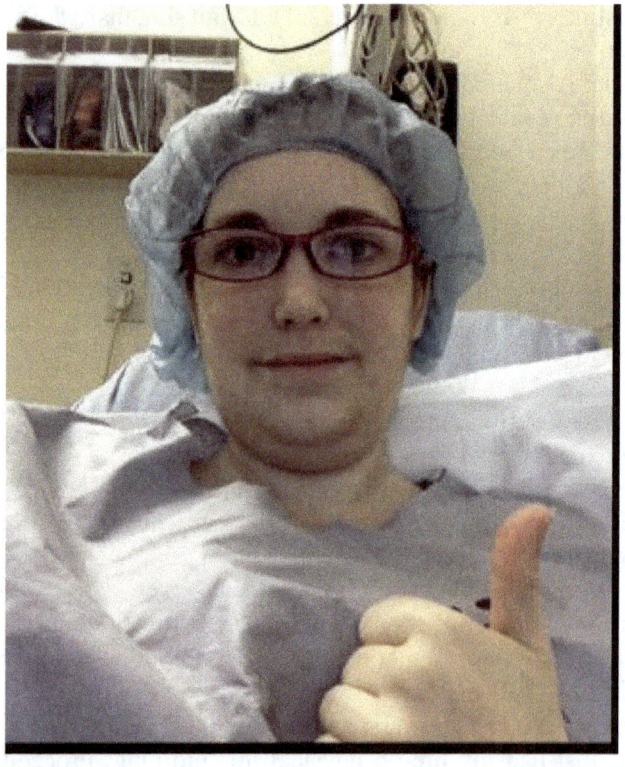

August 21, 2014 Facebook
Procedure was successful! Stent will come out in 8 weeks, and my esophagus SHOULD (knock on wood) then stay open. And I only

have to do liquid diet until tomorrow evening. By 6:00 tomorrow eve: pizza, get in ma belly!

August 24, 2014 Text
Krystin to dad: Went to hospital at 3:30 this morn. Very dehydrated, throwing up, dizzy and light headed. Was admitted, but hopefully only for the day, so all kitties should be fine. Just wanted to let you know. And of course I got a roomie who snores incredibly loud. That'll raise my blood pressure . . .
Dad: Do well. Just taking off for Moorhead
Krystin: Have fun! They moved me to a single room. :-)

August 24, 2014 Text
Pat to Gary: When's last time you were in K's apartment?
Gary: Several months. I can imagine why you ask. Not sure I want to know.
Pat: I fear she is not capable of living alone. Not sure what the solution is, as there are no adult versions of sorority houses with den mothers. It's total garbage. I feel sorry for the cats. They don't deserve this. Not expecting you to have a solution. Just throwing it out there as a serious concern.
Gary: Yeah, I said to Kathy before I texted you that I think she's not competent to live alone. I have no solution either. Staff at Anna Westin house.
Pat: It's not even a year and she's on her way to duplicating the Pig House. So sad.
Gary: I don't know what we can do.
Pat: I don't either, but I think it's gonna involve holding her cats hostage. I cut 14 mats outta Gabi and there are more. Poor little cat has tender spots from all the pulling. Maybe I need contact adult social services?
Gary: Is there such an agency?
Pat: I dunno. Sounded good.
Gary: I don't either. Sigh.

August 24, 2014 Text
Dad to Krystin: What happened?
Krystin: Apparently very mild dka. Even though I hadn't eaten anything since Wednesday, when you don't eat, the liver pumps out glucose. So I wasn't doing insulin because I wasn't eating, but my liver

was producing glucose. Even though I was still testing and my numbers were fine. I don't get it! But being discharged in next half hour.
Dad: Good luck! Keep me posted.
Krystin: Yup. All should be good now. Still taking pain meds cuz esophagus still burns where stent is. That part sucks, but at least I can swallow.
Dad: Should get better, right?
Krystin: So they say, yes.

August 25, 2014 Text
Krystin to dad: Ugh, I'm still taking my Dilaudid, but it makes me sleepy! Still feels like heartburn in my chest. I thought that was only supposed to last for the first 48 hours so I will call the nurse tomorrow.
Dad: Hope it gets better!
Krystin: Thanks! At least I can eat and drink normally.
Dad: Well, that's good. So some positive.
Krystin: Yup. But I'd like to be able to sleep comfortably, too!

September 3, 2014 Facebook
I've been having chest pain and back pain for the last 2 weeks (when my esophageal stent was put in), and hiccups feel like I was stabbed in the ribs. It's so bad that I've been taking painkillers every day. So, instead of the stent coming out in October, it's coming out tomorrow! No more pain please, thankyouverymuch.

September 4, 2014 Facebook
It's a good thing I don't write fantasy, because if I did, this is how LOTR would go:
> Bilbo Baggins leaves a special ring with Frodo Baggins. Years later, with the help of Gandalf, Frodo and Gandalf realize the ring is one of evil power and needs to be destroyed. Gandalf hops on one of his birds and flies to the summit of Mount Doom, tossing the ring into the lava and thus ending the potential and attempted rise of Sauron. Easy peasy. The End.

September 5, 2014 Facebook
OK people, time to REALLY try and stay as healthy as I can, becaaaaaaause, today I'm FINALLY being reactivated (hopefully for

the last time) on the pancreas wait list! Maybe I'll even get the big call before the New Year.

September 5, 2014 Text
Krystin to dad: You know that upper abdomen pain I've been having? I blew my nose this afternoon and felt the most horrible pain I've ever felt, and it hasn't gone away. Went to ER at 4:30, just now brought back to a bay. I am not waiting until October to figure this pain out. I almost started crying today, it was that bad.
Dad: Oh my. Let me know what happens.
(later) Dad: So what's up?
Krystin: Well, there's not much the ER can do about chronic pain. I just need to keep working with GI on that. But an ultrasound showed I have a lot of gas in that area, so I may have at least learned what causes the pain. That's a step. I will ask doc when she comes in again if there's something I can do to prevent or relieve upper abdomen gas.
Dad: One would think you could do a lot. Part of it could be the food you eat. Good luck with doc.
Krystin: Maybe, but I eat a pretty balanced diet, believe it or not, and I have the pain every day, so it would be hard to narrow it down. I think it might just be the gastroparesis still acting up. Who knows. I see Dr. Kandaswamy on the 22nd, so will talk to him about if my gastric pacer is working.
Dad: All you can do is keep on experimenting, I guess. Keep me posted. Try to get a good night sleep!
Krystin: I will, when they let me out!
Dad (10:20 p.m.): They're releasing you yet tonight?
Krystin: Yeah . . . like the doc said, not much they can do here. She can't expedite my colonoscopy or anything.
Dad: Get home safely!

September 6, 2014 Text
Dad to Krystin: You there? Ok?
Krystin: Yup. Doing fine. Was discharged at 1am, so slept in pretty late today. They discharged me very suddenly and quickly, which I saw was because the ambulance brought in someone and they just needed my room!

September 8, 2014 Blog

A spoonful of sugar still makes nothing go down

You like what I did there, with the subject?

OK, so it has been way, WAY too long. I fear I have lost many of my readers, but I promise I have not forgotten about you. I guess it's just been a pretty hectic month (even though I know it's been longer than a month since I posted last).

The biggest thing I've been dealing with lately is my throat. Well, more specifically, my esophagus. It doesn't want to stay open. It started probably a little over a month ago, when it started becoming hard to swallow. First, it started out that I could swallow my food, but it would sit in the upper part of my esophagus, like it was stuck, and I'd have to drink a bunch of water to push it down to my stomach. That lasted about a week, and then it became hard to even swallow. I could still eat food, but again, it would just sit in the upper part of my esophagus, and when I tried to drink water, it felt like my esophagus closed up altogether, and I would gag back up the water and the bites of food that were sitting there (pleasant, huh?). I talked to the GI clinic, and within a couple days, they did an endoscopy. Unfortunately, it was because I had gone into the ER on a Friday evening, because I wasn't able to eat or drink anything, even my pills. So I was both getting dehydrated AND not getting my very important transplant meds.

I was admitted overnight, and on Saturday I had an endoscopy done. My esophagus was so narrow, they couldn't even get a baby scope down there. The GI doc decided my esophagus needed to be dilated, but that couldn't be done that day because they didn't have the equipment available that they needed, and the doc who performs esophagus dilation was not working, since it was a Saturday. I don't remember if I stayed in the hospital or not, but it wasn't until Monday or Tuesday that I had the dilation done, by Dr. Amateau. Below is a picture of my esophagus before and after the dilation. [same as the one earlier]

WARNING: Some viewers may find the picture graphic, as it is a picture of inside my esophagus. Proceed with caution!

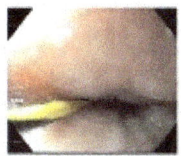 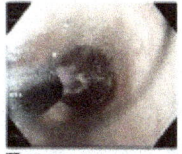 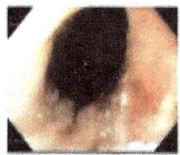

1 Wire in the esophagus   2 Dilation to 15mm   3 Post dilation

On the left is my esophagus before, in the middle is my esophagus during the procedure, with the scope down there and Dr. Amateau dilating it, and on the right is my esophagus once fully dilated. You can see why it was so hard to get a scope down there, let alone eat or drink anything! The dilation was done under anesthesia, but the first endoscopy was done under just sedation, like they always are.

It went fine and dandy for a while, but about a week later, I felt my esophagus narrowing again. I called Dr. Amateau's nurse and told her what was going on, she talked to Dr. Amateau, and they decided to put in an esophageal stent. It's like a mesh tube that sits in the esophagus, slowly dilates it over about 2 days to a normal size, then stays in for 2 months for the esophagus to "heal" around the stent, so when the stent is taken out, ideally the esophagus will stay that width. I think it was a Tuesday that I called his nurse, and we had the procedure scheduled for that Thursday. The stent placement procedure was also done under anesthesia, but I went home that evening, even though I was having a lot of pain and discomfort coming right out of surgery, with lots of pain meds and some antacid meds, we got it under control. Dr. Amateau suggested keeping me overnight in the hospital to make sure we could manage my pain, but I knew I had oral pain meds at home, and said there was nothing they could do there that I couldn't do at home. So I went home.

Below are two pictures. The first is of what the stent looks like, and the second is the device used to insert it into the esophagus. I have spared you a picture of what the stent looks like once inside the esophagus.

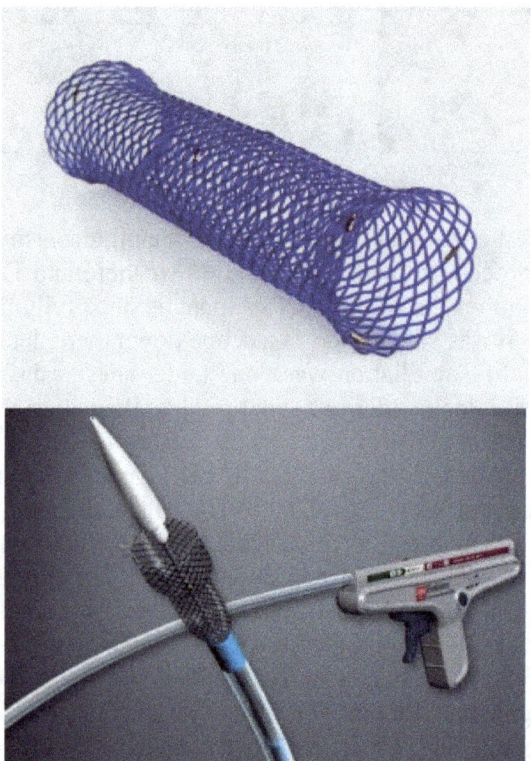

Pretty cool, huh? It's tight enough against the esophagus that food doesn't get stuck in there or anything, it just passes right by it. Well, my only food restriction was any leafy greens or salad, since I guess that CAN get stuck in the mesh, which makes sense. Other than that, my normal diet.

It is expected that for the first 24-48 hours, there would be some discomfort in both the throat, where the breathing tube was during surgery, and where the stent was placed, since it was dilating my esophagus slowly, and my body had to get used to it. Well, let me tell you, the pain and discomfort did not go away after 48 hours. Oh no, it lasted almost 2 weeks. I felt like I had really bad heartburn all the time, in my upper abdomen. The stent was placed right at the bottom of my esophagus, where it meets the stomach. It hurt all the time, and even more so when I would be in anything but an upright position. Sleeping was almost impossible, and some nights I actually tried to sleep sitting up in bed, leaning against the wall with a pillow behind my head. It was a sharp, burning pain, and even my Dilaudid pain med, which is one of the strongest there is, wasn't helping much. It was even sharper when I inhaled. Yawning, sneezing, or blowing my nose felt like I was punched in the gut, and hiccupping? Oh no no, that felt like I was stabbed in the gut with a fire-hot blade. So finally, almost 2 weeks later, I called Mary (Dr. Amateau's nurse) and said I can't take it anymore, I need it out.

2 days later (just last Thursday, 9/4), Dr. Amateau removed it. Like I said, normally it would stay in for 2 months, but I could not tolerate that pain for 2 months. Dr. Amateau said my esophagus had reached its full dilation, and he still thinks I made the right decision to put it in, even if it was coming out very early. The weekend was fine, I ate normally, yadda yadda yadda. But then on Sunday, guess what? I noticed that my food was starting to just sit in the upper part of my esophagus again, and I would have to drink later to push it down. Uh-oh. So, yesterday early evening I called and left a voice message for Mary, for her to talk to Dr. Amateau, and see what he thinks and what he wants to do about it. Obviously I can't be going in for esophagus dilation once a week, and my body didn't like the stent. So I will be curious to see what he has to say. I honestly don't know if there are any other options. I doubt esophagus transplant has made its way into the medical field . . .

As of 11:03am on Monday morning, today, I have not yet heard back from Mary, but the problem has not gotten any better (although it hasn't gotten worse, either). So this is an ongoing issue that we have yet to find a solution for. I was joking over the weekend that maybe all these problems are new to the medical field, and I'll be like a guinea pig and will be the one they use to find a cure or treatment for such-and-such problem, and even name something after me. That'll be my claim to fame. HA! A girl can dream, can't she? Well, not exactly the kind of dream that one has, but if it makes the issues better, let them do to me what they need to do! As long as it doesn't kill me, obviously. When I left the message for Mary, I told her that I may be willing to try the stent again, and just makes sure I'm always carrying my pain killers with me (even though it's not super effective, it helps take the edge off).

At the same time that all this esophagus nonsense is going on, I'm still having the upper abdominal pain that we also still don't know what it is. It was SO bad just this last Friday, I even had to leave work early. I went home and laid (lay?) down on my bed for a bit, but it didn't get any better, so I decided to go to the ER. I have a colonoscopy scheduled for the first week in October, because a different GI doc thinks the pain might be something wrong with my upper colon, but I couldn't wait until October. The pain was excruciating NOW. I didn't know what they could do for me in the ER, but maybe something sooner. Especially if I were admitted, they can always do stuff faster for inpatients than they do outpatient.

After a 2-hour wait in the waiting room, I was finally brought back. I was discharged at 1am, and the only thing that came out of it was that there was nothing the ER could do to help chronic pain, that I would need to keep working with the GI team, and good luck, OK goodbye go home. They discharged me very suddenly and very quickly, and I realized as I was leaving that it was because an ambulance was bringing someone in, and they needed my room. It was a very busy night at the Fairview University ER. Even when I left at 1am, there were still about 8 people in the waiting room, waiting to be seen. The only good thing I got out of it was that I got some IV Dilaudid, which always makes me feel great, and free parking, since at that time of night there is no one on duty in the parking ramps, so the security guy lifted the gate for me and I got to leave.

OH, I guess I did learn one thing while in there. I had an ultrasound done on the upper part of my abdomen, and the tech lady who did it said that I had a lot of gas up there, which could be causing the pain. I don't feel gassy or bloated when I have the pain, but maybe a person doesn't start to feel that gassy, bloated feeling until it's further down in the GI tract? Who knows. So maybe it's related to my eating and it's still a gastroparesis thing, which means perhaps my gastric pacer isn't working as well as it should be. I have an appointment set up with Dr. Kandaswamy (remember, he's my surgeon) at the end of this month, on the 22nd, to talk to him about my gastric pacer. If that's what's causing the severe pain, then it's an easy solution! He'll just have to go into the system and turn up the power, since obviously that's not something I can mess with. If it's not related to my pacer and is indeed an upper colon thing, then I need to wait until my procedure in October to show any results. And if THAT doesn't show anything, then I'm going to cry, because I think we're exhausting all our options as to what it could be. All I know is that when I get the pain, it's paralyzing, I can't stand up straight, and sometimes I even cringe and close my eyes and say to myself "stop stop stop stop." That doesn't work, of course, but it's an impulse thing.

As far as how I'm feeling. Hmmm. Well, I guess it depends on the day. Sometimes I feel really discouraged and pessimistic, especially when I'm [in] pain, or when I think about everything going on right now. I don't want to be that person who always has something wrong. I know I went over all this in a previous post, so I won't go into all again, but my spirits are definitely not as high as they used to be. I'm still happy, I still have so many things I want to do and places I want to go, but with all these issues going on and none of them being fixed, it's hard to imagine me being able to do any of those things. Know what I mean? I'm almost 30 and this is NOT where I'm supposed to be in life! But, as long as I keep telling myself that the life I want is not out of reach, it's just on hold. I'll be alright. :)

Alright, to completely change pace, and to save the best for last.

I'm reactivated on the pancreas wait list!!! Hopefully for the last time. Dr. Young talked to Dr. Kandaswamy and told him that me getting a pancreas should not be contingent on my EBV level. So this is great, since it was my EBV level that was keeping them from reactivating me. I know I'm at the top of the waitlist, but it could still be a while until I get a perfect match, since I have a lot of antibodies in my blood. I don't think there's anything that can be done to lower my antibody level, otherwise they would do that. So fingers, toes, and butt cheeks crossed that I may get one before the end of the year! So that's pretty exciting.

That's all I got for now. Now that I'm reactivated on the waitlist, the waiting resumes. Hopefully (knock on wood) no hospital stays between now and then (whenever then is), unless it's to fix my throat or abdomen pain. Then I'll willingly go. Other than that, nothing too exciting. I live a pretty boring life these days! But I guess that's not really new news, is it?

September 8, 2014 Facebook
Due to my upper abdomen pain, I have to keep my Dilaudid pain pills on me at all times. Just had to take one at work. Aaaaaand there goes my motivation to do anything else the rest of the day. I can haz nap nao?

September 9, 2014 Facebook
Krystin Engstrand is feeling conflicted.
Abdomen pain . . . need a Dilaudid . . . but can't get sleepy at work, can't leave early again . . . what to do!?

September 13, 2014 Facebook
Last night I took 2 Dilaudid for my abdomen pain, and chased it with some ZzzQuil to help me sleep. I slept so hard and so well, I may have even drooled a little. It was beautiful.

September 14, 2014 Facebook
I GOT A CALL FOR A POTENTIAL PANCREAS!! It's not for sure yet, I have to run to the hospital and give a blood sample, but as of now everything looks good on paper and it's a really good match. Stay tuned!!

September 14, 2014 Email
    It's a go!!

Krystin to dad:
    Surgery at 9:30. If you want to visit me in the late afternoon or after work, I'll be on the 6th floor, I forget what unit. The recovery unit. I'll be there for one night before moving to 7A. Same drill as last time. Send good thoughts my way around surgery time!!
    And if I die, my buried treasure is hidden in-
    Just kidding. I don't have any treasure.
    Love you lots!!

Dad to Krystin:
    Great! Love you, too! I will come see you later.

September 15, 2014 Facebook
AND IT'S GOOD! This is it guys. A whole flood of emotions are going through me right now, I can't even process this. I've waited almost 26 years for this, and now it's happening. I'm getting a pancreas. Send me good vibes starting about 9:15am - transplant time!! Here we go.

September 15, 2014 Email
Fwd: It's a pancreas!
Pat to Gary:
Did she send you one like this?
Begin forwarded message:
From: Krystin <kengstrand227@yahoo.com
Date: September 15, 2014 at 5:31:18 AM CDT

To: [many family members]
Subject: It's a pancreas!
My dear family,

It is with great joy that I announce the arrival of a new, healthy pancreas! I got the call on Sunday evening that there was a pancreas coming from out of state that was a good match for me. From a 31 year old male with no past medical problems. And I don't have any antibodies against him!! That's a very good thing, it means much less of a chance for rejection. Another patient is getting his liver and kidney; a double organ transplant!

I arrived at Fairview University hospital around 3am, after getting the call at 2:30am that the organ was removed and looked good. So at least they looked at it this time before having me come in. Surgery is scheduled for 9:30 a.m. Monday morning (9/15), so if you want to send good vibes my way, that's a good time. I'll be on the recovery floor for one day, then move to unit 7A, where I'll be for about 5-7 days before going home. If you want to come visit me, all are welcome!

I am beyond words as far as how I feel. Nervous, excited, scared, hopeful. . . . You all know how long I've struggled with my diabetes, so the fact that it could be gone 24 hours from now, well, I'm speechless. It will be a long recovery and lots of follow-up visits and tests, but I'm feeling good about it.

Keep your fingers crossed all goes well! I'll be in touch again with updates in a couple days, when I'm out of the post surgery fog.
Love,
Krystin

P.s. A big THANK YOU to my mom for driving me to the hospital in the middle of the night!

September 15, 2014 Text
Dad to Krystin: You rejoined the world or still pretty woozy?
Elliott to dad: Mom says K doing fine, pancreas working. So she no have diabetes any more. Let's hope other problems can be dealt with.
Krystin to dad: Bela has hiccups.
Elliott to dad: Bela has hiccups. Pretty funny. He puzzled.
Krystin to dad: Rejoined the world. Omg I wish I could hear him hiccup! Funny. You're up early!

Chapter 13

No Diabetes, Losing the Cats, and Opioid Addiction

September 16, 2014 Text
Krystin to dad: Stent placement still scheduled for Friday. Will be able to eat after that. Tube will stay in nose until the procedure, and can't eat while tube is in nose! Gah. I'm so hungry!"
Dad: But if hungry, probably healthy, too!
Krystin: Yeah I 'spose!

September 16, 2014 Facebook
My Foley catheter tubing got disconnected somehow, while I was taking a nap. I woke up drenched in my own urine. That was awkward. I felt like I was 3 years old again. Good thing I'm in the hospital, where this is a normal and frequent occurrence!

September 19, 2014 Text [Friday]
Krystin to dad: Just fyi, discharge Monday most likely. Going to do some work stuff on the computer now.
Dad: Hope it went well! How you feeling overall?
Krystin: Hungry. I'm feeling fine. More pain yesterday and today than the first couple days cuz the pain block is wearing off.
Dad: Hope that can be ameliorated some way.
Krystin: I have no idea what that means.
Dad: Hope pain be relieved.
Krystin: Oh. Yes, me too. All I have though is my button I can push every 10 min.

September 20, 2014 Text
Krystin to dad: Getting the tube out, but I only get to eat ice chips today. Maybe home Tuesday. Sigh.
Dad: Get more sleep without noisy roommate? Assume you squawking about needing food!
Krystin: Of course I keep telling the docs I want food, but what I want doesn't matter. It's what's best for the pancreas, and they want to make sure things are moving through before giving me food. At least last night I finally started passing gas. And yes, better sleep.
Dad: But are you receiving any nutrition at all?

Krystin: Not really. Just saline. Sometimes they drip in some potassium or magnesium. My stomach is probably the size of a pea by now.
Dad: That cannot be healthy. I'd sure be asking about getting some kind of nutrients!

September 20, 2014 Facebook
I haven't had anything to eat since last Sunday, and today I only get ice chips. It's hard to not get frustrated when they're starving my body. I am getting NO nutrients via my IV. Looks like discharge on Tuesday. I just want a cookie.

September 21, 2014 Text
Krystin to dad: Does Elliott even know I had transplant?
Dad: I told him. You doing ok?
Krystin: Yes, but can't swallow, so still no food. Need to find out if GI can put a stent in without blowing a lot of air into my GI tract, which could upset the pancreas. If they can't, then I go home on a feeding tube for 2-3 weeks until pancreas has healed enough for stent procedure."
Dad: Hoping for stent!
Krystin: Yes me too! I want to eat SO bad.
Dad: When you know?
Krystin: Maybe today, if Dr. K can talk to the GI guy. Otherwise tomorrow. So now home on Tuesday possibly. At this moment we're at a stand-still.
Dad: Let me know.
(later) Krystin: I go on full liquid diet starting tomorrow plus nutritional shakes, and will go home with nutritional shakes and stay on liquid diet until stent procedure. No tube.
Dad: Good!
(later) Dad: So, can you tell if you'll have more energy now that you have a pancreas?
Krystin: Can't tell yet. Probably though.
Dad: Hope so! I'll be over later this morning.

September 22, 2014 Text
Dad to Krystin: You got food! Feeling at least a little better?

Krystin: Yeah, a little. Will move to full liquid tomorrow, so will at least get soup and oatmeal and yogurt and pudding. More substantial in my stomach.
Dad: Good luck! Those can all constipate, of course :-(
Krystin: My colon is clean and empty. Had a procedure to see if there's a twist in the upper part of my colon, and in the process they empty me out. And no twist.

September 22, 2014 Facebook
The goods new is, the new pancreas is working SO well that they actually are giving me a medication to slow it down and not work so hard, so that it can rest and heal. The bad news is that the medication makes me toss my cookies. Yay but ick.

September 23, 2014 Facebook
Disconnected from the insulin drip yesterday. Hank the Panc and I are flying solo!

September 23, 2014 Text
Krystin to dad: Soft food diet for dinner! I get mushy meatloaf! ^_^
Dad: Wow, that progressed fast from nothing to liquid to real food!
Krystin: I know! But it's all going down fine, so I'm ok with that. And they said home Thursday at the earliest. As I suspected.
Dad: Uff da.

September 25, 2014 Facebook
Honey, I'm home!

September 25, 2014 Text
Dad to Krystin: Doing ok?
Krystin: Yes. About to make some soup. Had a Boost.
Dad: And feeling good, now out of hospital? Able to eat soup?
Krystin: Can't swallow. Shit, I dunno what to do.
Dad: Call your coordinator ASAP.

September 26, 2014 Text
Dad to Krystin: So?
Krystin: Need to go back. But can't drive. Or walk. Too dizzy.
Dad: I can get you in a short while. Will text.

Gary to Kathy: Going to get k, bring to hospital. She weak, dizzy, they want her back.
(later) Dad to Krystin: I take it you don't know anything new.
Krystin: Not really. Getting feeding tube soon.
Dad: Feeling any better?
Krystin: Yes, now that I got pain and nausea meds.
Dad: That's good, at least. I hope no threat to pancreas in all this.
Krystin: Me too! I don't think so though, or they wouldn't do it.
Dad: I meant also dehydration and lack of food.
Krystin: Oh, yeah that too. No tube today. Someone dropped the ball and now they can't fit me in today. Tomorrow between 1-4pm. Geez.
Dad: So how do you get food and liquid???
Krystin: IV fluids. Will try broth and jello.

September 28, 2014 Text
Dad: News?
Krystin: Tube & Temp of 103.
Dad: You ok?

September 29, 2014 Text
Krystin to dad: Too long to text. You could come visit. Can explain all, then. If you have time.
Dad: I will come over. Talked to your nurse last night after opera, so got some info. Watered and fed your kitties yesterday, they fine. Is your temp down? BTW, any chance they release you today? If so, I would come over then.
Krystin: No release today. I'm on antibiotics and they wanna get me more stable. Temp down to 101 I think.
Gary to Kathy: K much better, temp 98, alert and talking. Said she can already tell, despite this, she will have more energy.
(later) Dad: How you doing? Be able to sleep tonight?
Krystin: Tube is triggering my gag reflex and making me gag. Can maybe sleep. Nurse can give me something to help sleep.
Dad: Good luck. See you tomorrow.

September 29, 2014 Facebook
Krystin Engstrand is feeling broken.
I'm trying not to get discouraged, but I've about had it. Been here since Friday [September 26], not out until probably this Friday. Feeding tube stays in until the 7th, when I have the smaller stent put in. Getting

a blood transfusion because my hemoglobin is only 7 (should be between 12-15). I'm miserable, I feel like shit, and I have to have a CT scan because Hank may be a gymnast at heart. Hold on Hank, don't cry; we'll get through it together.

September 30, 2014 Text
Krystin to dad: Two small clots in the two veins connecting pancreas (one in each vein). Not a big deal, short term will get a Heparin drip, then will be on Coumadin for 6 months.
Dad: So not serious. I guess that's good. What next???
Krystin: Dunno. Observation for a little while to make sure everything is going ok?
Dad: You wrote on FB that you don't get out until Friday. Ugh.
Krystin: Well that's my guess. I have that home feeding class on Thursday because that's when they can fit me in, so. . . . Friday seemed a legit guess!
Dad: Let's hope no later than that!
Krystin: Omg yeah. No thanks.
(later) Dad: Did you ask about Coumadin and stent procedure?
Krystin: I start Coumadin today, but I'm also getting Heparin in my IV, so it will be fine.
Dad: I thought heparin also blood thinner.
Krystin: Hmm, I dunno the medical reasoning, but Sheri explained it to me and it works out.

September 30, 2014 Facebook
Esophageal stent placement on Friday! Everything will be SO much better after that! I haven't eaten anything more substantial than jello in 2 weeks. I just want an effing pizza already!

October 1, 2014 Facebook
Home today!! Home care nurse will come show me how to do the tube feeds, and tube will come out on Friday for my stent placement procedure. I'm so excited I get to be reunited with my kitties!! Yes, that is the best part about being discharged, and I'm not ashamed to admit it. #crazycatlady #freedom #letsblowthispopsiclestand

October 2, 2014 Facebook
I have so much happiness in my heart. I am beyond happy to be home with my kitties, to be having the stent placed tomorrow, and to have 2

perfectly working transplanted organs. I am also so overwhelmed with all the love and support that I have from everyone I know, and even from people I don't know. You're amazing, love you all.

October 4, 2014 Text
Dad to Krystin: What's going on????
Krystin: Sorry, been napping all day. At home. Infusion because magnesium level was low, that's all.
Dad: You're ok? Feeling good? What's it mean your magnesium level was low?
Krystin: I dunno, I don't know what magnesium does! Just feeling tired. Dunno if that is normal. Body very tired. Hopefully stent doing ok!
Dad: Can you eat and drink?
Krystin: Yup
Dad: Good! Progress!
Krystin: It's pretty exciting for me!

October 5, 2014 Text
Dad to Krystin: Better today?
Krystin: Kinda
Dad: That's not too enthusiastic.
Krystin: My body is just really tired, and I'm sleepy tired all the time. But at Pizza Ranch with mom now, so maybe some real food will help me feel better.
Dad: Hope so!
(later) Dad: Bet you tired cuz blood transfusion effects worn off and you still not producing enough red blood cells.
Krystin: Yes, very tired. Was in today for another magnesium and fluids drip.
Dad: How long that go on? Is this unexpected or normal?
Krystin: I dunno if normal. Will get 2 liters of fluids Weds and Fri when I go in for labs.
Dad: I would ask that question.
Krystin: Might you be able to bring my bag and computer to me tonight? I'm too tired to come get it, but I need to do some work. My body is so tired! Maybe tomorrow I will ask for another iron infusion
. . .
Dad: I can bring it over. Maybe ask for a blood transfusion. I think that's what gives you energy!

Krystin: Yeah, not sure why body so tired. All my lab results look good, so it's not like I'm super low on anything. Will talk to Dawn (my new coordinator) tomorrow when I'm in clinic.
Dad: Low hemoglobin? They said that would be a problem for a period.
Krystin: Yes, but it's going up. In the 8 range now.
Dad: Not high enough!
Krystin: I know, but up from 7. Ideally will keep going up and eventually will be in the 12 range or higher! It's weird; I WANT to go out and do things, just don't have the energy yet! May still be too close to surgery anyway, still need to rest up.
Dad: Very likely.

October 6, 2014 Facebook
Over the past 3 weeks, I have not been able to put into words how it feels to finally be free of the chronic illness I've struggled with essentially my whole life. Then, the other day, I was listening to this song, and I found myself crying. The lyrics say it all. Dreams really DO come true.

October 7, 2014 Facebook
I have reached the recovery phase of tiredness. My body is tired, my mind is tired. I get tired just thinking of moving around. Lots of sleep the past few days. But I know it's because my body is busy healing. Gotta keep Hank happy!

October 8, 2014 Facebook
If anyone wants to cook me a full dinner and deliver it to me, I would not be opposed. Or, if you're not much of a cook, and steak and sides from Murray's would be acceptable. :D

October 8, 2014 Facebook
Today's 2 hour infusion turned into a 5 hour infusion turned into being admitted to the hospital and getting scheduled for the G-J stomach tube to be put in tomorrow. Just another Wednesday. So bring my Murray's steak to 7A at the hospital instead of my home. ;)

October 8, 2014 Email
BP
Krystin to dad, mom:

After being at SIPC for 5 hours, getting 2 liters of fluids and an infusion of magnesium, my blood pressure still dropped when going from sitting to standing. And even my sitting was under 100 for both top and bottom number, which is low for me, considering I'm usually around 125/80. My nurse is paging the doc to see what she wants to do. Fingers crossed no admit. *sigh*

Dad to Krystin:
Sent text. No blood transfusion?

Krystin to dad:
I don't get service down here, so no see text. No, no blood transfusion. Maybe Dr. Liu will order one now . . . [SIPC was in the basement of the building.]

October 8, 2014 Email
Well, no surprise there . . .
Krystin to dad, mom:

I'm being admitted, and having a procedure tomorrow to have a G-J feeding tube put in my stomach. Joy. My gastroparesis is making me throw up again, and I've been throwing up the little bit of food I've been able to eat the past few days.

I don't get to go home first, because my BP is so [low] that they don't want me driving. Would someone be able to go to my apt and get some things for me?

I'm not sure if they'll want to keep me an extra day or after the procedure (with my luck, they will), so having these things will be nice. Especially the fresh underwear. O.o

Thank you so much to whomever (whoever?) can do this. I know it's not very convenient, and I definitely was not expecting to be admitted. But now they want to get this tube in my stomach ASAP, so that I can start getting proper hydration and nutrients. I have no idea how long I'll have to be using it.

October 8, 2014 Email
status report
Pat to Krystin, cc dad:

I missed going to my Volunteer Recognition Event. You needed help, so instead, I went to your apartment to gather your requested items so that dad could bring them to you in the morning. That means that I was in your apartment. . . .

You probably already know what I'm going to say, but for the record I'm going to say it anyway.

Bottom line: if I enter your apartment one more time and find the cat box in the state I found it in tonight, I'm crating up the cats and taking them to the Humane Society. Period.

I know you "love" them with hugs and kisses. I know there's always an "excuse" that you are unable to tend their box. You're tired. You're sick. You're throwing up. You're whatever. It's always been "something" for the past year and we need to accept the fact that there always WILL be "something." If your forever-recurring illnesses mean that you are unable to tend to the cats, then you simply cannot have them. Period.

When you were a baby, I had the 3-day flu and was about as sick as a person could be without being dead. Dad was out of town at an annual AIAW Conference and I had no one else to help me. I crawled across floors and up and down steps in between vomits in order to tend to you. It wasn't easy, but you were dependent on me, and I was totally responsible for you. It's just what a person does.

I'm not saying this for sympathy. I'm saying it for fact. Those cats are your "kids" as you call them, and they are dependent on you. If you are unable to tend to their needs from day to day for WHATEVER reason, then you are not able to be responsible for them and you simply cannot have them.

The question has come up any number of times whether or not you are capable of living on your own. I don't know the answer to that question. What I do know is that I'm witnessing, time after time, two innocent cats living in an unacceptable environment. I have no choice but to remove them if you cannot provide for them.

I had considered cc'ing my sibs and some others on this email so I'd have proof-of-purchase, so to speak, of my conditions presented. I'll spare you of that, and just cc your dad for now. It's obvious that you are not doing your duties as a cat owner. Either figure out a way to do it, or accept the fact that we have no choice but to remove them.

I cannot, in good faith, close my eyes to it one more time.

Gary to Kathy:
FYI. She's right.

Kathy to Gary:
I know she's right. And I know Krystin is very attached to those kitties. She shouldn't have gotten them at all. It's just sad.

October 9, 2014 Email
Pat to Gary:
No clue what this "yes" reply means. Maybe it means she'll just never allow me in her apartment again. Who knows. I just feel sorry for the cats ;-(

---------- Forwarded message ----------
From: Krystin
Date: Thu, Oct 9, 2014 at 8:41 AM
Subject: Re: status report
To: Pat
Ok.

Gary to Pat:
Nor, of course, do I have any idea.
I agree with you on this, in case you wondered. She either cleans up as needed or the cats must go.

Gary to Kathy:
Yup. But she's an adult living on her own, so you certainly well understand that neither Pat nor I get the final vote. Not to say she makes good decisions—she does not—but she does have the right as an adult to make them, good or bad. Pat is asserting the right to intervene if the animals are not properly cared for, which I think is also correct.
I would like play Pontius Pilate in this, but I can't, unfortunately.

October 9, 2014 Text
Krystin to dad: No tube today. The GI people are hesitant about putting it in, saying these are just transplant issues and I'll get better, blah blah blah. Like they know better than the transplant docs?? So

today I will push drinking 3 liters on my own and eating full meals and see how that goes, like if I have any nausea and/or vomiting.
Dad: Good luck. Docs don't always know what the problem is.
Krystin: Just kidding. Tube placement tomorrow. I only ate half a banana at breakfast before throwing up, and that was AFTER having taken an anti-nausea med. :-(

October 10, 2014 Text
Krystin to dad: Going down for procedure now.
(later) Dad: How you doing?
Krystin: In pain.
Dad: Sorry. Expected to get better soon? We come by and visit tomorrow afternoon.
Krystin: Hopefully, although I already got Dilaudid and it's not helping. Putting warm packs on it now.
Dad: Assume they being very attentive. I feel bad for you. Wish I could help.
Krystin: I just need more pain med, but you know how it is, they can't give me more than a certain amount within a certain time frame. It sucks.
Dad: I understand. Sigh.

October 11, 2014 Text
Dad to Krystin: Any better this morning?
Krystin: No. Pain so bad during the night, I was crying. I get my pain meds every couple hours, but nothing else can be done until I see the docs. It hurts so bad. :'(
Dad: That's terrible. Hope you see docs soon and they can do something PDQ.
Krystin: Me, too. I'm so miserable. Gopher game today, right?
Dad: Yes but we going to opera. Will be out of touch noon to 400 probably. But let me know if anything improves. We will come visit after opera unless you still in pain and not need visitors.
Krystin: Ok. You can visit. Will be a nice distraction.
(later) Dad: You get dinner, and it stay down? Feeling a bit better?

October 11, 2014 Facebook
All throughout the night and this morning I have been in some of the most agonizing pain I've ever been in. It's even brought me to tears. Where the tube is going into my stomach, it feels like someone

punctured through my skin with a shotgun, and then fired. Let me tell you: ow, ow, OW. Please let this pain be over soon, because even the painkillers only take [the] edge off, they don't relieve the pain completely.

October 12, 2014 Text
Krystin to dad: Dinner yes, but didn't eat much because pain so bad. Didn't get much sleep either, cuz pain so bad. Still bad today. Need talk to docs about a better way to manage the pain. Even the Dilaudid isn't doing much the past day. :-(
Dad: Yuck.
(later) Krystin: Switching to morphine.
Dad: Better? Anything wrong with incision? We stop by about 5 on way to dinner.
Krystin: Not much better, and no, nothing wrong with incision. It's the tube going I to my stomach. This pain is normal, but it sure is unpleasant.
Dad: If normal, at least that relieves worry about problem with it.
Krystin: Right. It's just not fun to wait out, especially when no pain killers are relieving the pain.
(later) Dad: Doing any better?
Krystin: Yes, am now. Will try to go to sleep early, too.
Dad: Good. See you tomorrow.

October 13, 2014 Text
Krystin to dad: Pain doing better this afternoon. Went back to Dilaudid, so also a little itchy, but we're trying a new anti-itch med.
Dad: Good. No talk yet of release?
Krystin: Possibly tomorrow.
Dad: Really. I am amazed. But glad if it can work. Can you eat?
Krystin: Yes, I can. Ate a good sized lunch today!
Dad: And it stayed down, I assume. You should try walking around a bit.
Krystin: Yes, it did. Umm, maybe walking. Mom is coming soon, so will maybe walk with her.
Dad: Good idea. If you can't walk hardly at all, that's not good.
Krystin: Right. I'm sure it will just be a short walk to start off with.
Dad: But might as well try to get your strength back up.
Krystin: Course.

October 14, 2014 Text
Dad to Krystin: How you doing?
Krystin: A tiny bit nauseous but the pain is better managed. They're still saying discharge tonight. Might you be able to pick me up later? Obviously not REALLY later. . . .
Dad: What about your car?
Krystin: Good point. I will have to call campus security to get it out of the ramp for me. So you know what, never mind. I'll get my car and then drive home. I can leave this floor without an escort.
Dad: Good heavens, don't unless you are sure you can drive!
Krystin: Doesn't matter, not going home tonight.
Dad: Why am I not surprised. You OK?
Krystin: It was my decision to stay. Still a little unsteady on my feet, also want to get more fluids tonight to make sure I'm good and hydrated for going home tomorrow.
Dad: Sounds like smart decision!
Krystin: Yeah, I've made that mistake too many times. I'm gonna play it safe and make sure I'm really ready! I got a walker to push when I go on walks, so that helps a lot with walking.

October 15, 2014 Facebook
Today marks the 1-month anniversary that Hank the Panc and I have been together! It's been a rocky month, but not because of any problems between the two of us. To celebrate, tonight I will treat Hank to one of our favorite dinners: salmon!

October 15, 2014 Text
Dad to Krystin: Terrible meeting day, can't get over until after 3:00. Maybe you already out by then!
Krystin: That's ok, I can wait. That will get me through lunch, and more opportunities to walk around with my walker.
(later) Krystin: Now I dunno if home today. I had a liter of IV fluids, fluids through my tube, and I've been drinking water, and my blood pressure still drops almost 40 points when I go from sitting to standing ☹
Dad: Ugh.
(later) Dad: I come over now?
Krystin: Sure, I'm just hanging out.
(later, after she got home) Dad: You doing okay?
Krystin: Yeah. Getting settled in and giving scratches to the kids.

Dad: Feeling okay, under the circumstances?
Krystin: Yeah, as good as can be I suppose!

October 16, 2014 Text
Pat to Gary: Did you drive K in this morning? Home Health called cuz can't find her.
Gary: Yes. DK if she back home yet.
Pat: Did she say what she was going in for?
Gary: Labs.
Pat: How did she look? Home Health says her HgB is 6.2 and that's not good. That's why they wanted to visit her. How would she get home?
Gary: Thought she might be able to drive herself. Assume medical folks will say something about that.
Pat: Well she's MIA somewhere in the hospital then. I'll keep trying find her.
Gary: She can't get texts because labs are way down basement. Can do email.
(later) Gary: Did you ever find her?
Pat: No. I left text and email, HomeHealthCare left voice message. Nothing so far.
Gary: Gad. Hope she didn't try to drive home and crash.
Pat: I worry about that too. On the other hand, she would be good about telling them she couldn't do it if not feeling strong enuf.
Gary: One hopes. If the alternative was being readmitted to the hospital, she might not have.
Pat: She said last night that she was surprised they discharged her. She could hardly get up the steps to her apartment and she was shaking like a leaf.
Gary: I know. She went in this morning in a wheelchair.
Pat: She's getting blood.
Dad to Krystin: Where are you?
(later) Pat to Gary: Any idea where Krystin is?
Gary: No.
Pat: I worried. She not respond to call or text.
Gary: We going to her apt.
Gary: She at apt, very tired.
Pat: How did she get home?
Gary: Drove.

Pat: So she has a car. Can drive in if needed. Or cab both ways. I don't mean to sound cruel, but I can't keep changing my schedule when others are involved. And she was too tired to answer her phone?????

October 17, 2014 Text
Dad to Krystin: What's going on?
Krystin: What a waste of a day at the clinic. They found nothing to explain the pain. I left with no answers.
Dad: Good grief. Couldn't you have let me know sooner? Kathy, I, and Kathy's mother have been worrying the last few hours. Anyway, what's next? I take it they not worried.
Krystin: Well, they're worried about me. It's a long story. I can explain when you get home.
Dad: If they are worried, why not put you back in hospital?
Krystin: Because nothing they can do! My xray was normal, the tube looks fine. They think I've become dependent on my pain killer. They can't raise the dose because I'm already at a dangerous level. Doc said the high level of narcotics can actually make my nerves more sensitive to the pain.
Dad: Uff da. Sounds like all can do is wait.
Krystin: I guess. That doesn't make the pain better. I'm not making up the pain, but I fear without my pain killer, it will get worse. I was crying in pain. This morning. It hurts too much to make food and eat. All I want to do is sleep all the time. I'm always so tired.
Dad: I am so sorry. Wish I could help. Too bad something stupid like aspirin doesn't work. We would be glad to have you in Elliott's room for awhile. We think you should come over.
Krystin: Ok. I think that's a good idea.
Dad: But you have to be nice :-) you can go spend time with your kitties.
Krystin: What do you mean I have to be nice??
Dad: Agreeable. Friendly. Nice. Not a grouch. :-)

October 18, 2014 Text
Dad to Krystin: You any better today?
Krystin: Eh. Can't really tell.
Dad: Oh. Will let you know when we arrive home. [We were visiting Kathy's relatives in Wisconsin.]
Krystin: Ok. Gonna try and find some food now.
Dad: Good idea. You should have something you can eat around there.

Krystin: Well yeah, what did you think I meant? I'm starting with a banana.
Dad: I knew. Bananas are good. Had one myself this morning.
Dad: Bunch of cousins not seen each other in years all having big gabfest here in Poy Sippi, WI. No idea when end. Then 4 hour drive.
Krystin: Ok. I'm just hanging out. Lots of naps today. Do you think there's a chance you'll stay overnight again? Tell them you have a daughter at home who needs your help! I don't wanna be alone tonight. I need company.
Dad: We're at least two hours away from home. You can go over anytime, but Elliott's room isn't ready.
Krystin: That's ok, at least I know you're on the way. I don't need his room right away.

October 18, 2014 Facebook
For the last month, I have put my body through so much, and have tried to be superwoman and deal with it on my own and take care of myself. I finally reached the end of my strength. Going to my dad's for a little while, so I can get the help and care I need to fully recover.

> Krystin: I think it will be good for me to not be alone and be with family and getting help. I've tried to do this alone for too long.
> Krystin: My mom is already having a hard time dealing with this. It's hard for her to watch. She's trying to be as supportive as she can, in her own way.

October 21, 2014 Text
Dad to Krystin: Did you eat your banana today? How you feeling?
Krystin: Yup, peanut butter toast with banana! I am at my apt now. Visiting with kitties and gonna do some work. Will find a good lunch to have. I think I will call Dawn (my new coordinator) about the tube pain.

October 23, 2014 Text
Dad to Krystin: How doing today? Pester anyone about the pain?
Krystin: Not yet. Just got to my apt. Feeling nauseous this morning, I think I need to lower the feed rate on my tube feeding. Is too fast, upsets my tummy.
Dad: Good idea. Getting enough liquids?

Krystin: Trying. Dawn is going to make a few calls to see if there's anything we can do about the pain.
Dad: Good!!!!

October 25, 2014 Text
Dad to Krystin: You eating leftovers with us or assuming you'll get food at Chris's party?
Krystin: I dunno yet if going to Chris's. Threw up earlier. No idea why. Have slight headache now. Still have an hour to decide though.
Dad: That's not good. You should go if you can.
Krystin: I know. I want to go.
(later) Dad: So, what you doing?
Krystin: I'll be home for leftovers. What time are you eating?
Dad: No idea. Not in any rush. You not going to party?
Krystin: I don't wanna be there if I throw up again. The nausea comes and goes. And I still have the slight headache. I talked to Chris. She understands.
Dad: Ok. Too bad.
Krystin: I know . . .

October 27, 2014 Facebook
First day back at work. Kinda nervous, but here we go. . . .

October 27, 2014 Email
Dad to Krystin:
    You still at work?

Krystin to dad:
    Yes, still at work. Got in about 9:45. Probably going to leave around 4. I'm going to go to my apartment before coming back over, to get clothes for tomorrow and see my girls for a bit.

Dad to Krystin:
    Sounds good. Glad you could make it 10-4.

October 29, 2014 Text
Krystin to dad: A nurse never came!
Dad: Call clinic!
Krystin: Dawn calling me back after talking to Dr. Liu.
Dad: Hope you were emphatic! Let me know what happens.
Krystin: Going to SIPC at 1

Dad: Good. Going to work?
Krystin: No
Dad: Ok
Krystin: I dunno how I'm gonna get there. Don't think I can drive.
Krystin: Can you help me?
Dad: Ok. I will leave now.
Krystin: Thank you.
Gary to Kathy: Going to bring Krystin in to clinic. More later.
Pat to Gary: Was she throwing up all the time at your house?
Gary: Yes, last night and this morning. She home now. Going back tomorrow.

October 29, 2014 Facebook
Nausea for the last 3 days. Throwing up randomly for the last 4. Dehydrated and exhausted. Headed to the clinic to see what's up. Happy early effing birthday to me. >:(

> Krystin: I get 2 liters of fluids and they're ready to send me on my way. No addressing the nausea and vomiting, or the pain in my side I've had for the last day, or my weakness and shortness of breath. They're setting me up for a trip to the ER in the next day or so. I'm not leaving here w/o answers.

October 29, 2014 Facebook
Nothing a little tomato soup, a heating pad, and 4 Oxycodone can't make better.

October 31, 2014 Text
Dad to Krystin: So you doing well today?
Krystin: Eh. Was nauseous all morning. who knows why. Just got back from lunch, feeling ok now.
Dad: Did you do the tube feeding liquid last night? Or maybe you were just hungry! Was it just this morning or also last night, maybe from dinner? Glad you better, anyway.
Krystin: No tube feeding last night. I was nauseous for like 5 min on the way home from dinner, but then was fine. But woke up really nauseous this morning. At least it went away now.
Dad: Where you going tonight? Here or apt? We out for dinner and play.

Krystin: I think I will be at my apt tonight, but will be around there tomorrow.

November 4, 2014 Facebook
Krystin Engstrand was voting in the 2014 U.S. Election.

November 5, 2014 Text
Dad to Krystin: You ok? No response to Kathy re dinner.
Gary to Pat: You heard anything from Krystin? Kathy emailed her about dinner here tonight and got no response. I texted her and got no response.
Pat: Not since yesterday morning. I've stopped worrying about her. Sounds cold, but really? A 30 year old who lets 24 hours go by without checking email or texts? Might we think it's a power game? I dunno.
Krystin to dad: Did she send a text? If so, never got it. Doing good though. Took a Xanax and it knocked me out!
Dad: Glad to know you're ok.
Gary to Pat: Got text from her simultaneously with yours. She fine.
Pat: And what was her excuse for not responding earlier? I invited her over for a movie last Saturday nite and she didn't respond until Monday. That's just rude.
Gary: I didn't ask.

November 7, 2014 Text
Dad to Krystin: How you doin?
Krystin: Not too bad. Was nauseous from after lunch until I got home, but no throwing up, and I feel better now.
Dad: Good. Wonder why nausea.
Krystin: I dunno. I had it ALL day yesterday, and was even throwing up a lot yesterday. I had to leave work at 3 and threw up twice on the way home. :(I think it's cuz I'm "backed up" if you know what I mean.
. . .
Dad: You talk to docs? Maybe you need to review your diet. Kathy says is lots of meds you can get to be not backed up.
Krystin: Oh I know, I have a pharmacy of those. And yes, the docs know I've been having this problem for years.
Dad: Sigh.
Krystin: Yeah . . . not fun. And sadly, nothing makes the nausea goes away. Hopefully, once I've had the pancreas a while, that's one thing being healthy will fix. Since the gastroparesis issues were caused by diabetes.

Dad: Hope so!

November 7, 2014 Blog
Meet Hank . . . and then some

Oh boy, I don't even know where to start. It has been a very chaotic month and a half, and for those of you who are friends with me on facebook, you already know most of what I've been dealing with. For those of you who don't, well, sit back and get ready for a rollercoaster of thoughts. Like with many of my posts, things may not necessarily be in any good order, and transitions may not be the best, but that's because I type it as I think it. So, here goes. I warn you, this is long, probably one of my longest posts, so if you need to go to the bathroom or grab some popcorn, do that now . . .

I got the call on Sunday September 14, about 5pm, that there was an available pancreas that was a good match for me. The call was from Dr. Patty Liu (pronounced like 'loo'), who is a surgeon who assists Dr. Kandaswamy during surgery, doing the surgical procedure. I asked her what Dr. Kandaswamy thought about the pancreas (how good a match it is, the condition of it, etc.), and she said that this pancreas is pretty much the best pancreas we could ever get for me. So I said I'LL TAKE IT! I quickly drove to the hospital to have some final cross-matching blood drawn. The good news is that I had no antibodies against the pancreas, which means no part of the pancreas will make my white blood cells angry and start to attack it. After my blood was drawn, I returned to my dad's house, where I was visiting for dinner, and waiting for a phone call. I was told that it would be late before I heard anything more.

It wasn't until about 10pm when I got a call from my social worker. By that time I was at home, but not asleep. She told me that my final cross-matching looked good, and the only thing left was for the surgeons to actually see the pancreas. It was coming from out of state, and wouldn't be here until about 1am. Dr. Kandaswamy and Dr. Liu would then look at it to make it sure it was healthy, no damage was done to it, and that the veins/arteries on the pancreas that they would use to attach it to me, were also not damaged. The pancreas was coming from a 31 year old male who had just died in an accident. He was healthy with no medical issues except . . . he had a history of IV drug usage. However, they screen the blood over and over for all the hepatitises, HIV, and other stuff. He was completely clean, so there was no risk that I would get anything from it. I told Dr. Liu on the phone that if they felt comfortable with me getting it, then I felt comfortable.

My mom would be the one to take me to the hospital if it was good, so I kept her on alert. She kept her phone on loud when she went to bed, and kept a quick, easy change of clothes at the end of her bed. I would only call her if we needed to go. If she didn't get a call from me, and woke up at her usual time in the morning, then she would know it wasn't going to work out. I got another call from my co-worker a little after 2am. She said it didn't take them long to look at the pancreas, and it's in very good condition. So it was a GO! Although I had been in bed, I hadn't really been sleeping at all. I was too anxious. I even had my phone volume as high as it could go, so that I didn't miss the call. I called my mom, said goodbye to my kitties, and drove over to my mom's house. I wanted to leave my car there, where she could keep an eye on it, instead of leaving it unattended in front of my apartment. We then got in her car and drove to the hospital at the U, my home away from home. She just dropped me off at the front door, since we had done this drop-off thing many times, and I knew where I was going and what I was doing. I headed right up to 7A, where they got me checked-in and started the whole pre-surgery process. Even though it was the middle of the night, I had to have an EKG, an abdomen Xray so the surgeons could figure out where exactly they wanted to cut/put the pancreas, and go through the millions of questions the nurse asks. Again, I didn't really sleep. I think they came to get me around 6:30am to bring me down to the OR. Before I knew it, they were rolling me into the operating room and giving me the wonderful cocktail of sedation meds into my IV, and soon after that, the oxygen mask went on, and I was fast asleep.

For a pancreas transplant, my defunct pancreas stays in. The new pancreas went on my right side, and is connected to my bowels. Sometimes it's connected to the bladder, but usually the bowels. The benefit of connecting it to the bladder is that it's easier to tell if there's any rejection, because it's easier to see in the urine. I'm honestly not sure why they prefer to attach it to the upper part of the bowels. Maybe less risk of rejection? Easier surgery with less risk of surgical complications? Hmm, perhaps I'll ask the doc one day. During the surgery, they make a very long incision right down the middle of my stomach, because they need lots of room to stretch open the skin and have plenty of working room to get the new pancreas in there.

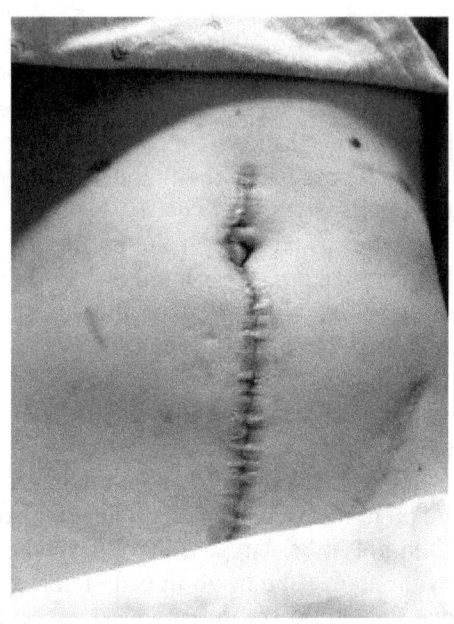

When I woke up in recovery, I actually had very little pain. During surgery, they gave me pain block shot which is a long-term pain blocking medication. It can last anywhere from days, to weeks, to months, to forever. It differs with the patient. The area around my kidney incision is STILL numb, but I found out it's probably because during the kidney surgery, some of my nerves were most likely damaged, so that area of skin will always be numb. Hmm, cool. That won't be true of the area around my pancreas incision, because the numbness has, by now (over a month and a half later), pretty much completely worn off. But it was really nice to have gotten, because it pretty much eliminated any post-surgery pain. I had discomfort, of course, but I was able to move around and get in/out of bed a lot easier, without wincing or cringing.

During that time in the hospital, I decided to name my new pancreas Hank the Panc. Hank was working SO well right off the bat. So well, in fact, that they had to put me on a medication (temporarily) to slow Hank down, because he was working a little too hard, and the docs didn't want him to work himself to "death." He needed to calm and relax and heal, and that wouldn't happen if he was working at full speed. But either way, go Hank! I considered that a really good sign. I was still on an insulin drip for the first 5 or 6 days, which is normal for pancreas transplant patients, while they make sure the new pancreas is healing and working. Right away though I was on a very low dose, .25 units an hour, which is about as low as you can get on an IV insulin drip. All my blood sugars were absolutely perfect, between 90-130 all the time. The next week, when they finally took me off the insulin drip, and let Hank do his thing, my numbers were still perfect, and in an even tighter range, between about 100-115. Sweet! And they have been ever since. ^_^

I was still on the clear liquid diet for another week, and the full liquid diet for a few days after that, because of the stricture in my esophagus, which was still causing me to have trouble swallowing. I went home on a Thursday (a week and a half after transplant), still on the full liquid diet. Dr. Kandaswamy didn't want me having the stent placed in my esophagus for at least 3 weeks post-transplant, because to put the stent in, they need to blow a lot of air into my esophagus, which travels down past my stomach and intestine, which is where my pancreas is connected. All that air would not be good for the pancreas, so I needed to give it a few weeks to heal.

I won't go into all the details, otherwise this will turn into a 10 page short-story, but I got home from transplant surgery on Thursday Sept. 25, and was back in the hospital on Friday Sept. 26. Again, I was back to not being able to swallow anything, not even liquids. This was a problem because I needed to be able to take my important transplant meds. Of course I was admitted, and I'm not sure which day it was, but I think it was over that weekend that I had a feeding tube placed in my nose, so that they could give me nutrients through that, and give me fluids through my IV, so that I would be both fed and hydrated.

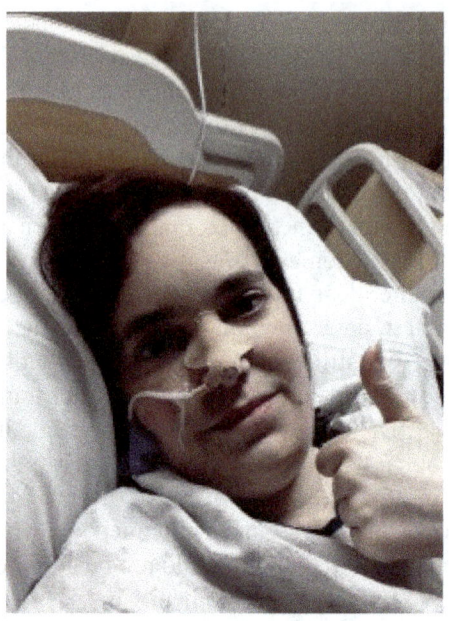

Dr. Kandaswamy still wasn't ready to let a stent be put into my esophagus, so I stayed in the hospital another week. I went home on Thursday Oct. 2. I was to do the tube feeding on my own every night. I got the supplement mush stuff to give myself, the bags to put it in, and the little pump to connect it to. It would all go in a little backpack that I could just sit next to my bed at night, and the tubing was long enough that I could toss and turn all night and I wouldn't pull it or anything. I was scheduled to have the stent put in the next day, on Friday Nov. 3, since by then I was over 2 and a half weeks out from transplant, and Dr. Kandaswamy decided that was good enough. So I only had to do the tube feeding for one night. Obviously I don't have a picture of the stent in, because I can't stick my camera down my throat to take one!

I still had the tube in my nose, so after I put under anesthesia, the GI (gastrointestinal) surgeon, Dr. Amateau, so has done all my other GI procedures, took out the tube before putting in the stent. So when I woke up in recovery, the tube was out of my nose, and the stent was in my esophagus. Remember, this time a smaller stent was put in, in the hopes that it wouldn't cause me as much pain and discomfort at the larger, first one had. Nope, no pain! I sat in recovery eating a popsicle and drinking some apple juice, then went home. Unfortunately, my stomach had shrunk so much, that I was having a hard time eating, and my appetite was almost non-existent. I still felt nauseous a lot, and even had frequent vomiting. The next week, on Weds. Oct 8, I was in SIPC to get some labs drawn and get some fluids. My blood pressure was so low, and I was so dehydrated, and having a hard time getting enough calories and nutrients in, that when Dr. Liu came to see me and check in, she decided right then to admit me again. Ugh.

Oh, if you're wondering about my kitties, don't worry, my mom and dad took turns going over the doing food/water/litter box duty each time I was in the hospital.

This time the docs decided to put a G-J feeding tube in, which is a more long-term feeding tube that is more discreet, and not hanging out of your nose. It is connected to the upper part of the intestine, so anything that goes in skips the stomach altogether, so there's less chance of nausea and vomiting. The procedure is NOT done under anesthesia, which I was not too happy about, since they have to make a small hole in the abdomen, for the tube to come out of. Yes, this means a tube would be hanging out of my abdomen, but that's easier to cover with a loose shirt or dress than it is to cover a tube hanging out of my nose! I was given a small dose of Ativan before the procedure, to help calm me down. The first part of the procedure is just like an endoscopy. They put a thing, flexible tube into my nose and down my throat; which is why I needed to be fully awake, because I needed to be able to swallow the tube so they can get it down my throat and into my stomach. After that part was done, THEN they gave me a heavier sedative. The rest I don't remember. When I "came to," I was back in my room. And in pain. Lots of it. It hurt right at the site where the tube went into my abdomen. As I commented on facebook right after the procedure, I imagined that's what it felt like to be stabbed with a butcher's knife.

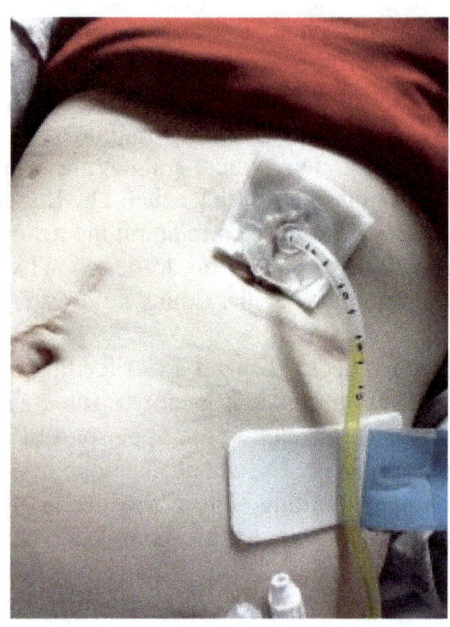

I was given tube feedings every night. I still had very little appetite, so even though I could swallow normally, I wasn't eating much during the day. I went home the next Wednesday, Oct 15, with directions to do my tube feeding every night. It would run for 12 hours, and I would be getting Iso Source, which is a calorie dense, fiber-containing formula to be used in tube feeding (although it is vanilla flavored, so it could be drunk if you want). Like with the nose tube, I put the formula in the bag, hook the tubing up to the little pump, put it all in the backpack, and let it run while I sleep. I would have to sleep at a slight angle, using a triable pillow, because if I slept too horizontally, I would wake up in the night with some indigestion feelings in my chest.

The plan for the tube was for it to stay in for at least 6-8 weeks. It's not an easy procedure, and IR (interventional radiology, the department that does the procedure) does not like to just take them out and put them in left and right. It took the docs a lot of convincing before IR finally agreed to do the procedure. I'm not sure why they don't like giving people G-J tubes, but I'm sure if I looked it up I could find out.

The G stands for 'gastro' and the J stand for 'jejuno,' which means the tube has access to both the stomach and the jejunum, which is the middle part of the small intestine. Everything that goes into my tube goes into the J port. Nothing goes in or out of the G port. I won't even go into what comes out of the G port if you take out the stopper. Being that it's the port to the stomach, you can probably figure it out yourselves. It's not pretty. Nor does it smell pretty. Yeah, made that mistake only once. I'm not even sure why they put in a G-J tube, and not just a J tube, which does exist. ANYWAY, I was to keep doing the feedings at night, as well as continue my normal eating during the day, until I was able to show the dieticians that I could eat each day to meet my caloric and nutrient needs. I wasn't excited about this tube hanging out of my stomach, especially with the pain that it was causing, but I knew the pain wouldn't last forever, and I would get used to it being there.

Well, 2 weeks after the G-J tube was put in, I was still having a lot of excruciating pain, even with the liquid Dilaudid I was taking (which, since it was in liquid form, I could put into the tube, which would make it work faster, since it didn't have to go through the whole digestion process in my stomach). Everyone has their own pain scale, based on what types and what levels of pain they've experienced in their life. A woman who has given birth might rate giving birth a 9. Since I have never given birth, I can't compare the pain from my G-J tube to that, so my 9 on the 1-10 scale is different from her 9. You know what I mean? Well anyway, it was bad. Paralyzing, at times, where I wouldn't even be able to move. The pain could be so bad, it would even make me cry. I feared getting out of bed or even getting up off the couch, because I knew the tiny bit of strain and stomach muscle needed to sit up would cause searing pain. Some pain and discomfort is normal for the first few days, but not after 2 weeks. So when I was in the SIPC clinic 2 weeks later, I told my nurse about the pain. One of the guys who helped put the tube in came and saw me to examine the tube site. I even had a chest Xray done to make sure everything looked OK on the inside. On paper, everything was perfectly normal. There was nothing there to explain why I was having such bad pain. It left me very frustrated and feeling defeated. How long was I going to have to put up with the pain? And was I really just going to have to "put up with" it?

The Dilaudid (pain killer) I was taking was doing nothing anymore. The normal dose of Dilaudid for people is 1-2mg every 4 hours. My dose was up to 4mg every 3 hours. One of the physicians who was on my medical team and following me when I was in and out of the hospital, Karin, came to see me as well, and talk to me. She told me that she, and the rest of the team, were concerned that there were other underlying issues about my taking Dilaudid. She didn't say it outright, but the message was clear: they were afraid that I was becoming addicted to it, and that my body was becoming dependent on it. My high dose wasn't even working anymore, and it would be too dangerous to increase my dose. It would just put me at higher risk for becoming addicted, which means I would want to take even more, and more frequently. She told me that what many people don't know is that when taking high doses of Dilaudid, it can actually make the nerves more sensitive to pain, and make pain even worse, which could make me want to take more, to make the pain go away, but the pain would just get worse, so I'd want to take even MORE. It's a vicious cycle, and a high enough dose can be fatal. Especially for people with kidney problems. Dilaudid's half-life (how long it stays in the system) can be up to 40 hours, so if I'm taking it every 4 hours, it can cause an excess buildup of the drug in the body, and result in fatality. No bueno.

When I got home from the clinic, I looked up Dilaudid on Wikipedia. I had been taking it for quite a while already, so I'm surprised I hadn't already looked it up. I've looked up all my different transplant meds when I started them! Let me tell you a little bit about Dilaudid. Also known as hydromorphone, is a narcotic, part of the morphine family, and of the opioid class. It's basically like the heroin of pain killers. It's 8 to 10 times more potent than morphine, and 3 to 5 times more potent than heroin. It's serious stuff. You can get a prescription to take home, but the doc can't just send the prescription to the pharmacy via the computer system. He/she has to physically walk the prescription paper to the pharmacy and give it to them. This is what Wikipedia says about the side effects of Dilaudid (hydromorphone):

> *Like other opiates, hydromorphone can be used recreationally. Its reinforcing effects are mediated via its strong affinity for the µ-opioid receptor, inducing euphoria, sedation, reduced anxiety, respiratory depression, and other prototypical morphinian effects. Although such effects make it particularly susceptible to abuse, many patients using it for analgesia are able to use it for extended periods of time without developing drug-seeking behavior. In abusers, there can be a strong psychological dependence, thus creating an addiction with repeated use. While physical*

dependence causes <u>withdrawal</u>, psychological dependence can create strong compulsions to use the drug which can persist for days or weeks after the physical dependence is broken, and has been known to induce anxiety, insomnia, depression, and a range of other persistent mental illnesses. For this reason, psychotherapy is often included in detox programs, sometimes augmented with pharmacological therapies. Despite producing similar effects, hydromorphone is more expensive on the illicit market than heroin is, causing the abuse rates of hydromorphone to be lower than heroin and similar opiates in many areas. Even in the medical community, hydromorphone is quite scarce; opiates like <u>hydrocodone</u>, <u>oxycodone</u>, and <u>fentanyl</u> are typically prescribed more often, due in part to the fact that most doctors are more familiar with those medications and the side effects and interactions thereof.

I felt like the conversation with Karin, and reading about Dilaudid, was the straw that broke the camel's back. After the discussion with her, I realized that she was right. I WAS becoming addicted to it. I craved that euphoric, warm, and happy, yet calming and relaxing sensation I would get as the drug hit my system. The problem was, I would only get that feeling when I got it via IV, because it would go straight into my blood. If I took an oral pill, or squirted it in liquid form into my mouth and swallowed it, or even put it into my G-J tube, I didn't get the same effect. My body craved that feeling, and when I was in the hospital, as soon as I was due for my next dose, I asked for it. Whether or not I was in extreme pain. I didn't realize that this was happening to me until she pointed it out, and that the medical team was concerned about me. I cried. A lot. Even on the way home, and every day for the next week. But that day, when I had been in clinic and talking to Karin, I stopped taking Dilaudid right then and there, cold turkey. It's not advised to just stop taking it, but after my realization, I didn't want it in my system anymore. After my talk with Karin, and after reading about it on Wikipedia, it scared the shit out of me. Don't worry, I didn't have any withdrawal symptoms or anything. The pain did ease up over that weekend, which made me think it WAS the Dilaudid that was making the pain so bad, but then I woke up Monday morning with the pain again, so who knows. That was frustrating.

I had also become depressed, that I knew for sure. After the pancreas transplant, everything was supposed to be better. I was supposed to be a new person. But with everything that was going on in the proceeding weeks, it completely broke my spirit. I had been so strong and so optimistic for so long, but I couldn't hold up the wall on my own anymore. With the pain from the G-J tube, and not seeing any light at the end of the tunnel as to when it would end, I felt defeated, overwhelmed, alone, and just overall down on life. I would go through these waves where I felt no hope for the future, and that would scare me and make me sad, and I couldn't stop crying. There was never any risk that I would hurt myself; I wasn't scared that I was going to do harm to myself, I was scared that I had no hope for the future. There were times when I said to myself that I don't want to be here anymore. Why me, why is this happening to me. I felt alone. My body ached, I lost my appetite, and all I wanted to do was sleep all the time. My body was tired, and my mind was tired. Every time I was discharged from the hospital, the medical team didn't like that I was going back to my apartment, where I lived alone. Although both my mom and dad live very close to my apartment, I didn't have any live-in support to help me, both physically and emotionally.

So the Saturday after I was at the clinic and had that talk with Karin, I moved back to my dad's house. Both Karin and my transplant social worker, who also came to see me when I was in the clinic that day, both asked if moving in with one of my parents for some time would be a possibility. I told them I think that's a good idea. I admitted defeat, that I definitely needed help, and that I couldn't do this whole recovery thing on my own anymore. I told them that I would talk to my dad and see if I could come stay with him and Kathy for a while. That Saturday, the day after I'd been in the clinic, before I could even text my dad, he texted me first, asking if I wanted to come stay with them. He beat me to the punch! I hadn't texted him on Friday after I left the clinic because he and Kathy had gone to Wisconsin, and were going to be home later Saturday evening. It was actually Kathy's idea to have me come stay with them. It really warmed my heart that they, too, had thought that was a good idea. I stayed in Elliott's room, since he's away at college. Early evening on Saturday, before going over there, I had another wave of depression and hopelessness wash over me. I didn't want to be alone. I needed to be around people. I couldn't stop crying, just sitting on my couch hugging my knees. I actually felt scared for my life for a little bit, scared for my future. I was scared because I had lost hope for my future. I wanted my dad and Kathy to come home quick, so that I could pack my bag and go over there. My mom was also out of town, so she wasn't home, and I seriously considered calling my aunt and uncle, who live in Richfield, and ask if I could come over and hang out with them for a little bit before going to my dad's. But I made it through, and after dropping Kathy off at the house, he came and picked me up at my apartment, because I didn't think it was a good idea to drive.

I stayed at my dad's full-time for a week, but went home to visit my kitties for a few hours every day. I was alone during the days while my dad and Kathy were at work, so I didn't do very well with breakfast and lunch, because I didn't have the energy or motivation to make anything, and I was still having blood pressure issues, so mostly all I want to do was rest. But at least I was getting good, nutritious dinners. At least, on the nights I felt hungry, I did. Many days I never felt hungry at all, at any time. I quickly figured out that the tube feeding was making me ill. I remember it doing that when I had to have a tube in my nose back in 2006. It made me lose my appetite, I because feeling nauseous and throwing up more and more often, until one day I threw up and the tube came right up and out of my throat, dangling out of my mouth. That wasn't fun. This time it wasn't in my nose, so I wasn't going to throw it up, but the formula was making me sick again. I had the same symptoms. So I started doing the tube feeding less and less. As of right now, Friday 11/7, I have not done the tube feeding in 9 days. And you know what? The nausea and vomiting has ceased, and I've begun feeling hungry again, and am eating a lot more. Huh, imagine that. The tube is still in, and I told Dr. Ibrahim on Wednesday that I stopped doing it, so if they want me to keep using it, they'll have to find something else, like another formula, to use. And even then, I'm sure it will still have the same effect. I think they should just take it out and let me eat on my own, since that is greatly improving.

The next week I started back at work, but not full-time. Most days I went in a couple hours later, and/or went home early. One day that week I even took the whole day off because I was too exhausted. This week was much better, although I was out on Wednesday again, but have still been pretty good at coming in at my regular time. Not every day have I made it all the way to 5:00, but I made it as far as I could, usually around 3 or so would be time for me to go home because my body was telling me it was time to be done for the day. I'm actually listening to my body and not trying to push it this time. This week I started a medication that is meant to help me retain water and raise my blood pressure, since it has been running low for a long time, like months. I'm also back at my apartment, have been all week, although the option to go to my dad and Kathy's for dinner is always open. I suppose one of these days I could go over and get the rest of my belongings that are still there. . . .

Things are currently going alright, but not perfect. I still have a long road ahead of me, that's for sure. I'm sure I have forgotten to mention many things, but I have been working on this on and off for 3 days now, so I'm just going to publish it. If you've made it all the way this far, congrats! You are a trooper and a loyal reader. I applaud you. :D

If you have any questions or want to know more about something, don't be shy! I am very open about everything, as I've said before, and also like I've said, if you're wondering something, chances are good that someone else is, too. Thanks for reading. Bye for now!

November 10, 2014 Facebook
Why is everyone complaining about the snow and not going to work because of the snow? This is Minnesota, people! We've known it was going to snow for like a week now, everyone should have been prepared! Why weren't y'all getting out your snow tires and shovels and window scrapers over the weekend? Sheesh. #mondayrant #sorrynotsorry

November 13, 2014 Email
so how you doing?
Dad to Krystin:
    Haven't heard from you for a bit. Things going OK?
    LY

Krystin to dad:
    Yup.

Dad to Krystin:
    Good! Are you still having to use the feeding tube, or can you get enough food and liquid so you don't have to? Would be nice if you could get rid of it.

Krystin to dad:

I haven't done tube feeding for 3 weeks. I see Dr. Kandaswamy on Monday and will talk to him about when the tube can come out, since I'm not using it for anything except Dilaudid, which I'm not even really taking anymore either. I'm doing pretty good, I think, on eating on my own. Can still use improvement, but my appetite is coming back more and more, so, we'll see what he says.

Dad to Krystin:

I am so pleased! And glad for you!

November 14, 2014 Text
Krystin to dad: Went home at 2:30 yesterday cuz I had been throwing up since about 1:45. Am home today, still throwing up. :-(
Dad: Damn. Call your coordinator?
Krystin: Yup, good idea. And of course no idea what triggered it. Or what is keeping it going.
Dad: That is the $64,000 question.
(later) Krystin: You home?
Dad: No, out to dinner and then theater in St Paul. You ok?
Krystin: No but nm
Dad: You going in to hospital? Did you check to see if mom around if you need help?
Krystin: She already brought me.
Dad: Where are you? ???
Krystin: ER
Dad: I am so sorry. Let me know what happens. I will have phone off 7:30 but will check at intermission and later.
Gary to Pat: You know what's up with k?
Pat: I drove her to the ER about 6:00. She said she'd been sleeping and barfing since 1:30 yesterday. Finally called somebody named Barb and was told to go in. That's all I know. She said she tried you first but no response so tm'd me. I was gonna TM you once I had more info.
Gary: Out to dinner and theater. Thanks for letting me know.

November 15, 2014 Text
Pat to Gary: She received fluids and apparently took taxi home at 1am.
Dad to Krystin: Where are you and how you doing?
Krystin: Home. Doing ok.
Dad: Any doc ideas how to deal with throwing up?

Krystin: Nope. All that happened was I got fluids. And a chest xray to see if my stent has moved, but it hasn't. That was all.
Dad: Nausea now?
Krystin: Luckily no, but not hungry either. Head feels a little funny, I'm guessing I need food since I haven't had any since noon on Thurs. :-/ (November 15 was Saturday)
Dad: So eat a little! And keep on drinking.
Krystin: I have Pedialyte too, so that should help. Starting with applesauce to make sure it will stay down.
Dad: Good idea to go slow, but would think should just keep on eating little bit at a time. I need to run to highland. You need any food?
Krystin: I'm going to. And no, I think I'm good. Thanks though.
Dad: Bananas? Grape tomatoes? Those both good for you.
Krystin: Maybe some bananas and cinnamon Life cereal.
Dad: Ok and when I bring them in, litter box will be clean, right? :-)
Krystin: Of course.
Dad: Is partial box of the cereal in bag of your food I'm bringing. Is that enough or you want additional box? Milk? Mango juice smoothie?
Krystin: Oh, I still have some Life cereal? More would be good. 1/2 gallon of milk please. Mango smoothie? Sure, sounds good.
Dad: You like potato salad or any other Lunds deli salad?
Krystin: Oh, and more Pedialyte? Mixed berry flavor. Will probably be in the baby aisle. I will pay you back, that stuff is kinda expensive.
Dad: Salad?
Krystin: No, can't eat lettuce with stent in. It can get stuck. Those things should be enough.
(later) Krystin: Great, feeling nauseous again. What the hell is going on in me?? This is irritating.
Dad: Darn.
(later) Krystin: Well, just threw up. I dunno what to do. All they would do at ER is give fluids, which I don't need. Something else must be going on.
Krystin: Called for coordinator on call. Will see what she says. I will ONLY go back to ER if they have other plans/ideas other than just fluids.
Dad: Keep me posted. Wish I could help, but doesn't seem like there's much I can do.
Krystin: Talked to coordinator. I need to really push the fluids. Unfortunately, dehydration can cause the body to not feel well, and to throw up. I just peed for the first time since yesterday, which means

even with the fluids last night, I'm still dehydrated. So I have to push past the nausea and keep sipping my Pedialyte for the next 6 or so hours. Will call back if it gets worse. So, that's the plan. Good thing you got me more Pedialyte!
Dad: Keep on drinking!

November 17, 2014 Text
Krystin to dad: If you saw my email, never mind. I going home first. Need wait for a bed on 7A anyway.
Pat to Gary: Sounds like she's going home first cuz 7A room not ready yet. I'll drive her in and keep her car at my house.
Dad to Krystin: Ok. Mom also told me. Give her your keys.
Dad: You're back on 7A?
Krystin: Yes 7A, room 213, by the door. My roommate burps and sniffles constantly. Probably a snorer, too.
Dad: I come see you 3:30 or bit thereafter?
Krystin: Sure, I'll be here!

November 17, 2014 Facebook
Krystin Engstrand is at Fairview University Medical Center.

I'm not sure how open about it I've been on my blog, but for about the past month and a half, I started developing severe depression, and it has only seemed to have gotten worse. I now understand how debilitating a mental illness it can be, and how it affects your daily life and keeps you from functioning normally. My doc does not feel like I should be home right now, and I agree. Being completely honest, I have had saddening and scary thoughts, and right now, being here and getting help is what is best and what I need. Sometimes you just need medical help because there's no more you can do on your own. I'm not OK right now, but I will be. My spirit may be broken, but I'm strong and will bounce back.

And I'm telling the docs I don't wanna be on Xanax anymore. The other night I had this genius idea to create a device that lets you blow bubbles in the shape of llamas. Or llamas in the shape of bubbles. Could be fun.

Anyway, here I am.

November 18, 2014 Text
Krystin to dad: They really do love me here. Moving me to a single room in about half an hour, and I didn't even ask for it! ^_^

(later) Dad: How you feeling?
Krystin: Well, after you left, I spent the next hour filling up 3 of those blue bags. I think my stomach just wasn't ready for the big bfast and lunch I ate. Now I know for tomorrow. Still a tiny bit nauseous, but I don't think anything will happen.
Dad: That's the problem you should be asking them to address! If you could eat, the world would be better!
Krystin: I can eat, I just have to take it slow. I'm still expanding my stomach, remember.
Dad: So go slow! I guess you just have to eat all the time, in little bits.
Krystin: I know that now.
Dad: Starting tonight, right?
Krystin: Well kitchen is closed now. Didn't eat dinner. So starting tomorrow morning.
Dad: Ok! Gnite Speed. Do well tomorrow.

November 19, 2014 Facebook
I saw a psychiatrist yesterday, and he put me on a drug called Remeron (also known as Mirtazapine) to help me sleep. Last night I was given the smallest dose possible, and within 10 minutes was deader than a log fast asleep. I slept for 12 straight hours and woke up with a sleep hangover and extremely sedated still. No fun. Good thing I got Ritalin this morning, to counteract it.

> Krystin: I could hardly open my eyes, talk, or lift my head this morning. I just stared at my nurse with my mouth hanging open. She probably thought I had a stroke or something at first! Definitely not worth the dead-like slumber.

November 19, 2014 Email
Dad to Krystin:
You doing well today?
Krystin to dad:
> Yeah, doing alright today. Once I got the Ritalin and woke up more this morning, that is. Before that, it was rough. I seriously felt like a zombie (or how I imagine a zombie would feel, I guess?). Ate lunch and that has stayed down. No bfast because I was just too out of it. I took it slow, and then had a snack recently. No nausea, so that's good! I still have a lot of, um, "stuff" impacted in my colon, so I have to do another enema today, but I keep telling myself for the best. I'm

pretty sure it's when I get backed up that causes the vomiting. Not to be blunt, but it's a case of no more can go in before something comes out.

Anyway, that's what I have to look forward to on my agenda for the rest of the day. Woohoo.

Dad to Krystin:
So, if your hypothesis is correct, once the colon gets "unimpacted," and you can keep it that way, then the nausea and vomiting should not recur. Have you tested this hypothesis on any of the docs? And is it possible to prevent colon impaction in the future?

Krystin to dad:
Well, yes, and that's what the gastric pacer should be helping with. Dr. Kandaswamy checked it out today with this little portable device, and apparently when I saw him a few weeks ago and he turned up the setting, it reset and went back to its lower setting. He thinks there is something wrong with the program, cuz he's seen other patient's pacers have the same problem. So he's calling Medtronic.

Probably more fiber in my diet, too. Will probably need a supplement for that. Or just a daily stool softener. I will write the question on my board for tomorrow!

Dad to Krystin:
This all sounds positive! Let's hope it works out.

November 19, 2014 Text
Dad to Krystin: So what's up? Still keeping food down and over morning grogginess?
Krystin: Yes and yes. They gave me Ritalin for the drowsiness, so helped greatly. And all meals stayed down, no nausea.
Dad: So smaller dose of Remeron or whatever it is? Any idea how long you will be there?

November 20, 2014 Text
Krystin to dad: Mom coming to get me, as I'm sure you've seen. Have a good evening!
Dad: Thanks!
(later) Krystin: I'm home and all settled in! Happy to be back with the furry kids.

November 21, 2014 Text
Dad to Krystin: You ok today?
Krystin: Day went well. Went in at noon and didn't feel exhausted or anything.
Dad: Good! So you doing ok. Still feel fine?
Krystin: Yes to both. Feeling good in both mind and body. Even after only 3 days of being on Ritalin, I think it's helping.

November 23, 2014 Text
Pat to Gary: Has K been staying with you?
Gary: Nope. Coming for dinner.
Pat: Ok. I thot doc had said she should stay with someone for a bit but she must be ok?
Gary: Seems to be. Who knows. I thought she was going to stay a couple of days, but hasn't said anything further about it.

November 27, 2014 Text [Thanksgiving day]
Krystin: I need to go in.
Krystin: Bad timing, I know.
Dad: Can you ask mom?
Krystin: Yes.

Joan to Gary: What is going on with Krystin?
Gary: IDK about Krystin. Texted, said she needed to go in. I asked her to ask Pat cuz was in middle of cooking. Have not heard since.
Gary to Pat: What's up with Krystin?
Pat: Said had diarrhea all night. Drank water and put some in tube but "I just can't keep up." She was weak. Dropped her off. She knows she will need cab home. I'm due at sis at 11:00 (that ain't gonna happen) and you have gig at 4. I agreed she on own now.
Gary: Thanks
Dad to Krystin: So what's going on?
Krystin: I had to come in because I had diarrhea that started yesterday and went ALL night. No sleep. Couldn't keep up with fluids, no food, so very weak and dehydrated. This sucks big time.
Krystin: Am going to get another liter of fluids, and have some juice and crackers. Doc will talk to Dr. Kandaswamy. MAY not need to be admitted since I have appt at SIPC tomorrow morning. Fingers crossed. I will still miss dinner though.
Krystin: I get to leave, but hold onto my ipad. I'll just get it tomorrow.

Dad: When you leaving? You can't come up to dinner?
Krystin: Prob 20 minutes. I suppose I could, but I'm a mess.
Dad: Up to you. [She didn't come.]
(later) Krystin: I'm finally home.
Dad: Ok! Feeling better?
Krystin: Yes, much, thanks.

November 28, 2014 Text
Krystin to dad: Weak again, even after all the fluids and food yesterday. Dunno what's going on.
Dad: Sigh. Let me know.
Krystin: Yup
(later) Krystin: Am in room 216. They must be really worried about me, because I have a "babysitter." This guy who just sits in my room with me. Kinda awkward, but whatever. My phone has 23% battery life left, so if I don't get charger tonight, may or may not last until tomorrow. Will give you my room phone number when done with all the admission stuff.
Dad: Ok
Krystin: 273-0798. Phone at 17%! So text sparingly.
Dad: Ok. If you want to, you could still come tomorrow night to dinner, even if back to hospital after. Ask about that if you want.
Krystin: Ok. Good idea. I would be going in my sweatpants and sweatshirt and looking like a bum, but I'm sure they don't care. I will definitely bring it up with the docs in the morning.
Krystin: You going to send me a pic of the tree? Peggy might be willing to take my kids.
Pat to Gary: I've got the cats and will go over tomorrow and gather rest of cat items. Not sure how that will sit when she gets home; will you go to hospital tomorrow with her stuff? Tablet & charger and a phone charger. She's on 7A.
Gary: Yes. Thanks. Peggy may take cats.

November 28, 2014 Facebook
Krystin Engstrand is feeling sad.
This is really, really hard for me to do, and it breaks my heart, but I think I need to find a new home for Gabi and Molly. With all my health issues and hospitalizations, I can't give them the proper care they need. I love them more than anything, but they deserve better. So if you or

anyone you know wants 2 loving, affectionate kitties, I would be glad to talk to you. I will NOT bring them to [the Humane Society]

> Christine Hinz Lenzen: My mom is going to foster them - Cecilia Cécile this is one step in the right direction.

November 29, 2014 Text
Dad to Krystin: You coming with us today? I have pair of black pants of yours I could bring for you.
Krystin: No, I can't leave then come back. Liability issues. Especially since I'm here for psych reasons. Am going to stay one more night though. Can leave tomorrow, but doc wants me to stay with you again for a little bit, if that's ok.
Dad: That's too bad. Ok
Krystin: He also wants you to be here tomorrow morning to meet with him and me and discuss a plan.
Dad: Ok

November 30, 2014 Text
Dad to Krystin: You have any idea of time this morning?
Krystin: No, because now I'm having stent procedure today instead of tomorrow, cuz it has moved. Dunno what time that is, haven't seen docs yet.
Dad: Solves tomorrow's problem! Wonder if they'll release you today. If so, not until later in day, I bet.
Krystin: Yup, most likely.
Dad: Just keep me posted.
(later) Krystin: Just saw Dr. Kandaswamy right now. Have to stay overnight again before procedure, which will be tomorrow morning, as originally planned. I need stay here and be NPO cuz stent has moved (slid) into stomach. They will keep me clear liquids and IV fluids. Food could cause the stent to be pushed into upper intestine, which would mean a more difficult procedure to remove it. So that's the plan.
Dad: Ok. So that's that. Any indication stent did its work? Just one damn thing after another! You feel ok?
Krystin: Guess I will find out within next week or so. Well, actually, probably right away! Doing ok now. Was nauseous and throwing up earlier. Probably cuz some of my meds need be taken with food, and there's no food in me. :(
Dad: Oh boy. Hang in there.

(later) Dad: How you doing?
Krystin: I'm doing alright. Hungry, since all I get is clear liquids.
Dad: Thanks. And good!

December 1, 2014 Text
Dad to Krystin: You let me know what's going on, when you can go home? I can get you any time after 1:00.
Krystin: No going home today. Not sure why exactly, but Dr. Kandaswamy said "within the next day or so." He wants me to see psych one more time before going and to make sure I really feel good and safe about leaving, so this doesn't happen again. So, yeah. That's the new plan.
Dad: Ok. I stop over this afternoon.
(later) Dad: Able to get food down and it staying down?
Krystin: Yes.
Dad: Good sign.

December 2, 2014 Text
Krystin to dad: Discharge today! But don't know when yet. I still have people I need to see before leaving. I'm guessing early evening.
Krystin: I need to go to my apt to get some stuff, and your house to get key. What are you doing for dinner? Should I find my own?
Dad: We think it will be Mings palace night.
Krystin: Ok. My discharge orders are in, but I have to wait for meds to be filled at discharge pharmacy. Not sure how long that will take. I will come there from the hospital though. Chicken chow mein for me, please, if you order before I get there. I will let you know when I have a better idea of time.
Dad: Kathy has to deliver humidifier to Spence after work, and she in meeting until 5. So who knows when we get food. Maybe we order and keep it warm.
Krystin: Ok. Either way, I will be there eventually for chow mein!
Dad: Ok!

December 3, 2014 Text
Dad to Krystin: All ok with doc? In meeting until 10:30.
Krystin: Yup, all is good. Was a short visit, since both my EBV and CMV levels are negative!
Dad: Great! Back to work?

Krystin: Yup. Feels good to be back. Dave welcomed me back, too, and asked how I'm doing.
Dad: Now, let's just hope you're where you're going to be!
Krystin: You mean like how I'm feeling?
Dad: Yes. Feeling good permanently!
Krystin: Then yes, let's hope that! Aside from being a little tired, I feel good today. More days like this would be quite alright with me! The Ritalin really helps.
Dad: You with us for dinner? DK what. At coop, may get something here.
Krystin: No, going to mom's tonight for chicken dinner and see my girls.

December 4, 2014 Facebook
This weekend my girls will move in with their foster auntie, Peggy Hinz. I am so grateful, and could not have asked for a better foster home for them until I am healthy and ready to be their mommy again. And the best part is that I can go visit them once in a while. ^_^

> Krystin: My only fear is that they'll forget all about me and won't want to come back home with me when that day comes. Or that they'll change, and won't be the same kitties that they are now. BUT, it's better than losing them forever!

December 6, 2014 Text
Pat to Gary: Have you seen or heard from K today?
Gary: Not today, no. Should I or we expect to?
Pat: Hmmmmm, I thought she was staying with you. Have sent a couple texts today but no reply. I give up. We can't live like this.
Gary: She been staying at Jeff and Randy house. I sent her email this morning, but it didn't require a response. I will try texting.
Dad to Krystin: You ok? Mom worried you not respond to texts. She thought you staying here.
Krystin: I'm ok! Just slept in late today.
Dad: Good! I worry. Let your mom know, too.
Krystin: I did.

December 8, 2014 Text
Krystin to dad: Shit, having problems swallowing again. UGH. Calling G.I. ASAP.

Dad: Yeah, better get in there fast. Damn.

December 9, 2014 Text
Dad to Krystin: So what does FB post mean? You back in hospital?
Krystin: Nope. Just got a cold.
Dad: And the esophagus problem? Your FB post is misleading cuz makes it sound serious!
Krystin: I edited it to clarify that.
Dad: And esophagus?
Krystin: And esophagus issue not solved. Both Dr. Kandaswamy and Dr. Ibrahim said to see this other doctor. When will I see him? Who knows. Dawn is going to try to get me in as soon as possible, but who knows what that means either. That other doctor could have other ideas cuz he specializes in that kind of thing. So ok, I see him, then more waiting until something can be done. This is all very frustrating how much time it takes, when this is an urgent matter!
Dad: Sigh. Just keep on pushing, I guess.
Krystin: Yup.
Dad: Meantime, you can still eat and drink, albeit slowly?
Krystin: Yeah.

December 10, 2014 Text
Krystin to dad: Appointment next Friday [December 19] with the throat doc. Great. Hope it doesn't get worse before then, but I know it will in that amount of time. I will try my hardest to stay out of hospital but it may be inevitable.
Dad: Too late. Best they can do? What if you have problem sooner?
Krystin: Then I have to go in. They would have to do tube feedings and IV fluids to keep me stable until appointment. But like I said, I'm not there yet.

December 12, 2014 Text
Krystin to dad: Can I stay over tonight? I know E is home. I am perfectly comfy on a couch. I just need that extra support around right now.
Dad: Sure.
Krystin: Thank you.

December 18, 2014 Facebook
Krystin Engstrand is feeling frustrated.
Well, the esophageal stent that was taken out a few weeks ago, that had been in for 8 weeks, was totally pointless. My esophagus has narrowed again, to the point that I can't swallow anything, not even a sip of water. It's extremely painful to swallow, and I can't open my mouth all the way without my jaw hurting. Tomorrow I see a special surgeon to discuss possible surgery options to permanently fix the problem. I already missed Thanksgiving. If I have to miss Christmas too, I am NOT going to be a happy camper. Well, more unhappy than I already am. Grr.

December 15, 2014 Email
how you doing?
Dad to Krystin:
    Back to work and doing OK on food and liquids?

Krystin to dad:
    I'm doing alright. My right eye is all blurry again, because a blood vessel must have popped, so I can't see at all out of my right eye. Everything is just a big blur. Driving to work was OK since it was light out, but I'm leaving early today so that I can leave before it gets dark, because there's no way I feel comfortable driving with only one good eye when it's dark out.
    Eating/drinking is going fine. Still hit-or-miss, but so far I've managed. Like I said, chew thoroughly, and small, slow sips. I may just make it to Friday! But really it's not just until Friday, because nothing is going to be done Friday. Really I gotta make it until whenever he decides what he wants done, if that's something they can do here, and then when. Ugh. This esophagus narrowing thing is probably my least favorite of all the health stuff I've encountered in the past year.
    This week is a busy week for me. Tomorrow is the health psychologist, Wednesday is the chiropractor, Thursday is Monica, and Friday is the throat surgeon. But at least that's pretty much it for the rest of the month.

Dad to Krystin:
    Uff da. So does the eye just gradually fix itself? I can't remember how that gets repaired. Or do you have to go back to the eye doc?

I can understand that the esophagus problem is the most annoying. I wonder if you shouldn't get a second opinion, like maybe go to Mayo. You might inquire about that.

I hope you make time for work this week!

Krystin to dad:
The eye problem fixes itself. I just have to wait for the fluid to drain/get soaked back up. Usually takes 3-4 days. It'll be really blurry like this for the first 2 days, then by the 3rd day I can notice it getting better, by the 4th day it's 90% better, and by the 5th day it's all cleared up. On average, that's how it goes. This is starting to happen more and more often, like once every couple months. I need to make an appointment with Dr. Bennett anyway, so when I see him next, he can look at my eye with his magic machine and will be able to see the blood/fluid/whatever pooling there in front of my vision. I'm guessing he'll want to do the eyeball shots again. Which I'll take over the laser treatment any day! The laser treatment is not pleasant at all, as I'm sure I've complained/cried about in the past.

I could get a 2nd opinion from Mayo, but who knows how long THAT will take before they can even get me in to see them? The only reason I'm getting in to see Dr. Agrade on Friday is because Dawn called and gave them a referral for me and pushed the clinic to get me in asap. I bet with Mayo it would be months before I got in. I'd be dead by then. O.o (OK, maybe I over exaggerated a little on that one.)

Yes, it's a lot of appointments this week, but I'm still able to work, and actually, I'm not missing that much work. All my appointments are late afternoon, so I'll need to leave early only half an hour one day, an hour the next day, and on Friday I'm just taking a long lunch from 11-1. So it's not too big of a deal.

Dad to Krystin:
It can't hurt to ask about Mayo.

December 19, 2014 Email
Dad to Krystin:
You'll let me know about the discussion with the doc today?

Krystin to dad:
Of course. I know I've told other people, but I don't remember if I told you - depending on what kind of plan he comes up with, and a

timeline, if nothing can be done until after Christmas, then I'm going to request that we do the endoscopy with the balloon, where they inflate the balloon inside my esophagus, then take the balloon out. Last time they did that, my esophagus stayed open enough that I could swallow well enough to eat, even if only for a week. At least that would get me through Christmas. If I'm not able to swallow, obviously I'll still come to dinner, I'll just have to sit there and be part of the conversations while everyone else eats. :-/

But I'm really going to push him on the esophagus dilation thing.

December 20, 2014 Text
Dad to Krystin: So what happened with doc?
Krystin: He will do dilation on Tuesday, to get me through Xmas and can work on a long term plan. At same time, my left tonsil is infected and had abscess that a nose/ear/throat doc poked to drain. So, a needle into the back of my throat. That was real painful. Now on a strong antibiotic for 10 days. The infection is not related to the esophagus thing.
Dad: One damn thing after another. BTW, you and E invited to Jensen Xmas on January 1.

December 31, 2014 Email
Friday night
Dad to Krystin:
    You at work today?

Krystin to dad:
    Yes, of course I'm at work today!

Dad to Krystin:
    Good--glad you're able to be at work with some regularity now!

Krystin to dad:
    Yes, I am doing very well these days. The past 3 or so weeks now have been consistently good, with no days of feeling down and sad. Now that the meds have had their full period of time to fully get into my system, they are working well. I generally feel happy all the time, even though this esophagus issue is frustrating. Even though the meds are a big part of the reason why I'm feeling better, I think it's also because I can finally see a light at the end of the tunnel. This esophagus

issue is the last big thing that needs to get resolved. After that, it's pretty much smooth sailing toward getting my life back and getting healthy, and getting this stupid tube out of my stomach and the picc line out of my arm.

Dad to Krystin:
    Yes! I am soooooooooooo glad for you.
    I take it no news on the esophagus.

Krystin to dad:
    Yes actually, some news on the esophagus. I have an appointment next Friday for the barium swallowing study, where they video me swallowing the barium, and not just take x-ray pictures. It's like an x-ray video instead. Then, immediately after that, I have a follow-up appointment with Dr. Andrade (the thoracic surgeon guy), so he'll be able to see the results of the study right away. I hope that from there, he can decide what course of action to take. If he wants to do more tests, I'm going to first make him do the esophagus inflation procedure again, because I can already feel it slightly beginning to narrow again. I can still eat and drink and everything, but I can feel just a tad of narrowing. Fingers crossed I can make it to next week. I need to take a break on the tube feeding, because I can feel it's starting to affect my appetite. It's not making me nauseous yet, but I'm going to avoid that altogether by not doing it for 2-3 days. So good, healthy, carb and calorie-filled eating I must do!

January 2, 2015 Text
Krystin to dad: Ugh, my esophagus is starting to narrow again. Not completely, but it's starting. And my swallow test appointment isn't until next Friday. Sigh.
Dad: Can you eat with us tonight and tomorrow night?
Krystin: Yeah, pretty sure.
Dad: Good. And rats.

January 5, 2015 Text
Dad to Krystin: How's throat doing?
Krystin: As far as swallowing, still doing alright. As far as my cold, my throat is scratchy and it constantly feels like I'm going to cough. When I do cough, it hurts. Usual cold symptoms. Nose is runny and itchy, too.

Dad: Sigh. Keep your chin up.
Krystin: Yup. Hopefully a good night's sleep tonight will let me feel well enough to go to work tomorrow. I'll be buying some cough drops and DayQuil on the way in.

January 9, 2015 Text
Krystin to dad: Dr. appt at 2:45. I got here a little after 3 cuz was doing swallow test. Just got brought into a room now. Doc is STILL 30-40 minutes behind, until he sees me (2 patients ahead of me to see). Wtf?? That's a bit irritating.
Dad: Let's talk tonight.
Krystin: 4 and I'm still waiting. Omg.
Dad: You should have raised a stink. Politely.
Krystin: So, there is no permanent solution to my esophagus narrowing. I will have to keep doing the dilation. We are going to start with doing it every 3 weeks, and hopefully at some point it will get to the point where we can make it longer between dilations. It's not an ideal solution of course, but that is the only option without doing major surgery, and he said that is a bad idea, with my health history, and he's not even sure what could be done surgically. Great. So that's the plan, I guess. Next dilation will be one day next week; won't find out when until Monday, when it gets scheduled.
Dad: Well, I guess that's what you have to do. A pain, but maybe as you say it will eventually get stretched out and stay open longer. Wish there were a better solution.

January 10, 2015 Facebook
Yesterday I had my follow-up appt. with the thoracic surgeon, after having done a swallowing test with barium syrup. Verdict is, there's no permanent solution to my esophagus narrowing. I have completely stumped the medical field. So, I have to go in every 3 weeks for the esophageal dilation procedure. The hope is that over time I won't need to go in as often, if my esophagus starts to stay open longer, but for now, this is what I'll have to do indefinitely. Fabulous.

January 12, 2015 Email
Esophagus dilation procedure
Krystin to mom, dad:
Hi mom,

My procedure is going to be this Friday, 1/16. It's scheduled for 10:15, so I have to arrive at the hospital at 8:15. I'm hoping that since it's in the morning, the guy won't be TOO far behind schedule (unlike last time, where I went in 2 hours late). Dad and Kathy leave for India on Thursday, and as you know, since they'll be putting me under anesthesia, I can't drive myself home, which means I wouldn't be driving myself there. Is there any way you could bring me in on Friday? I would be going right to the hospital, not to work first. And then would you also be able to pick me up after work? If you can do one but not the other, or can't do either, I can take a cab. And in the afternoon, if I'm done way before it's time for you to leave, I can hang out there. It's not like they're going to kick me out or anything.

When I saw the doc last week, I asked why they put me under anesthesia for this, since the first time it was done, like 5 and a half months ago, it was done under sedation, they didn't put me all the way to sleep. I learned it's because under anesthesia, they can be a little more vigorous than if I were awake. They can also dilate the esophagus wider if I'm asleep, and can hold the balloon device thing in there longer as well, which ideally means the esophagus will stay open longer if the balloon is in there longer. That makes sense. I just hope that this time I don't have such a bad anesthesia hangover like I did last time. At least it's on a Friday, so I don't have to worry about getting up for work the next day!

I told you that, to start off with, we're going to be doing this every 3 weeks, right? I don't remember who I told and who I didn't.

Anyway, let me know your thoughts. Happy Monday! Love you.

Dad to Krystin, Pat:

That's unfortunate, in one way, because it means you have to take a day out of work every 3 weeks. Would be nicer if they could do it on a Saturday. I guess I understand the need for anesthesia, but sure would be better without it.

Good luck!

Krystin to dad:

They don't like to do it on weekends because no one is there on weekends, so if anything went wrong, there's limited staff there to help. Or if I had a problem once I got home, then it's better to be during the week because everyone is there if I needed to go back in for something. Yes, it sucks as far as having to take a day off work, but I do understand their reasoning. Oh well. Dave understands, of course.

January 20, 2015 Facebook

For my esophagus procedure last week, the doc didn't just dilate it, he put in a stent again, also! (Per my request). This means that, for now, instead of going in every 3 weeks for dilation, I don't have to go in now for another 8 weeks, when the stent comes out. Then we'll play it by ear from there! So in the meantime, time for some major nomnomnoms.

February 4, 2015 Blog

Catching up: Part 1

It has been so long since I posted last, and things have just been so busy (read: chaotic) and I just haven't had the time to properly sit down and focus my mind on posting. Being that there are many things to update you on, I'm going to do it in stages, and each post will focus on one particular aspect of my life the past few months.

Part 1: Addiction

I realize that I am friends with a handful of my co-workers on facebook, and when I post an entry on here, it automatically cross-posts it to facebook. Some people may send me private messages (ahem, dad, ahem) about how I shouldn't be talking about this publicly, but I said from the very beginning that I was going to be open and honest about everything that was going on in my health care endeavors, and this issue has become a much bigger one than I ever expected.

On and off since my kidney transplant in 2013, whenever I was in and out of the hospital (which, let's admit, was a lot), if I was ever in pain, I would get Dilaudid through my IV. No biggie, just getting it here and there, and only while I was in the hospital. After my pancreas transplant last September, and the placement of the G-J tube in my abdomen, I had been on liquid Dilaudid consistently, every day, since then. That's almost 5 straight months of being on one of the strongest narcotic pain medications available. My daily dosing was 2-4mg every 4 hours as needed, and it was measured out so that I could take it 4 times a day, say 9, 1, 5, and 9. 20mg total for a day.

I should mention: I needed the pain medication because of the tube. Since the tube hangs out of my abdomen, which is an area that we're constantly moving during the day, and even at night if we toss and turn, the area around where the tube in inserted can't heal. Scar tissue can't form because the area isn't still enough for long enough for it to heal. If I had stayed in bed, not moving at all, for a week, then maybe it would've healed. Ain't nobody got time for that. And in reality, nobody CAN do that. We need to go to the bathroom, we need to eat, etc. etc. Since the area around it never heals, I have chronic pain from it. Sometimes the pain would be so bad that it would be paralyzing. Especially for the first month/month and a half after it was put in. It was especially hard getting out of bed. Not so much getting in, since I can just plop into bed. Getting OUT is another story, since we have to use stomach muscles to pull ourselves up and off the bed. Same with couches. So, any time I'd go from a lying or sitting position to an upright position, well, let me tell ya. OW. The Dilaudid couldn't help with that pain, but at least that was temporary, maybe for a minute or so after standing up. It did greatly help, though, with the daily pain of moving around and doing whatever I was doing. You know, living.

Here's the problem: After being on it for a while, I started building up a tolerance to it. I needed a higher dose to make the pain go away. Here's the other problem: I also needed a higher dose to give me the nice, happy side effect that it has on me that I was starting to crave. Euphoria: intense mental and emotional feelings of well-being, contentment, happiness, joy, and relaxed body and mind. Those feelings may only last for 10-20 minutes, but I was thoroughly beginning to enjoy those minutes. Since I had it in liquid form, I was putting it into my tube, which is how I was supposed to be giving it to myself anyway. For pain medication, I don't do well with pills, thanks to my gastroparesis. It would take a pill what seemed like FOREVER before my stomach finally broke it down and started to absorb the medication. And because of the gastroparesis, who knows how much of it I was actually getting. For example, I may take a 4mg pill, but only end up absorbing 2 or 3mg. With the liquid form going into the tube, it skips the stomach and digestion process altogether. The tube was going into my upper intestine, in case you didn't know that. So I would absorb it faster, and all of it, instead of sitting and waiting in pain, wondering when the pill would get digested, and if it was even going to help.

Let me be honest now. I didn't necessarily need to take more for the pain. My 4mg dose probably would've been just fine to get rid of the pain. But I was beginning to need more and more to get that euphoric feeling. Instead of taking one dose of 4mg, I would take a 10mg dose in the morning, then not take any all day, and then in the evening, when I was in my sweatpants and sweatshirt and settled in for the night on my couch with a TV show on, I would take another 10-12mg dose and enjoy the feeling while it lasted. On the weekends I would do that a few times, since I was pretty much sitting around at my apartment all day. Once, I ran out before I was due for a refill, since my primary care doctor had given me a 30-day supply. I was desperate, so I called the primary care clinic and talked to my doctor's nurse and said that I had accidentally spilled the bottle and that I now didn't have any. She said she would talk to Monica (my primary care doc). Monica approved the refill for another 30-day supply, but a lady from the pharmacy called me and said that insurance probably wouldn't let it be refilled, since it's a narcotic and they don't refill narcotic pain medications before they're due to be refilled. She called Medica, and turns out they will allow 1 early refill per year on narcotic medications. So I used my free pass.

I knew what was going on this whole time, and I knew what was happening to my body. I recognized all the symptoms of addiction. Most addicts won't acknowledge their addiction, they'll deny it, say they can stop any time. I was fully aware of it, of my thoughts and cravings; I wasn't denying anything. Yet I wasn't DOING anything to stop taking larger doses. I could sit on my couch and look at the bottle sitting in front of me on the table, and know that I didn't need to take 12mg, I could get by just fine with 4mg. But I would do the 12mg anyway. I knew that I didn't want my growing dependency to get any worse, and that I needed to come off this medication. Yet at the same time . . . I didn't want to. I was afraid of being honest with my doctors about it, because I was scared that they would discontinue the order and that I would never get any again, and I wasn't ready to completely let it go. Again, another red flag.

After my most recent esophageal stent was placed (that drama is going to be its own post), they gave me a prescription of liquid Oxycodone. So now I had both Oxycodone AND Dilaudid. Since I knew I was going to run out of my Dilaudid again before the prescription was due to be refilled (like, 2 weeks early I would run out), when both bottles were down to half full, I combined them into one bottle, so I had a Dilaudid-Oxycodone cocktail. I call it Oxylaudid. I was still taking the same dosages. 8mg here, 10mg there, 13mg when I was bored. Only instead of being straight Dilaudid, it was the Oxylaudid mixture. I figured that would get me through until the Dilaudid was due to be refilled again. When that ran out, it still wasn't time to refill the Dilaudid, so I needed to refill the Oxycodone. I couldn't call my primary care doctor or any of my transplant doctors, because they would ask me why I needed a refill on the Oxycodone when I was SUPPOSED to still have Dilaudid left. So I called the thoracic surgery clinic, since they are the ones who put the stent in. Again, I told the nurse on the phone that I had spilled my bottle (since she hadn't heard that excuse yet) and was still having pain from the stent. One of the surgeons prescribed me a 10-day supply, which would get me exactly through to my appointment just this past Monday with Dr. Kandaswamy, which was also the day that the Dilaudid could be refilled, although I had decided that I didn't WANT to refill the Dilaudid, but did still need a refill on the Oxycodone, legitimately. Even though I was using the narcotic pain medication partially for recreational use, because I like the effect it has on my mood, I also do actually have pain that can't be cured by Tylenol. I have very bad back pain that has been getting worse over the last couple years. Things like putting away groceries makes it really bad - really anything that involves bending over, or carrying something heavy, especially up a flight of stairs. It's partly genetic; my dad has had back pain his whole life, too. I also think I need to regularly see a chiropractor.

Well, let me tell you something. Even though both Oxycodone and Dilaudid are narcotics, Dilaudid is much, much stronger than Oxy. Once I stopped taking my Oxylaudid mixture and was just on the Oxy, the Dilaudid withdrawal began. A constant internal shaky feeling throughout my whole body as well as physical shaking of my hands; agitation; tension building up in my shoulder that would make it spasm; sweating; and not having that feeling of normalcy. Not good.

I met with Dr. Kandaswamy on Monday to discuss my G-J tube, and how much longer he wanted to leave it in for. We discussed the pros and cons of leaving it in longer vs. taking it out sooner, and I agreed with him that it could/should stay in for at least another month, maybe a couple months, just to make sure I am really on a good path now. I've been doing really well the last month and a half now with eating and not needing to do any tube feeds. But we all know, given my history, how quickly things can change. So he wanted to give it another 1-2 months just to make sure. I guess he didn't realize that I was still on a narcotic pain medication, and had been this whole time, since the tube was placed. He asked me if I could manage the pain without a narcotic pain medication, and I told him no, not really, and that I had tried Tylenol in the past and it just didn't work. Right then and there he decided the tube was coming out. Now. So out it came.

Even though the tube was out, we all agreed that it wasn't a good idea to just quit the pain medication "cold turkey." Dr. Kandaswamy didn't want to be the one to write another prescription for it because he wasn't the one to prescribe it in the first place, and the clinic who prescribed it the first time should do it again. Well, thoracic surgery gave it to me after the stent was put in, but they won't refill it because they said they only give patients enough to get them through the first week after the procedure, because after that most people don't have any pain or discomfort any more. Well, I'm not most people. Either way, they said that if I needed more, I needed to talk to my primary care doctor. So I go up one floor to the primary care clinic and ask if either my primary care doc or her nurse were in, for me to talk to. Neither of them were in that day, and the girl at the front desk said that for narcotic pain medications, they can't have some other doctor refill it, it has to be my doctor, so there was nothing that could be done that day. Great. It was already after 4 and I had to get back to work. I called my coordinator, Dawn, and left her a panicked message about how my doctor wasn't in and I don't have any medication left and I was scared about how I was going to make it through the night. I knew that a rough night was ahead of me. The last dose I had taken was around 11:30 that morning, so it had been hours already since I'd had any. Fortunately and surprisingly, I wasn't feeling any of the withdrawal symptoms yet. I think it's because I had so much adrenaline running through me from how the afternoon went and the worrying and anxiety about what I was going to do that evening. My brain wasn't allowed any time to remember that I hadn't taken anything in hours. I cried in my car on the way home, feeling helpless, anxious, scared, and worried all at the same time.

I wasn't actually completely out of Oxy. I had 7mg left. I decided to split it up, to help get me through the next day, when my primary care doctor would be back in clinic. By 9:30, I was finally starting to feel the tension building in my shoulders, once the adrenaline had started to diminish and I was calming down. I took 4mg, along with 2 Tylenol and 1 Xanax, to help relax the muscles. I knew that only 4mg alone wouldn't stop the side effects. It helped me fall asleep, and I pretty much slept right through the night. In the morning, right away I took the last 3mg and 2 more Tylenol (but no Xanax during the day. I'm on the lowest dose possible, and even 1 tablet makes me drowsy, so night time only!). Monica's nurse called me first thing, right at 8, and let me know that she got the message about needing a refill, and that she would talk to Monica. She said that Monica might not want to prescribe Oxycodone because she had been prescribing me Dilaudid in the past. But she would talk to Monica and see what she wanted to do, then call me back. I was torn. A small part of me secretly wanted the Dilaudid again, but more of me knew that I can't go back on it. Weaning off it would just be too hard. Luckily, when Monica's nurse called me back, she said that Monica agreed to fill the prescription, a 10-day supply, 200mg. Which gives me 20mg a day, or 5mg 4 times a day. I can do that. Then I have an appointment with her next week and we will discuss further plans for what to do, like if I stay on the Oxycodone for my back pain, or what. I've been very good with the Oxycodone and not taking more than my directed doses. Perhaps it's because the Oxy doesn't give me the fuzzy, euphoric feeling that the Dilaudid did, so there's really no point in taking a higher dose of the Oxy, because it wouldn't benefit me at all. Well, except that 5mg doesn't help with my back pain at all. It still hurts really bad, all the time. I forgot about that part.

    Today marks 1 week and 1 day since my last dose of Oxylaudid, and I still get the shakes and the tension/spasms in my shoulder if I push it too long between Oxycodone doses. After being on Dilaudid for almost 5 months, I know that for the rest of my life there will always be a tiny part of my brain that will miss the "high" feeling I got from taking it. Since Dilaudid is fast-acting, the withdrawal period is also brief, but intense, peaking in 14 to 21 hours, and resolving in 36 to 72 hours. That's 3 days. That's also for low dosage users. Higher dosage users, which I think I fit into, can experience painful withdrawal for up to 2 weeks, and long-term users, which at 5 months I am also considered, can experience symptoms for months, even years after. I'm on day 8. This blows. And that's a drastic understatement. I'm trying to get in with the pain management clinic, because they help patients with chronic pain, but they aren't taking new patients right now. So I'll be curious to see what Monica says next week when I see her.

And so concludes part 1. It's a struggle I'm going through right now, but I'm staying strong. I'm a trooper, and I'm doing really well with not taking more Oxycodone than I need to make the side effects stop. Sometimes I can go 5 or 6 hours between doses, and sometimes I'll already start to feel shaky again after only 2 and a half hours. It's a process, but I know I'll get through it.

February 6, 2015 Email
Back pain
Krystin to mom, Kathy, dad:

I had an epiphany on the way to work this morning. I think I know why my back hurts SO bad. How long has it been hurting so bad? About 3 weeks. How long has the stent been in? 3 weeks. DUH. I'm pretty sure he put the larger of the 2 sizes in this time. I guess before the procedure, I didn't indicate that I needed the smaller one. I have a chiropractor appointment this afternoon, so he can hopefully help with the long-term, chronic back pain that I have, but not the temporary, REALLY bad back pain that I have while this stent is in. :-(

February 6, 2015 Email
First A1C test since pancreas transplant . . .
Krystin to Page, Dad:

5.6!!!!!!!!!!!!!!!!!!!!!!!!!!!!!! ☺ [times 10]

February 7, 2015 Facebook
Apparently having 2 transplant surgeries and numerous hospital stays, all within a year and a half, and all of which require long recovery periods of sitting/lying around being a bum, isn't good for the spine. I want to bend over, and my spine says "haha, nope, how about some pain instead?" Chiropractor visits 2 days a week for the next 3 weeks it is. Time to crack some bones and make them pop!

February 9, 2015 Facebook
Krystin Engstrand is feeling positive.
The bad thing about having a chronically low hemoglobin level (basically a measure of iron in the red blood cells) is that I always feel tired and energy-less because of it. The GOOD thing about having a

chronically low hemoglobin level is that I now get to go in for an iron infusion, which always makes me feel great afterward! So even though this is yet another 1/2 day of sitting in a clinic hooked up to a tube, it's a good thing, so it makes me happy knowing I'll feel better and have more energy.

February 9, 2015 Facebook
Taking off leggings that you're wearing UNDER a pair of sweatpants. It can be done. I got skillz like that.

February 13, 2015 Facebook
Krystin Engstrand is feeling appreciated.
I got a comment this morning from a co-worker about how the bright colors I wear make the office a happier place. And a few weeks ago, I was told that one of our managers (who is one of THE people to have on your side, and who I work closely with often) said in a meeting that she likes and appreciates the way I dress; that I look professional and brighten up the workplace. I've actually been told that I'm like a mini her, which means I have great potential around here. It's the little things like this that can really make your day.

February 19, 2015 Email
(no subject)
Krystin to dad:
    What is your work schedule like next Thursday (2/26) at 3:40pm?

Dad to Krystin:
    It's not bad. What do you have in mind?
    And how you doing? Haven't heard from you in a bit.

Krystin to dad:
    Well, I have an appointment with Monica, and the whole reason for the appointment is to talk to her about detox/treatment options for getting off my pain medication. I saw Nancy the other night, and we spent the whole hour discussing this. The plan for my next appointment with Monica was to discuss weaning me off my pain medication, but Nancy and I both agreed that just weaning me off won't be enough. The mental aspect will need to be dealt with, too. I mean, I've been on a very highly-addictive narcotic pain medication for 5 months now. It was inevitable that my body would become

addicted to it. I'm actually surprised, as is everyone else who I've talked to, that NONE of my doctors realized that I was still on a narcotic pain medication, even though I was still legitimately having pain. So although weaning off it will help prevent major withdrawal, my body will still want it. A small part of my brain will still want it. So I think I'll need more help than just weaning off it.

This is not my fault, that over time my body became dependent on Dilaudid, and now Oxycodone. It was inevitable. Dilaudid is one of the most highly addictive pain medications out there. Now that the tube is out, I really have no reason to be on pain medication anymore. I'm really only still taking the Oxycodone so that I can avoid the withdrawal effects.

I would like someone to go to that appointment with Monica with me, not just for support, but also because you and mom are good at asking questions that I don't think to ask. Mom won't go with me. Just like she wouldn't go to my last appointment. She said it's too hard for her, but of course she won't talk to me about it. I realized at that point that of my whole support system, which includes pretty much everyone I know, she actually isn't part of it. At all. Yes, she still loves me, and yes she comes and visits me when I'm in the hospital, but she can't support me, for her own personal reasons. So I'm not talking to her right now, because that upset me.

If you can't make it, or don't want to for your own reasons, or think I need to do it on my own, or whatever, I've also considered asking uncle Jeff.

Well, that turned into a longer explanation than I intended. At least now you know the situation and what I'm facing. I have no idea if treatment means something inpatient, and if so, how long, I have no idea. That's what I will find out.

Other than that, things are going pretty well. Not much exciting happening from day to day, just working during the week and hanging out on the weekends. Now that the Remeron is completely out of my system (I think), I'm feeling better, and not so tired all the time. I can make it through a whole work day! The Ritalin helps with that a lot, even though I'm on the smallest dose that's prescribed. I must have missed putting it in Wednesday's slot when I fill my pill box last, because I didn't get it yesterday (I take my pills when I get to work, and noticed it wasn't in with the others), and I was SO tired yesterday. I never realized how much the Ritalin really was helping. I guess it can be attributed to what you have told me numerous times about medications: you don't know how you would feel if you DIDN'T take it. Well, yesterday I found out! Yes, this morning I made sure I had it before going to work.

I had an Xray this morning, because I think the stent has slid down again. Dr. Andrade's nurse will look at the pictures then let me know what's going on. She also said Dr. Andrade wants to do another endoscopy, so that may be done in the next week.

The chiropractor visits are going well. Monday was my 4th treatment, and I go again tomorrow. I am definitely noticing a difference.

OK, that's all I got. Talk to you soon. LY.

Dad to Krystin:
Well. To be honest, I'm not quite sure what I should do here. I can attend the appointment and ask questions that occur to me, but I'm not sure it's wise (for either of us) for me to play any significant role beyond that. I wonder if it might be a good idea to invite Jeff as well as me, and then as you have issues or questions, you can contact him. (He'd have to be at the appointment, obviously, or he wouldn't know what's going on. Do you have any idea if he'd be willing to be involved?) I'm worried that if I play any more significant a role, it could cause division between us. If you want to ask Jeff, and he's willing, you should perhaps forward him the pertinent part of this email you sent me.

What do you think?

Glad to hear other things going well. This stent slippage is annoying. Would be nice if that problem went away.

February 20, 2015 Email
Dad to Krystin:
You still want me to show up?

Krystin to dad:
Oh, sorry, I thought I replied to you. I must have just thought it and not actually typed it. Happens a lot.

Ummm, well maybe you're right. I don't want any part of my care plan to cause discord between us. I'm not sure how looking into treatment options could cause discord, since I'm not asking you to check on me and make sure I did this or that or hold me accountable for anything, like we used to do with my blood tests and insulin. But if you can see any reason how it might, then I understand your hesitation, because like I said, I don't want it to result in me just getting frustrated (and probably you, too)!

I think I'm not going to ask uncle Jeff. I know he really wants to help me in some way, but I feel like bringing an uncle to an appointment to talk about painkiller treatment is kinda weird. A parent, not weird, but an uncle, weird. I dunno, that's just how I feel. But I'll see. I'll think it over this weekend. If I go to the appointment by myself, that's OK. I've gone to all my appointments alone for the past 2 years, I'm sure I can handle this one. The main reason I wanted someone along is to ask the questions I don't think of. Again, it's OK if I go by myself.

Happy Friday! LY.

Dad to Krystin:
K--

I'm happy to go with you to the appointment--I have no reservations about doing that. My concern, which you echoed, is about being involved in your care plan AFTER the appointment.

So let's say I'll come with you, and we can chat after that.

Is it OK with you if I share this email string with Kathy? As you might guess, we do talk about our kids. . . . But I don't generally share your emails with her (unless they're jokes or not personal stuff).

Krystin to dad:
Of course.
And that sounds good. We can chat after the appointment.

Krystin to dad:
Oh, and thank you. *:) happy

February 20, 2015 Facebook
I wish Raj's character from The Big Bang Theory were a real person. We'd go together like kitty litter and pooper scoopers.

> Krystin: Like ice cream and sprinkles.
> Like cops and donuts.
> Like eggs and bacon
> Like Bonnie and Clyde.
> Ok I'm done.

February 27, 2015 Email
Autobiography
Krystin to dad:
    I'm going to work on my writing this weekend, finally. Do you think I should write it in past tense, since it was in the past, or write it in present tense? I can't decide.

March 9, 2015 Facebook
When you have an amazing weekend, Monday doesn't seem so bad. Bring it on Monday, I'm ready for you!

March 10, 2015 Facebook
Krystin Engstrand is feeling happy.
I can't stop smiling today!

March 10, 2015 Facebook
I'm not a very patient person. I'm all about instant gratification. That being said, how do I get the proper education and training to become an astronaut and go to space in about, oh, 2 weeks?

March 10, 2015 Email
Next week
Krystin to dad:
    having the stent removed next Wednesday, 3/18. The procedure is at 9:15 (supposedly), which means I have to be there at 7:15, or around then. Is it OK if I ride in with you that day? I haven't figured out how I'm getting home yet, since we never have any idea when I'll be done and ready. But can I at least get a ride in the morning?

Dad to Krystin, Kathy:
    Sure. You come to the house about 7:15? I could probably get you home later in the day, as long as it's lunch time or later.

Krystin to dad, Kathy:
    I will have my pre-op nurse call you when I'm actually going in for the procedure, and give you a time estimate as well as to when I'll be done (approximately, of course). Based on all my past

surgeries/procedures, I probably won't end up going in until 11 or later. Not to jinx myself or anything; it's just a fact. Ugh.
P.s. Thanks!
Dad to Krystin, Kathy:
   You're welcome. See you then.

March 15, 2015 Facebook
Happy 6 month pancreas transplant anniversary to me!! This is a BIG and significant date, because the first 6 months are the most crucial for whether or not the body will reject the new organ. We did it Hank the Panc, I love you! 😁👍

March 16, 2015 Facebook
Krystin Engstrand is feeling pumped.
For as long as I can remember, I've wanted to make a difference, to help people, to make a change, especially in third world countries. However, as a now double-transplant patient on immunosuppressants the rest of my life, that will never be an option. Luckily, there is so much that can be done here at home, even in ways that are close to my heart.

I have joined the National Kidney Foundation's Patient and Family Council advocacy program. I will be able to help patients waiting for a transplant, their friends and family, potential donors, and patients who have recently received a kidney transplant. I will get to share my story and experiences (of which, as you know, there have been a LOT). I am very excited to provide support and encourage them, and assure them that, even when things seem like they can't get ANY worse (and you know I've been there, too), that there IS a light at the end of the tunnel.

March 18, 2015 Facebook
Krystin Engstrand is at Fairview University Medical Center.
This stent has been in my esophagus for 9 weeks now. Time for that baby to finally come out! Bring on the anesthesia-induced "nap".

March 19, 2015 Email
how you doing?
Dad to Krystin:

How's it going minus the stent? Did they have anything to say about what might happen?

Krystin to dad:

It's going alright. They must have blown a LOT of air into my stomach yesterday while removing the stent/dilating, because last night, my stomach was SO distended. I felt and looked like I was 15 months pregnant. My stomach felt so tight and stretched, it was so uncomfortable, and it really was hurting my back. I could've sworn my stomach was going to burst open like a balloon. It was a little better this morning, but still pretty "fat" looking, and still hurting my back. Nothing that can really be done, either, to get the air out, except wait. Sucks. Swallowing is normal. I'm crossing my fingers I can get at least 3 weeks w/o having to go in for a dilation. What do you mean by what do they think will happen? Nobody knows what will happen. It's all just a waiting game, to see what my esophagus will do next/when it will start to narrow again.

But other than that, I'm fine. Super tired again these days. I'm on so many medications, and some of them keep switching, that it's almost impossible to narrow it down to which one/s causing the tiredness. I don't even feel like the increased dose of Ritalin is helping me. So, that sucks, too.

Ly.

Dad to Krystin

Well, good and bad news.

Maybe the esophagus won't constrict again.

One would hope that at some point the docs COULD pinpoint which drug might be causing drowsiness.

LY2

March 23, 2015 Text
Krystin to dad: I'm doing an overnight sleep study at the sleep clinic on Thurs 4/9.
Dad: Is this good? They pay for parking? :-)
Krystin: Yes to both. The room is like a hotel room, too. Not a hospital room. So patients can be more comfortable. It will hopefully help them

determine why I have sleep problems. It's not medication related, cuz I've had these problems since high school.
Dad: Let us hope they discover something of practical use for you! One problem, of course, is that you are not in your own bed at home. And there is the Hawthorn effect.
Krystin: They do this study on people all the time. I'm sure they take that into account.
Dad: Maybe I should do it, too!
Krystin: You have sleep probs, too? For me, it takes 1.5-2 hours to fall asleep, I have restless sleep and wake up numerous times, and I wake up way early and can't fall back asleep. And I have a hard time shutting off my brain when I should be going to sleep. Oh yeah, may also have sleep apnea. You should do it if you think it will help! At least go to the sleep clinic and see what they say when you tell them your sleep issues.
Dad: Based on your description, I don't have sleep problems!
Krystin: Lol, ok!

March 25, 2015 Facebook
My transplant social worker is amazing!! She got me a $2,000 medical grant that will pay for all my monthly transplant medications. It goes right onto my Fairview pharmacy account, which means I pay nothing out of pocket for them, for the rest of the year! Now I can buy groceries AND pay my rent on time. Winning.

March 26, 2015 Text
Krystin to dad: Sorry that was so long!
Dad: Good for you! That's pretty good :-) [The first few messages are cryptic, but presumably related to Krystin weaning herself off opioids. The "pretty good" was a standing joke in the family: the highest compliment I paid the children for anything was "pretty good," in the spare Scandinavian/"Prairie Home Companion" manner of offering a compliment.]
Krystin: Pffff. But thanks.
Dad: It only goes one more week? Sounds like you might even be done earlier if you want to. And you are feeling good?
Krystin: It's nice to not be scared anymore about going off it. My brain is much clearer and in more control. It makes me much more optimistic and ready to be done with it. No, I will then go down to 2mg for a couple weeks, then 1mg for a week or so.

Dad: That is wonderful. But I was pretty sure you'd succeed. Ok. Makes sense.
Krystin: So at least a month left planned, but yes, I could actually be done earlier!
Dad: Just depends on how you feel, I guess.
Krystin: I was not as confident about it for a while there. When the drug had really taken over my brain.
Dad: I have great confidence in you.
Krystin: On another note, I'm having a real hard time swallowing again. Luckily I see Dr. Andrade tomorrow morn.
Dad: Crap. Good luck. You need an esophagus transplant!
Krystin: That's what I'm sayin! There's gotta be another option than these stupid stent and dilations. Especially if they don't work! I will be very adamant about it tomorrow. May also have dilation, if they can fit me in. I won't make it through the weekend, that's for sure.
Dad: You tell 'em!

March 27, 2015 Facebook
Actual warning on hair dryer packaging: 'Do not use in the shower.' Well there go my weekend plans. Party poopers.

March 29, 2015 Text
Dad to Krystin: You coming over to do laundry today?
Krystin: Oh yeah, I forgot. Maybe. Not being able to eat or drink much is making me feel weak.
Dad: I understand. Whatever works. You be ok?
Krystin: Do you think you might be able to get me a few things? There are still some things I can swallow better than others.
Dad: You can't go out? Kathy just got back from the grocery store.
Krystin: My head hurts and gets light headed when I'm up too long. I'll just drink water, it's fine.
Dad: I can get a few things. What? How you get to work tomorrow?
(later) Krystin: Thanks again for the groceries. I'm starting to feel better. The Pedialyte really helps.
Dad: Good! Glad to get them for you. Good luck tomorrow. Let me know what happens.
Krystin: Just booked my taxi for 5:15am. Blah.
Dad: Ugh
Krystin: At least I'm the first patient of the day, I think, so I SHOULD go into the OR on time. Key word being should.

Dad: Let's hope so.

March 29, 2015 Facebook
Since the stents and dilations aren't working to keep my esophagus open, an esophagectomy, or removal of the esophagus, may be the only option left. So, great, yet another possible surgery (it's not definite that this will happen, yet). I don't have esophageal cancer, but re-occurring esophageal narrowing, or dysphagia, which prevents me from swallowing foods and liquids, can also lead to this surgery. Scary.

March 30, 2015 Facebook
What better way to start off a Monday than waking up at 5 am to catch a cab to the hospital for yet another esophageal dilation, only to find out they can't do it until Thursday because my blood is too thin from my Coumadin. Looks like another 3 days of not being able to consume anything. #fml

March 30, 2015 Email
Krystin to dad:

I made it to work by 9:30. I've been up since 4:30. Since everyone was expecting me to be gone today, I may have to leave early if I start falling asleep at my desk. Obviously I'm going to make it as long as I can, and my guess is that I'll actually make it all day. I hate missing work when I absolutely don't need to. Cab driver took the River Road to Cretin, Cretin to Cleveland, then to Yorkshire. Total, including tip, was $21. I never know how much to tip for a cab driver, and the total fare was $17. So $4 tip; that's decent, right?

Still haven't heard anything from the thoracic clinic about rescheduling. It BETTER be on Thursday, that's all I gotta say! Even though it's all my fault for forgetting to stop taking my Coumadin on Friday, so the only person I can be upset with is myself. Pfff. Oh, and yes, I did tell mom she doesn't have to pick me up!

March 30, 2015 Email
Dilation
Krystin to Pat, dad, Kathy:

My dilation procedure has been rescheduled for Thursday. And guess what? Same time! So once again I have to be there at 5:30. I'm assuming you'll all want me to take a cab again? Will someone be able to bring me home around the lunch hour? NO more Coumadin until after the procedure!

Dad to Krystin, Pat, Kathy:
   I think a cab would be an excellent idea.
   [Pat picked her up after.]

April 3, 2015 Facebook
Krystin Engstrand is feeling amused.
During my esophagus dilation procedure on Thursday, my surgeon not only did the dilation, but also gave the emptying valve of my stomach a shot of Botox. Well. I hope that spoiled little valve enjoys looking young, pretty, and wrinkle-free for the next 3 months.

April 5, 2015 Blog
Update on Part 1

   I know I haven't even gotten to part 2 or 3 of my 3-piece catching-up series, if you'll call it that, but I wanted to give an update on part 1, because I know you're all curious. If you remember, it was about my pain killer medication and my body becoming dependent on it, and me starting/wanting to wean off it altogether. It has now been, what, about a month and a half since I posted the last entry?? Whatever the time, I have since been working with Monica, my primary care doctor, to wean off it, and it has been going VERY well.

   About a month and a half ago, or right after my last entry, is when Monica and I started my 'weaning off' schedule, I guess you could call it. When we started, I was on 5mg 4x/day. We would slowly decrease from there, not only the dosing, but also the frequency with which I take it, until I get to such a low dose, and take it so infrequently (ex: 1mg 1 or 2 times a day), that I feel comfortable stopping completely. Instead of writing me a 2-week or 30-day supply, however, she has been writing me a weekly prescription refill, so that I would have to be much tighter with my dosing, and so that I didn't run out before my next refill the next week. This idea scared me at first, because it meant I couldn't do what I had been doing before, which was taking more on one day, then just take a little less another day, or take more than I should each day, or any other tactic to manipulate my dosing that would allow me to take a bigger dose once a day; even though this meant I would often run out before I was due for a refill. Which then, a couple times in the past, led to me calling one of my clinics and lying to my doctor, making up an excuse as to why I needed a refill sooner than scheduled. Now, each week when I go in to meet with Monica or Margaret (her nurse), I bring in the bottle from the previous week, and give it to them, even if there's still some left, so that they can keep track of how much I'm going through versus how much they prescribed me. One of the first weeks, I think Monica even tested me, by prescribing more than was needed for the next week, and to see if I would follow my directed dosing (which means there should be some left when I brought the bottle in the next week). Besides the fact that I figured out quickly that I had more than needed, I DID stay on track and didn't take any more than I was supposed to!

I know what you're probably thinking. That if I had some left over each week, I would keep it in an extra, secret supply bottle at home, and then bring in the empty bottle for them, right? WRONG! I have been SO good, that each week when I go in, there is always some left in the bottom, which means I'm actually using less than I'm allowed. And I NEVER keep any extra at home before going in. In fact, 2 weeks ago when I went in, I still had about 1/3 of the bottle left. Over the past week and a half, I've gotten to the point where I really only need it once a day. Sometimes I've even gone longer than 24 hours, and the only reason I take a dose, is because I'll start to feel the uncomfortable tension and restlessness in my legs and feet. Even though, at that time, I was allowed 3mg 4x/day, I only took one 3mg dose a day. Well, some days 2 doses, but rarely 3, and never all 4 anymore. Last week when I stopped in, Margaret came out to give me my next week's prescription refill. It was still for 3mg 4x/day (I still had one more week on that dosing until we took the next step down). I showed Margaret my bottle from the previous week, which still had quite a bit left, again, and told her that I didn't really need to still be on the 3mg 4x/day dosing. I told her exactly what I just wrote above, and suggested 3mg twice a day. So she went back to talk to Monica, and a short while later came out with the updated prescription. This time it was for a 14-day refill! Monica must be proud enough of me and realize how dedicated I am to this, that she's willing to write a prescription for 14 days instead of 7. (Well, perhaps also because I complained to Margaret that each week I refilled it, I had to pay a $10 co-pay for it, and that was adding up fast). I feel good about this dosing. I think I'll even see how it goes just doing 2mg twice a day, since I'm pretty sure that would be the next step anyway.

Monica has been working with me on physically weaning off of Oxy, but she referred me to a psychiatrist to work on the whole mental/emotional weaning aspect. When I discussed with Monica, about a week after my previous post, and told her that I was going to need help weaning my mind off of Oxy, too, whether it be a detox/treatment program, or what, she said that she is not the best one to give advice on that, and that I should see a psychiatrist. I told my mom this later, and she said "duh, I could've told you that." (Then why didn't you tell me that when I first told you I was going to talk to Monica about this??) Primary care doctors aren't ones to talk to about narcotic/opiate pain medication withdrawal, a psychiatrist is, since they specialize in those kinds of psychiatric issues.

Remember back at the end of November, when I was in the hospital with depression, and I was told I should start seeing a psychiatrist? And my doctor even put in a referral for me for the psychiatry clinic, but the clinic was full and not taking new patients until March of this year? Well, luckily, when Monica put in another referral, and I called the psychiatry clinic in late February to set up a new-patient appointment, they were all ready for me and could get me in within a week of calling, which happened to be the beginning of March, just like they told me back in November. Would ya look at that, for once Fairview actually held up their end of the bargain and could me in when they said they would! Well done, Fairview. Well done indeed.

I have seen my new psychiatrist, Dr. Leabhart, twice now. For my first appointment, naturally we discussed a lot of my history, and what issues I'm currently concerned about, and what it is that she and I should focus on. Of course I told her about the whole weaning and withdrawal thing, and after getting more details from me, she decided to put me on a medication called Clonidine. It is used for a wide array of things, but the main reason she prescribed it to me was to help with any withdrawal symptoms, and help ease the weaning process by reducing the sympathetic nervous system response such as tachycardia and hypertension, sweating, hot and cold flashes, and restlessness. Basically, if I were going to feel any of those symptoms, the Clonidine would help reduce the extremity of them, perhaps even mute them altogether. Luckily for me, it also helps treat other medical ailments that affect me, making the Clonidine even more of a benefit to me, such as helping with certain pain disorders, anxiety, blood pressure.

It can also work as a mild sedative. Therefore, I take 2 at nighttime, and only 1 in the morning. The dosing is small enough, that it doesn't make me feel sedated or drowsy in the mornings, and the 2 at night, although still a low-ish dose with the 2 combined, it just enough to help give me a little nudge towards falling asleep faster. She also increased my Ritalin from 20mg a day, to 30mg a day, which I always take in the mornings to help me get going. Last week when I saw her again for a follow-up, she increased it again to 40mg, since I mentioned that I didn't really notice any difference, i.e. finding it any easier to get going in the mornings, than I had on the 20mg. Remember, Ritalin is used mostly in children to treat ADHD. For adults, it's processed differently in the body. For children, it helps them be able to settle down and focus. For adults, it makes them (me) feel more alert and awake, and be able to function and focus on work. So even though I don't have ADHD, I'm taking a widely-known ADHD medication to help me get up and get going in the morning, since that seems to still be a big struggle for my body. Many mornings I find myself pushing my snooze button at least once, sometimes up to 4 times, and then just dragging when I finally get out of bed. No bueno. Since I saw her last week, I think the increase has been helping. I decided that what I need to do is to set 2 alarms. One for when I want to get up, and one for half an hour before that. When the first one goes off, I'll get up and take my Ritalin, then lay back down. Hopefully that half an hour between alarms will be enough time for it to get into my system and start kicking in, so when my 2nd alarm goes off, I'll be able to get out of bed, even if reluctantly, withOUT pushing snooze. I'll keep you updated on that one. . . .

My brain isn't scared anymore of not being on Oxy at all. My brain is finally stronger than the addiction, and I can completely control my thoughts and urges. For example, I was watching the show Criminal Minds the other morning, and they were discussing on the show how one of the suspects is addicted to Dilaudid, and he kills so that he can get a fix, or get money to buy it off the streets. 2 months ago, hearing them talk about it would've made me want to take some of my Dilaudid. This morning, I thought about it, but not about wanting it. I thought about how I was hearing them talk about it and that I DIDN'T want or need it. Well, want it? Maybe 5% of my brain thought that way, but the rest of my brain is stronger, and says "shut up, you don't want or need it, you're just being a greedy little baby." Or something like that. It feels really good to not have that cloud of fear over my head anymore. I was so worried about stopping, and how I would deal, and what my brain might convince me to do, but I don't think that way at all anymore. The cloud is gone. Now I'm READY to be done, ready to leave that in the past and move on with my life as a non-narcotic pain killer user. Yay for progress! I feel very proud of myself, and very accomplished, with how well I've done and how far I've come, and how much progress I've made.

That's all I got for now. I hope everyone has a good Easter Sunday, for those of you who celebrate it. Be well and take care!

Chapter 14

Miscellaneous Months of Medicine and More

April 7, 2015 Email
just out of curiosity
dad to Krystin:
   Krystin, now that you're by the worst of the medical matters (except for the darn esophagus), do you feel less subject to depression?

Krystin to dad:
   Oh, yes, very much so. I haven't felt down or sad since around the New Year or shortly after. I am feeling much better these days! Now if only we could figure out why I'm still so darn tired all the time, that would make life even better. One step at a time, I guess.

Dad to Krystin:
   Good! If you're still on an antidepressant, maybe you could cut that down.
   Fatigue--don't know about that.

Krystin to dad:
   But then there's always that issue of, am I feeling this good BECAUSE of my dose? If I cut down, will I start to feel down again? I suppose I could always cut down from 90mg to 60mg (it only increases/decreases in 30mg increments), and see how I feel, and if I start to feel those icky feelings again, then go back up to 90mg. I'll bring it up with my psychiatrist when I see her next, which is in a couple weeks.

Dad to Krystin:
   Heavens, yes, bring it up with the psychiatrist. I didn't mean to give you medical advice, I meant (but didn't write) that maybe you could bring it up.

April 8, 2015 Text
Krystin to dad: Today I walked to and from another work meeting way down University, AND to and from my dr. appt in PWB. Good for my stamina!
Dad: And you held up ok?

Krystin: Yup! No problems at all. Legs didn't hurt either during or after walking.
Dad: Well, you ARE getting healthier! I am delighted.
Krystin: And a nice walk across campus is always a refreshing break for me.

April 9, 2015 Text
Dad to Krystin: Good luck! Hope they learn something useful. [From the sleep test.]
Krystin: Thanks, me too! Then tomorrow morn I go for my esophagram at hosp on east bank! Then to work. They have showers here, so I don't have to go home first.
Dad: What's an esophagram?
Krystin: Where I drink nasty barium shit and they watch how well it doesn't/does go down and take xray pics and video. It's essentially a swallowing test. And then they try to figure out what to do next. So Dr. Andrade can see how my esophagus is doing right now.
Dad: Email me when you know anything! Meantime, hope you sleep badly tonight so they identify something to do. If you fall right to sleep and sleep like a rock, that won't be helpful!
Krystin: Haha, thanks. Don't worry, I'm sure I won't. I never do! But they'll also be measuring my breathing and movements and such, so at least they'll also see that I sleep badly and wake up often. I'll for sure let you know what I find out! A doc will call me mid-morning to let me know preliminary findings.

April 10, 2015 Facebook
Krystin Engstrand is feeling defiant.
Oh hellllllllll nah. My thoracic doc wants me to get a feeding tube in my tummy again, since the esophageal stents and dilations aren't working to keep my esophagus open. Oh hellllllll nah.

> Krystin: And the thing is, if he won't do surgery, does that mean he expects me to have a tube in indefinitely, like years? And be on pain medication the whole time since it causes chronic pain at the insertion site?? Ummmmm no. Nothankyou.
> Gary: crap
> Krystin: My sentiments exactly.

April 10, 2015 Email
(no subject)
Krystin to dad:

Obviously I'm not putting this on facebook, but I'm really stressing to Teri (the nurse) that a tube requires a pain killer due to its chronic pain that it causes me. Going back on a pain killer would absolutely destroy all the progress I've made over the last couple months with weaning off the Oxycodone. The tube would result in a backwards landslide right back into my old pain killer habits. Which means when it came to weaning off it again, it would be even harder a 2nd time. I just know it and I do NOT want to go through all that again. I've made it so far, and am almost off it completely! So, surgery is out of the question for Dr. Andrade; a tube is out of the question for me. Which leaves us with no other options than the stents/dilations . . . which clearly aren't working. Soooooo. . . ?? I have no idea what's next. I'll be interested to see what Teri says after she's consulted with Dr. A again. Sigh. This is very frustrating.

Dad to Krystin:
"Sigh" is right.
What's the barrier to surgery, other than he just won't do it?
Maybe it's time for a second opinion, like from Mayo.

Krystin to dad:

He doesn't want to do the surgery because it's an abdominal surgery. There are a few different surgeries they could do, but they're all through the abdomen. He says that there are risks doing yet another abdomen surgery, after the 5 I've already had. Whether they remove part or most of the esophagus, it would mean pulling the stomach up and attaching it to the remaining, upper part of my esophagus, where the narrowing/stricture isn't. Doing that kind of surgery, and moving more organs around like that, could affect my kidney and pancreas, too, since pulling up my stomach would most likely those organs being shifted around, too. Plus the pacer in my stomach, they wouldn't want that to dislodge or get moved into a position that either causes discomfort or pain for me, or so that it doesn't work properly. He says there are just too many risks. Doing it may fix my swallowing problem, but in return may cause new problems in other areas of my body.

It makes sense, but I dunno, at this point I'm willing to do it and see how it goes. Being able to eat and drink and take my medications is pretty damn important. Otherwise, if I just have a tube, does that means I won't be able to eat or drink anything ever again?? Does that mean my esophagus could just keep getting narrower and narrower until I can't breathe anymore?? I don't know. I know these questions need to be asked, don't worry.

I can see the pros and cons of a tube, and I can see the pros and cons of surgery. There are only cons to the stents/dilations. This is why I'm negotiating.

April 11, 2015 Text
Krystin to dad: I haven't needed/taken ANY Oxy in 48 hours now.

April 15, 2015 Text
Krystin to dad: I haven't had ANY Oxycodone since Sunday (maybe even Sat. eve?), and I've felt NO withdrawal symptoms at all. My body may just be done with it for good!
Dad: Great!

April 16, 2015 Email
second opinions
Dad to Krystin, Kathy, Pat:
   Just an FYI: http://minnesota.cbslocal.com/2015/04/15/good-question-when-should-you-get-a-second-opinion/

Krystin to dad, mom, Kathy:
   I'm debating whether or not to get a 2nd opinion, even though I did put in an online request for an appointment with Mayo. That was last Friday, and still no one has called me, so I'll have to give them another try.
   BUT, I have already been doing a lot of research online, at medical websites and other Universities medical sites and other websites, and it looks like the options that Dr. Andrade has presented to me are the only options available for this kind of issue. Dilation, stent, G-J tube, or surgery. I've even come across a couple forums on the topic, and people from all over the country talk about those things I mentioned. I haven't seen, on any website or any forum, other procedures or treatment being done. I can still get a 2nd opinion, but I have a feeling they'll just say the same thing. I trust Dr. Andrade, he's very good at

what he does, and is one of the best thoracic surgeons in the state. And I know he cares about helping me, because he says he does NOT want to do the surgery. He's not just looking to bulk up his wallet - he actually cares about my health and knows that if he did the surgery, it could cause other problems in my body. Dr. Robiner, my health psychologist who I saw yesterday and talked to about this, said that's a really good sign when a surgeon says he's not comfortable with surgery, especially coming from Dr. Andrade (who Dr. Robiner is familiar with because he has other patients who are also patients of Dr. A's, and they've all had good things to say).

So, I don't know. Is it worth taking half a day off work to go to Mayo in Rochester, just to find out the same thing? I honestly don't think they'll find anything new or different.

What do you (all) think?

Pat to Krystin, Gary, Kathy:

It sounds like you trust your doctor, he's part of a good team, and he's not interested in using you to suck up insurance money. It also sounds like you've done enough research to know that he has diagnosed you accurately and given you all the options out there, at least all that are currently available in medicine. With all that, and the situation at hand, seeking a second opinion would be of little benefit. IMHO.

Just remember: you get what you pay for and my opinion is free ;-)

Krystin to mom, dad, Kathy:

I should find out if I can do a sort of phone consultation with someone at Mayo, and see what they say, like if they think I should come. They may yes just because they want my (insurance) money, but it couldn't hurt to call, right?

And yes, it's with my throat. Been having trouble swallowing since the day after my previous dilation 2 weeks ago. Luckily I see Dr. Andrade tomorrow morning, and boy do I have a bunch of questions for him!

Dad to Krystin, Kathy, Pat:

I think at least having a telephone conversation cannot hurt, although I doubt they'll give you any consultation without seeing you and seeing your medical record.

My view is that a second opinion can, AT THE WORST, do no harm.

April 17, 2015 Facebook
I can't stop laughing. I just saw my thoracic doc, and turns out that my duodenum (the smallest, shortest, and very beginning part of the small intestine) has a funky kink in it, and could be getting squished by one of the many arteries that crosses it, thus causing so much acid reflux, which is causing my esophagus narrowing. It's a very rare health condition. It can be fixed, but it's very complicated. Bahahahahahaha! Of COURSE it is! When it comes to me, would you expect anything to be easy?? Fixing it would mean surgery where they'd have to work around all the other parts of the digestive system. Seriously, at this point, all I can do is laugh.

> Krystin: I'm living life around this; I'm not letting it keep me from living my life. I'm taking a crochet class, in May I'm going to start training to run the 5k Kidney Walk with Anjeanette in October, and I'm looking at classes in the fall for nursing school! So this SNAFU of a rare health condition is just going to have to keep up with ME!

April 19, 2015 Facebook
Krystin Engstrand is feeling smart.
I decided I should skip nursing school and go right for med school. By now, I'm pretty much an expert at the skeletal, muscular, immune, urinary, endocrine, nervous, and digestive systems, specifically but not limited to, nephrology, endocrinology, psychiatry/psychology, gastroenterology, radiology, ophthalmology, thoracic, vascular, endoscopy, infectious disease, and rheumatology. I practically have a medical degree already anyway! Just not on paper.

April 19, 2015 Text
Krystin to dad: Well, officially can't swallow. Haven't eaten all day. I hope my dilation is early in the week!
Dad: Me, too. Ugh. Hope you getting liquids down.
Krystin: Barely.

April 22, 2015 Text
Dad to Krystin: Are we bringing you home?

(later) Dad: How you doing?
Krystin: In some pain, but able to swallow normally. I got stent put in, not just dilation.
Dad: I knew about the stent. Hope they diagnose pain. Assume I bringing you home tomorrow. Keep me posted. Just so you don't have to be on pain meds again!
Krystin: Oh, may actually be going home tonight! Pain no go away, but it's bearable. Just have to wait it out, for all the air to get out of my tummy over next couple days. But I can at least swallow well again!"
Dad: How you getting home?
Krystin: I dunno. I'd have to come there, to get my car.
Dad: If you released, I give you $10 toward cab fare. I not drive over there again. Ok? Or maybe mom?
Krystin: I'll ask mom. You know they won't let me leave in a cab!
Dad: I didn't know that. Why?
Krystin: They need to release me to a family member or friend, so they not liable for anything. And cuz someone is supposed to be with me next 24 hours, even though I don't need that and we don't do that.
Dad: Good grief. What do they do when there's no such person? You don't have to answer that.
Krystin: Yeah, I dunno! And they know I have such people, so can't lie about that one. I think mom busy tonight. I can't get hold of her.
Dad: When they thinking they release you?
Krystin: Now
Dad: I going to eat first. So it will be half an hour at least.

April 23, 2015 Text
Krystin to dad: Been throwing up all night and morning.
Dad: Crap. Called doc office?
Krystin: No
Dad: Why? You should!
Krystin: Too nauseous
Dad: Well, it has to be you. Or you need to go in.
(later) Any better?
Krystin: No. Need help.
Dad: What you want? Coming to apt.
Pat to Gary: Did Krystin get hold of you? I'm in a website class. . . .
Gary: Krystin in ER. DK what going on except she was throwing up last night and today. Went to her apt, she gone. Talked to ER, they said she was talking to doctor would call me back.

Pat: Keep me posted.
Gary: K in observation. Seems they nicked something when put in stent, caused bleeding, made her sick. Am in her room, says she's feeling better. Don't know when release, she hopes today. If do, I can bring her home. We have dinner plans tonight.
Pat: Ok thanks. I'm scheduled to have dinner with her so I'll just be in touch with her at some point to see if she's still up for it.

April 24, 2015 Text
Krystin to dad: Getting discharged! Not exactly sure when, but sounds like soon-ish. Within the next hour maybe. Doc said he would get things started, so whatever that means. . . .

April 25, 2015 Text
Dad to Krystin: You feeling back to normal?
Krystin: Yeah, I mostly am. Felt just a tiny bit nauseous for a little while earlier, but I think it has gone away. No, no throwing up or anything, and have been able to eat and drink normally.
Dad: Good!

April 27, 2015 Facebook
Krystin Engstrand is feeling pumped.
First lunch meeting next week with a delegate from the National Kidney Foundation (Midwest division), to share my story and talk about the many ways I can be a NKF advocate. Woohoo! Super excited to finally start helping others and making a difference!

April 28, 2015 Facebook
Krystin Engstrand is at Health Partners Medical & Dental.
Procedure of the day: crown lengthening. Google it. Read the description, enjoy the pics. Imagine a scalpel cutting into the entire upper row of my gums. At least I got nitrous oxide (laughing gas), so I didn't impulsively kick a dude in the face.

April 28, 2015 Text
Krystin to dad: It's swollen and painful, but you know me, I'm a trooper. Even Dr. Raab said so. He was impressed with how well I did.
Dad: Great!
Krystin: Ok, all the Novocain has worn off now.
Dad: And how you doing?

Krystin: Ow.
Dad: Oh. Hope you get better fast.
Krystin: Me too.
Krystin: Hahahahaha, my u of m email auto-corrected Kandaswamy to kinda swampy. Hahaha. I think I have to tell him that. It gave me a good laugh. Then it gave me a mouth hurt.
Dad: Chuckle. I guess you can't laugh.
Krystin: I guess so.
Dad: Until tomorrow.
Krystin: Hopefully. Right now is the worst it will be, so at least it only decreases from here.
Dad: Good. Hope you can sleep.
Krystin: Dr. Raab just called to check in. That was very nice of him! Yes, me too. I may need to take some Zquil tonight.
Dad: What comes next?
Krystin: In a few weeks I go see Dr. Luis, who will fit me with the temporary, removable crown model, to slowly widen my jaw to comfortably fit the crowns. Then a couple months after that, he'll put the permanent crowns on. So, it's a long process, but worth it in the end. And today was the hardest part, so at least I've made it through the worst!
Dad: Wow.
Krystin: Yup. But in the end, I'll have a nice, new, bright, beautiful smile. No more being self-conscious about smiling!
Dad: Good. Hope it all turns out to be worth it!
Krystin: Oh yes, absolutely. Funny story. Yesterday morning I had my gastric emptying study, where I ate radioactive eggs, then they watched how fast it moved through my stomach over 4 hours. At 1 hour, there was still 88% of the eggs still in my stomach. At 2 hours, 83%. At 3 hours, 92% remaining. Hahaha, WHAT.
Dad: Back up?
Krystin: Must have! My bum duodenum wouldn't let it through! Even 7 hours later, I still felt like I'd eaten an elephant, from only an egg and piece of toast at 8 am. Dang.
Dad: Gotta fix that!

May 5, 2015 Email
Stent
Krystin to dad, Pat, Kathy:

My stent is being removed next week, on Thursday. It burns and hurts so much, I can't take it anymore. By next week, it will have only been in 3 out of 8 weeks, but I can't handle it anymore. Constant, 24/7 back pain and intense burning in my chest, and nothing I take or do relieves it. Unfortunately, I have to deal with it for another week, so hopefully I'll manage through until then.

Pat to Krystin, Gary, Kathy

Do they have any recommendations? What do other people with stents do?

Krystin to Pat, Gary, Kathy:

No recommendations, because I'm special, and these problems DON'T HAPPEN for other people! They do for the first 2-3 days, while the stent expands and the body adjusts to it, but then the discomfort goes away. For me, because I'm me, the pain and discomfort lasts the WHOLE time the stent is in. Yes, this has been an issue with my past stents as well.

May 6, 2015 Email
Krystin to mom, dad, Kathy:

OK, I will plan on taking a cab there, then have dad being primary to bring me home, and mom being back-up. Per usual, I'll have one of the nurses call you (dad) when I'm going INTO the OR, and then again when I'm moved to recovery. When I'm in recovery, then you know it'll be about 2 hours until I'll be ready, but I'll text you when they get me in the post-recovery room and have me sitting up and eating some crackers, etc. I'll give you another time frame from there. (Again, as long as everything goes normally - HA!)

Dad to Krystin, Pat, Kathy:

How is it you're going to eat after the stent is removed?

Krystin to dad, Pat, Kathy:

No idea. All I know is that the stent needs to come out. I'll discuss eating with Dr. Andrade (not eating WITH him, but I will discuss ME eating, with him. In case you were confused). I already told him and Dr. Kandaswamy that I'm not doing another G-J tube. I'm hoping that by next Thursday, the esophageal conference will be over and he'll have an answer for me as far as what we're going to do. He may not be able to do anything that day, but perhaps in the near future. Post stent, I will eat food for as long as I'm able, then I may need to switch over to supplement shakes. I guess I'll have to play it by ear.

Dad to Krystin:
    Sigh.

Krystin to dad:
    Yup, pretty much.

May 6, 2015 Facebook
Krystin Engstrand is feeling ecstatic.
    I am overjoyed about all the volunteer opportunities with the NKF that I learned about at my lunch with them. Not only will I get to help run fundraising and awareness events and be the speaker at 'Your Kidneys & You' presentations, but also be a mentor to someone who is in the very beginning stage of kidney failure. My heart swells knowing how much I get to help make a difference and make a change, and possibly even save lives. Just one of the ways I plan to leave a mark on the world. #payitforward #shareyourspare #savealife

May 7, 2015 Text
Krystin to dad: Officially been off Oxycodone for 1 week now, and NO desire to get more!!
Dad: !!!!!
Krystin: My sentiments exactly!

May 7, 2015 Blog
Catching Up: Part II
    I am finally getting to the next best part that has been consuming my life for the past 9 or so months. And by next best I actually mean very long, drawn-out, and way beyond complicated.
    It all started back in late summer/early fall of 2014, before my pancreas transplant. I'm thinking possibly July or August. I noticed one day that it was starting to get hard for me to swallow food. It felt like food was getting stuck, and I had to take some big gulps of fluids to push it down. I didn't think much of it at first. Only when it got to the point that I couldn't swallow at all, and was many times gagging

back up whatever I just tried to eat/drink, that I got worried. I don't even remember who I first contacted. Probably Pat, who was my transplant coordinator at the time, before I got my pancreas and got a new coordinator who has kidney-pancreas transplant patients (which would be Dawn, who I also frequently talk about now).

I was referred to the G.I. (gastroenterology) clinic. There I saw Dr. Amateau, who had me get an endoscopy done. It showed that my esophagus had narrowed. He soon after schedule me for an esophageal dilation, where they put a little balloon in my esophagus and blow it up, so expand my esophagus so that I can swallow again. Should have been end of story. Oh no, of course not. Come on, it's ME we're talking about here! I think it stayed open for about a couple months before I noticed it starting to get hard to swallow again. I talked to G.I. again, and that time Dr. Amateau decided to put in an esophageal stent, which is basically a mesh tube that sits in the esophagus, slowly expands over about 2 days, then stays in for 8 weeks for the esophagus to "heal" at that width. A stent only stays in for 8 weeks because after that there's the risk that the stent will start to grow into the esophagus. And that wouldn't be pleasant for either doctor or patient to have it removed. Ouch. Again, ideally, for most people that's all they need. Something will have caused their esophagus to narrow that one time, and the stent will fix it and they'll never have the issue again. But, I'm not most people, am I?

I had the stent removed after only 2 weeks of being in. It caused me so much pain in my chest and back, that I couldn't bear it anymore. There are only 2 sizes of stents: small or large. They had put the large stent in, which turns out was TOO large for how narrow my esophagus was. My esophagus still stayed open quite a while after that stent, close to 2 months I think. When I started to feel it narrowing again, it was becoming obvious that further tests and investigating was needed to determine what was causing this chronic narrowing. Dr. Kandaswamy, my surgeon, referred me to the thoracic clinic, which is actually in the same clinic as G.I. There I started seeing Dr. Andrade. Whereas gastroenterology deals with gastric stuff, like stomach and digestion, thoracic deals with issues of the esophagus and lungs (including esophageal and lung cancers).

Over the next few months, I worked with Dr. Andrade to figure out exactly what was causing it. When no apparent cause was immediately clear, his plan was that I would just keep having dilations done every couple months, in the hope that over time, the time between dilations would be farther and fewer in between, and eventually get to the point where I need one maybe once a year, or even not at all. Well, let me tell you how well THAT plan worked out. Hint: it didn't. After each procedure, my esophagus was beginning to close quicker and sooner than the previous time it was dilated. So instead of me needing a dilation further and further apart, the OPPOSITE was happening, and I needed them even more frequently! He said there is a surgery that can be done to fix the problem, but it would be an abdominal surgery involving removing the part of my esophagus that has the narrowing, pulling up my stomach, and attaching it to the remaining part of my esophagus. He wasn't comfortable with doing yet another abdominal surgery on me, considering all my previous surgeries. On any other person, he wouldn't even hesitate, but for me, it could be complicated. Pulling up the stomach means other things (like new organs) could also shift, and that could cause problems in itself. So even though the surgery may fix my esophagus problem, it could potentially cause other problems elsewhere in my body, and he was not willing to risk that. That's why he set out the long-term dilation plan.

He decided he wanted me to have another number of tests done that would give him a better, more detailed look not just at my esophagus, but also at my stomach and small intestine, since he realized that the problem may not be solely in my esophagus, but could be caused by a different problem lower down. In the meantime, I was having more dilations, and another stent, which did stay in the whole 8 weeks, even though it still caused me minor chest pain (burning) and back pain. It wasn't AS bad as the first one, because the second time he put in the smaller stent, so I was willing to put up with it. For these kinds of procedures, I am put under general anesthesia. Since the OR schedule for the thoracic and G.I. docs fills up quickly, often I would get to the point where I wasn't able to swallow anything, not even water with my medications, for a few days before I was finally able to get in for a procedure. My esophagus was very unreliable and unpredictable. Even during those few days prior to dilation, I could SOMETIMES swallow. I didn't know when in the day food/fluids would be allowed to go down, so if I was hungry, I'd just have to wing it and find out. Many times I'd be at work, and nope, it wasn't going to be allowed down. Luckily my trashcan sits nearby.

Finally, after 2 more months and an esophagram, CT scan with contrast, and gastric emptying study, it has been determined that I (most likely) have a very rare esophageal condition called SMA, or Superior Mesenteric Artery syndrome. From Wikipedia, which is where I get a lot of my knowledge, it is a "rare, potentially life-threatening gastro-vascular disorder characterized by a compression of the third portion of the duodenum by the abdominal aorta and the overlying superior mesenteric artery." Translation: My duodenum is being squashed by one of the many large arteries that surrounds it. The duodenum is the first, and smallest, part of the small intestine, so it is the first little sac that the stomach empties into. If food can't empty into it, it can't be digested (and therefore can't enter into the bowels to be gotten rid of by the body), so instead it sits in the stomach. And causes acid reflux. The acid reflux causes scarring in my esophagus.

Since my duodenum has been squashed for quite a while now, the acid reflux has been an issue also for quite a while. On a daily basis, in fact, which means the esophagus is not getting any time to heal, and the scarring and scar tissue keeps building up and building up, causing my esophagus to be very narrow. Which is why a few months ago, if I had a stent taken out or a dilation done, I could go 3 or 4 weeks before I would notice it starting to get harder to swallow. Now, I'm lucky if I can even get a week. With the stent before my current one, since it had slid down my esophagus a bit, I could actually feel my esophagus narrowing before the stent even came out! And after the last dilation, even the next day I could feel food trying to squeeze down. So really, forget a week; I'm talking A day. My 3 important transplant medications I now have in liquid form, for when this happens and I can't swallow pills. That doesn't help with eating, but at least I'm keeping my kidney and pancreas from failing on me! And really, that's the most important, isn't it? I could die from starvation, but dammit, I'm going to die with healthy organs!

So yes, I have another stent in right now, that has been in a little over 2 weeks. However, I'm having it removed next week because, even though it's the small one again, it is causing me just as much pain as the first, large one did. My chest burns ALL the time - it feels like I have 24/7 heartburn. Same with the back pain, starting below where the shoulder blades end, and going across my whole back. It's seriously unbearable. I can't sleep at night, it affects me during the day while I'm at work, I'm hesitant about eating because that makes the burning worse, and nothing I take for it helps relieve the pain, not even putting a hot pack on it. I've tried putting those Icy-Hot patches on my back and in front where it burns the most, but to no avail. I weighed the pros and cons of taking it out early, and decided that, even though my esophagus will start to close up again right away, it's not worth sacrificing my comfort, and my sanity, to put up with it for 6 more weeks.

You're probably wondering what other treatments are available for this kind of syndrome, other than stents and dilations (since that is not a permanent solution - the duodenum needs to be specifically worked on). Well, one option is an abdominal surgery that is very time consuming, and very complicated. The surgeon would have to do a lot of digging to get to the duodenum, since it's nice and tucked in there behind the stomach and surrounded by many arteries. He would have to be VERY careful not to accidentally cut anything that could cause major internal bleeding. No bueno. There are different kinds of surgery, depending on what it is exactly that they'd want to do. Actually, I think they can all be done laparoscopically, although Dr. Andrade made it sound like the kind of surgery he thinks would need to be done would have to be an open surgery in my abdomen.

This week there is an esophageal conference going on, where thoracic and G.I. and other doctors gather to discuss new discoveries and techniques and such, and also to discuss complicated cases. Dr. Andrade happens to be presenting at the conference, and guess what, he's using my case! Because let's face it, if I'M not a complicated case, I don't know what is. (I'm not sure whether to be proud or sad about that . . .). They'll put all their smart, brainy minds together to discuss what a good plan of action for me should be, considering the stents/dilations aren't working. So forget getting a second opinion - I'm going to get 50! Next week, when Dr. Andrade takes out my stent, he'll have some feedback from the conference that we can discuss while I'm still in pre-op. Even if we don't do anything other than take the stent out that day, it would be nice if he had a plan of attack for what will happen in the near future. I mean really, like NEAR future, since I won't have very long after the stent comes out. On Tuesday of next week I'm having another swallowing test done, where radiology will focus directly on the duodenum, and get some good close-up shots of it as the barium contrast goes through it, so they can get a much more clear idea of how well/fast the contrast does/doesn't move through. That will really give Dr. Andrade a good idea of what needs to be done. He'll have a couple days to look over the results, so I suppose it's possible that he may even decide to change my procedure on Thursday and take a different course of action than just removing the stent.

A couple weeks ago, I did see Dr. Kandaswamy to get his opinion on another surgery. He looked at all my test results, and said that for SMA Syndrome, he probably wouldn't need to do a whole complicated surgery, but laparoscopically go in and put a couple tiny stents into my duodenum, to hold it open so that the artery can squish it, and one where the kink is, so food can successfully make it around the curve without any problems. Which would therefore mean that food wasn't sitting in my stomach creating so much acid, so I wouldn't have the reflux issue, which would allow my esophagus to heal. Which would ideally mean that my esophagus can get back to its normal width, and stop narrowing, and I could eat normally again. Let's NOT jinx it and talk about all the ways this could go wrong, OK? He and Dr. Andrade are going to be in communication with each other over a plan, since, I found out, Dr. Kandaswamy would most likely be the one to do this kind of surgery! IF surgery is what they decide on. If they decide on the little duodenum stent thing, probably either of them could do. Dr. Kandaswamy has done every single one of my other surgeries (aside from the dilations/stents), so I would feel comfortable with either of them doing it.

On a side note, if you remember waaaaaay back late last summer, before I even had my pancreas transplant, I had to go in to the infusion clinic to get that infusion of Rituxan, because my EBV (Epstein-Barr virus aka mono) labs came back elevated. Rituxan, even though normally used in chemo, can also be used in patients to blast away EBV, which in transplant patients, it's pretty crucial to get that taken care of PDQ, instead of waiting for it to run its course. Being immunosuppressed and all, it could actually do a lot more damage on the body and the new organ than someone who isn't immune-suppressed with an organ transplant. When I got the Rituxan infusion, however, after only about 20-30 minutes I noticed my throat getting itchy, then it started to swell. The nurses immediately stopped the infusion, and gave me a nice swift jab in the outer thigh with an Epi pen. I had been starting to have an anaphylactic reaction, so Rituxan was put, and remains, on my allergy list. Anyway, it was shortly after that reaction that all this narrowing in my esophagus started. I thought it HAD to be related to the reaction I had to the Rituxan, considering the coincidental timing of it all, but no, apparently not. It really was just a coincidence that it started right after that infusion. OK then!

This has all been a huge pain in the ass for me. I'm tired, mentally and physically, of all this. I know it takes a long time, and a lot of tests, to finally narrow down exactly what the problem is, instead of guessing what the problem is and doing something about that, only to discover that that wasn't the underlying problem in the first place. So, at least now they know the source of the problem, and we can all finally see that bright shiny light at the end of the tunnel. This whole ordeal has been going on just under a year now, and it has definitely taught me how to be patient. Well, most like it has forced me to be patient, and I am NOT a naturally patient person!

There you have it. I think I have exhausted this subject, but please still feel free to ask me questions. Sometimes I mindlessly leave out big details because I already know about it, but forget that you all don't, so I may not mention it. Fingers crossed that next week is a productive week, and I'll keep you updated when I learn something new!

Bye for now.

May 8, 2015 Emails
TGIF
Krystin to dad:

I don't know what it was about this week, but I am mentally and physically exhausted. I think mentally because it's dealing with the whole esophagus/duodenum thing, and being conflicted about it coming out next week. It hurts so bad, I can't take it anymore, but I know my esophagus will narrow up again right away, because it's already doing that now, even with the stent IN there. It's like it's not even there at all. So it's not working AND it's causing me pain. That's physically exhausting, too, having to deal with the pain and discomfort 24 hours a day. And it's pretty close to 24 hours, since it causes really shitty sleep, too. AND, since the food just sits in my stomach for days and days, I'm not hungry very often, so I'm not eating much, and the food is just sitting there not getting digested, so I'm not getting any nutrients, either. Ugh. I know this why Dr. Andrade and Dr. Kandaswamy both want a tube put back in, but I don't care how crappy I feel, I am NOT going back there. Nothankyou.

On Tuesday morning I'm having another Barium swallowing test done in radiology over at the hospital, but this time they're going to focus directly on my duodenum, and watch how the contrast does/doesn't flow through the duodenum after leaving my stomach.

That will give Dr. K and Dr. A a much clearer idea of what exactly to do to my duodenum to fix the problem. Sounds like surgery may not be needed, but a laparoscopic procedure where they put little tiny stents in my duodenum, one to keep it inflated so that artery can't squish it, and one where the kink is in last section of the duodenum that leads into the jejunum, to hold the kink open so food can get around that curve. I'm getting so good at anatomy! (This will be very helpful in nursing school, so in a way, it's a blessing in disguise, eh?) Anyway, with that test being done on Tuesday morning, and my stent removal not being until Thursday morning, that gives Dr. A a couple days to look over the results with Dr. K, and maybe, hopefully, FINGERS CROSSED, they can come up with something by Thursday and then perhaps Dr. A can do a little more on Thursday other than just remove the stent from my esophagus, like even put the little stents in my duodenum! I can only hope for the best, even though it hasn't gotten me very far in the past. ONE of these days I'll get good news, right??

It's all just . . . frustrating. OK, end rant. I didn't mean for this to be this long. At least it's Friday, so I have the weekend to relax and rest, and hopefully feel refreshed by Monday. No big plans for the weekend for me, except tomorrow morning I might meet Anjeanette at Michael's again. She's taking a beginner's knitting class, with the same woman who taught our crochet class last weekend. I wouldn't join in, since I didn't sign up for the class, and have no interest in learning knitting, but I would bring my crochet project and sit and talk with them, if that's allowed. It starts at 10, so at least it would give me a good excuse to get up out of bed and not sleep in. We'll see how well that happens!

Dad to Krystin:

I wish I could help. All I can say is, "hang in there." We'll hope things take a turn in the right direction next week.

May 11, 2015 Text

Krystin to dad: I. Am. So. Tired. I dunno how I'm gonna get any work done this afternoon.

Dad: Uff da. Have cup of coffee with milk and a little sugar.

Krystin: I dunno if that will help. My Ritalin this morning didn't even help. I'm sure it's due to the stress and my very poor nutrient absorption. My body and brain are both exhausted. I just wanna sleep, but the stent pain keeps me from sleeping. Ughhhh.

Dad: I am sorry.
Krystin: I talked to Dr. Ibrahim today. He thinks I should take 2-3 days off work, because my stress is so high. It's not good for my new organs, either.
Dad: Will that help? You do what docs say, of course. What about duodenal front?
Krystin: I won't know more about that until Thursday. Tomorrow morning is my swallowing test to look at my duodenum.
Dad: Oh.
Krystin: Yup. I just want to be put in an induced coma for the next month. Or at least until this is all over and fixed and healed.

May 11, 2015 Email
As a random side note . . .
Krystin to dad:
   . . . You would be proud to know that I have not gone shopping (other than for groceries and necessities) for a long, long time now. I can't even remember the last time I went clothes shopping. Maybe all these health issues are a blessing in disguise (in a very morbid way). They're taking all my time, money, and energy!

Dad to Krystin
   I suppose that's one way to look at things!

May 12, 2015 Text
Dad: I don't blame you.
Krystin: It hurts so much. If a doctor were in pain like this, they would never let it go on this long.
Dad: You should say that to them!
Krystin: Believe me, I HAVE. It hurts all the time, but worse when I eat, obviously, cuz that's when the stomach produces more acid. Which is keeping me from eating much. Great diet this is, whether I want it or not. I've lost about 8 lbs in the last week.
Dad: Not good.
Krystin: Not at all. Especially when you love food as much as I do. I sent an email to Dr. I this morning, joking to him about the induced coma. If only they could really do that for things like this that take lots of tests and time, so the patient doesn't have to live in misery while they figure out the problem and its solution! Even when they do

whatever they're gonna do, it will still take time for my esophagus to heal.
Dad: I suspect it wasn't a solution he endorsed.
Krystin: Well he didn't respond, but I wasn't expecting him to. But no, I would be surprised if any doc ever endorsed that!
(later) Uh oh. I feel nauseous.
(later) May be going in. Waiting for thoracic doc on call to call me back. I hate my life right now.

May 13, 2015 Text
Krystin to dad: Been dry heaving all day, except now I think I just threw up a small glob of blood.
Dad: Ugh.
Krystin: I will call Dr. Andrade's nurse.
(later) Dad: So what's up? I just leaving campus, could come get you. Or you going out tonight?
Krystin: Nothing is up yet. I had to leave a message for Teri. She's with a patient right now but will call me back when she's done.
Krystin: You were right, Teri thinks the nausea is from food not emptying my stomach, and the blood from irritation from the stent. It was red, not dried black, so it was fresh and not from my stomach. And I actually feel a little better since that. So I'm comfortable with waiting to talk to Dr. Andrade tomorrow morn.
Dad: Good to hear.

May 14, 2015 Text
Krystin to dad: I feel so much better. I took a little nap when I got home. And I have no more pain. Even ate some of my Chinese left over from last night. I didn't even have any pain when I woke up from anesthesia. You'd never know they were digging into my throat earlier.
Dad: Great!

May 20, 2015 Email
Ugh
Krystin to Pat, dad, Kathy:
    With all the pain and discomfort from the stent, I didn't eat very often while it was in, since eating only made it hurt more. Which means my stomach shrunk a lot. With food sitting in there forever and not being able to move through, I hardly ever feel hungry. When I WOULD eat (when the stent was in), I would only eat a little, because 1) it hurt, and 2) I got full fast. Now, with the stent out, it doesn't hurt

to eat, but it's still hard, and I'm still not very hungry much. I've lost almost 10 pounds in the past couple weeks. NOT an ideal diet. (And I didn't even want or need to be on a diet!) :-(

Dad to Krystin, Pat, Kathy:
   So when do you learn about the possible duodenum solution?

Krystin to all 3:
   I see Dr. Andrade on Friday.

Dad to Krystin:
   None too soon! Tell him you're losing weight. That should be a motivator, if nothing else is!
Krystin to dad:
   Yes, absolutely. I can tell you this though, that I know for sure - he's going to recommend, again, a feeding tube. UGH. Unless he has a solution to the whole problem and can fix it soon. Which would be ideal, of course.

May 21, 2015 Text
Krystin to dad: I'm so angry and frustrated. I can't swallow again, but no matter who I tell, nothing is done quickly. None of the doctors are listening to me! I don't know what to do anymore, I am at a complete loss. I have complained and stressed to everyone on my medical team how urgent this is. A person can only go 3 days without water. I literally can't swallow anything. Why are they not taking more action?? Uuuuuuuugh I want to screen and cry at the same time.
Dad: I don't know what to tell you. Maybe go to ER and get admitted. They would have to admit someone who could not ingest liquid.
Krystin: Yeah. . . . They've had to do that for me before. I wonder if I called the on-call transplant coordinator or thoracic resident to get their opinion. They could at least let the hospital know I'm coming, if they say I should be admitted.
Dad: Yes
Krystin: Talked to the on call dude. He's going to talk to the thoracic team and get back to me. He said if I really feel like it's an emergency, I can go to the ER, but he agreed with me that probably nothing would happen quickly. Sigh. Fml.
Dad: Even if you can be there overnight before you see the doctor tomorrow, that would be good.

Krystin: He said the team thinks it's best if I just keep my appt. with Dr. Andrade tomorrow and talk to him then. They think that's actually the quickest way to do anything. Whatever. I'm so fed up I'm just gonna go to bed.

Dad: Sigh. Get a little water down and try to sleep, I guess.

May 21, 2015 Email
Subject: Swallowing

Hi Dawn and Teri,

Again, I'm emailing you both at the same time so that you can both get this at the same time, and relay my message to Dr. Kandaswamy and Dr. Andrade as you see fit.

I'm in a bit of a predicament again. My esophageal stent came out last Thursday, and today, a week later, I am at the point where I can't swallow again. Every time this happens, I tell thoracic, and they'll schedule a dilation or stent placement, but it's usually not for a week or so later. When I ask what I'm supposed to do in the meantime, all I get is a "hang in there" or "do your best." I don't think they really understand the severity and the urgency of the problem. I can't swallow ANYTHING. Not even water. Which means I can't take my meds, I can't stay hydrated, and I can't eat to keep up my nutrients. I've already lost close to 10 pounds in the last 2 weeks from not being able to eat normally. I have an appointment with Dr. Andrade tomorrow, but that's only an in-clinic appointment for a discussion. Who knows when any action might be taken. I'm not sure what to do at this point, because I need to drink, I need to take my meds, and I need to get nutrients. I feel like it's kinda ridiculous to walk into the ER and say "I can't swallow anything." I mean, what are they going to do? They're going to tell me there's not much they can do about it.

I have sort of an idea, but I'm not sure if it's even a possibility. Both Dr. Kandaswamy and Dr. Andrade want me to get a G-J tube put back in. The ONLY way I would do that, is if Dr. Andrade and Dr. Kandaswamy talked and came up with a solution to my problem, and agreed on something that could be done in the near future. Like I told Teri earlier today, I don't think any medication is going to fix this. I am pretty sure it will need to be some kind of procedure. I don't care WHAT it is, as long as it's an attempt to fix this. IF I had a tube put in in the meantime, I would want to be inpatient while it's in (like on the transplant floor, since they would be most familiar with my transplant meds) - assuming something was scheduled to be done about my esophagus/duodenum. That way, the staff can regulate my medications, regulate feeding through the tube, keep me on IV fluids, and, mostly importantly to me, help control any pain that the tube causes, especially considering the tube I had before caused me chronic pain. I just don't see any other option at this point, since I would NOT want to go home and go to work with a tube in. And obviously I don't want to be inpatient for weeks, which is why I'd hope that some kind of procedure or something could get scheduled soon. Not being able to eat or drink makes me weak and dehydrated, which makes my body ache and my head dizzy, which in turn makes it harder and harder for me not only to get out of bed, or get off a couch, but also move around. This is greatly affecting my daily life, both home and work. Please let me know your thoughts. Thank you.

May 22, 2015 Facebook
Today: feeding tube placed in my nose so that I can give myself fluids and Ensure supplements over the weekend. If they can't get it placed because they can't get the tube past my esophageal stricture, they'll admit me on IV fluids and supplements, and try again tomorrow.
Tuesday 5/26: Nose tube removed, round 2 of getting a G-J tube placed in my stomach.
Mid June: G-J tube removed, surgery to cut open the bottom of my stomach so that food can successfully move through it. Ideally. It's not even guaranteed to fix the problem, but as Dr. Andrade said, "it works for most patients."
My duodenum? It's fine. It's not being squished by any arteries after all.
If there were ever an FML moment, this is it. Srsly.

May 24, 2015 Text
Dad to Krystin: I home if you want to call.
Krystin: After an hour and numerous attempts, they got the tube in my nose. Home now. It's very uncomfortable in my throat cuz of the narrowing. This weekend is gonna suck.
Dad: Rats. I guess you can only put up with it. I sorry.

May 25, 2015 Text
Krystin to dad: I have an appt with Monica tomorrow morn at 8:45, before I have to be over at the hospital. I can drive over in the morn

and leave my car at the house, if that's ok. Just let me know what time to be there.

Dad: Would be good if you can be here at 715 tomorrow morning. You need ride home later also, I assume.

Krystin: Well, I will be inpatient for a few days, so not home tomorrow.

Dad: Didn't realize you would be there that long. Do any work while there? I have hand surgery Thursday, so Kathy has to bring me home that day.

Krystin: Yes, I can do some work while there. I not going home until any pain from it is under control. I absolutely do not wanna go home with narcotic pain meds. I'm not going through that again. I did request to be on 7A, so hopefully I can see some of my favorite nurses.

Dad: I see you there at some point!

May 26, 2015 Text
Krystin to dad: 7A, room 210, first bed.
Dad: Tomorrow. How you feel?
Pat to Gary: Any word from K?
Krystin to dad: Ok. Drowsy, and the tube site hurts, but sadly, I'm used to that.
Gary to Pat: She just texted, on 7A. She just texted, drowsy and site hurts. But otherwise ok.
Dad to Krystin: I come see you on way in. I have 830 meeting.
Krystin: Ok

May 27, 2015 Text
Krystin to dad: Pain finally under control and relieved. Maybe now I'll be able to take a nap.
Dad: Good! Heavy drugs?
Krystin: Absolutely. Dilaudid.
Dad: Addictive?
Krystin: Just a higher dose. What I'm used to.
Dad: My question is whether it is addictive?
Krystin: Well I won't be on it for a long time this time around, so hopefully not.
Dad: Good.
Krystin: Well it's a narcotic, so yes, it can be. It's what I became addicted to last time.
Dad: But not again, right?

Krystin: But like I said, it's only for a short while. And this time I know how to manage it.
Right.
Dad: I'm not worried. You know how to handle it this time.
Krystin: Exactly. And I WILL manage it correctly, because I am not going through again what I went through before, with withdrawal and weaning and such. No thank you!
(later) Krystin: They moved me rooms.
Dad: How you feeling now? Any talk about release?
Krystin: I am feeling much better now that pain is better. No talk of discharge, I assume still tomorrow.
Dad: But pain returns without drugs, I assume.
Krystin: Yes
Dad: Ugh
Krystin: Yup. And the Dilaudid makes me really itchy.
Dad: Ugh
Krystin: Yup

May 29, 2015 Text
Krystin to dad: Oh, apparently I'm being discharged right now. But nurse said no rush, I can stay as long as I need to. Might you be able to pick me up at some point? Or Kathy?
Dad: Someone will get you at 11:00. Text when you ready to be down there.
(later) Krystin: Home sweet home.
Dad: Good. On drugs?
Krystin: Some. But I can manage it.

May 30, 2015 Text
Dad to Krystin: How you doing? You still able to eat?
Krystin: I'm doing alright. Tube not too sore. Only when I'm in bed and try to turn over. Yes, still able to eat. Will do a tube feeding overnight tonight, though. To get the extra calories and nutrients.

June 11, 2015 Text
Krystin to dad: Been seen by the triage nurse, waiting now for a room. Pat J called ahead, so they were expecting me and know what the problem is.
Dad: Keep me posted.
(later) Dad: I take it no more news.
Krystin: Everything came back normal. Going home with no answers.

Dad: At least normal. Now what?
Krystin: Now I don't know what. I sit and wait some more for no answers.
Dad: Are they puzzling over doing anything?
Krystin: I dunno. Nobody tells me anything.
Dad: Sigh. Keep your spirits up.
Krystin: The ER is for emergencies and I'm not an emergency.
Dad: Hope you hear something tomorrow.
Krystin: Yeah, good luck with that one. But me, too.
Dad: Meantime, sleep well. Love you. Let me know if anything changes tomorrow.
Krystin: Ok. Good night.

June 11, 2015 Email
I'm sick and tired of this bs
Krystin to dad, Pat, Kathy:

    Great. I'm at that point again where, even if my esophagus is open enough to let me swallow tiny bits, nothing is staying down. Not even the couple sips of apple juice I took this morning. UGHHH this is getting SO frustrating. I've about had enough of this. Especially since whenever I tell anyone, nobody does anything about it. I'm SICK of nobody doing anything. I'm doing my tube feeding when I'm home, but that's not enough; there's not enough time in a day to run it with water to keep me hydrated, AND the supplement to give me some calories and nutrients. I'm sick of throwing up (literally). I feel nauseous all the time, even when I haven't tried to eat or drink anything. I throw up when I haven't tried to eat or drink anything, so where is all that fluid coming from that I'm throwing up? Even through the process of elimination, I still can't figure out what's causing this nausea and vomiting. I don't know what to do anymore. I got nothin'. I can't "hang in there" or "do my best anymore," because hanging in there and doing my best isn't keeping me hydrated; it isn't giving me calories and nutrients. I'm sick of this health care system taking their slow damn time with this. Don't they realize I could lose my new organs? Or that without proper hydration and nutrition, I could DIE? I feel like I'm already being pretty aggressive with everyone. I could march over to the ER, but nothing would come out of that. They could give me some IV fluids and then send me on my way. They wouldn't have a medical excuse to keep me since I have the G-J tube, and that's "supposed" to get me by until . . . what? I don't even know what is next, yet. Dr. Andrade is out of town until tomorrow, and who knows if he and Dr. Kandaswamy have even talked yet.

That's all for now. I just needed to rant. Plus I have to throw up in my garbage can now, so I'm gonna go. Maybe this afternoon another round of emails to Teri and Dawn are in order. :-/

Dad to Krystin, Pat, Kathy:
You are right. Reiterate your frustrations (and difficulties). I don't know what more you can do, other than planting yourself in the clinic and refusing to move until they figure something out. Which they may not be able to do. Push them on the stomach option?

Krystin to dad, Pat, Kathy:
Going into the ER. I talked to coordinator Pat, and she thinks there could be something wrong with the placement of my tube, since this nausea and vomiting should not be occurring with a tube in. And Pat said that looking at my labs from yesterday, I'm clearly dehydrated, and she agreed with me that my kidney probably hates me right now. She's also concerned about how much of my meds I'm keeping down.

So, once again, it's off I go. I shouldn't have even asked; I knew this was going to be the answer. I'm going home first, because if they decide to keep me, which Pat wasn't sure if they would or wouldn't, I want to make sure I have everything I need for an overnight stay. I'll keep you all updated as things progress.

Dad to Krystin, Kathy, Pat:
Better that than dehydration and further weight loss.

I suppose one can have some sympathy for the medical folks: you present them a problem they just don't know what to do about! (Because one must assume that if they did know what to do, they'd have done it!)

Keep us posted. Don't forget your chargers :-)

June 12, 2015 Text
Gary to Kathy: Bringing Krystin to house. She called and asked if I would. Not want to be alone. I think she scared. Nothing from docs.
Gary to Pat: Krystin called a bit ago, asked I would come get her, bring her to house. I did (was on a vacation day, so easy). She not doing well and I think she scared. She not wanted to be alone. Docs have no answers.

(later) Gary to Pat: Took her to the hospital. They admitted her, 7A. She was very weak. No news since I got her in and settled. Did not stay.
Gary: Talked to nurse. She now on IVs, resting comfortably. There at least through the weekend. They see no problem with the transplants.
Krystin to dad: Starting to feel slowly better. Pretty tired still, but getting fluids and pain med. Will be over the weekend at the least. I can update mom tomorrow.
Dad: Glad to hear. I talked to nurse about hour ago. I see you tomorrow.
Krystin: Ok. Good night. Ly.

June 13, 2015 Facebook
Krystin Engstrand is feeling drained at Fairview University Medical Center.
I'm alive, but yesterday I would've said barely. Back in the hospital after my trip to the ER on Thursday was fruitless. My condition only worsened, and quickly, throughout the day Friday. I've now been admitted and am getting lots of fluids, I've stopped throwing up, my breathing is back to normal, and they're doing their best at pain management. Maybe now they'll actually listen to me and be more proactive about fixing this stomach/duodenum issue, although from talking to the doc it doesn't sound like anything significant is going to happen swiftly.

June 14, 2015 Text
Krystin to dad: Still throwing up. Once last night and again about 10 minutes ago. Wonderful.
Dad: They trying to deal with it?

June 15, 2017 Text
Krystin to dad: My eye surgery is rescheduled for next Tuesday instead of tomorrow. 7:30am procedure, 6:15 arrival. Ew.
Dad: In meeting. Will drop over a bit later.
(later) Krystin: As I suspected, no Dr. Andrade today. No surprise there.
Dad: Unfortunate. Hope you see him tomorrow and press him on doing SOMETHING!
Krystin: Yup.

(later) Krystin: He finally stopped by. Fuck my life, that's what I have to say. I basically get to be connected to this stomach tube indefinitely and rely on it to get my nutrients and fluids, since nothing that goes in my stomach will stay there. Not even my own bodily fluids. So I have to be committed to being hooked up to tube feeding every night, and draining the G-port of stomach juices so that I don't throw them up; ideally. What kind of life is that? My life is over. I'm gonna lose my job. Nobody is ever gonna wanna marry me. I guess someone from some department is gonna come by to talk to me about how to adapt and change my lifestyle to accommodate tube life, cuz they still don't wanna do a major procedure that may or may not fix the problem. Fan-fucking-tastic. Fml.

Dad: I'd still think about Mayo for another opinion. But it's not a great message, I agree. Rats.

But I don't think your life is over. Don't think that way. I see you tomorrow and we talk. And talk to mom.

Krystin: I. Can't. Afford. It. $150, and that's just a new patient consultation. I texted mom, too.

Dad: We will talk.

June 16, 2015 Facebook
Krystin Engstrand is feeling disappointed.
After many, many months of tests, scans, procedures, stents, and lots of pain, discomfort, and frustration, I finally have an answer to my stomach issues: There is no solution. Damaged nerves in the stomach can't be healed, so I have to learn to manage my symptoms and try to work and live as normal a life as I can around it. And with the G-J tube staying in indefinitely.

> Krystin: It's things like this that really make me wish I had taken better care of my diabetes all those years. I can't feel sorry for myself, and it's hard to accept sympathy from people, because I know I brought this on myself. BUT, I've spent too much time looking back and having regrets. Looking back doesn't do any good; gotta look forward and stay positive and not let it keep me down!
>
> Krystin: I do allow myself pity parties, too. I allow myself to cry, and to hate the situation, and to feel bad/sad. I learned the hard way that keeping it in and pretending to be strong, even when I

was alone, was never a good idea. Thanks so much for your support, it truly does mean a lot to me. :-D

June 17, 2015 Text
Dad to Krystin: So what's going on?
Krystin: Possibly go today, if lunch goes well, and if I can poop, since I haven't since Friday when I came in. They don't wanna release me if I haven't gone.
Dad: Let me know.
Krystin: I was just told that we're having a care conference at 3, with Dr. Andrade, Dr. Kandaswamy, and the palliative care team to discuss and come up with my care plan upon discharge. You are welcome to come, if you want, so that you can be in the loop and know the plan. Of course you don't have to come, and I won't be disappointed if you don't! Just want to give you the option.
Dad: I can come over.
Krystin: Ok. Great!
(later) Krystin: I'm having a lot of that burning, acidic pain, and I realized it's probably cuz I had spaghetti with marinara sauce for dinner. Duh, marinara is tomatoes! I'm really going to have to be more aware of what I'm eating. Bed soon. I'm tired. Thanks for coming today to our little makeshift meeting. Guten nacht! Ich liebe dich.
Dad: But he said you could eat whatever you want. Wonder if it's more a matter of volume than content. Guten Nacht to you, too. Glad I could hear the docs. See you tomorrow.

June 18, 2015 Text
Dad to Krystin: How it going?
Krystin: Just fine. Same as yesterday.
Dad: Release today?
Krystin: Hopefully. Haven't seen any docs yet.
Dad: I have 11:00 meeting, otherwise free.
Krystin: Ok. I highly doubt I would be discharged before noon, anyway. Probably this afternoon some time.
(later) Dad: Any update?
Krystin: I'm getting more fluids before going, to make sure I'm good and hydrated. What time are you planning to leave work? If it's your usual 4-4:30, I can be ready by then.
Dad: Ok. Let know. Will you stay hydrated???
Krystin: Yes. It has to become one of my top priorities.

(later) Dad: How you doing?
Krystin: Good! Watching a movie on TV and relaxing. I'm sure I'll sleep well tonight!
Dad: Glad to hear that. I home tomorrow but want to hear how things going.
Krystin: Of course! I'll stay in touch.

June 19, 2015 Text
Dad to Krystin: So it going ok?
Krystin: Yup. Had no probs getting up and going. I even brought a lunch to eat.
Dad: Hydrated? Good luck with lunch.
Krystin: Yes, staying hydrated, and finally eating lunch now. It's going just fine. About as well as can be expected, and probably as good as it's gonna get with my "condition".

June 19, 2015 Facebook
Krystin Engstrand is feeling happy.
Believe it or not, I'm glad to be back at work after my little "vacation". I hate sitting on my bum in a hospital room doing nothing, so now it's actually nice to get into my routine!

June 23, 2015 Facebook
Woke up in the middle of the night to find that the tube that's connected to the bag filled with my nightly feeding formula, had disconnected itself from my G-J tube, leaving me in a pool of wet, gooey, sticky mess of formula. That's cool, it was probably about time I replaced my mattress anyway. And who doesn't love 2am showers??

June 24, 2015 Facebook
Krystin Engstrand is feeling sad.
I've had my fair share of crying lately. It's been hard for me to grasp, and accept, that nightly tube feeding and stomach draining is now part of my life, and that there's nothing the doctors can do to fix this. I'm especially having a hard time finding the strength that I've had all this time. I have nothing in the future to hold on to or look forward to that's going to make this better, because nothing CAN make this better. It's discouraging and depressing to know that I have to adjust almost every aspect of my life in order to accommodate this G-J tube and the long-

term lifestyle that comes with it. As my docs say, I have to "get used to it."

Fri, Jun 26, 2015 at 1:53 PM
From: Kathy Jensen
To: Krystin Engstrand
Cc: Gary Engstrand

Hi Krystin,

I wanted to let you know about something I talked about in a meeting I was in yesterday. Our office invited a group of about 30 staff people who work in communications to attend a brainstorming meeting about finding heroes at the University. A lot of what our office does is write stories about the amazing research and discoveries being made at the U and we hoped we could get campus communicators inspired to help us find and write these stories.

We started the meeting by sitting in a big circle and introducing ourselves. Ann, my boss, also asked people to talk a little about a hero they have in their life. I thought, oh great, the introvert has to not only speak in front of a bunch of strangers, but now I have to come up with a hero, too?!

Well, there were about 6 people ahead of me, so I had to think fast. A few people went through my mind - my dad, my uncle, Freddy Mercury (just kidding) . . . but I really didn't want a dead hero. As soon as I stopped concentrating on dead people, the first living person who came to mind was . . . you!

When my turn came, I told everyone that my step-daughter was my hero. I told them about how you were diagnosed with diabetes at a young age and that over the last few years, you've been challenged almost every day. I told them about the transplants, the many visits to the hospital, the feeding tube, and the fact that even though you have this and so many other things going on that I didn't mention, you go to work and you keep a good attitude and don't let it all get you down. I said I thought that took a really strong person and that I admire you for your bravery and your stamina.

I'm telling you all this because I know things are pretty tough right now. Well, I would have told you regardless, but I wanted you to know that I think you've been remarkably strong through all of this and I really think (and hope) the funk you're in now is going to be temporary. So come on over tonight and hang out on my comfy couch.

We want you to be well and it's absolutely no good being alone when you're sad. The kitties will help fix that. ;-)
    Kathy

June 30, 2015 Text
Dad to Krystin: How you?
Krystin: Been nauseous and throwing up all day. While I was at work and everything. And still am, and of course I have no idea why.
Dad: I am sorry. Call doc?
Krystin: I'll see if it's any better tomorrow. I'm so tired and my eyelids are so heavy, I'm going to bed. I'll keep you posted in the morning though.
Dad: Ok. Sleep as well as you can. I will be around.
Krystin: Thanks.

July 11, 2015 Facebook
Krystin Engstrand is feeling peaceful.
"The mystery of human existence lies not in just staying alive, but in finding something to live for." - Fyodor Dostoyevsky.
It's time to start applying this quote, which is one of my favs, to my life. Now that the funk and fog of the last few weeks is dispersing, I'm finally able to accept that my life is not over because I have a G-J tube. I am NOT my tube, and the tube and pain will not define me. I still have a lot of fight and strength in me, and I have so much to live for. Onward march! But after a short nap, k?

July 14, 2015 Facebook
"Oh my goodness Krystin, what happened to your eye??"
"Oh, well, sometimes I volunteer with an animal rescue group. This past weekend we joined some local police to break up an illegal loon-fighting ring, which is actually a big problem here in Minnesota. A nasty brawl broke out, and this is my souvenir. But this is nothing; you should see the other guy!"
That's my story and I'm sticking with it.

July 17, 2015 Email
Plan for tonight
Krystin to dad, mom, Kathy:
    I'm working until 3 today, and then I'm going to the ER.

Don't worry, it's nothing too serious, but I've been nauseous and throwing up on and off for the last week and have been having a hard time keeping anything down again. Over the past 2 days, between Tuesday and yesterday, I've lost 8 pounds all in throw-up fluids. And I haven't had a poop in probably 6 or 7 days. Not good. So Becky, the coordinator who's covering for Dawn this week, said that it's serious enough that I need to go in. They'll do a scan of my belly to see if there's any bowel blockage, and for sure start an IV and get some fluids going. Depending on how my labs look, and what the scan shows, she said it is possible, as usual, that I could be admitted. So I should probably plan on being admitted then.

Which is why, after work, I'm running home first to get stuff for when I'm admitted. Just in case! I'll keep you updated later after I get there and know more.

Dad to Krystin:
Please do. Just never ends, does it?

Krystin to dad:
Nope. And since this a chronic, ongoing issue, this won't be the last time, either. I really hope this isn't a once-a-month occurrence.

July 17, 2015 Text
Dad to Krystin: So what's up?
Krystin: Getting fluids now. Still waiting to get scan. I actually don't think I'll be admitted.
Krystin: Of course. I always do!
Dad: I know. I hope you not getting charged for emergency room charges each time!
Krystin: Hmm, I dunno! I don't think so. I would definitely know if I were.
Dad: Hope not! Argue strongly if you do!
Krystin: Scan showed lots of stool. Got an enema. Resulted mostly in a lot of gas. Urine sample showed something, because I'm getting an antibiotic in my IV that runs over an hour. Plus more fluids. And I threw up about 30 mins ago. But still no plan to admit.

July 18, 2015 Text
Krystin: Finally got home at 2:30am. I got 2 liters of fluids and 2 enemas that only made me poop a little. Didn't help my nausea.

Dad: So now what?
Krystin: Now I have 2 liters of fluids in me and am minus a bit of poo. That's about it.
Dad: I assume you continue to use GJ tube, etc. Hope the nausea goes away.
Krystin: Oh yeah, and I have a UTI. And yes, I will still use it.
Dad: Great. I just hope you get better.
Krystin: Absolutely. Me too.

July 21, 2015 Facebook
I am very excited that next week I will be giving my first presentation as a National Kidney Foundation advocate, at a diabetes support group at the Native American Community Clinic in Minneapolis! I finally get to start sharing my story, and the fact that my first presentation will be at a diabetes support group is pretty much perfect.

July 30, 2015 Email
how'd it go?
Dad to Krystin:
> How did your presentation go?
> LY

Krystin to dad:
> I wasn't able to go on Wednesday. Starting Tuesday afternoon, my back started hurting REALLY bad. I even had to leave work a little early to go home and lie down. Then Tuesday night I threw up in the middle of the night. So Wednesday morning, between that and my back still killing me, I wasn't doing too good. I quickly contacted Jordan, who is the coordinator for this region of the NKF, and told her what was going on, and she was able to go do the presentation. I felt so bad about missing it, but Jordan said that Camille, the woman who is in charge of that group that I was going to give the presentation to, said she would still love if I'd be willing to come back and talk to the group and talk about my story and journey, because it's a diabetes support group. Camille said usually just women, 4-5 of them, between the ages of 40-60. Of course I said absolutely, I'd still love to talk with them. So, hopefully that can get set up at some point.
> No plans this weekend, except dinner tomorrow. I have been so incredibly exhausted this week, and I don't know why. I've pushed the snooze button at LEAST 4 times, if not more, every day. It has been so hard to get out of bed, and when I'm at work, my head is elsewhere. Both Wednesday and yesterday I got in to work late - noon one day,

10:30 another. I don't know what's wrong. I emailed coordinator Dawn, and cc'd Dr. Ibrahim, to let them know what's going on. We'll see if either have any ideas.

 Ly.

Dad to Krystin:
 Well, that's too bad about missing the event and being so tired.
 You going to be OK for dinner?
 Good luck with the advice from the docs.
 See you tomorrow night.

Krystin to dad:
 Yeah, I'll be fine. Mornings and getting going is the hardest part, so by dinner I should be alright to go.

August 8, 2015 Text
Krystin to dad: Actually going for MRI shortly. Dr. Kandaswamy also wants liver biopsy.
Krystin: Just kidding, no MRI. My gastric pacer can't go in the machine. I'm in room 207, btw. Across from the nurse's station.
Dad: Ok. E and I may come by and then go to big ten for lunch.
(later) Dad: So how's it going?
Krystin: Not too bad. Got a good nap in. Just saw Dr. Kandaswamy. No biopsies on weekends, so I'll be here at least until Monday, and they'll do it then. Great. Now deciding what to order for dinner.
Dad: Too bad about staying. Can't they release you and have you come back Monday?
Krystin: I wondered that too, but they want to manage the pain, and make sure it doesn't get worse. I guess I understand that, but it sure does suck.
Dad: Yeah.
Krystin: They have charging stations now down in the lobby, with different charger types, so I can take my devices down and charge them if need be.
Dad: Yep. So, that's pretty convenient! You have to sit down there and wait, though, I would guess.
Krystin: Yeah . . . but it charges pretty quick, and I can wander the gift shop while keeping an eye on it.

August 8, 2015 Facebook
Krystin Engstrand is at University of Minnesota Medical Center.
So yeah, getting admitted happened last night. Excruciating mystery pain in my upper right abdomen that had me in tears. May be my liver now; blood work showed my liver enzymes are elevated. Ultrasound and Xray were normal (of course), so liver biopsy today. Oh joy. I've settled into a sort of melancholy that this is my life now. I'm just destined to be one medical disaster after another.

August 11, 2015 Text
Krystin to dad: Will be here another night. They want to keep me until they get biopsy results. Liver enzymes still abnormal, and esophagus is thickened (not new news), so if biopsy comes back normal, G.I. may do biopsy of esophagus. Biopsy and EBV lab results may be back tonight, if not then tomorrow morning. Either way, I stay until they find source of pain and come up with treatment plan. I sure wish I had packed an extra pair of underwear. . . .
Dad: Well rats. I come by this afternoon.
Dad: Maybe I grab lunch and eat in your room.
Krystin: Ok! That would be quite alright with me. About what time, do you think? I could order my lunch now, since it can take up to 45 min to get here.
Dad: Leaving Burton now, will pick up food and come up.
Krystin: Okay!

August 12, 2015 Text [and an example of a recurring pattern]
Krystin to dad: Sounds like I PROBABLY get to go home today, if Infectious Disease says they're ok with it, but we still waiting for biopsy results. If GI wants to do an endoscopy, it will be outpatient.
Dad: Let me know.
Krystin: Will let you know if/when I have more of a timeline. Oh, and I'm negative for Hep C and CMV, but EBV positive, which is why I have mono. Nothing to do about that, except they lowered my immuno-suppressant so that my body can fight it off quicker, which I think you already knew.
Dad: How is liver?
Krystin: Dunno yet!
Krystin: Ok, now it looks like GI is going to do the scope today. But if they can do it in a timely manner, I should still be able to go home

today, the doc said. It all depends on when they can fit me in, but they do want it done before discharging me. Will keep you posted.
Krystin: Going down for endoscopy now!
(later) Dad: What's up?
Krystin: Back in my room, took a little snooze after procedure.
Krystin: I do get to go today

August 14, 2015 Email
how you doing?
Dad to Krystin:
    You manage to get to work? And how you feeling?
    Do you get some test results today?
    Keep me up to date!

Krystin to dad:
    Yes, I made it to work both yesterday AND today - and the whole day! Well, today isn't over yet, but I WILL be here all day.
    I'm feeling not too bad. A little tired this morning, but I was able to get up out of bed and get to work, so at least that says something, right?
    I won't find out any test results until my appointment with Dr. Young on the 4th; so not for 3 more weeks. Like I said before, though: if my biopsy returns something serious, they'll call me if they want something done.
    So, that's all I know!

Dad to Krystin:
    Well, it sounds positive.
    You should try a cup of coffee at work--does your shop provide coffee to employees?

August 16, 2015 Text
Krystin to dad: I'm having a hard time getting up. Would you be able to pick up a prescription from the discharge pharmacy for me.
Dad: At the hospital? What do you mean, you're having a hard time getting up? I am not sympathetic.
Krystin: Nm I'll figure it out.
Dad: You should contact Peggy.
Gary to Pat & Peggy: Took Krystin to ER. Diarrhea and dehydration.

Pat: I wondered about that. Peggy called me earlier asking about her. I've been out of town so knew nothing.
Gary: Called me also. We finally went over there. Brought her to hospital.

August 17, 2015 Text
Pat to Gary: Any word from K?
Gary: No. Will call hospital in awhile if I don't hear anything.
Pat: Ok thanks.
Krystin to dad: On 7A again
Dad: How you doing? I will come by later this morning.
Gary to Pat: Just got text from her. On 7A again. Don't know anything else. Will go over later this morning.
Krystin to dad: Doing alright. Not sure what is wrong with me.
Pat to Gary: Ok. I'll try go over the noon hour. Or after work, depending on her discharge status. Keep me posted after you see her.
Krystin to dad: If you're coming over, can you stop at the 3rd floor pharmacy beforehand and get my Rx for me?
Dad: Ok
Krystin: Thank you. When were you thinking of coming? It actually might not be ready.
Dad: 1030 or so.
Krystin: Ok they're starting to work on it now, so it won't be ready when you come. I'll pick it up when I discharge.
Gary to Pat: Any possibility you could bring her home when she's discharged later today, as expected?
Pat: Yes
Gary: Thanks.
Pat: Well, not like you haven't done your share of transport. Much appreciated.
(later) Dad: You must be feeling better!
Krystin: Yes, I am! Now I gotta be very diligent to keep it this way.
Dad: Yes!
Krystin: I have Pedialyte and apple juice that I'm drinking, too. And even though I'm eating dinner, I'm still going to do a tube feeding tonight, also, so I should still feel good when it's time to get up tomorrow morn.
Dad: Let's hope you can keep that pattern going.

Krystin: Absolutely. Even though I can't control diarrhea, I need to make sure I can still get in fluids and nutrients if/when it happens. Like, hook up my tube feeding when it starts.
Dad: And eat a banana.

August 21, 2015 Email
Krystin to Christine Lenzen, Peggy Hinz:

Hi Chris and Peggy,
 I wanted to send you gals a message to let you know what's going on, because you are both important people to me. As you know, over the past few years I've had many surgeries and procedures, and am on my 2nd G-J tube. Therefore, I have been on a narcotic pain medication, Dilaudid, for quite some time. Unfortunately, and this is common, people who are put on narcotic pain medications long-term, for real medical reasons, can become addicted to their medication. Well, my name is Krystin, and I'm an addict. I have gotten to the point where I am WAY overusing my medication, taking much more than is needed on a daily basis, and frequently running out of my medication before it's due to refill. I have, on numerous occasions, manipulated my doctors and nurses into refilling it early, coming up with excuses as to why I'm out so soon. Dilaudid is like the heroin of pain medications. It's highly addictive, and the strongest pain medication out there. It's an opioid, like heroin. I didn't know before exactly how opioids work, but I read something just yesterday on Hazelden's website about opioids that really explained it. I'll give you the brief version, because it actually is interesting:
 "When opioid molecules travel through the bloodstream into the brain, they attach to receptors, specialized proteins on the surface of certain brain cells. The binding of these molecules with their target receptors triggers the same chemical response in the brain's reward center that occurs with anything that causes intense pleasure or is intended to be reinforcing to survival itself. This is the part of the brain that ensures our survival -- by reinforcing acts such as eating, drinking fluids, caring for our babies and having sex (for survival of the species).
 All rewarding and survival-based activities result in release of dopamine in the brain's reward center. But opioids, like all drugs of abuse, trigger the release of dopamine in excess amounts, far beyond what is needed to provide pleasure or keep us alive. The brain has been

signaled: something extremely important has taken place, and it needs to be repeated.

Prolonged use of increasingly higher doses of opioids changes the brain so that it functions more or less normally when the drug is present and abnormally when the drug is removed. This alteration in the brain results in tolerance (the need to take higher and higher doses to achieve the same effect; "chasing the dragon") and dependence (susceptibility to withdrawal symptoms).

Euphoria is the effect that most opioid users seek, but it's also the effect most likely to diminish with regular use. The opioid receptors have changed at a cellular level, trying to protect themselves from overstimulation.

An addict then is taking his or her drug of (no) choice in order to feel "normal," a concept that is difficult to grasp. Many people assume addicts enjoy the daily use of their drugs, but most opioid addicts cannot recall the last time their drug use was enjoyable. After a certain point, daily use becomes a drudgery and its own form of torture."

I have gotten to the point where it is not fun anymore. I do not enjoy taking it, and I don't like what it's doing to me, how it's making me think, and how it's affecting my work and daily life. I'm constantly thinking about it, and worry when my next refill is going to be, and if I have enough to last until then, etc. etc. Like the article said, the euphoria effect is gone, and I don't experience it anymore. Taking it has just become something I do to avoid withdrawal, which I've experienced before, and am already experiencing now.

At the U, on the Riverside campus, there is a detox program for adults with opioid dependence. It's a 3-5 day intense inpatient program, where they completely rid your (my) system of opioids, while at the same time treating withdrawal. After the program, I will need to find another alternative to managing my chronic pain, because my pain management nurse will not ever prescribe me Dilaudid. I'm trying to get in today, but so far they do not have any open beds. I have to just keep calling every couple hours and asking. If nothing tonight, I'll start trying again tomorrow morning. This is something I need to do, and although the addict part of my brain is really scared, I'm going to keep calling until I get in. I know I'll feel so much better on the other side, both in mind and body, to not have this consuming my life anymore. Obviously I'll still need to work with someone on the mental/emotional aspect of the addiction, but at least the physical part will be over.

Peggy, if I'm still around at noon tomorrow, I would still love to come see my kitties. If I get in before then, of course I will let you know. I assume there are no phones allowed in the program, and no contact with the outside, so once I'm in, I'll be out of touch for a while.

Love you both, and I'll keep you updated as I know more.

Christine:

Krystin, as always I'm proud of you for being strong enough to recognize there is an issue and to take charge and do something about it. And as recovery programs say, admitting you have a problem is the first step to recovery. I'm sorry that you are having to deal with this. But I'm glad that you are recognizing a pattern of addiction - hopefully this acknowledgement can help you avoid similar situations in the future. I love you and know that I've always got your back. I'll support you in any way that I can. 🧡

Peggy:

Ditto what Christine said. See you tomorrow at noon unless I hear from you earlier. Love you. XO

August 22, 2015 Text
Krystin to dad: Are you home right now?
Dad: In car just coming from highland. What's up?
Krystin: Was wondering if you could bring me over to riverside.
Dad: When? Now? I can. Forgot something in Highland anyway. How soon you ready?
Krystin: 10 min?
Dad: Ok. I be there.
Gary to Kathy: Taking Krystin to riverside so be a bit.
(later) Dad to Krystin: What's going on?
Gary to Pat: Took Krystin to ER for detox, no bed yet, but on way BG numbers fell, nurses had to get her out of car, rushed her in, put on IVs, etc. She was recovering a bit when I left. That was noonish. Not heard anything since. I have cat house key.
Krystin: Being discharged. Can explain why in car. You able to get me in about 25 min?
Dad: I will come when you discharged.
Krystin: I am. I'm ready. Same place you dropped me off.
Gary to Kathy: Going to get Krystin. She being discharged. I dk story. Back in a bit.

(later) Dad to Krystin: Doin ok?
Krystin: Yeah, but my back hurt SO bad a little bit ago. Almost unbearable. I had to take a bit more of my med, even though it wasn't due yet. Obviously I wasn't taking more for fun, I legit needed it. Back significantly better now. Will head over to cat house soon.
Dad: Ok. Do well. Let me know tomorrow night how you doing.
Krystin: Will do. Thank you for taking me in today, even if nothing came of it. Well, except them treating my low. At least now I know what the next step is that I need to do Monday morn. I left a voicemail for Dawn in the pain management clinic to give me a call first thing, when she has the chance.
Dad: You're welcome. Hope she has an intelligent plan.

August 24, 2015 Email
Krystin to Christine, Peggy:

Peggy, you already know this, but I wanted to update Chris real quick, then give you both another update.

Chris - I didn't end up going into the detox program. A doctor in the ER was talking to me on Saturday, and she wasn't quite sure why the pain management program suggested I do that. They don't give you any pain medication while in detox, obvs, and they wouldn't send me home with any. So yeah, I could get it out of my system, but I'd also be in pain the whole time, and have to deal with my pain upon discharge. So, detox isn't really for people who still need to take pain medication for legit, chronic pain needs. Back to the drawing board.

This morning I talked to Dawn, my pain management nurse, and she's going to have me go see a doctor at a different Fairview pain management clinic. Unfortunately it's way out in Burnsville, but this doctor, Sherri Haas, has special prescribing privileges. If she agrees to take over, maintain, and prescribe my pain medication, she can also prescribe this medication called Suboxone, which acts as both a pain medication AND a deterrent from over-using. It even comes in a patch, so there's nothing to put in a tube or swallow; it's time-released, and is good for 7 days before needing to be replaced. Dawn can't prescribe it, because she told me you have to have certain training, based on a law passed by congress, and so only some physicians can prescribe it. I'm not sure what all Dr. Haas and I will discuss tomorrow, but it sounds like I have some options for managing my pain. Fingers crossed!

Christine:

I'm glad you didn't let the mix up with detox deter you from finding a solution. Seems like this, like all things for you, is going to take a little patience to solve. Thinking of you, love you. Just remember that you are worth it! And it is worth it to feel good about yourself again!

Peggy:

Hang in there Krystin! You're going in the right direction by continuing to pursue a solution. Keep us informed, please. I do worry. Love you both! XO

August 26, 2015 Email
so what's up?
Dad to Krystin:

Haven't heard from you about your most recent interactions with the medical establishment. Any news?

Krystin to dad:

I had my appointment down in Burnsville yesterday morning. It was to see a doctor in their pain clinic, Dr. Sherri Haas, who has special prescribing privileges. She is prescribing me a medication called Suboxone. It's a film that you put under your tongue and it dissolves, so it gets absorbed differently than would a pill or injection. It will be taken instead of my pain medication, so when I get it, I will stop taking Dilaudid and start taking Suboxone. It acts as a pain killer AND prevents withdrawal symptoms, so even though I'll be stopping Dilaudid cold turkey, with the Suboxone I shouldn't experience withdrawal. It's only taken twice a day; once in the morning and once in the evening. She did warn that some patients found immense pain relief from it, while others found it didn't help with pain at all. So I guess I'll find out if it'll help with my pain or not. If it doesn't, I'm not sure what I'll do, because I don't think anyone will put me back on Dilaudid. There's special training a doctor has to go through to be able to prescribe and administer Suboxone, so not many doctors can prescribe it, which is why I had to go to Burnsville. I won't get the medication for a few days or so, because it has to go through insurance, and then the pharmacy has to specially order it. It'll go to the pharmacy here, in PWB, so I won't have to drive back to Burnsville to pick it up or anything. But I do have another appointment down there next week to check in and see how it's working, since Dr. Haas only wrote me a 7-day prescription. If it's working well, she'll write me a longer script. In the meantime, she did fill my Dilaudid for 7 days, to get me through until whenever I get the Suboxone.

I admit that I do fear that because of this, if I ever have to have another surgery or procedure, or if/when I'm inpatient, they won't give me pain medication anymore. Obviously there's going to be a note on my chart now that notes opioid addiction, so if I'm in the hospital and in extreme pain, then what, I just have to deal with it?? I'm guessing that since there it's monitored and administered on a schedule, they wouldn't withhold it; they just wouldn't send me home with any. Oh, well Dr. Haas did say that if I have anything done that requires a doctor to send me home with a pain medication, that that's OK, but to call them first and let them know.

Dad to Krystin:

Well, that all sounds very encouraging if the Suboxone works. Does it have side effects? I'm sure they would not withhold pain medication if you're in the hospital--but you're right, they might not send any home with you.

August 27, 2015 Email
pain killer
dad to Krystin:

After reading a couple of articles in the paper about it, I think you should inquire of your docs about medical marijuana--it apparently is an effective pain-killer without the addicting properties of current meds on the market.

Krystin to dad:

I know, a couple different people have sent me articles about it.

Dad to Krystin:

So ask your docs about it! It sounds to me like you're the perfect candidate.

How you doing?

Krystin to dad:

I'm doing alright. Jeff and Randy come home Sunday, so I'm still at the cat house until then. I still haven't started the Suboxone, but I'm calling the pharmacy today to see what the status is on that. A little hard to see how it's working, at my appointment next Tuesday, if I haven't had any time to try it out!

September 1, 2015 Facebook
Had an emotional breakdown at the infusion clinic today. Being a double transplant patient living with chronic pain, and no answer as to why, is tough, folks.

September 1, 2015 Email
Hydrating
Krystin to mom, dad:
    Staying ahead of the ER and getting some fluids at the infusion clinic this morning. I forgot that I have standing orders and cannot [see below] go in whenever I need to, without prior doctor orders. This may be a weekly thing. . . . Except that 2 liters takes 3 hours, since they have to run it slowly due to my tiny veins. So maybe weekends from now on will be better.

Dad to Krystin:
    That would be good. But I don't understand: you have standing orders but can't go in whenever you need to. Can't you get an order from the doc that you can go in whenever you need to--or at least once per week?

Krystin to dad:
    I CAN go in whenever I want! I don't need doctor authorization each time.

September 15, 2015 Facebook
Today Hank the Panc and I celebrate one year together! Many aspects of my life over the past year have been rough, but if one thing has stayed strong and true, it's Hank. Here's to 1 year being diabetes-free, and to many, many more!

September 16, 2015 Facebook
Aside from a couple areas that are healing a little slower than the rest, for a year later I think it looks pretty good! It'll never look pretty, but I don't care. It's organ transplantation, not plastic surgery!

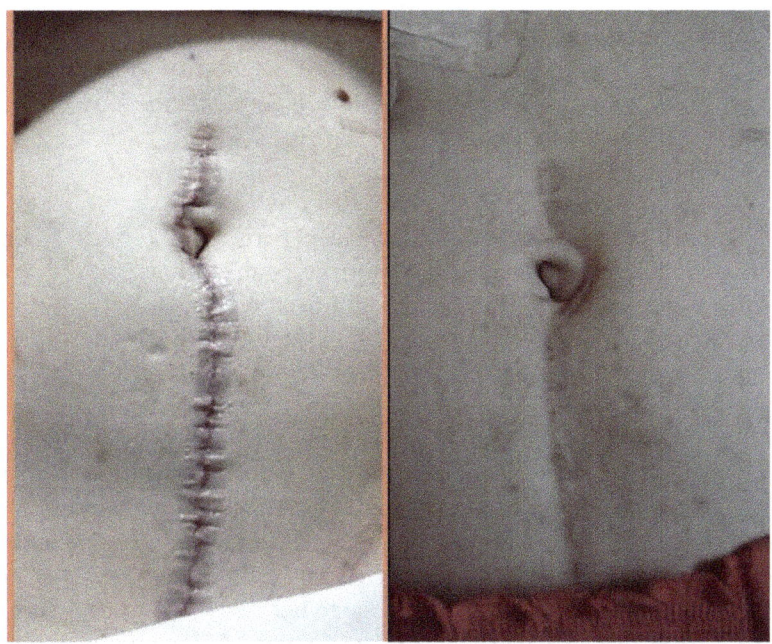

September 17, 2015 Text
Krystin to dad: Called for transplant coordinator on call. Not doing well over here. Bad cold kicking my butt, pain, and just not feeling well. Will keep you posted.
Krystin: Missed work today and most of yesterday, and Monday.
Krystin: This is the pattern of my life. I do better for a while, then for reasons beyond my control, something goes wrong and I decline quickly. Trust me, it's depressing.
Krystin: I really hate my life sometimes.
Dad: So what you going to do now?
Krystin: I don't know.
Dad: You want to go to ER? I can take you, but I don't want to hang around there, which I think you can understand. If they not admit you, then you need to take a cab home.
Krystin: Mom said if I'm not throwing up and can keep pushing fluids, to wait until tomorrow and go to SIPC to avoid ER fee. That makes sense, but I know I'll just keep sleeping all day.
Dad: You need to not do that. I can call you. So I not going to take you in. I'd say you could come here and sleep on couch if you want to, but

not sure what that would accomplish. You can if you want to, however.

Krystin: I would feel more comfortable being over there, knowing I'm not alone if I suddenly need help.

Dad: You drive over or I get you?

Krystin: I come over. Soon.

Dad to Elliott: Krystin coming to sleep here tonight. Sick again, probably to some medical place tomorrow. Sigh.

Elliott: Not a lot changed in the month I been gone then.

Dad: No, and I fear it never will. I think there's no treatment for the damage to her body. At least not yet. Stem cells could, but that's a ways off.

Elliott: She could make an attempt to be healthier. I know she not diabetic anymore and so damage from that no longer accumulating but she still smokes, doesn't exercise in any way, and not eat particularly healthy. Even if she had never had diabetes she wouldn't be a picture of health. And I know her doctors probably tell her that every day so not something that would be a surprise to her.

Dad: All true. I think, however, biggest problem is being immunosuppressed, which makes her vulnerable to every bug that comes around. That's her problem now, sick from a cold.

Krystin to dad: Going to bed very shortly.

Pat to Gary: Thank you for helping her. Again.

September 21, 2015 Email
SIPC
Krystin to dad:
 WTF, SIPC is full both Saturday AND Sunday already! Who are all these people needing infusions and stuff? Jeeeeez. She said to call back on Wednesday and see if they have any cancellations, so I guess that's what I'll do. . . .

Dad to Krystin:
 What about the other place? Is odd.
 Did you make an appt for 2 weeks?

Krystin to dad:
 No and no. I'll call Riverside.

September 23, 2015 Text [evening]
Dad to Krystin: How you doing?
Krystin: I'm ok. I'm still sick, so I feel like crap, but I'm getting by.
Dad: Ugh. I'm sorry. Nothing you can take to help, I gather. If nothing else, rest a lot.
Krystin: Nope, nothing can help but time. I wanna sleep a lot, but I've already missed a lot of work. Most of last week, and was 3 hrs late today. I was so tired and weak, but I don't have the time in my vacation or sick bank to take off.
Dad: Go to bed.
Krystin: I will at 9 when my show is over. It's a 2 hour season premier and I've been waiting months for it.
Krystin: I know . . . we'll see, maybe I'll go to bed early.
(later) Krystin: Ok going to bed. Good night!

September 28, 2015 Text
Dad to Elliott: Just took k to hospital. Tube not working, not getting fed, has lost 20 pounds. But she in good spirits because they think they can fix a number of problems. Sigh.
Elliott: Holy crap that's a lot of weight for someone her size.
Dad: No kidding. She's a little gaunt.
Pat to Gary: Just happened to text K about random kale project and she said was being admitted. I asked if she needed transport. She said you already did. Thank you for that. Again.
Gary: You're welcome. Your turn comes from time to time. She's lost 20 pounds, she reports. But she fairly chipper because Kandaswamy apparently thinks can fix a number of problems and she'll be better. One can only hope.
Pat: Didn't seem to me she had 20 pounds to lose and still be alive. I think we need keep in mind that we're only hearing her side, and I suspect much of that is what she wishes and not what she's really told. If Dr Kanda can fix her then he deserves the Nobel prize this year.
(later) Krystin to dad: Room 12. Have a roomie, but too soon to tell how she is.
Dad: Good luck with sleep.
Krystin: Thanks. Will be in touch tomorrow after I see docs.

September 28, 2015 Facebook
Krystin Engstrand checked in to Fairview University Hospital.
Let's see, what's wrong this time. . . . My G-J tube is misaligned, resulting in my stomach pulling back up into itself whatever goes into the tube, further resulting in my throwing up or draining from my tube whatever went in it, even FURTHER resulting in me losing 20 lbs. in 3 weeks. So thoracic has to go in (through my mouth and down my esophagus) to realign it. Next, interventional radiology will put in a PICC line so, along with overnight tube feedings, I can do overnight PICC line feedings of this high-calorie liquid stuff to help bulk me back up. And my esophagus needs a dilation cuz I can't swallow. And my plague cold still hasn't gone away. At least I look cute? (My favorite nurse, Shelley, says I do!)

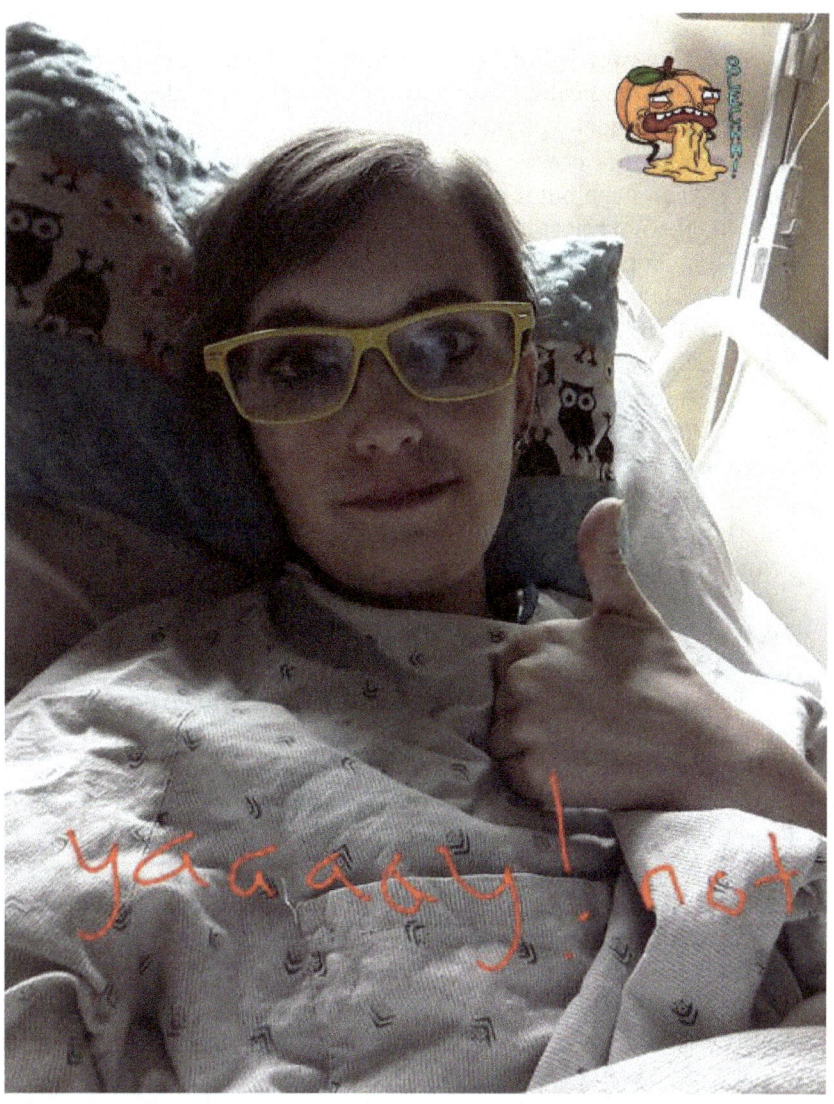

September 29, 2015 Text
Krystin to dad: Today I get picc line, and scan of tube. If they can see the problem from scan, then no need for a more complicated study. Then at some point thoracic will come see me and tell me if they wanna do anything. Also, scheduled for panc biopsy tomorrow.
Dad: Ok. May stop over around lunch time.
Krystin: I NPO all day. Boooo. :(

Dad: Chuckle
Krystin: They worried that cuz of reflux, I not getting (absorbing) all anti-rejection medication, and may be having an episode of rejection.
Dad: They can deal with that, right?
Krystin: Yup. For now I'll get it IV, so no chance I don't get it in my system. Then I can put it in my picc, for same reason / result.
Krystin: No, not rejection!! Pancreatitis. My bad.
Dad: Ugh. Hope they can treat that. Can be nasty.
Krystin: Yeah. Pick your poison, I guess.
Dad: I walking over. I get lunch and eat in your room. Ok?
Krystin: Ok!
(later) Krystin: Scan showed tube def needs to be adjusted. Pancreas shows lots of inflammation, so biopsy tomorrow will determine if rejection or pancreatitis. In meantime I get broth and jello. Bring me pizza!!! Just got picc line in, too.
(later) Krystin: In bed, going to sleep, so don't text back tonight. Will be in touch tomorrow. LY

Tuesday, September 29, 2015 Diary
10:30 a.m.

Today I sit in a hospital room, and I'm waiting to go down to have my tube scan. Over the last 2 hours I've had to put 600 ml of liquid contrast in my tube parts, so they can see what's wrong with it. We know it's misaligned. Possible coil? I go down for the scan at 11:30. Fear: 0 Anxiety: 0

I'm hungry. I went down to the gift shop and bought a salty snack for later, if/when I can eat (I'm NPO now), and a blue Airhead. I've been sneaking eating it, and I can feel it getting stuck. I hope the IR (interventional radiology) people don't bust me. My esophagus needs a dilation. Later I get a PICC line put in my arm so I can get extra nutrition at night. Last time one was put in, it was painful. I want to ask for some kind of sedation, but I doubt it. Fear: 8 Anxiety: 10.

I hope this is not my life: hospital stay after hospital stay after another. What kind of life is that, seriously? I feel so shitty all the time, is the problem. Always need fluids. Always malnourished and losing weight. Always have pain.

12:50 p.m.

The scan went fine. The contrast in my IV stung, as usual. No results yet. I know the docs especially wanna see my pancreas: how it looks, and if there are signs of pancreatitis. They don't seem to seem to be worried about rejection, though. So I won't be. Pancreas biopsy tomorrow for sure. I tried to sneak in an Airhead chew and some pretzel combos; they got stuck so I gagged them back up. Still feels like something is in there. Stuck. Bummer.

Dad came to visit over his lunch! That was nice. He always tries to visit at some point every day. Which really shows he cares. Mom never visits. I don't expect her to. I mostly want to eat! And to be able to!!

1:35 p.m.

I refused the first round of getting the PICC line. I decided I need something to calm the nerves, especially after last time. Hurt too much! Sounds like they've ordered something oral. Better be crushable, yo, cuz I can't swallow any pills! Not if I can't even swallow water. I did tell the doc, though, when he was in, that I need a dilation. PFFFF—they did, in fact, order oral Ativan! Back to the doc my nurse goes. #2. . . .

[In a box on the page:]
Fears of getting PICC line:

- pain   - having 2 ports
- discomfort   - ugly
- time consuming
- care responsibility
- time of obligation
- needle
- I DON'T WANT OR LIKE IT!

Nancy [Krystin's therapist] says I need to start focusing more on positive writing, if I indeed want to get back into it. Negative writing, like my blog was becoming, only helps me dwell on the issues and stay in that sad, depressed, hopeless state of mind. Same with imagery. I need to focus on, and write about, Korea! That was a good, happy time of my life, even if it didn't seem like it at the time.

Things I gained in Korea

- Independence   - Friends
- Confidence   - Memories/experiences
- Self esteem   - Self worth (after)
- Accomplishment in myself ← and proud!

Now what do I do with myself? I sit in a hospital bed.

October 1, 2015 Text
Krystin to dad: It's a rejection, due to elevated lipase levels. It's not great, obviously, but treatable. And just now finally going down for procedure
Dad: Just am glad it treatable!
Krystin: Of course
Dad: They can deal with it and no further risk?
(later) Krystin: Well, there is always risk my whole life as a transplant patient, but for now, yes. Steroids, so on Prednisone again, and high dose anti-rejection infusions. So, I'm not losing Hank yet. There are a lot of preventative measures these days, so I'm still far from losing it. I'm back in my room and clear headed.
Dad: Glad to hear no problem, at least not now. Hope not ever! I take it you feeling reasonable, all things considered.
Krystin: yes, feeling good now. I can swallow! And since no pancreatitis, I'm on regular diet. I can finally order my soup!
Dad: Great! I really hope the rejection issue was minor and fully treated.
Krystin: It WILL be treated. Not fully yet, since we just started treatment. And I think minor. They would be more worried and urgent about it if it were major.

Thursday, October 1, 2015 Diary
7:22 a.m.
　　Yesterday was the biopsy. I got enough sedation this time that I don't remember, but the site where they did it REALLY hurts now. Of course the Nubain pain med doesn't even touch any of my pain. I really want something stronger, and have the whole time I've been here. When I'm home, I don't care about Dilaudid at all, but when I'm in the hospital where I know it's available, that part of my mind says "I want,

I want, I want!" And I can't turn it off easily. I do think I actually deserve something, though, for the actual pain I have.

Today I go down to the OR for EGD with dilation, and tube adjustment. Actually looking forward to that, so I can eat again. Dr. Andrade came to see me in my room yesterday. He is so nice, and you can really tell he cares, by the way he takes my hand and holds it instead of just shaking it, both when he greets me and bids goodbye. He always tells me to "hang in there" and I can tell he understands how frustrated and impatient I am with everything. But [the] procedure today should really help!

- Still no prelim. results on it yet this morning.

Mom never comes to see me when I'm in the hospital, but I guess that doesn't surprise me, for a couple reasons. For dad, working on campus, it's super easy for him to stop in on his way in or out of work. Still, he doesn't HAVE to, so it really shows he cares. He also texts to check in occasionally. Mom just texts occasionally. Oh well. I honestly wouldn't expect any less from her! [I think Krystin meant "more," not "less," in that sentence.] Yeah, it's kinda sad. I dunno what's inside her head that prevents her from opening up about these things. All she says is that she's protecting herself. Ok then.

I went to the gift shop here at the hospital a couple days ago and spent $30—something which to me is ironic considering I just told my dad last weekend that I hadn't done any pleasure spending in a long time. Which is total bull now that I think about it more. I'm addicted to eBay, and the hospital gift store. They both just have so many tempting things! At least these days I'm using my check card more and more, and not credit. I seriously need to lower my debt if I want to find a bigger place to live in and get my furry babies back.

9:00 a.m.

I either have a rejection or pancreatitis. If rejection, treatment includes Prednisone and high anti-rejection meds, probably including Thymo, like after transplant. Pancreatitis treatment involves no eating and an intense/strict bowel regime. Obvs a rejection would suck, but I wanna eat so bad. I love food too much to not eat for like another week. If they send me home on meds for the pancreatitis, I know I'll eat. Even if lightly, just a snack here and here to satisfy my hunger pangs and need to taste.

Had a nice long convo, like 20 min, with my nurse, Jessica, all about books we read. Loved that!

Getting the PICC line put in this time around wasn't as painful. Maybe because I had some IV Ativan beforehand. I remember the whole procedure, but I think I was able to stay calm during it.

Had a convo with one of my other favorite nurses, Becky, for like 10 minutes while she changed my roomie's bedsheets, about our cats. Whenever I'm here and I see her, we always talk cats. One of things I like about [hospital station, solid organ transplants] 7A (sadly or not?) is that the majority of the nurses, I know, and they know me, by first name. They know my history and are supportive and understanding and sympathetic and all that. It's bittersweet, but also a blessing in disguise. I admitted to my therapist and coordinator that I actually enjoy being admitted to 7A. I'm taken care of. I get all my meds, my pain is dealt with, I get meals when I want, I get to see my favorite nurses, and just overall I feel emotionally good/better being here. Is that sad? It's a double-edged sword, having to be here, because I feel like shit. It's all kinds of clichés, 7A is!

It's 9:59 a.m. and supposedly I'm supposed to go down at 10 for my procedure. Ha! Yeah right. Either way, taking a writing break now.

Except for one more last thought. . .

I've been updating on FB, and using humor to inform people what's going on. The metaphor I'm using is being in a marriage with Hank (the Panc, duh), and how we had our first fight and he's all mad and inflamed, like a typical male, and we're in Prednisone steroid couple's therapy and such. I've gotten numerous compliments on it and how my humor through all this is amazing. How else am I supposed to get through this??

OK, now writing break time, before transport comes at 10:30. . .

(Future note: new pain regimen.)

5:00 p.m.
Dinner selection:
- whole grain wrap w/:
- ground beef
- roasted vegetables
- diced tomatoes
- shredded cheddar

- sweet corn
- apple pie
- skim milk

Because . . . I can swallow now!

October 1, 2015 Facebook
I'm doing fine; I had enough sedation during the biopsy that I don't remember it. Now Hank is hurting real bad, though, from being snipped, and there's nothing I, or any medication, can do to help him feel better. He sure is being a real wimp about it and letting me know how much he hurts. We started Prednisone steroid therapy yesterday, so hopefully that will help him man-up and get his s**t together. Today we go to the OR to get my tube adjusted and my esophagus dilated, so I can finally swallow solids, and make Hank happy with real food again. Like I said before, we aren't out of the woods yet, but we're keeping it together. We go to well together to lose it all!

Chapter 15

Pancreas Rejection

October 1, 2015 Facebook
Some conflicts in a relationship are rougher than others, because Hank is handing me a rejection notice. We're not breaking up, and through treatment our relationship can be fixed and strong once again. But for now, we're doing 2 different couple's therapies: Prednisone steroid therapy, and high-dose IV anti-rejection therapy. We still love each other and I KNOW we belong together for life, so even though it will take probably a couple or so weeks, we WILL get through this. Let's do this, Hank the panc!!

October 3, 2015 Text
Dad to Krystin: What's going on with you? Hope you feeling better.
Gary to Pat: You hear anything about Krystin? Elliott and I stopped to see her yesterday but didn't stay because she was in rough shape from vomiting and nausea. Nurse said she ate too much, but otherwise all indicators were fine.
Pat: I've sent a text both yesterday morn and this morn but no reply.
Gary: Me, too. That's why I asked you. Let me know if you learn anything.
Pat: Ok. And WTF? They're giving her FOOD? She told me Wednesday they said NO food for a while to give Panc a rest.
Gary: Idk.
Pat: I'll stop by today or tomorrow.
(later) Krystin to dad: Doing ok. Can only lay on back, otherwise pain and nausea. Dunno when discharge. Lipase is elevated again, so need more steroid treatment.

October 4, 2015 Text
Krystin to dad: Me neither, but it's how they measure for rejection. [She must have been responding to a question not in the text exchanges.] I think the steroid is what is making me feel so sick and crummy. And dunno about pain treatment. Not much helping right now. :/
Dad: Argh.
Krystin: You're tellin me. . . Finally taking a shower today, so that should help me feel better. Haven't had one all week. I stink.

Dad: Wonder if you getting out today.
Krystin: Highly unlikely. Also . . . let's cancel bed order. You right, now not good time for it, financially. Unfortunately. I'll just have to keep dealing with the back pain til I can afford new bed!
(later) Dad: So where are you healthwise and release wise?
Krystin: Feeling significantly better this afternoon/evening. Restless, even. MAYBE discharge tomorrow; it all depends in how my labs look, of course. Probably more likely Tuesday.
Dad: Well, at least glad you feel better. Hope you can nudge them to let you go if you feel okay!
Krystin: Well yeah, but If labs still too elevated, it doesn't matter how I feel! But I agree with you. You guys home now?
Dad: I understand. Yes. Just going to eat. I see you tomorrow.

Sunday, October 4, 2015 Diary
2:30 p.m.

Haven't written in a couple days because I've felt so shitty since my tube replacement and esophageal dilation. I think something was hit in there and I've been bleeding into my stomach a bit. I've been nauseous and throwing up (continuously nauseous, occasional throwing up) since the procedure. [This, massively, is what led to her death in 2017—bleeding from the aorta into the esophagus and into the stomach.] Today is the first day I've been able to actually sit up and feel normal. I've been trying to rest and sleep for the last 2 days. I think I also over-did it with dinner on Thursday night, eating almost a whole taco and some sweet corn. Too much for my stomach at once after not eating much prior to that. And I haven't eaten anything since due to no appetite.

Dunno about discharge. Maybe Tuesday?

Did I mention it's a rejection issue that Hank the Panc is having? Yup, so it's steroids and anti-rejection meds up the wazoo for me. Doing what we gotta do. These days, it's highly unlikely that someone would completely lose a transplanted organ. So if the docs aren't worried, I'm not. I mean, any level of rejection is serious, but it can be handled.

Dr. Kirchner increased my Dilaudid from 2 to 3 mg every 4 hours, since the 2 was doing jack shit. Finally. Obviously, I would prefer like 10 mg, but that's never going to happen. Under hospital roof, at least. I just want that high, even if minor, one more time. Even if one more time in my life, is better than never again.

sigh

Mom is actually coming to visit this afternoon. First time since I've been in.

I should probably order some food, even if only yogurt or pudding. No taco for this girl. I do actually feel a little hunger, for the first time in days. . .

My dad and Elliott stopped by Friday morning, but they soon left cuz I was feeling so crummy. So, I got to see E for about 15 seconds. Oh well. I'll see him at Thanksgiving, maybe (?).

I just now, in the last hour, started feeling "normal" again, like not so tired. I went down for an ultrasound of my pancreas about 3 pm and tried to rest when I got back, but noticed that I wasn't that tired. So I watched Scandal (damn! Can't wait until next week!), went for a walk about the 7 unit (all 4), and am now writing and watching Empire. Feeling pretty good. Mom should be here soon. I actually feel . . . restless!

It's strange, when Dr. Kirchner told me about the rejection, I had no emotional response. Not sadness, or grief, or whatever. I was indifferent. I wonder what that means.

6:30 p.m.

My visit with Mom went well. She was here about an hour and a half! But then her parking meter was about to run out. We had a real good visit, even walked down to the gift shop to get a new pen, since I broke my other one. Oops. Even got some necklaces off the $5 rack. There's some good shit on there! Even if it's cheap, I love it, and I get compliments.

Ordered dinner:
- winter squash (ate 1/5) w/brown sugar FORGOT IT! –(
- sweet corn w/butter & pepper ate half
- chocolate pudding finished
- apple juice finished

Hopefully it goes better than my last burrito meal!

7:35 p.m.

It's 7:37 and I don't get Dilaudid next until 9:15 and I want it now; I'm trying not to count down the minutes.

I'm definitely restless. I dunno what to do with myself. I went on another walk through 7A-7D, and don't wanna sit still trying to watch a movie. Oh damn, I could have watched OUAT! Now I have to wait until tomorrow. That's OK, though, then no commercials. Just from the first episode of the season, I can tell it's gonna be a good one.

8:15 p.m.
One more hour. Try for a nap, maybe?

8:46 p.m.
Half an hour. I'm anxious with anticipation, even though I don't know why. It's not like I get anything from it anymore. No nap happened. So maybe a walk instead.

9:15-finally! I even get a very slight, very brief "good" feeling. Nothing like I used to, but I'll take what I can get.

I wonder if I'll be able to convince the docs to send me home with some, until I can see Dawn again—which is Friday, actually! And if I ever have any withdrawal symptoms, I have a patch left, as well as a Suboxone strip and my Clonidine Rx.

I'm not tired at all tonight. I've been on many walks around the floor. I hope I'll be able to sleep tonight! I'm even getting hungry, since I had very little dinner.

I'm already planning breakfast: (may be too much food for one meal?)
- egg & veggie scramble   - apple juice
- Rice Krispies   - pineapple
(but with milk & Splenda, or mix w/yogurt?)

October 5, 2015 Text
Krystin to dad: When do you think you will stop by today? Just wondering.
Dad: I'm not on email right now.
Pat to Gary: Not sure if you stopped this morning but last night she looked good. Chipper, although she did ask for pain meds and they gave them to her. We walked to the Gift Shop and then she walked me to the street entrance an hour later when I left. Far from the 'near comatose' state that E described from Friday. Ok but I think she not sposed to eat.

Gary: I just eat my lunch and talk with her. Done that a couple of times, even though she couldn't eat. She fine with that.
(later) Dad to Krystin: Just getting food, will be up shortly.
(later) Dad: Know anything more than you did at lunch today?
Krystin: Nope. I would have told you if I did!
Dad: Thought so. Just checking!

Monday, October 5, 2015 Diary
4:40 a.m. – wide awake, watching The Theory of Everything

5:15 a.m. – more Dilaudid time! Where is my damn purse?
    The unit pharmacy is out and waiting to get it sent up from main pharmacy downstairs (24 hr.) Figures

5:35 p.m. – great, got another roomie, who isn't even a transplant patient.
    The 5th floor was full I guess? I hope they move her down at some point, since I'll still be here awhile. She has a daughter who has no inside voice and was shouting children's rhymes. Now mom is eating what sounds like rocks. OMG what is that? So. Much. LOUD. Chomping. And I'm already crabby cuz got no sleep last night. Although did nap quite a bit today, luckily. Even after she arrived. I can't take it anymore. I have to go for a walk. After I pee and order dinner. . . .
    - winter squash w/brown sugar hopefully they remember it this time!
    - cream of mushroom soup
    - applesauce
    - apple pie
    - apple juice

. . . And it all settled down well! Woot woot. I am TIRED now.
Time to change the bag of tube feed.

8:45 p.m.
    I have Benadryl for tonight if I want that extra help sleeping. I may not, cuz so tired, but my roomie snores, I swear even while she's still awake, so I may need the Benadryl AND my earplugs [sad face]
    Oh yeah, so, the team visited today.

May need another liver biopsy tomorrow, to see if the EBV has infiltrated my liver tissue. If so, we can't do the Thymo steroid therapy for my rejection, and could have to ride it out and see what happens. Um . . . no thank you? Dr. Kandaswamy doesn't think the EBV is in my liver tissue, cuz it wasn't from my biopsy back in August, but things can always change. We know that for sure! Fingers and toes and buttcrack crossed. <u>DOUBLE</u> crossed, if that's possible. Haha. Doesn't sound
comfortable. . . .

But if we can't do Thymo and I have to face total rejection, that means back on insulin. FUCK THAT. Just . . . no. I can't do that. Not after having a taste of not having to do it all. Not like I really did before. . . . And again, I felt a little twinge of panic, but no big reaction when Dr. K told me the news. Am I become my dad and turning into an emotional robot?

I did find out that if we do the Thymo steroid treatments, that can treat the rejection, but it also leaves my system wide open for the EBV to run amok, and could become strong, resulting in a 30% chance of me developing lymphoma of the liver. Which is also pretty scary and serious. I'll have to Google or Wikipedia about that, like I do with everything. I said I want to treat the rejection, though, and so I suppose am willing to risk the elevated EBV.

I DO see that Dr. in hematology, this month, so I can work with him on the EBV thing, and hopefully nip that in the butt, cuz we can't let the EBV get out of control, either. . . .

Now I wait, NPO, to find out if I'll be having the biopsy tomorrow =)

I got a couple pages of Sudoku puzzles from one of the visitor lounges, I think 7B, so at least I have that to keep me occupied as needed. Tried starting a puzzle, but there were like 3 different puzzles in the box! Lamesies. I did some work instead.

6:45 a.m.

Just got switched rooms, for some reason. Not complaining, just odd timing. Still have a roomie in new room but at least she's not snoring.

Back to sleep.

ZZzzzz

October 5, 2015 Facebook
Still battling and treating this rejection, which means still in the hospital, and will be for a few more days. More steroids tomorrow if another biopsy of the liver shows that the EBV isn't in my liver tissue. Good times for all! Getting bored, and this Glamour magazine is from May. Lamesies. But I think Hank and I are slowly reconciling and will be ok!

October 6, 2015 Text
Gary to Pat: I can't get over to see Krystin today. If you can, that would be nice. But if not, so it goes. I like to go to talk to docs myself.
Krystin to dad: Of course, no prob! I'm hoping no biopsy. My liver enzymes are down, so that's a good sign! Maybe even discharge later. If so, I will see if mom can get me. Gee, I hope the people in my apt building don't think I died, like Jim did! O.o
Gary to Pat: She might get discharged today. I'll get her.
Pat: Ok. TY
Krystin to dad: No biopsy! But starting the Thymo steroid IV treatment today, and if that goes well and I have no initial reaction, discharge tomorrow with the rest of the Thymo I do at home through picc line. They don't like to discharge people on day of first Thymo dose cuz of the risk of any side effects, like fever or whatever. So, that's what I know. We chat more later if you want.
Dad: Great! That mean rejection threat will go away?
Krystin: Theoretically and ideally yes. Now we just risk, in return, getting lymphoma if the EBV gets out of control, since this will pretty much wipe out my immune system for a bit. Well and I do see that hematology doc in a couple weeks, who specializes in elevated EBV, so he can tackle it if it gets to that point. It will all be ok, I like to believe.

Tuesday, October 6, 2015 Diary
10:45 a.m.
    No biopsy today! My liver enzymes are down. So Dr. Kandaswamy is comfortable with not doing a biopsy. Yesssss. Which means we'll start the Thymo treatment today, as well as take Prednisone on the side. Yay for becoming marshmallow face again! But I remember how much energy the Prednisone gave me before, and I liked that energy, so I'll put up with the puffy face in exchange. I will still be here one more night, because they don't like discharging

patients on their first day of Thymo, in case of any reactions like fever or whatever, since the Thymo pretty much kills off my white blood cells!

October 7, 2015 Text
Krystin to dad: Discharge today, about 4 or 5. I'm getting another Thymo infusion, that my nurse will start when it comes up from pharmacy, and that's a 6 hour infusion. Discharge after that. I am going to pick up my meds beforehand, so I will already have them.
Krystin: Will do. We're actually going to run it over 4 hours and see how I feel, and turn it down if need be. So I'm pretty sure it will be before 5 when I'm ready. I'll keep you posted, as usual.
Krystin: Woohoo, up to 115 pounds today! Slowly gaining the weight back. The Prednisone will help with that, too. And give me energy! That will feel good, especially for the walk on Saturday. I'm still asking around for a wagon, for when I need a break and Anjeanette will pull me.
Dad: Great!
Krystin: You at work today? If so, what time you plan to leave? I be ready probably at 4:30. Infusion started right at noon, so will be done at 4, so would be ready soon after that. Just gotta get dressed. Got all my meds, and will have gone through discharge papers with my nurse.
Dad: At home. If you can be ready shortly after 4, Kathy can bring you home.
Krystin: Ok.

Wednesday, October 7, 2015 Diary
1:15 p.m.

Discharging today, after my Thymo infusion! I am so ready to go home, and really want a cigarette. Dad is home today, but Kathy is at work, so she'll pick me up a little after 4, on her way home. How convenient that works out! I already got my meds from the pharmacy—I got a 2-day Rx for liquid Dilaudid, to get me through until my appt. at the pain management clinic on Friday. Woohoo! It's only 30 ml in the bottle, but I also have Benadryl at home, so maybe, hopefully, it will give me a little extra bump. Unfortunately, my tolerance has become so high (no pun intended), I hardly have any happy side effects anymore. A little more relaxed maybe, but not high. Honestly . . . bummer.

Dr. Ibrahim stopped by [my] room yesterday. He was actually here to see Diane, my roomie, but since I was here, too, he sat and chatted for a bit. When he first came in and realized it [was] me, he walked over, took my hand in both his hands, and gave me a kiss on my forehead! That was very lovely and made my day =)

My eyes are so heavy and droopy from my pre-Thymo 50 ml of Benadryl . . . Nappy time. Zzzz

October 10, 2015 Facebook
Krystin Engstrand is with Anjeanette Roy.
Today was one of the best days I've had in a long, long time. The NKF Kidney Walk 2015 was a big success. I had so much fun, got lots of free swag, talked to other transplant patients (and I made sure to high-five other fellow transplantees), felt good, was in great company, the weather was chilly but beautiful, AND I got in some good exercise! So all in all, a wonderful day, and I am so proud of myself for accomplishing it!

October 11, 2015 Text
Krystin to dad: My temp has been elevated all day. Right now at 101. Hmm. What breaks a fever? Tylenol? Benadryl?
Dad: Just a second. Use Google!
Krystin: I thought maybe personal knowledge and experience would have a good idea.
Dad: Tylenol. But call your coordinator or nurse to make sure no reason not to take. Or Advil.
Krystin: Ok. I know those are safe to take.
Dad: Kathy says should also drink a lot.
Krystin: I am. Got big bottle of water.
Dad: And coordinator or nurse should know.
Krystin: I talked to my nurse from when I was at SIPC today. She's afraid I may need to go in. I'm due at SIPC again in the morning, and she said she has a feeling that even if I wait until tomorrow, they'll still send me to the ER. I will drink lots of water and test my temp again in half an hour. BP also 84/47 and 121 heart rate. Ugh.
Dad: Can you drive in if you have to go?
Krystin: BP little low, pulse too high. Sigh. Yes, I will. Ok to drive.
Dad: Ok. When you know?
Krystin: I'll test again about 830

Krystin: 101.2 Damn. I really don't wanna go in, just to sit there and wait for hours.
Dad: Don't know what to tell you.
Krystin: I think I'm gonna wait. If it gets REALLY bad then I'll consider going in. But for now I keep drinking fluids and testing every 30 min.
Dad: Going up to bed, but let me know if any big news.
Krystin: Ok. Good night.

October 13, 2015 Email
Dad to Krystin:
    How you doing?

Krystin to dad:
    I'm doing well. Only got about 3 hours of sleep last night, because I just couldn't fall asleep for some reason, so I'm a little tired today, but not too bad, surprisingly. I have enough work to do to keep me consistently busy, so of course that helps.
    Did I tell you that tomorrow morning I'm getting an infusion of Rituxan? That wonderful stuff that made me have an anaphylactic reaction last year? Yup, Dr. Kandaswamy wants to try it again, so we can do something about my EBV level. Last year I didn't get any kind of pre-treatment, because we thought I was still allergic to Benadryl. This time, I'll be getting Tylenol AND Benadryl beforehand, as well as a small dose of a steroid, and then one other thing, but I don't remember what it is. Then they'll give me a very small test sample of Rituxan, and wait a little bit to see if and how that affects me. If I'm fine and have no reaction, then they'll slowly start giving me more, at an increased rate, until I reach whatever the normal rate is that they give it to people at, as long as I don't have any effects as it's increased. It will be a slow process, and closely monitored, but they know how I reacted last year, and will be ready at the quick, just in case. I have no idea how long this will end up taking if I do get the whole infusion. I'm guessing I'm going to be out from work the majority of the day, because even once the infusion is done, which alone will be a few hours I'm sure, I have a feeling they'll want me to hang out for a little bit after, to make sure there are no lingering side effects. Ugh.
    Ly.

Dad to Krystin:
   Well, if it works to combat the EBV and lets them forestall any pancreas rejection, then I would say it will be worth it.
   I'll keep my fingers crossed for you.

October 14, 2015 Text
Krystin to dad: Got to the infusion clinic at 9 this morning, and just got home, finally, about 45 min ago. Long day! (the time of this text was 7:56 p.m.) And no side effects this time, too.
Dad: And what's the result? You feel ok? This addressed what issue?
Krystin: I dunno what the results are. I guess my next labs will tell if the infusion worked. Feeling fine, though.
Dad: What does it mean to say it worked? Stop EBV? Stop rejection? That's what I don't remember.
Krystin: To kill off the EBV.
Dad: Ah. Let's hope it works
Krystin: Absolutely!
Dad: They give you odds? And rejection not an issue now, right?
Krystin: Dunno the odds. I think very good odds. And the rejection is still something we're working on treating. That's why I have to get labs drawn 3 days a week. So they can closely monitor how my new medication regime is working. Next lab draw will be on Friday. Dunno today's lab results.

October 23, 2015 Email
Today
Krystin to dad:
   I think I'm going to go over to the ER. I got NO sleep last night, first because the withdrawal symptoms that the new patch was causing were so intense, then my back pain got SO bad, and is still very bad today; so much that it's making me nauseous and throw up. So I've been feeling miserable for the past 12 or so hours. I'm not sure what the ER can do for me, but maybe give me something to at least make the withdrawal symptoms stop. I still find it stupid that a pain med patch would have a side effect of withdrawal symptoms, but I was warned that it would. I'll have my phone and will keep you posted.

Dad to Krystin:
   Ok. Good luck.

October 23, 2015 Text
Krystin to dad: I'm home. I got a 2 day Rx for Dilaudid, to give the patch time to reach its max, and so I'm not in so much pain in the meantime. Feeling much better now, my back pain is finally under control and it's not killing me anymore.
Dad: Great! Hope you don't have to pay ER charge.
Krystin: Of course I do. That will bring my UMPhysicians bill to somewhere in the 800 range. But I was so desperate this morning, I felt miserable.
Dad: You should go to Primary Care Clinic. I've always been able to get in the same day.
Krystin: Primary care can't give me fluids and pain medication right there. They would probably just tell me to go to the ER!
Dad: But if they refer you, seems to me you can argue you didn't choose to go there. In fact, I went to PCC and they referred me to ER and I didn't have to pay ER charge.
Krystin: Good point. I'll remember that for next time. Because we all know there WILL be a next time, unfortunately. . . .
Dad: Yes, but no sense paying the charge!
Krystin: Absolutely.

October 25, 2015 Text
Krystin to dad: I have $2 in my bank account, and I need a few groceries to get me through payday on Weds. Could I borrow $20? [There is no record of my response but I'm sure I gave her the money.]

October 28, 2015 Facebook
Krystin Engstrand is feeling bummed at University of Minnesota Medical Center.
Went in for routine labs yesterday, and ended up being admitted to my favorite hospital unit. Had a CT scan after complaining about my pain, that showed I have air pockets and inflammation in my colon, due to a hole in either my stomach or large intestine. Am on lots of antibiotics and can't eat anything, in the hopes that my body will heal the hole closed. If not, then surgery to remove a chunk of my intestine. Oh, and the reason I was originally admitted? Hank is having a tantrum again and acting up. So I'll be here for a while. Aaaaaand Friday is my birthday. Wonderful. Happy effing 31 to me.

October 29, 2015 Text
Dad to Krystin: So what's up?
Krystin: For sure no discharge by tomorrow. They want to keep monitoring me on IV antibiotics. The only good news is that it's not getting worse.
Dad: Oh. Good, I suppose. I stop by tomorrow. Maybe mom bring you party :-)
(later) Krystin: Which one of you has my extra apt key? If I'm going to be here for a while still, I could use some things.
Dad: We do. But can do nothing today. If you want mom to get stuff, I can leave key for her somewhere.
Krystin: Mom can tomorrow over noon hour. So tomorrow morning, put key in mailbox, k?
(later) Dad: Still up for a short time. How you doing? Any news?
Krystin: Doing fine, just "hanging out" I guess. No new news today. Still just watching things on a daily basis. Still no idea of a timeline.
Dad: Argh. Glad you doing fine but frustrating is no time line or idea what comes next.
Krystin: Yeah, that's exactly how I feel, too.

October 30, 2015 Facebook
This birthday has not started out well. I found out I'll be here through the weekend, and I still am not allowed to eat, so I don't even get the milkshake my mom was going to bring me tonight. But the nurses are trying to make this shifty day less so. They ALL came in together and sang happy birthday, and one of my fav nurses, who isn't even working today, called me on my room phone, from home, to wish me happy birthday. I'm still sad, frustrated, hungry, and crabby from being hungry, but I am truly thankful for how much they care around here. Now let me have a damn chicken sandwich.

October 31, 2015 Text
Krystin to dad: Saw the docs, but nothing to report yet. Had another CT scan this morning, so they are going to look at the scans and decide where to go from there and what kind of antibiotic regimen to have me on. No word on discharge, but only because they have to figure out the plan first. So, that's all I know for now. Happy Halloween! Whenever. As far as I know, no more tests or anything today.
Krystin: When were you thinking of coming?
Dad: I dunno. Early afternoon?

Krystin: Ok. Found out I still can't eat, and won't be able to until at least Monday, when I'll have another scan and they'll see how things are then. So, no discharge this weekend, no food this weekend, and more work to miss next week. I fucking want to discharge myself and be done with this. I'm sick and tired of this.
Dad: I can understand. But I suspect discharging yourself might not work out too well. Unfortunately.
Krystin: Just long enough to go eat a pizza. Then I'll come back. So really, instead of discharge I'll just break loose, then go back. I don't care if it makes things worse. I'm too damn hungry to care.
(later) Krystin: Nope, no food. Dr. Kirchner is being stubborn and said that colorectal people don't know about immunosuppressed patients and it's better to wait and see how things are tomorrow. Great. Yeah, no soup for me today.

November 1, 2015 Text
Krystin: I was put on full liquid diet! I can finally have my soup.
Dad (Kathy): Your dad is driving. He says great! Any idea when you get out?
Krystin: No, I haven't actually seen a doc yet today. My nurse just came in and told me my diet was changed. My guess is not today. They'll probably want to see how I do (and by me I mean my colon) after a day on the liquid diet. Like if my pain gets worse or if the inflammation gets worse, or something like that.
Dad: So you eating liquids? Any pain? I stop by tomorrow.
Krystin: Yes, no more than usual, and ok. I'm thinking afternoon nap time now.
Dad: Ok. Rest well.
(later) Krystin: Hmm, still no docs today. Maybe Changing me to liquids was all that needed to be done so they don't feel the need to see me. Either way, nothing to report on.
Dad: Ok. Keep me posted.
(later) Dad: How things going? I stop in on way in tomorrow. Have a.m. and noon meetings
Krystin: Things going same as they were yesterday. Dr. Kirchner made it sound like no discharge tomorrow, either, cuz she said start tube feeding tomorrow and see how I handle that. Ugh. I had no idea how big a deal this colon and air thing is!
Dad: Ugh is right. Wish you could get another opinion.

Krystin: Yeah, even if they say the same thing. I hate how much work I'm missing. Everyone there tells me not to worry about it, but I'm starting to anyway.

Dad: Let's hope something positive happens. You might tell the doc you're worried about work.

Krystin: For sure I will tomorrow when I see them. Work has been supportive for so long about me being gone for medical reasons, but there's a line, and it can only go on so far, you know? I'm just really lucky management loves me!

November 2, 2015 Text

Krystin to dad: Dr. Kirchner said one or two more days here.

Krystin: I'm on regular diet! And if all goes smooth I can discharge tomorrow. So, fingers and toes crossed that no problems arise from eating regular food!

Dad: Great!

(later) Dad: So, how's it going?

Krystin: Same ol same ol. Nothing really to report. Had chicken Florentine for dinner. Now just hanging out and watching a show on my tablet.

Dad: But pain, problems seem to be gone?

Krystin: I guess I don't know if pain is gone. It's being managed by medication. I'm sure without it I would have pain. My back does still hurt a little though, even with meds. But it's manageable.

Dad: So maybe we take you home tomorrow!

Krystin: Yup, I hope so. But you won't need to bring me home. My car is still here from when I had my appt last week. I'm gonna ask if I can get a parking voucher, so I don't have to pay for having my car in the lot for a week.

Dad: Oh. Ok.

Krystin: Were you looking forward to bringing me home or something?

Dad: No, no. Just wanted to be sure you could get home.

Krystin: Ok. Yup, I can. And now you don't have to wait for me to discharge and go to the pharmacy and get all impatient and everything.

Dad: :-)

November 3, 2015 Text

Krystin to dad: I KNEW it. I jinxed myself. Because of my elevated lipase level, no home today. I start tube feedings today, too.

Dad: Is that good or bad?
Krystin: Neither. It's more just a statement. To help get my weight back up and get back into that routine, since I'll be doing them at home.
Dad: Likely discharge tomorrow? You mentioned your job?
Krystin: Who knows, and yes I did. She said exactly what I predicted - don't wanna send me home too early, otherwise could just end up back here again and miss even more work. Better to miss one more day than another week in the future. (Read that with a female Russian accent, cuz Dr. Kirchner is Russian)
Dad: Sigh. Ok.

November 4, 2015 Facebook
All my morning meds, that I put through my G-J tube. And this is just morning. I also have afternoon and evening meds to take. Ahh, the joys of being a transplant patient facing a small rejection episode and being treated for inflamed intestinal issues. Good times.

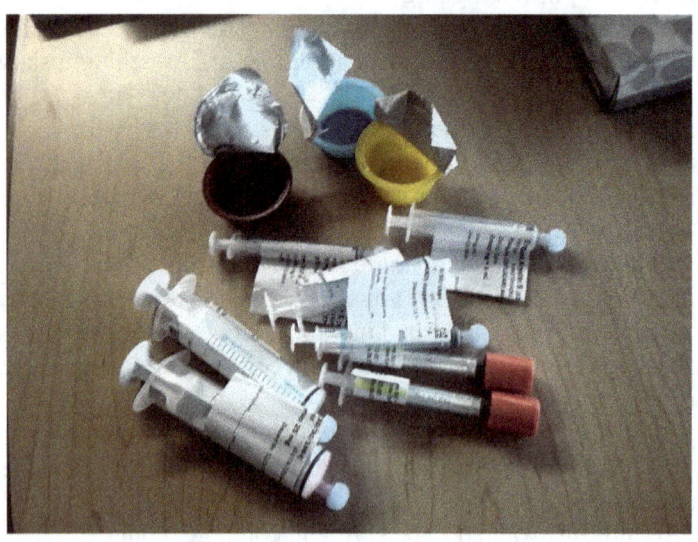

November 4, 2015 Text
Dad to Krystin: I not on campus today. You getting out?
Krystin: Pretty sure.
(later) Krystin: For sure getting out today! But later this afternoon, cuz my potassium drip still has 3 hours left.

(later) Krystin: Great, they don't have or give parking vouchers, so I'll have to pay for parking for 8 days. There goes like $40 that I don't have.
Dad: No! I'll give you some money if you want to stop by on way home.
Krystin: Ok, that would be helpful. The social worker was just here to discuss options for paying for parking, but there's not really anything they can do. On the upside, she said they're working on discharge stuff and hope to let me go in about an hour.
Dad: Stop by whenever. We're leaving about 5:30.
Krystin: Ok. If I don't get out before you leave, maybe put it in an envelope in the mailbox?

November 5, 2015 Text
Krystin to dad: Thanks for the $$. I really appreciate it. After paying all my monthly expenses, I have very little left for other things. Especially not a $51 parking fee! I got up an hour early today, cuz I forgot to change the time on my alarm clock. Oh well, better being up an hour early than an hour late!
Dad: Chuckle. You're welcome. You can go in early to work!
Krystin: I plan on it! Depending on workload, may stay late, too.
(later) Dad: So how you do after a long day at work?
Krystin: Doing good! I stayed an extra hour to make up some time. I still have a lot to catch up, so it was a busy day today, but it didn't wear me down, luckily!
Dad: Great!

November 5, 2015 Email
How you doing?
Dad to Krystin:
  Now that you're back at a work day?

Krystin to dad:
  I'm doing well. It feels good to be back at work! (How often do you hear people say that about their job??)

Dad to Krystin:
  Glad to hear. Hope you don't get too fatigued.
  Actually, many people who work at colleges and universities say that!

November 7, 2015 Text
Dad to Krystin: Hello?
Krystin: Doing fine, just tired today.
Dad: I can imagine. Rest and make sure you get lots of liquids!
Krystin: Easier said than done, considering I can't swallow anything again
Dad: Great. You have dilation planned?
Krystin: Teri is going to check the schedule and get back to me.

November 9, 2015 Email
Dad to Krystin:
    How you doing? You at work? Get esophagus taken care of?
Krystin to dad:
    I'm at SIPC getting fluids and my picc line dressing changed and labs drawn, but going to work after that. I haven't heard anything back, yet, from Teri. I'll call her if I don't hear from her midday or so.

Dad to Krystin:
    Good and good.

Dad to Krystin:
    You ok and get to work?
Krystin to dad:
    I was at SIPC this morning getting my labs drawn and my picc line dressing changed, and had them throw in a liter of fluids while I was there. I have my dilation procedure bright and early Wednesday morning, at 7:45, which means I have to be there at 5:45. But really if I don't arrive until 6:15 or so, it's not a big deal. I may drive myself in, so I don't have to pay for a taxi.

November 10, 2015 Text
Krystin to dad: I spent the whole day in the pre-op assessment clinic, for my procedure tomorrow. Not only did I have to see 3 diff docs, then I had to get a chest xray cuz my deep breaths are wheezy. Then I waited 45 min for valet to bring my car. Ugh. I've never been so exhausted from so much waiting.
Krystin: No, no work after. Even if I felt fine, I think once I got there I would quickly feel tired. Anesthesia hangover of sorts.

November 11, 2015 Facebook
Krystin Engstrand checked in to University of Minnesota Medical Center.
Esophageal dilation # . . . well, I've lost count.

November 12, 2015 Text
Krystin to dad: I'm being admitted today. About 1:00. All that pain I had just this last time I was admitted, is back, and it's even more severe. So it's the colon issue again. I dunno if the antibiotics I've been taking aren't working, or what, but I'm in a lot of pain, which started last night and kept me up practically all night. It's so bad it even made me throw up a couple times in the night, and the pain med they sent me home with yesterday didn't work at all. Wonderful.
Dad: Sigh. I'm sorry.
Krystin: Me too. This sucks. I'm starting to think I'll never feel "good", and my life is destined to be like this. I'll never catch a break!
(later) Krystin: All admitted and settled in. I get the window side again at least.
Dad: So how long you there for?
Krystin: No idea.
Dad: In pain?
Krystin: Yes. Very much so. At least the doc put in orders for some meds. Now waiting for pharmacy to fill them and send them up.
Dad: Do well.
Krystin: I go for a CT scan at 6, and all the contrast I have to drink is giving me a tummy ache on top of the other pain. Good times.
Dad: Ugh
(later) Dad: How you doing?

November 13, 2015 Text
Krystin to Dad: Got a suppository put in 30 or so minutes ago, and I'm still waiting. I don't feel the urge to go at all yet! Either today or tomorrow I'm having an endoscopy done. The good times just keep rolling in, don't they?? THAT'S how I'm doin.
(later) Dad: Know anything new?
Krystin: Nope.

November 15, 2015 Text
Krystin to dad: I'm going to be in isolation for the rest of the time I'm here.

Dad: How long you be there?
Krystin: Again, no idea. The docs haven't said anything about course of action or discharge. Hopefully early in the week!

November 16, 2015 Text [missing message]
Krystin to dad: Good, and not really the G.I. Doc stopped by; he's the one who has been monitoring me this week. He said I need to get up and walk more, so that I'm not so sleepy all day long. He's also trying to adjust my pain med regimen, but I'm arguing on that one. What I'm doing now is working perfectly fine! So why change it, huh?!?
Dad: So when you get out?
Krystin: Still no idea.
Dad: Gad. I assume you're pushing them.
Krystin: Of course. But I also want then to figure out this pain, so I'm not here AGAIN next week. . . .
Dad: True. I'll see you tomorrow morning. If you're still there. :-)
Krystin: I'll still be here, so ok, see you then!

November 16, 2015 Email
Disability
Dad to Krystin:
   I talked to [ ] in Human Resources about you going on disability. (They do not contact your department.)
   She said you should give her a call and she can have you talk with someone about what your options might be.
   You didn't by chance have the foresight to sign up for disability insurance when you came to work for the U, did you? You could have then, without medical check; you can't now, unfortunately.
   So call her and at least find out what your options might be.

Krystin to dad:
   Ok, I'll give her a call tomorrow. The only issue, and I'll tell her this, is that I can't take off any time UNPAID. I just can't afford that.

Dad to Krystin:
   Disability is with pay. Idk how much. Did you sign up for the insurance? It would show up as a deduction on your paycheck. If not, you're in tough shape, I fear. But talk to whomever she refers you to. You can just be laid off, you know.

November 17, 2015 Text
Krystin to dad: Finally got home about 30 min ago.
Dad: Good. How you doing?
Krystin: Alright. I still have the same pain as when I was admitted, but it's cuz no one is sure what is causing the pain. I was put on an extra acid blocker, in the hopes that that will decrease the pain, if it's reflux related. I still plan to go to work tomorrow.
Dad: Well, I hope the blocker and pain meds together eventually help.

November 18, 2015 Text
Dad to Krystin: How you doing?
Krystin: Not too bad. When my alarm went off this morning, I was ready to get up. I slept like a baby last night!
Dad: Great! Let's hope that goes on and on and on and on!
Krystin: Yeah, well, considering I can't eat anything and have to rely on tube feeds . . . but I'm gonna do my very best!
Dad: Food will return. Just get through this.

November 20, 2015 Text
Krystin to dad: What are you guys doing tonight?
Dad: Nothing. But probably don't want to do anything. Kathy just home late Wednesday from Chicago, we went out for dinner last night. Why you ask?
Krystin: I'm in a lot of pain, have nothing for it, and don't wanna be in pain alone tonight. Could I stay over?
Dad: Sure. Why nothing for it? You talk to docs???
Krystin: I've left a msg with both my coordinator and the coordinator's office, haven't heard anything. Pain doc won't prescribe anything unless she sees me.
Dad: Call back again!
(later) Krystin: A doc agreed to fill a prescription for me. I'm at the pharmacy now, and the order was never even brought over!
Dad: Do you still get it?
Krystin: No. It has to be handed to a pharmacist, it can't be called in, cuz it's a narcotic. I'm on hold with a coordinator now.
Krystin: Sounds like it. It's being filled now! I guess the doc could call it in. I just heard them on the phone filling it. Maybe there is a god after
all. . . .
Dad: Chuckle. Good.

Krystin: Btw, I won't be able to eat anything over the holiday. I'm NPO for 2 weeks.
Dad: Sigh
Krystin: I know.
Gary to Pat: Krystin is here. Waiting on pain meds prescription from u pharmacy. They got it all screwed up. If they get it ready, could you drive her over to get it?
Pat: Yes, I can
Pat: I just hate this pain med game. I still suspect some of it is addiction based. What ever happened to the rehab issue?
Gary: No, it isn't. I know, I've talked with docs. Something easier to talk about than text. It's a very complicated matter. They have rx ready, but she says you not need drive her, but I think otherwise.
Gary: Never mind. She's going, will get and go home.
Pat: What is her plan for the car then?
Gary: Sigh.
Pat: I know. She called me to say don't come. She did NOT sound like a woman in pain so severe that she needs Rx meds beyond her fentanyl patch (this a.m. she claimed pain so severe she threw up and couldn't sleep all nite). But if the docs keep giving it to her, there's not a thing we can do.
Gary: I told her to call you. I don't understand this pain issue.
Pat: Well, call or email any time (if texting too cumbersome) re: doc views on the complex pain issue.
Gary: Will do.
Pat: Pain issue is she's addicted. Phantom pain is real, and I've suspected that's what's been happening. Was hopeful about pain Rx rehab but then that fell apart somehow.
Gary: I'm going to talk to docs about Munchausen.
Pat: I'll have to Google it. . . .
Pat: Yup, worth discussing. She does have some actual physical issues, of course, but this all seems so ridiculously suspicious.
Gary: Yes. But Kathy wondered about Munchausen and it turned on a light for me. We'll see what I learn.
Pat: A couple years ago I made a statement about K having a mental illness and I think you were taken by surprise. Plain and simple: she's just not right in the head. Goes back to toddlerhood if I recall. . . .
Gary: Yeah, what I'm thinking.
Pat: And have docs EVER asked us about her medical history? Constant constipation in infancy to the point of me (as advised by Dr

[ ]) putting molasses in her formula bottle. Her projectile vomiting. Her telescoping intestine incidences.

Gary: Her constant tummy aches.

Pat: Me telling her at the Freeman condo not to put her hand on the stove burner, to which her response was to reach up and put her hand on the [thankfully not turned on] stove burner and saying to me, with pure defiance in her eyes, "see? I no get burned." Still chills my heart to think about it. And waking up crying nearly EVERY morning thru toddlerhood. That's just not normal.

Pat: Damn, I've just perd'n'near convinced myself that I'M perhaps mentally ill! Just kidding. . . .

Gary: Tell you what. I'm going to email the transplant doc tomorrow about Munchausen. I will cc you and suggest that you also email him about what you just put in those messages. Maybe that will put them on a new track. Ok?

Pat: Ok. It's just odd to me that with all the thousands they've invested in her healthcare that they've never contacted us re: history. Sure, she's an adult and they can't tell us stuff, but they could always just ask . . .

Gary: Half joking: HIPPA. But we can foist ourselves into the process.

Pat: But you'd need also support as many of my remarks as you can otherwise they WILL suspect me crazy. I know HIPPA. That's what had in mind when I said they can't tell, but they could ask.

Gary: I will. I remember, although only because you remind me. I remember less and less as the years go by :-(

Pat: Right. I will tell Kandaswamy that I am not asking him for information, I am GIVING him information. He doesn't have to violate HIPPA. And at what point after hundreds of thousands if not a million dollars in care might they think the parents could perhaps have some insight to contribute to the cause?

Gary: Idk. I don't run the place.

Pat: I know. We're all just so frustrated.

Gary: Yes, and I think Krystin is, too, and if it really is something like Munchausen, it becomes more understandable.

Krystin to dad: Home, and feeling much better.

Dad: Good! Glad things finally worked out.

Krystin: Oh yes, me too, very much so! Finally no more agony. ☺

Dad: :-)

November 24, 2015 Text [missing messages]
Dad to Krystin: Are you in hospital, or was that just appt for something?
Krystin: It was just from 2:30 - 3:45am. I'm at work now.
Krystin: Absolutely!! I knew it wouldn't be, though.
Krystin: Same 'ol issue. My pain med ended, and since I didn't taper off, last night I was having super intense withdrawal effects. I couldn't take it anymore, couldn't sleep, felt miserable. I was supposed to have appt at pain clinic this morning but they called and my nurse is out sick. BUT she approved for another doc to write a scrip for a week's worth, then my rescheduled appt is next Monday, so I'll be good through then.
Krystin: Yup, of course. But I'm guessing you've never experienced withdrawal. It can be almost as bad as or worse than the actual pain. It's horrible, and you just can't wait until the next day when clinics are open. I think I got about 2.5 hours of sleep last night. But, I'm at work!

November 24, 2015 Email
Tomorrow
Krystin to dad:
    What time do you plan on going into work tomorrow, if at all?
    If you go in, could I get a ride from you? My lipase level has doubled, and they're insisting I go in for a pancreas biopsy. The next available opening isn't until next Tuesday, and apparently a lot can happen with a transplanted organ in a week. I strongly pressed how it really isn't a good time for me to miss almost a whole day of work AGAIN, but she wouldn't really let up. So I figure maybe I can get a couple hours of work in before I have to be over at the hospital at 11:30. I have no idea how long the procedure will take. I don't get anesthesia or anything for a biopsy, but heavy sedation, so I will need a drive home. The lady on the phone guessed probably around 4-4:30, since after the biopsy I have to lie there on my back for like 2 hours after.
    Ugh. I understand how important this is, but the timing really sucks. Anyway, let me know. Ly.

Dad to Krystin:
    I am not going in tomorrow. I will see what Kathy's plans are.

Krystin to dad:
  OK. And actually, I'm supposed to go over to mom's tomorrow night, so I'll see if she can pick me up after work.

Dad to Krystin:
  Kathy can take you in. You come to the house?

November 25, 2015 Text
Dad to Krystin: What's the scoop on your hospital visit?
Krystin: What visit? It was just a biopsy. Cuz of the holiday I probably won't hear preliminary results until next week.
(later) Pat to Gary: Krystin just left. She ate a LOT for having such a tiny body. Hopefully she keeps it in.
Gary: I thought she is NPO
Pat: NPO?!!! Why?
Gary: She was supposed to be NPO for 2 weeks after she was last in the hospital, which included thanksgiving.
Pat: She never told me!
Gary: Maybe she got them to change. She was going to ask. It was just an experiment to see if it affected the pain. They really don't know what they're doing.
Pat: Well damn! If they're trying something new in uncharted territory, why would they let her convince them otherwise?? I'll ask her.
Gary: Ok, ask. They weren't even sure this would work.
Pat: Well for sure it wouldn't work if she doesn't do it.

November 26, 2015 Text
Pat to Gary: I asked K about being NPO. Her reply: "Ummm, well, yeah, I am. The 2 meals I've had with you is the only food I've had since discharge last week. I've cheated a little bit. I've been hungry and desperate, and if it interferes with anything, well then it's on me, I know."
Needless to say, I'm not surprised, but still pretty unhappy with her for being dishonest with me as well as continually being dishonest and destructive with herself. How can the docs help her when she won't help herself?

November 30, 2015 Facebook
Thanksgiving was really hard for me this year. Not only have I not been "allowed" (doc's orders) to eat for the past 3 weeks because of

this never-ending intestinal inflammation and infection, but also because my esophagus has become so narrow I can't even swallow my own saliva. Sitting around watching your family enjoy the meal that you look forward to for 364 days a year is quite depressing. Nightly tube feedings just doesn't do it for me.

December 2, 2015 Email
more on marijuana: expanded use
Dad to Krystin:
http://bringmethenews.com/2015/12/02/minnesota-will-allow-medical-marijuana-for-treating-intractable-pain/?cid=etemail

Krystin to dad:
    I'm not forgetting this option, but remember, for transplant patients, it hasn't been tested on us, so they don't know what long-term (or even short term) effects could be, and how they'd interact with transplant meds. And I think we've both agreed, I don't want to be part of the guinea pig trials!

Dad to Krystin:
    Right--but I'm not so sure you should be wary about being a guinea pig. It isn't like the stuff isn't already known. I'm sure they'll be testing it with all kinds of other drugs to see if there's an interaction effect.
    But maybe your pain will be gone by then and you won't care :-)

December 4, 2015 Text [she must have had a stent put in]
Krystin to dad: The nurse is gonna call you and go over all the discharge info, like last time. Just nod and agree, like mom always does.
Dad: Ok. But will I need to be there when you leave?
Krystin: No. They will bring me down to the entrance, where Kathy could pick me up then drop me back off.
(later) Krystin: It should after a couple days. [I assume this was in response to a query about whether the pain would decrease.] If not, it comes out. At least in the meantime I can finally swallow.
Dad: So just don't eat too much all at once!
Krystin: DUH, I don't wanna barf!
(later) You got home ok and got the meds? And how you feeling?

Krystin: Yes and yes! The pain is much better now with my meds working. Now just tired, so will probably go to bed early and get a good night's sleep.

December 10, 2015 Text
Dad to Krystin: How you doing? Haven't heard from you. Hope no news is good news.
Krystin: Yeah, doing fine. Really struggling to get up and going in the mornings. And no, coffee won't help. My body is just exhausted and wants to sleep all day.
Dad: Sigh. How stent doing? Hope you get energy back. And btw, you descended from William the Conqueror.
Krystin: Stent is working well, and no discomfort from it anymore.
Dad: Well, that's at least good!

December 11, 2015 Email
Debt
Krystin to dad:
 I know you guys talked me out of it last year, but seeing how finances have only gotten worse, I'm seriously reconsidering filing for bankruptcy. Unless you'd agree to be a co-signer on a Wells Fargo personal line of credit (not a loan) with me, like you did that one time a number of years ago. They won't approve me for it as an individual, since my salary doesn't meet their minimum standards. Just like last time, the monthly balance due would be auto-deducted from my checking account, so you would never have any financial responsibility in it. I asked mom if she'd be my co-signer, but she said no, which I pretty much knew anyway. For the past number of months, my account has over-drafted just a couple days before payday, and for the past few months, I haven't been able to pay my rent on time, so now I'm getting charged late fees, too. A line of credit would let me pay of ALL my remaining balances on everything, and just have that one balance due each month, which would be about $360 (I did the math), which is much lower than what I pay now to all the different entities.
 I'll understand if you say no, but I wanted to ask before I start looking into filing for bankruptcy.

642

December 14, 2015 Email
finances
dad to Krystin:
    Joe Dixon is going to get the name of someone you can talk to about bankruptcy versus other options. Within a day or so.

December 15, 2015 Text
Dad to Krystin: So how you doing with the pancreatitis? I assume you home, not in hospital. Meds helping?
Krystin: Yes, I'm home. Nothing is being done about the pancreatitis. I wasn't even put on antibiotics or anything. I was told I have pancreatitis and that was that, no follow-up or anything. Which seems odd. I will email Dawn tomorrow and ask if anything is gonna be done about it.
Dad: Hmm. Maybe you on enough meds to take care of it. But contacting Dawn is good idea. How you feeling?
Krystin: None of my meds are meant to treat something like pancreatitis. I'm not on any antibiotics or anything.
Dad: Then maybe you should be. But how you feeling?
Krystin: I've felt better. Pancreatitis is painful, and I feel exhausted all the time. Ok. Off to bed. Love you.
Dad: Ok, good night! Ly too.

December 26, 2015 Text
Dad to Krystin: How you doing? How was Owatonna? [Where she had gone to celebrate Christmas with Pat's family.]
Krystin: Doing alright. The pancreatitis pain has been pretty bad the last couple days. I think it's (the pancreatitis) getting worse. I talked to Dr. Kirchner on the phone tonight, and she said to call SIPC first thing in the morning, and get some labs drawn. She said she will also be at the hospital tomorrow and could bring over an Rx for me. She said it's unlikely there's anyone around tonight who could write an Rx except in the ER, but I told her I'm not going there just for an Rx and having to pay the $100 copay. So she said if I can make it through the night, she'll come see me tomorrow at SIPC. Owatonna was good. I started feeling nauseous after lunch and had to go lie down for a little bit, but it got better, and nothing happened
Dad: Hope all goes well tomorrow. Glad you can go in on Sunday and get dealt with.

December 27, 2015 Text
Dad to Krystin: Any news from today for you?
Krystin: Not really. Was at SIPC this morning for lab draws. My lipase is down quite a bit, so the pancreatitis must be getting better.
Dad: Well, I guess that's good. See you at some point this week.
Krystin: I still have quite a bit of pain, so the upper colon infection/inflammation is still hanging around, I guess.
Dad: Ugh.

December 28, 2015 Text
Dad to Krystin: What did you say before disconnecting???
Krystin: It doesn't matter. I wasn't disconnected, I hung up. I won't be ready. So I guess I'm not going to work today.
Dad: I'm trying to help you out. I just paid your car insurance. It would be nice if you were a little accommodating with our plans.
Krystin: Well I dunno what to tell you. I can't be ready in that amount of time, whether you paid my insurance or not. I'm not going to work looking like a homeless bum.
Dad: How fast can you be ready?
Krystin: From now, half an hour. MAYBE 25 minutes. Someone would have to bring me to riverside pharmacy after work, and wait while I wait for a prescription to be filled. And I can't leave before 5.
Dad: Ok. We pick you up at 9:05.

December 28, 2015 Email
Law School clinic
Dad to Krystin:
    Did you contact the Law School clinic?
    I am getting pessimistic that I can help you.

Krystin to dad:
    Aside from asking if you'd be a co-signer on a line of credit with me, I never asked you to help me, you did that yourself. I told you guys I was ready to file for bankruptcy, and you and mom are the ones who told me to hold off. Yeah, you paid my car insurance, and of course I greatly appreciate that, but you didn't HAVE to. I was ready to drive around with no insurance until I was able to make a payment, and deal with the consequences if anything happened until then. There's nothing a clinic could do to help me except look at my finances and say "yup, you need to file bankruptcy." Like the document I made

up shows, my expenses each month are more than I make. I deposited the money that I got from you guys for Xmas, and that I got from mom. After my monthly Wells Fargo loan payment was auto-deducted for the month of December, and my Affinity Plus car loan was auto-deducted, I have $641 in my bank account. $639 of that has to go to pay my rent on the 1st. So, I have $2 to cover everything else until payday next Wednesday. There goes all my Xmas money; so much for buying something for myself. And what if I hadn't gotten any money from you guys? I would be even deeper in the hole. You see why bankruptcy is really my only option left? I'm waiting to hear back from Joe, but I don't expect he's going to have some eureka idea that we haven't thought of. And come January, my paychecks will be even less, so I'll be even more screwed when it comes to paying my bills.

I'm open to other suggestions, of course, but I just don't see there being any left.

December 29, 2015 Email
Finances
Pat to Krystin, Gary:
Sounds like you have some challenges ahead. Just remember: everything is doable if you follow the paved path and take it one day at a time.

Dad mentioned that you might be seeking legal counsel (which I agree is a good idea). I can't help you with your debt, but I would be willing to help you with the legal fees. Just be sure that either dad or I (probably dad since he knows more legal lingo) know what you're doing and who you're seeing/talking with before you incur any legal bills. There are some out there who would gladly take you for a ride.

I've copied him on this email so we're all on the same page.
Love
Mom

Krystin to mom, dad:
I don't see how any counsel would help me, though. Most of the time people see a financial counselor to help them re-budget their finances, make better/smarter spending choices, etc. etc. That's great for people who have a little wiggle room with their money, but I have NO wiggle room. My monthly financial obligations add up to more than I make in a month, so I'm always in the hole. For the past number of months, I've been late paying 2-3 of my bills every month;

otherwise I'd overdraft my bank account, which has also happened several times over the past 4 or so months. I have to look at each bill and figure out how many days late it'll be before I can pay it, and which ones have the lowest late fees. I can only ever pay the minimum balance due, which pretty much means I'm paying off the interest, and not much of the balance. I already have monthly payment plans with 2 different collection agencies, because I wasn't able to pay those particular institutions' payment obligations for a number of months in a row. I don't think I've paid my rent on time for probably 4 or 5 months now. It gets paid eventually, but often I am only able to pay for a chunk of it, then have to wait until the next paycheck before I can pay the rest. Which, in turn, means I'm taking away money for last month's rent and not saving it for next month's rent. And that's how it is for most of my bills. ALL the Xmas money I got from you guys goes straight to my rent payment that's due Jan. 1. I didn't get to buy ANYTHING for myself. I think I told one of you this already, but this financial stuff is stressing me out so much, that my hair is literally falling out. In the evenings, I look around my apartment for things I could sell on eBay, as a way to add a little extra income. I have yet to sell anything.

So yeah, that's all I got for now. I'm open to any and all suggestions, but I fail to see one.

Gary to Krystin, Pat, Kathy:
Krystin,
If you look at that material I sent, you will realize that financial counseling is REQUIRED by law before you can declare bankruptcy. You don't have any choice.

And for Pete's sake, contact the law clinic. At least you can get free legal help to start with. I don't know how far they take you in the process, maybe not far, but they can get you going, if this is what you intend to do. And there's no reason to dawdle--getting it all done, if it's to help, will relieve the stress on you.

Dad to Krystin:
Krystin, (just to you),
I will help you out A LITTLE with immediate bills. Find time to talk to me. But first of all, pay your rent. I could also perhaps take you on a grocery trip, if you need food. I'm not an endless fount of money,

but I can help a little if you get your butt in gear and do something about the bankruptcy proceedings.

As for a little extra money: what about Merry Go Round (or whatever it's called) in Highland? Is that still there? If so, surely you must have clothes you can get rid of. I know, that won't be immediate cash, but it could be in the near future, no?

Krystin to dad, Pat, Kathy:
I remember now why I didn't end up filing for bankruptcy last year, and I think it'll be the reason why I don't this year. If I discharge my Wells Fargo loan, the entire remaining balance would go to dad, since he's a co-signer on it. If I discharge my car loan from Affinity Plus, I lose my car. These 2 loans are at the top of my list of bills I wanted to discharge the most, but discharging both would have some not-so-good consequences.

So that puts me right back at the beginning, and stuck. If I don't file bankruptcy, and if I can't keep up with the monthly payments, really the only solution left is to win the lottery, and I'm not holding my breath for that one. That's why I suggested a personal line of credit; I could use it to pay off ALL my debts, and have only one bill payment due each month (aside from rent and my electricity bill), and I wouldn't anything, like my car. I do, however, see why you were hesitant about being a co-signer, dad, and fearing that I may at some point find myself unemployed, and the payments falling on you. Obviously that would not be ideal.

So once again I'm stuck and don't know what to do. And YES, dad, I'll call the law school clinic.

Dad to Krystin, cc Pat:
Krystin,
I don't want to talk to you again about this until after you talk to the clinic--not because I don't want to talk to you, but because I think you're (we're) kind of flailing around in the dark. Let's get some advice from people who know more about all this than we do.

If you want to tell them to call me, if they do such a thing, I would be glad to talk to them as well.

Pat to Gary:
She wants a magic wand. Ain't gonna happen.

December 29, 2015 Text
Dad to Krystin: Krystin, stop fretting about money for now. I will help you get through this and we will get it figured out. Just don't worry about it for now. Ok?
Krystin: Ok, I'll try my best. And thanks.

December 30, 2015 Email
Gary to Pat:

There is one element of all this that weighs on me but perhaps not on you. Obviously, this should not be forwarded.

I'm not sure Krystin has all that many years to live, frankly. She's certainly medically precarious. Given that I think that, I would like whatever time she has left to be at least modestly pleasant. Yes, she's screwed up her finances, but at the same time I'd like her not to be fretting and stressed the entire rest of her life.

I hope I'm wrong about this, of course.

Pat to Gary:

Yes, I've thought about that many times in the last year. That said, it can't change how we approach her finances. We've offered to help her with her legal fees and given her every tool to help her with this but so far she simply sits on the information. Given that, what would paying her debts do? We'd be poorer and she'd continue her out-of-control spending. Say she lives longer than we calculated: do we bail her out again? And again?

Until she learns the steps needed to be more responsible, I'm not sending any money her way. Legal fees yes, but to just cover expenses, no.

Remember when I said I'd spent a weekend in tears and was so upset at the thought she'd be bankrupt and homeless? You were surprised, then, when I'd done a complete 180. Here's the key: she's given us every indication since that time that she she's not interested in putting forth any effort to help herself. Until she puts forth that effort, I cannot. Where's her part?

December 30, 2015 Email
clinic
dad to Krystin:

    If you'd like me to go with you to the Law School clinic, I will be glad to do so. My calendar is pretty clear next week, if you can get a time set up.

January 1, 2016 Facebook
Happy New Year to all!!! Goodbye 2015, hello 2016. May this year be significantly better than the last!

January 2, 2016 Text
Krystin to dad: I'm going to the ER at some point this morning. My pain has gotten significantly worse. It's excruciating, and paralyzing, and sometimes it's so bad it makes me cry. And it's constant. I can't wait for Monday for my CT scan. I need it done now, and hopefully put on some antibiotics, if it's the inflammation and infection again. Owie.
Dad: Let me know. Maybe postpone brunch.
Krystin: Maybe. Right now I'm waiting for the on-call transplant coordinator to call me back. I'll see what she says before I do anything.
Krystin: Nurse said to absolutely go in and get checked out and evaluated. So I'll head over there soon. Hopefully not too long a wait.
Dad: This is another $100? You really need to talk to Medica about this, if so.
Krystin: Yes, unless I get admitted. And I know.
(later) Dad: I cover cab for you. Let's decide on brunch tomorrow.
Krystin: Ok. I won't know until I wake up and see how I feel.
Dad: That's fine. Sleep well, if you can. Ly
Krystin: I doubt I will, but I'll try. Lots of ZzzQuil to make me sleep, hopefully.

January 3, 2016 Text
Krystin to dad: Nope, can't do it today. Still so much pain. This is miserable.
Dad: I understand. I feel so bad for you. Surprised the docs could not do anything. Abbott Northwestern has a well-known pain clinic, wonder if is worth contacting. Could you get a referral?
Krystin: It's definitely something worth looking into.
Dad: Contact whoever you need to. I could take you there.

Krystin: Ok, it'll be at the top of my list of things to do tomorrow. If I can get out of bed. I dunno how going to work is gonna go. . . .

January 4, 2016 Text
Dad to Krystin: What's going on?
Krystin: I've been admitted, although I don't get anything for pain except Tylenol. No idea what the plan is. Apparently my stent has slid down into my stomach, so that needs to be removed.
Dad: So you in great pain? Mom said stent has slipped.
Krystin: Yes and yes.
(later) Dad: I stop by tomorrow.
Krystin: It'll be a fun night.
Dad: I bet. See you in the a.m. Kathy will drop me off on the way in.

January 4, 2016 Email
help with finances
Dad to Krystin:
Krystin,
  Would you like me to take over your finances, at least for awhile? If you'd like me to do that, here's my proposal.
  1. I will give you cash every payday to cover gas and groceries and incidentals. Perhaps I can squeeze out $125-130 each pay period.
  2. You agree to charge absolutely nothing on any account anywhere--the one exception would be for pharmaceutical needs you have. Otherwise, if you can't pay cash for it, you can't buy it. (So no web purchases of any kind.)
  3. You would need to give me password and ID access to all your accounts (including your checking account) so I could make payments on them for you (car, visa bills, UMP, etc.). And info about where to send the rent and to whom it is to be paid.
  4. I might need a power of attorney from you, but we can do that later if need be.
  5. You need to change your cable/internet to internet only. Kathy says you can get everything you need on her Netflix account--there's no reason to be paying as much as you do for cable TV and internet (we don't--we only have internet service).
  The advantage for you is that you can quit worrying about money. The disadvantage, of course, is that you can't spend much. This wouldn't have to go on forever, but it would save you grief for the time being.

Finally: I think you may have some funds left through Marcia. If I'm right, I will use that money to help pay some bills. Please contact Marcia to see if I'm correct, and if so--and if you want me to handle your finances for awhile--tell her to contact me about releasing the funds.

I'm sorry you're back in the ER and in such pain. Get back to me when you can and let me know if you wish me to do anything along these lines.

LY

Gary to Pat, Kathy:
FYI

I know she's probably not in any state of mind to think about this right now.

Pat to Gary:

I sent her a text a couple hours ago asking what was happening but I've not heard back yet. Like I said, I brought her in, so if they don't admit her, she'll be stranded and in need of a ride. I'll plan on staying here until I hear from her, and be available for transport.

IF there is any money sitting with Marcia, maybe don't put it all towards bills? Not sure when she last had her car serviced, but I suspect it might need some work and she does need a working car. Would be nice to have a few hundred dollars on hand for that.

Just a thought. Maybe the funds are gone and it's a moot point.
Gary to Pat:
Let me know if I have to get her.
I did just get her car serviced (and paid for it, although she volunteered to give me money).

I didn't plan to spend it all at once. Rather spread it out in smaller increments to get bills caught up and perhaps get rid of 1-2 of the smaller ones over time. And yes, reserve some for emergencies.

January 5, 2016 Text [message missing]
Krystin to dad: It worked for a little while, but pain started coming back after 2 hours, and I get med every 4 hours. :(
Dad: :-(any news on stent?
Krystin: Dunno when, yet. Still saying some time this afternoon.
Dad: Would be nice if taking it out and replacing it eliminated pain.

Krystin: Yes, I absolutely agree. If pain not gone, I dunno what I'm gonna do.
Dad: Wait to see what happens. If still pain, squawk loudly to docs!
Krystin: Yup. I just found out my dose was raised, and every 3 hours, not 4. That should help better.
Dad: Good. Read your emails from me, please.
(later) Dad: Any news?
Krystin: Pain even worse than before procedure.
Dad: Do they know that?
Krystin: Yes
Dad: They doing anything about it?
Krystin: Nope. Just my regular pain med routine. Which does nothing.
Dad: Are you protesting?
Krystin: Yes, but to no avail. Nothing will change.
Dad: Oh. We need to look at Abbott. Or get to mayo.
Krystin: Ok
Dad: You have to take action. I can't do it for you.

January 7, 2016 Text
Pat to Gary: K says she also needs insulin shots. You mentioned Coumadin, but did you know about the insulin? She's pretty depressed.
Gary: Did not. Going to see her in few minutes. Why insulin??
Pat: Says has only half pancreas function since infection last fall.
Gary: Great. Is care conference with all the medical folks tomorrow at 2. I can attend. If you can, too, would be good. She tells me they recommending she not work full time or live alone. I in her room now.
Pat: I can be there. Just tell me where.
Gary: Some conference room on floor, I guess. DK right now. Yes, she very depressed.
Pat: Hugs from me. I assume she'll stay admitted thru then?
Gary: Yes
Pat: Fine for them to recommend x and y but having a suggested alternative would be helpful. I suspect they won't have that.
Gary: Idk
Dad to Elliott: There is a care conference for Krystin tomorrow at 2. Do you wish to attend?
Elliott: I don't know what that is and I have plans all day tomorrow
Dad: Ok. Docs are saying she needs to stop working for awhile and should not be living alone.

Elliott: Took them this long to come to that conclusion. This isn't a good plan. How she get insurance? How she pay for it? How she pay for anything with no income?

Dad to Krystin: How you doing? I will come over early with a power of attorney form for you to sign so I can deal with marcia and get your finances under control, if that's ok with you.

Pat to Gary: I said I wouldn't let you sink financially for those things you've covered (rent, car payment or whatever you said) and I won't, but please don't pay any more stuff until we can consult, ok?

Gary: All I'm paying is the charges that are auto deducted from her account. Car, affinity visa, etc. Those have to be paid for now or there are big nsf charges.

Krystin to dad: Been a rough day. Never really got a nap in. Pain has been slowly increasing since early afternoon, but of course nothing can be done about it. So, another long, painful night is in store.

Dad: I am so sorry. It amazes me that they cannot or will not do something for you. See you tomorrow. Love you lots.

Krystin: I said almost the exact same thing to my nurse. The nurses should be the ones who decide what to give, since they have the most exposure with us. See you tomorrow.

Dad: Well, I guess you can only keep on pressing them.

January 8, 2016 Text

Pat to Gary: Do we need to pow-wow or are we on the same page?

Gary: For the short term, she can come here, while we explore options.

Dad to Krystin: At least for the short term, you can come here while we explore options, ok?

Pat to Gary: NO! She'll drop off the radar screen then. We need keep their feet to the fire. There IS no short term. She needs intensive therapy. Are you qualified to do that?

Gary: For the short term, there is no other solution. They will release her next week. This is not THEIR problem to solve. They can make recommendations, and get information for us, but they don't decide. I will talk to HR on Monday and find out disability options. We will also pursue options with the social worker.

Pat: No, they can't discharge her until they have a place for her. I thought the social worker was going to call HR. Yes, this is their problem. They heard us when we said coming home with is wasn't an option. Don't back pedal now. We've said for YEARS that she needs inpatient mental health treatment. We're so close.

Gary: I do not believe there is any way to pay for that, at least not in the next two or three weeks. If ever. Any options are going to take some time.

Pat: What if we weren't here? Would they put her out on the street to die?

Gary: Who knows.

Pat: Well, I can't support your decision. They truly will not put her on the street if we don't take her in. Is Kathy in agreement with you?

Krystin to dad: Ok. I told Sherri, who came to see me later, that for now, that would work the best, until whatever. So, she knows that. And, thanks.

January 9, 2016 Text

Krystin to dad: Would you still be able to go to my apartment and get me some things?

Dad: Yes. Ok. Tomorrow, I'm guessing? I emailed you about it, too.

Krystin: I know. I replied. Yeah, tomorrow. And sent you message with info. I saw msg with rehab info, but not about getting stuff. So, give me a call when you're there and I'll walk you through where things are. I've even made myself a list!

Dad: Will do. Just sent you email.

What's your opinion about what I just wrote in email? I've had the sense that you don't want to stop working. If you have strength to do so, I will support you.

Krystin: I replied to email. I agree with you.

Dad: Got it. We may need to discuss with Sheri.

Krystin: Ok. I wrote note on my board that you want to be in touch with her and social worker.

Dad: Ty. See new email. Did your mom stop in?

Krystin: Yes, she was here from about 10:45-noon. Now my lunch of chicken Florentine and sliced pears just got here, so I will eat lunch and watch a show on my tablet.

Dad: She say anything about what's going on?

Krystin: No, we didn't talk about that at all. I think she wanted a visit just to talk and visit and not discuss medical stuff. Which was just fine with me.

Dad: Good. Plenty of time for all the other stuff.

January 9, 2016 Email
Dad to Krystin:
   Thanks.
   I think I should cancel Xfinity. Kathy also thinks that in the future you could just do with the internet connection--much of what you might want to see could be on Netflix. (We don't have cable TV--just internet.)
   We can talk about the rest of these as needed.
   For now, don't pay any of them without letting me know. I need to keep track of the balance in your checking account.
   LY too

Krystin to dad:
   About the Xfinity- yes, to an extent. A lot of shows still aren't on Netflix, and if they are, they're a season or two behind, so you can't watch current stuff. If you want to watch shows that are on a cable channel, it can be found on the web, but not the best quality. I dunno, I'm torn. I have a whole schedule of shows I watch, and channels I turn to that play marathons of shows I watch that I like to put on, but I'll definitely think it over, k?
   I won't pay any of those things, just stay away of the due dates, of course.

Dad to Krystin
   Would you please have Sheri call me? I'd like to talk to her about arrangements. And if you know the name (and number) of the social worker, we'd REALLY like to talk to him/her.

Krystin to dad:
   I will let my nurse know that you'd like to be in touch with Sheri, and the social worker, whose name is Beth.
   I sent a text about getting some things from my apt for me. Whichever day you are able to come, could you bring me some things? Especially since I'm still going to be here for who knows how many more days. You could call me from my apt and I'd walk you through it.

Dad to Krystin:
   It sounded to me like they are talking release Monday or Tuesday.

January 9, 2016 Email
Rehab places
Kathy to Gary:

These both look like they'd be appropriate, but no mention of price, of course, or insurance coverage. [List of places.]

Here's what the Medica site says about mental health coverage. The second column is in-network and the third column is outside network. Your guess as to what it means is as good as mine.

Inpatient services . . . .

Dad to Krystin:

Krystin, find a way to get this info to Sheri and Beth! It MAY be that Medica will cover something.

Kathy to Pat:

I'm forwarding a couple messages I've sent to Gary. I've been looking into what I can online and this is some of what I've found. I think all three of us should be aware of these things.

The Medica table didn't copy in to email very well. The first section is in network, the second is out of network. No idea how to interpret it.

Pat to Kathy:

Thanks for doing all this research. I'm just sorry you have to be going through all this with us 😔

January 9, 2016 Email
Working
Dad to Krystin:

Everybody seems to believe you should stop working, at least for a few months. I have a different view. I think you spending all your waking hours on health issues is itself not particularly healthy. But question is, do you have enough energy to work some of the time? If you are getting regular nutrition and regaining muscle strength, could you be at work?

Krystin to dad:

Yes, I could work, and yes, I want to. Like you said, I don't want to be sitting around all day doing nothing or focusing just on health stuff. I NEED work in my life. Even if I work part days, or part days or some full days at work, other part days at home, since I can do

FFATA from home. It would help keep my mood up, too, because I would feel like a contributing and productive member of society, instead of a useless bum. Yes, with good nutrition, I would absolutely have the energy to do some work. I've already noticed a little difference after these 4-5 days of feedings. Obviously I still have a long way to go, but this is a good start.

January 9, 2016 Email
Being at 4020
Dad to Krystin:
    One absolute condition on you being at the house: you do EVERYTHING medically you are supposed to do. Meds, feeding, and you start doing modest exercise. Like use the elliptical in your former bedroom 2-3 times per day for 10 minutes. I'm no PT expert, obviously, but that could not hurt.

Krystin to dad:
    Agreed, to all. Even the elliptical! I think that's a very good idea.

Gary to Kathy:
    Big talk. I guess we'll see. If she actually does this, and works, she should be a moderately pleasant person to have around for awhile.
    I am still wondering about keeping the apartment. I assume Pat could talk them into releasing her Feb 1. What I don't like is that she has no place to go from here. Except I suppose a new apartment. And meantime we'd have to pay to move and store her stuff. But if she didn't have rent or utilities, she could afford that.
Dad to Krystin:
    I am wondering about dumping the apartment. Does not mean you live with us permanently, just for couple of months you no have rent or utilities. We need to look at numbers.

Kathy to Gary:
    I think part of our job will be to make sure she does it. That's what the docs are saying needs to be done. Someone needs to be cracking the whip since she won't do things for herself. If she does stay with us, I'd like to get some kind of indication from the docs about how much we should expect of her. Yes, exercise is a good idea, but would they recommend that she do that right away? I don't know. I'd like to hear from them about how much we need to push her to do anything, from

exercise to working to doing her own laundry (yes, I think she needs to do that, too) to making her own food, etc.

Gary to Kathy:
 I agree with all of this.

Dad to Krystin:
 I am going to cancel your Comcast/Xfinity account. You may not be going back to your apartment. No reason to pay that bill. You can always resume internet whenever.

Krystin to dad:
 I think it would not be good for me to return to live in THAT apartment. Like with alcohol and drug rehab, it's not good to return to the old environment, where the same conditions exist that make it easy to relapse. In a way, I think that could apply to my apartment. I need a new environment with no history for me. You know? And probably seriously consider a roomie, if and when that time comes.

January 9, 2016 Email
Comcast
Dad to Krystin:
 Will our account let you see at least some of what you like to watch? I don't mean to subtract from your enjoyment of life, but I also want to try to get your finances to the point where you can manage.

Krystin to dad:
 Right. I understand. I'll check it out later on my tablet app.

January 10, 2016 Text
Krystin to dad: You don't need to bring my shampoo. It can stay at your house, the stuff here is fine until I leave. Are you able to bring a nail file for me, though? I really need one. If you guys don't have one lying around, I can get a few for super cheap at the gift shop. What time you think you come?
Dad: Ok on shampoo. I can bring file. As for time, midday sometime.
Krystin: WTF, I've been on the tube feedings every night that I've been here, and order food from food service, and my weight has gone DOWN. Only 100.9 this morning. How does that happen?? That's disappointing.

Dad: Have you talked to nurse or whoever about this? Maybe you need exercise to build up muscle mass.
Krystin: Not yet, my weight was just taken literally 4 minutes ago. I make a note on my board, though. And yeah, I'm sure exercise would indeed help!
Dad: You like flannel sheets?
Krystin: Yeah, I think so! I can't imagine why I wouldn't. Why?
Dad: We need to make up the bed. I think that's what you have in your apartment.
Krystin: I dunno, they're a sheet set from Target. I guess I don't get my mattress and sheets anymore. . . . Although, we COULD bring my air mattress to the house and put it on E's bed. It might look a little funny, but at least I'd have my mattress. At least consider it. It would be something of mine to have, that I'm used to, in a foreign room.
Dad: For now, it's Elliott mattress. We'll see how things go before moving yours.
Krystin: Ok

[A long text colloquy with Elliott about Krystin]
Dad to Elliott: So, after lotsa talk with your mother, what your thoughts about Krystin? Are we idiots for hoping she can get back to some kind of normal life? And trying to help her do so?
Elliott: I wouldn't use the word idiot. Mildly delusional perhaps. And I absolutely agree with mom that you should only let her move back home as a last resort. Don't let the medical establishment off the hook and just take her in. You are not equipped to help her the way she needs. But no, she forfeited the ability to ever live a normal life years ago. She's going to need help for the rest of her life. And I wouldn't jump up and volunteer to start that if I were you.
Dad: The only problem with your mother's analysis is that the medical establishment has some responsibility for ensuring some outcome. I don't believe it does. We will help to the extent possible for her to achieve something approaching normal for her. At least you know this: I'll be here for you no matter what. And the magical funding fairy hasn't shown up yet.
Elliott: Mom's point though is that you should not let her move home yet. If she has to move back to her apartment, that's her problem. Moving out solves money problems in the short term but you not taking into account the man hours and the value of that that it will take to move her out, and then back in somewhere else. Also as mom

pointed out, they will let her stay in her current place as long as she keeps paying rent. But trying to move into a new place with her current medical state, and possibly lack of job? And if she would have roommates, why would they ever pick her over someone else? Staying in her apartment maybe expensive but alternatives grim at best.

Dad: The apartment question remains open. Costs need to be figured. No, roommate is impossible. But sending her back to apartment now is saying "let her go to die." I cannot do that. Neither can Kathy.

Elliott: As mom would point out: she does not and has not for many years exhibited the behavior of someone who wants to live. She says she does but all her actions run contrary to that. It's not a lack of motivation. If she just needed a wake up call she would've started fixing this ten years ago after Paris. But she didn't. She just doesn't seem to really care. Every time you've ever told her what she needs to do to fix her situation, she says "I know". She has known her entire life. She just doesn't do it.

Dad: That is the psychiatric problem. The disconnect between very much wanting to live and the inability to do what is required to make it happen. The question is whether it can be overcome. She can't do it alone. What I am concerned about is whether anyone can. I don't know, but I'm willing to take steps to see, rather than simply let my child die.

Elliott: As I said before: she's going to need her hand held for the rest of her life. As soon as anyone lets her go, she'll resume the exact same behavior she's exhibited for 20 years.

Dad: And we have to take her in for a short time because the hospital can't keep her and there's no magic solution on Tuesday or whenever.

Elliott: That may be, and then the question is where such a place might be.

Dad: But for the immediate moment, I'm not going to send her to her grave. You think I should?

Elliott: I think you should let her go back to her apartment. She's not going to be any better off at 4020 and once she settles in there, especially now that you've cleared out my room to make it more homey for her, she's going to feel like she's got a safety net and will not try as hard. If you absolutely need to let her move in to save her life, fine, but make her think she could fail. She needs to have that risk. If that doesn't motivate her, she will never have the motivation. By jumping up and letting her move home you're just enabling her learned helplessness.

Dad: This is too difficult for texting. She comes here with rules we've laid out. But the "learned helplessness" phrase suggests a misunderstanding of the problem, I think. She has a constitutional failing. I don't know if it can be treated or if there are ways she can learn. If not, she either must die or be somewhere with a minder. You assume risk creates motivation in her. Evidence says no. So what am I to do? No loving parent will EVER knowingly let their child die without doing everything possible to prevent it. You are thinking rationally. A mistake in this case.

Elliott: I'm thinking rationally because I'm not her parent so I am able to step back and analyze it critically. For better or worse you are biased by your parental instincts.

Dad: You can analyze it--but not from her situation. I can analyze it the same way you do, although I think you not recognizing the psychiatric issue, and even reach the same conclusion. But as a parent, I must reject it out of hand.

Elliott: I recognize the psychiatric issue. The difference is I think it's not treatable. Which means you either let her go home and die or you put her in some institution for the rest of her life. She will hate that.

Dad: Ok, we need to go to bed shortly. Am trying to get meeting with medical and social work folks ASAP to find out what options are. And in response to your last message, I'm not sure there are such institutions any more. What we need to find out. Perhaps THAT alternative would finally be strong enough force to overcome the problem, although I nor optimistic. Even if you right, and not treatable, am I to just let her curl up in her apartment and die? I cannot do that. And as I have said before, who is going to pay for this institutional care?

Elliott: If you are right and those options not available any more, and you refuse to let her die, then the only option left is you personally take care of her for the rest of her life. And incur all the financial consequences. I personally don't think there is a best case scenario here anymore.

Dad: I know. It is a dilemma no parent ever wishes to face. I'm hoping there are some realistic options in between institutionalization and lifelong parental care. There may not be, but we're sure going to look for one. Besides, I not live long enough, forget the money.

Elliott: You not going to live long enough to what? Care for her? You think she going to outlive you?

Dad: I suspect that if she has adequate care, she could live some time. I could also die tomorrow. Ok, I just got in bed. We can continue tomorrow. I will keep you posted on what we learn. Hope you enjoy your work this semester.

January 10, 2016 Email
house understandings
Dad to Krystin:
Krystin,

There are a few things I hope we can agree on about your being at the house.

One, no mess spilling all over the house. Remember that this is our house and we do make an effort to keep it reasonably neat. Having stuff of yours scattered everywhere will just irritate both of us.

Two, if you feel down and need to talk, you know we're here to listen and will do what we can to understand. But if you get into a grumpy or sullen mood, please keep it to yourself. We do not generally get into moods--and if we do, as adults we don't let it show to others. I know you're depressed and this is a lousy situation, but being grumpy about it won't make it better and will just annoy us.

Three, it is still Elliott's room. Please treat it with respect. And that means keeping clothes picked up/hung up/in drawers. I do not want the room to look like a disaster area while you're in it.

Four, depending on what your docs say is necessary for your recovery, we will expect some degree of housekeeping from you. This means, as I wrote, no mess all over the house, putting dirty dishes in the dishwasher (or emptying it first, if necessary), and making your own breakfast and/or lunch (assuming you'll be able to eat). For the time being, I'll do the laundry, but will expect you to start doing it yourself in a bit. (In theory, one idea is that you get back to doing things anyone needs to do when living on their own, right?) Of course you can eat dinner with us when you're here.

Finally, I assume you will engage in the normal personal hygiene--brush your teeth, take a shower most every day, etc. Again, we will talk to your docs to see how much of this we can expect and when during your recovery we can expect it.

I don't mean to seem harsh, just want to set out some understandings about what will happen while you're here.
LY

January 11, 2016 Email
talking to boss?
Dad to Krystin:

    Are you going to talk to your boss at some point? I can't presume to tell you what you should say, but seems to me you could say you expect to be back full time within 3-4 weeks and can be part-time up until then, and want to cover the other time with sick/vacation time. (If that's possible. Or maybe disabilities office can get you some kind of help.)

Krystin to dad:

    Yes, of course I'm going to talk to Dave! I won't just leave him hanging in the dark or anything. What you suggested to say sounds very good to me. And even when I'm out, I stay in touch with him frequently. I don't know if I'll be able to cover it all with vacation time, since I don't accrue it that fast (AND I still have 50 something hours to claim from before this hospitalization), but I'll find a way. If not with a disability policy, I may need to change my appointment time to 50% pay, or something like that. We'll see. I'll look into it more, too.

January 11, 2016 Text
Krystin to dad: Sheri should be calling you soon. Would you guys be able to come over today? Everyone is here and available today.
Dad: Yes.
Krystin: Also, left a voice msg for Dr. Robiner [psychiatrist] if he can see me earlier tomorrow. Will let you know after I hear back.
(later) Krystin: Shari said probably no discharge until Weds, while endocrinology figures out a good insulin regimen for me after discharge. So we'll keep our scheduled appt.
Gary to Pat: I received today a statement for Krystin's gift trust. Comes due in 2044. What you think about seeing if can get the $2600 now? She be alive in 2044? Better to use the money now. Would help me a lot getting her finances in order. Only getting 2200 from other funds. I also going to get car doors fixed. Kathy got trapped inside her car yesterday cuz could not open doors from inside or out once she got in. Was scary.
Pat: As for 2044 funds, I believe those were my dad's intended "retirement" funds for the grandkids and I do believe there's a "major medical or life hardship" clause in there. You have POA, so check with Marcia. [Pat' sister, a financial advisor who originally set up the

funds.] Not what dad "intended" but none of this is what dad intended. I believe he would agree it's needed now vs later. Same as when we took the college funds early to pay for Sylvan.

Pat: I would just like to know where the funds are going before they are gone. I know you will hate this, but since they are originally my dad's contribution to the kids, I'd really like it if you shared with Marcia the financial obligations and let her share an opinion on the best bucket to put the funds in. It would just be a respectful move.

Gary: I am happy to share them with you. I would prefer that you share whatever you wish with Marcia. I intend simply to bank the funds for now and use them to supplement her income as needed to pay bills. I think that wiser than spending it all down. I think I sent you already a list of her financial obligations / payments. I don't know anything more than that and will deal with those. Canceled her Comcast account, so saved 100 month there.

January 12, 2016 Email
Neal
Dad to Krystin:
Krystin,

Neal [from the University's Disabilities Services office] and I are going to meet in your room around mid-day tomorrow. He's looking into some options to help you, getting FMLA forms finished, and talking to your boss, I guess.

See you then.

Krystin to dad:

Ok then! Good thing I plan on taking a shower today, so at least my hair will be clean and I won't smell. . . .

January 12, 2016 Email
expenditures
Dad to Krystin:
Krystin,

Why am I seeing charges like this on your checking account? [Not included.] I am NOT going to have anything to do with your finances if you keep spending money.

For now, I don't want to see any charges that you haven't checked in with me about first. I just can't get things in balance if you keep spending money.

Most of the balance in your account is MY money, that I put in to avoid overdraft charges. It is not yours to spend.

Dad to Krystin:

The more I think about these the angrier I get. Please do whatever you need to to reverse these charges. And I think you better give me your debit card. You do not have money to spend.

Krystin to dad:

Then don't think about them. Some of the money in my account IS still mine. But I'll do what I can about reversing some.

I'm sorry, but I'm not going to give you my bank card. I will, though, let you know beforehand if I need to make a small purchase here or there. I do have a much-needed appointment at Riverstone on Saturday that'll be about $20. I willingly gave up my cable and Internet at my apt. My once every 2 months salon appointment, I'm keeping.

January 13, 2016 Facebook

Krystin Engstrand is at University of Minnesota Medical Center.

I haven't posted anything yet on this, but I'm ready to now. I am being discharged today after being in the hospital since last Monday, 1/4. I've been getting treatment for partial acute cellular rejection of my pancreas. Translation: my body recognizes that there's a foreign object hanging out in the there, is suspicious of it, and has started taking action. This does NOT mean I'm losing the pancreas, don't worry. I've been getting high-dose IV steroid treatments, and will now continue on a Prednisone taper. I will need to do blood tests and insulin again for a while, but not forever. The next month or so will be tough, but I have so much support, I know I'll do great.

January 13, 2016 Email

Dad to Krystin:

I'm fine with the hair appointment.

Right now there is $989 in your checking account. Of that, $1000 is mine. So no, there is no money of yours in the account right now.

I will also point out to you that thus far I have spent: $368 to get your brakes fixed and 2 new tires, $468 for 6 months of your insurance, ~$350 to fix the door on your car and replace the rear light (don't know the exact total because the car is at Geller's right now). You might say I didn't have to spend the money on the door, but you cannot have a car that you might get trapped inside (as Kathy did).

So your car has taken about $1100 of my money, apart from the $1000 I put in your account.

OK, you keep your bank card--but make absolutely NO, ZERO purchases on it. There is no money in your account for anything.

Thanks.

Dad to Krystin:

In the future, would you let me know of any bills you get before you pay them off? If I have to manage money, I need to manage both inflow and outgo!

Krystin to dad:

Of course. I've never had to confer with someone over my purchases before, so it was easy for me to automatically make those payments. I will do better now.

Dad to Krystin:

TY. I do really want to help you, but I do need your cooperation!

January 13, 2016 Email
reflections
Dad to Krystin:
Krystin,

A few thoughts as you leave the hospital.

I think you need to look on coming to stay with us as your last chance. We're willing to be your safety net for a short while, but you'll need to get control of your life at some point soon. Living with us permanently is not part of the plan.

To be extremely blunt: what will happen if you don't stick to the medical protocols (and what we ask of you around the house) is that you'll end up back in the hospital, or your apartment, to die. Right now, I infer, the chances of reasonable recovery and normal life are good-- but only if you do everything needed to maintain your health. If you don't, you'll lose your job, lose health insurance, and heaven knows what will happen--except that I'm pretty sure you won't survive long.

I do not mean this to be hostile; I am trying to be as straightforward as possible. You need to fully understand the consequences of failure this time.

You may not realize how draining this recent set of events and your coming to the house has been for us. We don't have the

psychological or financial ability to support you and attend to your medical needs if you fail again.
Love you.

Krystin to dad:
No guilt trip there or anything, though.

Dad to Krystin:
Ultimately the responsibility must be yours. Whether you feel guilty or not is irrelevant--you just have to DO what is needed.

January 14, 2016 Text
Dad to Krystin: Sleep and tube feeding go ok? Didn't know if you wanted me around this morning. You take all your meds? Let me know how things going.
(later) Dad: What's up? You need to sign a release form for the program Neal was talking about. They will have it at the 7A station desk.
Krystin: Ok, perfect. Yes to meds, and yes to both sleeping and tube feeding. It took me a while to fall asleep, but that's normal. I slept well once I fell asleep!
Dad: Call me. Just to chat.

January 17, 2016 Text
Dad to Krystin: You doing ok?
Krystin: Ya. Took a nap at my apt. Gonna pack some stuff then head back over.

January 18, 2016 Text
Krystin to dad: Left a voicemail message for Suzanne at the psych program to call me. I'm going to ask her about the 3 days/week half day program instead. Hopefully she calls back today, since I'm scheduled to start tomorrow
(later) Krystin: She just called back. She's going to talk to the people at the half day program and see what their availability is for a new patient, then will call me back to coordinate a start date. So, no, I'm not starting tomorrow. She said even she wondered if the partial day program was going to be too much for me. So she understands.
Dad: Good. Now: elliptical!
Krystin: Yup. For like 3 minutes and I'm done.

January 19, 2016 Text
Dad to Krystin: What's up with you?
Krystin: I'm at work.
Dad: Yes, I saw your email. Feeling ok?
Krystin: Yeah, ok. Mostly tired already. Only been here 2 hours.
Dad to Krystin: Don't you have to get tube feeding going and all meds taken? So you can get up in the morning? You do theoretically have a full time job, no?
Krystin: Yes to all. They need support staff more in the afternoon than the morning, so I'm not going in first thing in the morning. Probably around lunch time. Dave is ok with that.
Dad: Ok. But do you have as a goal getting back to full time at some point?
Krystin: Yes, of course.

January 24, 2016 Text
Dad to Krystin: Know anything?
Krystin: Blood sugar coming down with fluids, but still being admitted, of course. I'll let you know what room when I get up there later. Mom walking there now to get apt keys to get cat house keys.
Pat to Gary: She's being admitted. I'm gonna dry my hair and walk over for her keys and will then do cat duty.
Gary: Ok. Ty.
Dad to Krystin: Forgot had volume off from last night. Think is pancreas issue? Any idea if they going to keep you overnight?
Krystin: Yes pancreas, and yes, that's usually what happens when I'm admitted. Getting a CT scan to see if blood clot is an issue and causing panc to not work properly, or if it's an issue of needing more insulin again, like before tube feeding and/or meals.
Krystin: Finally upstairs. Room 6, by window. No roomie so far. Kitchen closed now of course. Ordered food from outside hospital. Had to use card. I'll give you the cash later.
(later) Krystin: Uuuugh omg, this figures. First CT pics messed up, need to do again. Can't eat til after. Sigh.
Dad: Ugh.

January 25, 2016 Text
Dad to Krystin: So, any news?
Krystin: Ya, kinda. No one is sure how my BG shot up so high in just the one day, but I'll be doing blood tests again before meals, and doing

any necessary BG correcting with insulin. Also doing the one dose of NPH before tube feeding. Discharge tomorrow. Sorry I was so tired this morning. What time were you here? I wonder if it was the Seroquel from last night that made me so drowsy this morning. Hmm.
Dad: Nbd. Just so you can get back to some kind of normal life!
Krystin: Yup. I left a voicemail this morning for Suzanne at the psych program. If discharge tomorrow, ideally start program on Thursday, if they'll still have me!
Dad: Good.
(later) Krystin: Sorry if I disappointed you by ending up here again. I clearly made a mistake somewhere along the way. This was not an intentional step backwards. I now have a clear(er) path/instructions laid out for me as far as management. The team is worried, though, about how it will go when you're gone. But, I'm brainstorming some ideas of things and other people that/who could help.
Dad: Thanks! Kathy and I will come in tomorrow morning to talk with Shari, too, about arrangements.
Krystin: Ok. Hopefully she's here at that time.
Dad: . . . and what are you thinking as far as arrangements?
Krystin: Home health care nurse? Idk.

January 26, 2016 Facebook
After only 16 months, Hank and I are breaking up. He's still gonna hang around and maybe help out a little here and there, but essentially I'm back on blood tests and insulin. We tried to make it work, but I guess it wasn't meant to be. [Several responsive posts omitted]

> Christine Hinz Lenzen: Does this affect your kidney at all?
> Krystin: Yes. Kidney still doing great, but like before Hank transplant, I need to manage my blood sugars well to keep kidney happy and healthy.
> Christine Hinz Lenzen: I just wanted to make sure that with Hank bailing, it wouldn't cause a trigger reaction with kidney. Like "look that dude just jumped off that bridge. Looks like fun, let me try".
> Krystin: Lol, no, kidney is doing its own thing, not being influenced into jumping ship.
> Jennifer Woodard: Hang in there sweet girl. You're amazing. Seriously.

Krystin: Thanks dearie, that means a lot. Truly, all the love and support I have is a huge factor in how I keep on keeping on.

Crystal Lescault: Sorry :(If another pancreas becomes available do you get another try?

Krystin: That option isn't even on the table right now, since my transplant still has "partial function." Hank is like the unemployed cousin living on your couch who keeps promising he'll get a job and help out more soon. IF he completely moves out, then MAYBE down the line I can go back on the transplant list, or perhaps even look into islet cell transplant??

Laura Doberstein: Aww nuts. Sorry to hear this, but we missed you in the "diabetics only" club!!

Krystin: Yeah, me too . . . ?? Haha.

January 27, 2016 Email
form
Dad to Krystin:
    Krystin, you need to gather whatever info is needed for that form you filled out earlier. Your mom is going to contact the agency and get you applied, so it covers your copays and provides personal care assistance. We need to get that ball rolling as soon as we can. (And we need the medical records.)

January 28, 2016 Text
Krystin to dad: I start the day program next Tues, since Monday is my stent procedure.
Dad: Anything tomorrow?
Krystin: Just speaking at that diabetes support group. Then going to work.
Dad: You should be able to give a good talk!
Krystin: For real. And I only have an hour to talk! I should make a note card of main points I wanna talk about, and in what order, so I don't end up blabbing and sounding all chaotic and unorganized!

February 1, 2016 Text
Dad to Krystin: So how you doing?
Krystin: Not too bad.
Dad: Uh, no more info? Fix stent? Can you swallow solids?
Krystin: I dunno what they did. No one comes to talk to me in post-op. I know there's a new stent in there. Having some extra pain, but

that always happens. Yes, can swallow again. Just have to take it easy with eating for the next couple days cuz it's pretty sore in there.
Dad: I sure hope this one lasts awhile! We enjoying temps in 70s :-)
Dad: When you get released?
Krystin: About 4:45. I'm at mom's now. Of course now that I can swallow, I'm not very hungry.
Dad: Eat anyway! Gain weight!

February 2, 2016 Text
Dad to Krystin: In case you going to work and don't see my email before you leave, I suggest you move Kathy's car across the street this morning, before snow comes. Will be easier then! LY
Krystin: I can hardly move. Any movement sends shooting pains throughout my whole back. Are there spine nerves in the esophagus that they might have hit?
Dad: I have no idea. Contact your mom. I'm so sorry for you. Contact the docs.
Krystin: It hurts so much, even to breathe.
Dad: Do you have discharge instructions about who to contact if something is wrong?
Krystin: I'll call Teri, Dr. Andrade's nurse. I have her direct number.
Dad: Just got a text from the city. Kathy's car needs to be moved by 9:00 tonight. Can you do that?
Gary to Pat: Would you please make sure Krystin gets Kathy's car moved across the street? I've been telling her since last night to move the goddam car. Thank you.
Krystin: Yup
Pat: Will do.

February 3, 2016 Text
Dad to Krystin: Feeling better today? Ever get medical records? If so, work with mom and Neal to get that program application in.
Krystin: Nope, no records yet. It's getting a little irritating, since they said 5-7 business days. It's been what, 3 weeks?? I will call them again. Feeling ok. Pain is better, and I'm at work, but today feeling a little nauseous on and off. AND, I stepped on the scale this morning, and I'm losing weight instead of gaining, even with tube feeds. Down to 95. Hopefully now that I can swallow, I can make some of that up with actual food. No fat, carb, or calorie spared!

Dad: Good to eat lots! Yeah, bug the records people. Shari volunteered to help, so maybe leave a message for her, too.

February 11, 2016 Email
Ramsey County program
Dad to Krystin, Kathy, Pat:
Krystin,

I faxed in your application for that Ramsey County program. I talked this afternoon to someone in that office; she said the application will get into the system in a couple of days and assigned to someone--who will then call you. But she said they are about a month behind, so it will be some time before they call!!!

February 15, 2016 Text
Dad to Krystin: Just heard from Dawn. News is not good. You aren't taking meds or doing tube feeding. You are to see Kandaswamy today, right?
Krystin: She gave you wrong info then. That's the problem with people talking to each other but not to me. YES, doing all tube feeding. I didn't do it overnight last night cuz I [did] it for a long time during the day. If I did it at night, too, I would feel too full and icky. I didn't miss out on any. I AM getting my meds. I didn't get in my Coumadin the last few nights cuz we didn't test INR last nurse visit and call Coumadin clinic to get dosing. I now have dosing for this week cuz we tested it this morning. Yes, I have appt this afternoon. Dawn talked to me, too. She said it may seem like things are going better, but still not going well. My weight still isn't going up, even with tube feeds. Will see what they say at appt.
Dad: I gather you will get to the appt this afternoon. Want me to come? I have a big meeting at 330, so hope is before that, if you wish my presence.
Krystin: It's at 4:20...
Dad: What you want?
Krystin: Well you have meeting during that time! I wouldn't want you to miss that if it's important. I've been to many appts by myself.
Dad: Dawn thinks it might be helpful if I'm there. What you say? I can leave meeting early.
Krystin: Ok, if you want. Appt actually at 4:15. Clinic 2A in PWB.
Dad: Ok. Might be a tad late.

Krystin: Could you come get me? I talked to Dawn. It's ok if I'm late, but I'm not able to drive myself in. But she really wants me to go.
Dad: Ok, but will take me awhile to get to car. Let Kathy know asap, she also coming.

Chapter 16

Three Months in the Hospital

February 16, 2016 Text
Gary to Kathy: Just leaving ER. She in room, getting wired up, etc.
Gary to Pat: In case you not see email. Took Krystin to ER half dead. They got her right in, all hooked up. She said while we were getting her to the car, "this feels like death."
Pat: I did get your email and it's so very sad. You've done all you can do Gary. Kathy too - heavens knows more than she could ever have been expected to. If not death this time, it will be very soon. Her little body just can't take her abuse much longer. I'm sorry
Gary: Thanks. I am afraid you are right.
Pat: Just sent a reply via email. Reread it and I sounded like a calloused bitch. I'm not. Just trying to stay realistic and strong. Not so easy to do.
Gary: Then I won't read it.
Pat: It's not that bad. I just came across as casual. I'm far from it. I'd rather nothing but to be there with/for her. Asked about what phone numbers they had.
Gary: Call ER, I guess. I don't have a number. They're to call me when they transfer her to 7A.
Pat: So you'll keep your phone on? I'll keep mine on too, but you'll have to relay any updates. No need for them to call both. That was my Q in the email.
Gary: Yes. I have it with me and will keep it close. Will let you know right away if I hear anything.
Pat: When you made it sound like she could be on her deathbed (and therefore maybe never make it to 7A) I was just wondering if I should go be with her or if this was perhaps same as her other ER trips. I assume they will tell you if things take a turn for the worse and would be nice of someone came? (and yes, we'd be fighting for a parking space)
Gary: She was in worse shape than she's been that I can recall. Barely conscious. But will it turn out like other ER trips? Maybe. I make the same assumption you do.
Pat: You could call and find out and let me know.
Gary: Oh yeah, and like *I* could talk to someone on the phone right now?

Pat: I understand.
Gary [at 8:10 p.m.]: If I haven't heard anything by 9, I will call.
Pat: I called and said I wanted to get a status report on my daughter brought to the Fairview/UofM east bank Emergency Room. She connected me. I sat on hold for 15min 9seconds. I wish you better luck.
Gary: Ugh. Ok. I will try in a bit.
Pat: I'm trying (not very successfully) to step back from your report that she said "this feels like death." If the ER staff felt she was in that severe a state they would call us to come, yes? Like they did with Inez?
Gary: I certainly hope so!
Pat: Then they probably don't have much to tell us and a call to them would just take them away from what they need be doing. Or chatting with the nurses at the desk. I dunno. I've seen worse.
Pat: Since you didn't say anything, I assume you don't know anything.
Pat: Talked to the nurse tending her. Shared my concerns. Said she'd be around for a few days (no, she's not gonna die tonight) but that she was refusing some things. Said might be helpful to them if someone intervened. Could I go? Is her car at your house? If this is an all night thing then I might want her parking card so I don't get towed for expired meter.
Gary: Oh boy. Yes, car is at our house. Her parking card is good for reciprocal parking in eastern river road ramp but not hospital ramp.
Gary: Kathy putting together bag of stuff for Krystin, since we took nothing with.
Dad to Elliott: Thought we were on a death watch for Krystin tonight. Was barely conscious when got home from work, got her into car and to ER. She apparently going to survive, but is refusing some meds. Mom just went over there now, will let me know what happening. It may not be much longer. No, she won't be moved out when you home, will put her on sofa. Been draining evening.
Elliott: So mom said. Re the couch that is. Had not heard anything since mom say you take her to ER.
Dad: At some point her body is going to give up. But we all seem to have iron constitutions. We need to clean out her apartment because she never going back there.
Elliott: That's sort of what I was saying in the weeks before I left for school.
Dad: Don't remember that, but you were right. Going to bed, try get some sleep. But wired.

Gary to Pat: Going to bed, but text any time if news. If you leave hospital late, ask for escort to ramp.

February 17, 2016 Text
Gary to Pat: Did they give any indication re: how long they would keep her sedated? Or what prompted it?
Pat: No and they may have but I either didn't catch it or forgot. I will be going in tomorrow morning and will ask.
Dad to Elliott: They not release Krystin back to us, too dangerous for her cuz we not medical people and not here 24/7. Was experiment that didn't work. So you get your room. She going into nursing facility long term, Social Security pays for.
Elliott: Unfortunate. But may be only thing that works for her.
Dad: That's what medical people say. May allow her to lead decent life.
Elliott: She not likely to be happy about it
Dad: Want to talk with her so it's her decision. Still may not like it, but she wouldn't feel like she was being committed--and thus imprisoned. Even medical people say that unless she's committed, she still has final authority over what happens to her. I want to avoid commitment if at all possible.
Elliott: And if she says no?
Dad: Will cross that bridge when we come to it.
Dad to Elliott: Is all very sad and painful. But I still not hold her blameworthy. She got the wrong set of genes. If you'd had diabetes, you would have toed the line without fail.
Elliott: And she may very well have had the same issues, only not accelerated so because of the diabetes. We cannot know.
Dad: Would maybe have been other issues, but not major. She was sociable, enjoyed the variety of life, was excellent student, excellent employee. All gone because of her constitutional inability to deal with the disease. I was teary-eyed in 3 different conversations today telling people about her, after they asked.
Elliott: I hope you not think it your fault due to any failure as a parent
Dad: Not really. Doubt could have done more, and could do nothing when she not living here. We managed her well when she was little, then lost control when she teenager. Just wrong personality for diabetes. But death or debilitation of one's child is 1 of 2 worst disasters in any human life. Other is loss of beloved spouse.

February 20, 2016 Text
Dad to Krystin: I will fill out your rent credit tax form but I need your 2015 tax return.
Gary to Pat: At Wells Fargo doing Krystin checking account business, then will go to apartment.
Pat: I'll be there too off/on today.
Gary: Ok. I bringing 2 big suitcases and will start packing clothes. And whatever.
Dad to Krystin: Am retaining bankruptcy attorney. Do NOT pay any bills. Will continue to pay car loan and Wells Fargo but nothing else. Ok? Going to apartment to start packing clothes, etc. Dragged down those big suitcases we used for Scotland. No, will not throw away anything except what is clearly trash.
Pat to Gary: Try pack "like" things together, so when she tells her she needs a pair of pants we don't have to look through a suitcase of dresses. I'll be doing the kitchen. Ick
Krystin to dad: Well pretty much all my bills are auto-pay each month, so they pay
themselves. . . .I'll go in and see if I can turn that off. Except WF and car loan. Then we need to go over what we're going to submit to be expunged, or whatever you call it.
Dad: Yep. Thank you for turning off autopay. You are going to have to spend some time with us sorting clothes. And get copy of fed, state tax return from turbo tax if you can.
Krystin: Umm, ok, with my clothes, get what's in my chest of drawers, my underwear/sock/leggings/pajamas/etc. bins in my closet, and hanging stuff if you have room. You may need another suitcase! There are a couple grocery bags in closet with clothes in them. Those are to donate. HOWEVER, I may have a piece of clothing or two draped over the bags that I'm NOT donating, so maybe send a pic msg or call or something first, k? Don't do too much more digging around and packing up. There's a lot of stuff I wanna go through.
Dad: I'm not going to try to do this by text. You'll need to go through stuff once you out of hospital.
Dad: Well, we need to get things packed up so can get apt cleaned.
Krystin: I don't like that all these things are being done without me! I understand it, I just don't like being stuck here and not involved.
Dad: Well, not much we can do about it. But you'll have time to decide about stuff. We not toss anything except trash.
Krystin: Ok

Dad: I come over in a bit and have lunch with you, ok?
Krystin: Ok. Tell me when you're leaving and I'll order lunch then. Maybe you get here at same time!

February 21, 2016 Text
Dad to Krystin: Do you use a mouse with your laptop? If so, where is it? And I need your credit union account number. It's not on their website.
Krystin: The mouse should be in the bag. It's turquoise. And I dunno the account number. I'm sitting in a hospital. How would I be able to find it easier than you?
Dad: I thought you might have it written down somewhere. Boy, no sign of mouse. I will look again. Anything else you need immediately?
Dad: You want empty Furrybones boxes?
Krystin: No, and no.

Gary to Pat: Got any more boxes? I'm down to one.
Pat: I don't. I'm still looking at this list. Gonna eat lunch and go see K. Then to apartment. I'll see if I have more of those black tubs.
Gary: We will go buy some at the store in Highland. Not much we can do here without boxes.
Dad to Krystin: Do I keep all those blue plastic med bottle screw on tops with flip open cap?
Krystin to dad: Better for now, until I look at them.
Dad: I don't mean the meds, I mean all those top doohickeys.
Krystin: I have no idea what you're talking about, so yeah, better save them.
Pat to Gary: Do you have kitty house keys? I can do Monday Tuesday Wednesday.
Gary: I'll get back to you
Pat: When you meet with Rena [hospital social worker who proved to be largely unhelpful] tomorrow, ask which facilities actually have an opening for Krystin. No reason for us to look into a lot of places if they don't have an opening.
Gary: Will do. I can get cats tomorrow.

February 22, 2016 Text
Krystin to dad: I FINALLY finished those forms that Rena gave me, the adult disability worksheet. Whew! That was a lot of busy work. But it's all done and ready.

Dad: Good! Did you let her know? Make sure you get a copy. Now, FFATA and tax returns, right? ;-) Hope you're not too depressed about the plans. The trick will be to turn your lemon into lemonade.

Krystin: Talked to Heather [I do not recall who Heather was; she clearly had some role in determining eligibility for medical assistance]. I don't qualify for medical assistance. I'm just over that line of I make too much money to qualify. Bummer.

Dad: Well, that's not good news. Did you mention that your income will go way down? Do you have a contact for her? Did you tell her about bankruptcy? You need to talk to Rena ASAP about this. All the plans are out the window if you don't get medical assistance.

Krystin: I will get the number to call Heather back. Rena still hasn't been in to see me and get the paperwork, but she knows to come.

February 22, 2016 Email
This week, and next
Krystin Engstrand to her office:
Hi guys and gals,

So, I'm still in the hospital, and I have no idea when I'll be discharged. Maybe tomorrow, maybe Wednesday. Upon discharge, we aren't even sure yet where I'll be going. My body has been very sick lately, and my transplant team want me to go to a sort of assisted living type place. Not like ones for the elderly, but for people with chronic health issues who need a little extra help in keeping up with everything involved in their health care and keeping them healthy. My team is still looking into options, so I can't really give you much of a timeline. For the first little while that I'm there, I most likely won't be able to drive and come to work. Luckily, I can still do FFATA stuff remotely, and keep in close contact with Jon about it. But I have a feeling that for a little while, it will be like how it was after my transplants, where I was out for a number of weeks. I hope that's not going to be the case, but I wanted to put it out there that it may be a possibility. As always, I will keep you up to date as I learn more. This is not the definite plan yet, so things could change; mostly this is a heads-up of what could be.

I am so sorry this is happening, and that I haven't been a very good or reliable co-worker. It breaks my heart that I can't be there to do the job that I was hired to do. I thought I was going to get my new organs and get healthy and move on with my life, but I've never had that kind of luck, so here we are. I even had to give up the lease on my apartment. :-(

Anyway, please stay in contact, and I will do the same. I'll still be on email and working on FFATA. Thanks so much for all your support through all this. I hope that one day I will actually be healthy enough to work all day, every day, and to make it up to you and prove that I really do love my job and want to do it well and be a strong member of our awesome support staff team. Best, Krystin

February 23, 2016 Facebook
Krystin Engstrand is feeling stressed.
I'm on the verge of an emotional breakdown. I feel it coming.

Krystin: I found out yesterday that I lost my job, too.

February 23, 2016 Text
Dad to Krystin: Rena talked to her [presumably Heather]. It's ok. You forgot to tell her you can't work full time for awhile.
Krystin: I'm getting very stressed and anxious. Too many things are being done, and decisions are being made, without consideration for how I feel about it, or that I don't like. I'm not being heard or listened to. Docs are changing things based on what THEY want and think is best, even if I argue about it. My mood is souring and I am not happy with where many things stand right now. Too many changes and things are happening all at once and I can't take it.
Dad: I will come over in awhile and we can talk.
Krystin: Ok.
Dad: I will go up to 8 [the 8th floor was the location of the hospital cafeteria (which was really quite good)] first and get something to bring down to your room. Leaving Burton in 5 minutes or so.
Krystin: Good timing; I just ordered lunch.
Gary to Pat: If you just called, I didn't quite get to the phone in time. Sorry. Got the message. I will cancel parking contract.
Dad to Krystin: Don't get your hopes up too much, but I am going to push VERY hard on this requirement of passes and no car at the care facility. LY
Krystin: Ok, thanks. Dunno if that'll save my job, though. LY too.
Dad: Don't know about the job. Just would like you not to feel trapped. But like I said, not sure how successful I can be. But will give it my best shot.

February 24, 2016 Text
Dad to Elliott: Am in hospital. Did not give them my statement because OBE [I had drafted a statement on why Krystin needed institutional care; "OBE" = overtaken by events]. No nursing home because Krystin too healthy, does not qualify. So now we dk what happens.
Elliott: How on earth can she be considered too healthy for anything.
Dad: To qualify for nursing home care, must be mentally or physically unable to take meds, etc. She clearly not in that category anymore.
Elliott: Not specifically unable to take meds but clearly psychologically incapable of self-care long term. Don't see how that doesn't qualify.
Dad: One is immediate, one is not. Difference is what determines eligibility. This whole area of health care rules and programs is mind bogglingly complex. And we all have college degrees!
Elliott: Also our broken health care system and lack of institutions for psychological disorders. System doesn't care enough about people who don't have immediate, "solvable" problems. So you just get dumped back onto the street until you need a hospital again, or in prison.
Dad: Yep.

February 25, 2016 Text
Dad to Krystin: Ask for notary again. They seem to have forgotten. TY
Gary to Pat: The key is in the mailbox.
Pat: Ok. And I'm sorry you had to spend the whole day filling out forms.
Gary: Me, too. And I get to do it again tomorrow. In addition to faxing info across the planet.
Pat: Our system certainly sucks. I suspect they do it so people get discouraged and then just don't apply. Great to have a system that nobody uses.
Gary: I was just saying the same thing to Kathy. How anyone gets through this without an advanced degree is beyond me. And I do have an advanced degree and am befuddled by it all.

February 26, 2016 Text
Elliott to dad: Anything new with K worth mentioning?

Dad: Yeah, a bazillion things, almost all good, but huge questions on financial assistance that don't get answered until the wheels of state and federal agencies grind to a conclusion. I will send you an email either later tonight or tomorrow. I am guardedly optimistic.
Elliott: Define optimistic in this scenario.
Dad: That there will be sufficient funding that she can be in a place where she has health care support and meals but also have at least a part time job. She really wants to work and be a contributing member of society. Did I tell you she lost her job? That was the most devastating blow she's received. And it would help her a lot if you, of all people, send her the occasional message of encouragement.
Elliott: Yes you sent me that email three days ago.
Dad: I thought so but was too lazy to look. We--yes, both Kathy and me--are really hoping we can get her in a place where she can have a happy and productive and satisfying life. What every parent wants. I want it for you, too, but Krystin has been more of a challenge.

February 29, 2016 Text
Gary to Pat [at one minute past midnight on the 29th]: Nurse just called. Transferring Krystin to ICU. Believe she has blood stream infection from pic line. Fast pulse, low BP, on oxygen. They putting her on antibiotics. Nurse in ICU will call me at 6 a.m. with update if nothing else happens. When stabilized, she go back to 7A. I guess that's why we not heard from her.
Pat: Saw your text at 3am. Kinda hard to sleep after that - this is serious stuff. I'll stop at hospital on my way to work.
Gary: Yeah, I know. I didn't sleep well either. I'll be going in also. Nurse hasn't called yet this morning.
Gary: She stable, alert. They doing stent, something else today. Last night was disoriented. Station 4C, 4304. Will be there in 5 minutes.
Pat: I'll be about 45min.
Gary: Ok. She out of it right now.
Dad to Elliott: You there? Krystin in ICU. Got infection, very sick, got a call last night at midnight. Didn't go in cuz they sure could stabilize her. In hospital now, they say she better, but is sleeping.

March 3, 2016 Text
Krystin to dad [5:52 a.m.]: I'm wide awake. If you're gonna come see me this morning, I'm on 6B now. Room 226.
Dad: Ok. Will be a bit later.

(later) Dad: Stent fixed?
Krystin: Yup. And actually get ice and water now.
Dad: Step in the right direction!
Krystin: Did you stop by at all today?
Dad: Yes. You were in surgery and weren't expected back on the station for a couple of hours. I didn't want to sit there that long. I see you tomorrow.
Krystin: Ok. Bring a big ol bottle of water. Cuz you can now. Kathy must have one?

March 4, 2016 Facebook
Krystin Engstrand is at University of Minnesota Medical Center.
I entered the hospital through the ER on Tuesday February 16. I spent approx. 12 days on my fav transplant unit 7A, getting hydration and nutrition. During that time, I discovered that my esophageal stent has slid into my stomach, AND my G-J tube popped out of my stomach (don't ask). A day before the procedure to fix both, I suddenly came down with 2 nasty infections that put me in the ICU for 2 more days, most of which I don't remember. I returned to 7A for one night, they decided they didn't have enough nursing staff for my supervision needs (no food, ABSOLUTELY no water IN NO WAY - and believe me, I tried, and a couple times found, ways to sneak it), and was moved to 6B, the medical observation unit, where I've been for another 2 days now. Today I finally had the procedure to fix my stent and tube, and am allowed ice chips and water. One of these days I'll move back up to 7A, but I don't know when, then I don't know how much longer in the hospital. I was very sick. I will need to live in an assisted living place, but it's very hard to find a place that I qualify for. It's still a long journey ahead. This pic is from when I was in the ICU. A reminder to myself, never again.

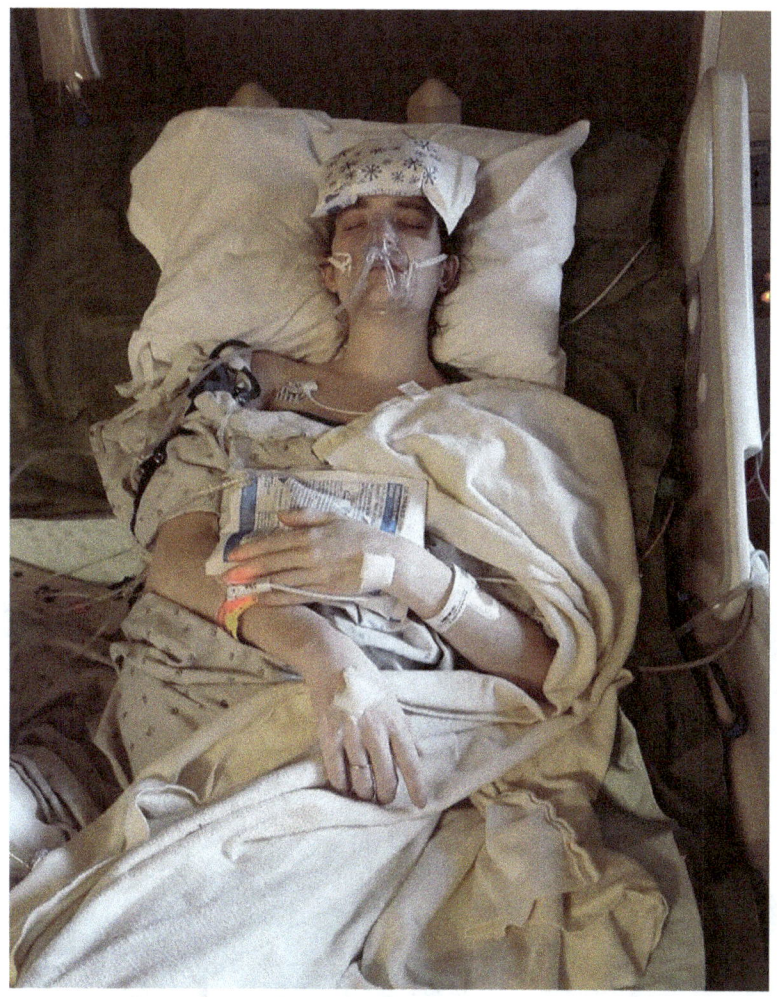

March 5, 2016 Text
Krystin to dad: Thanks for coming to visit today. Mom just left, so with both of you having visited, it ended up being a good day.
Dad: Good! I be in touch.
Krystin: Ok. I hope for good reasons, and I'm not in trouble?
Dad: No, no. Just in touch in general!
Krystin: Oh ok!

March 6, 2016 Facebook
They allowed my mom to kidnap me and take me outside for some sun and fresh air today. The first time in 19 days I've been outside. Sounds like tomorrow will be another good day to go outside. I tell ya, it sure does the mental health good.

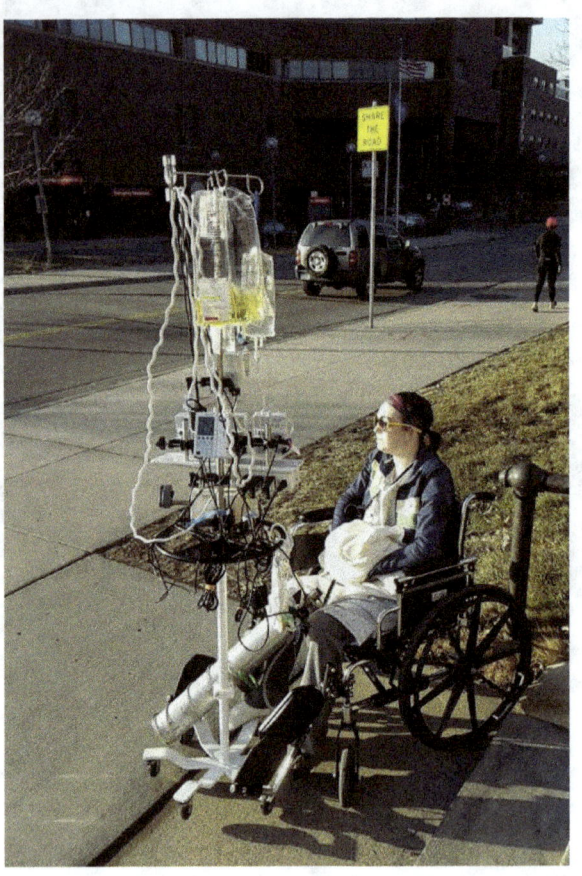

March 7, 2016 Facebook
A young lady from volunteer services here at the hospital just came by with a cart full of all kinds of different stuff for patients, for free! Donated by mostly nurses. So I got a soft blanket, a fun pillow case, a magazine, a little notebook, and some Sudoku puzzles. It's like Christmas in March! It truly made my day.

March 7, 2016 Facebook
Today I got to be Little Miss Sunshine again. Thanks for taking my Christmas tree and me outside, dad!

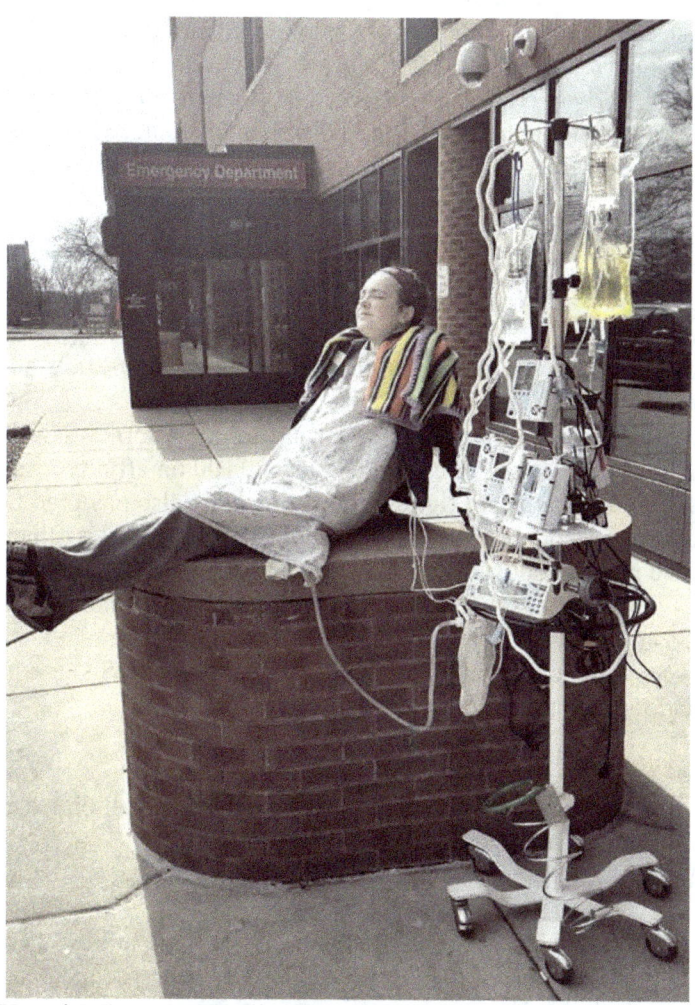

Krystin: I'm on TPN (liquid nutrition, for those who don't know - the yellow bag that looks like beer!), potassium, magnesium, 2 antibiotics, my immunosuppressant, and a saline drip. There's a pump for an insulin drip, but that's currently not in use because I've moved back to shots. The tube coming out of the bottom on my gown is attached to my g-tube in my abdomen, and is draining my stomach. Aaaaand for good measure during all this, sometimes a little bag of Ativan is hanging up there, too. ;) And every 6 hours my nurse adds a bag or Toradol, for my pain.

March 7, 2016 Facebook
Krystin Engstrand is feeling overwhelmingly thankful.
I get to keep my job! Whether in a month, two months, or five months, when I'm ready to return to work, even if only part-time starting, I will still have a position there, as long as there's an opening. My supervisor is beyond amazing, that's all I gotta say. I knew they loved me.

March 9, 2016 Text
Krystin to dad: I'm on liquid diet!!
Dad: On my way over. You see emails?
Krystin: Yes
Pat to Gary: Why don't you visit Krystin and I get Elliott at train station?
Gary: I in hospital now. Told her car has to go. Attorney said worth about 2300, she owes 3900, and also owes 1100 on affinity visa--and he said credit unions are rigid: to keep car, must also pay credit card. So, attorney said, she'd be paying 5000 for car worth less than half that. We no got 5000 anyway, so no real choice.
Pat: I was planning a visit tonight. She knows that. Just not sure when. I could still get E. I'm sure she's not happy about the car.
Gary: So why don't I get Elliott and you visit Krystin. She not happy but understands the arithmetic. Seems to be ok.

March 10, 2016 Facebook
I got put on a regular diet today. After a week and a half on ice chips, I CAN EAT!! I had French Toast for breakfast.

March 12, 2016 Text
Krystin to dad: Ugh, woke up this morning and my left eye is really watery and painful, and hurts even more when it's open, and is sensitive to light. Not red or puffy or anything, just tears and pain. Told doc, he put in order for saline eye drops. I don't need eye drops, my eye is already really watery enough!
Dad: Hope you told doc!
(later) Dad: How is eye?
Krystin: Still hurts.

Dad: Any treatment other than eye drops? They going to get ophthalmologist involved?
Krystin: No, and I dunno. No mention of that. Just keeping an eye on it.
Dad: You should ask for ophthalmologist.

March 12, 2016 Email
$$
Krystin to dad:

I've been thinking about my funds a lot lately. I've gotten quite a bit of "extra" money lately, between the 2 cat jobs, my tax refunds, and if we're going to sell my car. That's all MY money. I know I'm going through bankruptcy, but even if I weren't, yes I would use most of that for bills, but I would also keep some for myself. I think I deserve at least a couple hundred dollars of all that. And that's on the low side. That still leaves plenty for other stuff. I know I gave you permission to help handle my finances, but like I said, it is my money, and I'd like a chunk of it. I don't like this getting $10 at a time from you here and there. I need some of my own money. I could always take back control of everything, but I won't, as long as you and I can agree on a reasonable amount to give me. We can discuss this further, of course.

Ly.

Dad to Krystin:
Krystin,
Your message tells me why you got your finances so messed up. Here are a few points to consider.

1. There is about $2700 in "your" funds right now. Of that, $1000 is money I put in to your checking account to prevent charges from bouncing. That also includes about $2300 in funds from your grandfather. So of the $2700, none of it came from you.

2. I spent about $700 on your car, to keep the insurance in force and to keep it running.

3. Your mother and I just spent $1635 on a bankruptcy attorney for you.

4. I received a check for $400 from Jeff and Randy. You didn't earn it, your mother and I did. But we'll put it toward your funds.

5. Your health insurance costs right now are $41 per paycheck. Once your FMLA leave expires (early April), the full cost of your health insurance will have to be paid, $645 per month.

6. We don't sell the car. It get repossessed and someone comes with a tow truck and hauls it away.

I am trying to shepherd your money to the greatest extent possible because we do not know what expenses you will have to incur in the upcoming months. If you don't get the CADI waiver quickly, and get Medical Assistance and Social Security disability income, there will be some big living expenses.

So you have no, -zero- money. Yes, you'll get the tax refunds and the money from American Century. But that money cannot be used in anticipation of upcoming costs.

You don't have to spend money on anything right now. There is virtually nothing you need. You certainly don't need material things. You have boxes and boxes and boxes of stuff from your apartment. Nor do you need any clothing. For about 20 years.

Your mother and I have talked about perhaps providing you $50 per month for now; you can spend it on whatever you wish. You do not need $200 for anything.

Of course you can take back responsibility for your finances. But I'll take back my $1700 before I give you the money. Your mother and I are not a source of endless funding nor should be we be expected to start laying out hundreds or thousands of dollars for you. And if you do take back the responsibility, you deal entirely yourself with the bankruptcy attorney and everything else. I will not wish to hear anything more about money from you.

We can talk about this further if you still wish.

LY, too.

Krystin to dad:
If you and mom are paying for all those things, then where is my money (like my tax refunds) going?

Dad to Krystin:
None of it has come yet! (Well, $229 or something like that came from the state.) Remember that I've also been paying bills as I have to--the apartment rent was $639, for example, and we'll have to pay the cleaning person (no, we are not going to spend 2 hours each over there cleaning).

There was only $3400 to start with, before the rent, and that included the $2300 from your grandpa and the $1000 from me.

Krystin to dad:

Did you get the security deposit back for my apartment, or no, since we ended the lease early? I seriously have NO money of my own? I've never been good at math, but I feel like I should have at least some. I just hate all this having no money/funding source/bank account. It makes me very uncomfortable. I would feel much better having some cash in my wallet, since I have no credit or debit card. You've never been in this situation, so you don't know how it feels. I know I don't NEED anything right now, but that's not the point. But, since I'm not in charge of my finances anymore, I guess I don't have a choice!

See you about 5.

Dad to Krystin:

I assume we'll get the security deposit back--but they don't return it until after they've inspected the apartment and made sure it's cleaned up and cleaned out. We expect to get all of it back, and we'll put that in your funds.

Why don't I give you some money (actually, right now *I* don't have much, either, and I don't want to go out tonight without some cash). I'll get you some by Monday, OK?

And it's not true that I've never been without money. Back in the day, when there were no ATMs and credit cards were used far less than now, there were times when I had little or no money. Between rent and food and car and insurance, there wasn't a lot left over. So your assumption is not true!

Krystin to dad:

I know you said you don't have much cash on you right now, but between you and Kathy, do you have any, even a little bit, that you could give me tonight? What you gave me last time is almost gone (I think I have about $1.95) because a couple days now I've bought my Mello Yello, and a magazine, and one of those delicious cinnamon rolls from upstairs, because the ones from food service suck, and some deodorant from the pharmacy. If not, I can wait until Monday to get my Mello Yello again, I suppose . . . (read that in a light, sarcastic tone). See you soon.

March 13, 2016 Text
Dad to Krystin: How is eye?
Krystin to dad: Eye all better today. Don't forget you said you'd bring me $$ today.
Dad: Glad to hear. Wonder what happened. Ok. Since we're mid-month, how about $25.
Krystin: I suppose. Better than nothing.
(later) Krystin: Called Dick. He was with a client, so his secretary took a msg for him to call me. Haven't heard back, and I dunno how late he works, so may not be tonight. Hopefully tomorrow morn, then. Do you want/need my case # from Henn Co? One of us could call tomorrow to find out status of my case. When are we going to get a court date? I called SMRT a little after 5, thinking they were open until 6, cuz that's what their automated system says for their hours of operation, but when I called, I got another animated message saying they're open until 4:30. Wonderful. So I'll try again tomorrow morning, first thing. They open at 8. Tummy ache all better. I'm NPO again, since my lactic acid lab was elevated, and apparently food can affect the level. Lab will retest every 4 hours, and can't eat until the level comes down. Hopefully it doesn't take TOO many hours! Ah, lab guy here now. We'll see how it turns out. . .
Dad: Yes, I need case # if you faxed that form back telling them they can talk to me. Only Dick knows court date info. Good luck on tummy!

March 16, 2016 Text
Krystin to dad: Small care conference with some of the team docs and Dr. Andrade tomorrow, mid-morning. Don't know specific time yet. You're more than welcome to attend, if you're available. I can let you know specifics when they let me know.
Dad: Ok. Let Kathy know, too. I have a 9:00 meeting that I have to be at, but should be done by 9:30.
(later) Dad: I come over and have lunch? You talk to Dick Pearson yet?
Krystin: I guess not a conference. Just Dr. Andrade coming to my room to talk. Of course you're still welcome to come and hear what he has to say, provide input, ask questions, etc.!
Krystin: Do you have my social security card somewhere? I need to know exactly how my name appears on it. This is for applying for unemployment benefits.

Dad: I do. At home. On my way over to visit for lunch.
Krystin: Ok! See you soon then.
(later) Krystin: Meeting is at 10am tomorrow morning. Will just be the 3 of us and Dr. Andrade, and his PA.
Krystin: Someone stole my money! I had it in that panda case, and I just looked and it's not there. Must've been when I was gone for PT, or on one of my walks. Nothing else taken, luckily. Just my cash.
Dad: Tell the nurse.
Krystin: Oh I'm going to for sure.
(later) Krystin: The charge nurse is going to talk to someone, I forget who. Management maybe? I mean, I won't get it back, that I'm sure of. Technically it's my responsibility to keep track of my belongings and valuables. Goodbye $30. Damn.
Dad: I'm sorry.

March 17, 2016 Email
Housing option
Leota to Gary:
Hi Gary!
It was great to talk with you this morning! Attached is a picture and brief summary of the home we talked about.

Gary to Leota:
Thanks for the picture and the additional information. It sure looks like it could be workable for Krystin.

Dad to Krystin, Kathy, Pat:
Krystin: here's the additional info.

Gary to Kathy:
I think you know the story.

Gary to Pat:
In short, I received a call this morning from Leota in response to a message I'd sent to Meridien (on recommendation of [   ] at Dependable Home Care, who's been providing me with much useful guidance). Leota told me about this site, and that they have a space for Krystin, a lower-level (it's not a basement) apartment with bedroom, bath, and living area (more than she had in Highland!). Krystin could have her job at the U and she can have a car there. Leota was actually

fairly excited about the possibility that Krystin might be able to take the space because they have a hard time filling it: they need to have someone who can live fairly independently and who has no physical disability (because it requires stairs). Brooklyn Center isn't exactly close to us, but it's near Mae, so it's not terribly far away, either.

I've tentatively set an appointment to see the place on Monday afternoon at 2:00.

That's what I know at this moment.

March 20, 2016 Text
Dad to Krystin: We at Highland Grill for brunch, then to half price books where Kathy's bringing 3 bags of books to sell, then we come visit you for short bit. So probably noonish or a little later.
Krystin: Ok! Don't forget to stop at Lunds for my cereal. And if they have the coolers with pop by the registers, a 20 oz. bottle of Mtn Dew. Unless you already have the cereal, then you can get a 20 oz bottle of Mello Yello at the gift shop here.
Dad: I'm not keen on getting you food or drink. Especially not non-diet soda, which at least one nurse said you should not be drinking. What's with you and eating stuff you're not supposed to?
Krystin: You don't have to get the pop. I can have cereal to snack on. Call and ask my nurse. I have Maren again. As long as we cover it with insulin, it's fine. These days there's nothing I CAN'T have. Things I shouldn't have, probably, but nothing I can't have. And it's not like I need to be watching my weight. . .

March 21, 2016 Text
Dad to Krystin: So did you read and look at the pictures? [about the home in Brooklyn Center, Logan House]
Krystin: I did! Looks very promising and like it would be a good fit.
Dad: Ok, I will tell Leota that if they agree, so do you.
Krystin: Sounds like a good plan to me.
Dad: Ok! see you at some point tomorrow.

March 23, 2016 Email
Money
Mom to Krystin cc Gary:
　　Dad and I continued the conversation we started before I left for St. Louis. I've copied him here so we're all on the same page.

After comparing notes, it sounds like you got $20 from dad just a couple days ago, $8 from me tonight plus a few dollars from staff. You have to agree that this is a trend that cannot continue.

I'm going to bring you $10 when I visit this weekend. We will then alternate dad/mom giving you $10 once a week. That is more than enough for a hospital patient that has access to food and beverages (not to mention magazines and other items from the Goodie Room or whatever is on the 5th floor).

Also, please do not ask staff for money. Do not accept "you look like you're having a bad day" gifts from people shopping in the gift shop. Just keep repeating to yourself "I do not need more stuff, I do not need more stuff, I do not need more stuff" and then believe what you say.

Let's make this work, ok?

love

mom

March 23, 2016 Text
Dad to Krystin: You hear from Leota?
Krystin: Yup! They're coming to visit tomorrow.
Dad: Great! Did they tell you they could take you? I've heard zip.
Krystin: No, just that they want to visit and meet me and put a face to my name. Them meeting me must be a good sign though, yeah?
Dad: One hopes.
Krystin: Of course I will let you know all about it afterwards.
(later) Krystin: You know, I almost wonder if we SHOULD get rid of my car, and get a newer (but used) one that is more eco-friendly, that gets better gas mileage. I forget what those kinds of cars are called. I mean, especially if I'm going to be driving back and forth to and from Brooklyn Center every day. With my current car, that's a LOT of money going towards gas. OH, a hybrid.
Dad: We can chat about it.

March 24, 2016 Email
managing finances
Dad to Krystin:
Krystin,

I've been meaning to bring this up and I keep forgetting when I see you. So I'll send an email and we can talk more whenever.

I know you're not excited about being on an "allowance" but even you have to confess that you're a pretty lousy money manager. Most people don't have to file for bankruptcy. You have an unstoppable urge to buy things, it seems, so you have an incredible amount of "stuff," most of which you just don't need. Buying all that stuff ran you into debt you could not handle.

You can, of course, take back control of your finances whenever you wish, but I would strongly urge you not to because you'll run the risk of again getting into financial trouble. Let me give you some amount of money per month (spread however you wish--weekly, bimonthly, monthly), and that's all you have. Yes, it can include money for gas for the car whenever you regain your driver's license. We can certainly talk about how much money you will have to spend, but we can't really know that until we know what your financial situation will be once everything gets settled in terms of living and disability income and so one.

You will, however, have to learn to overcome your urge to buy trinkets and stuff, or you'll run yourself out of money very quickly every month. Wouldn't you rather have it for entertainment--going out with friends, etc.--than more little things that you don't need?

That's all.
LY.

March 24, 2016 Text
Krystin to dad: We didn't talk about my car! Also, still no sign of Dr. Andrade. Which doesn't surprise me. And I won't be surprised if he doesn't come at all today. Sigh. My nurse did put in a page to thoracic, though, to see if they'll be able to tell us whether or not he'll actually be able to come. Double sigh.
Dad: Sigh is right. We talk about car later. Is not urgent at the moment.
(later) Krystin: Ok, well, he just stopped by! Dilation hopefully Monday or Tuesday. He can't do it, but he thinks another thoracic surgeon, Dr. Podgaets, who has also done a number of my procedures, will be able to. Should know by tomorrow. Fingers crossed I can get in early next week! It'll be a rough weekend for eating, but at least I now know that a plan is in the works, which is always reassuring.
Dad: Great!
(later) Dad: G'nite Speed. Not sure I'll be on campus tomorrow, so may not see you. But we'll be in touch. LY

March 27, 2016 Text
Pat to Gary: Really? The hospital called you about K trying to get drugs from the pharmacy and now she has to have a 24/7 baby-sitter?
Gary: Oh yeah, that was yesterday. Hard to believe she could think that was ok.
Pat: Yet the baby sitter was standing right there today when I handed her cash. WHY ARE WE DOING THIS? No more cash. Period. There is nothing she needs that they can't provide. I'm feeling pretty deceived and abused right now ☹
Gary: I know. It does not make me a happy camper, either.
Pat: How can the Meridien house [Logan House] trust her if she has car, income, and deceit?

March 31, 2016 Text
Krystin to dad: Just had my meeting with Laura the nurse [from Meridien]. It went really well, just like last week. She said they are all very excited to have me there! P.s. where is Dick in the bankruptcy process? Are we moving forward at all? I keep getting emails from the different institutions telling me I'm overdue!
Dad: Glad to hear about the nurse! Yes, Dick told me yesterday things are moving along. Idk how fast this goes.

April 1, 2016 Text
Gary to Pat: New social worker a dynamo. They did NOT conclude Krystin can make good decisions. The opposite. All fronts now being pursued vigorously, they want to get her into Meridien asap. Am feeling much more confident about actions being taken.
Pat: Thank goodness! My nervous breakdown yesterday was apparently a major waste of time.
Gary: Take this the right way: I hope it was! But the bureaucracies still have to play out. Liz is optimistic.

April 4, 2016 Text
Krystin to dad: I'm in room 207 now. It's closer to the front desk, and in return I don't have a sitter anymore. Better window view. Still a single room. Downside is that there are 2 doors into the room, and outer door doesn't stay open, so I'm kinda shut off from everything/one. Inner door propped open by a chair.
Krystin: Oh, and a door alarm, so I can't sneak out and walk around without an escort.

Dad: I'll see you tomorrow. Probably afternoon. Have meetings in the morning.
Krystin: Okey dokey. Have a good night. Ly.

April 4, 2016 Email
RE: Life
Krystin to dad:
   I'm late responding to this.
   I made one bad, impulsive decision to make a point to the docs, and clearly didn't think it through at all. I'm paying the price now.
   I'm not going to take things. I don't have that urge anymore.
   At some point before I'm discharged, if you want to get a head start on me packing for the house, you could bring me a suitcase, and one box of clothes at a time (or two, if you and Kathy do it together. Or get a wheelchair when you get here and put some boxes on that and wheel it up, so you don't have to carry any of them, aside from getting them from the house to the car). That way I can pack in the suitcase what I want to take, then bag back up stuff I want to keep but don't need at the house, and stuff I want to donate. It'll be like spring cleaning of my clothes! It's just an idea, and something else for me to do to keep me occupied.
   Ly.

-------- Original message --------
From: Gary Engstrand
Date: 03/26/2016
To: Krystin Engstrand
Subject: Life
   So what's with buying drugs? Have you lost your senses?
   It occurs to me that with your incurable desire to acquire stuff, with not enough money, you might revert to taking things. If you do, there will be felony charges and we will start legal commitment proceedings. Then you will be confined at a site, lose the car, and lose the job. Just sayin.
   You seem to have an unstoppable urge to continuously get yourself in trouble. That doesn't bode well for your life.
   Sorry this seems harsh. It is. Because you could easily go off the tracks, and it would be extremely difficult for you to recover.

Dad to Krystin:
 I wish I could agree with you.
 You've been making a series of bad decisions for almost 20 years. You have consistently acted in such a way that you are committing suicide (although I know that's not your intent). You could be as healthy as Jeff and leading a fully normal life, even married with kids if that's what you'd wanted. But instead you chose consistently, for years, to not do the things you needed to do to maintain your health. This was not just one bad decision, it reflects your entire life.
 The same is true with money, by the way. The need to file bankruptcy suggests rather strongly that you cannot manage money, that you make bad decisions consistently over a long period of time.
 It is for these reasons that decision-making power in matters of health and money have been removed from you.
 I'm actually not blaming you, even though this message sounds like it. My view is that you have some neurological defect that doesn't let you make sound decisions like other people can. For some reason, you can't make wise choices. I have no idea what caused it or when, but the evidence for it is rather stark, wouldn't you say, based on the last decade or more?

April 4, 2016 Email
Dad to Krystin:
 Ugh. Your car was $700. I told him to go ahead.
 This is why you need an income! I will want to get that money back at some point after you have money coming in.

Krystin to dad:
 I thought you were going to have them fix it at no cost??

Dad to Krystin:
 They did fix the door at no charge. But the seat belt part alone cost $250 from Honda (awk!) and your driver's seat is rocking, so there's something loose that cannot be safe. There was also a considerable "clunking" every time I hit a small bump driving it to Geller's that also required a fix.
 Isn't owning a car such fun?
 Actually, I hate owning a car. It is like tearing up $100 bills and throwing them out the window every month.

Krystin to dad:

I have never noticed any of those issues with my car, so they must've developed in the last 7 weeks sitting out front! I swear cars just develop issues all on their own, even when they're not being driven. I've never heard that clunking noise, or noticed the seat rocking. Are you sure you didn't need to just push it backwards or forwards to lock it into a notch? Sometimes if I move the seat, I don't pull it all the way forwards, so it rocks a bit, but then I'll pull it forward harder and it'll click into place. Did you try that first?

I'm beginning to have the same sentiments about having a car.

Dad to Krystin:

Car report.

Seat belt fixed. Front and rear links were bad, made noise, now replaced. Do not ask me, idk. Car has gone through car wash, inside is now being cleaned.

April 7, 2016 Facebook

You see this tubing? It's about 2mm wide. That's how (not) wide my esophagus is. The esophagus is supposed to be 15mm wide. Imagine trying to swallow a bite of burger, or pizza, or your vegan stir fry, or whatever, and make, no force, it down an opening that small. That's how my eating has been, on and off, for the past year and a half. I was supposed to have another procedure done yesterday to widen my esophagus, but no, they cancelled on me, and now can't fit me in until Friday (and I've just passed 7 weeks in the hospital, btw.). So all evening, and this morning, I've been pissed, and angry with everyone, cuz I'm pissed and angry over the situation.

Then I took a deep breath and told myself this isn't forever. It's just until tomorrow. It's not the nurses' or doctors' fault; it's the stupid thoracic surgery department's fault for over-booking the surgeons. But I can make it through another day of soups and cream of wheat; it won't kill me. No use in letting my mood sour, it will only ruin my day. So, let's all put on a smile, remind ourselves that today is only one day, and proudly stick out your arm for the lab tech to draw your blood. Well, maybe only 2 out of 3 for y'all.

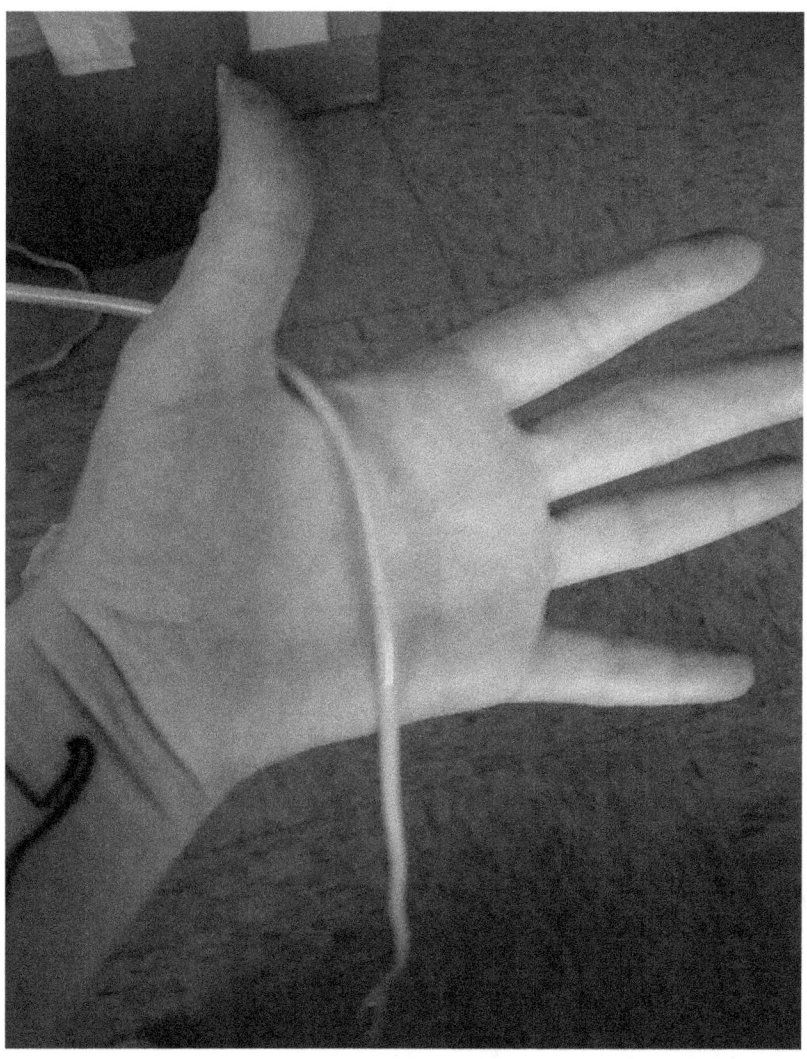

April 8, 2016 Texts
Krystin to dad: Woke up with fever of 102. Oh, and transport just came to bring me down to pre-op. Most recent temp 99.2, so it's coming down; charge nurse is gonna run it by docs and see if they're ok with me doing procedure. Fingers and toes crossed. . .
Dad: Good luck!
Krystin: I'm going! Just waiting for pre-op orders to get in so transport can come back and get me. Tonight, hello chicken fingers!

Dad: Thumbs up!

(later) Krystin: It went well, but I have to be on clear liquid diet until next week when they'll go in again and dilate it more. Only got to 10mm today, not 15 yet. This sucks, and I'm so hungry.

Dad: Do they expect it miraculously to stay at 15 by doing it twice?

Krystin: Probably. He wants to do a procedure every 7-10 days, dilating it a little more each time until he gets it to 20mm, which I guess is normal size. I think he then thinks it'll just stay open. Wishful thinking.

Dad: Well, nothing else has worked, so worth a try, I guess.

April 10, 2016 Facebook
Not that I'm starting to feel bitterness towards still being inpatient or anything. . . .

Discharge : ☐   Meet Specialty Pharmacy: ☐

DISCHARGE PLAN: Nunca. Estoy un prisonera...

Belongings: In Room ☐   With Family ☐   Security ☐

April 10, 2016 Facebook
Happy siblings day to my favorite bro, Elliott Engstrand. There's no lack of evidence that we're related, and I wouldn't have it any other way!

April 13, 2016 Text
Krystin to dad: Just got back from procedure. Still clear liquids for rest of the day. Full liquids tomorrow, then soft diet. Ugh, this sucks. If I were at home I'd be eating regular diet now.
Dad: At least things getting better.
(later) Krystin: Temp of 102.9 and in a lot of pain and all they're going me is Tylenol. It hurts so much I'm crying. I hate this place right now.
Dad: Ugh. I'm sorry.

April 14, 2016 Text
Krystin to dad: Sorry I missed you. Had an esophagram this morning, then thoracic going back in this afternoon with a camera to see if there are any tears or perforations from yesterday, and I believe putting in a stent. Sounds like Maren updated you on that, though.
Dad: Yep, she did. Hope no tears and you get the stent!
Krystin: Thanks, me too.
Dad: Make sure to call back the guy from Hennepin County. I think he's evaluating you for the CADI waiver.
(later) Krystin: I never got a call from Henn Co. . . . But they coming on Tuesday to do assessment. Liz told me that.
Dad: Good. Kathy, mom, and I will be there.
Krystin: Ok, so Liz gave you info? 1:00.
Dad: Yep
Krystin: I'm NPO for like a week cuz of small tear in my esophagus. The leak is contained, but no food or drink until it's healed. I'm very angry and irritated, since I was expecting my diet to be advanced, not taken away altogether. So obviously no procedure today.
Dad: Sigh. I feel bad for you.
Krystin: I feel bad for myself, too. I hate this life I'm currently stuck in.
Dad: Yes, have to get the esophagus problem dealt with. That's the biggee right now. Once past that, you should be good to go.
Krystin: Hopefully.
Dad: See you tomorrow. Probably late morning.

April 15, 2016 Facebook
Krystin Engstrand is feeling weirded out.
2 weeks ago I got a blood clot that ran up my left arm, getting dangerously close to my heart. If I hadn't said something about my arm being all swollen, it could've been fatal. Now I have a small tear

in my esophagus that is leaking, but contained. So I just have to wait for it to heal, which could take up to a week, and which means no eating or drinking absolutely anything; it could cause the tear to open more, requiring surgery to open my chest to fix it. Or, if not acted upon quick enough, could be fatal. Huh. So, twice in the last 2 weeks my body has tried to kill me. What.

April 16, 2016 Facebook
The floor above me is the hospital cafeteria. What on earth could someone possibly doing up there at quarter to 2 in the morning to make such a racket? They should be at home, sleeping! Don't they know I'm trying to concentrate on my adult coloring book down here??

April 17, 2016 Text
Krystin: Question. Do *I* have ANY money to my name in the new bank account? Like, if I needed some necessities at Target or whatever, and it was for things I needed, not like clothes or "stuff".
Dad: No. But we can talk tomorrow about how to get you money.
Krystin: Ok, cuz there are some things I legit need, and if I order them on Amazon before the 30 day free Prime trial runs out (I'll cancel it before the 30 days, so no charge for it), I get better deals and free 2-day shipping. I can have it shipped to me here, so that I can have the stuff already when I go to Meridian. The total would be $60. Just something to consider.
Dad: Or buy it at Target when you actually move. That makes more sense to me.
Krystin: Cuz it would be nice to already have it, and I could already use here, too.
Dad: We talk tomorrow.
Krystin: Ok. Remember I won't be able to drive or have a money source when I get to Meridian, and who knows when I'd be able to get to Target. I'm just saying it would be nice to already have it, that's all. But yeah we can talk tomorrow.

April 19, 2016 Text
Krystin: Thoracic moved my procedure to Friday. I am so effing mad right now I wanna cry. This is bullshit. 3 more days now being NPO. I'm so sick and tired of this. I want to be out of here and eating and moving on with my life. My blood pressure is super high right now cuz of how angry I am.

Dad: But I am not surprised. I am sure they want to be certain you won't get an infection. Better safe than sorry in this case. Be calm. This will pass.

Krystin: It's because a different, more important case came up. Because my issue isn't important, apparently. And I can't be calm when I'm starving and want to get the hell out of here.

Dad: I'm just sorry.

Krystin: What do you do when you have so much anger and frustration and irritation but you're stuck in a hospital and can't go anywhere or do anything with all that? I'm just speculating. I don't know how to handle all these feelings without losing my mind.

Dad: Talk to one of the nurses. That will help a little.

Krystin: Maybe in a bit. Right now I just wanna be alone.

Dad: Talk to someone at some point.

Pat to Gary: I thought that went well [a conference with the medical staff]. He made it sound like it's almost a done deal. Anything important happen after I left?

Gary: Yes, it went well. Just more of same after you left. I did walk out with him and expressed our concerns that at some point the hospital might just let her go. He said there's no way they could release her to anywhere except a care facility. The hospital itself has her on high security alert, so how could they expect anyone else (family/general public) to do that? That made me feel a little bit better.

Pat: Krystin did tell me that they moved her throat procedure to Friday, so NPO for three more days. She's pretty depressed. Okay I'm at class now for the next two and a half hours so I won't be able to reply after this for a while.

Gary: Yeah, I know. But I don't think they moved it. They were going to do an exam today, not promised procedure. They want to wait. Better safe than sorry, but no consolation for her.

April 20, 2016 Email
Medical assistance
Krystin to Kathy, dad, mom:

I was approved! Activated as of 4/1/16. So it will cover the medical costs I've accrued since my insurance ended on 4/8. Insurance card will be sent in the mail, so dad, keep an eye out for that so you can give it to me when it arrives.

So, now we wait on the CADI waiver. As soon as that gets approved, I should be good to go to Meridian and get the hell outta this hospital, FINALLY . . .

April 22, 2016 Text
Krystin to dad: Procedure is done. They didn't find a tear, so it's all healed up. On clear liquid diet for now.
Dad: Better than NPO! When next dilation? Or did they do one?
Krystin: They did end up doing one. I dunno about next one.
Dad: Why liquid diet?
Krystin: Because I haven't eaten in a week, so they have to start slow. But I'm going to talk to Heidi and ask if I can go to full liquid diet if lunch goes well.
Dad: I see. Hope you can. They may want to wait to see what happens with dinner.
Krystin: Yeah, probably.
Dad: So don't be surprised. You can certainly ask, but I bet tomorrow is more likely.

April 26, 2016 Text
Dad: So how you doing?
Krystin: Same as usual. In pain and starving.

April 26, 2016 Facebook
Krystin Engstrand is feeling grateful.
One of my favorite nursing assistants is also a kick-ass cosmetologist, so this weekend, she's going to bring her materials, devote an hour for just for me, and give me an awesome, much-needed new haircut/style, and some color highlights in the front. Her gift to me. One of the few silver linings to being inpatient so much and getting to know, even getting close with, many of the staff here.

April 27, 2016 Text
Krystin to dad: Figures, thoracic has delayed my procedure until late afternoon or early evening. Probably won't even end up being today. I'm not at all surprised, yet still just as infuriated.
Dad: Be calm. Nothing you can do.
Krystin: I can't calm down. They've done this to me over and over. And I'm starving. And by the time they finish, if I'm put on a diet, food service will be closed.

Dad: I can't help you!
Krystin: I know, I wasn't asking you to.
Dad: I know. Wish I could.
(later) Krystin: Back from procedure. Stent in and sutured in place. Quite a bit of discomfort, but not too painful. On clear liquid diet tonight with potential to advance to full liquid tomorrow. Food service closed by now, but they have chicken broth up here, so at least I can have a little something. Sadly, no jello up here, so that has to wait until tomorrow.
Dad: Glad it went well! Did they say it went well? So at least some food now.
Krystin: Yup, they said it went about as well as it could. Hopefully up to regular diet by the weekend.
Dad: That would definitely be an improvement.
Krystin: Absolutely.

April 28, 2016 Text
Dad to Krystin: So are you on the full liquid diet? And how you feeling?
Krystin: Not yet, but I think it's gonna be changed this afternoon. I'm alright. Still having the pain and discomfort of having a stent put in, but I'm putting up with it.
Dad: The pain dissipates eventually?
Krystin: After a few days, when the stent has finished stretching.
Dad: Good. Hope it happens fast.

May 1, 2016 Facebook
Krystin Engstrand was reading The Hot Zone.
What better time than when you're sitting in a hospital than to read a nonfiction book about a virus (the strains of Ebola) that makes people hemorrhage out of every orifice of their body, while their entire insides liquify, resulting in a horribly painful and bloody mess. Good times.

May 1, 2016 Email
Intake Mtg
Leota to Gary, Krystin:
    Fingers crossed that everything falls into place with the funding this week or next! Would it work for the both of you to do the intake meeting this upcoming Wednesday (5/4) morning at the hospital? Liz said that we could use a conference room. We can get all of the

necessary intake forms signed and plans created, so that you, Krystin, can move in as soon as we get the green light from Hennepin County.

May 4, 2016 Email
Today
Dad to Krystin:
    So how did you come away from the session today feeling? Good? Bad? Ok?

Krystin to dad:
    I assume you're referring to the meeting with the Meridian people? If so, I felt good about it. Excited, even, to go there. I think it's going to be a really good fit, and from the way they were talking, it sounds like I can stay there as long as necessary. So this place could be long-term, and not short-term, which would be OK with me. I don't like that it's so far away from you guys and work, but I'll get used to it. I think once I get all moved in and settled, I'll be really happy there.

May 7, 2016 Facebook
When you have a set number of footsteps you want to get in each day (gotta keep those calves in shape!), sometimes you have no other option but to plug in those earbuds and have a solo dance party up and down the unit hallway. #hospitalgrooving #noshame

May 8, 2016 Email
Order
Krystin to dad:
    Can I make ONE more, final purchase from Amazon Prime Now? It's not just for stuff I want; I'm thinking ahead to things that I'll want/need at the Meridian house, so that I won't have/need to go to Target within the first couple days, so that I can focus on unpacking, sorting, and moving in. I know that you don't want me spending any more money until we find out about SSDI/SSI, but the things on my list are things I'm going to have to get at some point (like some toiletries that I know I didn't have at my apartment), and I'd rather know that I have them when I move, and, like I said, not have to think about going shopping during my first few days there. You could add it to my IOU list. It's under $50.
    Did we ever get a security deposit back for my apartment? Also, Liz said I should reapply for unemployment once I discharge, so that could be some extra income, too, if approved; she thinks I will be.

Hope you're having fun playing in the dirt with your flowers. *:) happy

Dad to Krystin:
Wouldn't it be just as easy to stop at Target on the way there on day 1? Security deposit is in your funds. Good idea to reapply.

Krystin to dad:
We absolutely could, but what's the likelihood that we're going to go Target shopping that day? We are going to have so many other things to focus on. Plus, if I order now, I can include my pop, which is cheaper than me getting cash from you and buying bottles at the gift shop.

Dad to Krystin:
How does price of other stuff compare with Target?

Krystin to dad:
I've actually done some comparisons already, when I was first ordering from Prime. Amazon Prime ends up being a bit cheaper; one of the benefits of being a Prime member. Plus their whole free same day, 2 hour delivery window thing. That's why I wanna order now. I'd get it, and my pop, tomorrow morning.

Dad to Krystin:
Ok. Keep in mind finances.

May 11, 2016 Email
Retail therapy - it's a real thing
Krystin to Pat, dad, Kathy:
I was reading an article about mindful shopping, and how to avoid impulse shopping, which I seem to have a problem with, and learned that it's a LEGIT psychological issue, like part of the brain's defense system.
"Factor in a rough day at the office (OR SEEMINGLY NEVERENDING HEALTH ISSUES) and you are particularly vulnerable, as you look to escape your emotional funk. . . . Buying actually elevates feel-good chemicals in the brain. . . . More than half of Americans admit to retail therapy - shopping to boost mood . . .

which has been proven to increase dopamine levels, ease life transitions, and reduce stress and anxiety."

Hmmm, interesting. Just sayin.

Pat to Krystin, Gary, Kathy:
Yeah but the temporary satisfaction from the dopamine rush can't compare to the constant stress of being in debt or the expense of having to declare bankruptcy.

Now that you know you're clinically dopamine-dependent, you can recognize it when it's happening and stop it in its tracks. "Down With Dopamine!"

Just sayin ;-)

May 12, 2016 Facebook
Since I already have my 4-year degree, I found out I can go through an accelerated nursing program and get my BSN (Bachelor of Science in Nursing) in 2 and a half years instead of 4. Then I can continue on my way to becoming a transplant coordinator! The dream is real.

May 13, 2016 Text
Krystin to dad: How is it going to work with my hearing on Monday? [bankruptcy hearing with the court] Will I do a phone interview from here? Assuming I'm still here, that is.
Dad: Yes.
Krystin: Call me when you are able. Ok. It's about registering for the debtor education class I need to take.
Dad: Call Dick Pearson about it. Idk anything. I just talked to him, so call quick. He will be at your hospital room 12:45 Monday.
Krystin: No, it just needs to be paid for. I figured you could log into my account and enter payment info, then I'll log in to take the course online. Takes about 2 hrs. Right now I'm eating a late lunch though
(later) Krystin: CADI waiver was approved!
Dad: GREAT! Let Leota know asap! Maybe moving this weekend is possible.
Krystin: What about SSDI? Don't I need that, to supposedly pay room and board?
Dad: Idk

May 14, 2016 Facebook
Krystin Engstrand is feeling fresh.
My "3-month hospital anniversary" gift from one of the nursing aids was finally getting my hairs cut. AND, if all goes well, I could be looking at discharge this coming week!

May 16, 2016 Facebook
My latest attempt at a little hospital humor.

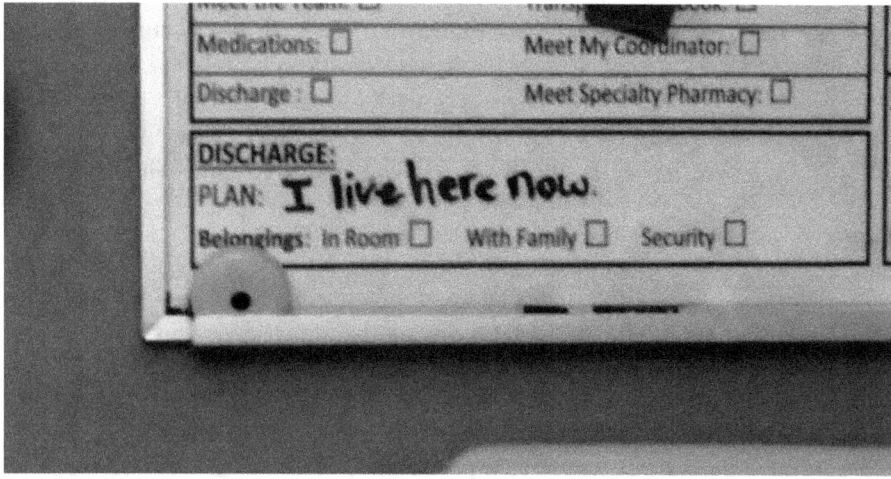

May 16, 2016 Text
Krystin to dad: Hearing is done! Took all of 2 minutes. It went as well as you'd expect. Dick is a nice guy. You on campus today? I know we don't know when exactly I'm moving, but I have a bag of dirty clothes that I'd like washed before I move, if possible. I could even come down to the entrance and hand it to you.
Dad: I am not. Message Kathy and see if she could pick it up. Dick say the hearing went well?
Krystin: Ok, I will ask her. Yes, he said to tell you it went well! It was literally a 2 minute call. Question question question, boom boom boom, done. All yes/no questions. Super easy.
Dad: Good. See you tomorrow morning.
Krystin: Okey dokey.

May 18, 2016 Email
Hear me out . . .
Krystin to dad:
    I have a question, and I hope you aren't appalled that I had the balls to ask this again, considering my history, but. . . . Would you be willing to pay for one more Amazon Prime Now purchase? I know I said the previous one would be the last one, but now since I'm gonna be here a little while longer, I have a few snack items I'd like to

replenish, and finally get my pop, and some organization items, like a box of sheet protectors and a couple binder pockets, for the 3-ring binder I already have. I'm organizing ALL the paperwork I have for, well, everything. Also the things I've torn out of the magazines I've read. It's the best way for me to keep everything together, and I know I didn't have these things in my desk at my apartment, so they aren't things in any of the boxes. The purchase total is under $30. Well, maybe a little over once tax is included. I know I don't really have any money for stuff like this, but having my snacks that I like and staying occupied helps me stay sane and in a good mood.

I know mom said a while ago to give you guys a list of things I'd want and then you guys could get them for me (instead of me going to the gift shop), but this way, I can get them NOW, and not have to wait for you or mom to be able to go to Target or wherever. I would not save payment info, and I absolutely promise never to make any purchases without your consent. Well, and I wouldn't be able to anyway, since I wouldn't save the info. I learned my lesson from last time, and I ESPECIALLY learned now not to watch stuff on Amazon Video.

No hard feelings if you say no. Considering what happened before, I would understand. Mom already turned me down.

I'm guessing no visit tomorrow, since you guys will be moving?

Ly.

May 18, 2016 Text
Dad to Krystin: See email.
Krystin: I don't have anything yet, but I'll keep an eye out for it. I'm guessing it's about my car.
Dad: No. About how you getting to Logan house tomorrow. Who's transporting you?
Krystin: I'm under the impression that the move has been pushed back! Everyone here thinks so, too, since I was denied SS. Since I need that to pay room and board, right?
Dad: Well, we're moving all your stuff tomorrow because Leota said we should.
Krystin: Ok, that's my stuff, not me. But I dunno, it's up to the docs.
Dad: I guess we'll see.
Krystin: I don't know if everyone is on the same page. I mean, Leota knows I was denied SS. But we're gonna appeal it. I need to talk to Beth, here, asap, and see what she knows and who she's been in touch

with. Apparently a lot of people are denied the first time, but approved the second time. Manuel mentioned that today, too. But yeah, like you said, we'll see. At this point we won't know anything until tomorrow!
Dad: Going to bed now. Sleep well! And maybe move tomorrow!
Krystin: Guten nacht!

May 19, 2016 Facebook
Hallelujah, it's discharge day!!

May 19, 2016 Facebook
FREEDOM!
I sure did accumulate a lot of stuff over 3 months.

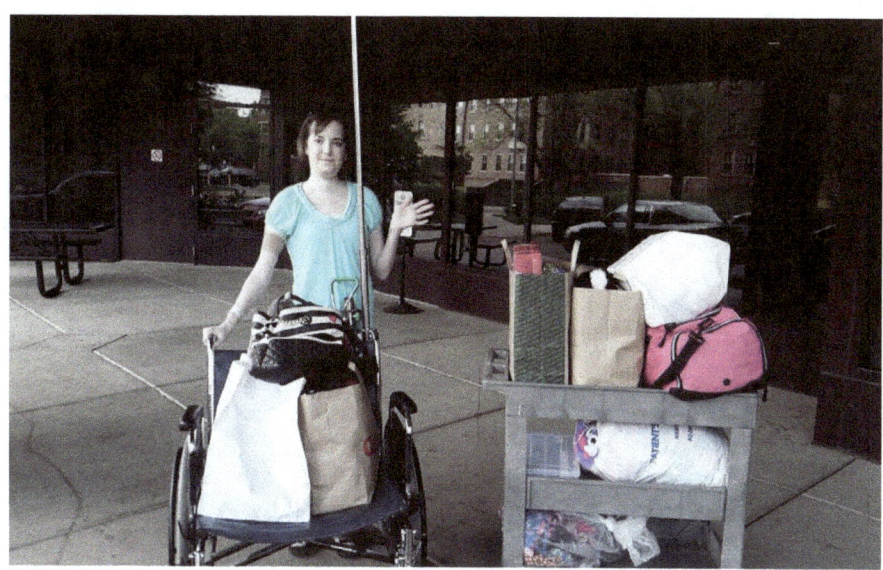

Chapter 17

Life at Logan House

May 19, 2016 Email
dope
Dad to Krystin:
   You're moving! Finally!
   We brought all your stuff to the Logan house (just got back to 4020) — but I kept out the clothes from the hospital, thinking I would bring them to you tomorrow. Argh. So you'll have to dig out new clothes to wear.
   Talk to you later. Let me know how things go!

May 19, 2016 Text
Dad: Are you moved?
Krystin: I'm at the house. Making up my bed now.
Dad: Now that you've seen it, look ok?
Krystin: Yeah, it does! Very crowded with all my stuff, but I'll slowly get everything in its place.
Dad: And get rid of some stuff, right? Glad you like it.
Krystin: Yes, I have a lot of sorting to do!
Dad: You eat your first dinner there?
Krystin: Yup. Chicken and pasta noodles with some kind of pesto-esque spicing. It was really good.
Dad: Great! Tomorrow more unpacking and sorting. Have fun!
Krystin: Yup. Fun stuff. And thanks!

May 20, 2016 Text
Dad to Krystin: So how things going today?
Krystin: Pretty good. Was a busy morning, but now I have time to do more unpacking.
Dad: What made it busy?
Krystin: Meds, breakfast, paperwork, chatting, got low, going over protocols, got low again, lunch, more talking about house stuff.
Dad: Oh. Hope you don't keep getting low!
Krystin: Us, too! First time was 48.
Dad: Hmmm. Too much insulin.
Krystin: We calculated and measured everything out exactly. It shouldn't have happened.

(later) Krystin: Are you going to give me some money when I see you next? And my clean laundry. ☺ I was invited to go get nails done with Jane, the other female resident, and one of the managers, tomorrow.
Dad: I can give you some money but wasn't planning on coming up until Sunday.
Krystin: Ok, I'll just go to be social.

May 21, 2016 Text
Krystin to dad: Do you think $100 is a reasonable amount to give me? They moved the nail outing to tomorrow, so I can get my nails done, too.
Dad: Ok. What time is outing?
Krystin: Afternoon. Sometime after lunch. It was going to be at 2 today, so I'm guessing same time tomorrow. But we can go whenever really, we don't have to make an appointment or anything.
Dad: Just wondering when I should get there with money. I'll aim for late morning.
Krystin: Okey dokey. Also, I think we should set up that shelving unit in my living room area, and I'll put my books and some other stuff on that.
Dad: They have facility guys who can do that for you.
Krystin: Who has my bulletin board? And trash can from my kitchen?
Dad: Not me. Ask your mother. We come up about 11.
Krystin: Ok, see you then!

May 24, 2016 Text
Krystin to dad: I made stir fry dinner tonight!
Dad: Just for you or for everybody?
Krystin: Everyone. They all said it was good!
Dad: Good for you!

May 27, 2016 Text
Krystin to dad: Going to the ER for emergency scope of my esophagus. Stent has migrated slightly, but still sutured, so it's pulling on the sutures, which is extremely painful. Can hardly eat or swallow my pills cuz of the difficulty and pain. Will keep you posted.
Dad: Oh gad. So this wasn't a cure-all. Damn.
Gary to Pat: K in hospital until Tuesday. Meridien hopes they can take her back when stent issue dealt with.
Krystin to dad: Fml.

Dad: I am so sorry. Will come see you tomorrow. Talked to someone from Meridien. They hope to have you back after Tuesday.
Krystin: I don't know why they wouldn't.
Pat to Gary: Hopes? What does that mean??
Gary: I am not sure. Apparently depends on the outcome of the hospital stay. I really do not understand what is going on.
Pat: And why until Tuesday?
Gary: Because that's how long she'll be in the hospital. I gather. I will go see her tomorrow and try to find out what's going on.
(later) Krystin to dad: Still in ER waiting to go upstairs. I will let you know room when I get there. Someone at the house is bringing me some stuff.

May 28, 2016 Facebook
Krystin Engstrand is feeling frustrated at University of Minnesota Medical Center.
Well, this is happening again. The stent in my esophagus has decided to defy gravity and move UP my esophagus. It is extremely painful; like one of those sticky, spiky burr balls that stick to your clothes is sitting in my throat. Until it's repositioned and sutured back in place, no swallowing anything (too painful), and back on tube feeds.

May 29, 2016 Text
Krystin to dad: Going down for the procedure shortly.
Dad: Wow. Good.
(later) Krystin: They replaced the stent.
Dad: Really??? That's great, right? So you are on what kind of diet? Can you go back to Logan house now?
Krystin: Don't know timeline for going home. Still on soft diet, I'm sure.
Dad: I'd sure be asking to get out fast! But is this good? They have some reason to believe it will stay in place?
Krystin: I certainly hope so!
Dad: Hope you go home tomorrow!
Krystin: Me too!

May 30, 2016 Text
Dad to Krystin: Any news about getting out?
Krystin: Nope, none. I'm hoping tomorrow.
Dad: You staying in touch with Logan house?

Krystin: Yup. I'm convinced I have lung cancer. I decided that, today.
Dad: Good grief. I hope you get a medical opinion about that before you jump to any conclusions!
Krystin: Lol, of course. Of the dozen or so signs and symptoms, I only have 2. But, it's my upper right abdomen, and I've already had my gallbladder removed, so all that's left up there is ribs and a lung. And the pain is even sharper when I inhale; especially if I take a deep breath. That's the lungs! And yes, my nurse put a note in to the docs.
Dad: Good!

May 31, 2016 Text
Dad to Krystin: At clinic, will now walk to hospital to see you!
Krystin: You must've just missed me.
Dad: Left your room after was there 30 minutes. So what's up today?
Krystin: Discharging soon!
Dad: Today? Great!
Krystin: Hold that thought. Discharge will depend partly on results of the ultrasound I just had on my arm, where that clot was. They're deciding if they need to send me home with Lovanox (blood thinner) shots, or just Coumadin. So, may be tomorrow at this point. *sigh
Dad: Ugh. But why could it not be later today or early evening?
Krystin: Taking longer to schedule damn procedure than it did to talk to doc. All is fine, nothing bad. It very well could be, if they look at the pictures and make a decision before leaving for the night. My nurse is pushing them.
Dad: Good. Hope you go!
Krystin: One more night here. (unhappy)
Dad: That's too bad. You get out early tomorrow?
Krystin: Hopefully! I will talk with the team and decide if I'll go home with the shots.
Dad: I won't be on campus tomorrow, so keep me posted.

June 1, 2016 Text
Krystin to dad: Nope, not today. (unhappy)
Dad: Well crap.

June 2, 2016 Text
Krystin to dad: Sigh. Not today, either. Maybe Saturday. The house management decided that they want the hospital to get my INR to a therapeutic level before going home, so that they don't have to worry

about the shots. This stay is going to end up being longer than it was supposed to. Again.
Dad: Shit.
Krystin: My sentiments exactly.

June 3, 2016 Text
Dad to Krystin: Any update?
Krystin: No, nothing new. Just waiting for my INR to reach 2, and today it was still only 1.25. Was 1.06 yesterday. At this rate, 3-4 more days. (unhappy)
Dad: Ugh

June 4, 2016 Text
Krystin to dad: INR 1.54 today. I know it won't hit 2 by tomorrow, but maybe home on Monday!
Dad: Too long. Why can't you just have shots for couple of days at Logan?
Krystin: Idk, their reasoning doesn't make sense. They don't want to have to worry about me getting a clot, and the staff not knowing what having a clot looks like or what to do, or making sure I actually get the shot when it's due, etc. They feel safer having the hospital get me to my goal INR level.

June 4, 2016 Email
RE: now what?
Krystin to dad:
    This is late finally getting back to you, but my answer hasn't changed
    First I'm going to focus on finishing unpacking all the boxes.
    I haven't had time to sit and ponder my future. Going back to SPA, yes. Writing, yes. And I'm serious about going to nursing school. I'll have to find a way to pay for it and work around my work schedule, but I do really want to pursue that.

-------- *Original message* --------
From: Gary Engstrand
Date: 05/24/2016
To: Krystin Engstrand
Subject: now what?

Now that you seem to be settling in a place where your meds and nutrition will be handled, what are you going to do with your life? Try to get back to writing? I know you want to get back to work at least part time, but that won't take up all your life. I guess my question is whether you've thought about what you want to try to accomplish. Just wondered if you've thought about this yet.

Dad to Krystin:

Unpacking makes sense.

SPA and writing, good. I had an exchange with Pamela about lunch and my retirement; she said they'd love to have you back part-time this summer because they've got 3 people going out on maternity leaves. So you're supposed to contact David when you're ready. I guessed you might be able to return mid-July.

You can get 75% of tuition covered by Regents Scholarship. But you also have to be admitted to the School of Nursing; I don't know how stringent their requirements are. And man, you're going to have to take a lot of science courses. If you haven't, you should take a look at the curriculum--I assume it's posted somewhere on the web.

June 6, 2016 Text

Krystin to dad: Supposedly leaving around 1 today!

Dad: Good!

(later) Krystin: Nope, now not today.

Dad: Well crap. Driving now. Let me know more later.

Krystin: There's a care conference here tomorrow at 10, and the team wants you there. Can you make it?

Dad: Not easily. What are they going to say?

Krystin: Tube feeding, my diet, overall plan. I don't know what else exactly, but Beth said she'd like you there.

Dad: That will be difficult. How about your mom? Or Kathy? My last day of work is Tuesday and I have a couple of final meetings this week. One is tomorrow at 10.

Krystin: Ok. I'll ask mom, and can you ask Kathy?

Dad: What about Liz or Tanya? They should be there.

Krystin: They will. It was their idea.

Dad: Not sure why your mother or I need to be there.

Krystin: Me neither, really. They want everyone on the same page, since the discharge summary they (the house) got in their email is different from the one I was handed, because one thing changed, and a new med was ordered. But because they were different, Tanya wants

to hear from everyone involved in my care this round what their discharge expectations are. I dunno, it's dumb that I couldn't leave today, I think. Should I have Beth call you?
Dad: No. Tell her to call your mother, since I can't be there.
Krystin: I'm already texting with mom. No Kathy?
Dad: That is an unnecessary imposition. This is silly. Neither your mother nor I can be at Logan to have anything to do with meds. What role could we possibly play?
Krystin: I don't know! That's why I asked if Beth should call you. I assume it's for times when I'm with one of you for more than just a few hours. So that you know the plan, too. That's my guess. It's more than just meds.
Dad: Your mother can talk with us about what she learns.
Krystin: Ok

June 8, 2016 Text
Dad to Krystin: You getting out today?
Krystin: Got out yesterday! Been back at the house since about 4:15 yesterday afternoon. Sorry, I guess I thought you knew! Getting many more boxes unpacked and sorted today. Already making good progress
Dad: Great! And stick to the rules. You don't want to get kicked out!
Krystin: Oh, yes, of course, absolutely! I want them to trust me. No rule breaking.

June 10, 2016 Text
Gary to Pat: Krystin let you know she's in ICU at Abbott?
Pat: Did not. What happened?
Gary *(forwarded message from Krystin): Tanya said I needed to go in, since I hadn't had anything to drink or eat all day. So, she called for an ambulance to bring me to the hospital. Right now I'm at Abbott Northwestern hospital. I have a bowel obstruction, along with dehydration and tachycardia. And at North Mem they put a port line in my neck. It hurts. By my abdominal and back pain is a bit better. No idea how long I'll be here. I'm in the ICU, getting fluids and antibiotics for a urine cultures. That's all I got for ya. Ly.*
Pat: Great.
Gary: Yeah.
Pat: ICU for IV fluids? There's something here we don't know. A person doesn't lay in the ICU for that.

Gary: She said also tachycardia.
Pat: Common with dehydration. Sounds like it might be more than that.
Gary: I guess we'll see.
(later) Dad to Krystin: What's going on?
Krystin: Being transferred to the U this evening, so I can be under the care of my transplant team.
Dad: Good, I suppose. No idea when out, of course.
Krystin: Nope, of course not.
Dad: Keep me posted, as usual.
Krystin: Made it to 7A. Room 210. Nice view in this room.
Dad: And any diagnosis?
Krystin: Just got here, so haven't seen the docs yet. I still need the CT scan with contrast, to verify if it is actually a bowel obstruction or something else. That will probably be tomorrow.
Dad: Well, let me know. Hope you're feeling better.
Krystin: Yes, much better than yesterday.
Dad: Well, at least one thing better!
Krystin: True.

June 11, 2016 Facebook
Krystin Engstrand is feeling defeated at University of Minnesota Medical Center.
My spirit has really taken a hit lately. How am I supposed to pursue any of my ambitions and aspirations if I keep ending up here for unforeseeable and unavoidable reasons? What kind of life is being an inpatient frequent flyer? This blows. I just wanna go home, and stay there.

June 11, 2016 Text
Dad to Krystin: I take it no news.
Krystin to dad: They wanna keep me one more night, of course, to make sure things have cleared up, even if I'm pretty sure they have, since I've now been having runny stools all night and day.
Dad: Well, that's better than 2 weeks! You must be feeling much better. Were you also dehydrated?
Krystin: Yes to both.
Dad: How you get dehydrated? Seems odd. Staff not let you drink enough? ;-)

Krystin: Thursday, I didn't eat or drink anything cuz was too distended, nauseous, and in pain."

June 12, 2016 Text
Dad to Krystin: Hope the plan remains that you go home today!
Krystin: Me too. I'm going to push them.
Dad: If you feel good and systems seem to be working, no reason to stay there!
Krystin: I never should've been here. The issue worked itself out within a day without their help.
Dad: Tell them that, although the Logan people understandably get nervous when you ailing. They don't want anything bad to happen on their watch, and who knew the problem would work itself out?
Krystin: If I do discharge today, who knows what time. If you wanted to come visit and bring me some more money, that would be ok.
(later) Krystin: Well, I'll be here all day. Logan house won't take me back today cuz it's a weekend and none of the regular staff are working. So, I can never be discharged on a weekend day.

June 12, 2016 Email
Proposition
Krystin to dad:

Now that I'm close to being done unpacking at the house, I have a list of things I'd like/need that the house won't buy for me. Such as a clothes steamer (yes, I actually want one of these, and I'm guessing you'd believe I need one to get wrinkles out of my clothes), a shower mat, a robe, some things for hanging my art safely on the walls, and a small lamp for my nightstand. Amongst a few other things. I can get them on Amazon Prime Now, for similar prices as Target, but Prime will deliver it to me within 2 hours for free. Since giving me a credit card number isn't an option, what about you buying me an Amazon gift card online, and I can use that? The total is about $81. I know it sounds like a lot, but these are things that would be greatly helpful to have. Let me know what you think. If I order soon enough, I can get the items on my list. If I wait until tomorrow, and have it delivered to the house, I don't know if the Amazon warehouse closest to Brooklyn Center will have all the items.

Dad to Krystin
    I don't want to do this amazon prime routine. We'll talk about this stuff.

June 17, 2016 Text
Krystin to dad: Dumbest thing ever: I have to go to the ER by ambulance cuz my blood pressure is elevated. They're afraid I'm gonna fall and hit my head. Even though I feel completely fine.
Dad: Jeez. Good luck. Hope you get back home today. We just about to leave campus to go north.
Krystin: Can you leave me a little more cash, if possible?? We have a few activities this weekend and I don't think I have enough for it all.
Dad: We're leaving town. I cannot today. I don't know if you can borrow any. You may be in the hospital :-(
Krystin: No, can't borrow any. Maybe mom can, even though she usually says no. I'll ask anyway.
Pat to Gary: I'm on the road but if you have a chance to call me, please do. Meridian called re: k. Need share info. Thnx.
Gary: In Walker at grocery store. Will call a bit later. Just don't tell me they're kicking her out.
Pat: Not yet.
Gary: Do we have to talk before end of weekend? I'd rather not think about this while at the lake. . . .
Pat: No. Just please contact me before you next see her.
Gary: Will do. No plans to see her before sometime next week anyway.
Pat: Enjoy the lake. I'm camping and it's pouring. These are the happy times!!
Gary: If Krystin texts me?
Pat: She might. In hospital.
Gary: She told me that. Didn't sound serious, but who knows from her.
Pat: Bingo. But stop thinking about it now like you wanted to and enjoy your time away. Just call me end of weekend.

June 18, 2016 Text
Dad to Krystin: How you doing?
Krystin: Doing ok. I have a sitter with me at all times again, so I don't steal people's shit, cuz mom told them I have a history of stealing. Not once has the thought even crossed my mind to go into one of the other bedrooms and take something. Thanks mom.

(later) Dad: You must be back home!
Krystin: Yeah, back home same day. Blood and urine tests all came back clean and normal. I've been trying to tell Tanya that it's stress that's raising my blood pressure, but she doesn't believe me.
Dad: What stress?
Krystin: Uhh, from everything going on the last month. All the hospitalizations, moving into the house, all the rules, etc. It has all been very stressful.
Dad: I see. Hope that stops!
Krystin: Me too!

June 23, 2016 Text
Krystin to dad: G-J tube replacement day! 12:15 check-in.
Dad: Great!
Krystin: Were you thinking of coming to visit me later today?
Dad: No. Have social event with old friend at 430 in Woodbury and bunch of errands before that. Now waiting to get computer reconnected to umn [University of Minnesota email service, umn.edu] Got kicked out because retired!
Krystin: When would be a good time to get some money, then? I feel like I've been trying all week. What if we stop by after my procedure, even if you're not home? Will E be home?
Dad: I'm curious why you need money right now. I don't know if Elliott will be home.
Krystin: Because I have none. I like to have some for outings and activities. The house doesn't cover anything we do. There's an event this weekend I want to attend. Wouldn't you feel uncomfortable if you had no money on you, and no way to get any? It's not like I'm spending it on clothes. It's all been on activities or things I need for my room or the house (that isn't covered by the house budget).
Dad: Ok
Krystin: So . . . what should we do? I want to go see Finding Dory on Saturday with Jane. Did Tanya call you today?
Dad: Come tomorrow before 11.
Krystin: If someone can bring me, then ok. You are a very busy guy now! Tanya has been trying to get hold of you.
Dad: I know. She tried twice to call me and the connection was horrible. She may have called when I was out but I don't interrupt a conversation with a friend over a beer to take calls. I am not available 24/7 to whomever may want to talk to me!

Krystin: I know, but lately you have been hard to get hold of and take a long time to respond to things; longer than you used to. And someone can bring me tomorrow.
Dad: She [Tanya] said she'd email me. She hasn't. And I don't have to be here tomorrow anyway.
Krystin: Damn. I'm getting a cold.
Dad: Take care of yourself.

June 25, 2016 Email
feeling good?
Dad to Krystin:
    You seemed to feel better yesterday than I've seen you in some time, and you looked better, too. Are you feeling better? I sure hope so!
Krystin to dad:
    Yes, I am feeling better. Thanks for noticing! Of course seeing the kitties had a big part in that, too. I know I came to pick up money, but I was looking forward more to seeing the furry kids. No offense to you, of course. I've seen you occasionally. I haven't seen the kitties in months. And tomorrow I get to see MY girls! =^.^=

June 30, 2016 Email
Visit
Krystin to dad:
    When you come today, can you bring me some money, like $100? Tanya brought Jane and me to get our nails done, and I didn't have enough, so I owe her $25. Then on Saturday we have an activity that's about $15. And Tanya wants me to do something on the 4th, though I don't know what yet. I'm done buying stuff at Target that I need for my room, so what's left over should hop last me a while.
    Thanks,

Dad to Krystin:
    I will do this, but you must remember that you're quickly going to run out of money unless you find some alternative income source.

July 4, 2016 Text
Dad to Krystin: How you doing?
Krystin: Doing ok. Been napping most of the day, cuz I was super tired all day. Been sleeping horribly lately. And my stent has moved, I think

up again, cuz it hurts to swallow and has been causing really bad, painful heartburn. Going to try to get in for an xray tomorrow.

July 5, 2016 Text
Krystin to dad: Are you free for a phone chat?
Dad: No. Out shopping. Not home for coupla hours.
Krystin: Ok. Can you give me a call when you get home?
(later) Krystin: If I ever needed a break from the house and was approved for a leave, could I spend a weekend with you guys? I'm not saying this weekend necessarily, just in general.
Dad: Probably. Would obviously have to be some understandings with Logan house.
Krystin: Of course.

July 8, 2016 Text
Dad to Krystin: Could you go out to lunch today with Elliott and me?
Krystin: Yes, I can!
(later) Krystin: Thanks again for lunch. It was really good to get out, and to see you guys. Also, Tanya approved visiting some weekend. She said it's actually encouraged.
Dad: Glad you enjoyed it. So did we. And not spend the whole time talking about medical issues! You can come over, but if before Elliott goes back to Moorhead, you get the couch! LY

July 12, 2016 Email
Dad to Krystin [I don't have the message that prompted this reply]:
    As for Friday: Krystin, I would rather not come. I've tried to be there for you when you've needed me over the past many months, but I think that daddy can (should) begin to bow out of your treatment/life regimen--you are 31 years old and I would hope wouldn't need me to be so deeply involved in your life now that things seem to be stabilizing and you're getting back to a reasonably normal life (he says keeping his fingers crossed). Does that make sense? LY

July 16, 2016 Text
Krystin to dad: Are you around today?
Dad: I am now.
Krystin: Do you have any cash on you? Tanya has a few activities planned over the next number of days and I don't have enough for the ones that require money. And mom and I are going to go to a movie

and I don't know if she's going to cover ticket and/or snack cost. And next week I'm finally going to get a valid state ID.

Dad: I could give you a $100 bill.

Krystin: It would be tomorrow. A staff comes in at noon, so it would be after I eat lunch. Early afternoon? Then I could also get that box you still have. And see kitties! And Kathy, if she's there?

(later) Krystin: The meeting went really well. They decided I don't need constant supervision anymore, so I can move about the house on my own!

July 18, 2016 Text

Krystin to dad: Could I come stay at the house until Weds morning?

Dad: Why? What's up with docs? If just to get away from Logan house, not sure that's a good idea.

Krystin: Well, yes, it is. Meridien won't let me have my pain med at their house, even though a Meridien nurse approved it. Mostly it's Tanya who made that decision. And she's not a doctor. The whole reason I went to the ER on Saturday was cuz of pain. I have an appt with thoracic on Weds morning, and I am not willing to put up with this pain anymore until then. And they won't admit me to the hospital just for that reason. But I've had enough. Yes, I do need a break from this house, and I also don't want to be in bad pain for the next 2 days. It's cruel and inhumane.

Dad: I'm guessing there could be difficulties with you leaving. Not sure what's going on with denying meds a doc prescribed. Have Tanya get in touch with me if you wish.

Krystin: If Meridian isn't equipped to handle my health care needs, then maybe I don't belong here. I want to be in charge of my health care again. The whole medical establishment is ignoring my pain. They're driving me off a bridge, I hope they realize that.

Dad: I don't know what to say. If you have a prescription, you should be able to take it.

Krystin: Exactly. But it wasn't written by the pain management team themselves, so I don't get it at all. And Tanya already disposed of it.

Dad: The only thing I can say is that maybe you should be more forceful. Meridian wants to keep you as a client, and I don't know how it would look if you said you wanted to move. Problem is that options are really limited.

Krystin: I need a nap now after 5 hours of sleep last night, so will get back in touch a bit later.

(later) Krystin: Oh, and it would be pointless to talk to Tanya. She'll just argue and make everything my fault and tell you all the things I did wrong.
Dad: I don't know there's much I can do.
Krystin: Yeah, that too. There's not much anyone can do, really, if they're going to make me deal with the pain.
Dad: I'd be talking loudly to the docs on Wednesday.
Krystin: Yup. Although it's all up to Dawn with pain management, and I'm not seeing her on Weds. However, I CAN send her a message on MyChart and "talk" loudly to her. Yeah, I'll do that tonight. Maybe she'll be sympathetic for me and make an exception this time as far as pain med.
Dad: Good idea.

July 18, 2016 Facebook
Krystin Engstrand is feeling pissed off.

I am suffocating, and I just need to breathe.
I'm smothered under pain and pressure, I must be relieved.
Nothing I do is right, nothing they say is fair.
I cry and scream and throw a fit, but no one seems to care.
Nobody will listen, to what I have to say.
My life doesn't seem important, but I'm living every day.
I'm angry and alone, lost inside my mind.
No one will look beyond my face, to see what they might find.

July 19, 2016 Facebook
Krystin Engstrand is feeling surprised at University of Minnesota Medical Center, East Bank.
Apparently my blood is so thin that one little paper cut and I'll bleed out and die in like 2 minutes. Or something like that. Anyway, my docs didn't think it was a good idea for me to be out in the big dangerous world. At least until it's under control. Oh and maybe an infection in my liver? So, this will be an interesting stay.
This is how I feel about it, btw.

July 20, 2016 Text
Dad to Krystin: Are you there? Can we still plan on you for cat care and plant watering or should we ask Spence?
Krystin: Sorry, I'm here. I still plan on doing it! I'm here cuz when the home care nurse came to the house yesterday to draw my INR level, it was through the roof. Monica said to go to the ER right away. Pain is

still the same, and still nothing is being done to manage it. Tanya is pissing me off cuz even the ER doc said he'd give me something but Tanya said no. ARGH. Plus, she answers the doctor's questions FOR me, won't even let me talk. It's like, I can answer my own health questions. She's not me. Or she'll butt in to say something, or cut me off, or after I've answered the question, she'll add some additional information that wasn't what he asked about, to ME. She feels like since she's the manager, she always has to add to the question, as if she knows my health info better than I do. Uhh, excuse me, but no. This house is giving me more stress than I need in my life

Dad: I will get back to you later about all this.

Krystin: Ok.

Dad: I think I should write to Leota. But I can make it gentle.

Krystin: Ok. It will be obvious to Tanya that it's about me, though, if and when Leota talks to her. But she's just TOO aggressive, and literally NONE of my docs like her. Which reflects badly on me.

Dad: None of the docs like her? How do you know that?

Krystin: Word goes around the medical staff. They talk, they exchange messages. And nope, none of them. She's too mean and aggressive. She has shouted at almost all of them at some point. Actually shouted. And a couple different docs have told me.

July 21, 2016 Email

Dad to Krystin:

    I sent a message to Leota. I think, however, that it is best you do not know that.

Krystin to dad:

    Can I see the email you sent her, so that I can know what it is that I don't know?

Dad to Krystin:

    No. It is best that you NOT know, so you can in all honesty say you have no idea what I said if you are asked.

    But you know what you've told me. . . .

Krystin to dad:

    Ok, fair enough.

Dad to Krystin:
   Where are you? How you doing? What's up?

Krystin:
   Still at the hospital. Absolutely nothing happened today. Now I'm stuck here over the weekend, too, with nothing happening. Doing alright, but in pain and they're doing nothing to help it, of course. Slept almost none last night. Now just waiting to see what thoracic wants to do about my stent. Part of it isn't right up against my esophagus, so things (mostly liquids) are going between the stent and my esophagus, pooling there, then being pushed back up and over the side of the stent, and down my esophagus via the stent. Does that make sense? So maybe they'll need to suture it in. It's on the right side, which would definitely explain the pain on my right side!

Dad:
   Uff da. I'm sorry. We have a wedding tomorrow at W A Frost, so maybe we stop by on way. Then off to Nebraska on Sunday morning. I better have Spence plan on doing cats and plants.

Krystin:
   Yeah, now I'm thinking he probably should

Dad:
   Well, that's a new twist. Hope they get in on Monday and fix it!

Krystin:
   Last time I was here they did it on a Sunday, so who knows, maybe this weekend. I'm on the neurology unit, cuz that was the only unit with an available bed. I wanna be up on 7A!

Dad:
   Will keep fingers crossed.

July 23, 2016 Text
Dad to Krystin: I'm sorry we didn't get over to see you. I hope everything goes well while we are in Nebraska. Keep me posted on developments. LY
Krystin: It's ok, I know how life happens like that sometimes. Docs think there's actually some food particle stuck in the stent, and that's

why it feels narrow. Food has a hard time passing that particle. I'd be happy to see what it is! Nothing happening this weekend, of course, so I won't know the plan until Monday. Hopefully they'll even do the procedure on Monday! (Yeah right). At least the stent isn't coming out. AND the doc finally put in a one-time order for Dilaudid, for when I'm ready to go to sleep, so hopefully I'll actually get some sleep tonight!
Dad: Hope so, too! Will be in touch. Long boring drive tomorrow :-(Sleep tight.

July 23, 2016 Email
your bankruptcy has been approved
Dad to Krystin:
    Came in the mail today.

July 24, 2016 Facebook
Krystin Engstrand is feeling aggravated at University of Minnesota Medical Center, East Bank.
I am so fed up with the pain management team. I'm in their care, and they're doing nothing about my severe pain, except give me Tylenol. The first rule of pain management is to treat the patient's pain. How can a person have quality of life when they're in constant, untreated pain? They can't, that's how. I'm on day 3 of almost no sleep because of my pain. What is wrong with these people??

July 29, 2016 Text
Dad to Krystin: Any news?
Krystin: On our way to the house!
Dad: So you're all better and happy!
Krystin: Yes! "Happy" is relative, but essentially yes; especially since I'm back on my soft diet!
Dad: I am hoping happier increases. Enough said. Eat away!

August 2, 2016 Text
Dad: How's life back out of the hospital?
Krystin: Much better than IN the hospital! It's fine though. Back to same 'ol group home living. I wish I were back at work, and had a car to drive, and an income, and was able to go out alone with friends. But none of those things have been discussed yet. Good news is that I FINALLY have an appointment with Dawn @ pain management

tomorrow! Maybe something good and helpful will actually come out of it.
Dad: You can always start the discussions.
Krystin: yeah, I'm gonna bring up work tomorrow with Tanya. I NEED to email Dave soon. Eventually they aren't going to be able to hold a position for me anymore. They've waited a long time for me!
Dad: I think that's right. I would not delay much longer.

August 3, 2016 Email
not to tell you your business, but . . . .
Dad to Krystin:
    if I were you, I'd contact Dave now and tell him you're trying to figure out details related to returning to work part-time--and ask him, by the way, is there still a position for you to return to?

Krystin to dad:
    That's a good idea. I'll do that tonight after dinner!

August 6, 2016 Facebook
Krystin Engstrand is with Peggy Hinz and 2 others.
What a wonderful day to celebrate the marriage (the wedding was a couple months ago, in Michigan; today was the reception for us MN folk) of one of my closest friends. Yay for one of the most perfect couples I know!

[L to R: Christine Hinz Lenzen, Pat Engstrand, Krystin, Peggy Hinz (Christine's mother)]

August 8, 2016 Text
Dad to Krystin: Going off to bed shortly, but thought I'd inquire I'd things going ok there. And if any news on job front.
Krystin: Things going alright still. Dave has been in touch with Neil, to start discussing my return. Tanya and I even discussed it more today, so hopefully that means I could be back at work by the end of the month!
Dad: Great!

August 29, 2016 Facebook
This is how bad my acid reflux is: every single tooth on the top row needs a filling. Today was round 1 of about 5 or 6. I can feel the novocaine numbness all the way up to my eyeball!

September 1, 2016 Text
Krystin to dad: Got weighed at the doc appt on Tuesday. I've gained 10 pounds since moving to the Logan house! Today I saw thoracic and he said I can discontinue the nightly tube feeding since I'm eating so well and not having problems with my stent!!!!!!!!!
Dad: Great!!!!
Krystin: Today I learned that I should be dead. Apparently it's in my medical chart that when I was in the hospital for that 3 months, my whole body was failing and like none of the docs expected me to make it through. Did you know that? Tanya and I were talking about it today and she didn't realize that I didn't know that. She said oops, maybe I wasn't supposed to know that everyone thought I was going to die. Wonderful. Guess I showed them. No one ever told me to my face how bad things really were at the time. Tbh, I'm a little bit in shock. *I* didn't realize how bad things were, health wise. It's a very weird and indescribable emotional feeling that I have, once again, cheated death.
Dad: I did not know. Glad you showed 'em! Now presumably you are a long way from that point!
Krystin: Yes, I absolutely am.

September 13, 2016 Text
Krystin to dad: So, I'm going back on an insulin pump around the end of October. The OmniPod.
Dad: Glad for you if it's what you want.
Krystin: Yeah. You know as well as I do how much I hate doing so many shots.

September 24, 2016 Facebook
Krystin Engstrand is registered to vote.
No way in hell would I miss voting in this election, even if someone paid me to!

October 2, 2016 Facebook
Krystin Engstrand shared a memory — feeling nostalgic.
I wish I could go back to this time, when I still had my kitties with me and Hank and I were still together. I remember how happy I felt. I may not have those things anymore, but I do believe I can get back that happiness. I just have to find other (legal) ways of achieving it! In fact,

I'll start today, with a visit to see and cuddle my furry girls! =^.^= <3
^_^

> See Your Memories
> Krystin Engstrand
> October 2, 2014 · Saint Paul ·
> I have so much happiness in my heart. I am beyond happy to be home with my kitties, to be having the stent placed tomorrow, and to have 2 perfectly working tran . . .

October 10, 2016 Facebook
Krystin Engstrand is feeling proud.
I graduated from physical therapy today!! Yay for some enormous progress on the whole 'getting healthy' thing!

October 11, 2016 Facebook
Krystin Engstrand is at M Health Clinic and Surgery Center.
Taking my new insulin pump home from the clinic today for the first time.

October 20, 2016 Email
Krystin to dad:
Hey,

 Sorry I've been so unresponsive. It's not even like I've been that busy, so I have no excuse! Just procrastination.

 Things are a bit better with Tanya, but we still bicker a lot. I won't go into details in an email, but I had an appointment with Nancy on Tuesday, and I told her that Tanya and I seriously need couples therapy. I also told her that if things with Tanya continue like this, that I don't know how I'm going to live here long-term without losing my sanity. Tanya and I will always butt heads over a lot of things, and she's still young and immature and thinks she's always right. And what pisses me off the most is when something she says or does is contradictory and hypocritical because it'll be something that she has scolded staff or me for doing. And she pulls rules and shit out of her ass randomly. It's like she has an obsession with needing to exert her superiority over everyone.

 I better stop now or I'll just get myself riled up. I know this is the best place for me to be, and I have no intention of leaving. Tanya and

I need to better understand and respect each other, and find our median.

In other news . . . I have scurvy! Which I learned is a scary word for vitamin C deficiency. I have what looks like chickenpox, all over my body. Even my face. I have Clindamycin gel that I apply pretty much everywhere, twice a day. I started it Monday night, and I haven't seen any improvement. In fact, the spots are growing in number and spreading. I certainly hope that the gel starts working soon.

Straight from the doctor's mouth, I'm officially a 'rare medical case'. I'll probably be the one person diagnosed with scurvy in the state of MN in 2016. Yay, I'm a statistic!

That's about all for now. Tonight is the company Halloween party, so we'll all dress in our costumes and go. No idea what it'll be like. And still no update on the work front. Sigh.

Enjoy your last couple days! Ly.

Dad to Krystin:
Thanks. Scurvy? Heavens. Are you also getting vitamin C?

October 28, 2016 Message to a friend
I would absolutely love to get together. I'm STILL not back at work, so my schedule is pretty open. I want to tell you, I'm living in a group home now, in Brooklyn Center. Having many health issues, and not being able to work because of them, is considered disabled by the state. So, I'm living here, but I'm otherwise completely independent. I get help taking all my meds at their designated times, managing my diabetes, and nutrition, so I don't become malnourished again. I have pretty much my own living area on the lower level, and I get to cook meals, and I'm even the one who gets to do the grocery shopping for the house!

November 2, 2016 Text
Pat to Gary: Did you talk to Tanya?
Gary: No. What's up?
Pat: Can you call me?
Dad: Sure.
Dad to Elliott: Krystin in psych ward at U hospital. Sigh.
Elliott: She still seeing bacteria everywhere?
Dad: Idk. Probably. She not say anything to me about it when I talked to her a bit ago. She seemed to be ok, but wants them to diagnose and

deal with issue. I wonder if it isn't pharmacopoeia of drugs she's on, messing with her brain.
Elliott: Or she's institutionalized and looking for any way to be back in a hospital of some sort rather than at that house.
Dad: Who knows. Beyond my pay grade to figure out.

November 9, 2016 Text
Dad to Elliott: Is your show [his senior art show, at Moorhead State, in Moorhead, MN] a coat and tie affair? Krystin might come, too, assuming she out of hospital, which is expected tomorrow or Friday.
Elliott: No not at all. You want to drag her 4 hours away from her primary care location?
Pat to Gary: Did Krystin talk to you about coming to Moorhead and staying with you two, and then we bring her back?
Dad to Elliott: She badly wants to come to see your work and school. She can travel.
Elliott: Well I didn't invite her because I didn't want to have her sit at dinner with us and freak out about bacteria but ok. That and every time she's left the cities to go somewhere with me and mom she always suddenly feels very sick and needs someone to stop what they're doing and take her to a hospital. If I didn't know better I'd say it was an attention seeking maneuver. But your call I suppose.
Dad: Sigh. I know.
Pat to Gary: She didn't. First off, we have a room with one queen bed so she'd have to sleep on the floor. Secondly, and more importantly, I'm not excited about the idea. I take her places around the cities but do not want to take her out of town.
Dad to Elliott: She's supposedly going to be beyond seeing bacteria.
Elliott: She said that or a doctor said that?
Dad: Doc, but he can only say what she tells him. She told me same thing. Couple of her psychotropic drugs eliminated or reduced, so seems entirely possible.

November 29, 2016 Email
Predicament
Krystin to dad:
Hey,
    So, I'm finally getting worried about my financial situation. I only have $5 on me, and I still owe the house about $45-$50), and would like to have about $75 spending cash. I'm not sure when I'll get the

checks from my GRH approval, and now who knows when I'll be going back to work. AND it sucks that I have to purchase some of my medical stuff because the house doesn't pay for it. The $75 credit you gave me, was that for a bday dinner, or present, or both?

What is my balance now? I think I accidentally deleted the email from you that had the spreadsheet attached. I'm guessing it's getting pretty low. Ugh, I hate worrying about money. :/ Ly.

Dad to Krystin:
Here's the bad news.

> Krystin's funds as of 6/23/16:
> $53   balance 11/29/16

Krystin to dad:
Oh, ick. That's unfortunate. Well I don't know what to do, then. I guess be broke until I finally go back to work? Maybe I can find stuff to sell on eBay.

Dad to Krystin
I could liquidate your money in MSRS, which is a couple of thousand dollars, but I don't know if that's a good idea (yet). I'll put in another $100 in your funds.

Krystin to Dad:
Isn't MSRS my retirement??

Dad to Krystin:
Yes. It has about $6K in it. Which won't do much for you. But let's leave it be. If you can ever get back to work full time at the U, you could begin to add to it.

December 2, 2016 Email
while I think of it
Dad to Krystin:
A little fatherly advice. I think you should stop FB posts about things you think you are seeing. Both Kathy and I find that a little weird, and when we see a crumb or piece of litter but you see something alive, it certainly conveys the impression on FB that you're not in possession of your faculties.

If you are seeing things that others are not, you should be in touch with the psychiatrist again about further adjustments to drugs.

December 6, 2016 Facebook
Krystin Engstrand is feeling accomplished.
It's amazing what can happen in a year. I started 2016 as a walking corpse, almost dying; I will end it being healthier than I've been in probably 15 or so years. This year was shitty, and [I was] frequently both mentally and physically exhausted. I spent about as much time IN the hospital as I did out, if not more. But, here I am now, metaphorically standing on top of a mountain yelling "take that, life, I win! I did it!" It's true that where there's a will, there's a way. Over and over and over, I found a way, and it feels so good, because *I* feel so good!
Next step, finally going back to work.

December 11, 2016 Text
Dad to Krystin: Haven't heard from you recently. How you doing?

December 12, 2016 Text
Krystin to dad: I'm doing pretty good. Keeping busy with all the arts and crafts stuff I've been making!
Dad: Any news re job?
Krystin: We're planning on beginning of Jan. Hopefully within the first week!

December 14, 2016 Text
Gary to Kathy: Krystin being admitted to hospital. Fever, vomiting, creatinine levels elevated.
Kathy: Oh crap. Who told you?
Gary: She called me. At hospital. Will call back later with update.
Pat to Gary: Has anyone there heard any more from Krystin?
Gary: Nothing beyond her call to me to say she was being admitted. Said she would call back later.

December 15, 2016 Text
Dad to Krystin: How you doing?

December 15, 2016 Facebook
Krystin Engstrand is feeling sick at Fairview University Medical Center.
Throwing up all night. Temp of 102.5. Too weak to walk. Not why I'd choose to be in the hospital, but eh, I've been here for worse.

December 16, 2016 Facebook
From when I was at the ER on Wednesday. I'm adding an amendment to the Constitution: Thou shalt not covet my pizza. [I think she meant an addition to the Ten Commandments.]

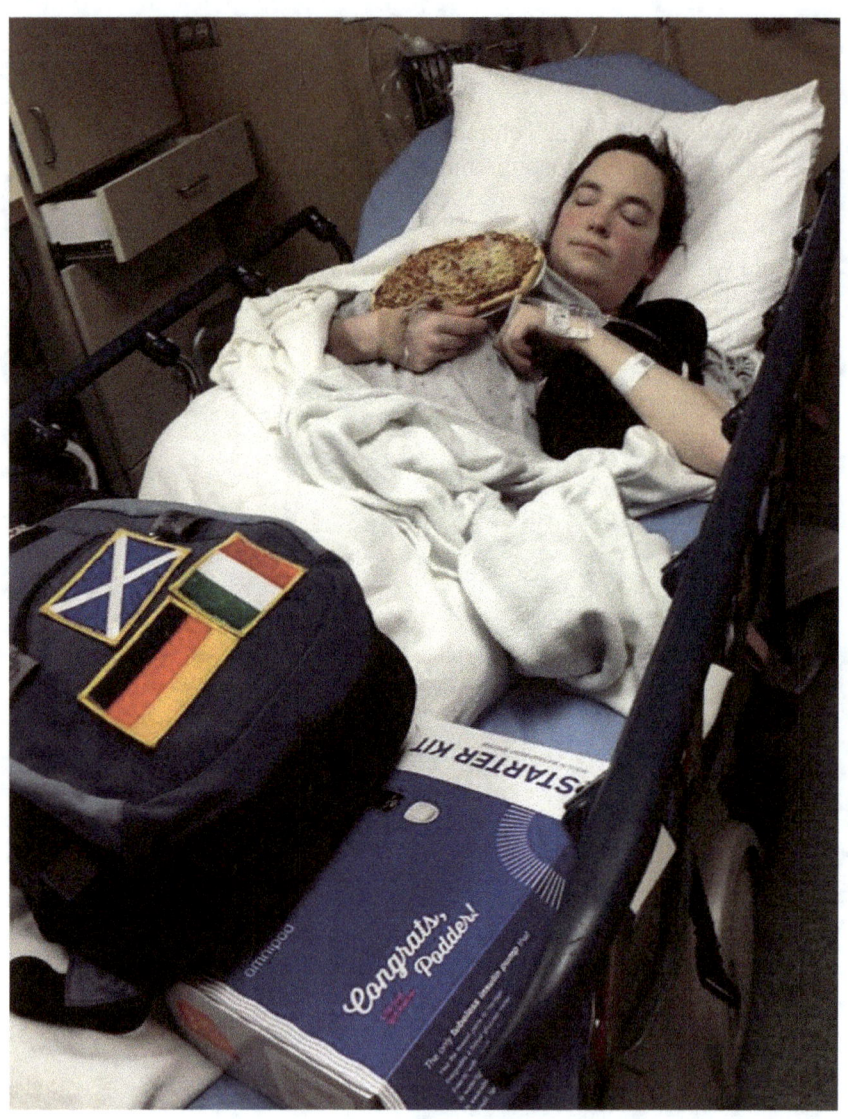

December 19, 2016 Facebook
I get to go back to work right after the new year!! I know people don't say this too often, but I'm so excited! After 10 months of hospitalizations, moving, and getting to a healthy state, this will be the best New Year ever.

January 8, 2017 Facebook
Krystin Engstrand is at Fairview University Medical Center.
I am resurfacing to the world of facebook. I have been spending my last 8 days in the ICU, after having a surgical procedure that left me with a brand new 10" incision to go along with it. Good times.

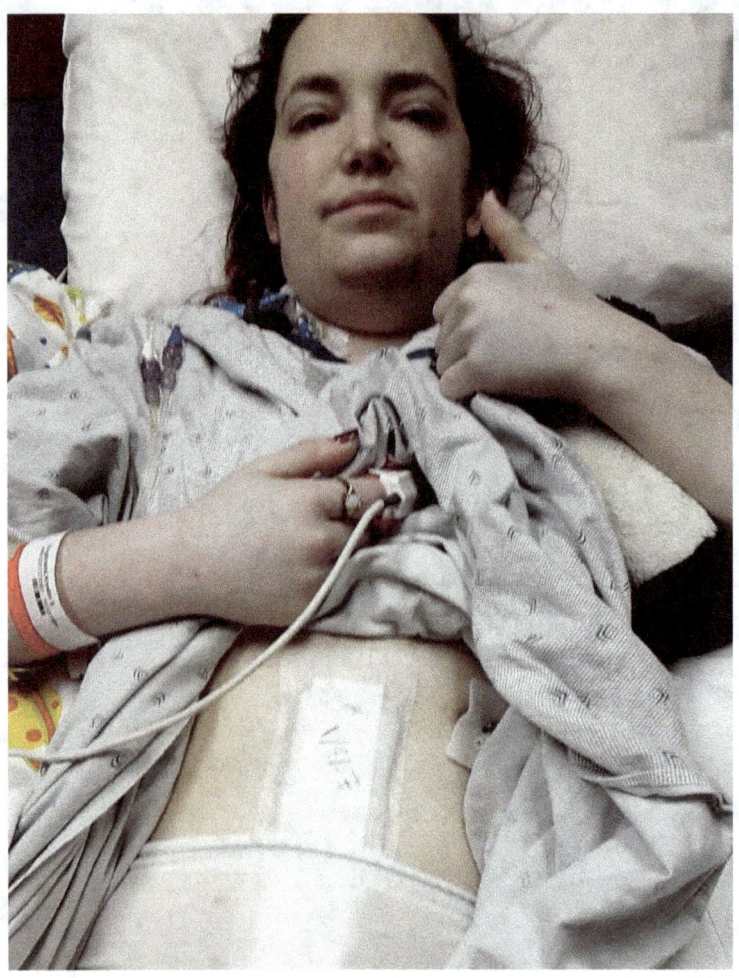

Krystin: Imagine taking a section of a garden hose, bending it in half, then also twisting it in a loop. So, a big 'ol mess of fun. That entire section of my small intestine was removed. Not gonna lie; it hurts.

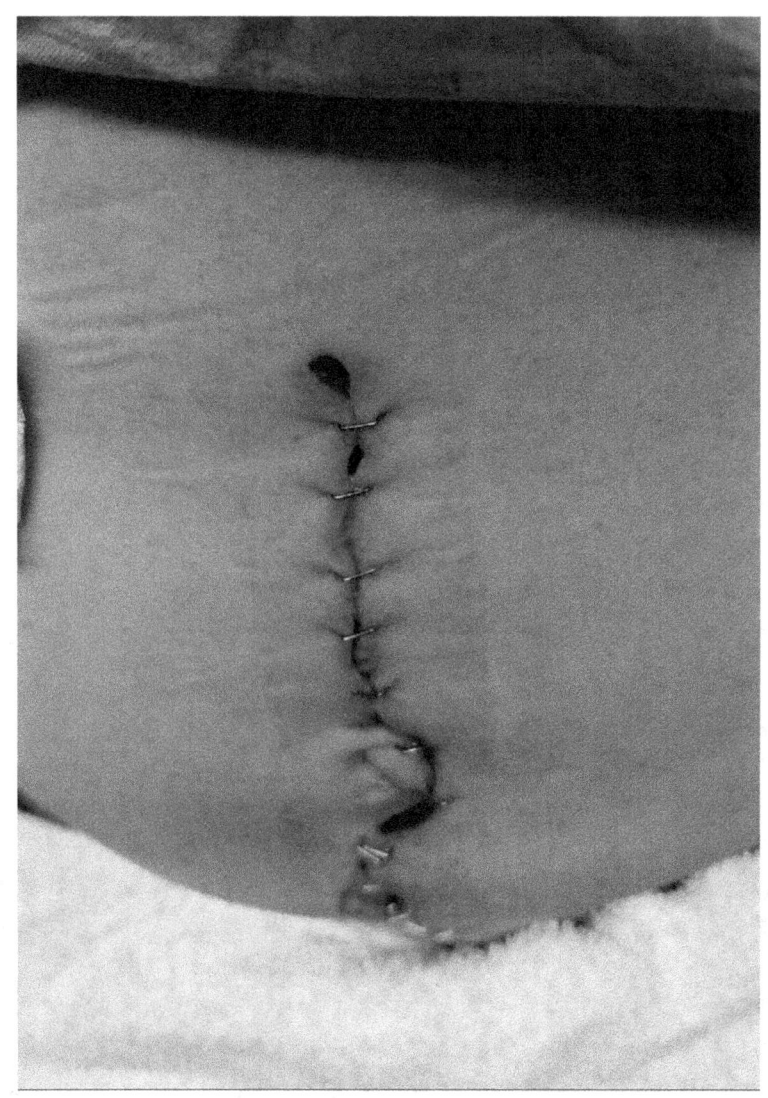

February 10, 2017 Facebook
Krystin Engstrand is feeling bummed.
Having all these medical ailments one after the other has made me miss so many important, milestone events for close, long-time friends, like showers and parties and weddings. I'll never be able to get that time back and be able to celebrate with them, and that saddens me.

Out of the 41 days of 2017 this far, I've been in a medical establishment for 40 of them. Not the best start to the new year. I hope it's not indicative of the rest of the year. . . .

February 15, 2017 Facebook
Today marks 1 year since I've been at work. Time flies when you practically live in the hospital. At least my position is still going to be there for me when I'm ready to go back. Love my job.

February 16, 2017 Email
where are you?
Dad to Krystin:
    Did you go back to Logan? Should I write to Amber?

Krystin to dad:
    Nope, not at Logan. Supposedly my CADI waiver expired 2/1, so I needs to be reinstated, and Tanya said I can't return to Logan until it is. And Cassandra, my Hennepin County caseworker, said it could take a week for all paperwork to go through and be approved. Wonderful. I think it's ridiculous that I can't go back yet. So now I'm just sitting here taking up a bed.

February 23, 2017 Facebook
Krystin Engstrand updated her status.
After almost 2 months of being first in the hospital for my surgery, then the transitional care center while my 10" incision healed, I'm finally home! I would be OK with not being in the hospital again for a while. . .

March 2, 2017 Facebook
Krystin Engstrand is feeling ecstatic.
It's official, the date is set, and I'm doing a happy dance like there's no tomorrow: I return to work on the 20th!!

March 13, 2017 Email
Krystin to dad:
    I don't suppose you'd be willing to give me a small advance on my tax returns? $60 or so. I know you're having my tax returns put into your bank account, then you can easily subtract it from my balance. If I don't have money, then I can't do some of the house activities, which

would mean another individual has to stay home, since 1 staff can't take out 3 individuals yes, I'm getting the small amount of SSI each month, but now I also have 3 bills to pay off.

Let me know what you think. I could swing by tomorrow, if you agree.

Dad to Krystin:
OK

P.S. They can't deposit the money in our account, so you'll have to wait for a check. I will advance you money, but I do expect you to return it to me when you receive a tax refund.

Krystin to dad:
Of course. Is $80 actually ok? That would def get me through until my first work paycheck. Do you want those deposited in your account?

March 17, 2017 Blog
I'm back!

Hello everyone. It has been almost a year since I last posted. I took a little break, but now I'm ready to start writing again. I'm not going to recall everything that I've been through in the past year; I'm going to start with now, with today. No use dwelling on the past! And tbh, you all already know anyway how rough 2016 and the beginning of 2017 were for me.

I have not made it public, until right now, that I now live in a group home, in Brooklyn Center. When I was in the hospital for 3 months last year, the doctors said that I should not return home, but instead live in a group home where I can get help with all my medical needs. And I couldn't leave the hospital until I had a place to go. So, here I am. It has been challenging at times, since I went from living alone in an apartment and being in charge of my life and having the freedom that comes with living alone, to living in a house with 3 other individuals (who are all blind), and that is staffed 24 hours a day. I feel like I'm being treated like a child sometimes. But, I know this is a good place for me, since I obviously wasn't doing very good living on my own and juggling all my medical needs.

I pretty much have the whole lower level to myself. Bedroom, bathroom, and living room area. Since the other 3 who live here are blind, they rarely come down for anything. I don't have my car anymore, so staff have to drive me when I want to go somewhere. That part sucks. But overall, this is a good place for me, and my health and well-being have both increased drastically.

All my hard work is paying off! I feel good, which is something I haven't felt in a long time.

This is going to be a short post. Mostly I'm just dipping my toes back into the blog pool. Another post will be coming soon!

Xoxo

March 20, 2017 Email
how was work?
Dad to Krystin:
    Did you actually work? :-)

Krystin to dad:
    No, not really. :)
Spent most of the time unpacking all my stuff and organizing everything in my new cube. Then we had a little 'welcome back' gathering with support staff in our file room, with cookies! So that was nice. Today will be work, though. I'll sit with Nancy and go over things that have changed in our daily tasks over the past year. Maybe spend some time up front with Michael, to go over proposal log-in stuff, but probably not until next Monday. It will be a busy day for sure!

Dad to Krystin:
    Not yet, and not until you have information for certain, but at some point--assuming work goes well and you manage to avoid docs and hospitals--you could inquire about increasing your work hours to 10 or 12. The key factor is any income limit with the state or the feds.
    Glad it went well! I hope that continues.

April 1, 2017 Email
Dad to Krystin:
    How as work last week?

Krystin to dad:
    Work was good! I've always been a quick learner, so I've been able to get back into the swing of things. Like riding a bike!

Dad to Krystin:

So as far as I can figure, you earned (before taxes) $288! So a little more spending money. We'll hope that this can go on indefinitely and you won't be side-tracked by hospital visits!

April 1, 2017 Blog

Welcome to prison

Living in a group home is tough. Since I used to live on my own for a while, living in a group home feels like going from freedom to captivity, Instead of the other way around. The other 3 residents are blind, and have some form of an intellectual disability, so their families are their guardians. I, on the other hand, have all my marbles and am my own guardian. Nothing I do has to go through my dad first. I make my own decisions; I'm in charge of my life. However, there are so many rules, that I don't feel like I get to make any decisions at all! Here are a number of rules that must be followed, some of which were actually created just for me:

(For anonymity, I'm going to refer to my group home manager as Callie.)

- No food or beverages of any kind can be in my room.
- I MUST be upstairs by 8am (7am on work days) to take my morning meds. Staff were complaining that I took too long to come upstairs.
- I can't go out and do things without a staff person driving me and staying with me. Unless it's with family. Then it's ok.
- If my mom or dad come pick me up, they must come inside so that staff can see that it's a parent, and not a drug dealer. Or whatever.
- I must always be courteous and respectful to staff. Even if I'm having a shitty day, I have to put on a smile and fake it. Staff were also complaining that I'm too rude. Whatever.
- My Ambien sleep med has to be taken by 10pm, or if don't get it at all.
- I can't even buy Tums unless I have a doctor's prescription for it. Pffff.
- No Mello Yello allowed.
- I can't make my own damn appointments. Callie does it.
- No snacks at movies.
- I don't even get to hold on to my own health insurance card. Callie does.
- Tuesdays and Fridays are the days I get to do laundry.

- I must clean my bathroom on Sundays. If I want to do it on Saturday, that's quite alright, but certainly not on Monday.
- Measure out all my meals down to the last teaspoon, so I can calculate the carbs exactly.
- Don't drink milk with every meal, or we'll run out before the next grocery run. Never in my life have I been told I drink too much milk!
- I need to be eating dinner at 5pm, with everyone else. No eating dinner hours later. What are we, 85? The U.S. is one of the only countries that eats dinner so early. In Europe, dinner isn't until 8 or so! After cocktails and hors d'oeuvres.

This isn't even close to being all of them, but I think you get a picture. It feels like I'm always doing something wrong, even if I don't know that what I'm doing is wrong. Don't worry, I'll get a nice lecture from Callie when she's next at the house. I am constantly anxious; especially if I hear Callie's car pull into the driveway, because my brain has been conditioned to expect something to be wrong. That's not the quality of life that anyone should have in their own home.

Callie is quite a bit younger and me. She's somewhere in her mid-20s. 25, I believe. She is always treating me and talking to me like I'm a child. I don't know if she's intimidated by the fact that I'm older and in possession of all my marbles, unlike the other 3. She can't pull shit on me and think that she'll get away with it and/or that I'll say something. I'm not blind, so I see everything that goes on. She must find a way to exert her authority over me by trampling all over me. She often talks to me like I'm a child, and with a condescending tone of voice, and that just ends up making me frustrated and irritated. She hates being pointed out for any error she may have made, and will make up excuse after excuse to try to put the blame on someone else. That's usually me. Even if it's something I have nothing to do with. She refuses to ever be wrong. How do you deal with someone like that?

Callie finds any and every little thing to pick on me about. She nitpicks. Many of the things she tries to correct me on, are contradictory to something she corrected me on a week before. With that kind of outlook on my life, how am I supposed to know what's right or wrong? What is a company rule and what are rules she invented? What rules are preexisting and what are ones that she made up there on the spot? I shouldn't have to adjust MY actions based on what mood she's in that day. Right?? Or issues that may have had a number of factors that resulted in this or that, 100% of the blame is put on my shoulders. After all, you can't scold inanimate objects, or traffic, or even another staff person. If another person or people are involved, well then I must have used my manipulative ways to get them to do something. Are. You. Kidding. Me. You can see why I'm so frustrated and irritated and other -ated adjectives.

The thing that bothers me the MOST is when she tries to lecture me about my diabetes and how I need to do this or that or else that or this will happen. Excuse me, but I've dealing with diabetes for almost 29 years, while she's only been dealing with me and my diabetes for not even a year yet. I have been getting lectures about my diabetes since high school. Just because I didn't take proper care of my diabetes while growing up doesn't mean I didn't know HOW. I knew WHAT I had to do to stay healthy; I just didn't WANT to. So please don't tell me that I need to drink some juice and eat some complex carbs when my blood sugar is 35 or else I'll die. She gets way more frantic over a low blood sugar than is necessary. Sometimes it's actually amusing watching her run around the kitchen like a chicken with its head cut off, pouring juice and trying to find the bread loaf. Chill, woman!

I also get blamed right away for things, without getting the benefit of the doubt. "Why did you put an empty pickle jar back in the fridge?" 1. I didn't, and 2. One of the staff wants the pickle juice. "Where did my Monster energy drink go that I put in the fridge?" I have no idea. I don't like or drink them. "Why is there a 2 liter bottle of orange pop in the fridge, when you know you're not supposed to drink citrus-y beverages?" It's not mine, and I haven't even touched it. A staff member bought and brought it. She picks every little thing, about which she will argue with me. I swear she lives for drama. I know that a big factor for the bickering is the age difference and maturity level. Some days I'm able to take a deep breath and try to be the adult, and tell myself it's not worth it, while others I want to pull my hair out, and can't help but put in my 2 cents. Sometimes we can go a week or more without arguing over anything, while sometimes we can go a week or more of arguing every day. I don't like having a 25 year-old run my life. I swear that when I signed a bunch of papers when I first moved in, I signed away my freewill and my soul. How was I to know that the documents I signed were going to be processed by a figure with 2 red horns.

Admittedly, I know that this is the best place for me to be right now. I clearly proved to friends, family, and everyone on my medical team, that at least for now, I cannot live alone and take care of myself. At least not well enough to stay out of the hospital. Of all the places that my mom, dad, and Kathy looked into, while I was having my 3-month staycation in the hospital, this was the best fit. I also admit that health has increased tenfold since I moved in last May. On the poor/fair/good/excellent charts that you see in doctors' offices, my health has gone from fair to good. Sure, in 2016 I was in the hospital more than not, and I spent the first 2 months of 2017 recuperating from a major surgery at the beginning of the year, but maybe that's what it took for me to move up on the health scale. *I* never get the credit that I feel I at least partly deserve for my good health. Callie tells me all the time of the praise she gets from administration on how well she's done with me. Um, excuse me, but the reason she looks so good in the eyes of everyone else is because *I* did all the hard work to turn my health around. She could've tried as hard as she wanted to make me healthy, but if I hadn't been, and still am, cooperative, then she wouldn't be receiving all this credit and praise. You're welcome, Callie, for me making you look so good. Now where's my balloon and gold star??

Pretty sure I've surpassed my quota of complaining in one post, so I'll leave it at that. It feels good to be writing again, and I'm optimistic that future posts will be more positive! I suppose I needed to get this all off my chest and over with.

Ta-ta for now.

April 10, 2017 Blog
The other side of the coin

In my last post, I only focused on the negatives about my living situation. Therefore, this time I find it fair to focus on the positives of living in a group home, because yes, there are some, despite my last post making it seems like there aren't any and like I was living in Hell itself. There are more things I would love to vent about, but I'll save that for a rainy day. I think Callie and I need couples therapy!

To start with, at my endo (endocrinology) appt last week, my endocrinologist was looking at my most recent set of blood work. She said my kidney is doing very well, my hemoglobin is within range, and my calcium and vitamin C levels are perfect. A clean bill of health! I'm pretty sure that I've never been given a clean bill of health in my life. Or at least as far back as I can remember. All my hard work is finally starting to pay off. Go Me!

I am so happy to be back at work. It has given me semblance of structure, normalcy, and routine. And, I feel, that it has restored some of my sanity. I'm a pretty quick learner, so even by the 2nd day, I remembered how to do everything that I do. I only work Mondays and Wednesdays from 8-12. The 3rd week of April I will switch to afternoons on Tuesdays and Thursdays 12-5. As the months progress, I will slowly add more hours. So it'll be awhile until I'm back to full-time, but, baby steps! Too many times did I try to return to work early, and that just resulted in me having to take more time off! This time around I'm going to be smart and responsible, and not rush into anything. For my very first day back at work on 3/20, Callie was a hot mess. Like a parent dropping their kid off at daycare for the first time, only being able to imagine all the ways something could go wrong. If some day she spontaneously decides to come into my office to make sure I'm there, and I'm not, she'll call the police to issue a missing person alert. Something about me being a vulnerable adult, and what if I jumped into an unmarked van after being offered candy. Cool your jets Callie, I'm in the restroom. Seems a little TOO extreme to me, but nobody asked for my opinion.

As far as the group home life, I do actually have fun and get out of the house. I've discovered that I really enjoy, and am good at, DIY crafts. Especially paper crafts, although I do dabble in other types of DIY crafts here and there. That means that one of my favorite outings is to Michaels. If not at a doctor appointment, running errands, or at work, I'm at the house. It's bittersweet, really, because sometimes I'm restless and bored out of my mind, but all that time at the house has also allowed me to really hone my crafting skills. I don't think I'll need to buy holiday decorations for the next decade, since I've been making them all! I've even had managers from other houses ask if I could come decorate their houses! Sometimes at the dollar store I can find something that I'll need for a project, too. My crafting inventory has, I think, quadrupled over the past year. I have a whole shelving unit just for my supplies.

I also watch a lot of Netflix. And play PokemOnGO.

I've been watching American Horror Story on Netflix. It's quite an interesting show; it plays on the supernatural. Each season has a different plot, so it doesn't matter if you watch the seasons out of order. What makes it interesting to me is that most of the same actors and actresses are in each season, but as completely different characters. It gives me a new perspective on and respect for acting, to see the very wide and different character types that the cast can play. Right now I'm on season 2, which takes place in an insane asylum in the 1960s. And since I didn't watch in chronological order, I'll be done with the whole series (of 6 seasons) after this. I actually started with season 5 (a haunted hotel) because Lady Gaga is in it, and I really like her, both as a singer and actress. Anyway, I digress.

Some days I go to Target, or out for lunch, or go with Callie to run some of her errands. On weekends, when all 4 of us residents are home, then we all go do some activity, such as bowling, going to the humane society, going to Underwater World at the Mall of America, or Comp Zoo during the warm months, or, when the weather is nice, going on walks. You get the idea. I told Callie that some weekend I'd like to go to the Science Museum.

If any of you reading this have recommendations for good weekend activities that are free, or cheap, I'm open for ideas! And remember, the other 3 individuals are blind.

Much to my surprise, two of my housemates, whom we'll call Danny and Janet, enjoy going to movies. Based on dialogue, they can create their own vision, in their minds, of what is going on on the screen. I almost wonder if that's a better way to "watch" movies, especially ones that were books, first. We imagine and create whole worlds in our heads while we read, then are disappointed when it becomes a movie and doesn't look the same as it did for us in our imaginations. Unfortunately, they also don't get to see how far we've come with movies as far as graphics and picture quality and design, and such. The only time I wonder about Danny and Janet at movies is when there are long scenes with no dialogue. I imagine it's difficult to create scenes in your mind if you don't have dialogue to build it off of. But, they love going to movies, so obviously they manage! I was jealous of Janet, who spent last weekend at her mom's, and they went to see the new Beauty and the Beast movie. I want to see it so bad! She goes to her mom's house every other weekend, which I think is wonderful, since my other 2 housemates don't really have family to visit and/or do things with. Not even on holidays.

The other day I learned that the wife of one of the staff, we'll call him Carl, had died. She was still living in Africa, and suffered a major heart attack. I feel so bad for Carl. Who knows when he even saw her last. I would guess that he went back to Africa maybe once in the past year. Now he's trying to plan a funeral, in Africa, from here. I bet he's racking up those frequent flyer miles with all his long distance phone calls. He's going to keep working right up until the funeral, so he can make money to pay for the funeral and plane ticket. It's actually pretty common in Africa that the male head of the house moves here to work and earn money to send home to his family still in Africa. I can't imagine losing a loved one and having to get everything planned via long distance phone calls.

It reminds me of when I was in South Korea, and was informed that my good friend Maria, who was like a sister to me, had passed away. I was on the other side of the world, and could do absolutely nothing. I didn't get to go to the funeral, or say a final goodbye to her. For Carl it's a little different, because it's his wife who passed, but the same concept. So I have a lot of empathy for Carl.

That's all I got for now. Off to Underwater World at the M.O.A., even though we were just there a couple weeks ago. Oh well. It's still fun to watch the sharks. I discovered that the mall has this huge arcade area, with go-carts! The other 3 can't do it, but I sure as heck want to!

Hasta luego!

April 27, 2017 Blog
A little of this, a little of that

Danny requested that we go to McDonald's for dinner on Wednesday of last week. I have now filled my McDonald's quota for the year, that being eating there once. I even got a salad, so go me for making healthy choices! Ok, so maybe I also had fries and a Mcflurry, but it's the thought that counts . . . right?

Anyway, when we got back to the house, while staff person Carl was helping Danny out of the van, I heard this high-pitch squealing sound unlike anything I've ever heard before. I thought some yippy little dog had wandered into the garage. Turns out it wasn't a dog. Carl had gotten a finger pinched in the van door, and it had made a nice slit on his finger. Ouch. I probably would've made unrecognizable sounds, too. It was bleeding pretty bad, even an hour later. He did end up leaving early to go get it checked out. Can't say I blame him. I'm guessing he probably needed stitches.

A couple weekends ago we went to Northtown mall; 4 individuals and 2 staff. As soon as we entered the mall, those of us in the front stopped to let the others catch up. We had Tim in his wheelchair, and a girl probably between 8-10 came over and stood right in front of us, staring dead at Tim, unblinking and not saying a word. After about 15 seconds, I felt that was long enough to be rude, so I asked her if she wanted to take a picture so it would last longer. She gave me a quizzical look and said "um, no thank you." I'm sure she didn't mean anything by it, and didn't know better, so I took it upon myself to teach her one rule of appropriate social behavior.

Janet likes to "watch" movies, and a number of months ago she asked if she and I could watch a movie together once in a while, down in my living room area. She really likes and values quality bonding time/hanging out time, so even though she can't see the movie, she is perfectly happy to sit there and listen to it. Saturday night (4/22) she and I finally watched a movie together. We watched Finding Dory on Netflix. She really enjoyed that. Every once in awhile I'll go with her to get our nails done at a local nail and salon place near the house.

There are so many questions I want to ask Janet about being blind, but I can't get a feeling of how she would react. Is it rude to ask a blind person about being blind? I want to ask her if she's been blind her whole life. If she has any education. If she can read braille. How it feels to have to put her life and ALL her trust in the staff and with the general population. I can't imagine that being easy to trust that we won't let any harm to her, that we'll protect her, and not let her walk into a tree, or fall down a curb, or walk out into a busy intersection, etc. etc. Maybe it's easier if one is born blind. If I suddenly went blind after 32 years of having vision, having seen what I've seen, I don't know if I could trust everyone! But Janet, if born blind, doesn't have anything to compare being blind with. Does that make sense?

I'm now on the Tuesdays/Thursdays shifts at work. Noon-5pm, 10 hours a week. I made it to work every day when I was working 8-noon, but I sure am glad to not have to get up at 6am anymore! For most of you, that's probably not that big of a deal, but I am not a morning person. At. All. Now I get up at 8 to do my blood sugar, morning meds, and breakfast. Then I kinda laze around until it's time to get ready to go. I really, truly do appreciate those 2 extra hours that I get to sleep! Work is going great, though. I'm pretty much back in the full swing of things, which I think I said my last post, so I guess by now I'm even MORE back in the swing! It feels like I'm finally back to being a contributing member of society, rejoining and being a contributing member of my work team, and being productive. For me, that's one of the best feelings ever. Anti-depression medication or not, being back at work greatly increases my mood.

I need to vent again, and I don't see my therapist for another week, so sorry guys, bear with me.

Last Thursday morning (a week ago today), for the first time since I moved in last May, I shouted at Callie. I was at my wit's end. Once again, because something put her in a bad mood this morning, I suffer the consequences, and new or existing rules suddenly change. I shouldn't be punished because she's having a bad day. She said something about how I'm not used to being told no. Um, actually, it's the opposite. I don't remember verbatim what she said next, but it was something about how I always react to being told no by getting mad and (sometimes) crying and going to my room.

Well, that's when teenage Krystin joined the party. I shouted "Because nothing is ever fucking consistent in this house." I definitely caught her by surprise, since I've never yelled at her before. And yes, I grabbed my stuff and went down to my room. Maybe I even shut my door a little harder and louder than usual. If I'm arguing with someone and I'm ready for the argument to be over, of course I'm going to remove myself from the situation. I'm not going to sit there and process everything right in front of her. Doing so would be very uncomfortable for me, and if I stayed, the argument would just get even more heated, and I was ready for it to be done. It sure felt good, though.

I'm surprised it took me so long to realize this, but I think one of the biggest reasons that she and I butt heads is because she treats me like she's my mother. I love my mom dearly, but I don't need another mother; I already have one. When Callie starts treating me like a child, it brings me back to my teenage years, when I fought with my parents all the time.

How do you deal with difficult people who you can't seem to please no matter what you say or do, and you can't avoid them forever, because they're your manager and you have to interact with them every day? If anyone has any experience or knowledge on this kind of thing, then I'm begging you, please share your insight! If I say white, she says black. If I say A, she says B. She's like a weather cloud looming over my head, and when I wake up each morning, I don't know if it's going to be rain or shine with her. And her mood can be one way, and then in an instant, like flipping a light switch, it's suddenly another way. It gives me anxiety and stress, and I don't know how to redirect that stress and anger into a successful solution. Maybe there isn't one most of the time, but I need consistency.

Many of you may be thinking that I need to bite my tongue and go along with whatever Callie says, to keep her happy and pleased, but what kind of effect will that have on my emotional well being? She also needs to know that it's not OK to treat me like this. She's not old, but I fear that in this case, she can't learn new tricks.

Whew, OK, I'm done (for now).

I have to toot my own horn for how good I've been doing with my soft/mechanical diet. The stent that's in my throat, keeping it held open so that I can swallow foods and such, so that I can, y'know, stay alive, has been in there for over 6 MONTHS! And it's still right in place. This is the longest I've had any stent in. The soft/mechanical diet entails nothing crispy or crunchy that could have a sharp edge, like potato chips. It could risk scraping my throat and stent, or even pull on the stent, to pull it out of place. This stent has a special coating around the outside, which prevents my esophagus from healing and growing around/into the stent. If the stent were to become part of my throat, AND it's sutured in place, it would be very difficult to remove. My surgeon would literally have to CUT the stent out of my esophagus, and that just doesn't sound like a good time for anyone.

When I was first told that I was put on a soft/mechanical diet (which is actually most common for people who have had, for example, jaw surgery, and can't chew anything), I was angry and upset. I had to give up some of my favorite foods! But over the last 6 or so months, I've realized that I really didn't have to sacrifice that much, and that there are improvisations and alternatives. For example, I'm not supposed to eat crunchy cereal, but if I pour milk on it, like people tend to do, and wait a little bit, the cereal with become softened, and I can eat it. With toast, once I put butter and jam on it, the bread softens up. I'm not supposed to do pizza, but Punch pizza is OK, because it's so floppy and soft, and nothing about the crust is crispy. I can still eat pie (yay!), just not the crust. So, I've found that this diet isn't really that bad, and I've found ways that I can still have some of my favorite foods and make it work with my diet. I'm not supposed to eat leafy greens, because it could get stuck in my stent, so no salads or spinach for me. Oh darn, I'm so broken up about it, can you tell?

That's all, folks. Until next time, cheers! ☺

April 23, 2017 Email
2 matters
Dad to Krystin:
    1. No TCF card here. Maybe you better call them on Monday.

2. You weaken your case for more independence considerably when you have benadryl that is outside your pharmacy regimen. What were you thinking???

Krystin to dad:
I'll call them tomorrow.

I was thinking that I wanted to get some decent sleep. I haven't had any in a while, anyway. Like, weeks. Clearly I wasn't thinking. Not thinking is part of what landed me in a group home in the first place. But Tanya and I have talked about it (taking Benadryl) extensively and are working on moving forward. And if you're wondering if I bought Benadryl whenever you've brought me to Walgreens, the answer is no. I really did, and do, need "girl stuff." I can promise you that.

I don't know what all Tanya told you guys, but I tell everyone to take what she says with a grain of salt. Yes, there is truth in the matter, but she also likes to exaggerate to make both me and the issue look worse than it is. It's just part of who she is, unfortunately.

Anyway, TTYL.

April 24, 2017 Email
Meeting
Krystin to mom, dad, Nancy [therapist], Meridien person
Hey mom and dad (and Liz and Nancy),

So, one of the downsides of Tanya's office being right next to my room, and having thin walls, is that I hear almost everything she says. Based on what she recently told a new nurse who was training here, we absolutely need to have a meeting with Tanya and Liz. Tanya thinks every single thing that comes out of my mouth is a lie, and that I have some undiagnosed mental disability. It's fine if she keeps that stuff to herself, but I feel very violated and disrespected when she tells all this stuff, stuff SHE believes is wrong, to a new person. That doesn't give me any chance to build a relationship with someone, when they come into the relationship with all these prejudices. The fact that she way over exaggerates doesn't help at all, either. She also thinks that I had my psychiatric medical records locked, so that Meridien can't see them, as if I'm trying to hide something from them. None of that is true.

I also greatly dislike that I'm not allowed to call or talk to any of my doctors. Only she can do that. And if I do communicate with a doc,

I get a nice lecture on how that's not allowed. So, aside from being at an appointment, I never get to talk to my docs again? What bullshit. Then if she talks to a doc on the phone, no info is shared with me, so I don't know what she and my doctors discuss. So what is SHE hiding?

I don't know how she can expect me to be open and honest with her, when she's not open and honest with me. A bit hypocritical, if you ask me.

We need a meeting so that we can get everything out on the table. I'm tired, and stressed, and frustrated and irritated, and all kinds of other -ed words, and for the first time, it's making me seriously consider my living here. I don't want to leave here, but I do need to be talked to and treated to like an adult. Mom, I love you with all my heart, but 1 mother is enough. I don't need another 25-year-old one.

I'm CCing Liz, the program director, and Nancy, my psychologist. I feel that they should be in the know about this, too.

Hopefully we can move forward from here.
Krystin

May 10, 2017 Blog
I don't ramble, I tell stories

Hallelujah, ask and you shall receive! A couple weeks ago I sent a somewhat nasty email to some of the administrative people, calling bullshit on how Callie talks to and treats me. A meeting has been scheduled, disguised as an annual review of my first year at Logan (house). Really what it is is a meeting to discuss my concerns, mainly with Callie. Attending will be myself, my mom, dad, and Kathy, Callie, the program director, the program administrator, and Cassandra, who's my Hennepin county caseworker. Just add pizza and it's a party! I feel like it will be a productive meeting. Callie may avoid me for a few days, but she'll get over it. Ideally the outcome of the meeting will be that I'll finally be treated like an adult. The meeting is set for tomorrow (5/11) morning.

Something that Callie said to me last week, in an argument, is how I'm not used to being told "no." She has a very skewed misconception of my life before Logan house. And I absolutely hate when people make presumptions about my life, even if they don't know anything about my upbringing. Her comment really offended me. It's actually quite the opposite of what she thinks. Growing up, both my parents worked full-time, and my dad was also getting his PhD while still working. Plus, the house that we moved into (and which is still my dad's [now my dad's and Kathy's] house, and still my home) needed a lot of repairs and other work done. We didn't have extra piles of cash just sitting around for toys and games and such. I don't think Callie realizes how little I was actually told "yes." I did chores, and when I was 15 I got my first job. I wasn't spoiled, and I didn't get everything I asked for. I worked for it. So I hope you understand when I say that I wanted to smack her across the face when she said that. Clearly she doesn't know as much about me as she may think.

I've been thinking about my job (of which I just passed my 5 year mark!) often over the past few months, and how my position was held for me for just over a year. I really want to ask my supervisor why. Why not replace me? It's a little bit of an ego and confidence boost, knowing that other people recognize my hard work as much as I FEEL like I'm working hard. Does that make sense? I really am a valuable member of my work team! Feels good. ^_^

In an attempt to keep me from hiding food in my room, Callie had a doorbell installed in my room. It's right next to my bed, attached to the side of my nightstand. If, at any time, I start to feel low, and going upstairs to test my blood sugar and eat something seems daunting, I can push my doorbell. The bell that rings is on the first floor, so staff can hear it when I push it, and know to come downstairs, blood sugar meter in hand (and hopefully some juice!). I've actually had it about a month now, but haven't pushed it once. Not because I haven't needed to, but because I feel weird pushing it. I feel like I'm ringing for my butler, or room service, or something. And how do I know that ALL the staff know what it's for if they hear it? What if they can't hear because of the TV or radio? I could be sitting down there for a long time, with my blood sugar continuing to drop. The doorbell is a good idea in theory, but in practice I just don't feel comfortable using it.

As part of Danny's intellectual disability, he has a hard time making decisions on his own. You can't ask him what he wants to drink with dinner, or ask him if he wants A or B. He'll get confused and stay silent. But if you ask him, "Hey Danny, do you want milk with dinner?" then he'll say yeah, and we all act like it was his idea in the first place. I'm not telling you this to make fun of Danny. It's more like the longer I live there, the more I learn about my fellow housemates. As another example, I love that some days Danny decides he wants to wear one of his Halloween costumes to work. His favorites are the bowling pin, or the hotdog. No rhyme or reason to it, some days he just wants to wear a costume! I admire that about him. We should all wear costumes whenever we want! There's no law that says we can only wear costumes on Halloween. So Danny, you do what you gotta do, buddy!

I also like how he LOVES books. I'm not sure why, considering he's blind, that his absolute favorite objects are books, but they are. A van picks up Janet and Danny for work every morning, and the driver, Thomas, always walks into the house and says to Danny, "Good morning professor," because Danny likes to bring his books to work with him, so he looks like he's on his way to teach a class, in which he has like 5-10 girlfriends, depending on the day. Right now I think it's a Gina, who is not yet his girlfriend, but will be after he impresses her with all this books. Or something like that. I love this kid, he cracks me up sometimes. He LOVES that he beat me in bowling last weekend. Granted, he gets the side bumpers put up, and has a ramp thing to put the bowling ball on, then all he has to do is give it a push, and down the lane it goes. He was cracking up when, at the end of the game, I said to him, "Danny, you beat me!" I think that made his day.

Janet is also really coming out of her shell. All 4 of us have 'outcomes' that we strive to accomplish. For example, one of mine is to cook dinner for everyone on Wednesday nights, or to clean my bathroom downstairs every Sunday. I think one of Janet's outcomes is to be more expressive, and speak up more. Each week when I'm making the grocery list, I ask her if there's anything she would like to put on the list, and she'll name off a few items. I think before, she didn't feel comfortable making food requests, but in just the one year I've lived there, she has grown as a person, and is more assertive. Go Janet! Another thing I love about her is that she lives her life as if she could see. She'll frequently tell staff members how she likes their shirt, or their super comfy sweatshirt. I really admire that about her. Why let life get you down, right?

Something curious yet funny happened to me last week. Some of you already know this story from when I posted it on facebook, but it's worth reading again anyway. Ok, so, last week I woke up in the middle of the night, probably in the 3:00 am hour, with a really low blood sugar. Eating some Lucky Charms cereal (dry, not with milk) sounded like a good idea, so I ate a bunch of cereal, felt much better afterwards, and went back to bed. I don't know if it was the next morning or a couple mornings after, but one morning I pull out the box of Lucky Charms, really looking forward to a big bowl, when I discovered that, to my dismay, that the night I was low, I had eaten ALL of the marshmallow pieces, leaving a bag of only cereal pieces. And everyone knows that without the marshmallow pieces, Lucky Charms is basically just Cheerios! I was both appalled and amused. It had to have taken some serious concentration to just pick out the marshmallows, which is surprising, considering it was both the middle of the night, and I was low. Huh. Curious. OH, so after all that cereal, you'd think that my blood sugar would be, understandably, through the roof the next morning, right? NO! My blood sugar was normal and within my range. Very curious indeed . . .

I have to give a shout-out to Elliott (my bro) for landing his first "real world" job. He'll be working at the U for the department of Research Animals Resources, or RAR. Which, btw, is where I worked for the summer before my junior year at the U. I worked with all the little mice, and he'll be working with large animals; goats, I believe. Hopefully none of them spit in his face or yell at him!

Alright, I'm outta here for now! Cheers.

May 11, 2017 Email
Meeting
Krystin to dad, mom:

Do you think the meeting this morning went well? Were all your concerns addressed? I think *I* did a good job at staying calm and not getting in a heated argument with Tanya. Now we'll see if there are improvements. . . .

Thanks for coming to the meeting. It means a lot to me, even though I'm my own guardian, that you guys were there.

Ly both.
Pat to Krystin, Gary

I thought it went well and yes, my concerns (only real one was the lack of communication at times) were addressed.

Gary to Pat, Krystin:

I also thought it went well. . . . Keeping calm served you well, Krystin, and it will continue to serve you well. (I know that it is sometimes very difficult not to get mad or peeved or raise your voice--but standing firm on calm almost always leads to better outcomes.)

Now let us see how events play out.

LY, too.

May 16, 2017 Email
Pain
Dad to Krystin:
How's the pain?

A random thought occurred to me. Maybe you and the docs have already considered this, but in case not--

Might it be one or more of your meds that is causing the pain? Either one med or some interaction effect between two (or more) of the drugs? I wonder if you shouldn't talk about maybe some experimental substitutions (if that's possible) for some of the drugs to see if there's any pain reduction.

Anyway, just a thought.
LY

Krystin to dad:
I just had an appointment this morning with Dawn, my pain management person. After showing her where my pain is, and how it feels, she went into my chart to look at past blood work, and saw that my liver enzymes were extremely elevated. She had me lay down, and pressed on my abdomen where my liver is. She said it doesn't feel swollen or inflamed, but she wants me to get in to see Monica ASAP. Monica can then decide which route to take, like if I should see GI or a hepatologist, or what. I left a message with Margaret, Monica's nurse, and am waiting for her to call back to see if she can squeeze me in anywhere this week.

Wouldn't that just be the cherry on top of the cake if I'm having liver problems now, too. Gah!

May 19, 2017 Email
how's the pain?
Dad to Krystin:
Getting any better? Any result from talking with medicos?

May 21, 2017 Email
Krystin to dad:
No, it's actually getting worse. Sometimes it even brings tears to my eyes and explicit words from my mouth. It burns SO much. This pain is worse than pain I've had waking up from a major surgery. ER docs can't find anything. Saw Monica, and she's going to refer me to someone in GI. In the meantime, I've missed work, I've missed

therapy, and I missed the weekend activities. I just want to sleep, because when I'm asleep, I don't feel the pain. It's misery, and nothing can be done about it. :(

May 23, 2017 Email
visiting
Dad to Krystin:
    You're welcome to come over this weekend. I have to confess that I'm not sure what that accomplishes when you're in constant pain--you don't exactly make a fun houseguest! But if you'd like to spend a little time here, away from Logan, of course you can come.
    When would you come?

Krystin to dad:
    You make a good point. Let's see how the rest of the week plays out. Not sure if they'll be able to fit me in for a procedure this week, but I certainly hope so. Last week, when I saw Monica, she put me on a specific diet, in case it's an ulcer that I have, so as not to irritate or inflame it. It actually worked pretty well over the weekend. That, plus the Tylenol, kept the pain to a minimum, and I only had occasional burning flare-ups. It would still be nice to have the problem fixed this week, but if not, I'm managing the pain alright, so I wouldn't be a complaining couch potato all weekend.
    I would probably come right from work on Friday (I work until 5). I have a therapy group Monday morning, at 9, over here by the U, down University a bit. If you could bring me there, then a Logan staff person can pick me up when I'm done, and head back to Logan. Would that be ok?

Dad to Krystin:
    Sounds good. You work on Friday? Thought it was Tues-Thurs. Or is this an adjustment for time you missed?

Krystin to dad:
    Support staff will be short-staffed on Friday. Michael is out on vacation and a couple other people will be out, so yes, I'll be making up the day I missed last week, but also to come in and help out. Otherwise you are right, I normally work T, TH.

May 25, 2017 Email
income
Dad to Krystin:

Have you learned anything about having to pay Meridien or any more about income limits?

Krystin to dad:

Nope to both. I've told Tanya that I would like my Meridian bill each month, instead of a huge bill plopped in my lap 6 months from now, but I haven't gotten anything. So, I'll just keep asking!

I will ask about the income thing at my official annual meeting in June, with Tanya, Liz, Amber, and I believe Cassandra, too. At our meeting a couple weeks ago, did I introduce you to Cassandra? Well, she's my Hennepin county caseworker.

Dad to Krystin:

I would not be surprised if you have to begin paying something out of your income to Meridien (reducing the state/federal obligation). We talked about that: you'd have to be paying for rent and food if you lived in an apartment, so this is no different. Just so they don't say they have to take most of your earnings!

Krystin to dad:

Yes, I've known all along I would have to pay rent. I'd just like a bill every month and not biannual!

June 3, 2017 Facebook
Had a doc appointment the other day with a new doc, who said to me (and I love when this happens), "I was looking through your chart, and I see you have some type 1 diabetes." Me, being a smartass, said "Still? I was hoping that this time I'd have less diabetes than I had before." Haha

June 9, 2017 Email
ulcers
Dad to Krystin:

Saw your FB post. It is my understanding that at least one cause of ulcers can be stress. Are you stressed at Logan by dealing with Tanya? If so, you/we may have to address that problem.

You should raise this issue when you see the docs. (Stress, that is, if you have it.)

LY

Krystin to dad:

It is very highly possible. Yes, dealing with Tanya makes me very stressed. Whenever she comes to the house, my anxiety goes through the roof. Even if I hadn't done anything wrong or had anything to hide. It has become a conditioned response to seeing her, sadly.

Ly, too!

Dad to Krystin:

Then this is something you MUST mention to both your docs and Nancy. If that's the problem, either Meridien gets someone else or you move. And I can explore good options with someone who owns a bunch of places like Logan where you might be happier.

June 12, 2017 Facebook

Krystin Engstrand is feeling optimistic at University of Minnesota Health.

Going under the knife today (ok, not really a knife, but I will get a scope down my throat) to finally figure out what's causing all my pain, and to fix what's "broken." Fingers crossed that when I come out on the other side, I'll be a pain-free Krystin!

June 17, 2017 Facebook

Krystin Engstrand is feeling crafty at Michaels Stores (Brooklyn Center, MN).

Splatter painting on canvas! Take that, Jackson Pollock. [I had this framed after Krystin's death and it now hangs in our house. I'm not a big fan of abstract art but I wasn't going to let it disappear.]

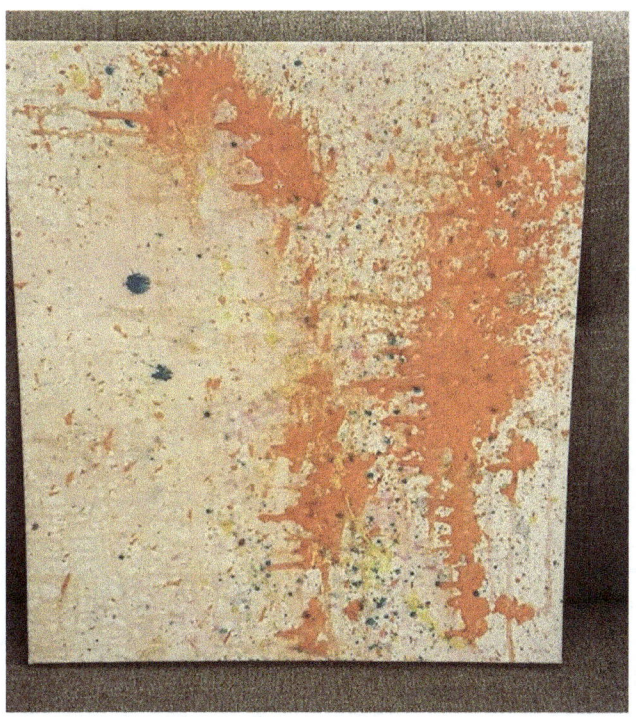

June 30, 2017 Email
Krystin
Tanya to Gary, Pat, Krystin, Meridien staff:
Hello,
I am writing you to let you know krystin has been admitted to the U of M for observation. Krystin had a CT yesterday and the results came back with the starts of necrotic bowel.

Krystin's does not show at this time any signs of necrotic bowel from lab work, so to stay on the safe side they want to keep her due to in the past things rapidly changing.

Krystin does not know yet what room/floor she is on. When we know for sure I will send a follow up email.

Thanks,
Tanya

July 5, 2017 Email
Cassandra to Tanya, Gary, Pat, Krystin:
Hi Everyone,

    Thank you for the updates. Has anything changed with Krystin's hospital stay?

Cassandra, MA, LPCC
Waivered Services Case Manager

Tanya to Cassandra et al, Gary, Pat, Krystin:
Krystin was released on Monday !
    We are to monitor her for signs of infection.

July 3, 2017 Blog
Don't you worry; here I am!
    Hello clan! I apologize for the long gap between my last post and now. It's like you wake up one day and realize weeks have gone by. Now that I'm working again, time flies. I mean, where did June go?? I'm sure you've all been sitting at the edge of your seat, waiting excitedly yet patiently for my next installment. Well wait no longer; here I am!
    Speaking of work, it's going really well. Last week I bumped up my hours from 10 hours a week to 12. For most of you, that's not a big deal, but for me, it's one more step closer to "normalcy." (But what is normal, really, and who sets the requirements? My mom and her sisters like to say "Normal is just a setting on the washing machine.") I know that I'm more of a medical roller coaster than I am normal, but, baby steps!
    I'm doing this thing with my blog where I make sure not to make it ALL medical related. That's what happened with blog last time, before I took the long break (over a year, I think?), and it made me depressed writing about it all, reliving it through my writing. So now I'm making sure to include happy stuff, too!
    My housemate Danny cracks me up sometimes. Once in a while, after his evening shower, he forgets that he's naked, and will walk around the house in his birthday suit, until a staff person tells him to go to his room and put clothes on. It's interesting that as one who was born blind, he never learned humiliation, or inhibition. I would guess that's true for most lifelong blinders. I personally admire that trait, not caring what people think of you. Birthday suit optional. I think we

could all take a page from his book, screw cultural taboos, and let loose once in a while, Lady Godiva style! Janet doesn't do that after her shower, but Danny has no problems putting it all out there for the world to see. Literally.

I think I've mentioned this before, but Danny is obsessed with the word 'tomorrow.' Everything is tomorrow! Recently he said something about 'last night tomorrow.' Most of the time we just smile and nod. Which he doesn't see, being blind and all. . . . It's like when Janet says she likes your t-shirt, then asks what's on it/what color it is.

The other day we went to Northtown mall, and almost lost Danny. One staff person was going to walk around with Janet and me, and the other staff with Danny and Jim. Danny always helps push Jim in his wheelchair, while the staff person holds onto one of the handles. We're about halfway down the corridor when the staff person realizes that he's the only one pushing Jim. We stop abruptly and the staff says "where's Danny??" We all turn around to see Danny still back at the entrance, standing alone, waiting for someone to steer him to the wheelchair. It sounds like a panicky moment, but actually we all got a good laugh out of it.

THEN, when I was in Bath & Body Works, out of the corner of my eye I saw a person who looked very similar to the staff person who was with Jane and me. But this guy was alone. I ALMOST spun around and exclaimed "where's Janet?? First we almost lose Danny, and now we've lost Janet?? Geez!" But alas, it wasn't him. All in all, it was an amusing trip.

Lately I've been thinking about group homes, what it means to me, and why it took me so long to make it publicly known that I live in one. Perhaps it's because it took me almost a year to realize and accept that there's no shame in it. I think I was me, being self-conscious about it, and not wanting to be seen as a disabled adult. So many people have prejudice feelings about group homes, because they don't know anything about them. Only how they are portrayed on tv and in movies. I didn't want to be molded into the kind of individual that is seen in the media It's a completely selfish way of thinking on my part, I know, but it's a feeling that, over the last year, has greatly diminished. I can't take good enough care of myself alone, juggling all my different health needs, and need a little help. There's absolutely NO shame and NOTHING to be embarrassed about, and I'm so glad I have reached that state of mind. My good health wouldn't be where it is today if I hadn't moved to the Logan house!

Callie and I still butt heads quite often. We're both proud and stubborn women who need to be right, and don't give in easily. So you can see why some of our arguments can be lengthy and intense. I haven't yelled at her since that first time, but I've certainly wanted to. I'm trying to pick my battles, but she doesn't make it easy. All the other staff and I are in a good place; she's the only one I have a strained relationship with. She has played a big role in me finally being healthy, but she has also been a big contributor of my stress. I need to find a balance, but even if I'm trying to, it usually helps if both parties and willing to change, and she's not. She's still young and power hungry. BUT, enough of this.

I've noticed that out here in the burbs, it's completely normal for a family to have, on average, 5 cars, give or take about 2. Everyone has a work car, and then a second car for everything else. One of the staff was telling me that a friend of his got 2 cars for his birthday. 2 cars at the same time?? Inconceivable! Especially for those of us who grew up in the hood of South Minneapolis (kidding). It's funny to drive down a street here and seeing 6 or so cars all in one driveway, parked bumper-to-bumper.

I was going to post this last week, but I ended up in the hospital over the weekend on my favorite floor 7A. I'd had a CT scan with contrast on Thursday, and I guess the thoracic docs didn't like something they saw on the scan, so on Friday morning Callie came into my room and told me that she talked with thoracic, and since it was a Friday, I should go to the ER to be checked out. Supposedly on the scan they saw what they thought was the beginning of a dying bowel. I already had 2 feet of my small intestine removed in January; I can't lose much more! When I was in the ER, I saw the ER doc, a thoracic surgeon, AND my transplant surgeon, whom in the past I think I have referred to as Dr. K (for Dr. Kandaswamy).

Dr. K examined me, looked at my CT scan right there in the room with me, and asked me a bunch of questions. He told Callie (who was with me) that I wasn't showing any signs of a necrotic (dying) bowel, and therefore didn't see any reason to keep me. Well, with Meridian rules, they can't take me back to the house unless I've been on observation for at least 24 hours. With it being Friday, and no management being at Logan house over the weekend, I would have to stay until Monday. Dr. K said that's fine, he'll admit me under 48 hour observation. I lose.

That didn't work well with my work schedule. My work days are now T/W/Th, but with the 4th of July on Tuesday, the U is closed, thus making me miss out on one day of work. I talked to my supervisor the week before and asked if I could work Monday instead of Tuesday, at my usual time of 1-5. You better believe that come Monday morning, both my nurse and I heavily pushed the docs to sign and put through the discharge orders. I had breakfast, washed and dried my hair, and packed up my belongings. I made it to work at 12:50. Woohoo! Yay for team work! Of course, after being at work for a little while, I began to wonder why the hell I said I'd come to work. . . .

If you wonder what I did all weekend, let me tell you that Netflix is a girl's best friend. And Jimmy John's (sandwich place) delivers to the hospital, so for a couple meals over the weekend I ordered a yummy, healthy sandwich. Which was counteracted by the BBQ chips I also ordered, but never mind that. It was a good attempt at eating healthy! :D

No 4th of July plans for me. But that's not new; we never do anything for 4th of July. Some years we would go to my aunt and uncle's lake cabin, and my dad and Kathy still go, but I think it's been a number of years since Elliott and I were there. When we were younger, we had our OWN lake cabin in Wisconsin to go to! I'm the only one in my family who still enjoys fireworks, so I was always outnumbered on that one. Now, at Logan house, from the picture window in the kitchen we can actually see fireworks in a couple different places above the treeline. So I can kinda get my fix that way. Well, *I* can see them. Not so much for Janet, Danny, and Jim. Actually for Jim, the loud firework noises scare him, like a squirrel or rabbit being scared. I think that's partially due to the fact that he falls asleep in his chair in the living room, then the fireworks wake him up, and he gets all mad over being woken up. I'm pretty sure the 4th of July is his least favorite holiday.

It's my furry Molly kitty's golden birthday on the 4th of July! Turning 4 on the 4th. They grow up so fast!

I have a tendency to let so much time pass between blogs because I convince myself that I'll have something else exciting or important to write about before posting. Usually I don't. So, in the spirit of not waiting any longer, I'm posting this as-is.

Happy 4th of July to all!
Cheers.

July 11, 2017 Email
Incident
Krystin to Meridien people (bcc to dad):
Hi Amber and Liz.

    I was recently approached and lectured about not writing my blood sugar on the whiteboard, and was very offended and angered by the accusation. I was having a good day, until I was blindsided by this. I have not written my info on the board in a very long time, but apparently staff are saying I do, when it's actually staff who write my blood sugar info. The accusation went even further by being told it was the markers from the board I used to have, so therefore I must still be writing on the board. DESPITE the fact that the markers are kept in the med closet. Soooo, I got them, how? The more I tried to explain how it couldn't have been me, the more Tanya got defensive and said she didn't like I was talking to her. Which is quite funny considering that's how I'M talked to all the time by her. And now I also have to deal with staff lying about me. I'm sure they don't trust me at all anymore, but now I'm quickly learning not to trust staff, when lies are being told about me and incidents like this happen. This does not make for a happy home environment.

    Perhaps we need to discuss this more, but I'll leave that up to you.
    Cheers.
    Krystin

July 12, 2017 Email
Stress
Krystin to dad:

    I did some research yesterday on long-term effects of stress. I found this list on WebMD, and highlighted the effects that I have/have experienced. No wonder my resting heart rate is still over 100.

    I'm conflicted, though. I'd like to stay at Logan. Tanya is the only one/thing causing me so much stress. However, they're not going to switch to a new manager at Logan because of one person. Tanya needs to learn how to treat and talk to someone who is actually competent and can think for themselves. She also needs to grow up.

    Ly.

Dad to Krystin:
    Did you receive a response to your message?

Krystin to dad:
From Amber or Liz? No.

Dad to Krystin:
Let me know if you do. One possibility you have to be aware of is that they suggest you find somewhere else to live.

Krystin to dad:
Yeah, I'm aware of that. I hope it doesn't come to that, because like I've said before, I'm otherwise happy at Logan. And I think it was you who told me at one point to be careful what I wish for, because I could end up somewhere that is even worse. The first and only time we had a session together with Nancy, Tanya and I were good, great even, for at least a solid 2 months or so. I dunno, maybe we need to schedule quarterly "couples counseling" sessions with Nancy! It couldn't hurt, and the worst it could do is nothing.

Dad to Krystin:
Why don't you suggest that?

July 24, 2017 Email
Dad to Krystin:
Back to work tomorrow?
Sorry for the dull weekend. We don't necessarily do all the much!

Krystin to dad:
Yup, back to work today! It's a very slow day. I think I've not had anything to work on more than having something.

No worries about the weekend. Even if I just laze around, like I probably would've done at Logan, it's nice to be in a different environment, especially coming home and being with family and getting in some kitty time! At Logan, everything is all about medical this and medical that. When I'm home at 4020, or at mom's, yeah we may discuss some medical things here and there, but it's not the main focus of everything. I like escaping that, too. (I escape Logan; I don't escape from still following my medication regimen!)

I absolutely understand about the book thing. I actually just recently got the next Camilla Lackberg book, so I know that once I start, I won't be able to keep my nose out of it, either.

Ly!

July 30, 2017 Email
how are you doing?
Dad to Krystin:

 I only saw your text very late last night--we were at a play so I had my phone turned to silent. Are you going in?
Krystin to dad:

 I hurt. A lot. A very sharp, burning pain. And it's been constant. And not a thing to do about it. Fml. Oh, and no, I didn't go in.

Dad to Krystin:
 I am so sorry. I wish I could help. No doc help, I take it.

August 1, 2017 Email
what to do
Dad to Krystin:

 I haven't come up with any novel ideas. I do think, however, that you should find another doctor/clinic to consult with. Maybe your mom knows people at HCMC. The other place to consider (other than Mayo) might be Abbott-Northwestern. They used to have a pain clinic (your mother was there as an intern when we first met); I don't know if they still do, but in any case it's a good hospital/clinic and worth talking to.
 Mayo would be my first choice, but getting in there might be a lengthy process.
 But you have to do this; I can't.

August 1, 2017 Email
Pain
Krystin to Tanya, et al, dad, mom:
Hey guys,

 I'm emailing you all to address my ongoing pain issue, which seems to be getting worse by the day. I have not found any position to sit in or anything to do that relieves the pain, which means that I'm in this pain literally all my waking minutes of the day.
 I don't think anyone understands just how bad the pain is. It's paralyzing; it can literally stop me in my tracks and bring tears to my eyes. I can't sit in one position for more than a minute. I can't sleep, and I can't eat because it hurts too much. It hurts when I breathe. I've missed work and outings because of it. Right now, my life is misery. I'M miserable, and no one should have to live like this, ever. Over the

past several years I've developed a pretty high pain tolerance, and this pain right now, although in a different area of my body, is right up there with the pain I experienced after my transplants.

I would like to heavily consider a 2nd opinion on what could be going wrong. Recently I was told that Abbott Northwestern, Mayo, or even HCMC might have good pain management programs/physicians. I know that my pain management physician, Dawn, will never again prescribe me anything stronger than Tylenol, and in this case I think that 1) an exceptions should be made, and 2) I'm clearly not just drug seeking. Right now my biggest concern is self preservation, so if going elsewhere is what I have to do, I'm going to do it, because the U isn't doing jack shit for me.

Let me know your thoughts. I would like to take action sooner rather than later.

Thanks,
Krystin

Dad to Krystin:
Good for you! Did your mom respond?

Krystin to dad:
Yeah, she said to get a referral from Dawn.

August 5, 2017 Blog
Organized chaos

You remember that awful pain I was having a couple months ago, that started around Easter time? In the 2nd week of June I had the procedure done to check out what's going on in my esophagus, and if it was something wrong with the stent that was causing me such pain. Nope, the stent was perfectly in place. It eased the pain, but it'll come back. And with a vengeance. That's a story for another time.

It drives me nuts when a certain staff member drives me somewhere, say to my dad's house or to go visit my kitties. I know very well how to get to these places. At every single stop sign or stoplight or corner, I'll be asked no less than 4 times which way to go. If we're coming up on a stoplight and I say "at the light, take a left" (and there's only 1 stop light coming up), again it will be a game of 20 questions. Here? Yes. This stop light right here? Yes. Turn left here? Yup. Right here? YES DAMMIT, turn the corner! He always seems surprised that I know directions to places, and they almost don't believe me when I give an instruction, hence all the questions.

One of the staff who took me somewhere on the 4th of July wanted to stop at the African food market by our house, owned and operated by an African family. It was closed. An African market. On the 4th of July. Give it a second, you'll get it.

Punctuality is very important to me. Anyone who know me well knows that I'm habitually early to everything. Not when it comes to waking up in the morning, I should clarify that I'm not early at waking up. But when it comes to having to be at a certain place at a certain time, I'm ALWAYS on time, usually early, even. Being at Logan is ruining my early bird reputation. Now I'm hardly ever early to anything! Different staff drive at different speeds, the places on 94 where there's construction going on keeps changing, and if it's a Tuesday or Thursday and Tim is home, it takes forever and a day to get him out to the van and buckled in. Knowing that, I try to leave extra time for Tim, but somehow we end up leaving the house late anyway, because of some reason or another. I thought that by now I'd have a car again and be driving myself to and from work/appointments, but alas, no such luck. Some day . . .

I notice a lot more people standing on corners holding signs asking for money out here in the burbs than I ever did while growing up in Minneapolis. Understandably, though. Stopped at a red light the other day, I saw the driver of the car ahead of us lean out and give the beggar dude a $50 bill. FIFTY! I'm in the wrong profession! But don't bother trying to offer them food - they just want money, presumably for drugs or alcohol. I only say that because if you actually get a good look at a lot of them (but still trying not to make eye contact), they're wearing new Nike Air or Air Jordan shoes, or a Ralph Lauren shirt. Hmm. Curious.

I was a good Samaritan on the 4th of July. Well, let me first say, I know that it's a day to celebrate our country and all that, but I hate it because of all the firecrackers people set off in their backyards. It scares the living daylight out of animals, domestic or otherwise. Parent animals get spooked and abandon their babies. Every year, it breaks my heart to think of all the animals out there that have to find safety from the loud noises and scary sparks and such.

That being said, I rescued a kitten that night! My room is on the lower level of the house, so my window looks out at a deep window well. I was sitting on my bed watching Netflix, and I started to swear that I heard mewing coming from outside my window. I went over to the window to listen, and sure enough, I heard the kitten. It probably got spooked and jumped in there for safety, but then was stuck, and too small to jump back out. I called 911 and told them there's a kitten stuck in my window well, and they passed the message on to animal control. Less than 10 minutes later, an officer arrived. Since it was dark out, and we had to walk around to the back side of the house, he had a flashlight. It was a little stray grey and white kitten that couldn't be more than about 4 months old. The officer found a large shovel from our garage, to scoop the kitten out. Of course as he's trying to do that, the kitten freaks out and becomes all spastic and jumping around in the well. We finally get it out, though, and it zooms across the yard into some bushes.

The next day or so, I learned that there's a whole family of stray kitties living under the deck in the backyard! 5 kittens. 4 grey and white, 1 all grey. I watched them pounce and play and roll around on the deck, probably waiting for mom to return with breakfast! My heart was very happy, even if they're strays. SO cute!!

Not sure if I mentioned this before, but I'm now working 3 days a week. T,W,Th 1-5. I love being back at work, and having that chunk of time out of the house. To be able to focus on something other than medical issues. When I went on my 3 month staycation at the hospital last year, I lost one of my biggest (and favorite) tasks to one of my co-workers. That's OK, I knew that since I was gone, someone needed to do it. Upon returning to work this year, I learned that I will not be getting that task back. Not because I wasn't good at it or anything. Quite the contrary. It was like my baby, my special project, because then I was given the task (from someone who left to work elsewhere), it was a big 'ol mess. I organized it, shaped it, made it more convenient. Plus it made me feel a little special, that it was a special task that was turned over to me, out of all the support staff, to manage on top of my regular tasks. Now I don't have any tasks that are just mine, that I'm in charge of. I know, I know, with time those kinds of things will come back to me. I guess the fact that I only work 12 hours a week makes it difficult to assign me anything that needs to be worked on every day.

I researched long-term side effects that stress can have on a person. I found a legit list on WebMD, which I consider to be a reputable website. In each different section, I highlighted the symptoms that I'm experiencing now. 90% of the cause of my stress? Callie.

Emotional symptoms of stress include:

- Becoming easily agitated, frustrated, and moody
- Feeling overwhelmed, like you are losing control or need to take control
- Having difficulty relaxing and quieting your mind
- Feeling bad about yourself (low self-esteem), lonely, worthless, and depressed
- Avoiding others

Physical symptoms of stress include:

- Low energy
- Headaches
- Upset stomach, including diarrhea, constipation, and nausea
- Aches, pains, and tense muscles
- Chest pain and rapid heartbeat
- Insomnia
- Frequent colds and infections
- Loss of sexual desire and/or ability
- Nervousness and shaking, ringing in the ear, cold or sweaty hands and feet
- Dry mouth and difficulty swallowing
- Clenched jaw and grinding teeth

Cognitive symptoms of stress include:

- Constant worrying
- Racing thoughts
- Forgetfulness and disorganization
- Inability to focus
- Poor judgment
- Being pessimistic or seeing only the negative side

Behavioral symptoms of stress include:

Behavioral symptoms of stress include:

- Increased use of alcohol, drugs, or cigarettes
- Exhibiting more nervous behaviors, such as nail biting, fidgeting, and pacing

What Are the Consequences of Long-Term Stress?

A little stress every now and then is not something to be concerned about. Ongoing, chronic stress, however, can cause or exacerbate many serious health problems, including:

- Mental health problems, such as depression, anxiety, and personality disorders
- Cardiovascular disease, including heart disease, high blood pressure, abnormal heart rhythms, heart attacks, and stroke
- Obesity and other eating disorders
- Menstrual problems
- Sexual dysfunction, such as impotence and premature ejaculation in men and loss of sexual desire in both men and women
- Skin and hair problems, such as acne, psoriasis, and eczema, and permanent hair loss
- Gastrointestinal problems, such as GERD, gastritis, ulcerative colitis, and irritable colon

I've discussed this situation with both of my parents, and they have both inquired as to whether or not I'd like to start looking at other structured living options. *Sigh. That's a very loaded question. I like being at Logan. I like the staff. I like my housemates. Even Danny, the human food vacuum. Callie is literally the ONLY one, in all of Meridian Services, who I have a problem with. I shouldn't have to pick up my life and move it elsewhere because of one person. But I know she's not going to change. She's like me in that we're both strong, stubborn, and sometimes even a little defiant, women. Sometimes you have to stoop to someone else's level to effectively communicate with someone.

Janet has been in the hospital over a month now, with no known discharge date. She must feel scared and out of place. She doesn't know her surrounding, or any of the nurses. It's like starting at ground zero for her, building up trust with all these new people. She's been at Logan house for many years now. She knows the lay of the land and all the staff. She knows she can trust them with her life. Being blind and moved to a hospital setting is a whole new ball game. I have gone with staff a couple times to visit her. You can see it on her face how happy she is to have people she knows come to visit.

No staff visit me in hospital. Callie said cuz I've never asked anyone to. Touché.

I will be back soon, so don't miss me too much!

Cheers for now.

August 11, 2017 Facebook
Krystin Engstrand is feeling ecstatic.
Today I'm putting in a full 8 hour day; my first 8 hour day since February 2016. Time to make it rain, y'all!

August 11, 2017 Blog
[her final post, two months and a week before she died]
A wee post

If anyone emails me with questions or comments regarding a recent blog post, and I don't respond, I promise I'm not ignoring you. I usually plan to address it in my next post. If you have a question, other people may have the same question!

That being said . . .

I was admitted to the hospital recently, following an EGD with stent alignment. My stent had migrated way down, and it had started to cause both pain and difficulty swallowing. The same procedure I've had done dozens of times in the past. This time, however, I was so tired after coming out of anesthesia; more so than would normally be expected. It landed in inpatient for 2 days to come out of the grogginess. I could hardly function because I was SO tired. I could hardly keep my eyes open or concentrate on things that people told me or asked me. I've never had this kind of reaction before! After a couple days, there was nothing medically keeping me there, so they had to discharge me, ready or not. It's amazing the healing powers of one's own bed! But the majority of my pain is gone, so overall I'd say it was successful.

Emmett has become one of my favorite staff people. He himself has a handful of now grown daughters, all older than me. I can tell he cares a lot about me, perhaps because I trigger in him the father role, in a way. Which is wonderful, because it's nice to have a staff person around who genuinely cares about the clientele, and doesn't just see it as a job. He's worked at Logan for something like 17 years! The other day he said "I don't like you being in the hospital, because then you are not happy. I like when you're home, because then you are happy and smiling, and we can all smile together!" Probably one of the sweetest things I've ever been told. But I digress. The point is, he's seen and heard it all, so it's nearly impossible to offend him.

A number of months ago, I was on my way upstairs and started smelling something funky. Callie was in the kitchen, so I asked her what was cooking, because it smelled like dog or cat food. She said "Krystin, don't be rude, it's Emmett's dinner." Awk. Ward. Callie later told me that stuff like that rolls right off his back. I still felt bad, and of course I apologized to Emmett.

I love that he can turn anything into a song. Kinda like my mom and her sisters. He'll make up a tune and sing away, impromptu. I always wanted a song to be written for/about me. Now I have 10.

After a year of dealing with Callie and "allowing" her to talk to me and treat me unfairly, I'm finally taking my voice back. I didn't feel like I had my own voice anymore, and I'm done letting her walk all over me. I'm being my own advocate and standing up for myself, making sure that when my health and well being are on the table, that my opinion is heard. I don't do it in a snarky way or anything. I do it out of respect for myself. If I talk to her in the same tone she uses when talking to me, she doesn't like the way I'm talking to her and feels disrespected, I point out that I'm only returning the favor, and that I learned it all from her. She doesn't like that, either. I know that I need to take the high road and be the adult in the matter, but sometimes she needs a taste of her own medicine. And I admit, that's childish, but sometimes it feels good.

She has become much more professional and less friend-like with me. The line dividing the 2 sides is much more distinct. Maybe it's better, in our situation, that she play the managerial role the majority of the time. I think that trying to be friends was the underlying cause of most of our arguments. It's probably hard to set/enforce rules, from a managerial role, with friends. For us, it has to be one or the other, but not both.

A couple people have brought up the idea of considering finding a new place, like within a different company. I'm still on the side of staying at Logan. A few different staff people at Logan have talked about other homes, because a lot of them have 2 jobs, the other being at a group home run by a different company, and I never hear good things. Altogether, Logan is the best, in many different categories. We have been staffing, better structure and supervision, better management (as far as actually working directly with residents on a daily basis), better structure and supervision of clients' medications, better management of doctor appointments and the manager being so involved in everyone's health care, running a tight ship at the house as far as laying out and enforcing rules and policies, yadda yadda yadda. No matter how angry/frustrated/irritated I can get with Callie, after looking at all this on paper, it's pretty clear that Logan is the best place for me to be if I want to be successful with my health care and helping me build those responsibilities and duties that I'll need to be ready to live on my own again, some day. I just need to suck it up and work hard, instead of keeping doing things that set me back. I love this quote that I read somewhere that says something about how you must do the thing that you don't want to do, to get to the place that you would like to be. Maybe it was a fortune cookies. Either way, I can dedicate a few years at Logan, so that I can have many years back out on my own. Yay for goals!

 A few weekends ago I spent a night at my mom's, because she was babysitting my furry kids. The next day, my mom drove me back to Logan. I went down to my room to unpack and relax. I do my dinner blood sugar around 5. 5:00 came and went, as did 6:00, and still nobody came to get me. A little after 7, I was sufficiently hungry, so I made my way upstairs. Whoever was sitting at the dining room table, was looking in my general direction, with an expression as if they'd just seen a ghost. They were very relieved to see me, so the ghostly expression turned into surprise. They had no idea I was home! I guess the other staff person forgot to pass on to the next person that I was there. Communication fail.

 If you've ever wondered, and I'm sure you have, if a kidney transplant person can still get a kidney stone, then wait no longer. The answer is yes! And if you also have a history of abusing your pain meds, no matter how long ago, then you get to pass the stone with naught but Tylenol and time. That sounds like a grand 'ol time. Said no one EVER while passing a kidney stone. I know that because of my history, I screwed myself over with my narcotic pain med, but come ON docs, you gotta be kidding me! I know people who have been admitted to the hospital because of a kidney stone. I'm tough, and

I can handle most medical-related things that docs toss at me, but this is one instance where I don't want to tough it out. I hurt and I want either 1) for it to hurry up and pass through already, or 2) help me out, docs. Does this count as sadistic, inhumane, cruel and unusual punishment? Because it sure feels like it. :(

As far as my chronic pain, well, that's what my Gabapentin (also known as Neurontin - a non-opioid pain med) is for, and it's something I'm going to have to learn to live with and get used to. Mostly because no scans or tests or anything can show docs the cause of the pain. Perhaps it's as easy as something like for someone who's had numerous major abdominal surgeries, it's a pain that will always be there. Well that sounds fun. Still no advances in the whole medical marijuana thing as far as it being used by diabetics and/or transplant patients. Please, by all means, I'll be a test subject! It's such a mellow drug, I can't imagine it could cause harm to my kidney. I've been through so many other medical procedures and surgeries and infections, and blah blah blah, and still it's going strong. As for my blood sugar levels, well, if I HAD to guess what medical marijuana could possibly do, is slightly lower my blood sugar levels, if not maintaining them within my goal range. I should bring this up with my pain management physician. . . .

(No, I'm pretty sure that medical marijuana doesn't have the same effect as the pot that people buy off the street and smoke. In fact, I WOULDN'T want any psychedelic effects! I gotta stay on top of my game.)

Omg . . . right now, as I write this, Danny is upstairs in the bathroom and has locked staff out, and it sounds like he thinks the situation is pretty hilarious. Have I told you how he likes to wear his Halloween costumes to work, no matter the season. Don't mind us over here, we're just taking our humongous hot dog for a walk.

I can't eat at the table at the same time as Danny. He's a human vacuum, and it's ridiculous how much food he can fit in his mouth. He's like a hamster, stuffing it all into the sides of his cheeks, makes one big swallow, and does it again with the next bite. I honestly don't know how he hasn't choked yet. He'll pop a whole hard-boiled egg into his mouth in one bite. A whole deli sandwich, fixings and all, in 3 or 4 bites. A regular size piece of pizza in 2. A hot dog in a bun in 3, maybe 2. You get the idea. I can't watch it, and I especially don't want to hear it! You know that with that much food in his mouth, he isn't chomping away with his mouth closed. Bleah. I don't know why eating is such a race for him. On occasion, I've told him that his food isn't going anywhere; it's not going to sprout some legs and run off. I think that behavior is so ingrained in him, it doesn't matter what people say. He's not going to change.

I haven't again seen any of the family of kitties living under our back deck. Callie said that she had to let maintenance know, by Meridien policy. Not kill them or anything. Just to catch them and bring them to a shelter or humane society or something. All very humane. I still can't help but look out the kitchen window every morning, just in case! And actually, if the kitties did get caught, that would explain why I'm seeing more
bunnies. . . .

Speaking of bunnies - I'm still looking into the possibility of getting myself a bunny and registering it with the county as an emotional/stress therapy animal. I would like one person to raise their hand and say my life isn't emotional or stressful enough for a therapy animal. Anyone? I'm not actively pursuing this right now, but every once in awhile I look up bunnies on the Humane Society website, over the years I've read up on how to care for a bunny (no loose cords on the ground!), and I've read up on Hennepin County's website about requirements for a therapy animal. I've wanted a bunny since kindergarten, so this isn't a new thing for me. I'm allowed to have a bunny at Logan, and although I love my furry babies more than words can express, it does break my heart a tiny bit when I have to leave them after visiting them. This way I know I'd have another furry baby waiting for me at home. And I'm PRETTY sure that Janet and Danny would love to come down and sit and hold/pet a bunny once in a while. See? This could benefit everyone! ;)

I work until 5 now, and sometimes Logan staff forget to come get me. The dudes earlier this week thought I was still in the hospital, despite the fact that they've both seen me since then. I was a little angry and impatient at first, but I was also slightly amused by the situation. I shouldn't have been surprised. After all, men.

We had a staff meeting at work this morning, and about halfway through, my insulin pod, located on the back of my arm, started beeping. It was giving me my 24-hour notice that I need to change my pod tomorrow morning. Oops, my bad, excuse me while I slip out and make my arm stop beeping at everyone. It's not really that awkward, though, because most of my co-workers know that I'm diabetic and I have some kind of insulin device attached to me somewhere. It's like

'Where's Waldo?' of the diabetic world. 'Where's Krystin's Pod?' Ha! I'm a genius. ;)

Yes, I'm working on a Friday; it's to make up the time that I missed last week from being in the hospital. This is the FIRST full, 8-hour I've worked since way back in February 2016! It went very well. At no time in the afternoon did I feel exhausted or like I needed to take a nap. 8 hour days are not the norm. Like I said, I only did it today to make up for lost time. Next week I'll return to my T-W-Th schedule. But yay for progress!

As is with any group of people who spend time together often, many people can adopt nicknames, usually bestowed upon them by someone else in the group. I call Tim 'Timiny Cricket' (after Jiminy Cricket in Pinocchio). Janet calls me Jelly bean lady, and 2 of the older staff call me Krys (and only 2 other people in my entire life have ever shortened my name), but that's about it. It's strange hearing my name shortened, because that's not my name, and I don't go by that name, and never have, so it's like wait, what, who me? The other 2 people in my life had earned the right to shorten my name. My 1st grade teacher, whom I absolutely adored, and the wife of a couple who have been long-time friends of the family. If I'm not called Krys by the aforementioned staff, then it's Krysti (like Christie). I guess it's too much work to add that 'n' at the end of my name? In the end, it doesn't really matter, and I don't feel the need to correct them, because I know they're talking to me and not someone else. I have much bigger issues to worry about than how someone pronounces my name!

Well my friends, that is all I have for you now. Enjoy the weekend, and here's hoping that it'll be nice in your neck of the woods.

Cheers!

August 11, 2017 Email
Unplanned absences at my work
Krystin to Tanya, dad, mom:
Hi all,

I didn't get in TOO much trouble about the day of work that I missed last week due to unforeseen circumstances after my procedure, but Laura did pull me aside today to ask me to really try and let her or someone here at work know if I'm going to miss more work than planned. They let it slide this time, but if it happens again, there may be some repercussions. Most of the time, I'll be able to contact people on my own. This past time, however, I wasn't able to do that because

I was still drooling and sleeping and spilling apple juice all over myself, and any speech sounded like mumble-jumble. Then there were times where I thought I was conversing with someone (who was in the room), but I was only thinking the words in my head and not actually saying them out loud. . . .

SO, I thought up the idea of a phone tree-type chart. 99.9% of the time, Tanya will be at the top, because she'll be the one taking me in (like to the ER, for example). From there, I am providing a list of who, in order, needs to be contacted. [list]

If NONE of these people are reachable, then run, because there's probably a zombie attack. Or a giant asteroid about to hit us. I could see it going either way.

I am open to any other thoughts/suggestions/questions/etc. about this plan. Happy Friday, and have a good weekend!

September 4, 2017 Facebook

When it comes to the state fair, part II: go JUMBO (cotton candy) or go home!

September 13, 2017 Email
Discussion topic for my quarterly
Krystin to Tanya, others at Meridien, dad, mom, Kathy:

Perhaps this is something to discuss at my quarterly, but we need to set clear and distinct rules and policies of Meridian. No more of something that I'd been doing for the past year suddenly being not allowed. One of the main things that we need to work on, TOGETHER, is what I actually do and don't have a choice of. I'm constantly being told that I'm my own guardian and that I can make my own decisions, but in reality, I don't. So the words "you can make your own decisions" needs to stop being said to me. I'm not asked about X or Y; I'm told. If I disagree with almost anything, I'm threatened with 911 being called. I want to know that, as the competent adult that I am, if I say I don't want to do something, I don't want to have to do it. Unless it puts myself and others around me in serious harm, which has never been the case during the time I've lived at Logan.

If I want to have a snack in my room while I relax, as long as it's part of my diet, why can't I do it? are you worried about spills? So, I'd clean it up. I highly, highly doubt that, while growing up, your parents, or anyone's within throwing distance parents forbade you to ever eat in your room because they worried about spills. There is nothing that I eat that would cause a major flood in the basement, or even require anything more than a couple paper towels and some Lysol cleaning spray. If say a dribble of this or that fell onto my bed or floor, it's not like I'm going to leave it there without cleaning it up, and spend the next week watching bugs infest my room. No. I'm going to clean it up, and knowing by now how much I absolutely hate anything creepy-crawly, you damn well know I'm going to get that cleaned up! So, I would honestly like an explanation as to why this rule is in place, since it affects absolutely no one, in any way. I'm not asking to eat a whole meal downstairs.

If you're worried about my insulin, then that's where a rule can be set. Say that I have to be back up within a certain amount of time to show that I finished my snack, and to clean up and dishes that were used. I'm not like all the other individuals at the Meridian houses; you guys tell me that all the time. So why can't special rules be made for me? It's basic psychology. If you give me a little slack, give me even just a couple exceptions, give me back a little control over something, then I wouldn't fight back and break the rules all the time. And a lot of the time, I don't even know I'm breaking a rule! Like I said, it seems like some things change daily, so it's almost impossible for me to keep track what is allowed and what isn't allowed on each day of the week. I went from 100 to 0 overnight, as far as what I'm in control of in my life. Even a year and a third later, this is still a very predominant issue. Maybe if I have a little control over some things, I'll be happier, and if I'm happier, then I wouldn't push back so much. More basic psychology.

Tanya, I know you don't like when I go over your head, and you like me to discuss my issues directly with you, but let's be honest, all that happens the majority of the time is we end up arguing in a power struggle. Sometimes we just need some mediation, and the viewpoint and opinion of someone outside the situation, in the hopes that an outsider could look at the situation unbiased, and not enter into it already having decided that I'm wrong, without even having heard both sides.

I'm not sure when my quarterly meeting got moved to, but I would definitely like this to be something that we discuss together, with Cassandra.

Krystin

September 14, 2017 Email
Theory
Krystin to mom, dad, Kathy:

I have a theory about what has been causing my alleged delusions and psychosis. I still truly believe that something is physically going on, and not just my brain making me think I see things on me. Hear me out and humor me before going to Tanya and telling her I need to go back to the psych ward. :D

I want Logan house to be tested for asbestos; especially the basement. I believe it started, however, way back when I lived in my apartment. You've mentioned before about how sick I always was while in my apartment. You attributed it to the cats, because that seemed like the most likely and plausible cause, but I don't actually think it was. I think it was either already an issue in the building (which I don't think), or it came in on that circular, dark blue rug that I had in my living room area. In rooms where there is constant airflow, and not just a dank room with sitting air, asbestos can live almost indefinitely. If on the rug, that would mean it came with me to Logan house. THAT could be why I frequently got sick and have been having many more health issues over the past couple years. Especially being someone with a very compromised immune system.

I have taken many pictures over the past number of months, and just recently I read something about asbestos, so I googled asbestos on ceilings/walls/carpets/skin/floors/cloths/etc. etc. The pictures that I've been taking? EXACT matches, in pattern and color, to the pics I've seen on google.

I want the house to get tested, but I'm afraid that if I tell Tanya, she'll think I'm going crazy again, laugh it off, and do nothing about it, hoping that the feeling would pass and I'd forget about it. I haven't forgotten about it even once over the past 10 or so months. I'm determined to find the root of the cause, because, like I said, I do believe it is something going on in the environment, and not in my head. I even looked up how to get a home tested. Minnesota has 2 licensed asbestos tester people, who can look at a home, take samples, test them, and officially "diagnose" asbestos in a home. I don't know if the initial visit is free, but I'm considering contacting both of them.

I'm attaching 2 pictures. The first is one of asbestos on carpet, that I found on google. The 2nd one is a picture I took of MY carpet at Logan house. I have many more pictures like this, from the walls, ceilings, furniture, clothing, floors, my skin . . .

Am I going crazy?

1 Asbestos on carpet.jpg
2 Asbestos on my carpet.jpg

Dad to Krystin, cc Pat, Kathy:

I have no way to judge whether or not your hypothesis is correct. Apart from a modest cost, I don't know what harm would be done by a test.

Kathy to Gary, Krystin, Pat:

The first picture is titled "asbestos on carpet," but it's clearly not. It's some kind of white spots that appear to have been under a tile floor. That dark part is the old glue that's still on the floor after removing the tiles. You can see the lighter colored tiles to the right in the pic and the same tile square markings where the tile has been removed.

Pat to Gary, Krystin, Kathy:

The one picture isn't carpet; it's the subfloor after tile has been removed. The other picture looks like cotton candy, but what do I know.

A group home needs to be inspected and certified annually. Just ask them to see a copy of the most recent report. Then you'll know.

September 22, 2017 Email
Work
Krystin to dad, mom, Kathy:

Starting next week, my work hours increase to 20 hrs a week!

M 8:30-12:30 (then therapy group 1-3)
T 8:30-1
W 8:30-11:30 (then therapy w/Nancy 12pm)
Th 8:30-1
F 8:30-12:30

Woohoo!

September 28, 2017 Facebook
Krystin Engstrand is feeling awful.

Had my routine esophageal stent replacement procedure yesterday. Still out of commission today, and possibly tomorrow. I have never had as much post-procedure pain as I have now. And this Tylenol is doing jack sh*t.

Sad

September 29, 2017 Email
how you doing?
Dad to Krystin:

It's 10 here, so going to bed in a few minutes [we were in Europe]. Saw your FB post; hope the pain is going away. LY

September 30, 2017 Email
Krystin to dad:

Honestly, I'm doing horribly. The pain is very close to unbearable. I can hardly take it. And of course all I get is Tylenol. Even went to urgent care yesterday. Not much he could do to help. He said to follow up with thoracic on Monday.

I've been sleeping a lot, to make time go by and because when sleeping I don't feel pain. 😢

But don't let this weigh on your mind, ok? This too, shall pass. Take in everything and enjoy every minute! Ly.

Dad to Krystin:

Well, heavens, I hope you get better quickly! LY

October 4, 2017 Facebook
Krystin Engstrand is feeling pained.
My body is one big smorgasbord buffet line that viruses and germs help themselves to, whenever they want to. Today, going in to get tested for strep.

October 6, 2017 Email
KE
Logan [Tanya] to Gary, Kathy, Pat, cc Krystin:
Hello,

I wanted to update you all on a situation with Krystin.

Krystin has been experiencing some pain after getting her stent replaced last Wednesday, September 27th. Krystin was seen on Friday, September 29th for the pain and prescribed Tylenol 3. During the weekend, Krystin's pain wasn't bad and was using chloroacetic spray to help numb the throat. Krystin was brought to urgent care, again, yesterday October 4th to get checked for strep throat. Her test came back negative, so I asked them to do an Xray of her stent to rule out any problems with her stent.

Krystin's stent had migrated upwards. We contacted the thoracic team, as Krystin did not want to be rushed to the ER right away and wanted to see what they had to say. Krystin agreed that if we have not heard back from them by this morning, October 5, that we would go to the ER. Krystin and I went to the ER this morning and the have determined to admit Krystin to the u of m so they can get the procedure done inpatient and hopefully get her in quicker for a procedure.

She will be on floor 7b. Once I know I a room I can email everyone!

Please let me know if you have questions.

Gary to Tanya, Pat, Kathy, Krystin:
Thank you, Tanya.

As Krystin probably told you, Kathy and I are in France, so I won't be able to visit her. But keep us posted.

Pat to Tanya, Gary, Kathy, Krystin:
Thanks Tanya.

Just FYI - Gary and Kathy are out of the country so it should be only my ## (612 799-8542) on Krystin's hospital room board for this admit. Might you let staff know that?

Funny, she JUST sent me a text telling me that October 6th is National Transfer Money to your Daughter's Account Day. She said nothing about being in the ER/hospital!!

Oh, second text just came: procedure probably sometime this afternoon. Still nothing about being in the hospital.

Wow.

As always, keep me posted.

Pat

October 16, 2017 Email (my final email exchange with her)
Krystin to dad:

Woke up around 5am this [Monday] morning feeling super nauseous. Even had to pull my garbage can over next to the bed. I especially feel nauseous after eating. Try as I might, I haven't been able to gain weight for the life of me. In fact, I've been losing weight, and my appetite has greatly decreased. I've had little energy, am tired most of the time, and frequently feel bloated.

Last time I had all these symptoms simultaneously was back in January, and required bowel reconstructive surgery.

So you can probably imagine why this is a little disconcerting for me. I do NOT want to spend another bday in the hospital. ☹

Dad to Krystin:

Ugh. I'm sorry. I trust you're in touch with the docs. LY

Krystin to dad:

Not yet. I haven't even told Tanya. I'm scared I might get admitted. It's too close to my bday for that. . . .

Dad to Krystin:

But you can't go on like this for days. Besides, you shouldn't ignore a medical problem that might get worse.

At lunch on Tuesday, October 17, I received a call that I was to get to the hospital as soon as possible.

Tod und Erinnerung†

Star-Tribune

Krystin Engstrand

Engstrand, Krystin age 32, Minneapolis, died 10/17/17 from complications of diabetes. Survived by her mother Pat, her father Gary and his wife Kathy, her brother Elliott, and many aunts, uncles, cousins, & friends. A proud graduate and employee of the University of Minnesota. She had much love for her cats, a lifelong ambition to become a writer, and a positive outlook for the future. We admired her strength through so many challenges and will miss her quirky sense of humor. A celebration of Krystin's life will be held October 29 at 4020 46th Ave So, Minneapolis, 55406, 2:00 - 4:00. Memorials to Animal Humane Society or American Diabetes Association.

Published on October 22, 2017

---

† "Death and Remembrance." After Richard Strauss's *Tod und Verklärung* (Death and Transfiguration), in acknowledgement of Krystin's German, which she studied for several years in college. As did I, in high school and college. We occasionally used German in our emails and text messages.

* * *

Let me begin this chapter with excerpts from a lengthy message sent to me by one of Krystin's friends eight months after Krystin died, a message she sent in response to a question from me on how she met Krystin. They met in South Korea teaching. Quoted with permission.

She wrote to me that she wanted me "to understand Krystin and know her from my point of view and how I knew her. It's not an attempt to canonize her as she would laugh out loud at the idea of people thinking her saintly, but she was a complex person and I want to do her justice by sharing my memories of her."

> Something that I always loved about Krystin was how observant she was. She really had a mind like a detective, and could infer things about people from their behavior or the circumstances at hand. She was always trying to maximize things at work and create better systems for organization or execution of plans. I remember being at the mall with her once in Cheonan, waiting to see a movie after we had lunch at a noodle place, and a Lady Gaga song came on. There's a part of the song that has a background vocal that is so faint, and I remember her pointing out that part of the song saying it was her favorite. The fact that she was so aware of subtlety and had a taste for things that were well done artistically is something that remains with me. After she left Korea she sent me a huge box of toys, candy, puppets, stickers so I could distribute it to the Korean students we taught. It must have cost her at least $200 to buy everything and send it. She was the only teacher that I knew of to do something so beautiful and generous like that. The kids were just crazy over all the new and interesting things. It was such a triumph!
>
> There are probably things about Krystin that you are surprised to read and know, because it doesn't seem to mesh with what you knew of her as your daughter. Kids don't want to disappoint their parents or feel that their actions are being disapproved of or not right for them, so a lot of times we don't tell our parents what we are feeling or thinking (or doing). I think a lot of the silence on how Krystin really felt about things in her life, especially regarding having diabetes, was deeply rooted in anger and shame over her own management

or mismanagement of having a chronic illness. She absolutely HATED having to have an insulin pump and having to deal with diabetes.

From my point of view I really don't think she ever got over being forced into a world that she had no choices. She would smoke socially, but when I would go visit her at her apartment she would never have to leave to take a smoke break, which makes me think she was not addicted to it. She would also only drink socially and not at home after work. The fact that she drank and smoke only socially leads me to believe that it was just another way that she wanted to be like everybody else and feel young and normal, even if it meant possibly hurting her own health. No one likes to be reminded of their mortality every day, and I think having to be so responsible all the time really stressed her out.

I think she tired of responsibility, a responsibility that was forced on her by life. As I said before in one of my posts, people without a chronic illness don't seem to understand the psychological drain it is to always have to be so aware of bodily functions and how it relates to day to day life. Take that, in combination with the everyday stress of work and relationships with families, friends and significant others, and it can be intense and hard to deal with sometimes.

I remember her telling me how it bothered her to try to have a physical relationship and be vulnerable for a guy to see the place on her body where her pump plugged in. She was very self conscious about it and I think it prevented her from pursuing relationships that she wanted because she felt like it made her unattractive or unappealing to men. She told me about the time she was in Europe and went into ketosis. She hadn't been taking care of her diabetes and she ended up in the hospital, I think it was Paris. She told me about how her mother took care of so many things for her and how guilty she felt that she had put her mother in that situation. She told me that she really felt like she understood a mother's love for her child after that experience, and she felt a lot of shame that she had let her mother down by almost dying due to her own negligence.

I think that Krystin flirted with the idea of dying because she fantasized it as a way of having control over her situation and being without pain or worry. She was never truly suicidal or anything like that but she did mention to me after the pancreas transplant started to go bad that she was really tired and sick of dealing with medical issues. She told me several times that she was not really afraid of dying but was more worried what it would do to you and her mom. I know that Krystin had a step mom, but she did not talk about her much to me other than to say she was "cool." She mostly talked to me about you and her mom and her brother. She loved her brother more than I have seen some siblings love each other, but it annoyed her that she felt that he was not using his full potential. I think that is something all older siblings feel about the younger one though, especially when we are in our 20s. She felt extremely appreciative of everything you did to help her when she got back from Korea. She told me often how you and her mom were her heroes. I know that you guys fought sometimes, but I want you to know that she had so much respect and admiration for you. I think she knew that most of the arguments were because you both believed you were right, and she knew she was stubborn and didn't like to admit when you were right and she was wrong. Again, it was kind of a perfectionist streak where she didn't like to be wrong.

 I wanted to tell you [about] a conversation she and I had around the time when she was trying to get a kidney transplant. She was super pissed at you because at that time you would not consider having her brother tested or checked as a possible donor. I remember her telling me that you didn't want to risk losing two children. She was just absolutely furious at you, but some time later she told me how hard it must have been for you as a parent to be in that situation, and that you made the right choice. She had so much respect for you to have made that decision, even though she had previously been so angry at you for it. I hope that me telling you this doesn't hurt you, but makes you understand how much she loved and respected you. And if that was something that ever upset or worried you, I hope that it doesn't anymore. [Elliott was never going to be a donor. As he put it to me recently, "I think we did talk about it and the entire talk consisted of you telling me I was not going to donate a kidney and me agreeing." I doubt it mattered what I said; he had seen for too many years how Krystin hadn't followed the protocols she was supposed to, so he had decided he wasn't going to go through transplant surgery for her. Krystin was upset with me because I wouldn't lobby him to be a donor.]

I know this was a long email, but it was sent with a lot of love and respect. I still feel a lot of pain at not being able to call her or send her a message. I still think about her a lot, and I always will. Even though she had what most would consider a short life, she was able to do more than most people, and she did it all with a chronic illness. I know that she wanted to do more to inspire others, and that she really wanted to use writing as a way to give people hope.

* * *

I was having lunch with a friend at the University of Minnesota's faculty/staff dining club on October 17, 2017. My cell phone rang but I ignored it during the lunch conversation. As we were preparing to leave, I checked my phone and retrieved a voice mail message. The message was from Tanya, Krystin's primary care-giver at her group home, telling me I needed to get to the hospital as soon as possible. Krystin was in intensive care. Krystin was in the University hospital, about two blocks across campus from the dining club, so I walked over there quickly.

Upon arriving at ICU, I met Tanya, and we were walked to a conference room by one of the physicians. We passed the room where Krystin was being treated; I could see that there were seven or eight people around her bed. When the two of us were seated, the ICU physician, Dr. William Browne, described Krystin's medical situation. He told us Krystin had been bleeding from her aorta into her esophagus; he drew us a diagram to illustrate and explain the situation. As a short-term measure, they had put in a stent. I asked what the long-term solution would be; he did not reply to that question at the time.

Shortly thereafter Pat arrived at the hospital. (Tanya had also called Pat.) Pat, Tanya, and I were convened in another conference room with Dr. Browne and a couple of other people on the hospital staff. One of those people, I assume a hospital social worker, took the lead in the discussion. He informed us that Krystin's medical condition was "not survivable," but that they would "clean her up" (I believe that was his phrase) and keep her alive long enough for us to say our goodbyes. I asked if they would bring her back to consciousness; he said they would not. I told him I agreed that they should not, if doing so would mean she would be awakened to learn she was dying. (Dr. Browne had not responded to my question about a long-term solution because he knew there wasn't one—I inferred he did not do so because he was not the person who should deliver the message that Krystin was in a terminal state.)

At this point I texted both Kathy (my wife) and Elliott (my son, Krystin's brother) to come to the hospital immediately. My text to Elliott read "CALL ME IMMEDIATELY WHEN YOU CAN. IMMEDIATELY!" Elliott worked on campus, at a building a few blocks from the hospital; after we talked and I told him what was going on, he left work to walk over. He commented that he didn't ask questions. He knew it was important because I never use capital letters in text messages.

Kathy also worked on campus and subsequently walked over following this exchange about 1:00.
G: Called to the hospital. Idk what this about.
K: I don't know what you're talking about.
G: Pat and I have been called to the hospital following Krystin surgery
K: When?
G: Now. I'm just getting to 4th floor icu.
K: Let me know what's going on when you can.

At about a quarter after the hour I texted her again.
G: Talked to doc. Waiting in lounge. Substantial internal aortic bleeding, they have tried but can't seem to stop. Sounds like she may not survive.
K: Should I come over?
G: Not yet.
K: Unless you don't want me there, I'd like to come. Where are you?
G. OK. 4th floor icu 4C. Ask for where parents are.

At 1:30 I texted Kathy again.
G: She dying. Will end today.

At 1:40:
G: We get a little time with her, but she not conscious, will not regain consciousness.

After which Kathy arrived at the hospital.

Pat had also alerted Peggy Hinz about Krystin's condition. Peggy asked if she could come to the hospital; Pat told her to do so.

Shortly thereafter Pat, Elliott, Kathy, Tanya, and I were ushered into Krystin's hospital room; Peggy joined us. As I had told Kathy in a text, Krystin was not conscious and was hooked up to equipment of some kind. It was clear that there had been blood in many places, although Krystin was clean. We remained in the room for perhaps an hour, hugging Krystin and talking quietly. We then departed.

Here is the summary of events that I composed within the week after Krystin died (in italics). Dr. Browne helped me by spending an hour on the telephone with me several days later and who then exchanged emails with me to confirm the accuracy of my narrative. What he told me to start with:

I know there were many physicians from multiple specialties who talked with you on the day Krystin died. I was not the surgeon who performed the procedures on Krystin. I am an intensive care specialist, and I only work in the ICU. I took care of Krystin only while she was physically in the ICU. Our gastroenterologists, anesthesiologists, thoracic and cardiovascular surgeons and interventional radiologists provided all of her care while she was in the endoscopy suite and operating room.

Dr. Browne told me that because Krystin came into the ICU, she was his patient, and even though she moved to the endoscopy suite and operating room, he received regular updates through the morning and then met face to face with the physicians who had been in the operating room.

First, I had to ask him what a fistula was. He described it as similar to two plumbing pipes running together in your house, and one of them rusts through to the other, so what they carry gets mixed together. If one of the pipes is carrying liquid under high pressure, it will immediately begin propelling liquids into the other pipe at the site of the fistula. This was the point of the diagram he had sketched when Tanya and I first met with him, although it took this later explanation for me to fully understand the situation.

Gastroparesis is the failure of the stomach to appropriately absorb food, causing acid reflux, which Krystin suffered from. Dr. Browne said gastroparesis is a big problem for those with diabetes: the stomach basically quits doing what it's supposed to do and just sits there.

Over the previous months Krystin had had a stent in her esophagus because it kept constricting, preventing her from swallowing food. The stent sometimes slipped down to her stomach and had to be replaced or repositioned. One such intervention had taken place earlier in October. In conversation with Dr. Browne, I learned that replacement or repositioning of the esophageal stent, in early October, is unlikely to have been the direct cause of the events that led to her death. (The word "direct" is mine, not his.) What he believed occurred was that as the esophagus built up scar tissue, from the repeated stent procedures, it constricted (just as a scab constricts skin until it falls off). The constriction of the esophagus brought it even closer to the aorta than it usually is (which is close, anyway). At some point a couple of days before she died, a fistula developed between the esophagus and the aorta—somehow, a hole in the esophagus led to a breach in the aorta, likely because of the scarring and stomach acid from gastroparesis (and the direction was from the esophagus to the aorta, not the other way around). As with a fistula in two pipes, one under high pressure (which, in essence, is what the esophagus and aorta are), once the aorta wall was breached, it started pumping blood into the esophagus, which is what caused the blood to get into her abdomen (and into one of her tubes, which is what alerted the staff at her group home that there was a problem).

Once that fistula developed, then the die had been cast. (That the fistula developed on October 15, rather than earlier in the month, was why the stent procedure couldn't have been the cause: if the aorta had been invaded then, because of suturing the stent into place or for any other reason, the aorta would have begun bleeding immediately, but it didn't.) Krystin had resisted going into the hospital in the day or so before she finally did go, even though she was in pain, because she didn't want to again be in the hospital on her birthday (October 30). The doctor said at that point the delay didn't make any difference. The fistula had already developed. (The death certificate lists "aorto-esophageal fistula" as the immediate cause of death, with "other contributing conditions" as "esophageal stricture.")

So, while the stent procedure didn't itself directly cause the breach of the aorta, it is likely the repeated stent procedures did ultimately lead to the fistula.

When Krystin went into ICU, they first removed the stent, because they could not get at the source of the bleeding without doing so. That is when they discovered the fistula. At that point they called in both thoracic and cardiac surgeons, who determined that they could not do anything. One possibility would have been an aortic stent—but inserting it where it was needed would have meant blocking the flow of blood to her brain, thus causing an immediate stroke. Even in order to do that, they would have had to remove the esophagus permanently, so she could never have eaten again (she would have been on a feeding tube permanently—something she would have detested!).

Dr. Browne said that before they removed the breathing tube after we had all left the hospital, he checked Krystin. He didn't do the full array of tests, but his judgment, from quick checks and eye examination, was that she was almost completely brain dead by the time they were finished trying to save her: that the low blood pressure she suffered from while they were trying to save her very likely caused brain death. He said he doubted seriously she would have ever again awakened, even if they had managed to fix the aorta. (He said one measure was that when they removed the breathing tube, she stopped breathing, which suggested that basic brain stem function had shut down.)

Dr. Browne reaffirmed what they told us on the day: Krystin said "let's get it over with" and went into anesthesia. She never felt any pain from the surgery and she didn't go into it with any thought of or terror about death.

When we were at the hospital, Dr. Browne had told us that it was highly probable that blood in her system (from the leak in the aorta) had shut down the liver and the kidney, so had she survived, she also would have been on dialysis (which she also would have detested).

He repeated what they had told us at the hospital: they had given her 52 units of blood. He said in most surgery, patients receive 1-2 units. They went to heroic measures to save her—until they realized they couldn't.

Dr. Browne expressed profound sympathy for us; he told me he has a 27-year-old daughter and he cannot imagine what we are feeling. He commented that it is impossible to be empathetic in this situation, because empathy requires putting oneself in another's position—which he could not do. (I told him he was right.) This isn't the first time he's had to face this with a patient's parents, and he said it breaks his heart every time he has to do so.

While the immediate cause of death was the fistula and the bleeding into her esophagus, the obituary was not incorrect: Krystin died from complications of diabetes.

I am ambivalent in a small way about not going to the hospital to see her when she went in late Monday, October 16. I had not seen her for over a month (because Kathy and I were in Europe September 27 – October 14), although I had, as usual, exchanged messages with her off and on throughout that period. Had I known the situation was terminal, I would have rushed to see her. On the other hand, it would have been out of the ordinary for me to have done so, because none of us visited her in the hospital during what were typically in-one-day-and-out-the-next events. A visit could have set off alarm bells. Moreover, had I or we known that it was terminal, then so likely would Krystin, and I can imagine that Krystin would then have been terrified. As far as I'm concerned, the most important thing the surgeon told me was that Krystin felt no pain during the events and that she went into the procedure with no foreknowledge of death, so no terror. I cannot have wanted her to face that, so—I tell myself—my absence when she went in avoided any extraordinary concern on her part.

* * *

[Posts to Krystin's Facebook Page in the days following her death (selections, through the end of 2017)]

October 18, 2017 Gary Engstrand
My daughter Krystin died yesterday afternoon at University Hospital. It was peaceful for her. She went in on Monday with blood problems; Tuesday morning they anesthetized her, started surgery, and discovered substantial internal aortic bleeding that they could not stop. Krystin said "let's get this procedure done" before going under; she never regained consciousness so she died without fear. We were able to be at the hospital to bid her farewell (although she did not know we were present).
--Gary Engstrand (her dad)

> [Many expressions of sorrow and sympathy]
> Gary Engstrand:
> Thank you all for your thoughts and kind words. They mean a great deal to us. As you can imagine, these are the saddest days of our lives.

Given her multiple medical problems, I have suspected for a number of years that I would outlive Krystin, assuming I achieved my predicted life expectancy. Being intellectually aware of a future devastating event is not the same as confronting the reality of it now; I cannot know if the shock was slightly mitigated by the foreknowledge. But shock it was, particularly because I didn't expect it to happen when she was only 32.

What is even more disconcerting and depressing is the disassembling of someone's life by the dispersal of personal belonging and emptying a residence. We have spent several hours in her apartment sorting and saving, and we will have to do more because we did not finish. I have done this twice before, for my great-aunt in 1989 and my father in 2005, both of whom were in their 80s; this is the worst case because she was my daughter and because she was so young. A few boxes saved, many more donated, and "poof," someone is gone. I rebel at the thought that Krystin will disappear. She will live in our memories and photos and letters, but her physical presence, in person and place, will not.

For now we're just numb. We are muddling along, dealing almost mechanically with the tasks required by social norms and legal procedures. We know that normal life will return, but it will take awhile and it will never be the same. There will always be a niche where grief resides. We will, however, retain the happy memories as well, of which fortunately there are many.

October 18, 2017 Peggy Hinz is with Krystin Engstrand
[Peggy was the only non-family member at the hospital when Krystin died, and she was the only one invited]
Gabi and Molly's mom, Krystin, died peacefully yesterday afternoon at the U Hospital. We will miss her forever. 😹 💔

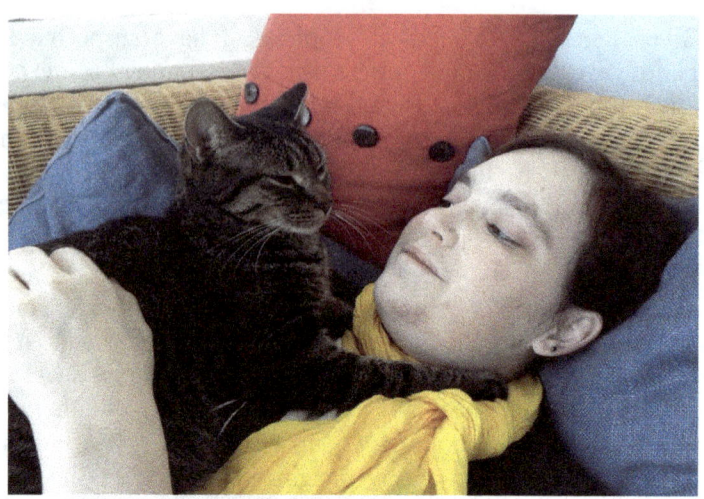

Amber Janssen: I had the honor to meet Krystin Engstrand through working at the Logan home for a few months. She was about the strongest person I have ever met. The lifelong struggle is over Krystin. So blessed to have been a part of your life even if only for a short time. ♥♥

Sherrill Naegele: OMG!!! I am at a loss for words! I know she struggled for so long, but this is coming as a shock to me! We knew each other for ten years, meeting at Remuda, and were instantly great friends! She will be sorely missed. I am so sorry for your loss! My deepest sympathy! 💔 We always had a saying since we met...I'll leave the window open for you". Tonight, my dear friend, I'll leave my window open for you! May you Rest In Peace.

October 18, 2017 Christine Hinz Lenzen is with Krystin Engstrand
I lost a good friend yesterday. Krystin and I met when we were 2 years old, she was my longest and oldest friend. I do not remember a time when she wasn't in my life. She struggled for the better part of a decade with health complications - but she was a fighter and even through all of her lows she always seemed to bounce back in better spirits, even more determined to get better. She would have been 33 years old in a couple weeks.

October 18, 2017 Crystal Lescault is asking for donations to We Are Diabetes — with Krystin Engstrand
Oh Krystin, do you remember that I told you not to eat the cake, that you weren't allowed??! We had a good laugh about that. Sorry it wasn't a lot, but I'm glad I was able to give you 4 and a half more years. You had the chance to fight, I'm proud I could help with that.
Eat all the cake you want now girl! We'll miss you.
#shareyourspare

> Honor Krystin's Birthday by donating to We Are Diabetes
> Fundraiser for We Are Diabetes by Christine Hinz Lenzen
> Krystin Engstrand passed away on October 17 due to complications from years of mismanaged diabetes. She would have been 33 years old on October 30.

We Are Diabetes is an organization founded by our friend Asha and is primarily devoted to promoting support and awareness for type 1 diabetics who suffer from eating disorders. Had an organization like this been around for Krystin when she started suffering, it could have made all the difference in the world.

October 18, 2017 Jessica Leigh
I am stunned and heartbroken to hear the news today that my dear friend Krystin has passed away from complications of diabetes. We became friends in Korea and became even better friends afterwards. I feel a little angry and frustrated that people are labeling her death as "mismanagement of diabetes". Krystin would be the first to admit that she struggled being a "good" diabetic, and we spoke many times on the struggles and guilt she felt at not being able to be consistent with the constant demands of the chronic illness that she never signed up for. It wasn't stubbornness or lack of trying--it was a constant battle to overcome such a rough hand of cards. Krystin told me about many experiences she had, how she nearly died in Scotland and the guilt of the stress she felt she placed on her parents, especially her mom. She was successful at times with being positive about her condition and transplants, but extremely tired at the physical pain. Krystin was deeply complex and to me she was a beautiful person and fierce friend. She loved her family and friends deeply and several times she told me of the joy and gratitude she felt to have such a supportive mother and father and brother. I will miss you lady, but I know you'll be with me every time we are lucky enough to have a spirit of adventure.

> Christine Hinz Lenzen: I'm sorry that you were hurt by the wording, but Krystin would have been the first to admit (and often did) that all of her health complications were due to the way that she dealt with (or rather didn't deal with) her diabetes. Please read

this article that she wrote in 2012 for We Are Diabetes, the organization that I'm asking people to donate to in honor of her birthday. I hope her words can bring you some comfort. http://www.wearediabetes.org/.../we-are-survivors-krystin...

> Jessica Leigh: Krystin always brought me comfort and now she is gone. I find it disrespectful that you say that she died because of mismanaging her diabetes. That's like someone who struggled with alcohol addiction their entire life and knew it was wrong but it wrenched their soul and wrestled with the struggle every day--yet upon their death you air it out in public as if to shame them. You never had to walk in her shoes yet it is easy to say that all her health problems were her own fault, and that is simply unfair. Growing up as a child and then a young woman with such a burden as diabetes and struggling with constant monitoring and physically painful injections and depression from never feeling fully adequate or "normal" is easy to marginalize when you're not the one in her shoes. Krystin was a strong and fiercely loyal friend and I would not be a friend to her if I didn't share or point out how much she expressed to me the burden she felt regarding her inability to achieve a "normal" life. Her physical pain was something the doctors never took seriously, and her mental pain was real. Saying that it was all her fault is not fair to Krystin at all. She never asked for diabetes. She did the best within her capabilities and felt constant guilt that it wasn't enough for those around her. I'm glad she's a free spirit now--free of the judgement of those who never walked a mile in her shoes.
> Christine Hinz Lenzen: I'm sorry that you are hurting Jessica, I am hurting too.
> Gary Engstrand: Jessica, I just read this carefully for the first time. I believe you accurately captured much about Krystin. She *wanted* to do the right things, but it was difficult for her to carry through, and that inability, over a decade or more, is what probably led to her death, I am sad to say. Yours is a marvelous recollection and story. Thank you so much for it.
>
> Jessica Leigh: She loved you so much, Gary. You were one of her heroes. Krystin and I were so close and shared a lot of the deep things people feel uncomfortable talking about--maybe

because we are both Scorpios, who knows. She really wanted to be a good diabetic, but it was a struggle for her that was mental, spiritual and physical. I would say it was analogous to an alcoholic who knows that what they are doing is wrong but they can't completely stop. She always wrestled with it and was aware of it as if it were another person in the room. The hand that Krystin was dealt was more difficult than over half of America. People accept chronic illness as if it is something normal because they hear the word "diabetes" and are familiar with it. But they never have to go home and live with it. K would talk about you and her mom and brother all the time and how important you were to her. She wasn't afraid of dying but told me she was only afraid of what it would do to her mom and to you. You raised a beautifully stubborn, intelligent, caring, empathetic and artistic human being who cared about the world. Everywhere I go for the rest of my life I know I am going to see her--every time I travel, see beautiful art, and all those things that we shared in Korea and delighted in. Sending you all my love, Gary.

Gary Engstrand: Jessica, I can't read many more of your posts; every time I do, I end up in tears. The word "hero" surprises me. I'll trust your judgment on its use, but I'm surprised. She knew that her mother, and I, and my wife Kathy (who cared deeply about Krystin as well, and had her in our home for several years of our relationship and marriage) all loved her deeply. Krystin and I made that clear to each other and I know she understood it. I'm glad you believe Krystin wasn't afraid of dying. It is reassuring to know that, because it's not a topic that ever came up with us—no parent talks to a child about the child's death (except may in the case of terminal illnesses, I just don't know). I was always afraid her death would come too soon, and I certainly wasn't going to make her think about it. She was right about the effect: it hasn't been positive, to put it mildly. In your exchange with Chris Lenzen, I have to come down on Chris's side: Krystin was forthright about her responsibility, as recently as a month ago with us. All of what you and your friend Angela have written is correct, but Krystin herself would say—did say, repeatedly--that she didn't manage the disease well in her teen years and into her early 20s. All those lovely adjectives include facets of Krystin that we sometimes didn't see fully (except the stubborn—we saw that one from the time she was a toddler!). In any case, I hope you do remember her from time to time over the course of your life. It is only in our memories that she will continue to live. Thank you, again, for your comments.

October 18, 2017 Serena Gragert
Krystin was a good childhood friend of mine from elementary school. She passed away yesterday from complications from diabetes. She was just shy of 33.

I remember walking to the nurse's office with her before lunch so she could take her insulin. I used to watch her poke her finger to take her glucose and ask her "doesn't that hurt?!" She would always shrug and just say "nope, not really", and we'd head to lunch. I always thought she had to be so strong for being able to do that everyday.

I remember playing over at her house, and the countless birthday parties. It's crazy how time flies...
Please consider donating in her honor. And give an extra thought and prayer to her family, who lost an amazing gal with a great spirit.
Honor Krystin's Birthday by donating to We Are Diabetes
Fundraiser for We Are Diabetes by Christine Hinz Lenzen

October 18, 2017 Amanda Eustice is feeling sad
My friend Krystin, who I was able to stay in touch with since elementry school (Dowling) Passed away yesterday. She fought a long hard battle with diabetes. She will be missed by many. She touched so many lives. This hits home, too young, too sweet, too caring.

Hug each and every one of your loved ones tighter, you never know if it will be the last.
Honor Krystin's Birthday by donating to We Are Diabetes
Fundraiser for We Are Diabetes by Christine Hinz Lenzen

October 18, 2017 Siheung, South Korea Adrien Poudrier
RIP Krystin Engstrand... You were one of the first friends I made in Korea and my very first Asian neighbor... While myself and so many others are mourning your loss, we are relieved to know you are no longer in pain... Tonight I'm listening to the Gaga CD you gave me

and remembering all the wonderful memories we shared together xoxox

October 18, 2017 Emily Berg
I am shocked and saddened to hear about the death of Krystin Engstrand. I met Krystin in high school and I don't think I've seen her since graduation. However through the power of Facebook I was able to follow the amazing, strong and funny woman she continued to be through adulthood. After spending a couple of days in the hospital 2 years ago I felt compelled to send her a message.

I wrote her, in part "it was my first time being admitted and I thought of you a few times. Hospitals are not fun as you know. I remembered all of your posts and humor and thought 'Krystin has had to do this so much, you can handle a couple of days.' I know we're not close friends but I just wanted to write and say the way you take everything and package it in a humorous way is really inspiring and helped me a lot too."

She wrote me back and I hope she wouldn't mind me sharing part of her response now.

"...It touches my heart to know that my experiences, and the way I handle them, is an inspiration to others. And it's nice to know that I have so many people supporting me and helping me through all this stuff, even if only with kind words, like yourself... I'm actually going to be a guest speaker at the Native American Community Clinic at some point. They have a group once a month for diabetics, and I'm going to go and talk with the women and share my story. I'm really looking forward to it because I hope that my story will be inspiring for them, too, and they can know that I know exactly what they're going through with their diabetes, and have been there, done that. If I can touch the life of even one of them, then I've made a difference."

I don't know if she ever did speak with that group but I do know she made a difference. My thoughts and love are with her close friends and family.

October 18, 2017 Mackenzie Owens is with Krystin Engstrand
Damn. I hadn't seen Krystin Engstrand as much as I would have liked over the past few years, but when I tell you she was my HOMEGIRL in high school and how many laughs we shared?? I mean it. Baby girl was hilarious! She battled Diabetes for as long as I can remember and although I'm truly sad to hear of her passing, what a relief to know she can finally rest. Rest In Peace Krystin, we love you girl, forever.

October 18, 2017 Crystal Lescault
My friend Krystin Engstrand passed away yesterday, ending her lifetime battle with diabetes. Her body couldn't fight anymore, and the doctors could no longer keep her going. She was a fighter though, right up to the end. Many of you know that I donated one of my kidneys to Krystin in June of 2013. I am proud to say that I gave her more time. I have no regrets. I only wish I could've given even more. Krystin and I also share a birthday, a year apart. This year, for our birthday on October 30th, I ask that you make a donation in her memory if you are able. I truly believe that had Krystin had the support of an organization like this early on in life she might still be here today.

Krystin, we know you are no longer suffering and that you are at peace. I believe that you and Maria Croy found each other again and that you will truly be able to rest. We love you.

October 18, 2017 Laura Doberstein is with Krystin Engstrand
My heart is heavy tonight after reading that my camp friend, Krystin Engstrand passed away yesterday. Gone. We met during one of the truly best years of camp, our LDP year in 2001. We quickly clicked and chummed together. She loved to write, loved her cats, loved crafting and her family and friends. Krystin, I will miss your laugh, and commiserating over our shared disease. Fly high dear one, swing by Hudson, WI for me, for I know I can always find your spirit there.

October 18, 2017 Anjeanette Roy is feeling drained
It was a very emotional day for me at work. Yesterday my friend/coworker Krystin Engstrand passed away during a medical procedure. She had a life long battle with diabetes, including a kidney and pancreas transplant. The past couple of years were filled with illnesses and long hospital stays. She was on medical leave for over a year, but was finally back to work part time and loving it. Through it all she remained strong and fought hard.

As I walked past her cube many times today, it really started to sink in that she would never be sitting there again. I won't be able to pop in and poke her and ask her what was new in her world anymore. There won't be anymore chats popping up asking questions or her just showing up in the entrance to my cube to say hi.

I have so many great memories with her. My work bridal shower, my wedding, Crystal Lescault's bridal shower and the Backstreet Boys concert we went to.

Even though she didn't feel good, I got her to my apartment for what she thought was a movie night, but was actually a surprise 30th Birthday party (her golden birthday) with just a couple friends.

I will miss her bubbly personality, sharp wit and huge heart. I will never be able to look at anything Hello Kitty related without thinking of her and missing her. There are Netflix shows that I might never find out what happens because watching them without her won't be the same. I know she wouldn't want me to be sad, but right now I am.

I will miss you my friend

October 18, 2017 Rachel Johnson is with Krystin Engstrand
Rest In Peace, Lovely Friend 💖 ⭐ 🌸

Rachel Johnson: Travel so safe, Lovely Girl ~~ as you have always been in the best of care ~~~
What a fighter. What a gal!

October 18, 2017 Jessie Pudil is feeling sad
I have a heavy heart today as I learned a friend of mine growing up in elementary school has passed away at the young age of 32 (almost 33).

Birthday parties, recess, and all the other great memories we created together back in our Dowling days are priceless. I will cherish them forever. We did have a chance a few years ago to catch-up and it was great.

I am sharing this to honor my childhood friend, Krystin Engstrand who made growing up that much more memorable. Please keep her family and those close to her in your prayers.
Honor Krystin's Birthday by donating to We Are Diabetes
Fundraiser for We Are Diabetes by Christine Hinz Lenzen

October 19, 2017 Gary Engstrand
Since I am laser-focused on a single topic at the moment, something a friend of mine wrote to me this morning. "Here is a phrase I have always loved: death ends a life, not a relationship." That's my solace for the day.

October 20, 2017 Gary Engstrand:
Here's a link to the Celebration of Krystin's life
https://www.facebook.com/events/476098329440989/
SUN, OCT 29, 2017
Celebration of Krystin Engstrand's life
4020 46th Avenue So

October 19, 2017 Crystal Lescault is with Krystin Engstrand
Today's memories. Krystin got me a Vikings crockpot (among other awesome things) for my bridal shower so she'd send me recipe ideas. She also knew my love for pups, pities in particular. We'd often swap pup and cat pics. Glad we all have so many happy Krystin memories to hold onto. I'm sure she's already gathered up all the cats in heaven to keep her company 🐱🐶💜💚✌️.

October 19, 2017 Christine Hinz Lenzen
I'm so amazingly touched by your donations in honor of Krystin's Birthday. We Are Diabetes is an organization that Krystin really believed in and I know she was proud to share part of her story with that community. Thank you to everyone who has donated, and to those of you who have shared the page with others. I know Krystin would have felt the love and support that you're sharing on her behalf. 🧡

I've spent much of the last two days in and out of feeling numb and uncontrollable tears. It is hard being far away from anyone who knew Krystin - and it feels like I am grieving alone. I know some of you feel the same way. It gives me comfort to read your stories and memories of her.

I know I shared this before, but in case you missed it:
Krystin was an amazing writer - she dreamed of publishing a book someday and told me that she hoped her story and her mistakes would be able to help others struggling with what she went through. Whenever she traveled, when she was in rehab, or once I moved away, she would send me letters that went on for pages about her life, what she was seeing, the things she was feeling. I've saved most of them over the years.

October 19, 2017 Jennifer Ewing is feeling sad
I'm so sad to find out that Krystin passed away. She was such a beautiful person inside and out who fought long and hard to overcome so many things life threw her way. You will be greatly missed 💜💜

October 19, 2017 Crystal Lescault is feeling emotional with Krystin Engstrand
When Krystin posted on Facebook a little over 5 years ago that she was going to need a kidney transplant I quickly commented and told her that I'd like to be tested. Something inside me at that moment said "I'm going to be her match". I firmly believe that "something" was Maria.
I still can't believe these two beautiful souls are gone...but I take comfort in knowing they are together and no longer in pain. Best friends in life, and in death.
Rest In Peace, beautiful angels, you are missed 😖🧡.

October 20, 2017 Sherrill Naegele to Krystin Engstrand
I am deeply saddened to hear of the loss of my dear friend Krystin Engstrand. We met at Remuda Ranch in 2007 and became instant friends. Over the years we would send each other little care packets now and then. We are currently in the moving process, and Last week I just happened to come across the last letter I got from her and I'd like to share it with you all. When I had read it, I started to plan out what I would send her this Christmas as a surprise. And to know that I can't grieves my soul. In the last package I sent her, was a Wonder Woman bracelet, because she truly was a super hero. My love goes out to all her friends and family. We use to have a saying..."I'll leave the

window open for ya". Well Krystin, my window will always be opened for you. ♥

    Jessica Leigh: She was an incredible friend, and so missed. She couldn't come to our wedding this weekend because she was too sick, but we will be thinking about her. It makes me feel good to read other memories of her friends. Thank you for sharing.

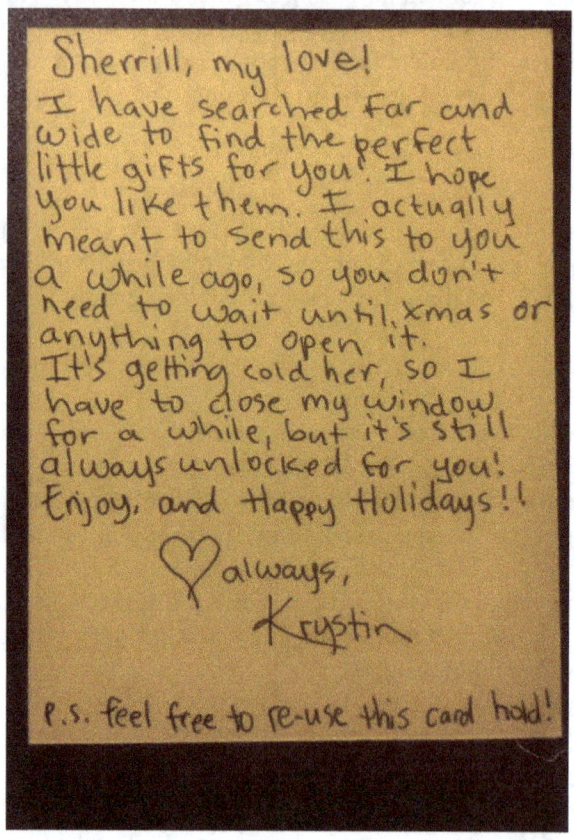

October 21, 2017 Cecilia Cécile shared a memory
happy belated birthday Krystin, and happy early birthday Christine!
[Cecilia thought Krystin's birthday was October 20.]

October 21, 2017 Christine Hinz Lenzen is with Krystin Engstrand
I was going through some old photos and found these gems. Remembering simpler times 🧡

October 21, 2017 Christine Hinz Lenzen is with Krystin Engstrand
Visiting old memories 🧡

with Hannah Mae, Krystin Engstrand, Cecilia Cécile, Jessica Maselter and Liz Fantastic

with Krystin Engstrand and Jessica Maselter

with Jessica Maselter, Sybby Hood-Dischinger, Sara Lofstrom, Krystin Engstrand and KJ Davis-Almquist

October 21, 2017 Jessica Maselter
I don't think you can ever prepare to say goodbye to someone, and especially not at the age of 32.

It's taken me a few days to write this post, and mostly because I can't put into words how to feel. Thankful is what I will go with today. Christine Hinz Lenzen thank you for bringing Krystin into my life almost 25 years ago, I can recall every sport, every sleepover (keeping Peggy Hinz awake while we giggled in the living room and stayed awake until the morning hours) and running amuck around the neighborhood like it was yesterday. These are the memories I am going to keep close and live everyday finding the good in everyone.

I'm so thankful you're no longer in pain Krystin Engstrand and you and Maria Croy are together again. I'm sorry I didn't visit, call or connect more; you're amazing and your passion for bringing awareness to the struggles of diabetes will be carried on through those that knew you.

This is a tough time for all of Krystin's family and friends, I look forward to coming together to celebrate the amazing woman Krystin was. 🧡

October 23, 2017 Gary Engstrand to Krystin Engstrand
Krystin friends, very-long-time friends of ours, Andy and Carolyn Collins, did a little remembrance for Krystin. When Krystin and Elliott were little, we visited Andy and Carolyn at their summer place on Prince Edward Island for a week (Krystin & Elliott got so sick of looking at lighthouses I think they never wanted to see another one again). Krystin participated in a study that Andy conducted of teenage kids with diabetes (he's a retired professor of child development from the U of M). Kathy and I just spent 4 days together with them in Paris; we were at the end of our trip and came home, they went on a river cruise on the Rhone. They sent me an email and pictures today which I share with you with their permission.

* * *

Dear Gary and Kathy,
We bought flowers for Krystin to send down the Rhône River in her memory on Saturday afternoon.

Some of them escaped our camera lens but we managed to catch a couple of them before the current took them away. All too soon ...

We know you will grieve her loss forever. We want you to know we remember her fondly and think of you every day.

Love, Carolyn and Andy

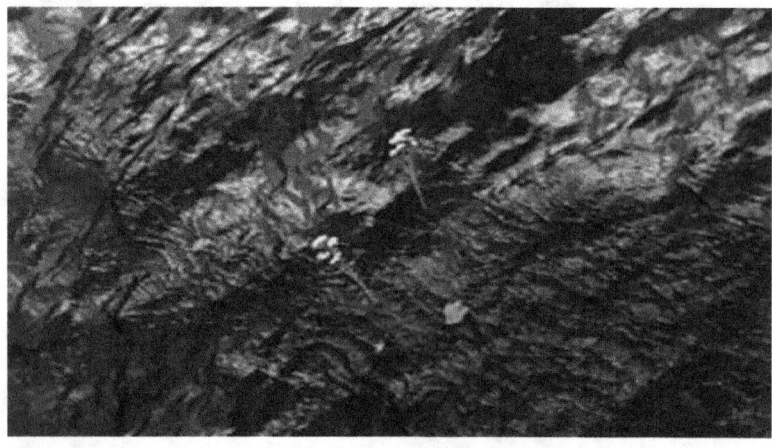

October 24, 2017 Gary Engstrand to Krystin Engstrand
To Krystin's friends, once again.

(1) I collected a number of small items from Krystin's rooms that we will put out for you to take as mementos (if you're planning on coming on Oct 29). For her women friends, I also brought home and will put out a number of her scarves (dress, not winter). Krystin loved scarves, and I'm certain she'd be pleased if her friends would like to have one. She was always generous with her friends and family. DO NOT BE BASHFUL about taking scarves or other items; the family has its mementos of her life, so anything you do not take will be donated.

(2) By and by I will write reflections on Krystin and on losing her. If any of you would like a copy, please send me an email. garyengstrand@gmail.com. It will be an MS Word document and too large to post on FB. I want to quote from a number of your FB posts (with attribution, of course); if you don't want me to quote you, send me an email about that, too. Some of you have written marvelous and touching posts and I'd like to memorialize them in my own remembrance.

Rachel Johnson: Thank you so much for taking the time and effort to write the reflections, Mr. Engstrand. As anyone could likely attest, Krystin's wit and humor was so delightful and poignant at times. I miss writing to her already.

October 24, 2017 Christine Hinz Lenzen is with Krystin Engstrand.
I can't believe you're both gone. You both played integral roles in my life, both together and separately. I don't know how it could be that I've lost you both so young, but I take solace in the idea that you're at peace now in each other's company.

October 29, 2017 Amanda Eustice
Today was emotionally heavy for me, as we gathered to celebrate the life of Krystin. It was so good to see friends and family get together and honor what a wonderful woman she was. She touched so many lives. We will always have a piece of her with us in the memories we share. P.s. Krystin, hello kitty is all you!

October 29, 2017 Asha Brown
I spent some of my day today sending a quiet and loving prayer to my friend Krystin Engstrand who recently passed away due to complications from diabulimia. An hour later I was notified another acquaintance of mine has also left this world due to the complications her body endured from years of Insulin omission.

I can't stress enough how dangerous this disease is folks. I've devoted the rest of my life to helping others GET HELP before it's too late.

If you believe that we need more resources to help the T1D community handle this deadly eating disorder please consider showing your support by donating to We Are Diabetes.

October 30, 2017 Crystal Lescault is with Krystin Engstrand
There's a giant Hello Kitty theme birthday party going on in heaven today 🎈

October 30, 2017 Molly Kubeczko-Schmidt to Krystin Engstrand
Especially thinking of you today, hoping they are throwing you one heck of a birthday party on the other side!!! Missing you each and every day 💙 💚

November 1, 2017 Christine Hinz Lenzen
Edit: We reached $1500!

Together we've raised almost $1500 for We Are Diabetes to honor Krystin's birthday.

Ultimately, Krystin died not just from complications of diabetes, but because she suffered from the eating disorder Diabulimia, too. We Are Diabetes is exactly the type of support that Krystin needed when she started struggling. Supporting this organization in Krystin's honor helps support others struggling with what Krystin went through. Thank you all for your support and donations. It means a lot to me, and I know it means a lot to her Mom and Dad. 🧡

November 11, 2017 Christine Hinz Lenzen
This is a very informative 30-min documentary on the eating disorder Diabulimia - the disorder that Krystin suffered from and for which she received treatment. This is from the BBC and highlights the issue in the UK - but I know from watching Krystin seek help, that a lot of these issues are also present in the medical community here in the US.

It was hard for me to watch this and not think of how isolated Krystin felt, too.

YOUTUBE.COM
Diabulimia: The World's Most Dangerous Eating Disorder

Peggy Hinz: Thank you for finding this and sharing. It's hard to watch, but helps me understand what Krystin went through. Most people have never heard of Diabulimia. I'm surprised at the percentage of Type 1 diabetics with an eating disorder. We all need to be more aware.

November 26, 2017 Jessica Leigh to Krystin Engstrand
Yesterday Isma and I put up our first Christmas tree as husband and wife. Every year I look forward to putting up the ornament you made me. It has been so hard this last month to not be able to pick up the phone and call you or send you a message. I know we will see each other again, but in the meantime it's going to be years and years for me and a fraction of a moment for you. Ever since the wedding I have been seeing butterflies everywhere. At first I thought it was just an unusual amount of butterflies but now that it is almost winter I am seeing them on paper, pinned in offices of important meetings...the most random of places. And then I remembered that we met at the Hampyeong Butterfly Festival. Of course! I know your soul is free and you're no longer limited by the physical pain and bullshit that you had to suffer through on Earth. But I will miss you until I'm an old lady, and no doubt I will still selfishly wish you were here with us, on this side. Thank you for the butterflies you send. They are great consolation and always make me smile. Love you and miss you.

December 24, 2017 Christine Hinz Lenzen to Krystin Engstrand

It's Christmas Eve! I know how much you loved Christmas and I've been thinking of you. Your Mom is going to come over tomorrow to help celebrate, so don't worry about her - she'll be with family 🧡. We all miss you, K.

My mom redid the basement (she put in a bathroom! Imagine how great that would have been during all of those sleep overs?!) and she's been encouraging me to take all of the things I've stored in her basement for the last decade and a half back to Michigan with me. LOTS OF PHOTOGRAPHS. I was looking through some today and found these two photos from some hang out session at your house. They're from the summer after we graduated from South.

Merry Christmas, Krystin. I'll love you forever, I'll like you for always, as long as I'm living my best friend you'll be. Xoxox — with Krystin Engstrand.

July 8, 2018 Gary Engstrand

> *Krystin Facebook post, July 15, 2014:*
> *I want to be a tree when I die! But I want to be a bonsai. That doesn't seem to be an option.*
> goodnewsnetwork.org

Biodegradable Urns Will Turn You Into A Tree After You Die - The Good News

I thought about getting a bonsai tree to memorialize her, even though I'm sure she was being partially silly in the post (as she was with many of her posts). I read about growing bonsai indoors, however, and it would not work (at least not in our house or in Elliott's apartment), because they require full, bright sun.

So the best I could do is lightly spread a few ashes around her maple tree.

www.ingramcontent.com/pod-product-compliance
Lightning Source LLC
Chambersburg PA
CBHW050259010526
44108CB00040B/1895